Social Constructionist Theories of Crime

The Library of Essays in Theoretical Criminology
Series Editor: Stuart Henry

Titles in the Series:

Anomie, Strain and Subcultural Theories of Crime
Robert Agnew and Joanne M. Kaufman

Postmodernist and Post-Structuralist Theories of Crime
Bruce A. Arrigo and Dragan Milovanovic

Biosocial Theories of Crime
Kevin M. Beaver and Anthony Walsh

Feminist Theories of Crime
Meda Chesney-Lind and Merry Morash

Cultural Criminology: Theories of Crime
Jeff Ferrell and Keith Hayward

Social Constructionist Theories of Crime
Stuart Henry and Ross L. Matsueda

Radical and Marxist Theories of Crime
Michael J. Lynch and Paul B. Stretesky

Developmental and Life-course Theories of Crime
Tara Renae McGee and Paul Mazerolle

Crime Opportunity Theories
Mangai Natarajan

Social Control and Self-Control Theories of Crime and Deviance
Joseph H. Rankin and L. Edward Wells

Social Learning Theories of Crime
Christine S. Sellers, L. Thomas Winfree, Jr and Ronald L. Akers

Social, Ecological and Environmental Theories of Crime
Jeffery T. Walker

Social Constructionist Theories of Crime

Edited by

Stuart Henry

San Diego State University, USA

Ross L. Matsueda

University of Washington, USA

Routledge
Taylor & Francis Group
LONDON AND NEW YORK

First published 2015 by Ashgate Publishing

Published 2016 by Routledge
2 Park Square, Milton Park, Abingdon, Oxon OX14 4RN
605 Third Avenue, New York, NY 10017

Routledge is an imprint of the Taylor & Francis Group, an informa business

British Library Cataloguing in Publication Data
A catalogue record for this book is available from the British Library.

Library of Congress Control Number: 2014938857

ISBN 13: 978-1-4094-1961-7 (hbk)

Contents

Acknowledgements

Ashgate would like to thank our researchers and the contributing authors who provided copies, along with the following for their permission to reprint copyright material.

Annual Reviews, Inc. for the essay: Joseph W. Schneider (1985), 'Social Problems Theory: The Constructionist View', *Annual Review of Sociology*, **11**, pp. 209–29. Copyright © 1985 by Annual Reviews Inc. All rights reserved.

Emerald Group Publishing for the essay: Glenn W. Muschert and Anthony A. Peguero (2010), 'The Columbine Effect and School Antiviolence Policy', *Research in Social Problems and Public Policy*, **17**, pp. 117–48. Copyright © 2010 by Emerald Group Publishing Limited. All rights of reproduction in any form reserved.

Lexington Books for the essay: Stephen J. Pfohl (1981), 'Ethnomethodology and Criminology: The Social Production of Crime and the Criminal', in Israel L. Barak-Glantz and C. Ronald Huff (eds), *The Mad, the Bad, and the Different: Essays Honoring Simon Dinitz*, New York: Lexington Books, pp. 25–37. Copyright © 1981 by D.C. Heath and Company.

David Polizzi for the essay: David Polizzi and Bruce A. Arrigo (2009), 'Phenomenology, Postmodernism, and Philosophical Criminology: A Conversational Critique', *Journal of Theoretical and Philosophical Criminology*, **1**, pp. 113–45.

The Rowman & Littlefield Publishing Group for the essays: Ray Surette and Charles Otto (2001), 'The Media's Role in the Definition of Crime', in S. Henry and M.M. Lanier (eds), *What is Crime?*, Boulder, CO: Rowman & Littlefield, pp. 139–54. Copyright © 2001 by Stuart Henry and Mark M. Lanier; Leroy C. Gould, Gary Kleck and Marc Gertz (2001), 'Crime as Social Interaction', in S. Henry and M.M. Lanier (eds), *What is Crime?*, Boulder, CO: Rowman & Littlefield, pp. 101–14. Copyright © 2001 by Stuart Henry and Mark M. Lanier.

SAGE Publications, Inc. for the essays: Stuart Henry (2009), 'Social Construction of Crime', in J. Mitchell Miller (ed.), *21st Century Criminology: A Reference Handbook*, Vol. 1, Thousand Oaks, CA: Sage, pp. 296–304. Copyright © 2009 by SAGE Publications, Inc. Reprinted by permission of SAGE Publications; Vincent F. Sacco (1995), 'Media Constructions of Crime', *Annals of the American Academy of Political and Social Science*, **539** (Reactions to Crime and Violence), pp. 141–54. Reprinted by permission of SAGE Publications; Sean P. Hier, Dan Lett, Kevin Walby and André Smith (2011), 'Beyond Folk Devil Resistance: Linking Moral Panic and Moral Regulation', *Criminology and Criminal Justice*, **11**, pp. 259–76. Copyright © 2011 Sean P. Hier, Dan Lett, Kevin Walby and André Smith. Reprinted by permission of SAGE Publications; Nicole Hahn Rafter (1990), 'The Social Construction of Crime and

Crime Control', *Journal of Research in Crime and Delinquency*, **27**, pp. 376–89. Copyright © 1990 SAGE Publications, Inc. Reprinted by permission of SAGE Publications.

Social Justice for the essay: Stuart Henry and Dragan Milovanovic (2000), 'Constitutive Criminology: Origins, Core Concepts, and Evaluation', *Social Justice*, **27**, pp. 268–90.

Springer for the essays: George Psathas (2004), 'Alfred Schutz's Influence on American Sociologists and Sociology', *Human Studies*, **27**, pp. 1–35. Copyright © 2004 Kluwer Academic Publishers; Ken Plummer (2011), 'The Labelling Perspective Forty Years On', in Helge Peters and Michael Dellwing (eds), *Langweiliges Verbrechen* [*Boring Crimes*], Weisbaden: VS Verlag, pp. 83–101.

Taylor & Francis for the essays: Helmut R. Wagner (1969), 'Phenomenology and Contemporary Sociological Theory: The Contribution of Alfred Schutz', *Sociological Focus*, **2**, pp. 73–86. Reproduced by permission of Taylor & Francis Group LLC (http://www.tandfonline.com); Philip Jenkins (1994), '"The Ice Age": The Social Construction of a Drug Panic', *Justice Quarterly*, **11**, pp. 7–31. Copyright © 1994 Academy of Criminal Justice Sciences; Mary deYoung (1998), 'Another Look at Moral Panics: The Case of Satanic Day Care Centers', *Deviant Behavior*, **19**, pp. 257–78. Copyright © 1998 Taylor & Francis. Reproduced by permission of Taylor & Francis Group LLC (http://www.tandfonline.com); Robert O. Keel (2001), 'Ethnomethodological Perspective (on Crime and Deviance)', in Clifton D. Bryant (ed.), *Encyclopedia of Criminology and Deviant Behavior*, London: Brunner-Routledge, pp. 148–53. Copyright © 2001 Taylor & Francis. All rights reserved.

University of California Press Journals for the essays: Malcolm Spector and John I. Kitsuse (1973), 'Social Problems: A Re-formulation', *Social Problems*, **21**, pp. 145–59; Kai T. Erikson (1962), 'Notes on the Sociology of Deviance', *Social Problems*, **9**, pp. 307–14. Copyright © 1962, The Society for the Study of Social Problems.

University of Chicago Press for the essay: Harold Garfinkel (1956), 'Conditions of Successful Degradation Ceremonies', *American Journal of Sociology*, **61**, pp. 420–24. Copyright © 1956 The University of Chicago Press.

Waveland Press, Inc. for the essay: Victor E. Kappeler (2011), 'Inventing Criminal Justice: Myth and Social Construction', in Peter B. Kraska and John J. Brent, *Theorizing Criminal Justice: Eight Essential Orientations* (2nd edn), Long Grove, IL: Waveland Press, pp. 185–94. Copyright © 2011, 2004 by Waveland Press, Inc. All rights reserved.

Every effort has been made to trace all the copyright holders, but if any have been inadvertently overlooked the publishers will be pleased to make the necessary arrangement at the first opportunity.

Publisher's Note

The material in this volume has been reproduced using the facsimile method. This means we can retain the original pagination to facilitate easy and correct citation of the original essays. It also explains the variety of typefaces, page layouts and numbering.

Series Preface

Because of its pervasive nature in our mass mediated culture, many believe they are experts in understanding the reasons why offenders violate the law. Parents and schools come high on the public's list of who to blame for crime. Not far behind are governments and legal systems that are believed to be ineffective at deterring offenders – too many legal protections and too few serious sentences. Some learn how to behave inappropriately as children, while others are said to choose crime because of its apparent high reward/low cost opportunity structure. Yet others hang out with the wrong crowd, or live in the wrong neighborhood, or work for the wrong corporation, and may get their kicks from disobeying rules in the company of like-minded others. A few are seen as evil, insane or just plain stupid. While such popular representations of the causes of crime contain glimpses of the criminological reality, understanding why people commit crime is a much more complex matter. Indeed, for this reason the quest to establish the causes of crime has been one of the most elusive searches confronting humankind.

Since the mid-19th century, following the advent of Charles Darwin's *The Origin of Species*, those who sought scientific knowledge to understand crime abandoned philosophical speculation and economic reductionism. In its place they founded the multifaceted interdisciplinary field of criminology. Unlike criminal law and legal theory that explored the logic of prohibitions against offensive behavior, and in contrast to criminal justice that examined the nature and extent of societies' responses to crime through systems of courts, police and penology, criminology's central focus is the systematic examination of the nature, extent and causes of crime. Criminological theory, as a subset of criminology, comprises the cluster of explanations seeking to identify the causes or etiology of crime. This *Library of Essays in Theoretical Criminology* is designed to capture the range and depth of the key theoretical perspectives on crime causation.

While there are numerous criminological theories, most can be clustered into 10 or 12 theoretical perspectives. Moreover, each of these broad theoretical frameworks is, itself, rooted in a major academic discipline. The most predominant disciplines influencing criminological theory include: economics, anthropology, biology, psychology, geography, sociology, politics, history, philosophy, as well as the more recent multi-disciplinary fields such as gender studies, critical race studies and postmodernist social theory.

Criminological theories are rarely discrete. Although they often emphasize a particular disciplinary field, they also draw on aspects of other disciplines to strengthen their explanatory power. Indeed, since 1989 a major development in criminological theory has been the emergence of explicitly integrative theoretical approaches (see Gregg Barak, *Integrative Criminology*; Ashgate, 1998). Integrative/interdisciplinary approaches bring together several theories into a comprehensive explanation, usually to address different levels of analysis; these range from the micro-individual and relational approaches common in biology and psychology, to the meso-level institutional explanations that feature in sociological analysis, to the macro-level geographical, political, cultural and historical approaches that deal with societal and global structures and patterns. Recent developments in criminological theory have seen an acceleration of this trend compared with that of single disciplinary explanations of crime (see Stuart Henry and Scott Lukas, *Recent Developments in Criminological Theory*; Ashgate, 2009).

Although there are now over 20 English-language criminological theory textbooks and numerous edited compilations, there is a need to make available to an international audience a series of books that brings together the best of the available theoretical contributions. The advantage of doing this as a series, rather than a single volume, is that the editors are able to mine the field for the most relevant essays that have influenced the present state of knowledge. Each contribution to the series thus contains many chapters, each on a different aspect of the same theoretical approach to crime causation.

In creating this series I have selected outstanding criminologists whose own theories are discussed as part of the literature and I have asked each of them to select a set of the best journal essays to represent the various facets of their theoretical framework. In doing so, I believe that you will receive the best selection of essays available together with an insightful and comparative overview placing each essay in the context of the history of ideas that comprises our search to better understand and explain crime and those who commit it.

STUART HENRY
Series Editor
School of Public Affairs
San Diego State University, USA

Introduction

Set within the interpretive tradition of sociology, social constructionism and the related interactionist and labeling theories each take slightly different but interrelated views of crime and deviance. Unlike positivist theories that see the phenomenon of crime as the outcome of a range of micro-, meso- or macro-level forces, theories within the interpretive tradition focus on social processes rooted in human interaction through which humans create, maintain and reproduce patterns of conformity, crime and deviance. At their simplest, social constructionist theoretical perspectives focus on the process whereby humans make conceptual distinctions based on perceived differences, evaluate those differences as good or bad, and classify people as more or less likely to engage in convention, crime or deviance, based on established stereotypes of those engaging in such behaviors. Importantly, primary labelers also create new negative stereotypes, or 'folk devils', based on moral panics about the potential threat of the signified behavior. As such, negative or deviant labels are social constructions of human types that exaggerate some characteristics and diminish others, producing caricatures of both conventionally behaving actors and offenders, with accompanying expectations of future likely behaviors. Audience interaction with those labeled limits the degree to which they can escape the confines of the label or its multiplicity of prescriptions and assumptions. Rooted in the interactionist insights of George Herbert Mead and Herbert Blumer, the extent to which individuals can resist incorporating collective social definitions of the other into their own self-identity, is dependent on their counter constructions of meaning, political power, access to media and strategies for redefining their situation; it also depends on the nature and form of state moral regulation of society.

Whereas positivist theories generally assume a passive actor, or at most a reactive actor, interpretive theories assume active human agents who can shape their own biographies as co-producers of their social world, while also being influenced by the world that they shape. Humans are relatively free to creatively engage with other humans but, paradoxically, in the process, are subject to the meanings that others construct about them, and impose on them through social interaction. In this process they incorporate the others' meanings into their own definitions of themselves (Mead, 1934; Blumer, 1969). Thus, rather than being static types, fixed in time, interactionist and social constructionist theorists see humans as dynamic, malleable and re-definable; humans are creative beings, acting according to meanings they impart to situations that confront them. Hence human activity is a socially creative process whereby human beings take other humans into account before they act. This occurs through a process of role play.

Mead's concept of the 'self' (1934) refers to how, in the process of role-taking, a person can play the role of the other and can act towards their own self the way he or she sees others acting towards them. In the process of human development this interactive taking-account-of-the-other becomes routinized and taken for granted. Matsueda (1992, 2001; Heimer and Matsueda, 1994) says that most behavior is habitual and doesn't require much thought until problems arise, then 'the person stops and engages in reflection, thinking or cognition ...

the person takes the role of the other, views the problematic situation from the standpoint of significant others, and evaluates alternative lines of action from the perspective of the others' (Matsueda, 2001, p. 234). He argues that this 'imaginative rehearsal of alternatives' is a 'serial process of cognition' that is repeated until a satisfactory solution to the problem is found (Matsueda, 2001, p. 234). The result of this process can be social control in the form of self-control:

> The self arises through role-taking, the process of taking the role of the other, viewing one's self from the perspective of the other, and controlling one's behavior accordingly … Moreover, because role-taking involves considering lines of action from the standpoint of reference groups, it follows that behavior is controlled by social groups. Self-control is actually social control. (Matsuada, 2001, p. 224)

Moreover, Heimer and Matsueda 'expanded the role-taking process to include learned definitions of delinquency, anticipated reactions to delinquency, and delinquent peers' and called this process 'differential social control', arguing that this can result in a 'conventional direction (e.g., when taking the role of conventional groups) or a criminal direction (e.g., when taking the role of criminal groups)' (1994, cited in Matsueda, 2001, p. 235). This development of the theory was also used to explain the gender differences in delinquency (Bartusch and Matsueda, 1996; Heimer, 1996) and life-course delinquency (Matsueda and Heimer, 1997).

Ironically, although social constructionism affords the human creative agency through the process of dynamic interaction, routine practices that consistently define persons in certain ways can ossify those persons as social types with relatively fixed statuses, a 'mortification of selves' (Goffman, 1963). This is a process, known as 'the self-fulfilling prophecy' in labeling theory or 'objectification' in social constructionist theory, that produces and reproduces the appearance of static types, that reifies human agency, masks its creativity and limits humans' ability to change.

These interactive social processes of meaning creation, shared meaning and taking the role of the other are the foundation of the constitution of society and its social order. Mead rejected the separation between philosophical 'realism' that saw social reality as unaffected by the ways humans think, and philosophical 'nominalism' that saw the world as ordered by humans' definitions and classification. For Mead the central question was 'to grasp *both* the nominalist and realist elements as "dialectically" related (co-producing), such that individuals create social forms that in turn recreate individuals' (Einstadter and Henry, 2006, p. 207). From this perspective society (and social order) takes on a more fluid and dynamic relationship to its members. For Blumer (1969) society is composed of acting units that are composed of people acting together in joint activity, as a group, in a situational context that is open to interpretation and negotiation; it is the collectivity of acting units that constitutes society. As Matsueda puts it:

> We should think of society not as a static structure containing functional positions, but rather as an ever-changing process. We should think of social order not as an unchanging property of society, but rather as an outcome of interaction and negotiation between members of society. Similarly, we should view members of society as not only adapting to a changing society and social groups, but also helping to constitute that society and those social groups. (2001, p. 223)

In short, the contribution of social constructionists is to explain how society appears to be a concrete objective reality while simultaneously being socially constructed through human actions and processes.

Building on the work of Edmund Husserl's phenomenological philosophy and Max Weber's sociology of understanding, Alfred Schutz (1932 [1967]) developed a sociological phenomenology that culminated in Berger and Luckmann's groundbreaking book *The Social Construction of Reality* (1966). This work describes how through routine practices of social interaction humans create social phenomena that appear to have independent, objective existence from the very humans who created them. As these social realities become solidified as representations in the minds of those who created them and as they lose sight of their own authorship of the phenomenon (a process called reification), the social constructions act back on their creators, shaping and channeling their subsequent actions. Berger and Luckmann explain that this separation of humans from their social constructions occurs progressively: first, the categories are externalized, then, as humans communicate with each other, the categories become, and are referred to, as though they had object-like existence. Finally these 'realities' are internalized as institutions, codes and practices. Thus society is an ongoing, constantly emerging outcome of human agents' interaction with one another that produces shared 'representations' (Knorr-Cetina, 1981). Representations are composite mental pictures taken to represent a reality assumed to exist and acted towards as though it does exist, regardless of whether there exists an underlying objective reality.

> When people's mental pictures of reality approximately correspond to each other, as assessed by communicated cues and signs which that they share and agree on, then they assume for practical purposes that a reality exists. Enough is held in common to produce patterns of behavior, whose very repetition serves to reinforce the original notion of reality and bolster the appearance of substance and structure. (Einstadter and Henry, 2006, p. 217)

The social constructionist perspective sees crime and deviance as the outcome of these same social processes. The deviance process starts with an audience of social actors signifying a behavior as different, perceiving that difference as meaningful action and then judging the action, and the actors committing it, positively or negatively. In the case of negative judgment of significantly different action, the outcome is likely to be collective reaction in the form of banning that behavior, ultimately through law. Consistent with Blumer's notion of joint activity, audiences banning behavior, who Becker (1963) refers to as 'moral entrepreneurs', invest considerable time and energy in seeking to elevate the symbolic meaning of the negatively judged action in order to convince those with power, and sometimes authority, to ban the behavior. They do this by generating both fear about the harmful consequences of the behavior in question and advocating the solution as social reaction to curb it, in the form of rules, laws and enforcement. While the fear may originally be narrowly perceived, and be little more than a 'private trouble', moral entrepreneurs embark on a series of social actions to elevate the fear to become a 'public issue'. This process is enhanced by creating a 'moral panic' (Cohen, 1972) about the behavior in question, which is achieved through a variety of claims-making using expert testimony and mass media that builds into a crescendo resulting in a ban, though ultimately declines as the myth-making involved is eventually revealed (Goode and Ben-Yehuda, 1994).

Participation in banned behavior has a variety of motivations, and for many actors may be a one time or an infrequent event with limited consequences or little likelihood of persistence. Labeling theorists distinguish between 'primary deviance' and 'secondary deviance' (Lemert, 1951). Primary deviance is often transitory, exploratory and not perceived by the rule-breaker as an indicator or marker of their identity. Primary deviance 'has only minor consequences for a person's status, social relationships, or subsequent behavior. Primary deviance tends to be situational, transient and idiosyncratic' (Matsueda, 2001, p. 225). In contrast secondary deviance is the direct result of societal reaction to primary deviance when humans take on others' negative definitions of themselves (Lofland, 1969). The secondary deviant is now more likely to break rules because of who he or she has become:

> Secondary deviance ... is explicitly a response to societal reactions to deviance and has major consequences for a person's status, relationships and future behavior. Secondary deviance occurs when society's response to initial deviance (e.g., stigmatization, punishment, segregation) causes fundamental changes in the person's social roles, self-identity, and personality, resulting in additional deviant acts. (Matsueda, 2001, p. 225)

As a result of a variety of social processes, including secrecy and transparency, the labeled deviant increasingly engages in the deviant activity, and associates with fellow deviants, which overwhelms the rest of his or her life. Goffman called this 'role engulfment', such that the deviant activity becomes a 'master status', defining the identity of the deviant actor. When societal reaction to the original deviance limits or totally restricts the opportunities for persons to engage in legitimate activities, their exclusion results in 'deviancy amplification'; as reactions become more severe, the deviance and crime also becomes more severe (Mankoff, 1971; Young, 1971).

Matsueda and colleagues (Matsueda, 1992, 2001; Heimer and Matsueda, 1994) also point out the important role played by informal labeling. They say that labeling comes not only from official control agents such as the police and the courts, but also from unofficial ones such as parents, peers and teachers. They argue that since 'the self is a reflection of appraisals made by significant others', such informal negative labeling 'would influence future delinquency through the role-taking process' (Matsueda, 2001, p. 235). Overall, then, Matsueda's contribution suggests that the informal labeling process starts much earlier than the formal, and may continue in tandem with it.

Organization of this Volume

This volume draws on essays selected to bring together the theoretical roots of the past with current theory in the social constructionist tradition. Stuart Henry's overview (Chapter 1) situates present-day social constructionist theory in the theoretical tradition and philosophical foundation of the perspective. He begins with a consideration of the concept of social constructionism in the context of an assessment of its impact, reach and significance. He then examines the roots of the perspective in Husserl's transcendental phenomenology and his exposure of the taken-for-granted assumptions underpinning the natural attitude of humans. Henry then goes on to explore Schutz's phenomenology of the social world and humans' experience of mundane existence as both objective and subjective experiences, which they share inter-subjectively, and in projecting purposeful action. Schutz's work led in two directions: the first was to Berger and Luckmann's *Social Construction of Reality* and the three interrelated processes of externalization, objectification and internalization; the second was to Harold Garfinkel's studies of how social order, institutions and social structure emerged from people's shared mundane interactions in everyday life, which he referred to as ethnomethodology. Parallel to Schutz's work, Henry's overview then explores the symbolic interactionist tradition of George Herbert Mead and Herbert Blumer and their focus on the ways meaning emerges from social interaction. This is followed by a review of the labeling perspective of Howard Becker and Edwin Lemert, showing how social reaction to minor deviance can create deviant and criminal careers that can become ossified through stigmatization and institutionalization as illustrated by the work of Erving Goffman. The overview identifies ten core themes of the social constructionist perspective before distinguishing between three types of social constructionist theory: radical, contextual and postmodernist. From here the essay examines the way social constructionism has been applied to explain crime and deviance, and focuses particularly on the importance of claims-making, moral panics and crime as a social construction and the role of power in the construction process. Henry concludes with an evaluation of the social constructionist perspective.

This book is divided into two parts, the contents of which are designed to reflect Henry's overview. Part I 'Social Constructionism, Criminology and Criminal Justice' contains sections on the theoretical roots of social constructionism in Alfred Schutz, on the social construction of social problems, on the mass media's role in defining crime, on the process of moral panics and on the social construction of criminal justice. Part II 'Social Constructionist Related Theories' includes sections on symbolic interactionism and labeling theory, ethnomethodology, and phenomenology, postmodernism and constitutive criminology.

Social Constructionism, Criminology and Criminal Justice

Theoretical Roots: Alfred Schutz

The section on theoretical roots contains two essays that both review and assess Schutz's contribution to the field. Chapter 2, by one of Schutz's students and his biographer, Helmut R. Wagner, is entitled 'Phenomenology and Contemporary Sociological Theory: The Contribution of Alfred Schutz' and explores the intersection of Husserl's philosophy and Weber's sociology of understanding (*vestehen*), and particularly Schutz's contribution to theorizing about social reality. For Schutz, says Wagner, this reality is in the minds of humans, but humans who are consciously aware of themselves in the realm of the social – that is, other humans, captured by his concept of 'intersubjectivity', expressing that the 'Individual and the Social are but two sides of the same process' (p. 14). Wagner explains Schutz's adoption of Husserl's concept of 'the life world' based on an interactively contingent and emerging set of biographical experiences that evolve as humans engage in purposeful situational projects together. In such projects humans draw on their stock of knowledge from past experiences and relate to others through knowledge of the types of people they are, or what Schutz calls typifications. Beyond situational typifications of the 'here and now' are cultural typifications that allow humans to connect to wider typifications that are part of the societal network in which they are embedded, if not directly connected, thus experiencing the total life world as a structured system of relations, including typifications of collective entities. Wagner points out that Schutz's contribution was to lay the foundation of society as a dynamic social system that emerges in and through social interaction and that is subject to changing interpretations of meaning and cognitive orientations to others. Social reality is nothing but the practical reality of the everyday world as perceived and interpreted by its subjects. Wagner goes on to assess Schutz's contributions to the foundation of sociology, sociological theory and methodology, and to establishing the roots of interpretive sociology.

Chapter 3, 'Alfred Schutz's Influence on American Sociologists and Sociology', by George Psathas, examines the significance of the contributions of three of Schutz's students: Helmut R. Wagner, Peter Berger and Harold Garfinkel. Psathas focuses on Berger's sociology of knowledge and Garfinkel's foundation of ethnomethodology, showing how these stemmed from Schutz's sociological philosophy. After reflecting on why Schutz's ideas were not widespread during his lifetime (he died in 1959), Psathas situates the direct influence of Schutz's work in the context of the 1960s when it was being discovered, translated and becoming made widely available. This was a period in which not only were society's established policy, institutions and practices being challenged, but so too were established orthodoxies in sociology that had traditionally presented functional analyses of structured and macro-forces that had excluded humans' creative and interpretive processes. Schutz's body of theory, rendered into new directions by his former students, made a considerable impact on the emerging students of those times as it resonated with their social reality and importantly gave them the philosophical and sociological tools to make a difference. In considering the influence on Helmut Wagner Psathas shows how he not only became Schutzian but also became Schutz's biographer, and he credits Wagner for presenting Schutz's ideas in a clear and systematic way. He then reviews Schutz's student Peter Berger and his sociology of knowledge, especially his teaming up with another of Schutz's students, Thomas Luckmann, to produce the 1966 classic *Social Construction of Reality*. This work marked a revolution in the sociology of knowledge that not only challenged the previous orthodoxy, but also provided the foundation for the application of social constructionst theory to studies of social problems, crime and deviant behavior. Psathas finally considers the work of Schutz's student Harold Garfinkel, who drew particularly on commonsense assumptions, the natural attitude and everyday life in his founding of the field of ethnomethodology.

Constructing Social Problems

The section on the social construction of social problems focuses on one dimension of the application of social constructionist theory and contains two essays. Chapter 4, Malcolm Spector and John I. Kitsuse's 'Social Problems: A Re-formulation', is foundational in introducing social constructionism to the field of social problems theory. Spector and Kitsuse reject as deficient both the functionalist and the conflict approaches to social problems analysis prevailing at the time. Instead they redefine social problems as '*the activities of groups making assertions of grievances and claims to organizations, agencies, and institutions, about some putative conditions* ... as a problem and asserting the need for eradicating, ameliorating, or otherwise changing that condition' (p. 146; emphasis in original). They describe a four stage natural history of the problem-making process, starting with the idea that social problems are perceived by social audiences as offensive, harmful or undesirable to some or many of the population, who make claims to that effect thus making the problem into a public issue.

In the second stage, official agents from public agencies react to these claims and demands. Third, the claims-makers respond critically to the efforts by official agencies to deal with the problem and challenge their procedures as being inadequate. Finally, in the fourth stage, the offended groups develop an alternative set of counter institutions, and alternative ways to respond to the problem.

In Chapter 5, 'Social Problems Theory: The Constructionist View', Joseph W. Schneider provides an overview and assessment of the social constructionist perspective some fifteen years after it had become the dominant paradigm in social problems analysis. He reviews the founding theoretical statements and research in the tradition around problem control and prevention, and the creation, ownership and processing of social problems, and he extends the constructionist view to consider how bureaucratic organizations and the law become part of the process that constructs a problem. He focuses, for example, on how deviant behavior has become 'medicalized', which is the process whereby rule violation is increasingly seen as having a biological or medically treatable root. The involvement of scientific/medical agencies removes from consideration that there is any problem with the social system or that the deviance may be a critique of that system; medicalization renders the problem individualized and non-political. Schneider considers the role of the media in the problem construction process. Finally he considers a range of criticisms of the perspective, including its seeming abandonment of consideration of 'objective conditions' in favor of a view that these conditions are the emergent social reality itself constituted by the claims, but contradictorily acknowledging that these conditions or social context generate alternative definitions of the problem. Overall Schneider provides a thorough evaluation of both the potential and the pitfalls of the social constructionist approach.

Constructing Crime: The Media's Role in Defining Crime

The section on the mass media's role in defining crime contains two essays. Vincent F. Sacco's 'Media Constructions of Crime' (Chapter 6) argues that while the media's role in influencing the fear of crime is important, the ways that the media is organized, and the way that the news gathering process is structured, have a major impact on the way crime is seen as an urgent problem, what kind of problem it is and how the crime problem should be resolved. He argues that the way news gathering excludes some sources and includes others has ideological implications for the way we think about crime and its solution. He documents how crime problems are screened through a series of filters, including law enforcement, advocacy claims, culturally resonant news themes and conventions and requirements of commercial media, before they become public issues. The result is not so much a conspiracy but a confluence of practices that lead to a consensus about what is and is not crime and what to do about it that excludes alternative approaches.

In Chapter 7, 'The Media's Role in the Definition of Crime', Ray Surette and Charles Otto argue that that the media plays a powerful role in the process of defining crime and is the primary engine in criminalization and decriminalization. They explore the movement of behaviors defined as deviant to behaviors defined as criminal and the role that the contemporary mass media plays in this definitional migration. They point out that work on the definition of crime has rarely considered the role of the media. However, the interests of the politically powerful are also seen as related to the commercial interests of the mass media and the coalescing of the media, business and politically powerful interests in turn contains and limits the definitional social construction of crime. Surette and Otto argue that the predatory crime featured in popular culture and the true crime genre 'simply crowds out other candidates from public consideration' (p. 119). They use the social constructionist framework to explain the effects of the media on the changing definition of crime, locating the media as the distributor of knowledge about crime that filters out claims and claims-makers, excluding those of the powerless in favor of those of the powerful. The media's visibility-raising energy though its crime image constructions is dominant in the definition of crime because these constructions are all most people experience.

Constructing Crime: Moral Panics

The section on the social construction of crime through moral panics contains three essays. In Chapter 8, '"The Ice Age": The Social Construction of a Drug Panic', Philip Jenkins uses the 1990 moral panic around 'ice' or smokable methamphetamine (crystal meth) to launch a study of the history of a drug panic from its origins to its eclipse. Jenkins emphasizes political divisions in Hawaii as playing a key role in the panic. He argues that this illustrates both how local problems are elevated to public issues and the limitations of this process. His essay explores the rhetorical devices used to create a sense of fear around the supposed danger, and the reasons why such an apparently plausible danger failed to gain more public attention or credence. This essay anticipates several of the arguments in Jenkins' 1999 book *Synthetic Panics: The Symbolic Politics of Designer Drugs* in which he states, 'the intensity of cultural reactions to a particular chemical does not necessarily reflect the actual social harm or individual damage it causes' (1999, pp. 2–3).

In 'Another Look at Moral Panics: The Case of Satanic Day Care Centers' (Chapter 9), Mary deYoung uses the moral panic of claims about satanic practices in US day care centers in the period 1983–91 to illustrate the structure and process of a moral panic. She starts by providing an overview of the concept of moral panic and its place in the sociology of deviance. Then she uses data from a sample of day care centers that were subject to charges of satanic ritual child abuse from 1983 through 1991 'to illustrate salient points about its timing, trigger and target, content, spread, and denouement' (p. 157). She traces the emergence, rapid rise and eventual demise of the panic which produced a litany of casualties among the communities involved and among the professional child care workers whose careers were destroyed. DeYoung then uses her analysis of the satanic day care moral panic to provide a critique of contemporary moral panic theory. She argues that the theory needs to be revised in order to explain 'empowered folk devils, pluralistic social reactions, and symbolic and contradictory social ends' (p. 157).

Sean P. Hier, Dan Lett, Kevin Walby and André Smith's 'Beyond Folk Devil Resistance: Linking Moral Panic and Moral Regulation' (Chapter 10) re-conceptualizes moral panic theory by linking it to criminological theories of moral regulation. The authors argue 'that moral panics should be conceptualized as volatile expressions of long-term moral regulation processes' (p. 179). They illustrate their argument by examining the claims-making activities of the British media about British youth who wear 'hoodies' in public places, examining what happened after a shopping mall banned hoodies and effectively excluded youth who wore them. The contribution of this analysis is to move moral panic theory from the view that it is a cyclical exceptional part of the deviance-making process, to show how it is a normal, rational, routine part of everyday life that is bound up with, and often resonates with, the state's moral regulation of society. The authors argue that while moral panic theory is correct in demonstrating that those demonized as folk devils engage in resistance to primary labels and struggle to redefine their negative labeling, this resistance is precarious and easily undermined. This is because the primary labelers are reinforced by the power of state-level moral regulation. Thus Hier and colleagues argue that 'moral panics represent episodes of contestation and negotiation that emerge from, and contribute to or reinforce broader processes of moral regulation' (p. 180).

Constructing Criminal Justice

There are three essays in the section on the social construction of criminal justice, each of which relates to aspects of the argument of Hier et al. in Chapter 10. Nicole Hahn Rafter's 'The Social Construction of Crime and Crime Control' (Chapter 11) examines the extent to which the field of academic study of criminal justice was impacted by the social constructionist theoretical position at the end of the twentieth century. She traces the constructionist tradition within criminal justice by examining work in 'social histories of criminal justice practice and theory; critical criminology; research on the victimization of females; and feminist theory about the contribution of criminal justice to understandings of gender' (p. 197).

In Chapter 12, 'Inventing Criminal Justice: Myth and Social Construction', Victor E. Kappeler argues that images of the media in popular culture 'are constructed mystifications of the reality of criminal justice in U.S. society' (p. 211). He describes a litany of examples of aspects of the real practices of criminal justice, such as prosecutors and defense attorneys bargaining to dispose of dockets of criminal cases, or the effects of prison on the children of those incarcerated. These realities and other omissions that sterilize the political and powerful interests operating within the criminal justice system are displaced by social actors and myths of the popular images: 'Criminal justice, like crime, is a social construction that shifts with intellectual perspective, political influence, social sentiment, cultural values, and the interests of powerful groups in society' (p. 212). Kappeler says that even the concept of the 'criminal justice system' produces a false sense of the reality, protection and comprehensiveness of criminal justice practices, and excludes alternative realties of social harm. In this essay Kappeler explores the multiple sources of the myths that produce cultural images of criminal justice, including parents, peers, governments and popular culture and the mass media. Government deploys statistics on certain kinds of crime, but not others, which feeds the media and this is enhanced through selected use of spokespeople using a crime control model rather than a crime causation model to disseminate 'a highly selective ideology of crime and justice … a hybrid product of government ideology and media distortion' (pp. 213–14). Kappeler then explores myths about criminal justice that mask its inherent contradictions and which tend to individualize crime, rather than see it as a systemic problem. These myths gain strength as they are retold and melt into our taken-for-granted knowledge. They are connected to broader cultural ideas about human behavior as being a matter of individual rational free choice and the myth that the law emanates from divine sources to protect society from individual evil and excess through its ability to deter offenders. Kappeler concludes by assessing the costs of the myths of criminal justice to a society that fails to attribute blame for the social conditions that cause harm, and fails to allow itself to imagine how society and its justice system could function differently.

Chapter 13, 'The Columbine Effect and School Antiviolence Policy', by Glenn W. Muschert and Anthony A. Peguero, examines how the media portrayal of an incidence of horrific crime, in this case the rampage school shootings, can generate fear and heightened emotions around social control policies, in this case antiviolence policies in schools. The Columbine Effect refers to the development of a set of policy responses, particularly those of zero tolerance, surveillance and the use of access policing, police presence and searches, that are designed to prevent or deal with the extreme case of an 'active shooter', as if this was a common rather than an extremely rare occurrence. The result of building justice policy in response to the extreme case is that the antiviolence policies themselves impose harm on all schools by subjecting them to measures that undermine trust and the educational process. Muschert and Peguero review six levels of antiviolence policies: crime prevention through environmental design, zero tolerance, anti-bullying programming, emergency management planning, peer mediation and school climate programming. Their analysis assesses the level of violence and efficacy of each type of policy. They then discuss the unintended consequences of school antiviolence policies that have been developed in the face of exceptional cases, such as rampage shootings, and show how these can produce negative and contradictory effects.

Social Constructionist Related Theories

Symbolic Interactionism and Labeling Theory

The first section in Part II, on symbolic interactionism and labeling theory, contains three essays. Kai T. Erikson's classic 1962 essay 'Notes on the Sociology of Deviance (Chapter 14) begins by questioning the prevailing Mertonian view of deviance as dysfunction caused by a normal response to some sociological strain in the social system, saying that a broader perspective is necessary. Erikson argues for a historical process approach that explains not only the origin of deviance but its persistence, social organization and social patterning. He locates the quality of deviance not in the quality inherent in the act but in the properties imposed on certain forms of behavior by the audience observing them. This became a cornerstone of the subsequent labeling theory, and reappears in Becker's *Outsiders* (1963). Erikson suggests shifting sociological attention to the community social screen that, for some people, filters out their deviant behavior as something significant compared to all the other conventional behaviors they also engage in. He asks how community members decide which behaviors are deviant and why they set up special institutions to deal with those who enact them. Erikson then suggests, like Durkheim, that what is selected as deviance has to do with what a social system decides is important to maintain its own boundaries. Moreover, he argues that what this is varies as it organically changes to reflect the accumulation of decisions over time, and it is through portrayals in the media of such boundary infractions and their consequences that society is able to inform its members about what norms it values: 'morality and immorality meet at the public scaffold and it is during this meeting that the community declares where the line between them should be drawn' (p. 258). The deviant is a reminder of the dangers that seem to threaten the security of the human group, providing occasion to distinguish between in-group and out-group. Thus deviance serves to preserve rather than disrupt stability. Indeed,

Erikson suggests that society may even seek out or recruit deviants in order to perform this function and observes that 'deviant activities often seem to derive support from the very agencies designed to suppress them' (p. 259). Why else, he asks, would we cluster deviants together in tightly segregated groups so that they become alienated and can learn skills, attitudes from each other. Erikson then discusses the negative effects and the stages of status degradation ceremonies performed by social control agencies and, anticipating subsequent developments in rehabilitative shaming and restorative justice, talks about the absence of the reversal of such ceremonies and why this persists in US society but not in others.

Leroy C. Gould, Gary Kleck and Marc Gertz, in 'Crime as Social Interaction' (Chapter 15), argue that rather than crime being an isolated event it requires us to examine the interrelationship of several factors that allow crime to occur as events. The issues they address are what comes together to make crime events or crime episodes. Even though they do not highlight the media, it is clear that their interactionist framework affords a role for the media, especially in the symbolic realm and the 'crime stories' that constitute crime episodes. They view crimes episodes as the outcome of interactions among three distinct elements: offenders, agents of social control and crime targets. The term 'criminal episode' includes 'various overt and symbolic interactions among these actors that precede and follow the event itself' (p. 265).

In his comprehensive overview essay 'The Labelling Perspective Forty Years On' (Chapter 16) Ken Plummer summarizes and assesses the contributions of labeling theory. As he states, labeling theory developed in the 1960s, reached its heyday in the 1970s 'and thereafter has more or less gently faded away' (p. 277). In this personal and reflective essay Plummer reviews its history, examines the current status of labeling theory and suggests some links to generational theory. He starts by pointing to the limits of its narrow version with its excessive focus on the career development of the labeled deviant and suggests that labeling theory has a fourfold problematic oriented to the social reactions to deviance: 1) What are the characteristics of labels, their variations and forms? 2) What are the sources of labels, both societal and personal? 3) How, and under what conditions, do labels get applied? 4) What are the consequences of labeling? Plummer, using his 1979 review essay as frame, says that by the time of its writing the critical criminological perspective of Taylor, Walton and Young (1973, 1975) had replaced labeling theory. After lamenting its loss, even though somewhat prematurely given its transformation into social constructionism, and after locating it as a generational theory locked into a particular generation's attempt to make sense of deviance and social control, Plummer moves to a review of contemporary developments. Here he recognizes that classic labeling theory has become infused into several other developments. Indeed he identifies and illustrates twelve such dispersals: moral panic theory; sociology of everyday crime and dramatization; studies of public attitudes to crime; research on discourses around crime; shaming and stigmatization studies; studies of stereotype; construction of social problems; social exclusion theory; crime, media and culture; cultural criminology; cultures of control and their impact; queer theory and postmodernism. He concludes that labeling theory brings an important and abiding set of concerns for sociologists and criminologists and here he outlines a preliminary number of issues where we can see how labeling theory's continuing problematic and questions remain central to understanding the phenomenon.

Ethnomethodology

The section on ethnomethodology contains three essays. It opens with Harold Garfinkel's classic essay 'Conditions of Successful Degradation Ceremonies' (Chapter 17) which provides an analysis of a ritual event – the moral degradation ceremony as an expression of society's condemnation of those designated as deviant. Degradation ceremonies reflect the moral indignation of a community and, as Durkheim recognized, they reinforce group identity and promote social integration. In the process, the public identity of the rule violator is transformed into something less than it was. The process of status transformation involves a series of stages that separates the person engaged in deviant activities from their conventional status by highlighting their negative status, and reducing their status in the eyes of the community.

In Chapter 18, 'Ethnomethodology and Criminology: The Social Production of Crime and the Criminal', Stephen J. Pfohl considers the theoretical, methodological and empirical contributions of ethnomethodology to criminology. He contrasts ethnomethodology with labeling theory and suggests connection with critical criminology. Consistent with the social constructionist tradition, Pfohl suggests that social reality is a product of social interaction. There is no reality in the interpretation of everyday life. Pfohl notes that ethnomethodology has 1) analyzed the uncritical use of official statistics on crime and deviance as accurately reflecting crime; 2) analyzed conceptions of what is criminal or deviant as historically specific, and 3) aided researchers in approximating objectivity. Pfohl argues that the ethnomethodological perspective is more radically interpretive than labeling theory because it is an analysis of the success of labeling. He argues that ethnomethodology discards the normativity in labeling theory. However, Pfohl acknowledges that ethnomethodology has ignored problems of power, self-identity and history.

Robert O. Keel's 'Ethnomethodological Perspective (on Crime and Deviance)' (Chapter 19) provides an encyclopedic overview of the perspective. He starts by asserting that there is confusion that lumps ethnomethodology with a variety of other perspectives but that ethnomethodology distinguishes itself because it is a study of how order emerges as a practical accomplishment of the shared experience of members of particular societies: 'This focus on order as a practical accomplishment of the everyday interactions of members of a group produces ethnomethodology's distinctive perspective on deviance in comparison to normative sociologies' (p. 317). Societal members ongoingly and interactively produce a sense of order for their world and deviance is a negotiated reality whose accomplishment contributes to that sense of order. Keel explores the basis of ethnomethodology in Schutz's sociological phenomenology by examining the concepts of intersubjectivity, common stocks of knowledge, shared typifications and recipes for accomplishing tasks. Shared understandings are used to understand our world and order our experience. Rather than a shared sense of deviance members have a shared sense of methods that are the interpretive procedures for making sense of others' behavior and it is through deploying these that deviance and order are accomplished. Drawing on the work of Stephen Pfohl (1994), Keel then proceeds to analyze the range of interrelated processes including reflexivity, indexicality, retrospective interpretation, rules of consistency and economy, and documentary interpretation. He concludes that 'deviance and the deviant do not exist independently of the social construction of meaning centered in the situational context of everyday life' (p. 320), which the social processes of interpretation, typifications and negotiation elucidate.

Phenomenology, Postmodernism and Constitutive Criminology

The final section, which considers phenomenology, postmodernism and constitutive criminology, contains two essays. Chapter 20 is a conversation between two leading theorists of this perspective, Bruce Arrigo and David Polizzi, which explores the relationship between phenomenology and postmodernism in the context of commenting on the underlying philosophical foundation of an essay by Arrigo and Williams entitled 'Existentialism and the Criminology of the Shadow' (2009). Their exchange first examines Eric Fromm's Freudian/Marxist perspective and then turns to a brief discussion of postmodernists Foucault, Derrida and Lacan in order to assess their positions on language and subjectivity. Polizzi and Arrigo then develop a general critique of the postmodern position relative to phenomenology, reviewing the work of Husserl, Heidegger and Merleau-Ponty. It is important to note that the overarching conversational concern is with the underlying philosophical foundation of the Arrigo and Williams (2009) essay. It represents a significant departure from those matters noticeably featured in criminology proper and exhaustively debated by its strident positivist adherents. The exchange takes us back to the philosophical roots of this perspective in exploring the ontological, epistemological issues underpinning this approach and by contrast the absence of these in mainstream criminology.

Stuart Henry and Dragan Milovanovic's 'Constitutive Criminology: Origins, Core Concepts, and Evaluation' (Chapter 21) clarifies the core concepts of their postmodernist theory, situating it in the context of its intellectual roots in a number of critical social theories, including Marxism and semiotics, and postmodernist, as well as critical race theory and topology. The article also reviews a variety of questions and criticisms that have been leveled at the theory in the twenty-five discussions it had received in the literature nine years after first being published. Henry and Milovanovic address constitutive criminology's core concepts: the discursive coproduction of crime, rejection of the idea that crime and offenders can be separated from social processes and the idea that constitutive criminology 'seeks to examine the relations that coproduce crime, as well as ways to intervene in that coproduction to reduce the harms that are its ongoing outcome' (p. 359). The constitutive approach furthers the postmodernist focus on knowledge as a political and subjective category and argues for the need to apply the deconstruction of discourse to crime. It also affirms the idea of applying 'replacement discourse' to address less harmful practices. Constitutive criminology is founded on the social constructionist idea that 'humans are responsible for actively creating their world with others' (p. 360) and analyzes the coproduction of crime in the relationships of individuals and society. In Henry and Milovanovic's conception crime is redefined as 'the power to deny others their ability to make a difference' (p. 361) and this definition applies to constitutive criminologists' interests in crimes of reduction and crimes of repression. Crime is also seen as a discursive construction. Endemic to this understanding is the concept that the criminal justice system is part of the problem of crime, not its solution. The authors also look at the reception of constitutive criminology by academic criminology. One critique of the theory is the lack of explicit research conducted in the area. Additionally, some critics have charged that the prose of constitutive criminology is excessively complex, which the authors express is the result of attempts to categorize the theory using modernist discursive and conceptual frames of reference. In terms of criticisms related to its integration, the authors argue for more integrative understandings of criminology and a lessening of the urge to understand theory in essentialized, separated and rigorous disciplinary senses. Further responding to critics who charge that the theory, due to its emphasis on social construction and discourse, sees crime as unreal, Henry and Milovanovic argue that strategic policy outcomes are a necessity. Included in their discussion are replacement discourse, reconstruction and dissipative structures.

Conclusions

Overall, then this volume captures the social constructionist, interactionist and ethnomethodological roots and traditions that form a dynamic theory of human action and its deviant and criminological outcomes. It is perhaps instructive to conclude by contrasting Plummer's early assessment of the field (1979) with where we are today. When first formulated in the 1960s labeling theory was seen as a radical approach not least because of its irreverence towards the system and established knowledge at a time when longstanding institutions and established knowledge were being challenged by emerging social movements, such as the women's movement, the civil rights movement and the anti-war movement. Yet, says Plummer (1979), by the late 1960s it had been co-opted into the mainstream and had become the theory of deviance, if not of criminology. However, between 1970 and 1975 there was, according to Plummer, a 'dethroning of its dominant position' such that 'in just ten years labeling theory has moved from being the radical critique of established orthodoxies to being the harbinger of new orthodoxies to be criticized' (1979, p. 85). In contrast, the social constructionist version of the perspective has not only survived but has become one of the transcendent theoretical perspectives of our time. As Stuart Henry notes in the following overview (Chapter 1), social constructionism has appeared in sociology, psychology, psychotherapy, women's studies, queer studies, the history and philosophy of science, narrative philosophy, literary theory and postmodernism, among others, and has even become part of popular culture; though the same cannot be said for its more esoteric ethnomethodological stepchild.

References

Arrigo, Bruce A. and Williams, Christopher R. (2009), 'Existentialism and the Criminology of the Shadow', in R. Lippens and D. Crewe (eds), *Existentialist Criminology*, Abingdon and New York: Routledge-Cavendish, pp. 222–48.

Bartusch, Dawn Jeglum and Matsueda, Ross L. (1996), 'Gender, Reflected Appraisals, and Labeling: A Cross-Group Test of an Interactionist Theory of Delinquency', *Social Forces*, **75**, pp. 145–77.

Becker, Howard S. (1963), *Outsiders: Studies in the Sociology of Deviance*, New York: The Free Press.

Berger, Peter and Luckmann, Thomas (1966), *The Social Construction of Reality*, New York: Doubleday.

Blumer, Herbert (1969), *Symbolic Interactionism: Perspective and Method*, Englewood Cliffs, NJ: Prentice-Hall.

Cohen, Stanley (1972), *Folk Devils and Moral Panics: The Creation of the Mods and Rockers*, St. Albans: Paladin Press.

Einstadter, Werner J. and Stuart, Henry (2006), *Criminological Theory: An Analysis of its Underlying Assumptions*, Lanham, MD: Rowman & Littlefield.

Goffman, Erving (1963), *Stigma: Notes on the Management of Spoiled Identity*, Englewood Cliffs, NJ: Prentice-Hall.

Goode, Erich and Ben-Yehuda, Nachman (1994), *Moral Panics: The Social Construction of Deviance*, Oxford: Wiley-Blackwell.

Heimer, Karen (1996), 'Gender Interaction and Delinquency: Testing a Theory of Differential Social Control', *Social Psychology Quarterly*, **59**, pp. 39–61.

Heimer, Karen and Matsueda, Ross L. (1994), 'Role Taking, Role Commitment and Delinquency: A Theory of Differential Social Control', *American Sociological Review*, **59**, pp. 365–90.

Jenkins, Philip (1999), *Synthetic Panics: The Symbolic Politics of Designer Drugs*, New York: New York University Press.

Knorr-Cetina, Karin (1981), 'Introduction: The Micro-sociological Challenge of Macro-sociology: Toward a Reconstruction of Social Theory and Methodology', in Karin Knorr-Cetina and Aaron Cicourel (eds), *Advances in Social Theory and Methodology: Toward an Integration of Macro- and Micro-sociologies*, London: Routledge & Kegan Paul, pp. 1–47.

Lemert, Edwin M. (1951), *Social Pathology*, New York: McGraw-Hill.

Lofland, John H. (1969), *Deviance and Identity*, Englewood Cliffs, NJ: Prentice-Hall.

Mankoff, Milton (1971), 'Societal Reaction and Career Deviance: A Critical Analysis', *Sociological Quarterly*, **12**, pp. 204–18.

Matsueda, Ross L. (1992), 'Reflected Appraisals, Parental Labeling, and Delinquency: Specifying a Symbolic Interactionist Theory', *American Journal of Sociology*, **97**, pp. 1577–611.

Matsueda, Ross L. (2001), 'Labeling Theory: Historical Roots, Implications and Recent Developments', in Raymond Paternoster and Ronet Bachman (eds), *Explaining Criminals and Crime*, Los Angeles: Roxbury Press, pp. 223–41.

Matsueda, Ross L. and Heimer, Karen (1997), 'A Symbolic Interactionist Theory of Role Transitions, Role Commitments and Delinquency', in Terence P. Thornberry (ed.), *Developmental Theories of Crime and Delinquency*, Advances in Criminological Theory 7, New Brunswick, NJ: Transaction, pp. 163–214.

Mead, George Herbert (1934), *Mind, Self and Society*, ed. C.W. Morris, Chicago: University of Chicago Press.

Pfohl, Stephen J. (1994), *Images of Deviance and Social Control: A Sociological History*, New York: McGraw-Hill.

Plummer, Ken (1979), 'Misunderstanding Labelling Perspectives', in David Downs and Paul Rock (eds), *Deviant Interpretations*, Oxford: Martin Robertson, pp. 85–121.

Schutz, A. (1932 [1967]), *The Phenomenology of the Social World*, Evanston, IL: Northwestern University Press.

Taylor, Ian, Walton, Paul and Young, Jock (1973), *The New Criminology: For a Social Theory of Deviance*, London: Routledge & Kegan Paul.

Taylor, Ian, Walton, Paul and Young, Jock (eds) (1975), *Critical Criminology*, London: Routledge & Kegan Paul.

Young, Jock (1971), 'The Role of Police as Amplifiers of Deviancy, Negotiators of Reality and Translators of Fantasy', in Stan Cohen (ed.), *Images of Deviance*, Harmondsworth: Penguin.

[1]

Social Construction of Crime

Stuart Henry
San Diego State University

According to social constructionists, what counts as crime varies depending on who is defining it: "There are no purely objective definitions; all definitions are value laden and biased to some degree," and what is defined as crime by law "is somewhat arbitrary, and represents a highly selective process" (Barak, 1998, p. 21). This social constructionist challenge to the fact of crime as defined by law is rooted in a history of critical theory.

The Concept of Social Construction

Social construction is a theoretical position that cuts across a number of disciplinary and interdisciplinary fields, including sociology, psychology, psychotherapy, women's studies, queer studies, the history and philosophy of science, narrative philosophy, and literary theory, among others. As Stam (2001) noted, social constructionism has not only permeated many fields of study but also has become part of popular culture (for overviews, see Burr, 1995; Gergen, 1999; Potter, 1996). Advocates of social constructionism argue that the social world has an existence only, or largely, through humans' routine interaction. By identifying some features of social life as significant, distinguishing those features from others, and acting as though they have a real, concrete existence, humans create social reality.

In its extreme form, social constructionism draws on the idealist/nominalist philosophical tradition that social reality has no independent existence outside the human mind. Humans interpret the world and make summary representations (images in their mind) that they believe reflect an underlying reality; at issue is whether there is any independent objective existence to the reality that these representations appear to reflect. Most social constructionists, however, are not total relativists but are more moderate. They believe that some fundamental reality exists; they also believe that even social constructions, once created, have a degree of reality in that they recognize that if humans define situations as real, then they are real in their consequences. Therefore, if we categorize behavior, events, and experiences as similar, and name or label them in specific ways, they appear before us as representations of object-like realities with real effects that can be experienced positively or negatively.

Although we create the realities that shape our social world, and are impacted by the actions of those who put energy into sustaining them as realities, we are also capable of changing these realities by recognizing our role in their construction. Crime is seen as one such social reality, one that we collectively construct and, by implication, can collectively deconstruct and replace with a less harmful reality.

There are different versions of social constructionist theory, depending on the extent to which theorists attribute independence to reality existing outside of the human mind and whether this attributed reality is seen a result of personal cognitive meaning creation (*personal construct theory*) or the result of shared symbolic social processes (*social constructionist theory*). There are also differences in regard to whether theorists believe that social reality can be changed depending on how far they believe humans can free themselves from their own social constructions.

Definition and Significance

From the social constructionist perspective, *crime* is a classification of behavior defined by individuals with the power and authority to make laws that identify some behavior as offensive and render its perpetrators subject to punishment. In Western societies, legislators and courts, enforced by state agencies, have the power and authority to define crime and administer punishment. What behavior they define as crime reflects both their own values and interests and the collective norms and values of the society, or at least the most vociferous segments of it.

The extent to which the norms and values of a society represent those of the whole society or some universal human values is questionable, because what counts as crime in different societies varies in content, with a few exceptions. However, as anthropologists Alfred Kroeber and Clyde Kluckhohn (1952) pointed out in their study of many cultures, there do seem to be some universals. Kroeber and Kluckhohn claimed that among its own in-group members, no culture could be found that accepts (a) indiscriminate lying, suggesting that all societies value honesty; (b) stealing, such that all societies value rights of property ownership; (c) violence and suffering, suggesting that all societies value peaceful coexistence; and (d) incest, such that all societies restrict sexual intercourse to nonfamilial adults.

However, what counts as acceptable or unacceptable behavior in these categories varies, not only culturally and subculturally but also historically. For example, in Western industrial societies, in spite of its enormous economic cost to victims, perpetrators of corporate and white-collar crimes were, until the late 20th century, rarely subject to punishment, because the crimes of business, and white-collar crimes in particular, were not considered "real" crimes, even though they typically produced multiple victims who each suffered economic losses of up to 100 times the cost of street offenses (the typical average robbery in the United States nets $1,200, and the typical bank robbery loss is $4,300, compared with the typical embezzlement, which is $17,000, and the typical corporate crime, which ranges from $5 million–$300 million). Whereas a bank robber typically receives a 20- to 30-year prison sentence, a bank embezzler can receive as little as 5 years' probation. The influence of juries in deciding whether to indict or convict a person for crime can also reflect local rather than national values, as in the case of a Texas man who shot to death burglars in his next-door neighbor's house who was not indicted by the grand jury for homicide.

Moreover, the ability of some interest groups to mobilize mass communications to influence the values of others through moral crusades targeted toward certain behaviors, such as drug use, homosexual relations, assisted suicide, smoking in public places, and so on, can significantly affect what kinds of behavior are defined as acceptable or criminal. This stands in comparison to the human attempt to create a moral social order in which some behavior is defined as acceptable and other behavior is defined as unacceptable or deviant, through the creation of rules that ban some behaviors and subject rule violators to sanctions. Whereas deviance is taken to be a violation of social norms, crime is seen as a violation of criminal law, and whereas deviance is behavior perceived as different and negatively evaluated as threatening and morally offensive, crime is seen as harmful—physically, economically, socially, and psychologically—resulting in victims who suffer some loss, reduction, and repression of what they were prior to the offense (Henry & Lanier, 2001; Henry & Milovanovic, 1996).

However, like the social reaction to deviance, the criminal justice reaction to crime can result in labeling effects that amplify the significance of the original law violation. This process can entrench the delinquent in a career trajectory that leads to greater rather than less involvement in the offensive behavior, not least because options to engage in nonoffensive behaviors are closed off, while attributes, qualities, and skills in relation to the law violating behavior are enhanced.

Thus, the social construction of crime, through its amplification by social reaction, can produce the real consequence of *career criminals* as the offender becomes engulfed in coping with the stigma of a criminal identity that ultimately might lead to his or her embrace of that socially constructed identity through identity transformation. No longer are these just persons who broke the law by, for example, being tempted to shoplift; instead they have become "shoplifters." Clearly the significance of the social construction process can be that more crime, rather than less, is the outcome of the attempts to control the original offensive behavior.

The actions of moral entrepreneurs to whip up public sentiment through the mass media into what has been called a *moral panic* about certain offenses is capable of producing the appearance of "crime waves" and can demonize certain categories of people. Social constructionists have focused on the practices of criminal justice agencies and moral entrepreneurs in creating moral panics through claims about the threats posed by some groups to the population as a whole.

A consequence of the social construction of crime and the creation of moral panics is that a society's crime rate, in particular increases in certain types of crimes, can be viewed less as a consequence of a real increase in crime and more the effect of the amplification of a problem through its public discussion in the media. Furthermore, it can reflect increased public awareness of behaviors that are then defined as problematic, resulting in more reports of crimes to the police and more arrests of alleged offenders by the police. Thus, real rises and falls in crime may reflect a combination of the following: (a) actual increases in the activity, (b) the socially constructed fear of its presence, and (c) a willingness of authorities to reclassify other activities as potential crimes. Because of crime's socially constructed nature, real trends in crime are difficult to establish.

Historical and Theoretical Roots of Social Constructionist Theory

Husserl's Transcendental Phenomenology

The roots of social constructionism can be attributed to nominalist philosophy. Although the nominalist philosophical tradition can be traced back to the 11th century and can be found in the 18th-century philosophy of Immanuel Kant and the 19th-century philosophy of Friedrich Nietzsche, it is Edmund Husserl's 20th-century *transcendental phenomenology* that laid the foundation for social constructionist theory. Husserl combined insights from philosophy, mathematics, and early psychology. He developed a method for suspending, or "bracketing," what was taken for granted as objects in the natural attitude (a commonsense, mundane approach to the world) in order to see how these are constituted in the human consciousness. The *natural attitude* is the taken-for-granted assumption that objects have material-like qualities. Husserl's phenomenological inquiry revealed how our acting toward objects as though they are real constitutes them as real; their apparent material qualities are, in part, a result of the ways in which we act intentionally toward them as real.

Schutz's Sociological Phenomenology

Husserl's transcendental phenomenology was a major influence on the work of sociologist Alfred Schutz. In his *Phenomenology of the Social World* (1932/1967), Schutz integrated Husserl's phenomenology with Max Weber's sociology, in particular with Weber's concepts of interpretive understanding and ideal-type construction, which are generalized types of behavior. Schutz saw that in their day-to-day mundane existence in the social world, humans experience both an objective and subjective existence. Humans both take this world for granted as a reality yet also see it as shared with others intersubjectively, while also interpreting it differently, depending on their past experience. Because human action is purposive, based on human interpretation and shaped as a project by past biography and social position, a socially constructed shared experience by people having different experiences produces multiple views of social reality, which leads to a position of moral relativity.

Berger and Luckmann's Social Construction of Reality

In the 1960s, during a time when Western industrial societies were undergoing significant social and political change and when protest against establishment institutions was rampant, from anti–Vietnam war protests to civil rights and women's movement protests, a social climate emerged that resonated with the intellectual view that social structures and their institutions need not be what they had always been and that they could be changed. Peter Berger and Thomas Luckmann's (1966) classic book, *The Social Construction of Reality,* captured the historical moment of liberation from our self-made social order by building on the insights of Schutz. In this work, they showed that although society and its institutions appear to be real, having an independent and object-like existence, its reality is the outcome of a series of social processes through which humans interactively create institutionalized social phenomena but in the process lose sight of the fact that they created those phenomena. The resultant reification leaves the created social world appearing through types and patterns of behavior as an object-like entity, acting outside and independent of the humans who created it. Berger and Luckmann said that reification involves three interrelated processes: (1) externalization, (2) objectification, and (3) internalization. *Externalization* occurs through communication whereby people create categories that define and classify the events that they experience, eventually becoming patterns that are institutionalized, formalized, and codified to stand objectified apart from those who created them, who then develop "recipe knowledge" about them and how to relate to them. The process of *objectification* and explaining the existence of these object-like social entities serves to further legitimate their independent existence. The process of *internalization* occurs when knowledge about these social institutions and structures is communicated back to members of society, who embody it as part of their knowledge of social reality. Not only do humans lose sight of their role in the creation of social reality but, importantly, they also lose sight of their ability to change the world.

Garfinkel's Ethnomethodology

Harold Garfinkel's (1967) *Studies in Ethnomethodology* contributed to the development of social constructionist thinking in that, like Berger and Luckmann, Garfinkel and colleagues, such as Harvey Sacks, David Sudnow, Don Zimmerman, and Melvin Pollner, focused on how social order, social institutions, and social structure emerged from shared mundane interactions among ordinary people in their everyday lives. In defining their world and acting toward its boundaries through routine practices of interpretation, people create and negotiate categories of behavior that are deemed acceptable and categories that are unacceptable or deviant. Exploring the ways or the methods, rather than the shared meaning, by which this everyday interpretive process produces realities is the contribution made by ethnomethodology. For ethnomethodologists it is the routine practices (called *methods*) that people use to classify other people as deviants or offenders that are important in considering what is and what becomes a crime, rather than the content of the activities of people whose behavior is classified as deviant or criminal.

In studying humans in the process of coconstructing their world through conversation, language, making distinctions, and taken-for-granted assumptions, ethnomethodologists are engaged in a form of radical social constructionism (discussed further in a subsequent section of this chapter), although some scholars maintain that the two are theoretically different (Bogen & Lynch, 1993). It is important to note that ethnomethodologists do not assume the constructions that they study exist independently of the discourse used by humans interacting; neither do they exclude their own analysis from the constitutive process.

The Social Interactionism of Mead and Blumer

Whereas ethnomethodologists were concerned with the ways of interpretation was accomplished through routine practices, Herbert Blumer, a student of social psychologist George Herbert Mead and influenced by pragmatic philosopher John Dewey's ideas about human's interaction with the environment, had been working on developing an interactionist perspective. His *Symbolic Interactionism* (1969) demonstrated that, instead of being fixed to objective roles, statuses, and structures in an interrelated system, as functionalist theorists had argued, social meaning was created through interaction and subjective interpretation with others. Mead, in his 1934 work *Mind, Self and Society,* showed that human identity was the outcome of both people's own emergent sense of self, derived from their individualized self-concept he called the *I,* and an internalized sense of the social self he called the *me,* which was derived from generalized views that others held of them that they perceived through "taking the role of the other." Blumer (1969) argued that people act toward others and the world around them on the basis of the meaning that they attributed to people, events, and structures. The meanings were not fixed but negotiated through a social process of symbolic communication both with one's self and with others, during which items were named or labeled.

From the interactionist perspective, crime is defined as a social event, involving many players, actors, and agencies. Thus, crimes can be characterized the following way:

> [Crimes] involve not only the actions of individual offenders, but the actions of other persons as well. In particular, they involve the actions of such persons as victims, bystanders and witnesses, law enforcement officers, and members of political society at large. A crime, from this perspective, is a particular set of interactions among offender(s), crime target(s), agent(s) of social control and society. (Gould, Kleck, & Gertz, 1992, p. 4)

Labeling Perspective in the Sociology of Deviance

During this same period, there emerged a perspective on deviance, later applied to crime, that drew on these concepts of the social process of meaning construction through interaction and the routine ways these were accomplished. The fundamental idea was that what became designated as crime and deviance was, as Howard Becker (1963) argued, not a quality of an act a person commits but a quality of the reaction of the audience who interprets it as deviant or not. In other words, deviance was not just the result of actions by a human actor; it depended on the audience, who signified a behavior as an act of importance and judged the act positively or negatively, labeling it good or bad. Labeling theorists argued that whether an issue becomes a public harm and/or ultimately a crime depends on a group's ability to turn private concerns into public issues or their skills at moral entrepreneurship (Becker, 1963). Creating a public harm from a private issue involves identifying and signifying offensive behavior and then attempting to influence legislators to ban it officially. Becker argued that behavior that is unacceptable in society depends on what people first label unacceptable and whether they can successfully apply the label to those designated as offenders. For example, prior to the 1930s, smoking marijuana in the United States was generally acceptable. Intensive government agency efforts, in particular by the federal Bureau of Narcotics, demonized marijuana smokers as "dope fiends," a campaign that culminated in the passage of the Marihuana Tax Act of 1937. As a result, marijuana smoking was labeled unacceptable and illegal, and those who engaged in it were stigmatized as outsiders.

Edwin Lemert (1967) made a distinction between *primary deviance* and *secondary deviance,* arguing that many people engage in minor rule violations, but only some of those people are selected to be labeled as "problems." When this occurs repeatedly, people may internalize the definitions that others have of them and undergo an identity transformation, coming to view themselves as deviants. Lemert and others, such as Erving Goffman (1963), argued that the result of this labeling could be secondary deviance, such that people who were stigmatized by the original label now act deviant because this is part of their deviant identity.

In this sense then, deviance—and, ultimately, crime—is a social construction, first because of the original process of labeling people and second as a result of the amplification of those people's deviant behavior and the interactive effects of others' actions toward them. People become deviant or criminal as a result of the iterative process between their own actions and the reactions of others to them.

Core Features of Social Constructionism

As precursors to social constructionist thought, the ideas discussed in the preceding sections formed into a theoretical perspective that some consider transcendent as a perspective across disciplines, in particular of sociology, psychology, psychotherapy, and feminism. Ten core elements have been identified as being more or less shared by scholars who take a social constructionist perspective (Henry, 2007):

1. Because of the way it is negotiated and created, "truth" about the social world or social categories in it, such as crime, should be challenged and seen as "truth claims" rather than as having any real or concrete status. Concepts such as what the real crime rate is, trends in crime, and who commits crime and why are claims about the truth rather than facts about reality.

2. Collective claims by groups about understanding social phenomena in the same ways, such as common views about what counts as crime or justice, should not be seen as evidence of an underlying reality; for example, if terrorism is a crime, then why do many nations think that U.S. foreign policy displays elements of terrorism? Does that mean that U.S. foreign policy is criminal?
3. The use of labels to classify social phenomena such as murder, theft, robbery, and rape need not reflect an underlying reality, even though the outcomes of these actions can be harmful to the victims; rape may be more an act of violence than a sex act, and food poisoning caused by systemically unhygienic restaurants may be more an act of robbery than a street mugging is.
4. What counts as reality—say, of crime, harm, and consequences—may be different across time, space, and cultures. Some examples include smoking, cocaine distribution, and environmental pollution over time and in different cultures.
5. Because of the process involved in its production, neither experts nor nonexperts have a privileged claim to reveal the truth about social phenomena such as crime; for example, the identification of a suicide or homicide depends on circumstantial evidence that coroners may know less well than relatives.
6. All knowledge is the result of social processes that are based on interaction and shared subjective meaning attached to a situation that are negotiated by the participants. These participants include, for example, robbers and their victims, as well as criminologists and their students.
7. Meaning is produced in an ongoing fashion and gains significance from the people who are attributing qualities to acts and events, as well as from the occasions when it is produced, performed, or acted toward. For example, occasional drug users may become "junkies" not through their use of drugs alone but by the way that others act toward them, label them, and limit them from normal behavior.
8. People who produce knowledge, such as criminologists, government statisticians, and professional practitioners, are no less subject to critique, and their claims are no more privileged than those of others.
9. Knowledge production about social phenomena such as crime is a political process, shaped by concentrated interests that are seeking a social or political outcome; consider, for example, claims for example that abortion is murder, homosexuality is a sin, and consumer fraud is a simply a sharp business practice.
10. Knowledge and meaning about social phenomena such as crime are not fixed but multiple, variable, and changeable through reconstructing the language and symbolic process and by altering the discursive methods that accomplish it.

Types of Social Constructionism

Although it is possible to identify the core themes that social constructionists share, there are a variety of different approaches to constructionism depending on the extent to which advocates accept or reject realism as well as the extent to which they subject their own analysis to a constructivist critique. Gergen (1994), in *Toward Transformation in Social Knowledge,* distinguished between the psychological version of constructionism rooted in Kelly's (1955) personal construct theory, which is concerned with how individuals cognitively construct their world by making sense of their own experiences of their environment, and the other view of social constructionism, which is rooted in the sociological interactionist–phenomenological tradition of the shared construction of meaning shaped by situational and social context, culture, and history. It is this second, social constructionist approach that has been adopted by scholars who examine crime and deviance. Within social constructionism there are three major positions: (1) radical, (2) contextual, and (3) postmodernist.

Radical Constructionists

Social constructionists such as Woolgar and Pawluch (1985), who completely reject the idea of an objective reality, are known variously as "extreme," "radical," "strict," "vulgar," or "strong" social constructionists. They see everything as socially constructed and reject the existence of an independent objective reality. Such perceived reality is seen as nothing more than the agreed-on assumptions of the specialized community that created the assumptions. Advocates of the radical version of social construction also reflexively consider their own theory as a social construction. They believe that people observe the world from different communities and make "truth claims" about constructions of the world but are not able to objectively verify the existence of the reality they perceive.

Radical constructionists also differ among themselves, with some seeing knowledge constituted by an individual's mental process as being closed to outside influence. Such radical individual constructionists see the world as composed of collections of individual worldviews, or *multiverses.* Other radical constructionists see the world as coconstructed or coproduced, whereby the social interaction of human agents through discourse—talking, language, gestures, and other communications—coproduces shared meaning about the world. This shared meaning depends not on qualities of the individual mind but on continual construction and reconstruction in the company of others, or *recursivity.* As a result, there is a relationship between the human agent and the social world such that each constitutes and is constituted by the other (Henry & Milovanovic, 1996).

Contextual Constructionists

In contrast, some scholars, such as Spector and Kitsuse (1977/1987) and Best (1993), take what is called a "contextual," "minimalist," "moderate," or "weak" view of social constructionism, believing that some underlying reality exists and that not everything is a social construction. They believe that by selecting from, interpreting, and classifying this underlying reality, humans build social constructions that have different appearances depending on the social and cultural context. Contextual constructionists accuse radical constructionists of relativism and nihilism (Best, 1989) and, according to Best (1993), the radicals misunderstand the task of analysis, which is to locate social constructions in real cultural–structural contexts; to avoid being exclusively reflexive; and to focus on the substance of issues, evaluating false claims, and even creating new claims. However, they also acknowledge that any underlying qualities that exist do not define an event, person, or action; instead, drawing on the symbolic interactionist tradition, they argue that humans do this through a social process of definition, based on what is relevant to their purposes, shaped by their past biographical positioning, in particular by social and cultural matrices. From these social contexts humans come to agree that some categorizations are more valid than others. In other words, constructions are meaningful only when they are placed in a particular social and situational context, one that specifies the criteria of definition, relevance, and classification. As a result, the concern of contextual constructionists is to understand social problems such as crime and deviance:

> [How they] are generated, sustained, taken seriously, and acted upon; and how certain claims of seriousness are advanced by specific agents and reacted to, or ignored, by different audiences. Their argument is that *by themselves* [italics added], conditions do not constitute social problems; what *makes* them social problems is how they are defined and reacted to by various segments of society. (Goode, 1997, pp. 60–61)

In contextual constructionists' opinion, to make changes for the better, people need to examine the generation and sustenance of social phenomena such as crime, describing how these phenomena are defined, defended, and reacted to. Those who take the contextual position are able to make judgments about which approach is better able to discern the nature of the construction process, how far it distorts any underlying reality, the extent of the discrepancies between objective reality and subjective experience, how realities can appear to exist and be sustained, and how changes may be made in the process to produce less harmful constructions.

Although this difference between radical and contextual constructionists is important insofar as it allows contextualists to use empirical evidence to support their claims that others are making fallacious claims (thus privileging their method of claims-making), commentators have argued that there is neither one constructionism nor many, but a cluster of core themes (as identified earlier) engaged in differently depending on the authors' aims and intent. In other words, social constructionism is itself seen as a politically framed claims-making process.

Postmodern Constructionists

In both the sociological and psychological literature, social constructionism resonates with postmodernism, discourse analysis, and narrative theory, in particular with the affirmative or reconstructive offshoots of postmodernism, such as constitutive theory in criminology with its emphasis on "replacement discourse" (Henry & Milovanovic, 1996).

Postmodernism involves a process of deconstruction of the truth claims of others, which is designed to expose their assumptions and their arbitrariness to prevent closure and certainty. It challenges all power and authority that is based on claims to superior or privileged knowledge. The deconstructive critique is designed to resurrect and celebrate silenced voices of the marginalized to reveal the presence of multiple realities, voices, and worlds as part of a multiplicity of resistances to the hegemony of others' claims to truth.

Affirmative postmodernism is based on the assumptions of social constructionism in that reconstruction is also possible through replacement discourse (Henry & Milovanovic, 1996). Such postmodernist constructionism believes that viewing a socially constructed world through deconstruction affords the possibility of reconstructing that world. Interestingly, this perspective has developed in applied disciplines such as psychotherapy (Parry & Doan, 1994; Rosen & Kuehlwein, 1996) and criminology (Henry & Milovanovic, 1996, 1999), where some form of intervention has been deemed necessary to transform the present harmful social constructions. Indeed, in criminology, Henry and Milovanovic's (1996, 1999) *constitutive theory* seeks to deconstruct harmful discourses of domination through the reconstructive process of *replacement discourse,* not least by actively engaging the mass media's construction of what constitutes crime and harm and what counts as the criminal justice system's response.

Postmodernist constructionism emphasizes contingency rather than certainty (Butler, 1992), and it takes into account the reflexivity issue raised by ethnomethodology. As Kegan (1994) wrote, what emerges is "a theory that is mindful of the tendency of any intellectual system to reify itself" and instead "to assume its incompleteness and to seek out contradiction by which to nourish the ongoing process of its reconstruction" (pp. 329–330). For Rosen (1996), "Reconstructive postmodernism goes beyond the differentiation of the anti-modernists' stance toward the reintegration of modernism into a transformative way of knowing" (p. 42). Thus, postmodernist constructionism is a humanistic form of social science that seeks not only to reflexively understand the way humans constitute their world and are constituted by it but also to use that knowledge to help them transform it into a better place.

Crime and Deviance as Social Constructions: The Importance of Claims-Making

From the social constructionist perspective, criminal behavior is a joint human enterprise between actors and audiences.

Crime and deviance are created by human agents making distinctions, perceiving differences, engaging in behaviors, interpreting their effects, and passing judgments about the desirability or unacceptability of the behaviors or people labeled as criminal, as though those behaviors and people possessed object-like qualities. Since Spector and Kitsuse's (1977/1987) original examination of the social construction of social problems, social constructionists have tended to examine the agencies involved in the claims-making process that produces the panic rather than individuals designated as deviant or their behavior.

Most constructionist work focuses on how people in authoritative positions create moral panics around the perceived fear of certain designated behaviors, regardless of whether these behaviors exist and whether there were persons actually engaged in them. Pavarini (1994) pointed out that what becomes defined as crime depends on the power to define and the power to resist definitions. This in turn depends on who has access to the media and how skilled moral entrepreneurs are at using such access to their advantage (Pfuhl & Henry, 1993).

Crime as Moral Panic

The original concept of moral panic was used by British sociologist Stanley Cohen (1972) in his book *Folk Devils and Moral Panics.* Cohen described the demonization through the mass media around the 1960s "mods" and "rockers" teenage rebel groups whose behavior threatened valued British cultural norms. In *Moral Panics: The Social Construction of Deviance,* Erich Goode and Nachman Ben-Yehuda (1994) argued that moral panics are societal reactions to perceived threat characterized by (a) volatility seen in their sudden appearance and rapid spread among large sections of the population through the mass media and other means of communications, followed by a rapid decline in further instances of the problem; (b) the growth of experts who are claimed to be authorities in discerning cases of the said feared behavior; (c) an increased identification of cases of the behavior that build into a wave; (d) hostility and persecution of the accused as enemies of society; (e) measurement of society's concern through attitude surveys; (f) consensus about the seriousness of the threat; (g) disproportional fear relative to investigations of the actual harm; (h) a backlash against the persecution; and (i) exposure of the flaws in identifying the problem. An excellent illustration is found in Jeffrey Victor's study of satanic ritualistic child abuse in his book *Satanic Panic* (1993); others include Philip Jenkins's (1998) book *Moral Panic: Changing Concepts of the Child Molester in Modern America.*

Goode and Ben-Yehuda (1994) explained the social construction of crime and deviance through moral panics by one of three models. The *grassroots model* proposes that displaced anxiety from societal stress among members of a population results in a spontaneous moral panic that scapegoats new categories of criminals and deviants. Here, control agencies reflect opinion rather than create it. The *elite domination model* holds that people in positions of power, whether government, industry, or religious leaders, are responsible for promoting moral panic as a diversion from problems whose solution would undermine their own positions of power. Finally, the *interest group conflict model* sees the creation of moral panics as the outcome of moral entrepreneurs seeking to gain greater influence over society by defining its moral domain.

Research conducted by Victor (1998), for example, pointed out that moral panics claiming crime or deviance need not be based in reality but in imaginary offenders whose existence gains credibility in the eyes of the public when authorities and those who claim expert knowledge (in particular, science or medicine) legitimize the accusations. These panics are likely to occur when bureaucratic interest, such as competing agencies, are vying for jurisdiction of authority; when methods of detection result in errors; and as Victor claimed, when there is a symbolic resonance with a perceived threat identified in a prevailing demonology—which serves as a master cognitive frame that organizes problems, gives meaning to them, explains them, and offers solutions. A key component of moral panics is the process of claims-making.

Social constructionists of crime, deviance, and social problems examine how interest groups, moral entrepreneurs, and social movements create claims about behavior. Claims-making involves four elements in a process: (1) assembling and diagnosing claims about behavior or conditions seen as morally problematic; (2) presenting to significant audiences, such as the news media, that the claims are legitimate; (3) providing a prognosis of how to address the problem to bring about a desired outcome by defining strategies, tactics, and policy; and (4) contesting counterclaims and mobilizing the support of key groups.

Crime as a Social Construction

Social constructionist views of crime reveal that there are multiple definitions, each of which suggests a different set of criteria as constituting the phenomenon.

Legal Constructions of Crime

The starting point of the social constructionist critique is to challenge the veracity of the legal definition of crime as "an intentional act or omission in violation of criminal law (statutory and case law), committed without defense or justification, and sanctioned by the state as a felony or misdemeanor" (Tappan, 1947, p. 100). Sutherland (1949) argued that existing crime categories are constructions that distort the reality of harm. He argued that a strict legal definition excludes white-collar crime. Others have pointed out that the strict legal definition of crime also ignores the cultural and historical context of law, such as laws on gambling and prostitution that vary by state and nation.

Powerful Interests and the Construction of Crime

Conflict between groups with different and competing interests can result in different constructions of crime such that groups in positions of power criminalize others' behavior depending on whether they threaten the interests of the powerful. The result is that powerless groups are generally the victims of oppressive laws:

> Crime is a definition of human conduct created by authorized agents in a politically organized society. . . . [It describes] behaviors that conflict with the interests of the segments of society that have the power to shape public policy. (Quinney, 1970, pp. 15–16)

Groups in society form around wealth, culture, prestige, status, morality, ethics, religion, ethnicity, gender, race, ideology, human rights, the right to own guns, and so on. Each group may fight to dominate others on these issues. Ethnic or cultural conflict is a good example: What is taken for granted as acceptable behavior by one subculture is defined as criminal by another, or by mainstream culture.

When the basis of power is wealth, the conflict is considered class based. Actions defined as crime are rooted in the vast differences of wealth and power associated with class divisions. Groups that acquire power through political or economic manipulation and exploitation place legal constraints on those without power. A definition of crime based on economic interests emphasizes that "crime and deviance are the inevitable consequences of fundamental contradictions within society's economic infrastructure" (Farrell & Swigert, 1988, p. 3). Crime is defined as the activities of those who threaten the powerful. Such a view explains why serious crimes are those of street offenders, whereas those of corporate or white-collar "suite" offenders are considered less serious. Theorists who challenge the social construction of crime through laws based on powerful interests argue that *any* behavior that causes harm is crime (Reiman, 1995). Michalowski (1985) for example, argued that we should include as crime "analogous social injury," which is harm caused by acts or conditions that are legal. For example, promoting and selling alcoholic beverages and cigarettes (described as "drug delivery systems"), although legal, produce considerable social, health, and psychological problems.

Perhaps the most dramatic call from social constructionist–oriented critics to expand the definition of crime comes from Larry Tifft and Dennis Sullivan (2001), who argued that the hierarchical structure and social arrangements of society produce harm that evades the legal definition. They believe that these acts should be criminalized, which will render criminal many contemporary legal production and distribution activities. It may also criminalize many of the criminal justice system's response to crime, because these also produce additional harms.

Conclusion: Evaluation of the Social Construction of Crime

In general, social constructionists have been criticized depending on how realist or nominalist their core assumptions are. Pro-realists accuse constructionists of being nihilistic and unscientific; anti-realists ridicule any attempt at science as just another truth claim that is using scientific ideology to claim legitimacy for its own political ends (Woolgar & Pawluch, 1985). Anti-realists argue that claiming to be able to observe and document the variability in claims about a condition assumes the objectivity (i.e., reality) of the condition without reflexively subjecting one's own analysis to the same questioning. Contextual constructionists counter that a strict anti-realist reading is an illusion that cannot be transcended by developing new language and discourse, because language is embedded in society (Best, 1995). Best (1995) called for a "weak reading" of the constructionist position, pointing out (a) that it is actually useful to locate social constructions in real cultural–structural contexts; (b) it is unavoidable and not helpful to be exclusively reflexive; and (c) that focusing on theory rather than the substance of problems may undermine and paralyze the critical edge.of their constructionist position, inhibit their evaluation of false claims, and even prevent their creation of new claims.

More broadly, pure or strict social constructionism has been criticized for implying that problems of crime and deviance are merely fabrications, which is protested by the individuals suffering their consequences, even though constructionists argue that there are often real consequences of acting toward constructions as though they are real. The point of constructionism is that revealing how what is taken to be real can be deconstructed enables the possibility of it being reconstructed differently through replacement discourse; when social problems, deviance, and crime are subject to a deconstructionist analysis, they can be reframed in ways that enable their reproduction to be slowed and even reversed such that they become differently and less harmfully constituted (Henry & Milovanovic, 1996). The question—indeed, the challenge—for constructionists is how to demonstrate the value of this kind of analysis in bringing about changes in objective conditions while maintaining that these conditions are only as real as we allow them to be. The value of social constructionism is that it seeks not only to understand the way humans constitute their world and are constituted by it but also to use that knowledge to help them transform the world into a more comfortable place.

References and Further Readings

Barak, G. (1998). *Integrating criminologies.* Boston: Allyn & Bacon.

Becker, H. (1963). *Outsiders.* New York: Free Press.

Berger, P., & Luckmann. T. (1966). *The social construction of reality.* New York: Doubleday.

Best, J. (1989). Extending the constructionist perspective: A conclusion and an introduction. In J. Best (Ed.), *Images of issues: Typifying contemporary problems* (pp. 243–253). New York: Aldine de Gruyter.

Best, J. (1993). But seriously folks: The limitations of the strict constructionist interpretation of social problems. In G. Miller & J. A. Holstein (Eds.), *Reconsidering social constructionism* (pp. 129–147). New York: Aldine de Gruyter.

Best, J. (Ed.). (1995). *Images of issues: Typifying contemporary problems* (2nd ed.). New York: Aldine de Gruyter.

Blumer, H. (1969). *Symbolic interactionism: Perspective and method.* Englewood Cliffs, NJ: Prentice Hall.

Bogen, D., & Lynch. M. (1993). Do we need a general theory of social problems? In G. Miller & J. Holstein (Eds.), *Reconsidering social constructionism* (pp. 213–239). New York: Aldine de Gruyter.

Burr, V. (1995). *An introduction to social constructionism.* London: Routledge.

Butler, J. (1992). Contingent foundations: Feminism and the question of "postmodernism." In J. Butler & J. W. Scott (Eds.), *Feminists theorize the political* (pp. 3–21). London: Routledge.

Cohen, S. (1972). *Folk devils and moral panics.* London: MacGibbon and Kee.

Farrell, R. A., & Swigert, V. L. (1988). *Social deviance* (3rd ed.). Belmont, CA: Wadsworth.

Garfinkel, H. (1967). *Studies in ethnomethodology.* Englewood Cliffs, NJ: Prentice Hall.

Gergen, K. J. (1985). The social constructionist movement in modern psychology. *American Psychologist, 40,* 266–275.

Gergen, K. J. (1994). *Toward transformation in social knowledge.* Thousand Oaks, CA: Sage.

Gergen, K. J. (1999). *An invitation to social construction.* London: Sage.

Goffman, E. (1963). *Stigma: Notes on the management of spoiled identity.* Englewood Cliffs, NJ: Prentice Hall.

Goode, E. (1997). *Deviant behavior* (5th ed.). Upper Saddle River, NJ: Prentice Hall.

Goode, E., & Ben-Yehuda, N. (1994). *Moral panics: The social construction of deviance.* Oxford, UK: Blackwell.

Gould, L., Kleck, G., & Gertz, M. (1992). The concept of "crime" in criminological theory and practice. *The Criminologist, 17,* 1–6.

Henry S. (2007). Deviance: Constructionist perspectives. In G. Ritzer (Ed.), *The Blackwell encyclopedia of sociology* (pp. 145–163). Oxford, UK: Blackwell.

Henry, S., & Lanier, M. (2001). *What is crime?* Lanham, MD: Rowman & Littlefield.

Henry, S., & Milovanovic, D. (1996). *Constitutive criminology: Beyond postmodernism.* London: Sage.

Henry, S., & Milovanovic, D. (Eds.). (1999). *Constitutive criminology at work: Applications to crime and justice.* Albany: State University of New York Press.

Jenkins, P. (1998). *Moral panic: Changing concepts of the child molester in modern America.* New Haven, CT: Yale University Press.

Kegan, R. (1994). *In over our heads: The mental demands of modern life.* Cambridge, MA: Harvard University Press.

Kelly, G. A. (1955). *The psychology of personal constructs.* New York: W.W. Norton.

Kroeber, A. L., & Kluckhohn, C. (1952). *Culture: A critical review of concepts and definitions.* Cambridge, MA: Peabody Museum.

Lemert, E. M. (1967). *Human deviance, social problems and social control.* Englewood Cliffs, NJ: Prentice Hall.

Mead, G. H. (1934). *Mind, self and society* (C. W. Morris, Ed.). Chicago: University of Chicago Press.

Michalowski, R. (1985). *Order, law and crime.* New York: Random House.

Parry, A., & Doan, R. (1994). *Story re-visions: Narrative therapy in the postmodern world.* New York: Guilford Press.

Pavarini, M. (1994). Is criminology worth saving? In D. Nelken (Ed.), *The futures of criminology* (pp. 43–62). London: Sage.

Pfuhl, E. H., & Henry, S. (1993). *The deviance process* (3rd ed.). New York: Aldine de Gruyter.

Potter, J. (1996). *Representing reality: Discourse, rhetoric, and social constructionism.* London: Sage.

Quinney, R. (1970). *The problem of crime.* New York: Dodd, Mead.

Reiman, J. (1995). *The rich get richer and the poor get prison.* New York: Wiley.

Rosen, H. (1996). Meaning-making narratives: Foundations for constructivist and social constructionist psychotherapies. In H. Rosen & K. T. Kuehlwein (Eds.), *Constructing realities: Meaning-making perspectives for psychotherapists* (pp. 3–53). San Francisco: Jossey-Bass.

Rosen, H., & Kuehlwein, K. T. (Eds.). (1996). *Constructing realities: Meaning-making perspectives for psychotherapists.* San Francisco: Jossey-Bass.

Schutz, A. (1967). *The phenomenology of the social world.* Evanston, IL: Northwestern University Press. (Original work published 1932)

Spector, M., & Kitsuse, J. I. (1987). *Constructing social problems.* New York: Aldine de Gruyter. (Original work published 1977)

Stam, H. (2001). Introduction: Social construction and its critics. *Theory and Psychology, 11,* 291–296.

Sutherland. E. H. (1949). *White collar crime?* New York: Holt, Rinehart & Winston.

Tappan, P. (1947). Who is the Criminal? *American Sociological Review, 12,* 96–102.

Tifft, L., & Sullivan. D. (2001). A needs-based social harms approach to defining crime. In S. Henry & M. Lanier (Eds.), *What is crime?* (pp. 179–203). Lanham, MD: Rowman & Littlefield.

Victor, J. S. (1993). *Satanic panic: The creation of a contemporary legend.* Chicago: Open Court.

Victor, J. S. (1998). Moral panics and the social construction of deviant behavior: Theory and application to the case of ritual child abuse. *Sociological Perspectives, 41,* 541–565.

Woolgar, S., & Pawluch, D. (1985). Ontological gerrymandering. *Social Problems, 32,* 214–227.

Part I
Social Constructionism, Criminology and Criminal Justice

[2]

PHENOMENOLOGY AND CONTEMPORARY SOCIOLOGICAL THEORY

THE CONTRIBUTION OF ALFRED SCHUTZ*

HELMUT R. WAGNER
HOBART AND WILLIAM SMITH COLLEGES

Introduction

From its inception, sociology shared a mostly ill-defined and often unruly border region with philosophy. Not only did the basic ideas and key problems of various sociological approaches issue from this region, it also gained permanent significance as the area in which the clarification of the preconditions of sociological reasoning could be attempted.[1]

Leaving earlier forms of the interplay between sociology and philosophy aside, this paper concentrates on the encounter of one branch of 20th-century philosophy with one branch of 20th-century sociology. Both demand consideration as radical new departures in their fields. They are: Husserl's phenomenology[2] and Weber's sociology of understanding.[3] The man who arranged this encounter and spent an academic lifetime exploring its implications and consequences, was Alfred Schutz.[4] His contributions were suspended between the poles of meta-sociological considerations and methodological applications, the preconditions of sociological theory and inquiry and the conceptual and propositional tools of sociological operations. While he did not develop a comprehensive system of sociology of his own, he contributed to substantive sociological theory. His work is replete with implications for several areas of sociological interest.

---

*This is an expanded version of a paper read at the session on "The Boundaries of Sociology" at the Annual Meeting of the American Sociological Association in Boston, August 26, 1968.

The Subject Matter of Sociology

Schutz, like other outstanding sociologists before him, ascribed methodological priority to the question, What is the "Social reality" with which social scientists concern themselves? In agreement with the exponents of such diversified approaches as the post-Hegelian historicists, the post-Comtean sociological positivists, and the neo-Kantian social philosophers, he considered it a reality *sui generis*: a reality existing not in the external realm of natural processes, but in the internal realm of human consciousness. Yet, he did not accept any of these traditions. He shared Wilhelm Dilthey's concern with the *meaning* of the social and historical reality but did not seek it in the spheres of the Objective Mind of philosophical idealism. He was intrigued by Emile Durkhein's suggestion that the "things" he called "social facts" exist in the minds of men. However, he objected to their interpretation as mere external and constraining elements which enter the thinking of individuals as collective representations on the coercive authority of a Collective Consciousness. Finally, he subscribed to Georg Simmel's suggestion that all phenomena of the social world should be traced back to their roots in the behavior of individuals. Yet, he did not accept Simmel's "formal sociology" which, while stressing the reciprocal psychological effects interacting persons have on each other, eliminated the "content" of reciprocal relationships (specific purposes, meanings, and motivations) in order to concentrate on their abstract "forms."[5]

Taking his cues both from Husserl's conception of intentionality and Weber's theory of subjectively meaningful action,[6] he went to the source of human consciousness: the conscious individual, a being endowed with volition. The consciousness of man, including the apprehension of his own self, issues from and expresses his social existence, and he understands his life as life among fellow men. The crucial point of the human mind is intersubjectivity; the crucial point of social interaction is understanding.[7] The Individual and the Social are but two sides of the same process.[8]

Focusing on the individual means focusing on the sphere of his social experiences, the "life world" of Husserl. This life world is subjective. Each individual builds it for himself, out of his personal experiences, expanding or revising it in the process of his ongoing life. Being subjective, it is unfinished and subject to change. It is different for each individual, because the life experiences of each are different; at any time he finds himself in a unique "biographic situation." Yet, this life world is intersubjective. All operate in it by orienting themselves upon others, whose existence they take for granted; and all find their bearing in it with the help of the only guide lines available to them: the given forms of a common language, the explanatory or normative ideas about the life they share, and any other components of the whole conception of the world of their cultural community.

Furthermore, the life world is interactional. Men act in it with or against each other, follow their interests and plan their activities under consideration of others, aim at making themselves understood by them and at understanding them. Such reciprocal understanding presupposes neither unusual powers of empathy nor concern with the intricacies of the other's personality as a whole. Rather, the understanding required is situational: it aims at grasping the meaning one's partner ascribes to the situation insofar as this meaning is relevant for the actual purposes at hand. It is a practical matter.[9] Individuals need to understand each other only insofar as necessary for the satisfactory conclusion of their common undertaking in a specific situation.

Situational involvements necessitate workable definitions of the situation[10] and, in their construction, the utilization of appropriate elements of an individual's store of experience and his stock of knowledge. His store of experience consists of those "sedimentations" of memories of, and conclusions from, past experiences on which he can draw when facing new situations. His stock of common knowledge consists of those common-sense generalizations and typifications which he has absorbed with his language, and those culturally provided patterns, explanations, or ready-made definitions which he has accepted for his own uses. As a coherent ideational structure, the life world is a typified world. The actors in it find themselves in situations which often resemble situations experienced earlier, and thus are considered "the same." Simultaneously, they largely recognize each other merely as types: student and professor, customer and salesman, housewife and letter carrier; and they deal with each other according to typified conceptions of situations: attending a lecture, making a purchase, receiving a letter.

The typifications of everyday life are relevant for the individual, first of all, within the immediate sphere of his involvement with others. This sphere constitutes the "world within my reach"; be it the actual reach of things and persons "here and now"; be it the restorable reach of situations in which he had been involved and which he can bring about again in the future; or be it the obtainable reach of objectives etc. which may be his when moving into another sphere of life than his present one. The world within actual reach is the sphere of direct face-to-face relationships, of "pure we-relations," of consociated action-partners. However, the network of cultural typifications allows the individual to transcend the boundaries of situational involvements. He finds himself linked to others of his fellow men indirectly but effectively: to the director of the corporation for which he works but with whom he has no dealings; people entirely unknown to him who are engaged in growing, processing, shipping, and retailing the food items he buys in the self-service store; the President of his country whose decisions may affect his pocketbook or compel him to risk his life in a far-away theater of war. The common-sense typifications of corporation executive, farmer, meat packer, trucker, store manager, head of government, etc., as well as the typifications of his own place in these relationships as employee, consumer, tax payer, etc., enable him to gain a practically sufficient understanding of the network of societal relations with which he is entangled. Thereby, he experiences his total life world as a structured system of relationships with fellow men who are close to or remote from him, and who are familiar with him or disappear behind the veil of anonymity. Finally, there are the typifications of collectivities, such as "the corporation," "the city," or the "Federal Administration," from which all allusions to fellow men as acting partners are deleted.

But, regardless of these scales of acquaintance and variations, men face their world of everyday life in a "natural attitude", a stance which allows them to accept it as it presents itself to them; they operate in it with pragmatic practicality; and they take if for granted as long as their established private and common definitions of situations, their recipes for action and conduct, and their common-sense expectations work sufficiently well for their purposes on hand. As long as this is the case, the life world is not only familiar to its individual inhabitants; it inspires confidence: what has worked in the past, will work again.

Yet, the individual is not simply the prisoner of custom or the puppet of structural-functional role expectations. Pre-given typifications are not automatic definers of situations; they are conveniently available aids in defining them. Likewise, semantic forms are not imposers of meaning but vehicles for their expression. Both remain subordinated to the cognitive activities of the individual: the life world is intentional and volitional. Its interpretative structure is created and recreated by each individual; acceptance of public definitions of situations is based on the individual's understanding and decision, which in turn issue from his personal life experiences. The utilization of public definitions of situations hinges on their workability in the individual's sphere of life. The public as well as the private stock of knowledge is subject to pragmatic test: if a formula works, it is accepted without further ado; if it doesn't work, the individual has a problem on his hands and must seek its solution. If established interpretations cease to make sense, the individual has to subject them to scrutiny, re-interpretation, revision, or even to reject them.

This, then, is a main contribution made by Schutz: the exploration of the ramifications and implications of subjective orientations, intersubjective processes, interactional-situational involvements, cultural typifications, and the common-sense public knowledge with the help of which the individual builds his image of the social world and locates himself in it. This exploration laid the foundations of a theory of the social system as social, i.e. intersubjective, process without sacrificing the interactional principle of interpretation and without abandoning the 'voluntaristic' starting point at any level of analysis.[12]

The outline of this theory of the "social world" suggests the answer Schutz has given to the question: What is the proper subject matter of sociology? It is the social reality given in the cognitive orientations of individuals involved with one another in the world of everyday life; it consists of the meanings which they attach to their interactions and relations; it exists in their interpretations and definitions of social situations; it comprises their interests, their motivations, and their objectives and purposes; and it is embodied in their stock of knowledge of gradually acquired typifications of self and fellow men, or courses of actions and encounters. The social reality of sociology is the practical reality of the everyday world as apperceived and interpreted by its inhabitants.

The Foundation of Sociology

However, if the social-phenomenological reality of everyday life is the proper subject matter of sociology, its position among the sciences becomes unique: it is not just separated from other fields by this subject matter; it is itself grounded in this subject matter.

The world of everyday life is the "paramount reality" of human existence and cognition. However, man has created other "provinces of meaning,"[13] set apart from everyday life by different "cognitive styles." The pragmatic "natural attitude" of the life world may be abandoned in favor of an attitude of detached observation and inquiry, the cognitive style of philosophy and science. By suspending his personal interests and involvements, a sociologist transposes himself into a "scientific situation," assumes a scientific stance in which he devotes himself to objective inquiry according to established rules of procedure.

As much as this attitude differs from the natural attitude prevailing in the life world, it is derived from it. Intellectual inquiry is rooted in the attitude of reflection which anyone must assume whenever he finds that his "recipe knowledge" fails in a given situation. Detached observation is related to the stance of any observer of situations in daily life which merely arouse his curiosity. The cognitive style of sociology, however, differs from doubt and reflection in everyday life by its objective. First of all, it does not seek a workable solution for a practical problem at hand. Rather, it makes the situations of the life world themselves problematic, seeks to explain what in this world is taken for granted. And, secondly, it differs from the attitude of the detached observer in daily life by transforming "idle curiosity" into systematic investigation. Passive observation is turned into active inquiry. These differences are crucial, but should not obscure the roots of a scientific attitude in ordinary doubt and reflection, and in observation which occurs in everyday-life situations. The cognitive style of scientific inquiry is constituted by the decision to make occasional "suspension of belief" and detached observation into dominant attitudes, and to discipline and systematize reflection based on them. Thereby, a new stock of knowledge is created, being an end in itself: knowledge for the sake of knowing[14] both content and forms of social orientations, motivations, activities, and relations.

The sociological stock of knowledge, then, contains statements about the paramount reality of the life world, couched in the "meta-language" of sociology. But more: the conceptual language of the field and its integrative frames of reference themselves are rooted in this reality. Substantive sociological concepts are concepts of a second order, erected on the basis of first-line constructs of common-sense thinking. This is most obvious in the case of terms for collectivities (family, clan, community, etc.), complementary role conceptions (father-son, ruler-subject, etc.), terms for social activities and relations (communication, collaboration, etc.), but applies also to all other concepts including those of interest, meaning, motive, etc. Insofar as sociologists are involved in typification, they not only imitate the processes of typification in everyday life, lifting it on the plane of sociological reasoning; they base themselves on the typification contained in everyday language, whether they denote types of people, types of situations, types of activities, types of groups and collectivities.

Substantive Theoretical Contributions

Schutz's sociology is closely related to that "interpretive sociology" which is linked to the name of Max Weber. Its foundations, in fact, were obtained by the super-imposition of a set of suitable components of Husserl's phenomenological psychology upon Weber's theory of action.[15] The resulting basic framework constitutes the major contribution of Schutz.

Weber's concept of social action refers to the conduct of persons who direct themselves intentionally to others in a way which is meaningful to both parties. Consequently, it involves a whole set of interrelated factors, such as those of intention, interest, motivation, means and ends, objectives, subjective meaning, understanding, etc. Schutz showed that most of these concepts are equivocal, and are used by Weber, often overtly and intentionally, in more than one way. In numerous cases, he argued, the investigation would have to be carried beyond the starting points elected by Weber. Thus, while accepting the action scheme of Weber in principle, he addended it in various ways.

Most of all, he clarified the problem of motivation. Motives, according to him, are of two kinds: there are "in-order-to motives," embodied in the goals, aims, and long-range plans of the actor; and there are "because motives" which are constituted by the "reasons" for which he focuses on his goals and works toward their realization. The subjective meaning of any action, that is solely and exclusively, the meaning it has for the actor himself, is essentially contained in the dual motives which guide him in his conduct.

Secondly, Schutz accounted for the volitional character of action in terms of the specific anticipatory mental activity of "projecting," the planning of particular acts or sequences of acts. Projecting starts from the goal, imagined as already being achieved, leads to the establishment of some broad guidelines for the execution of the planned action; it may lead to later interruption of the course of action itself for purposes of specification and possibly modification. Schutz's investigation of the complexities of the processes of projecting, in conjunction with the ramification of motivation, make it clear that action, and especially social action, is a matter of greater intricacy than Weber's scheme had suggested. Finally, Schutz paid considerable attention to the subjective processes of social interaction. In such reciprocal social action, the motives of the involved persons interweave in a characteristic manner: the "in-order-to" motive of the one becomes the "because" motive of the other, and vice versa. They "understand" each other in this process when they grasp each other's motives to a practically sufficient degree. Face-to-face interaction, in addition, lets a person witness the immediate process of the on-going experience of his partner, making for a possibly most vivid form of intersubjectivity.

One of the most stringent conclusions of Schutz's elaboration of the theory of action concerns the "subjective approach" in sociology. Since the subjective meaning of an action cannot be anything but the actual meaning the actor himself ascribed to his conduct, it is impossible to "understand" social action by means of outside observation and, even, to ascertain merely the beginning and the end of any human action without understanding the motives and interpretations of the actors. The "subjective approach" is indispensable for even the most elementary analysis of action.

Outside the central area of the theory of action, some of Schutz's substantive contributions to sociology offered starting points rather than developed frames of reference. Yet, these too are significant for social psychology, including the theory of social types and social roles. Still other contributions consist in the foundations for a sociology of knowledge, which, in contrast to the conventional focus on ideology, would deal centrally with social cognition as such, both on the individual level of a person's actual "knowledge" of "his" social world, and the collective level of the "relative-natural conception of the world" which forms the world view of a cultural community. A particularly challenging side-line of these investigations has been opened up by Schutz with his accentuation of the problem of a social "distribution of knowledge." Recently, it has been shown that such a comprehensive sociology of cognition can be developed from Schutz's beginnings.[17] Thereby, a significant new area of sociological investigation has been opened up.

Methodological Contributions

Schutz's methodological contributions concern concept formation, typification and model construction, and ideal-typical procedures.

According to him, sociological constructs are based on the commonsense constructs of everyday life. Thus, conceptualization is lifted out of the context of mere taxonomy, and returned to the sphere of substantive investigation—where it properly belongs, if we follow the tradition established by Weber and confirmed by Herbert Blumer, Anselm Strauss, and others.[18] Schutz was vitally concerned with the construction of sociological concepts by way of empirical investigations into the meaning structure of everyday social behavior in all spheres of social life.[19]

As concerns type concepts,[20] he concentrated on types of human actors and types of social actions. In both cases, he distinguished analytically separated aspects: There are types of social figures which are descriptively classified as past or potential actors; and there are types of actors-in-action which embody the typical dynamic schemes of motivating, projecting, and executing specific types of acts. Simultaneously, there are types of acts which, as past or future events, may be classified without reference to actors; and there are types of courses-of-action dealing with the typical dynamic aspects of action as process but cannot be treated independently from acting individuals.

The dynamic types embody Schutz's models or ideal types. Their construction proceeds from empirical observation to the establishment of "typical course-of-action patterns," which are coordinated with models of ideal actors. These actors are endowed with consciousness which, in turn, is restricted to the "elements relevant to the performing of the course-of-action patterns observed"; they display sets of "typical notions, purposes, goals, which are assumed to be invariant in the specious consciousness of the. . .actor-model."[21]

The model is activated by thought experiment. It is assumed to operate in whatever situations are selected for inquiry. The empirical application of these models-in-action, or "puppets," serves the same purposes as Weber's ideal types. As rational construct, the ideal type allows to compare actual behavior in actual situations to theoretical expectations in order to explicate sociologically significant components and tendencies within the situations under consideration. The procedure may also be used to measure, figuratively, both the sufficiency of a given actor's knowledge of those factors in the situation which are relevant for the achievement of his purpose, and the degree of rationality of his action, that is, the degree to which motivational factors irrelevant for the achievement of his purpose intrude the planning and execution of a course of action in such a way as to detract from its efficiency and consistency.[22]

Schutz's conception of ideal type represents a specific version of that of Weber. Like the original, it is two-pronged: an ideal type results from actual investigation, and becomes a guide to further study. As a sociological tool, it is a model in the technical sense of the term, suitable for the qualitative analysis of a pertinent yet difficult set of phenomena, those of subjectively meaningful social action and interaction.

Empirical Contributions

Schutz's main efforts were devoted to the construction of a theoretical-conceptual framework for what may be called a phenomenological sociology. His frequent references to empirical matters, within this undertaking, served illustrative purposes. On occasions, however, he applied aspects of his theory to the exploration of concrete problems, thus approaching the level of empirical investigation. One kind of these studies he devoted to the emergence of social types in situations in which individuals are unable to take the surrounding world of everyday life for granted. Foremost, he analyzed the cognitive acculturation problems of the newcomer to an established society, and the reorientation-problems of the returning veteran. Or he concentrated on situations in which becomes problematic what had been taken for granted, as in the study of the distribution of knowledge and the acquisition of additional knowledge in the case of the well-informed citizen in contrast to the expert on the one hand, and the man-in-the-street on the other. A concern with the foremost inner problem of American society led Schutz into the investigation of the meaning of the demand for equality and equal opportunity in the face of discrimination. Manifesting an astonishing range of interests, he also moved with ease on the rather esoteric level of musical communication, dealing with the flow of communication between composer and performer, performer and beholder, and composer and beholder, on the one hand, and the process of intercommunication among performing musicians on the other. Finally, he involved himself in the interpretation of the work of creative artists and writers. Thus, he treated Mozart's operatic works as a kind of musical phenomenology, and he showed Cervantes's Don Quixote as the man entangled in "multiple realities."[23]

These writings alone demonstrate the great scope of the possibilities for socio-phenomenological investigations of empirical significance.

Conclusion

Unavoidably, this survey cannot offer more than the bare outlines of the work of Alfred Schutz. It does not do justice to the depth of his analyses and the ramifications of his concepts, but it may indicate the scope and significance of his contributions.

His interpenetration of Husserl's phenomenological psychology and Weber's sociology of understanding has strengthened the foundations of that theoretical approach which Howard Becker called interpretative sociology,[24] and it has opened new vistas for substantive sociological inquiries.

For one thing, the resulting redefinition of the subject matter of sociology as that of the mental constructs issuing from intersubjective experiences supplies a most consistent justification of sociology as a field *sui generis*; it reaches the irreducible base line of all social phenomena understood as human phenomena. The methodological correlates of this redefinition, concerning the characteristics and procedures of sociological conceptualization, generalization, and typification, offer a strong inducement for applying ideal-typical methods instead of merely displaying them as methodological curios.

Substantively, the linkage between Husserl and Weber resulted in the development of a significantly perfected theoretical model of social action, a model which invites specification by way of construction of sub-types, and which awaits expansion through the development of sets of interactional models of varying degrees of complexity. It is in this area, next to that of the further development of a sociology of cognition, that I expect the most fruitful exploitations of the intellectual heritage of Alfred Schutz.

FOOTNOTES

[1] This concerns not only ontological and epistemological positions and implications, but also the basic methodological problems of theoretical reasoning and substantive inquiry.

[2] Husserl's phenomenology constitutes a radically new departure in philosophy; existentialism is merely one outcome of it.

[3] Weber's sociology of understanding, almost an afterthought to his broad historical investigations, marks a decisive break with the positivist tradition in sociology.

[4] Alfred Schutz's first and most fundamental publication appeared in 1932 under the title, *Der Sinnhafte Aufbau der sozialen Welt.* (Vienna: Springer, –2nd ed. 1960). It occurred in English only in 1967, in the excellent translation by George Walsh and Frederick Lehnert, under the title, *The Phenomenology of the Social World.* (Evanston, Ill.: Northwestern University Press, 1967). In addition, three volumes of *Collected Papers* are available in English (The Hague: Nijhoff, 1962-66). Footnote references to the *Collected Papers* appear under the abbreviations, CP I, CP II, (CP III).

[5] Wilhelm Dilthey, who belongs to the second half of the 19th century, aimed at the understanding rather than the causal explanation of historical events and processes, thus showing the way to later sociologists, such as Max Weber. Emile Durkheim, by contrast, remained in the positivist tradition established by Auguste Comte but did not see sociology as mere "social physics." Georg Simmel, the most unsystematic of all classical sociologists, remained in the tradition of Kant's critical idealism. It would take extensive investigations to expose the relationships, the points of contact, and the differences between Schutz's thoughts on the one hand, and those of Dilthey, Durkheim, and Simmel on the other.

[6] Husserl's conception of intentionality, in the nutshell, is based on the fact that all consciousness is consciousness *of* something. On the one hand, what becomes the object of our thought imposes itself upon us; on the other hand, we single out such an object by concentrating our attention upon it. While thinking cannot be separated from the object of thought, a sharp distinction must be made between the activities, the processes of thinking and their results. Weber's theory of subjectively meaningful action, although frequently misunderstood and misinterpreted, is better known to sociologists and does not warrant an explanation here. Of course, it would take a lengthy study to trace the trains of thought by which Schutz brought the two in conjunction.

[7] Clearly, this comes close to the social-psychological contributions of George Herbert Mead. We would have to turn to Mead in order to understand the processes by which an individual becomes that social being as which he is encountered later in everyday life. Schutz, in a sense, started where Mead left off.

[8] Needless to say, this position was developed, before Schutz, in the writings of Charles Horton Cooley.

[9] It is at this point that phenomenological theory makes contact with the pragmatic theory of behavior by John R. Dewey.

[10] Schutz, here, acknowledged his debt to William I. Thomas.

[11] It is clear that this pragmatism is not identical with the practicality of immediate material interests: a formula for human conduct will be maintained in the face of failure, if an explanation of the failure occurs which "explains" it to the satisfaction of the individual without necessitating to discard it.

[12] Max Weber had laid the foundations of an interactional interpretation of societal collectivities by insisting that the hypostatized conceptions of, e.g., "the State," are defined as interactional networks in which activities and effects must be reduced to those of individuals operating in terms of normative and functional expectations. He linked the individual cognitively to such collectivities in terms of expectations of a "chance" that a specific kind of conduct of members of them would or would not occur. Schutz, from this starting point, developed a theory of degrees of involvement with personally close relationships to such of complete anonymity. Accordingly, the typifications of everyday life are graded according to generality and anonymity, and fade into those which pertain to specific large-scale collectivities and even to more or less unspecific categories. The treatment of these aspects of the work of Weber and Schutz, so far widely ignored, warrants greatest attention. Yet, it must be granted that they constitute beginnings and direction signs rather than developed interpretive theories of, e.g., the "social system."

[13] Schutz, here, accepted William James' fruitful thesis of cognitive "subuniverses" or provinces of meaning, all of which are "real after their fashion." See William James, *The Principles of Psychology*. New York: Holt, 1890. Vol. II, 289-298.

[14] "Knowledge for the sake of knowing" constitutes one of the three basic kinds of knowledge in the pertinent exposition of Max Scheler, a philosopher who influenced Schutz's work to a considerable degree.

[15] This super-imposition was carried out within the confines of a thorough critical appraisal of Weber's theory of action, including its methodological foundations and its silent presuppositions. See *The Phenomenology of the Social World*, op. cit., pp. 15ff, 144ff.

[16] It is not possible, within the confines of the present paper, to enter a discussion of the phenomenologically highly important concept of "inner time" (Schutz) or "duree" (Bergson).

[17] Peter L. Berger and Thomas Luckmann, *The Social Construction of Reality.*

Garden City, N.Y.: Doubleday, 1966.

[18] Herbert Blumer's "sensitizing concepts' and the "grounded theory" by Barney G. Glaser and Anselm Strauss are crucially important in this respect.

[19] Schutz's own work contains a good illustration of this procedure in the paper on "The Homecomer." *American Journal of Sociology*, 5D, 4 (December 1945), 363-376. CP II, 106-119.

[20] Up to this point, we have consistently spoken of Schutz's type concepts. He himself, in most cases, was concerned with ideal types. We have preferred the more general term in order to cover all sociologically relevant cases of type construction, regardless of whether they show the characteristics of Weber's ideal-typical procedure or not.

[21] "Concept and Theory Formation." Journal of Philosophy, 51, 9 (April 29, 1954), p. 227, CP I, 48-66.

[22] This is based on Max Weber, "Die Objektivitaet der Sozialwissenschaftlichen Erkenntnis." In *Gesammelte Aufsaetze zur Wissenschaftslehre.* Tuebingen: Mohr. 2nd ed. 1951, 146-214.

[23] "The Stranger: An Essay in Social Psychology." *American Journal of Sociology* 49, 6, 1944; 499-507. CP II, 91-105.

"The Homecomer." Op. Cit.

"The Well-Informed Citizen: An Essay on the Social Distribution of Knowledge." Social Research 13, 4, 1946; 463-378. CP II, 120-134.

"Equality and the Meaning Structure of the Social World." In Lyman Bryson, et al., *Aspects of Human Equality.* New York: Harper 1957. CP II, 226-273.

"Making Music Together: A Study in Social Relationships." *Social Research* 18, 1, 1951; 76-97. CP II, 159-178.

"Mozart and the Philosophers." *Social Research* 23, 2, 1956; 219-242. CP II, 179-200.

"Don Quixote and the Problem of Reality," In Alfred Schutz, *Collected Papers II: Studies in Social Theory.* The Hague: Nijhoff, 1964; 135-158.

[24] We are referring here mainly to Howard Becker, Herbert Blumer, and the exponents of symbolic-interactional theory.

[3]

Alfred Schutz's Influence on American Sociologists and Sociology*

GEORGE PSATHAS
Department of Sociology, Boston University, Boston, MA, USA (E-mail: geops1@bu.edu)

Abstract. Alfred Schutz's influence on American sociologists and sociology in the 1960s and 1970s is traced through the examination of the work of two of his students, Helmut Wagner and Peter Berger, and of Harold Garfinkel with whom he met and corresponded over a number of years. The circumstances of Schutz's own academic situation, particularly the short period of his academic career in the United States and his location at the New School, are examined to consider how and in what ways he was constrained from exerting an even wider influence. The two major areas of influence in American sociology that are examined are the sociology of knowledge and the early development of ethnomethodology.

Introduction

I never met Alfred Schutz but I have come to know, respect and admire him through his writings, through his ideas and insights, and through his remarkable intellect and personality. His students, colleagues, family and friends have told me much about him, but the most personal testimony I can give is to say that he influenced and inspired me in my life as a teacher, a sociologist and as a person with philosophical interests. I cannot succeed in living up to the rich legacy he has left us but I will offer these thoughts at least as a partial acknowledgement of his profound influence.

It is difficult to trace his influence on American sociology because many years have elapsed since his thoughts and ideas burst on the American scene and these ideas have now been disseminated widely, become absorbed, incorporated and re-formulated by many scholars. But what I will try to do here is capture some of the beginnings, the times when his ideas were new on the scene, when American sociologists first became aware of him and through him of phenomenology, and when his ideas began to be read, discussed and absorbed. As this absorption continued, there is one main area of sociology which was transformed, namely the sociology of knowledge, and another new field of study for which his thought provided a foundation and beginning inspiration, ethnomethodology. I will consider both of these by focusing on the development of two major American sociologists whom Schutz influenced, Peter Berger and Harold Garfinkel.

The Context of the Times

It is hard now to recall the excitement which Schutz's work generated among a number of American sociologists, myself included, during the 1960s and 1970s. I personally discovered Schutz while reading the footnotes in Garfinkel's papers in the early 60's where Garfinkel not only praises Schutz but also borrows and incorporates many of Schutz's ideas and conceptualizations into his own work. And it was in these same footnotes that I discovered the name of Edmund Husserl and the term "phenomenology."[1]

As Bauman (1996, pp. 825–826) has written:

> The most seminal of departures that led in the course of the 1970s to widespread criticism and rejection of what Giddens termed the 'orthodox consensus' was the phenomenological revolution. Initiated by Berger and Luckmann (1966), the revolution was sustained by a spate of radical reformulations of the subject matter and proper strategy of sociological work. The posthumously published work of Alfred Schutz served as the main theoretical inspiration and authority . . . . The effect of the exposure to phenomenology was to shift interest from external, extra-subjective structural constraints to the interpretation of the subjective experience of actors; and from the determination to arbitrate between objective truth and prejudiced opinion to the effort to reveal the conditions of knowledge rooted in communally transmitted traditions. . .[2]

I could not agree more. But let me recall for you what that period was like and how phenomenological, interpretive and qualitative perspectives were emerging in sociology. Here are some of the books and papers that were appearing in the late 50s and the 60s:

1958 Peter Winch, *The Idea of a Social Science and Its Relation to Philosophy*
1958 Michael Polanyi, *Personal Knowledge*
1959 Harold Garfinkel, Common Sense Knowledge of Social Structures in *Transactions of Fourth World Congress of Sociology*, 4 (Milan, 1959) pp. 51–65.
1959 Erving Goffman, *The Presentation of Self in Everyday Life*
1960 Herbert Spiegelberg, *The Phenomenological Movement*
1962, 64, and 66. Alfred Schutz, *Collected Papers, Volumes I, II, and III*
1963 Peter Berger, *Invitation to Sociology: A Humanistic Perspective*
1963 Erving Goffman, *Behavior in Public Places*
1964 Harold Garfinkel, Studies of the Routine Grounds of Everyday Activities, in *Social Problems* (a paper that was published only with the active assistance of Howard Becker who was editor of the Journal)
1964 Aaron Cicourel, *Method and Measurement in Sociology*
1964 Thomas Kuhn, *The Structure of Scientific Revolutions*
1966 Peter Berger and Thomas Luckmann, *The Social Construction of Reality*
1967 Harold Garfinkel, *Studies in Ethnomethodology*

1967 Alfred Schutz, English translation of *The Phenomenology of the Social World*
1968 Burkhart Holzner, *Reality Construction in Society*
1969 Herbert Blumer, *Symbolic Interactionism*, a collection of his papers

The late 60's in American sociology was a time in which these perspectives were appearing in increasing numbers, when the dominant functionalist, positivist, and natural science paradigm was being challenged both from the left (by Marxist and conflict theorists) and from other directions (by symbolic interactionists, phenomenologists, and ethnomethodologists) and when younger sociologists were seeking alternative perspectives.[3] It was a time when phenomenology and Schutz's ideas might find a positive reception.

Schutz's Influence on American Sociologists and Sociology

There are several aspects to this question of whether and in what ways Schutz influenced American sociology. One is the influence he was able to have during his lifetime, particularly during the time he lived in America, on American sociologists and the field of sociology itself. A second is the influence he achieved after his death, first as mediated by his former students and contemporaries and secondly as exerted directly through his own writings and ideas.

Direct and Indirect Personal Influences

The matter of influence is not always easy to trace and there are various kinds and degrees of influence as well as different ways in which influence may be exerted.[4] One kind of influence is that which I shall call *direct personal influence* in which the person is in a face-to-face relationship with a mentor/colleague, may have studied with him or her and has, over time, had a number of occasions to interact directly with him or her.[5]

Included here would be the influence of the teacher on his or her students which affects them to such an extent they have become adherents, followers, or developers of their mentor's main ideas and theories (what Spiegelberg calls "total influence"); or they may be influenced in such a way as to seek to extend, expand, and develop what they believe to be the implications of their mentor's ideas. In so doing they may make some of their own original contributions and achieve a major transformation of the original ideas.

There is also what may be called a negative or counter influence in that the one being influenced seeks to argue against, negate, modify or overturn the ideas of the source of the influence. (I shall not have time to consider some of these in this paper but some examples are found in the works of Kurt Wolff and Erving Goffman.)[6]

Evidence for the kinds of influences I am discussing can be found in the works of those so influenced, not merely in the citations they may include in their writings which refer specifically to the influencer's works and ideas[7] but also in the content and form of their own intellectual contributions. Whether they are self-consciously aware of being influenced or not, they may have incorporated the influencer's way of thinking to such an extent that the influence is visible in the methods, theories, and approaches they use in their own work (e.g., the works of Maurice Natanson which have presented many of Schutz's ideas for philosophers as well as human scientists).

There is also the *indirect personal influence*[8] in which a face-to-face relationship is lacking but the person is affected through indirect contacts, by reading the work of the influencer, or being in direct face-to-face relationships with those who have studied with the person. The influencer may be a contemporary (or have become a predecessor) but the influence can be *strong* by virtue of direct involvement with others who once had direct contact with the originator of the ideas, or, *weaker* in that the influence is mediated by the written works and secondary literature dealing with the influencer's thought.

Under the heading of *direct personal influence*, there is no question that Alfred Schutz had such an influence on a number of persons who studied with him, who took graduate degrees under his tutelage, and who began their earliest independent scholarly writings following the same theoretical and methodological approach and perspective of their mentor. In sociology the names of Helmut Wagner, Brigitte Berger, Peter Berger and Thomas Luckmann are most important, and in philosophy, Fred Kersten, Maurice Natanson and Richard Zaner. Less direct were some who were his contemporaries, had direct face-to-face contact with him and may have corresponded with him but had not formally studied with him or done their graduate work with him, e.g., Harold Garfinkel.

There are those on whom he had an *indirect personal influence* mediated primarily through his written works or their direct contacts with his former students or colleagues. In such cases I would consider the influence to be demonstrated in their citations of his work and ideas, the incorporation of his conceptual frameworks in their own works, and their self-identifications as scholars working within a Schutzian-phenomenological perspective at various times and in various of their published works. Such identifications can, of course, be subject to change over the years and any naming of persons would need to be qualified in terms of the time periods during which their work showed such influence. (Here I would include, without specifying more exact dates, myself, and several other sociologists: Valerie Benz, Egon Bittner, Aaron Cicourel, Burkhart Holzner, Roger Jehensen, Louise Levesque-Lopman, Mary Rogers, David Rehorick, David Sudnow, and Frances Waksler among others; the list can be extended considerably.)

Direct and Indirect Influences on the Field of Sociology

A more extended study of Schutz's influence on American *sociologists* should also be a study of his influence on American *sociology*.[9] The latter kind of influence is perhaps the more significant question to be asked whereas the former may be easier to trace. The question for American sociology is whether certain substantive areas, fields, or sub-fields (e.g., the sociology of knowledge or deviance) or whether types and varieties of theories or methods (e.g., social problems theory), or whether general sociological theorizing can be shown to have been directly or indirectly influenced by Schutz.

The form of this influence could be *direct*, as when Schutz himself might advance work in a particular field or *indirect* when mediated by those who had been directly or indirectly personally influenced by Schutz. In the latter instances we would have to trace the impact of Schutz's ideas as these may have been extended, expanded or modified by those who had been so influenced. Secondary, tertiary and more extended influence may be claimed, but, as time elapses, if the influence has been substantial, the original ideas may have become so absorbed and incorporated into a field that their original source is no longer recognized (or alluded to) in subsequent writings (e.g., the sociology of knowledge in the late 1990s).

Schutz's Own Direct Influence on American Sociology: During His Lifetime

I will begin my inquiry by first focusing on Schutz's own unique position in American academia and the extent to which he was able to exert a direct influence during his lifetime; first, on particular American sociologists whom he seems to have influenced; and then on the field of American sociology in general. In the process I will refer to some of my own experiences since I received my graduate training in sociology in the 1950s in American universities and have taught and conducted my own research and writing in the 50 years subsequent to the time when Schutz's first sociology graduate students did their work with him at the New School. In addition, I have personally been influenced by many of Schutz's ideas.

Alfred Schutz was born in 1899 in Vienna and died in 1959 in New York. He was a refugee scholar who escaped the Nazi regime with his family, first to France in 1938, and then to New York in 1939. Employed most of his life in banking, he taught part time at the New School (beginning in 1943) for many years and only in the last three years of his life full time (when he left banking in 1956 and became a full time Professor of Philosophy and Sociology at the Graduate Faculty of the New School). His many publications scattered in several different journals but primarily in *Philosophy and Phenomenological*

Research and in *Social Research*, over a period of years, were collected into three volumes published after his death as *Collected Papers*, 1962, 1964, 1966. His first major work, *Der sinnhafte Aufbau der sozialen Welt* (The Meaning Structure of the Social World) was translated into English as *The Phenomenology of the Social World* in 1967 and the last of his major works, left unfinished, was completed by Thomas Luckmann (and published in English in 1973 and 1989) as *Structures of the Life World*.

Schutz's influence on American sociology during his lifetime was limited. I have long wondered why this was so and will offer what I believe were the major reasons.

1. For most of his academic career, he worked part-time in a graduate program which was not widely recognized in American sociology and was considered by some to not be part of the mainstream.[10] He himself taught courses in both sociology and philosophy, sometimes dividing his time equally between two departments. At a later stage he simultaneously chaired both departments. Although on the East coast and in a major urban center, it was small (some 3–4 members) all of whom were European trained and was overshadowed in the 40s and 50s by departments of sociology at Columbia and Harvard. The New School had originally been founded to provide a home for refugee scholars and it welcomed those who were trained in Europe to all its programs. The graduate sociology program and department did not follow the contemporary American model nor did its faculty manage to develop contacts and connections with other American institutions, professional and scholarly societies, or informal personal contacts and networks,[11] though, as we shall note, some attempts were made. Its students were generally fully employed and took courses in the evening though a few were able to become teaching fellows or assistants during their studies. There were no programs of sponsored empirical research which might provide research training for graduate sociology students.[12] The particular character of the New School and the Graduate Faculty (formed in 1935) was such that although there were many students, not all were enrolled in a regular degree program, and, of those who were, few completed their degrees.[13]

2. The academic department of sociology at Columbia, which gained strength in the late 1930s, came by the 1940s to be dominated by Robert Merton and Paul Lazarsfeld whose interests were in developing a distinctive empirical and research model of sociology. For example, although Merton had an interest in the work of Simmel, he was more interested, as Jaworski (1998, p. 4) contends, in "'using Simmel's ideas, to absorb them into a research plan and . . .to move sociology into empirical and applied research and away from a European model of textual study, exegesis and scholarship." Jaworski compares the New School and Columbia as representing two different ideal types:[14] Columbia favored what he calls the "research program" which consists of "sharing abstract empiricism's instrumentalism, its goal of utilizing a text for

some purpose, and . . . [in part] 'scholarship's' universalism, its desire to advance intellect and learning" (1998, p. 5). It also draws from a positivist philosophy of science and uses theoretical texts as the source of hypotheses and concepts.[15] The New School model was one of what he calls "scholarship" in which "intellectual work [is] in harmony with humanistic, intellectual traditions, . . . [which] link sociology to literary, philosophical and historical projects, [examining texts] historically and systematically, [and where] biography is accepted as relevant to understanding a thinker." Columbia shared institutional dominance in the East with Harvard and by the 1950s the mainly positivist model of quantitative empirical research, with research grants, and at times favoring applied sociology – what (Jaworski, 1998, p. 6) has referred to as the "natural science model" – had largely succeeded in capturing a major share of American sociology.[16]

3. His first book, *Der sinnhafte Aufbau der sozialen Welt*, although published in German in 1932 and involving an extensive critique and commentary on Max Weber's sociology, was not translated into English until eight years after his death in 1967. He himself had declined several requests to authorize a translation (made by Natanson and even Garfinkel), during his lifetime. This meant that Parsons' (1937, 1947) translations and interpretations of Weber's sociology were the primary sources of knowledge of Weber for most American sociologists in the 40s and 50s. Schutz's critical interpretations as well as appreciations of Weber, and his own Weberian perspective, were largely unknown and untranslated.

4. His various articles and papers could not become widely known in sociology. Though they eventually achieved widespread recognition and acclaim, they were originally published primarily in philosophical journals, e.g., *Philosophy and Phenomenological Research, Review of Metaphysics*, and the *Journal of Philosophy*, or the more eclectic New School journal *Social Research*[17] which was oriented to social and political research. (All of these papers were finally collected in the three volumes of his *Collected Papers, vols I, II, and III*, edited and published posthumously, in 1962, 1964 and 1966.) Thus, of the total number of 26 articles he published between 1940 and 1959, only 2 (The Stranger in 1944 and The Homecomer in 1945) were published in a sociological journal, *The American Journal of Sociology*;[18] 11 were in philosophical journals; 7 were in the journal published by the New School, *Social Research*, and 6 were in edited books of contributed papers.

5. Although he began to prepare a volume which would have been a systematic organization of his thought since his first book, Schutz was unable to complete and publish this in his lifetime and it remained for Luckmann to bring it to completion posthumously as *Structures of the Life-World* in two volumes. (Schutz and Luckmann, vol. I 1973, and vol. II 1989 in English) Such a work might have succeeded in bringing to the attention of the broader sociological community in "a fully organized and elaborate detail the main body of his

social theory" (Broderson, 1964, p. xii). But it was not until fourteen years after his death that the first of these volumes was published in English translation. In contrast, his first book had been well received in Vienna and, according to Broderson (1964, p. xi), "seemed destined to become a work of major influence among social science scholars in general. But (the war and his exile), destroyed the intellectual community where the book had been conceived and where alone it could have made its immediate impact upon the contemporary mind."

6. He had an ill fated contact and correspondence with Talcott Parsons, the leading American sociological theorist[19] and an influential member of the Harvard department.[20] Schutz gave a lecture at Harvard at Parsons' invitation and sent to Parsons in 1940 an extensive commentary on Parsons' *The Structure of Social Action* (1937)[21] but their correspondence ended in 1941. As Parsons moved farther away from a subjective and voluntaristic theory of action to develop a general systems theory, Schutz remained true to his phenomenological roots in insisting on the importance of the subjective dimension in human action.

Parsons misunderstood Schutz's commentaries on his work[22] and eventually rejected them by saying that to accept them would have meant making fundamental revisions of his work (Wagner, 1983, pp. 75–76). Thus, what might have been a fruitful opportunity to connect Schutz to other contemporary American social theorists turned into a rejection and disconnection.[23] Schutz refrained from publishing this critical commentary and assessment of Parsons' work during his lifetime.[24] His contacts with American philosophy were a bit more successful and he helped Marvin Farber (Buffalo University) in the founding of the journal *Philosophy and Phenomenological Research*, to which he contributed some 12 papers in the period 1940–1959.

Summary: Schutz's Influence During His Lifetime

Considering all of the above outlined factors, it becomes possible better to understand why Schutz's influence on American sociology did not occur during his lifetime but after his death. It would be mediated in part by the small number of students whom he influenced during his lifetime. Although he began teaching at the New School in 1943[25] his most well-known Ph.D. students in sociology did not complete their degrees until 1954 (P. Berger), 1955 (Wagner) and 1956 (Luckmann), each having begun their graduate studies some 3–5 years earlier. Thus, it is fair to say that his most productive years in relation to training graduate students were a relatively short 10 year period from 1949 until his death in early 1959. It is, of course, a credit to Schutz that the inspiration which he personally provided and the power and appeal of his ideas attracted several brilliant students who succeeded in making his ideas widely known and influential both in sociology and philosophy.

Schutz's Influence on American Sociologists

In this preliminary assessment of his influence I will look specifically at two of his sociology students, Helmut Wagner and Peter Berger, and then at one sociologist, Harold Garfinkel, who, although not his student, began to read Schutz in the 1940s and was stimulated by his thinking. Each of these is of interest in different ways: Wagner became a Schutzian social scientist, expositor of Schutz's ideas and later a biographer of Schutz; Peter Berger was one of the first to introduce a broad based phenomenological perspective to a generation of sociologists. Then, with Thomas Luckmann, Schutz's concepts and theories were introduced by incorporating them in their formulation of what became an influential version of the sociology of knowledge. Harold Garfinkel's development of ethnomethodology owes its origins to Schutz's remarkable insights into the world of everyday life, common sense knowledge, and the taken-for-granted.

Helmut Wagner (1904–1989)

Helmut Wagner, an emigré from Nazi Germany which he left in 1934, studied at the New School for his M.A. in 1953 and Ph.D. in 1955 where he did most of his work under the direction of Alfred Schutz and Carl Mayer. He taught briefly at Bucknell and then, for almost all of his academic career, at Hobart and William Smith Colleges from which he retired.[26] His "interest in sociology was awakened by his reading of the work of Max Weber" and was "influenced by Weber's insistence on the importance of interpreting social action from a subjective standpoint. Later he accepted Alfred Schutz's re-interpretation and deepening of Weber's micro-sociology and joined him in efforts to give sociology a consistently subjective foundation" (Psathas and Bittner, 1991, p. 225). For some 28 years in academic and scholarly work, he dedicated himself, in his words, to "the comprehension of Schutz's thinking in all aspects of his seemingly kaleidoscopic but internally, remarkably coherent pieces of writing. . . the critical evaluation of these pieces. . . (and to) carrying selected aspects of Schutz's investigations beyond his cut off points, deliberately chosen by him and ever pointed out in his writings or in letters to friends" (1991, p. 226)

Wagner published many articles about phenomenology and sociology and his books were instrumental in bringing Schutz's thought to the awareness of a next generation of sociologists. He collated under several topical headings Schutz's scattered writings in the Heritage of Sociology Series, titled *Alfred Schutz On Phenomenology and Social Reality*, 1970. He outlined the framework of Schutz's thought under the following topics: I. Phenomenological Foundations; II The Cognitive Setting of the Life World; III Acting in the Life

World; IV The World of Social Relationship; V Realms of Experience; and VI The Province of Sociology. In his introduction to this volume, Wagner provided a brief sketch of the scope of Schutz's conceptualizations and contributions to sociology, social psychology, sociological theory, and methodology and to what Wagner (1970, p. 47 fn. 44) aptly characterizes as "metasociology"; i.e., a concern with questions that are "logically prior to sociology" such as establishing, delineating, and interpreting the subject matter of sociology, the nature of 'social reality.'"

His intellectual biography of Schutz (1983) was an extraordinary work which traced Schutz's personal and academic development; the major traditions and predecessors that influenced Schutz; the relations between Schutz and his contemporaries; the student generation influenced by Schutz; and the ways in which Schutz's thought connected to Leibniz, Bergson, and Husserl.

In his own major work, *Phenomenology of Consciousness and Sociology of the Life World*, 1983, Wagner provides an introductory overview and entry into a social phenomenological perspective, borrowing and elaborating on Schutz's views. The book presents an orderly and coherent Schutzian sociology, one which can serve to introduce the student to this perspective. As Wagner says of his work:

> I am writing this book as a student of Schutz and as someone trying to apply phenomenology . . . . the form of this book, moving from consciousness to the life world, follows that established by Edmund Husserl. However, the application of his approach . . . is predominantly the work of Alfred Schutz. He was a critical student of Husserl. Thus he followed not the letter but the spirit of the original phenomenological investigations, and he opened them to the influences of other thinkers, notably . . . Bergson . . . William James, John Dewey, and George H. Mead. (1970, p. 5)

In addition he edited (with Ilja Srubar) a *Bergsonian Bridge to Phenomenological Psychology*, 1984, and translated and introduced *Life Forms and Meaning Structure*, 1982 (an editing of Schutz's early unpublished writings preceding his 1932 book). He was a "premiere custodian of the Alfred Schutz legacy... as well as advancing the cause of a phenomenologically oriented sociology through his own elaborations on this legacy." (Psathas and Bittner, p. 227)

At the time of his death he was editing a fourth volume of Schutz's papers (which was eventually completed by Fred Kersten and George Psathas and published in 1996) and planned to publish the more extensive intellectual biography of Schutz which the University of Chicago Press had forced him to reduce in size and scope when it was published in 1983.[27] Wagner succeeded in making Schutz's thought available in a more systematic fashion to an American sociological audience and to providing an important and influential study of the development of Schutz's ideas and perspectives in his intellectual biography.

Peter Berger (1929–)

Peter Berger, also born in Austria and an emigré to the United States at age 17, graduated from Wagner College in Brooklyn in 1949, and attended the New School where he received his M.A. in 1950 and his Ph.D. in 1954. The mentors he cites in his early work as having influenced him are Carl Mayer[28] with whom he studied Max Weber and the sociology of religion; Albert Salomon, who taught on Durkheim; and Alfred Schutz with whom he studied the sociology of knowledge and seminars on "Current Events and Everyday Situations in the Light of Sociological Theory." His involvement with those faculty at the New School who taught philosophy, and particularly phenomenological philosophy, was minimal. It was Thomas Luckmann, later his colleague and co-author, who became more familiar and involved with phenomenological philosophy.

He very early evidenced an interest in the sociology of religion. He attended the Lutheran Theological Seminary in Philadelphia briefly contemplating a career in ministry before resuming his doctoral studies and his first two books in this area, *The Precarious Vision*[29] and *The Noise of Solemn Assemblies*, were both published in 1961. He has gone on to become one of the most influential sociologists in the sociology of religion and has continued his interest and writings in this field for nearly 40 years.

His third book, the 1963 volume titled *Invitation to Sociology*,[30] had a major impact on the field of sociology. [31] The subtitle of the book is " A Humanistic Perspective." Of Schutz, Berger writes: "In so far as the humanities have always focused on the meanings of social life, Schutz's ideas have had an appeal to sociologists who consider themselves humanists."[32] *Invitation to Sociology* does show an indebtedness to Schutz both in its approach and in explicit citations by Berger in footnotes. For example, in the notes to chapter 1 he says:

> Alfred Schuetz (1899–1959) was a philosopher of the phenomenological school who devoted most of his life work to the philosophical foundations of sociology as a science. . . *His influence on contemporary sociologists is as yet limited but will undoubtedly grow as his work becomes more accessible*. (1963, p. 178, my italics)

And later in chapter 1:

> People who like to avoid shocking discoveries, who prefer to believe that society is just what they were taught in Sunday school, who like the safety of the rules and maxims of what Alfred Schuetz has called the "world-taken-for-granted," should stay away from sociology. (1963, p. 24)

In a distinct phenomenological turn, one of his basic themes in *Invitation* is that of "sociology as a form of consciousness." He proposes (1963, pp. 35–53) that sociology is a "way of looking"; being able to "see through" things;

"see(ing) through the facades of social structures"; "penetrating the smoke screen of official versions of reality"; a "debunking and unmasking" mentality; maintaining "an unrespectable perspective" i.e., an awareness of worlds other than those of middle class respectability; this includes appearing to be "detached," "distant from" the "respectable," powerful elements of society. It is a consciousness that is "in tune with the modern era[33]. . . in which values have become radically relativized." The modern age is characterized by "conversion," changing one's views, radically and frequently, (or "alternation") between different meaning systems and an awareness that ideas are relative to specific locations, a "relativizing motif." Thus, debunking, relativizing and unrespectability and a cosmopolitan and urbane attitude means that a sociological perspective is a "broad, open, emancipated vista on human life." (1963, p. 50)

In the final chapter, titled "Sociology as a Humanistic Discipline," he points out a number of values which are "endemic to scientific procedures": humility, effacement of self, honesty and precision in method, respect for findings honestly arrived at, patience, (and) a willingness to be proved wrong and revise one's theories." (1963, p. 166) He notes that there are other traits which assign it to the "vicinity of the humanities." These he mentions are "a concern with the human condition, the same subject of the humanities' fundamental question, what it means to be a man . . . in a particular situation" (1963, p. 167) This he says implies an "openness of mind, and a catholicity of vision." (And an ongoing communication with other disciplines especially history and philosophy. "The foolishness of some sociological work, especially in this country, could be easily avoided by a measure of literacy in these two areas." A disregard of history, he says, "is an offense not only against the Western ideal of the civilized man but against sociological reasoning itself – namely that part of it that deals with the central phenomenon of predefinition." And philosophy is important "because it would prevent the methodological naiveté of some sociologists" and enable a "more adequate grasp of the phenomena themselves that [one wishes] to investigate." (1963, pp. 168–169)

Berger's vision of sociology appears in this book, as well as others, to have been influenced both by Max Weber and Alfred Schutz. At times he also sounds and speaks like an existential philosopher. In fact, he cites Heidegger and the notion of *das Man* as well as notions of authenticity and inauthenticity.

> Society provides the taken-for-granted structures which allow us, by following the rules, to be shielded from freedom . . . The "okay world" (of the taken-for-granted) is precarious . . . and we know this . . . but may seek "shelter" in (ways of doing or believing) that make the world believable. The walls of society are a Potemkin village erected in front of the abyss of being. (1963, p. 149)

> Society provides us with warm, reasonably comfortable caves, in which we can huddle with our fellows, beating on the drums that drown out the

howling hyenas of the surrounding darkness. 'Ekstasis' is the act of stepping outside the cave, alone, to face the night. (1963, p. 150)

And, in the conclusion to the book, he says that it

> . . .is part of a civilized mind in our age to have come in touch with a peculiarly modern, peculiarly timely form of critical thought that we call sociology. [One can] become less stolid in one's prejudices, more careful in commitments, more skeptical about commitments of others, and perhaps more compassionate in their journeys through society. (1963, p. 175)
>
> We may become aware of the 'logic of the theatre' of the social world and be able to look up and see the machinery by which we have been moved. In this act lies the first step toward freedom. . . and the conclusive justification of sociology as a humanistic discipline (1963, p. 176).

This perspective, as he outlines it, is broadly humanistic and phenomenological. It is an open, receptive, and curious outlook; looking at "what is" rather than accepting official views. It means setting aside "what we all know to be so"; to use rigorous procedures, methodologies that have rules; to be logical and consistent; disrespectful of convention or received wisdom in order to "see through" to what is actually the case. The book has been widely read, often as required reading in introductory courses in sociology, though less so today. Its themes were perhaps more "radical" in the 60s and 70s[34] but it is interesting in retrospect to see how forcefully and extensively Berger drew on phenomenological insights in developing his viewpoint. His version of sociology was in direct contrast to that of the 1960s Marxist, politically engaged and committed sociologists.[35] Throughout his career Berger consistently critiqued both the positivists and the Marxists while drawing from and integrating the ideas of major thinkers from these camps, such as Durkheim and the early Marx.

The most important book, however, which brought Schutz's thought to the awareness of sociologists in the late 60s was the one he co-authored with Thomas Luckmann,[36] who had also been a fellow student at the New School and a student of Schutz, *The Social Construction of Reality: A Treatise in the Sociology of Knowledge*, 1966.[37] This work represented a direct challenge to the classical sociology of knowledge developed by Marx and Mannheim which Schutz had characterized as "the so-called sociology of knowledge" (Schutz, 1964, p. 121) and which Berger and Luckmann (1966) challenged and overturned.[38]

> . . . a sociology of knowledge will have to deal not only with the empirical variety of 'knowledge' in human societies, but also with the processes by which *any* body of 'knowledge' comes to be socially established *as* 'reality.'

> . . .[it] must concern itself with whatever passes for 'knowledge' in a society regardless of the ultimate validity or invalidity . . . of such 'knowledge.' And insofar as all human 'knowledge' is developed, transmitted and maintained in social situations, the sociology of knowledge must seek to understand the processes by which this is done in such away that a taken-for-granted 'reality' congeals for the man in the street. In other words, we contend that *the sociology of knowledge is concerned with the analysis of the social construction of reality*. (p. 3)

> We therefore exclude from the sociology of knowledge the epistemological and methodological problems that bothered both of its major originators. (they refer to Scheler and Mannheim among others) (pp. 12–13)

> *The sociology of knowledge must concern itself with everything that passes for 'knowledge' in society*. (italics authors')

> . . . commonsense 'knowledge' rather than 'ideas' must be the central focus for the sociology of knowledge. It is precisely this 'knowledge' that constitutes the fabric of meanings without which no society could exist. (p. 14)

> . . . what we are suggesting here is a far-reaching redefinition of the scope of the sociology of knowledge, much wider than what has hitherto been understood as this discipline.

> . . . We owe the fundamental insight into the necessity for this redefinition to Alfred Schutz. . . . he clearly saw that this discipline would have to focus on: 'all typifications of common-sense thinking (which are) integral elements of the concrete historical socio-cultural *Lebenswelt* within which they prevail as taken for granted and as socially approved. Their structure determines among other things the social distribution of knowledge and its relativity and relevance to the concrete social environment of a concrete group in a concrete historical situation. *Here are the legitimate problems of relativism, historicism, and of the so-called sociology of knowledge*.' (italics mine) (Schutz, 1962, p. 149)

and again:

> While we would not give the central place to the social distribution of knowledge that Schutz implies here, we agree with his criticism of 'the discipline thus misnamed' and have derived from him our basic notion of the manner in which the task of the sociology of knowledge must be redefined. In the following considerations we are heavily dependent on Schutz in the prolegomena concerning the foundations of knowledge in everyday life and greatly indebted to his work in various important places of our main argument thereafter. (pp. 14–15)

The view which Berger and Luckmann presented in this book is directly opposed to the earlier, classical formulations of the sociology of knowledge as developed from Scheler, Marx and Mannheim. It does not look for the social determinants or correlates of ideas and ideologies; it does not accept the notion that sociology should be primarily concerned with the ideas and ideologies of intellectuals or elites; it redefines the topic as "commonsense knowledge" which is found everywhere; and includes the ordinary, everyday 'knowledge' of the man in the street. This approach makes the topics of the sociology of knowledge broader, more inclusive, and more widely distributed, while privileging no sets of knowledge above any others. Though they themselves do not report any empirical studies in this book, they lay out a theoretical perspective which in the past thirty years has radically transformed the sociology of knowledge.

It is beyond the scope of this paper to document these influences in detail but in support of this conclusion I will only cite at this point one bit of evidence. This is an encyclopedia entry written by Volker Meja and Nico Stehr (1993) who have written extensively on the sociology of knowledge and edited more than one book on the topic. These authors had in their earlier writings given little or no attention to Berger and Luckmann. In this article, however, they write:

> The sociology of knowledge has recently experienced a reorientation in the direction of an analysis of everyday life and of natural scientific and technical knowledge (both neglected by the classical sociology of knowledge). Peter Berger and Thomas Luckmann's *The Social Construction of Reality* (1966) written in the tradition of Alfred Schutz's phenomenology and Arnold Gehlen's philosophical anthropology, represents a clear departure from the preoccupation of the classical sociology of knowledge with issues of epistemology and methodology. Everything that is regarded as knowledge in society is now accepted as a legitimate subject matter for sociological investigations.
>
> Inspired by developments in the history of science, the sociology of knowledge has also turned in the direction of empirical analyses of the social construction of scientific facts, frequently by way of ethnographic studies of laboratory life. Such research on the 'manufacture' of natural-scientific knowledge has led to a reassessment of traditional assumptions about the unique rationality of scientific knowledge. Seen through the lens of the 'strong programme' of the sociology of scientific knowledge, scientific knowledge and everyday knowledge are in fact extraordinarily similar in certain respects. (1963, pp. 638–639)

Thus, fields of study have developed which are now referred to as the "sociology of scientific knowledge" or the "sociology of science" rather than the sociology of knowledge.[39] It is this diffusion, particularization and focus on a variety of areas of commonsense knowledge that owes much of its original impetus to the ideas of Alfred Schutz.[40] This shift and transformation of a field, I believe, could not have come about without the work of Alfred Schutz. It was Berger and Luckmann's incorporation of Schutz's ideas in their formulations that enabled this transformation.[41]

Harold Garfinkel (1917–)

Harold Garfinkel, after graduating from the University of Newark (now the Newark campus of Rutgers University), began his graduate studies in sociology at the University of North Carolina in 1939. His sociological interests had first been in issues of race and inequality but at North Carolina he became more and more interested in theoretical problems and in how sociology might deal with issues related to understanding the actor's point of view. Here his readings in W.I. Thomas and F. Znaniecki on social action and Kenneth Burke and C.W. Mills on vocabularies of motives and theories of accounts were important as were his readings of the work of Talcott Parsons whose book, *The Structure of Social Action*, appeared in 1937. At the same time he was introduced to phenomenological philosophy in courses and in discussions with fellow students and to the thought of Husserl, Schutz and Gurwitsch.[42] His graduate studies were interrupted by service in the military after the completion of his master's degree in 1942. Subsequently, he pursued his doctorate at Harvard, beginning in the fall of 1946 where he came into closer contact with Talcott Parsons, whom he saw as providing an important development in sociology for the study of social order and social action. He had become interested in the problem of social order and the description of action as well as developing an understanding and critique of the actor's point of view.[43]

At Harvard he met Gurwitsch with whom he had many discussions while also reading with him *The Field of Consciousness*, which was in preparatory stages (eventually first published in 1953). From Gurwitsch he saw the ways in which empirical examples could be used in phenomenological studies and the significance of such notions as functional significations and gestalt complex.[44] Gurwitsch recommended him to Schutz and he then wrote to Schutz in 1949[45] requesting an opportunity to meet.[46] He said he wrote at the suggestion of Aron Gurwitsch, "friend and extra-curricular teacher . . . with whom I have had many conversations. . ." His dissertation topics,[47] he says, have taken him "rather deeply into your writings as well as into the writings of Husserl and Gurwitch. The orientation of the thesis has been taken principally from these writings but particularly from your article *On Multiple Realities* and your book *Der Sinnhafte Aufbau Der Sozialenwelt*." (sic)

The "particular problems" with which he was concerned in his dissertation he listed as "the theory of meaning, the theory of objects, the method of *verstehen*, the role of motivation theories in accounting for change, the logical character of the subjective categories, and so on." He also offered to translate Schutz's book into English and proposed they meet later that month during the time of the American Sociological Society meetings, saying, "I have felt for a long while the need to talk with you and I have been encouraged by Dr. Gurwitsch to ask for a meeting." He "traveled regularly. . . (to New York) to spend tutorial evenings" (Garfinkel, 2002, p. 84) with Schutz and also engaged in a correspondence with him. In the fall of 1950 Garfinkel went to Princeton where he was an Instructor for two academic years. He helped arrange for the Princeton Conference, held in 1952, at which Schutz presented his paper on "Common-Sense and Scientific Interpretations of Human Action."

By June of 1952 Garfinkel had competed his doctoral dissertation and received his degree. He then moved for two years to Ohio State University.[48] In October of 1953, he sent Schutz two additional papers written at Ohio State, having already sent him a copy of his dissertation – which he now requested to be returned. Of this work, he says, "the inspiration was drawn from what I have learned from your writings. Only the last section of the paper, dealing with some problems encountered with the (sociological) attitude in use, has much of my own in it." This latter (unpublished) paper, titled "Notes on the Sociological Attitude," he says, has "drawn without conscience" from your writings. Specifically, the "section characterizing the natural and scientific attitudes, with the exception of some additions from my own reflections, is a paraphrasing of your ideas as they are formed in your article 'On Multiple Realities.'" And the second section, he says, draws from Schutz's article "The Problem of Rationality in the Social World" and uses Schutz's "four postulates of social science . . . by turning them into basic procedural rules that are definitive of the attitude."[49] He also formulates a notion of a "sociological epoché" which he calls "the rule of sociological empiricism."

In his response, Schutz wrote a lengthy four page, single spaced, typewritten letter taking up several points in these papers. On the paper on the sociological atttitude, which he "liked very much" he says that he is in agreement with what Garfinkel says about the "attitude of daily life and the attitude of scientific theorizing" and on the "sociological attitude" if he would call it instead the "attitude of the social scientist." In a significant concluding sentence on this paper he says, "If you say that the study of the methodological decisions upon which the *actual* practices of sociologists are based are practically unknown territory you have my full approval and I hope you will be one of the explorers of this undiscovered treasure island."

This last sentence may be apocryphal because Garfinkel was already on his way, launched in part by Schutz, to the "undiscovered treasure island." The exploration turned out to be, for Garfinkel, the "methodologies of actual practices by ordinary members of society" which he had first formulated in this paper as the "actual practices of sociologists." The treasure perhaps is yet to be located in its entirety because as Garfinkel was to say at a later date, the findings are "inexhaustible;" but the nature of the treasure and the means for locating it was to take Garfinkel many laborious and still continuing expeditions, at first alone, but later with a small band of dedicated and intrepid explorers. The "exploration of the methodologies of actual practices" and the studies of work was to turn out to be "ethnomethodology."

In his letter of August 20, 1958 after he had been at UCLA for four years, Garfinkel offered to meet with Schutz during a trip to the East coast to tell him "what the state of 'Schutz-in-Sociology' is at UCLA, Berkeley, Chicago, Northwestern and other places where I have visited, gained adherents, or sent students." and again says "I want very much to talk with you. . ." However, Schutz's travels prevented their meeting that fall. Garfinkel had sent Schutz "a package of writings" as a "token of my seriousness about and continuing preoccupation with your work. Thus far, . . . I have managed to retain the freedom to work out my program using your work as a principal scheme for re-reading the theoretical and empirical concerns of the sociology of common sense situations, not to say the more frequently encountered common sense sociology of theoretical situtations." He adds that he is working on a book "on the study of norms and normative orders of activities. Your work on common sense informs every part of it. There is much to tell you."[50] In Garfinkel's view, at this point, he was continuing to be influenced by Schutz's thought but was, at the same time, working "out my program" using Schutz's work as a "principal scheme" to re-formulate what the study of common sense could be.

What was it that Garfinkel was trying to find and why did he eventually leave Schutz behind? At an early stage he appeared to be a Schutzian social scientist, had absorbed his main ideas, and paraphrased them in his own writings while trying to expand and add a few "reflections" of his own. But after leaving Princeton, he continued to head West and by the time he reached and settled in California in 1954, he was well on his way on an intellectual journey that would separate him from his East coast beginnings forever. The writings that he sent Schutz, most likely what he was working on while in California, may give us a clue concerning the new directions in which he was working. Rawls (2000) says that in preparing to present the work on the jury project to the ASA meetings of 1954,[51] Garfinkel came up with the term "ethnomethodology" to refer to what they had been doing in their research. It is not clear whether he sent a copy of this work to Schutz. Perhaps it is significant that this usage did not become prominent until after Schutz's death in 1959 though it does appear in unpublished papers in 1956 and 1960.

A Closer Examination of Garfinkel's Early Writings

In his doctoral dissertation, *The Perception of the Other: A Study in Social Order*, 1952, Garfinkel drew heavily on Schutz's analyses in order to explore a counter position to that of Talcott Parsons on the nature and sources of social order.[52] Schutz, as we have already noted, had become familiar with Parsons' earliest writings (1937), particularly his examination of Weber and his drawing on other European theorists, e.g., Durkheim and Pareto. Schutz's correspondence with Parsons is detailed in Grathoff's edited book (1978). But

Schutz's hopes for a productive relationship with Parsons were dashed as Parsons misinterpreted and rejected Schutz's commentaries and criticisms.[53]

In his early studies, Garfinkel used Schutz's insights to develop means to discover whether Parsons' formulations concerning the sources of social order could be empirically studied. His efforts resulted in various studies which disrupted, disturbed or undercut commonsense understandings and meanings. If Parsons' theorizing made sense, such situations would result in breakdowns of interaction, senselessness, or anomie, and total disruptions of the setting. Whereas Parsons assumed that "mutual understandings and rationality" undergird the "shared character of rules," when Garfinkel tried to make visible these shared understandings he found that persons used various means to make sense of the situation, to extend, modify or even suppress the rules, to ignore what happened, or to let events take their course and wait. He found that "the moral order of daily life exerts such a powerful presence that considerable lengths will be gone to in order to retain, if at all possible, the things-as-usual character of ordinary life." (Sharrock and Anderson, 1986, p. 32)

Garfinkel reasoned that the notions of a shared culture and the means/end rationality of action had to be suspended. It would be necessary to study what had been taken for granted. Further, he reasoned, the "rationality, sense, understandability . . . [of activities] must be treated as the outcome of those actions, their accomplishment. The achievement of rationality, understandability and so on takes place in and through the performance of the actions themselves." (Sharrock and Anderson, 1986, p. 32) The investigation of the ways that social actors display the knowledge and understanding they have would require direct studies of the "systematic, methodical and routine ways" that they do it. The name Garfinkel was to give for the study of such procedures was "ethnomethodology."

Part of the evidence for Schutz's influence is to be found in Garfinkel's own acknowledgments. Among his first published papers, Garfinkel (1956) cites Schutz's paper, "Common Sense and Scientific Interpretation of Human Action," first presented at the Princeton Conference in 1952 (and later published in *Philosophy and Phenomenological Research*, 1953). In his paper, "Aspects of the Problem of Common Sense Knowledge of Social Structures," (1959) he cites Schutz in a footnote as follows:

> Readers who are acquainted with the magnificent writings of the late Alfred Schutz will recognize the debt that anyone writing on this topic owes to him. The paper is respectfully dedicated to him as an esteemed teacher and sociologist. (1959, p. 51).[54]

In an unpublished paper presented at a meeting of a seminar on ethnoscience in April 1961, titled "Reflections on the Clinical Method in Psychiatry from the Point of View of Ethnomethodolgy," Garfinkel outlines as one of the methods which may be used that of the search for "the essential features of the psychiatric case history." He proceeds to outline, with extensive quotes (2 1/2 pages, single spaced) from Spiegelberg's chapter 14 on "The Essentials of the Phenomenological Method" what he calls "The Rules of Constitutive Phenomenological Procedure." He discusses the method of "free imaginative variation", quotes Dorian Cairns as well, and lists five steps which are to be "carried out within the procedure called 'the phenomenological reduction.'"

As a result of this analysis he then delineates what he presents as "The Distinctive Features of the Psychiatric Case History," including such features as "that [the case history] is concerned with persons; that time consists of time-in-the-account; that time in the account consists of historical materials; that the account is a 'time object' that the account is terminable; that 'psychiatric' refer to the rules that define a competent reading of the sentences that comprise the account, etc." This is the most explicit use of the phenomenological method that I have been able to find in any of Garfinkel's writings and although his paper is titled "from the Point of View of Ethnomethodology" it would seem to mean that he sees a close relationship between this point of view and phenomenology. It is clear that his views are still evolving. His audience at this seminar may have included Frake and Goodenough, two prominent ethnoscientists whose ideas he also incorporates. He seems here to place ethnomethodology as one of the ethnosciences (which include, for example, ethnobotany, ethnomusicology, ethnophysiology, etc.) which he claimed in later writings had furnished him with a clue as to what to name his project when he was trying to make sense of what jurors were doing (starting with his work on the jury project at the University of Chicago in the summer of 1954.) Later, of course, he distances himself from ethnoscience completely.

But, as is also true in some of his other early writings, while he cites particular persons and their ideas, he does not necessarily fully accept them. In this paper he actually rejects the approach of the ethnoscientists who ordinarily accept a person's definitions and meanings for a term when studying their usages,[55] and offers the phenomenological reduction as a means for the researcher to uncover the essential features of a phenomenon as it is meant, in this case, "the psychiatric case history."

In this paper he also mentions Wittgenstein (possibly for the first time that I can find) and assimilates him to his project as well.[56] This, to my knowledge, may be the last time Garfinkel cited (and utilized) the phenomenological reduction. He had already written, by 1960, several other papers which were later included in the 1967 collection, *Studies in Ethnomethodology* and which (retrospectively) were included under this heading while he was still exploring and using phenomenological methods.

His citations of Schutz continued as he drafted in 1962 what became published in 1964 as "Studies of the Routine Grounds of Everyday Activities" and later included in the 1967 collection.

The new associations he was developing on the West coast were undoubtedly contributing to the evolving nature of his approach just as his own researches were leading him to develop more extended statements of his program. He always worked in seminars and discussion groups and informal consultations with other persons, students and colleagues. He had met Harvey Sacks in one of Parsons' seminars in 1959–60 during a sabbatical year at Harvard and continued to collaborate with him until the time of Sacks' death in 1975. In 1958 he had met with Edward Rose[57] and others at Santa Fe and later at Colorado. He had formed a working relationship with Aaron Cicourel, with whom in 1957–58 he had organized a seminar that included Egon Bittner, Troy Duster, Peter McHugh, Kenneth Polk, and Gerald Platt. He had read the linguistic philosophers Austin and Wittgenstein. He had inspired Cicourel's (1964) book, *Method and Measurement in Sociology*, which was one of the first sustained critiques of sociological research methods drawing from both Schutz and Garfinkel without actually using the term ethnomethodology. Cicourel (1964, p. iv) notes "a two year collaboration with Harold Garfinkel introduced me to the work of Alfred Schutz and clarified my understanding of the role of theory in method and measurement in sociology." In his chapter on "Theoretical Presuppositions,' Cicourel (1964, p. 189–224) cites extensively Wittgenstein, Schutz and Garfinkel, and recapitulates many of Garfinkel's ideas.

I think it is fair to say that up until 1967, with the appearance of *Studies in Ethnomethodology*, Garfinkel and his students and associates still saw their work as not only drawing inspiration and conceptualizations from Schutz but as also being based on Schutz's foundational explorations of the natural attitude, multiple realities, common sense knowledge, and the distinctions he drew between common sense and scientific interpretations of human action. Thus, it is clear that by the time of his dissertation in 1952 Garfinkel had read Schutz's various papers published in the 1940s and utilized these in his examination of Parsons; by 1959 he had incorporated and acknowledged his debt to the many ideas of Alfred Schutz; and at the time of the publication of *Studies in Ethnomethodology* in 1967, which consisted of several of his previously published papers, he writes in the Preface:

> The[se] articles originated from my studies of the writings of Talcott Parsons, Alfred Schutz, Aron Gurwitsch, and Edmund Husserl. For twenty years their writings have provided me with inexhaustive directives into the world of everyday activities. (1967, p. ix)

Other collaborations are acknowledged in this and other writings.[58]

Summary: Garfinkel and Ethnomethodology

While ethnomethodology should not be considered a continuation of Alfred Schutz's sociology, it was stimulated by Schutz's achievements and is indebted to his many insights. Ethnomethodology extends, elaborates, modifies, and radicalizes some of Schutz's perspectives[59] in ways that would very likely not have been acceptable to Schutz himself, judging from the critical reception that Garfinkel's thought has received from Schutz's students and followers (e.g., B. Berger, P. Berger, Grathoff, Luckmann, Natanson and Wagner). Nevertheless, in my view, it is unlikely that Garfinkel's ethnomethodology would have achieved its beginnings without Schutz's prior theoretical and methodological explorations.

As such, ethnomethodology represents one extension and elaboration of a phenomenological foundation for studies of the world of everyday life. As various commentators have said, it is a perspective, an orientation, an approach, an analytic mentality, as well as a movement. It includes such features as: bracketing presuppositions and theories about the social world, or, at best, maintaining an "ethnomethodological indifference" toward them; requiring a "faithfulness to the phenomena of study"; accepting that human qualities of thought, reason, emotion, planfulness, judgment, and knowledge are involved in human actions; rejecting any pre-formulated and prescribed strategies or analytic methodologies; requiring methodological perspectives which are uniquely adequate for the phenomena to be studied; remaining faithful to the description of members' methods of practical reasoning and practical actions in the world of everyday life; and avoiding causal, motivational, psychological, and constructive-analytic, interpretations and explanations of human action.[60]

Ethnomethodology is oriented to the discovery and analysis of the produced orderliness of everyday life. There is a diversity among ethnomethodologists and in ethnomethodological studies such that it is difficult to define its "core," if there is such a thing. But that diversity is in one respect an indication of its vitality and its continual effort to differentiate itself from other perspectives most of which, in current sociology at least, are more dominant than its own.[61]

Conclusion

It is clear that Schutz left a remarkable legacy in what was after all a short and not full-time academic career of sixteen years in America. If his personal circumstances, collegial connections and institutional relationships in America had been more favorable, there is no question that he would have had an even greater influence during his own lifetime. Those on whom he had what Spiegelberg refers to as a "direct personal influence" include: Helmut Wagner on whom the influence can be characterized as a "total influence" since he then went on to become an "adherent, follower, and developer of his mentor's main ideas and theories;" Peter Berger, who together with another former student, Thomas Luckmann, went on to "extend, expand, and develop what they believe to be the implications of their mentor's ideas" into a new approach to the sociology of knowledge; and Harold Garfinkel, with whom he had extensive contacts – both face-to-face, in correspondence and through his writings – and who made "original contributions and achieved a major transformation" of Schutz's ideas in the development of ethnomethodology. With other persons and in other areas of sociology [62] Schutz also had a considerable influence which remains to be traced through subsequent developments in sociology in the latter half of the twentieth century.

Notes

* Presented as the Alfred Schutz Memorial Lecture, at the annual meeting of the Society for Phenomenology and the Human Sciences, Pennsylvania State University, State College, October 6, 2000, and co-sponsored by the Center for the Advancement of Research in Phenomenology, the American Philosophical Association, and the Society for Phenomenology and the Human Sciences.

1. Garfinkel had read Schutz's work in the 1940's, drew on Schutz in his doctoral dissertation (1952) and had organized a conference at Princeton held in 1952 to which Schutz was invited. He also met with Schutz many times and corresponded with Schutz over a number of years. (Garfinkel, 2002, p. 84)
2. Bauman adds (1996, p. 826) that "Harold Garfinkel's 'ethnomethodology' (that treated the social as the accomplishment of knowledgeable actors, in the course of their everyday work) added further impetus to the reorientation of sociology away from 'objective' systems and structures and towards 'social agency', self-reflexive, intentional action and its unanticipated consequences. . . ." I will discuss Garfinkel below.
3. Bottomore(1993., p. 635) points to a number of movements that also affected this change. "The decline of the functionalist paradigm began in the 1960s when a great transformation of sociology took place. International conflicts, and especially the Vietnam war, the emergence of new social movements, the growth of dissent and opposition in Western countries and in Eastern Europe, the widening gap between rich and poor nations, provoked a radical reorientation of social thought. Social change and conflict, instead of social integration and the regulation of social life by shared norms or a presumed 'common value system', now became central issues for analysis.
4. See Herbert Spiegelberg's excellent discussion of the forms of influence in his study of the influence of phenomenology in psychology and psychiatry (1972, pp. xxxvii–xliv)
5. An example is provided by Wagner (1983, pp. 36–37) who describes Schutz's early relationship with Felix Kaufmann with whom he studied Husserl's writings and who then "helped to shape the content" of *Der sinnhafte Aufbau.*
6. Wolff has written about his disagreements with the cognitive emphasis of much of phenomenology, including Schutz's views, as he developed his notions of surrender and catch. Goffman undertook a critique of Schutz's notions of multiple realities in his *Frame Analysis* (1974).
7. Although, as Speigelberg (1972, p. xxxviii) notes, the testimony of the "recipient of the influence who admits his 'debt' is prima-facie evidence of such influence . . . (it may be that he is) mistaken in his judgment and even may give credit for such irrelevant reasons as scholarly display or ingratiation. Hence mere footnote quotations should never be considered sufficient proof of influence. . ."

8. Spiegelberg (1972, pp. xxxviii–xli) refers to this as "influence . . . (by an) impersonal source (such as) an idea or a book." He goes on to distinguish different degrees of influence as: "total and partial, (which includes) stimulation, reinforcement and corroboration."
9. The question of who is an American sociologist and what is American sociology will have to be alluded to only briefly here. Some of those whom Schutz influenced as his students at the New School were European born and raised but went on to become American citizens and remained in the U.S. (e.g., Helmut Wagner, Brigitte Berger, and Peter Berger). Others were European born and raised and later returned to Europe to carry on their academic careers (e.g., Thomas Luckmann, Hansfried Kellner, Richard Grathoff) I shall include in this paper only those who remained in the U.S. and became contributors to the development of American sociology.
10. Rutkoff and Scott (1986, pp. 252–253) characterize its reputation as follows: "Critical distance from the mainstream of American academic life has frequently resulted in the New School's dismissal as an eccentric and maverick institution, while its political activism has at times led it to lose some of that same critical distance. In addition, its rejection of traditional standards and its openly skeptical attitude toward conventional professional canons have left the New School vulnerable to intellectual and artistic fads. . . . Defining itself as nondisciplinary, it has at times encouraged what appeared to be little more than confusing eclecticism, but it has also been the setting for some remarkable collaborative efforts. [Here they mention dance and music, John Cage, the structuralism of Levi-Strauss, Roman Jacobson, and Alfred Schutz's phenomenology] . . . all developed in the atmosphere of free exchange that characterized the school. Artists and intellectuals in twentieth century America have found few places as flexible and innovative as the New School."
11. Coser (1984, pp. 121–123), himself a refugee scholar, notes of the New School and Schutz that his "relative obscurity in America can be accounted for largely by his isolation from his native-born peers in sociology and philosophy, a common characteristic of the New School faculty, most of whom live in a world populated by fellow refugees." Rogers (2000, p. 356) says that a number of circumstances "disadvantaged" Schutz: he lacked "connections, contacts and networks" and the ways in which these can "interplay with organizational affiliation"; he worked "part-time in academe . . . not with an Ivy League institution, nor . . . with any . . . center of lively philosophizing and theorizing; he had no mentor promoting his ideas, helping him get published, or showing him the ropes of the American academic system (and) he worked in areas of social theory that are hard to define, if only because of their transdisciplinary reach."
12. In the late 1940s, following the end of the war, such programs began to develop at major universities in sociology and by the time I entered graduate school in 1950 there were research assistantships involving empirical research available at most major departments in the East, a model which Columbia had stimulated.
13. According to Fred Kersten, who was Schutz's teaching assistant and took attendance, (personal interview 9/19/00) there were many students in Schutz's classes with seminars of 20–25 students but not all were enrolled in a regular degree program. The special nature of the graduate program at the New School was one that was easy to enter but only a small percentage were ever to complete. After Schutz's death when two of his former students, Peter Berger and Thomas Luckmann, were hired, there was the potential for a Schutz legacy to be established at the New School. But by the late 60s both had left and the Graduate Faculty had been decimated by the 70s. Rutkoff and Scott (1986, p. 252) say that "with the deaths of Aron Gurwitsch and Hannah Arendt and the retirement of Hans Jonas, the once distinguished philosophy department was devastated. In sociology, Karl Mayer and Albert Salomon retired, and in the late 1960s its young stars Peter Berger

and Thomas Luckmann both resigned. Adolph Lowe retired from the economics department. In political science and sociology, Arnold Brecht died, and Hans Speier and Hans Morgenthau . . . re-retired, . . . Things became so desparate that in 1978 the New York State Board of Regents rescinded accreditation for the doctorate programs in philosophy, political science and sociology departments. . . ."

14. Jaworski (1998, pp. 4–5) outlines three ideal types: Abstract Empiricism, Scholarship, and a type which is in between these two which he calls the Research Program.
15. Here I can offer my own example of research I engaged in during the late 1950s and early 60s when I conducted small group laboratory experiments designed to test some of Simmel's notions concerning coalition formation in triads. Mine and other researchers' interests were limited to the development of hypotheses derived from Simmel's discussions and made no connections to the broader historical or comparative analyses engaged in by Simmel.
16. This is certainly the model within which I received some of my graduate training at Yale in the mid 1950s. When I was once observed carrying a book by George Herbert Mead by one of my empirically oriented professors, I was asked why I was reading philosophy rather than sociology. Jaworski (1998, p. 6) says: "In the American academy today, the research program and abstracted empiricism have largely supplanted scholarship. *Explication du texte* is a dying art, while methods that ape the natural sciences are *de rigueur* in graduate schools across the United States. European-style scholarship, with its ties to philosophy and literature, has been rejected as old-fashioned and replaced by an American brand of academic work tied to scientific advance and social improvement."
17. The quarterly journal, *Social Research*, founded by Alvin Johnson who was also the New School's founder, was established in the early 30s when the Graduate Faculty was first organized. It was at first designed to publish the works of the General Seminar, an interdisciplinary group of the faculty, as a way of making their work more widely known and available in English. "Every member of the faculty . . . had to agree to write one article a year. . . . with almost 800 subscriptions, it soon developed into a respectable organ for emigré scholarship." (Krohn, 1993, pp. 98, 104–105)
18. It is significant to note that this journal was founded and edited at the University of Chicago in a department founded in part by Albion Small, who had studied in Germany. The Chicago department remained sympathetic to the work of German sociologists, particularly Simmel, for many years. This department was founded in 1892 by Albion Small and was the first to offer graduate instruction in sociology in the world (Bulmer, 1984, p. 38). "In sociology, all the leading figures before 1915 . . . had spent a period of advanced work in Germany; Small studied at Berlin and Leipzig in 1879–81, W.I. Thomas at Gottingen and Berlin in 1888–89, . . . Henderson at Leipzig . . . in the later 1890s, and Robert E. Park at Berlin, Strassburg, and Heidelberg . . . between 1899 and 1903. George Herbert Mead studied at Leipzig and Berlin in 1888–91. . . . One important consequence of this experience, particularly for Small, Thomas, and Park, was the openness to European scholarship which it engendered. The Chicago School was characterized by an awareness of European social thought and social inquiry." The Chicago School flourished until the 1930s though its legacy continued for some years thereafter. It is regarded as the founding home of symbolic interactionism in American sociology. Louis Wirth was one of those who urged Kurt Wolff to undertake a translation of the works of Georg Simmel in the late 1940s. It would be interesting to speculate on what the consequences would have been if Schutz had become a member of the University of Chicago department when he began his teaching in the U.S. in 1943 since some aspects of the Chicago School tradition were still present among some second generation sociologists still there, e.g., Herbert Blumer, Everett Hughes, and Louis Wirth.

19. After Parsons' first book *The Structure of Social Action*, 1937, three major works appeared within three years and had a major impact on sociology: *Essays in Sociological Theory, Pure and Applied*, 1949; (with E.A. Shils) *Toward a General Theory of Action*, 1951, and *The Social System*, 1950, with its pattern variables and his general theory of social action.
20. Their correspondence is provided in full in Richard Grathoff, *The Theory of Social Action: The Correspondence of Alfred Schutz and Talcott Parsons*, Indiana University Press, 1978. Schutz's paper at Harvard in April of 1940, according to Grathoff (1978, p. 139), initiated the correspondence between Schutz and Parsons. The Harvard department achieved great strength beginning in 1945 (see Bulmer, 1984, p. 206) after Parsons reorganized it into a Department of Social Relations.
21. Wagner (1983, p. 158) reports that it was Hayek who had invited Schutz to write a review of Parsons' *Structure of Social Action* for *Economica* a British journal which he edited "thus unwittingly causing the Parsons-Schutz controversy of 1941." The review, which became an extended article, was never published and is now available in its original, lengthier form in Grathoff (1978, pp. 8–60) In the meanwhile, Schutz had sent several of his papers to Parsons including "The Problem of Rationality in the Social World" and "Phenomenology and the Social Sciences," and offered to send "William James's Concept of the Stream of Thought Phenomenologically Interpreted."
22. As Natanson notes in the Foreword to *The Theory of Social Action*, 1978, edited by Grathoff, "Despite serious differences in interpretation, both men are deeply concerned with the theory of social action, with the status of the subjective interpretation of meaning, with the relationship between common-sense and scientific constructs of social reality, with the problem of rationality in human action, and, despite everything which divides them, with the meaning of theory in social science. Why then did the discussion fail? . . . What divides the two men is not different philosophies concerned with different problems but rather the meaning of philosopy for social science. For Schutz, sociology cannot ground itself; epistemology is not a luxury but a necessity for the social scientist. Nor, from a phenomenological perspective, can science, if it is to be truly rigorous, provide its own conceptual foundation. For Parsons, the demand is for demarcating science and philosophy, for allowing philosophy to enter the discussion only when it is needed. It would seem that philosophy should speak only when spoken to! Yet Parsons is immersed in philosophical issues. . . ." (pp. xiv–xv)
23. Parsons had studied in Germany, was fluent in the language, and had translated Weber. Schutz's 1932 book was a commentary, critique and elaboration of Weberian sociology. One would have thought that they would have had common interests. But as is now known, Parsons' translations and interpretations of Weber were distinctively his own and his later work did not remain connected to the Weberian perspective. In his new translation of Weber's *Protestant Ethic and the Spirit of Capitalism*, Kalberg (2001, p. 41) notes that Parsons' translation of Weber was "profoundly flawed."
24. A major portion of the paper was published as "The Social World and the Theory of Social Action" in *Social Research*, 1960, pp. 203–221 and is in *Collected Papers*, vol. 2. Broderson (1964, p. x) notes: "this essay represents the last section, about one third of a longer paper, written in New York in the summer of 1940, the author's first work after his arrival from Austria. The paper was mainly devoted to a critical review of Talcott Parsons' *The Structure of Social Action* (1937), a work which Schutz had studied with the keenest interest. He originally intended to have the entire paper published as his first contribution to scholarly debate in America. However, he changed his mind when he realized that a critical piece such as this would scarcely be understood nor its constructive aspects appreciated unless readers were acquainted with the position in philosophy and social theory on which it was based."

25. According to Wagner (1983, p. 70) and Rogers (2000, p. 379) he began teaching one course a semester in 1943, increased this to two per semester in 1949, and only in 1956 did he finally leave his business commitments to teach full-time, dividing his teaching between sociology and philosophy. By today's standards (1990s), two graduate courses per semester would be considered full-time at the professorial level, but, since he divided his teaching between two departments, probably only half of his courses were in sociology from 1949 to 1959. In 1943 he taught "Introduction to Sociological Theory" and the "Theory of Social Action;" in 1944 he co-taught with Albert Salomon a seminar on Mead and a course in "Social Groups and Problems of Adjustment" followed by "Problems of a Sociology of Knowledge" and, in the following year, seminars on "Self and Society," "Problems of a Sociology of Language," and "Methodology of the Social Sciences."
26. He never taught in a graduate program and, to my knowledge, did not influence any students to pursue further work in a Schutzian sociology though his lectures which appeared in a major book (Wagner, 1983) and his personal contacts did influence, among others, Valerie Malhotra Benz.
27. He had prepared some 38 chapters and 2,400 manuscript pages, part of which was the basis for the 1983 volume. Michael Barber has completed this project, which is scheduled for publication in 2003.
28. In the Preface to *Invitation to Sociology* (1963, p. viii) he says: "In all my thinking on my chosen field I owe an immense debt of gratitude to my teacher Carl Mayer. I suspect that there will be passages that will make him raise an eyebrow. I still hope that he would not regard the conception of sociology here presented as too much of a travesty on the one he has been conveying to his students." Wagner (1983, p. 159) says that Mayer "...was probably the foremost expert on Weber's work both in Europe and the United States..." and that Salomon had studied with both Simmel and Weber in Europe (p. 163). Berger says that these professors, Mayer, Salomon and Schutz, were referred to as "the big three" at the New School at that time.
29. This book is described (entry in *Current Biography Yearbook*, H.W. Wilson Co., New York, 1983, p. 29) as one in which, "Berger, still believing in the divinity of Jesus exactly as defined in the Nicene (sic) Creed, did consider the Jesus encounter crucial. [The book] was an acidic, often satiric Kierkegaardian analysis of the function of the church establishment in America as contrasted with true Christian commitment. Equally anticlerical was A *Precarious Vision*, 1961, a sociological look at the institutional church's connivance in the perpetration of social facades and fictions that deprive the individual of personal authenticity, to trap him or her in what Jean-Paul Sartre called 'bad faith.' Berger's prescription for personal liberation from social masques and individual assumption of ethical responsibility was a return to a Christian faith rooted in the Bible. Whatever Christendom's elite thought of them, both books were popular with a younger generation of American Christians and became a common source of meditation readings in campus chapels."
30. It was reported in 1983 in *Current Biography Yearbook* that the book had sold over 1 million copies.
31. He also published several important papers, some co-authored, after *Invitation to Sociology* and before *The Social Construction of Reality*. These are: (with H. Kellner) "Marriage and the construction of reality," *Diogenes*, 46, 1964, pp. 1–24; "Identity as a problem in the sociology of knowledge," *European Journal of Sociology*, Spring, 1965; and a review of Tiryakian's book, *Sociologism and Existentialism*, 1962, in the *American Sociological Review*, 31, 1966.
32. I recall once in the late 60's when I introduced Berger to an audience as "a phenomenologist" he told me, "no, I am a humanist."

33. Berger also became one of the more influential theorists of modernity as evidenced by his writings such as *The Homeless Mind* (with H. Kellner), 1974; and *Facing Up To Modernity*, 1977. He turned to studies in this area beginning in the 70s after Luckmann had returned to Europe and the intellectual circle of colleagues and friends who had clustered around the New School had moved. This circle (personal interview, 4/24/00) included Thomas and Benita Luckmann, Hansfried Kellner, and Stanley Pullberg, all of whom moved to Germany and Maurice Natanson who moved to North Carolina. Berger went to Mexico on a trip in 1969, met Ivan Illich, and "discovered the third world." These contacts led to his interest in problems of third world development and modernization and his interests shifted. If Luckmann (and others of the cluster) had stayed in America they had planned to work on a book on social psychology and his work would have continued on its earlier course if "they had stayed."
34. But as Berger himself says in the Preface: "If other sociologists should read this book, especially in America, some will unavoidably be irritated by its orientation, disapprove of some of its lines of argument and feel that things considered by them to be important have been left out. All I can say is that I have tried to be faithful to a central tradition that goes back to the classics in the field and that I believe strongly in the continuing validity of this tradition." (pp. vii–viii)
35. I recall that when I first taught a graduate course at Washington University in the late 60s and drew heavily from *Invitation to Sociology* and *The Social Construction of Reality* the ideas of Berger and Schutz were criticized by Marxist sociologists as conservative, advocates of the status quo and guilty of static views of society. This was another way of saying they were neither political activists nor ideologists of the left. (Schutz was condemned for having been "a banker.")
36. The book had originally been intended as a collection of separate chapters by Berger, Luckmann, Kellner, Pullberg and Natanson but eventually evolved into a book by Berger and Luckmann who collaborated in writing, editing and revising each others' texts. Luckmann was responsible for the first chapter "The Foundations of Knowledge in Everyday Life" which is "based on Alfred Schutz and Thomas Luckmann's *Die Strukturen der Lebenswelt*" (*Structures of the Life-World*) (Berger and Luckmann, 1966, Fn 1, p. 194) Luckmann has written about their collaboration in a paper titled "Berger and His Collaborators" in Woodhead, Heelas and Martin, (2001)
37. Ritzer (1992, p. 387) calls this book "one of the most widely read and influential books in contemporary sociology. One of its main attractions is that it translated Alfred Schutz's sometimes arcane phenomenology into the terms of mainstream sociological theory. . . ." Appearing at almost the same time was Burkhart Holzner's study titled *Reality Construction in Society* (1968), completed, he says, in the spring of 1966 before the publication of Berger and Luckmann. Although he did not study with Schutz, his book adopts a Schutzian perspective on the sociology of knowledge and "integrates phenomenological, and traditional sociological, and social psychological perpectives." He felt that his work "complemented" Berger and Luckmann with the main difference being his "explicit concern with the structural distribution of knowledge in differentiated social systems, and the conditions of its maintenance and change." He acknowledges that "my analysis owes much to [Schutz]" and he cites *Collected Papers, Vol. I.* It is interesting that this book, a clear and consistent re-formulation of the sociology of knowledge without the Durkheimian slant that Berger and Luckmann adopted, never achieved widespread recognition.
38. Berger recalls that Schutz had said that "if the sociology of knowledge is to live up to its name it must deal with everything that passes for knowledge in society . . . rather than, as it had up to then, dealing with the history of ideas. And that was an "aha" experience for Luckmann and me, because in a way it was, you can call it in quotation marks the

'democratization of the sociology of knowledge', in other words the alleged knowledge of a truck driver is as significant as that of the philosopher from that point of view. And since there are more truck drivers than philosophers, the everyday knowledge is crucial for the sociologist, not for the philosopher. . . . in the end, what he thought the sociology of knowledge should be, in a way, Luckmann and I took that as sort of 'marching orders.'" (i.e., that a book on the topic should be developed. G. P.) (Personal interview, 4/24/00)

39. It is not possible to discuss here the development of what came to be known as "social constructionism." I asked Berger (interview 4/24/2000) why he did not title the book "the construction of meaning or meaning construction in everyday life" and he said that such a title might have been more apt, but it is now too late. Neither he nor I would accept much that is titled "social constructionism" as being an extension of the Schutz-Berger-Luckmann program. But it is too late now to retrieve the title. It only remains, as Ian Hacking (2000) has recently tried to do, to attempt to clarify the various uses and meanings of the term. Berger himself notes that he has had to "shy away from constructionism" because of the misinterpretations of the concept. Perhaps, he says, "we shouldn't have used the word 'construction' because that suggests construction *ex nihilo* . . . where what we said was 'all reality was socially interpreted' and what has been said since then is, two things: one, all interpretations are equally valid; and two, there's really no reality to begin with, there are only the interpretations. And, those two statements, from my point of view are crazy. That is not what we ever said." (personal interview, 4/24/00)
40. There is now no special section of the American Sociological Association with this latter title and the research section of the International Sociological Association which had this name, I am told, no longer exists.
41. Schutz himself did not write very much on the sociology of knowledge specifically and as Kurt Wolff has told me (personal interview, 2/10/00), when Wolff tried to discuss his own ideas with Schutz in the 1950s, ideas which were directly influenced by his having studied with Mannheim, Schutz gave Wolff a copy of his paper "The Well Informed Citizen." Wolff did not understand this to be relevant since it in no way continued in the Mannheimian tradition. It is interesting that a key phrase that Berger and Luckmann have quoted from this essay was Schutz's reference to the Mannheimian approach as the "so-called sociology of knowledge" (Schutz, 1962, p. 149; 1964, p. 121) which is some indication of Schutz's disdain for that approach.
42. Garfinkel (personal interview, 7/7/01) recalls these influences. He also writes (2002, p. 83) that ". . .at North Carolina, in the philosophy department, the phenomenological philosopher Louis Katsoff in his seminar introduced me to the scholarly texts of analytic philosophy in the social sciences. He also introduced me to the texts of transcendental phenomenological philosophy and while doing so emphasized their distinctive and critical rival relevance for the social sciences. Sigmund Koch and Alisdair MacIntyre provided tutorial guidance through the publication of gestalt psychology promoting the new writings of "field theory" by Kurt Lewin and his associates. It was at North Carolina under the initiative furnished by texts of Husserl's transcendental phenomenological philosophy and gestalt psychology that "the problem of meaning" in Ethnomethodology had its origins and early nurturing as a central subject in sociology."
43. Rawls' paper on "Harold Garfinkel" (2000) provides important biographical details which are drawn on here. I also interviewed Garfinkel (July 7, 2001) to learn about some of his earliest contacts with phenomenology and phenomenologists.
44. Garfinkel (2002, p. 84) says that Gurwitsch was an important influence in his thought. "From 1946 until I left Cambridge in 1951, I met with Aron Gurwitsch, who lived in Cambridge. We discussed subjects in phenomenology and sociology. Most particularly we discussed his (at the time) untranslated masterpiece, *Field of Consciousness*. In 1957,

at UCLA, with money from the Senior Research Fellowship, Aaron Cicourel and I hired Arturo Biblarz, a graduate student in sociology, to translate Gurwitsch's book. That gave both of us early textual access in English to Gurwitsch's argument on the functional significations and their coherence of figural contexture in its empirical perceptual details. That argument has been a foundational point of departure in all my teaching. It has lasted a long time. It has also been missed as Ethnomethodology's key resource in identifying Ethnomethodology's concerns to specify "the problem of meaning' with a program of certain positive empirical researches and instruction in sociology's identifying 'problem of social order.'"

45. All quotes are from Section IV 7 Correspondenz Schutz-Garfinkel, 585–594 in the Schutz archives. From Garfinkel to Schutz dated December 5, 1949; October 8, 1953; August 20, 1958; and from Schutz to Garfinkel, dated January 19, 1954; and October 21, 1958.
46. According to Mullins (1973, p. 183), Garfinkel "visited and studied with Alfred Schutz at the New School of Social Research" in 1950–52 while he was based at Princeton and engaged in writing his doctoral dissertation. It is clear from Garfinkel's writings that his contact with Schutz had begun earlier than this while he was at Harvard. In his curriculum vitae, Garfinkel lists for the years 1950–52, "Instructor, Department of Economics and Social Institutions, Princeton University, September 1950–August 1952; and Research Assistant in the Organizational Behavior Project." According to Wagner's biography of Schutz (1983, p. 242), "In 1949, Schutz was approached by Harold Garfinkel, a student of Parsons at Harvard, who was preparing his dissertation. . . One of his major themes came from Schutz, the other from Parsons. . . . Garfinkel sought a personal meeting with Schutz. But it is likely that they met first at the Princeton conference on methods in 1952 which had been organized by Garfinkel. The program included Schutz's presentation of the paper on "Common-Sense and Scientific Interpretation of Human Action." (Wagner is incorrect about the date of their first meetings.) "In 1953, Garfinkel mailed three mimeographed essays to Schutz. . ."(p. 239) Wagner goes on to detail the correspondence between Garfinkel and Schutz but there is no mention of any further meetings. According to Garfinkel (personal interview, 7/7/01 and Garfinkel, 2002, p. 84) he had already met with Schutz several times prior to the 1952 conference.
47. He had already prepared in 1949 a draft of a dissertation proposal very different from the one he eventually submitted. This earlier proposal has not been available to me.
48. Kurt Wolff, who had also been a participant in the Princeton conference, was instrumental in bringing Garfinkel to Ohio State where he worked, on soft money, on research studies of leadership. When funds ran out in the spring of 1954 Garfinkel was about to be out of a job for six months. He was recruited by Fred Strodtbeck, a former graduate student colleague at Harvard, to work on the "jury project" in Wichita on research he was doing with Saul Mendlovitz. This collaboration led to one of the first research studies in which Garfinkel referred to "ethnomethodology" to characterize the study.
49. Garfinkel has generously attributed ideas to others. Therefore, one must be careful in taking his acknowledgements literally.
50. Schutz responds in October regretting that they had not been able to meet and saying it was good to hear from Garfinkel "after such a long time." He says he has not yet received the "package" and whether he ever read this more recent work and responded is not known to me. Garfinkel never completed a book on the study of norms but it is likely that what he was referencing was some of the work on games and studies of other practical actions in what was later included in his paper, "Studies of the Routine Grounds of Everyday Activities" (1964, of which there is an original draft dated 1962).
51. Garfinkel (2002, p. 80 says that this paper was presented to the annual meetings of the American Sociological Association in 1953. (My analysis of the chronology suggests that it was probably 1954. G.P.) ". . .we recommended that there be added to anthropology's

guide to the "ethno" sciences, a guide that ran from Ethno-Astronomy to Ethno-Zoology, one more "ethno" side of social science preoccupation with science – Ethno-methodology."

52. According to Timasheff (1955, pp. 241–242), "The central theme of Parsons' sociological theory is 'the functioning of structures.' Structural-functional analysis requires systematic treatment of the statuses and roles of actors in a social situation as well as the institutional patterns involved. Status refers to the place of the actor in a social relationship system considered as a structure; role, which in any concrete instance is inseparable from status and represents the dynamic aspect of status . . . refers to the behavior of the actor in his relations with others, when viewed in the context of its functional significance for the social system. Institutional patterns are conceived of as patterned (or 'structured') expectations which define culturally appropriate behavior of persons playing various social roles. A plurality of interdependent role patterns forms an institution. . . . Institutions, Parsons holds, are the focal point of sociology. He defines sociology or social theory . . . as that aspect of the theory of social systems which is concerned with *institutionalization.*"
53. It is not clear whether Garfinkel had known of or read Schutz's commentary and critique of Parsons *The Structure of Social Action* which he had written in 1940 and never published. It is likely that he had read the part which was later published under the heading of "The Social World and the Theory of Social Action (*Collected Papers II*, pp. 3–19). It is interesting that both Schutz and Garfinkel had been engaged in lengthy critical reflections and commentaries on Parsons' theories. Garfinkel (personal interview 7/7/ 01) says that Schutz had hoped that Garfinkel could facilitate a re-connection with Parsons after Schutz had written his review of Parsons and had used the word "naive," a remark that bothered Parsons considerably but which Schutz had intended only as a use of the Kantian distinction between "naive" and "critical" philosophy where "the former begins inquiry with the object of knowledge; the latter turns to the conditions for the possibility of knowledge." (Grathoff, 1978, p. xii). Schutz thought that Parsons was philosophically "naive" in this sense while Parsons took the remark more personally as he indicated in his response to Schutz when he says "that is your opinion."
54. In footnote 1 he says, "The concept 'everyday affairs' is intended in strict accord with Schutz's usage in his articles, "On Multiple Realities," *Philosophy and Phenomenological Research*, 4, June 1945, pp. 533–575; and "Common Sense and Scientific Interpretation of Human Action," *Philosophy and Phenomenological Research*, 14, September 1953, pp. 1–37"; and in footnote 3 he cites "Schutz, Alfred, *Der Sinnhafte Aufbau der sozialen Welt*, Julius Springer, Wien, 1932; "The Problem of Rationality in the Social World," *Economica*, 10, May 1943, pp. 130–149; "Some Leading Concepts in Phenomenology," *Social Research* 12, February 1945, pp. 77–97; "On Multiple Realities; Concept and Theory Formation in the Social Sciences," *Journal of Philosophy*, 51, April 29, 1954, pp. 257–274; "Symbol, Reality, and Society," *Symbols and Society*, "Fourteenth Symposium of the Conference on Science, Philosophy, and Religion," edited by Lyman Bryson and others, Harper and Brothers, New York, 1955, pp. 135–202"; and in footnote 4, "The material in the following two pages is based almost entirely upon Schutz' writings. See n. 3" In footnote 13 he cites Marvin Farber, *The Foundation of Phenomenology*, Harvard University Press, Cambridge, MA 1943, pp. 237–238 from which he references Husserl's use of "occasional expressions." He also cites Felix Kaufmann's, *Methodology of the Social Sciences*, Oxford University Press, New York, 1944.
55. He says, in fact, "to do an ethnoscience job we cannot be looking for nor can we consider that our tasks can be solved by settling for the psychiatrist's definition of his term 'case history.'" (p. 8)
56. Citing Wittgenstein, he interprets him to say: ". . .(this) is like Wittgenstein's finding that to provide a definition is to furnish a program of procedures whereby the particulars of

the object are reproduced as a recognizable case of the general object 'illuminated from within'. . . by the general schema as an objective composition of universal features." (p. 8)

57. It was Rose who proposed to call Garfinkel's project "ethno-ontology" a term which Garfinkel rejected. Rose was more eclectic and came to refer to his field research oriented studies as "ethno-inquiries."
58. Garfinkel worked most closely over a period of more than 12 years with Harvey Sacks. Their collaboration was extensive and one of mutual influence. Sacks (who died in 1975) went on to develop, with Emanuel Schegloff, what has come to be known as Conversation Analysis, now considered to be one of the important offshoots of ethnomethodology. This field continues to be developed by Emmanuel Schegloff, UCLA, and Gail Jefferson, now in The Netherlands, and many other researchers nationally and internationally. In *Studies* (1967, p. viii) he mentions Egon Bittner, Aaron V. Cicourel, Lindsey Churchill, Craig MacAndrew, Michael Moerman, Edward Rose, Harvey Sacks, Emmanuel Schegloff, David Sudnow, D. Lawrence Wieder, and Don Zimmerman as doing ethnomethodological studies.
59. Incidentally, Garfinkel has never himself claimed to be a Schutzian or a phenomenological sociologist and has eschewed all efforts to categorize his approach as anything other than 'ethnomethodological.' Mary Rogers, (1983, p. 133) among others, says that: ". . .ethnomethodology does not represent a phenomenological sociology. Nonetheless, in several respects ethnomethodology hints at a phenomenological sociology, most obviously in its insistence on 'social facts' as members' accomplishments and its commitment to disclosing the practices that establish those accomplishments. Its processual emphasis also bends it broadly toward phenomenology, as does its concern with the 'forgetfulness' of social science, specifically sociology. But these phenomenologically relevant elements of the ethnomethodological perspective represent, at best, a narrow extraction from the phenomenological frame. Ethnomethodology does not build on or even make use of the far-reaching relevance of phenomenology. Indeed, one could scarcely infer the nature of phenomenology from ethnomethodology. Yet ethnomethodologists as well as commentators on their work frequently maintain that the ethnomethodological and phenomenological perspectives are substantially linked. . .". My own (Psathas, 1977) interpretation has been different and I have considered ethnomethodology to be part of the phenomenological movement.
60. "The ethnomethodological approach studies the *methods* actually practiced (used) by *members* of society for accomplishing (doing) whatever it is they are doing (including their ways of talking about whatever it is they are doing). A serious and careful study of the methods used by members for accomplishing practical actions in the world of everyday life would result in descriptions and analyses of *the methodology of everyday life* or of the ethno (member of a group- or the group's) methodology, or members' methods. The methodology part of the term ethnomethodology is to be understood as referring to the 'how', the *actual situated practices, the methods by which everyday activities are accomplished.*" (Psathas, 1994)
61. It has suffered in an important respect from years of benign neglect as well as the original hostile and exclusionary reaction which it received from mainstream sociology. This resulted in the inability of students to find employment and of departments to develop rigorous and funded programs which could advance scholarship and research in ethnomethodology. Nevertheless, a world wide movement of ethnomethodological studies has developed and is in part documented by international conferences, a web site, a bibliography of over 2,000 studies and formation of a Section on Ethnomethodology and Conversation Analysis at the American Sociological Association in 2002.

62. I am unable to consider in this paper Schutz's influence on sociological theory or on the meta-sociological or foundational issues which he explored. His thought in these areas provided important insights, influenced many social theorists, and over time became incorporated in various writings. These are the subjects of a much longer paper if not a book.

References

Bauman, Z. (1996). Sociology. In *The Social Science Encyclopedia*, 2nd ed. London and NY: Routledge.

Berger, P. (1961). *The Precarious Vision: A Sociologist Looks at Social Fictions and the Christian Faith*. Garden City: Doubleday.

Berger, P. (1961). *The Noise of Solemn Assemblies: Christian Commitment and the Religious Establishment in America*. Garden City: Doubleday.

Berger, P. (1963). *Invitation to Sociology: A Humanistic Perspective*. Garden City: Anchor Doubleday.

Berger, P. and Kellner, H. (1964). Marriage and the Construction of Reality. *Diogenes* 46: 1–24.

Berger, P. and Luckmann, T. (1966). *The Social Construction of Reality: A Treatise in the Sociology of Knowledge*. Garden City, NY: Doubleday.

Berger, P. and Luckmann, T. (1967). *The Sacred Canopy: Elements of a Sociology of Religion*. Garden City, NY: Doubleday.

Berger, P., Berger, B. and Kellner, H. (1974). *The Homeless Mind: Modernization and Consciousness*. New York: Vintage Books.

Berger, P., Berger, B. and Kellner, H. (1977). *Facing Up To Modernity: Excursions in Society, Politics and Religion*. New York: Basic Books.

Berger, P.L. (1983). *Current Biography Yearbook*. New York: H.W. Wilson Co.

Bottomore, T. (1993). Sociology. In *Blackwell Dictionary of Twentieth Century Social Thought*. Oxford: Blackwell.

Bulmer, M. (1984). *The Chicago School of Sociology*. Chicago and London: University of Chicago Press.

Cicourel, A. (1964). *Method and Measurement in Sociology*. New York: Free Press.

Coser, L. (1984). *Refugee Scholars in America: Their Impact and Their Experiences*. New Haven: Yale.

Farber, M. (1943). *The Foundation of Phenomenology*. Cambridge, MA: Harvard University Press.

Garfinkel, H. (1952). The Perception of the Other: A Study in Social Order. Unpublished Doctoral Dissertation, Harvard University.

Garfinkel, H. (1954). How Jurors Recognize the Correctness of a Verdict, Unpublished and Undated. (Later published (1967) as Chapter 4, Some Rules of Correct Decisions that Jurors Respect. In *Studies in Ethnomethodology*. Englewood Cliffs, NJ: Prentice Hall.)

Garfinkel, H. (1956). Conditions of Successful Degradation Ceremonies. *American Journal of Sociology* 61: 420–424.

Garfinkel, H. (1959). Aspects of the Problem of Commonsense Knowledge of Social Structures. *Transactions of Fourth World Congress of Sociology, International Sociological Association* 4: 51–65.

Garfinkel, H. (1964). Studies of the Routine Grounds of Everyday Activities. *Social Problems* 11: 225–250.

Garfinkel, H. (1967). *Studies in Ethnomethodology*. Englewood Cliffs, N.J.: Prentice-Hall.

Garfinkel, H. (Ed.) (1986). *Ethnomethodological Studies of Work*. London, Routledge & Kegan Paul.

Garfinkel, H. (2002). *Ethnomethodology's Program: Working Out Durkheim's Aphorism*. Lanham, Boulder, New York, Oxford: Rowman and Littlefield.

Garfinkel, H. and Sacks, H. (1970). On Formal Structures of Practical Actions. In J.C. McKinney and E.A. Tiryakian (Eds.), *Theoretical Sociology*. New York: Appleton Century Crofts.

Grathoff, R. (Ed.) (1978). *The Theory of Social Action: The Correspondence of Alfred Schutz and Talcott Parsons*. Bloomington: Indiana University Press.

Gurwitsch, A. (1957/1964). *The Field of Consciousness*. Pittsburgh: Duquesne University Press.

Hacking, I. (1999). *The Social Construction of What?* Cambridge, MA: Harvard University Press.

Heap, J. and Roth, P.A. (1978). On Phenomenological Sociology. *American Sociological Review*. Also in A. Wells (Ed.), *Contemporary Sociological Theories*. Santa Monica, CA: Goodyear.

Jaworski, G.D. (1998). Contested Canon: Simmel Scholarship at Columbia and the New School. *The American Sociologist* Summer: 4–18.

Kalberg, S. (2001). *The Spirit of Capitalism* Revisited. *Max Weber Studies* 2(1): 41–58.

Kaufmann, F. (1944). *Methodology of the Social Sciences*. New York: Oxford University Press.

Krohn, C.D. (1993). *Intellectuals in Exile: Refugee Scholars and the New School for Social Research*. Amherst: University of Massachusetts Press.

Luckmann, T. (2001). Berger and his Collaborators. In L. Woodhead, P. Heelas and D. Martin (Eds.), *Peter Berger and the Study of Religion*. London.

Meja, V. and Stehr, N. (1993). Sociology of Knowledge. *Blackwell's Dictionary of Twentieth Century Thought*, pp. 637–639. Oxford and New York: Blackwells.

Morris, M. (1977). *An Excursion into Creative Sociology*. New York: Columbia University Press.

Mullins, N.C. (1973). *Theories and Theory Groups in Contemporary American Sociology*. New York: Harper and Row.

Parsons, T. (1937). *The Structure of Social Action*. New York: McGraw Hill.

Parsons, T. (1949). *Essays in Sociological Theory, Pure and Applied*. New York: Free Press.

Parsons, T. and Shils, E.A. (1951). *Toward a General Theory of Action*. Cambridge, MA: Harvard University Press.

Parsons, T. and Shils, E.A. (1951). *The Social System*. New York: The Free Press.

Psathas, G. (1968). Ethnomethods and Phenomenology. *Social Research* 35: 500–520.

Psathas, G. (1977). Ethnomethodology as a Phenomenological Approach in the Social Sciences. In R. Zaner and D. Ihde (Eds.), *Interdisciplinary Phenomenology*. The Hague: Martinus Nijhoff.

Psathas, G. (1980). Approaches to the Study of the World of Everyday Life. *Human Studies* 3: 3–17.

Psathas, G. (Ed.) (1979). *Everyday Language: Studies in Ethnomethodology*. New York: Irvington.

Psathas, G. (1994). Ethnomethodology. In *Encyclopedia for Language and Linguistics*. Oxford: Pergamon Press.

Psathas, G. and E. Bittner (1991). In Memoriam: Helmut R. Wagner. *Human Studies* 14(2–3): 225–227.

Rawls, R. (2000). Harold Garfinkel. In G. Ritzer (Ed.), *The Blackwell Companion to Major Social Theorists*. Oxford and New York: Blackwell Publishers.

Rogers, M.F. (1983). *Sociology, Ethnomethodology, and Experience: A Phenomenological Critique*. Cambridge, London and New York: Cambridge University Press.

Rogers, M.F. (2000). Alfred Schutz. In G. Ritzer (Ed.), *The Blackwell Companion to Major Social Theorists*. Oxford and New York: Blackwell Publishers.

Rutkoff, P.M. and Scott, W.B. (1986). *New School: A History of the New School for Social Research*. New York and London: Free Press.

Sharrock, W.W. and Anderson, R.J. (1986). *The Ethnomethodologists*. London: Tavistock.

Schutz, A. (1932). *Der sinnhafte Aufbau der sozialenwelt*. Vienna: Springer

Schutz, A. (1945). On Multiple Realities. *Philosophy and Phenomenological Research* V (June): 533–576.

Schutz, A. (1953/1962) Common-Sense and Scientific Interpretation of Human Action. *Philosophy and Phenomenological Research* XIV(1) (also in *Collected Papers, Vol. I*).

Schutz, A. (1962, 1964, 1966). *Collected Papers, Vols. I, II, III*. The Hague, Martinus Nijhoff.

Schutz, A. (1960). The Social World and the Theory of Social Action. *Social Research* 203–221 (also in *Collected Papers, Vol I*).

Schutz, A. (1982). Life Forms and Meaning Structure, trans., introduced and annotated by Helmut R. Wagner. London, Boston: Routledge & Kegan Paul.

Schutz, A. (1969). *The Phenomenological Movement, I and II*. The Hague: Martinus Nijhoff.

Spiegelberg, H. (1972). *Phenomenology in Psychology and Psychiatry: A Historical Introduction*. Evanston: Northwestern University Press.

Stehr, N. and Meja, V. (1964). Introduction: The Development of the Sociology of Knowledge. In *Society and Knowledge*. New Brunswick, N.J.: Transaction Books.

Timasheff, N.S. (1955). *Sociological Theory*. Garden City, NY: Doubleday.

Wagner, H. (1969). Phenomenology and Contemporary Sociological Theory: The Contribution of Alfred Schutz. *Sociological Focus* 2: 73–86.

Wagner, H. (1975). Sociologists of Phenomenological Orientations: Their Place in American Sociology. *The American Sociologist* 10: 179–186.

Wagner, H. (1976). The Influence of German phenomenology on American Sociology. *Annals of Phenomenological Sociology* 1: 1–29.

Wagner, H. (1983). *Phenomenology of Consciousness and Sociology of the Life-World*. Edmonton: University of Alberta Press.

Wagner, H. (1983). *Alfred Schutz: An Intellectual Biography*. Chicago: University of Chicago Press.

Wagner, H. (with Ilja Srubar) (1984). *A Bergsonian Bridge to Phenomenological Psychology*. Washington, D.C.: Center for Advanced Research in Phenomenology and University Press of America.

Wolff, K.H. (1978). Phenomenology and Sociology. In T. Bottomore and R. Nisbet (Eds.), *A History of Sociological Analysis*. New York: Basic Books.

[4]

SOCIAL PROBLEMS: A RE-FORMULATION

MALCOLM SPECTOR
McGill University
and
JOHN I. KITSUSE
Northwestern University

A definition of social problems is proposed as a generic phenomenon: the process by which members of groups or societies, through assertions of grievances and claims, define a putative condition as a social problem. Then a four-stage natural history model of social problems is described. In Stage One, groups assert the existence and offensiveness of some condtion. In Stage Two some official agency responds to the claims; in Stage Three claims and demands re-emerge, expressing dissatisfaction with the official response. In Stage Four alternative, parallel, or counter-institutions are established.

> If we can get our social life stated in terms of activity, and of nothing else, we have not indeed succeeded in measuring it, but we have at least reached a foundation upon which a coherent system of measurements can be built up. We shall cease to be blocked by the intervention of unmeasurable elements, which claim to be themselves the real causes of all that is happening, and which by their spook-like arbitrariness make impossible any progress toward dependable knowledge.
>
> Arthur Bentley (1908:202)

Is a sociology of social problems possible? Is there any distinctive subject matter or phenomenon to which this term refers? After more than 40 years, the writings on social problems still lack definition and substance. A recent reader on approaches to social problems (Rubington and Weinberg, 1971) highlights this dependence of social problems on other fields of inquiry: social pathology, social disorganization, deviant behavior, value-conflict, and labelling theory.

In a previous paper, we reviewed two dominant approaches to social problems in order to ask why they have failed to produce a clear-cut vision of social problems as a generic phenomenon (Kitsuse and Spector, 1973). We found that the functionalist approach, exemplified by Merton and Nisbet (1961, 1966, 1971), contains two lacunae. First, in basing the study of social problems on the analysis of "objective conditions"—that is, the distribution of such phenomena as crime, divorce, mental illness, drug use, pollution, and violence—the sociology of social problems becomes merely the analysis of dysfunctions within the functionalist or social system paradigm (see Merton and Nisbet, 1971:819-820). Second, Merton's distinction between manifest and latent problems obscures methodological problems of identifying empirical cases in point. He fails to clarify who may or must decide that "substantial discrepancies" between widely shared social standards and actual conditions of social life exist (1971:799).

A second approach to the study of social problems, the so-called "value-conflict" school (Bain, 1935; Case, 1924; Frank, 1925; Fuller, 1937, 1938, 1939, 1942; Fuller and Myers, 1941a, 1942b; Becker, 1966:1-31), asserts that:

> *Social problems are what people think they are,* and if conditions are not defined as social problems by the people involved in them, they are not problems

> to those people . . . Sociologists must therefore study not only the objective conditions phase of a social problem, but also the value-judgments of the people involved in it which cause them to define the same condition and means to its solution in different ways. (Fuller and Myers, 1941b, 320-21, emphasis in the original.)

Thus Fuller and Myers (1938:419) attempt to explain the causes of the objective conditions and the process by which they become defined as social problems. In their view, value-judgments and value-conflicts play a crucial role in the causes of the objective conditions, in the process of their definition as problems, and in "preventing solutions" to social problems (Fuller and Myers, 1941a, 21). We believe that the attempt to explain both the objective and the subjective aspects of social problems deflects the originality and thrust of the value-conflict formulation. While Fuller and Myers take the position that objective conditions in themselves are not sufficient for the existence of social problems, they stop short of asserting that from a theoretical point of view objective conditions are neither necessary nor sufficient. To the extent that they attempt to explain the existence of the objective conditions themselves, they come to resemble the functionalist formulation of which they are so critical (see especially Fuller, 1939).

The Ideas of Process and Natural History

Our analysis of the two major approaches to social problems leads us to propose that the explanation of the "subjective elements" of social problems—the process by which members of groups or societies define a putative condition as a problem—is the distinctive subject matter of the sociology of social problems. Thus we define social problems as *the activities of groups making assertions of grievances and claims to organizations, agencies, and institutions about some putative conditions.* The emergence of a social problem, then, is contingent on the organization of group activities with reference to defining some putative condition as a problem, and asserting the need for eradicating, ameliorating, or otherwise changing that condition. The central problem for a theory of social problems, so defined, is to account for the emergence, maintenance, and history of claim-making and responding activities. Such a theory should comprehend the activities of any group making claims on others for ameliorative action, material remuneration, alleviation of social, political, legal, economic disadvantage, or other consideration.

Social problems so conceived are not static conditions, but sequences of events. These sequences of events will vary: every social problem has its own unique history. One task for the sociology of social problems is to search for common elements, stages, or processes among the histories of various social problems—that is, to determine if social problems have a "natural history," and if so, to describe its stages and the contingencies of its development. Park (1970:xvii) defined a natural history as

> nothing more nor less than an account of an evolutionary process—a process by which not the individual, but the type evolves . . . every social change that is capable of description in conceptual terms, will have its characteristic cycle . . . description of the cycle seems to be the first step in the analysis and description of social change everywhere.

The idea of natural history, like that of career or value-added analysis (for a somewhat more demanding formulation, see Smelser, 1963:12-20), is that a given phenomenon develops through a number of distinct stages, each characterized by different dynamics or processes, different casts of characters, kinds of activities, and dilemmas. Such development need not, however, be a linear progression, but may be conceived as a process in which progression from one stage to the next is facilitated or hampered by various contingencies. The utility of a natural history model may be assessed by the proper identification of stages and the set of contingencies that condition the development through those stages.

Fuller and Myers (1941b) invoked the idea of natural history in their analysis of the growth of trailer camps in Detroit. However, their use of this model, based on the case history of only one social problem was premature, leaving them vulnerable to the negative findings of Lemert's (1951) replication in Los Angeles. In addition, Fuller and Myers' (1941b:321) natural history model is too rigid in its specification of a "common order of development through which all social problems pass, consisting of certain temporal sequences in their emergence and maturation." There is no theoretical, and certainly no empirical basis for the hypothesis that *all instances* of social problems emerge and mature through the stages of "awareness, policy formation, and reform."

We propose a simple four stage natural history model for the analysis of social problems. The model should be regarded as an exploratory expedition presenting hypotheses and guides to empirical research. The model was derived from an extensive but informal survey of the histories of many social problems, and from detailed histories of six social problems compiled by graduate students in a seminar on social problems. Thus we have attempted to guide our passage between the Scylla of generalizing from a case study (as did Fuller and Myers and Lemert) and the Charybdis of basing our analysis on unsubstantiated facts and examples.

Stage 1: The attempts by some group(s) to assert the existence of some condition, define it as offensive, harmful, and otherwise undesirable, to publicize the assertions and stimulate controversy and to create a public or political issue over the matter.

Stage 2: The recognition by some official organization, agency, or institution of the group(s) legitimate standing. This may lead to an official investigation of the matter, proposals for reform, and the establishment of an agency to respond to those claims and demands.

Stage 3: The re-emergence of claims and demands by the group(s), expressing dissatisfaction with the established procedures for dealing with the imputed conditions, the bureaucratic handling of complaints, and the failure to generate a condition of trust and confidence in the procedures as sympathetic to the complaints, *etc.*

Stage 4: The rejection by complainant group(s) of the response or lack of response of the agency or institution to their claims and demands, and the development of activities to create alternative, parallel, or counter-institutions as responses to the established procedures.

The bases for this formulation are (1) that social problems develop over time and may be characterized by different activities at different times in their development and (2) these differences are not unrelated, but rather build on the previous development of the social problems. This led us to try to consolidate the different kinds of activities, which in turn led us to the four stages of development. Our presentation of them should be taken as an ideal type model of social problems. As such, it is a simplified version designed to highlight various aspects of the model, rather than to serve as an exact empirical description of any specific social problem. Its bias is to exaggerate the orderliness and linear development of any empirical example.

Another way of viewing stages One to Four is as distinct kinds of social problems activity. Then the natural history model is one possible order that may occur, perhaps the most typical, perhaps only one among many. If social problems develop different sequences, this would suggest several kinds of processes at work, and perhaps more than one social problems career or natural history.

STAGE ONE

Social problems activity commences with the collective attempts to remedy a condition that some group perceives and judges offensive and undesirable. The complaining group may or may not be the victims of the imputed condition; for example, the complaint that the welfare system demoralizes its clients may be made by an organization of social workers, clergymen, or other humanitarian group not directly subject to the condition. On the other hand, groups directly affected by the condition may take action in their own interests. The former type we might call moral crusaders, or "dis-interested" groups; the latter, interest groups—those who claim to have a real and material stake, something to gain or lose in the outcome of a given line of activity.

Initial social problems activities consist of attempts to transform private troubles into public issues.[1] Stage One is focused on the contingencies of this transformation process. Needless to say, not all such attempts are successful; a group's problem-defining activities may elicit no response—the group may lose its constituency, be ignored by the mass media, torn by internal dissension, fail to mobilize economic resources to sustain its activity, or give up hope.

We suggest that the critical concerns in this formative stage of social problems are the ways that complaints about the condition are raised and the strategies used to press the claims, gain publicity, and arouse controversy. The "objective seriousness" or extent of the condition itself, or its presumed dysfunctionality, may be relatively independent of the success or failure of this transformation. That is, the relationship between "objective conditions" and the development of social problems is variable and problematic. It is an empirical question whether certain types of conditions are correlated with or associated with certain types of claims. Since social problems are raised through the claims of dissatis-

[1] Our use of the terms "private troubles" and "public issues" differs from that of Mills (1959), who emphasized the individual and personal character of the former and the social structural character of the latter. He conceived of them on two different and independent levels of phenomena and provided no theoretical link between them such that private troubles might be transformed into public issues. As indicated below, we do not preclude the possibility of even the most idiosyncratic and private trouble becoming, through collective action, the basis for social problems activity.

fied groups, we turn now to examining the nature of these claims and the enterprise of making claims.

The Process of Making Claims

The making of claims and complaints is an integral part of social and political life. They are everyday activities in all societies and occur at all levels of government. While any sort of complaint *could* become the basis for a social problem, the vast majority of such claims are disposed of in ways that do not lead to the creation of social problems. Many may simply be ignored; others may dissolve when the claim is satisfied; still others may be bargained away, cooled out, or bought off.

Some claims, however, will not be turned aside so easily. These claims may lead to further actions culminating in the establishment of a social problem. We would like to venture a paradigm to explain the nature of such successful claims. We divide our discussion into three topics: the power of the group, the nature of their claims, and the strategies and mechanisms of pressing claims.

The Power of the Group

Other things being equal, groups that have more membership, greater constituency, more money, greater discipline, and organization will be more effective in pressing their claims than groups that lack these attributes. However, this is not to say that these characteristics "explain" the success or failure of a group in pressing its claim. For power to become an active part of the process, it must be expressed through the claims of the participating groups.

Power, conceived as the ability of a group to realize the demands it makes on other groups, agencies, and institutions, may be distinguished from a group's *claims of power.* The latter may be stated explicitly (e.g., threat of strikes, boycotts, withdrawal of political support) or implicitly conveyed (hints of plans to create embarrassing public confrontations, various forms of nuisances or harrassment). Groups may or may not be able to mobilize the power they claim; or if mobilized, it may be ineffective in producing the threatened consequences. Thus, a group may be bluffing; and if it's bluff is called, it may not be able to deliver. For example, a threatened demonstration may be ignored, forcing the group to reveal its inability to produce the threatened "mass;" a tough political boss may question the ability of ethnic leaders to deliver the "bloc vote." Alternatively, a genuinely powerful group may not be willing to expend its resources on a certain issue, hoping that the bluff or threat will produce results.[2]

The Nature and Variety of Claims

Groups may experience and express dissatisfaction in a variety of ways. They may feel only a vague, general, or amorphous sense of dissatisfaction; or they may experience dissatisfaction as specific complaints and pointed grievances. They may have no idea who created, is responsible for, or caused the imputed condition; or they

2 We wish to emphasize that we do not view the success of a group in pressing its claim as *ipso facto* evidence of their power. We have said that other things being equal, more powerful groups will have a greater chance of being successful, but only through mobilizing that power through the claims they press. As we shall stress in the following two sections, weaker groups may win out over stronger groups, or win where others have failed, through careful or fortuitous strategy in phrasing and pressing their claims.

may have a very specific notion of who or what is oppressing them. These conceptions may or may not be linked to an overarching ideology or theory about how the world works. Groups may have no idea of how to remedy their perceived situation, or they may have very specific programs of reform and proposals for change.

All of these dimensions of the experience of dissatisfaction will influence the kind of claims that a group will make. Let us consider some hypotheses generated by these dimensions.

1. The more vague the sense of dissatisfaction, the more diffuse and general will be the claim, and the less likely will be the recognition or response to the claim; and the less likely will there be a specific remedy enacted.

2. The more vague the sense of dissatisfaction, the less likely is the group able to affix responsibility or propose remedies for their discontent.

3. The less the group is able to affix responsibility for their dissatisfaction, the less able they will be to choose a target to which to direct their complaint.

4. The less the group is able to affix responsibility for their dissatisfaction, the less able they will be to counter the charge that they themselves are to blame.

This sample of hypotheses suggests that the experience of dissatisfaction may vary considerably and thus affect the kinds of claims a group constructs, as well as the way it expresses and directs these claims. Often a group may be aided in developing its claim by individuals or organizations that specialize in expressing protest. A group may be experienced in a vague and undefined way by some group; they may even voice complaints about it, but not effectively. Then the trouble may be picked up and seen as a classic instance of "exploitation," "discrimination," "corruption," etc., by such organizations as political parties, labor unions, professional radicals, or service organizations. Such groups may give oherence and rationale for the complaint, as well as offer the group aid and allies, sometimes in return for their support on other issues.

By entering into coalitions with others, a group may gain numbers, prestige, institutional authority, and other advantages. They may find, on the other hand, that the advantages are purchased at the cost of a diffusion of their issue and an involvement in others in which they have no interest. Or their own troubles may be considered "only a part of the larger problem" by their allies, thus given low priority in view of the "larger goals" they seek.

The importance of the more or less sophisticated ideologies that such organizations apply to the troubles is that they provide coherence and analysis to the troubles in question, and thus a rationale for the assertion of claims. On the other hand, a general ideology may be a disadvantage in making visible a *specific* claim. If such a complaint is couched in a framework that calls for a general restructuring of society or the destruction of capitalism, this may impede the effort by obscuring the specific claim or giving officials an excuse for ignoring the complaint.

The Mechanisms for Pressing Claims

Closely related to the nature of the claims is the way that claims are delivered, expressed, or made public. The fate of a claim may heavily depend on the channels through which it is pressed, the strategies used to achieve visibility of the imputed condition, and the auxiliary personnel who play a part in this process. One important contingency in the processing of complaints is identifying the party to whom the complaint should be addressed. If the group complains to the wrong party or office, they may get no results; they may get bad advice or directions as to where they properly should go; or they may inadvertently reveal their position to an opponent. Frequently there may be no office to complain to, since the substance of the complaint is that no one is doing anything about the imputed condition and that some organization or agency should be made responsible to deal with it. In such cases, long chains of referrals and buck-passing may occur with no organization willing to accept jurisdiction over the complaint.

Similarly, the way that the press and mass media are handled is recognized as important to the life history of any social issue by social problems groups. Such elementary devices as issuing press releases or informing the media in advance of a planned event may alter the course of the proceedings. Certainly knowledge and expertise in attracting and holding the attention of the mass media are important resources of groups airing complaints. Also the support of muckraking literature or the staging of a "national event" may be crucial in transforming private troubles into public issues and controversies.

Some methods of expressing or dramatizing complaints may come to be viewed as ineffectual, which may lead to their displacement by more dramatic means of protest. Thus, demonstrations and hunger strikes may give way to civil disobedience, which may in turn give way to insurrection and guerilla warfare. Protest groups may face the dilemma of insuring defeat through the use of ineffective methods, or risking disaster through use of organized violence.

Assertions of Claims and Social Controversy

We have said that social problems arise from the statement by groups that certain conditions are intolerable and must be changed. Such actions may provoke a reaction from other groups that prefer the existing arrangements or would stand to lose something if they were altered. Such groups may challenge the claims of the protesting group, mount their own campaign, lobby against proposed changes. The value judgments that led the protesting group to act in the first place may bring them into conflict with groups that do not share these values or with groups with vested interest in the condition in question. Such conflicts may escalate the visibility of the whole debate and facilitate the creation of public awareness of the imputed condition.

This controversy is the culmination of Stage One. A given social problem may remain at this stage interminably; or it may quickly be transformed into the next stage; or it may falter and die if no further activities are generated to gain recognition of the group's claims.

Stage Two

The idea that the natural history of a social problem is divided into stages suggests that the career of the phenomenon may be divided into several periods each characterized by its own distinctive kind of activities, participants, and dilemmas. Here we argue that when governmental agencies or other official and influential institutions to which claims might be put respond to the complaints of some group, the social problems activity undergoes a considerable transformation. This transformation begins when the agencies to which claims are being made begin to recognize the group and respond to their complaints. The bases of this recognition may be diverse. The group may have brought considerable pressure to bear on the agency either through confrontation tactics, mass media campaigns, demonstrations, or threats of such actions; it may have applied economic pressure such as threat of boycott, or manipulated political influence; or the agency may have recognized that it had something to gain by taking over the issue being raised in order to control it.

The formal recognition of the group may range from passive acknowledgment of the claim to active attempts to control, regulate, or eliminate the condition at issue in the claim.[3] Any of these responses is likely to give the protest group a degree of recognition or standing that they did not have before. The activities of Stage One, the attempts to call attention to a condition and define an issue, are almost entirely "unofficial," conducted without the sanction or seal of societal authority. With recognition of their claim, however, the group is likely to be asked to participate in official proceedings on the problem. The group may be asked to meet with the mayor or testify before a Congressional sub-committee hearing on the problem.

At this point they find that they are no longer just a protest group, but the *bona fide* "spokesman" for a constituency that may be much broader than their original group. They may find that groups that previously had shunned them now expect them to press *their* claims as well. They may be called upon for more documentation of their claims than previously, and they may be asked to offer solutions as well as complaints. Thus, even the simplest response to the claims may bring about a transformation in the protest group or create new organizational crises for it.

The response of an official agency may be the result of a long struggle to gain standing for the protest group. This may take the form of trying to convince some agency to assume jurisdiction over an issue; or it may take the form of convincing someone that the group has a real and material, rather than merely a theoretical, interest in the proceedings. In the process, the group's crusade may have become a cause celébre; and their achievement of standing may be viewed as their "finest hour." "Dis-interested" groups or moral crusaders may have particular difficulties in gaining standing because they are not affected by the condition they protest. Such groups may be told to mind their own business, or may have to attach themselves to someone actually affected by the condition in order to press their claim. The American Civil Liberties Union, for example, must find injured parties willing to go to court in order to raise constitutional issues because the courts will not take jurisdiction over debate only in principle.

While official response may give the protest group their "finest hour," it may also represent the beginning of the end of their control over the claims they raise. The response to their complaints may take the edge off their

---

3 Alternatively, an agency may respond by efforts to eliminate the claim through repressive control policies, as charged in the cases of the Black Panther Party and the Chicago Seven conspiracy trial.

protest that "nothing is being done." The establishment of a committee to study the problem may cool the controversy and make the issue less visible in the mass media. Although the group may be called to testify before the committee, they find that they are cast in the role of providing information rather than defining and negotiating the nature of the problem. The committee may seek out other and opposing views on the topic, reducing the original group to simply one voice among many. When the hearings are over, the members of the committee will be the new experts and authorities on the subject. While the original group may comment on the report of the committee, it is that report that will define the issues, summarize the facts, put various groups in perspective and in their places.

Thus, as official and powerful agencies or institutions begin to take part in the social problems activity, they may lend prestige to the original protest group, but at the same time may begin to overshadow and thus reduce the significance of its activities. Finally, the responding agencies may take over the issue, making it their own, and neutralize or eliminate the original protest group.

Social problems that reach this stage of development may still die or disappear. The commission and its report may disenfranchize the original protesting groups, which subsequently may become demoralized and fall apart. The commission may or may not recommend that actions be taken to satisfy the claims; and these recommendations, if made, may not be enacted. Studies of the activities and reception of commissions of inquiry in Great Britain and in the United States reveal vastly different patterns. Writing about the British Royal Commissions, Hanser (1965:45-7) says:

> I know of no student of the Royal Commission in the 20th century who does not regard it with the highest esteem . . . it is never charged with dishonesty or violation of civil rights, with being composed of "front" men for an anonymous staff which does all the work, or with being subservient to the government.

Further, the Royal Commissions have a reputation for producing significant (although sometimes unpopular) recommendations and for successfully getting their proposals adopted.

In contrast, Presidential and Congressional investigating commissions in the United States are notorious for their partisanship, their violations of civil liberties, their long-windedness, and their inability to influence governmental policy or get their recommendations adopted (see Popper, 1970; Marcy, 1945). Commenting in 1965 on U.S. attempts to build commissions equivalent to the British system, Hanser (1965:234) remarks:

> All would be in vain if the national leadership, whether from inertia, intellectual incompetence, or inability to stand up to vested interests, were consistently to ignore its recommendations. The dismal record of disregard of the rare advisory groups that have really performed well is ominous.

The reaction of the American government to the commission reports on obscenity and pornography, marijuana, and violence confirm this trend in the American system. This pattern fosters the belief that commissions are "reform by public relations," in which the commissions to study a problem are taken to be the substance of reform itself. While the commission may be set up in the heat of controversy when many protest groups are active, when the report is finally issued and ignored several years later, the groups may no longer be around or interested. Or they may have staked their hopes in the commission, and thus lose their battle when the commission itself loses. Thus, commissions may be the burial ground of a great many social problems.

In order for a social problem to continue to exist beyond this formidable hurdle, an institution must be created to deal with the claims and complaints concerning the condition in question; or some existing institution must be mandated to expand its jurisdiction to include this responsibility. When such institutions are created, the social problem cannot so easily disappear.

The creation of such institutions may require legislation of a special kind, and also the allocation of money, personnel, and physical facilities. Such agencies legitimate, institutionalize, and routinize the handling of complaints. Once created, they assume a life of their own. Those who staff them may develop vested interests in the operation of the agency, which may be directed more to satisfying the *complaints* about the imputed conditions than to their amelioration or eradication. Thus, agencies, in lobbying for larger budgets, may emphasize that they are doing their job of dealing with complaints about the condition but also claim that the extent of the condition is increasing and their agencies need more money. Stage Two is complete when the complaints about some condition have become domesticated and routinized by some agency that develops a vested interest in doing something about the complaints, though not necessarily dealing with the conditions the complaints are presumably about.

STAGE THREE

We have suggested that when social problems activities culminate in the creation and establishment of procedures to deal with claims, those activities may diminish and even disappear. The intent of those who negotiate with the social problems group to establish such procedures may range from a genuine attempt to work out a "solution" to the claims, to a cynical and disingenuous maneuver to mollify and defuse the social problems activities, with no intention of ameliorating or rectifying the imputed condition. Regardless of intent, however, the established procedures may be misconceived or inappropriate to the claims and demands they were designed to handle—the procedures may focus on remedies for the imputed condition but fail to satisfy the demands of group members *as complainants*. For example, an agency may establish procedures to rectify specific conditions raised by protestors, but claim that these changes "had been in the works" anyway and were not in response to protest. Agencies may do this to foster the image that all protest is ineffective, even when they are actually responding to it. In such cases protest groups may persist, even as reform is taking place, to force an admission from the agency to "get the record straight."

At the other extreme, the established procedures may in fact turn out to be a "public relations" solution in which the imputed conditions are ignored, on the view that the social problems activities can be "cooled out" by establishing a committee, creating a liaison position for "increasing communication," programming regular meetings to "decide issues" that are never resolved. Edelman (1967:39) has termed this process the "dissemination of symbolic satisfactions." He observes that "the most obvious kinds . . . are to be found in administrative dicta accompanying decisions and orders, in press releases and in annual reports. *It is not uncommon to give the rhetoric to one side and the decision to the other*" (emphasis added.)

As a consequence, assertions about the inadequacy, inefficacy, or injustice of the procedures may themselves become the conditions around which new social problems activities are organized. The groups engaged in these activities may not be the same as those involved in Stage One social problems; some will have disappeared after the negotiation of procedures in Stage Two. Other groups may find they lack the sophistication for dealing with the maneuvers of organizational personnel. Still others, however, may have set up "watch dog committees" to monitor the implementation of the negotiated procedures, and thus stand ready to press claims against them in renewed social problems activities.

The important and distinctive feature of Stage Three social problems, then, is that the claims are not concerned directly with the imputed conditions asserted in Stage One. Rather the claims are made against the organizations established to ameliorate, eliminate, and otherwise change those conditions. Thus, Stage Three activities are not concerned directly with the conditions imputed in Stage One, but about an organization's procedures and methods of dealing with their clients and their complaints. This may be illustrated by the difference between claims about unsanitary conditions in meat packing plants, and subsequent claims against the availability of control agents to complainants, their indifference toward the complaints that *are* registered, their corrupt practices with regard to their inspection of the conditions themselves, *etc.* It should be noted also that even with the best of intentions, the dynamics of bureaucratic processes are likely to generate new sources of complaints.[4] Agencies set up to consider all complaints equally and universalistically may later be charged with insensitivity or ritualism. Clients may claim that the agency is indifferent to the details of their particular case, and that they have become "just a number."

Our conception of Stage Three, then, makes a distinction between claims about conditions that characterize social problems activities in Stage One, and claims about the manner in which the procedures negotiated in Stage Two function to deal with those imputed conditions. Thus, the establishment of procedures in Stage Two provide for the routinization of claims; complaints about pollution are directed to the environmental control agency; claims about unfair business practices might be referred to the Better Business Bureau; complaints about suspected phone taps might be taken to the phone company or police. But Stage Three claims are generated when the environmental control agency itself is accused of licensing polluters of the environment, the Better Business Bureau is said to be in league with the local businessmen against consumers, or the phone taps asserted to be monitored by the phone company or police. That is, the complaints are against the very agencies that have been established to

---

[4] For a stimulating formulation of the bureaucratic problems attending the creation and development of regulatory agencies, see Bernstein (1955: Ch. 3) in which he presents a "life cycle" of regulatory commissions.

process the complaints in question. Stage Three activities may be intensified when responsibility for handling such claims are distributed among several agencies, creating a system of passing such claimants from one office to another, each of them denying responsibility for "that kind of problem."

The outcome of Stage Three social problem activity may be a re-negotiation of procedures, reform of existing practices, dismissal of a high level administrator, possibly the establishment of a new, more specialized agency. Such outcomes may effectively routinize Stage Three claims, but possibly with explicit "watch-dog" provisions to monitor the effectiveness of the claim-processing procedures. Alternatively, Stage Three activities may generate an atmosphere of fundamental distrust of institutionalized procedures, an attitude of cynicism, resignation, and despair, and a lack of confidence in established institutions in general. This distrust of various institutional attempts to deal with complaints may in fact be characteristic of contemporary social problems activities. The lag between the creation of a regulatory agency and the sense of doubt and cynicism among social problems groups about the intention as well as effectiveness of agency efforts is becoming progressively narrow. Classic problems associated with bureaucratic procedures and charges about unresponsiveness of "establishment" agencies generally to the clients they presume to serve has created a militancy in social problems activities that explicitly questions the good faith of those agencies. If this lack of confidence in institutional processes is indeed an historical trend, Stage Three social problems may increasingly move into Stage Four activities.

STAGE FOUR

A new stage in the development of social problems occurs when groups organize their activities on the contention that it is no longer possible to "work within the system." Their focus shifts from complaints and protests against the established procedures to creating and developing alternative solutions for their perceived problems. Such attempts are typically characterized by their focus on a local community and its problems—activities that appear in every area of social life. Minority groups who claim lack of police protection form vigilante patrols for their own communities. Underground newspapers emerge to provide news for and about populations ignored by the conventional press. Food co-ops are formed to fill the demand for specialized products at reasonable prices. Independent political parties are formed to express opinions rejected by the major parties.

These activities are organized by claims that challenge the *legitimacy* of established institutions and the procedures they organize for the processing of claims. The challenges may be generated by a group's experience of having been "given the runaround," of being mollified by "smooth PR types," outright dismissal of complaints as clients of control agencies, *etc.* Or they may be more direct expressions of the generalized lack of confidence in and distrust of "solutions" that established institutions are willing to consider and implement.

We suggest that social problems in Stage Four develop in two directions: (1) the creation of alternative institutions as a means of developing a social and political base for radically changing the existing procedures or (2) disaffiliation and withdrawal from the institutional system to create alternative institutions as limited solutions for group members. Both of these developments are contingent on the definition of established institutions as "hopeless," the rejection or disaffiliation from the established system, and the decision to "work outside the system."

The two lines of development, however, are consequences of a major difference in orientation. The first might be characterized as "value-oriented," the second "interest-oriented" social problems. The alternative institutions created by value-oriented social problems seek to establish those institutions not only for their members, but for the society at large. The primary concern of "interest-oriented" activity is to create a viable solution for the members of the group, requiring only a negative relation to the established system, i.e., to be allowed to pursue, without hassle or harrassment, the group's own solution.

The "free school" movement provides examples of the two types of orientation. One faction of the movement is engaged in radical criticism of the educational establishment through publications, manifestos, articles, and books, as well as by practicing new forms of educational methods with a view toward transforming the conventional system. The other faction is attempting to form free schools in rural as well as urban settings, taking their primary task to be one of providing alternative educational systems for its members.[5]

The "free school" movement also provides us with an example of one of the major hazards of Stage Four social problems—i.e., the possibilities of cooptation. Attempts to create alternative institutions outside the system may produce a new set of experts in the given field. They may be the leaders of various experiments in creating and running new kinds of institutions. Their experience may bring them credentials acceptable to establishment organizations, even though they are developed outside their jurisdiction. Successful and workable alternative institutions may stimulate the interest of the established institutions as they attempt to come up with answers to their critics. They may attempt to take over or to co-opt the alternatives developed and may make attractive offers to the leaders and experts of social problems groups.

For example, the government may invite leaders of the "free school" movement to participate in conferences, compile bibliographic references, accept grants to evaluate the alternative methods of education, *etc*. These invitations may serve the established systems in a number of ways: it can drain off leadership from groups that threaten its institutional dominance; co-opt leadership into its structure, enabling it to claim the innovations as well as to control its effects on the system; insulate that leadership from the members of the group, thus discrediting it and reducing its future effectiveness in organizing social problems activities.

The two types of orientations to Stage Four activities, then, are diametrically opposed with reference to relations with the established system. And insofar as each of them are "successful," they have markedly different consequences for that system. A successful value-oriented alternative would press for the establishment of that alternative as *the* institutional form and, thus,

[5] Kozol (1970) presents a lively discussion of the ideological bases of these alternative orientations within the "free school" movement.

radically transform the existing system. In contrast, a successful interest-oriented alternative would remain an alternative, always vulnerable to the possibility of the revocation of the tolerance of indifference on the part of the established system that is a condition of maintaining the alternative.

CONCLUSION

Building on a critique of previous formulations, we have tried to justify the conceptual category "social problems" as a generic phenomenon, independent of the concepts upon which it has historically depended. As a first attempt to build a theory of this phenomenon, we have proposed a natural history model of social problems in which we attempt to identify the "raw materials" for the sociology of social problems. We differ with previous formulations which spend the greatest part of their statement on the distribution and etiology of the rates or amounts of such "problem" phenomena as crime, divorce, drug use, or poverty. From our point of view, the evidence that there is, for example, a crime problem is not that there is a high rate of crime or that the rate is higher than it used to be. Rather the evidence is that there are many individuals and groups complaining about various aspects of crime—violence in the streets, burglaries in the suburbs, corruption in the police force, *etc.*—and the activities of the myriad agencies that are mandated to do something about those complaints. The so-called "crime problem" as a social problem, like that of the "generation gap," "pollution," "disadvantaged child," and others, is generated and sustained by the activities of complaining groups and institutional responses to them.

REFERENCES

Bain, Read
1935 "Our schizoid culture." Sociology and Social Research 19(Jan.-Feb.): 266-276.

Becker, Howard S.
1966 "Introduction," in Social Problems: A Modern Approach, New York: John Wiley.

Bentley, Arthur F.
1908 The Process of Government: A Study of Social Pressures. Bloomington, Indiana: Principia Press.

Bernstein, Marvin H.
1955 Regulating Business by Independent Commission. Chap. 3. Princeton: Princeton University Press.

Case, Clarence Marsh
1924 "What is a social problem?" Journal of Applied Sociology 3:268-273.

Edelman, Murray
1967 The Symbolic Use of Politics. Urbana: University of Illinois Press.

Frank, L. K.
1925 "Social problems." American Journal of Sociology 30:462-473.

Fuller, Richard C.
1937 "Sociological theory and social problems." Social Forces 4:496-502.
1938 "The problem of teaching social problems." American Journal of Sociology 44:415-435.
1939 "Social problems," pp. 3-59 in Robert E. Park (ed.) An Outline of the Principles of Sociology. New York: Barnes and Nobles.
1942 "Morals and the criminal law." Journal of Criminal Law and Criminology 32:624-630.

Fuller, Richard and Richard Myers
1941a "Some aspects of a theory of social problems." American Sociological Review 6:24-32.
1941b "The natural history of a social problem." American Sociological Review 3:320-328.

Hanser, Charles J.
1965 Guide to Decision: The Royal Commission. Ottowa, New Jersey: Bedminster Press.

Kitsuse, John I. and Malcolm Spector
1973 "Toward a sociology of social problems: Social conditions, value-judgments, and social problems."

Social Problems 20 (Spring): 407-419.

Kozol, Jonathan
1972 Free Schools. Boston: Houghton, Mifflin.

Lemert, Edwin
1951 "Is there a natural history of social problems?" American Sociological Review 16:217-233.

Marcy, Carl
1945 Presidential Commissions. Morningside Heights: King's Crown Press.

Merton, Robert K. and Robert A. Nisbet
1961 Contemporary Social Problems. New York: Harcourt, Brace and World.
1966 Contemporary Social Problems, 2nd ed. New York: Harcourt, Brace and World.
1971 Contemporary Social Problems, 3rd ed. New York: Harcourt, Brace World.

Mills, C. Wright
1959 The Sociological Imagination. New York: Oxford University Press.

Park, Robert E.
1970 "Introduction," in Edwards, Lyford P., Natural History of Revolution. Chicago: University of Chicago Press, Heritage of Sociology Edition.

Popper, Frank
1970 The Presidents' Commissions. New York: Twentieth Century Fund.

Rubington, Earl and Martin S. Weinberg
1971 The Study of Social Problems: Five Perspectives. New York: Oxford University Press.

[5]

SOCIAL PROBLEMS THEORY: THE CONSTRUCTIONIST VIEW

Joseph W. Schneider

Department of Sociology, Drake University, Des Moines, Iowa 50311

Abstract

This paper reviews and critiques the origin and development of a new specialty in sociology, the sociology of social problems. While social problems long has been a topic of sociological attention, it is only since the work of Blumer and, most especially, Spector & Kitsuse in the early 1970s, that a theoretically integrated and empirically viable tradition of writing and research has developed. The central proposition of this tradition is that social problems are the definitional activities of people around conditions and conduct they find troublesome, including others' definitional activities. In short, social problems are socially constructed, both in terms of the particular acts and interactions problem participants pursue, and in terms of the process of such activities through time. The founding theoretical statements are reviewed and the research is discussed in terms of the following categories: containing trouble and avoiding problems; the creation, ownership, and processing of problems; public regulatory bureaucracies and legal institutions; medicalizing problems and troubles; and social problems and the media. The paper closes with an overview of problems and insights of the perspective. There is a bibliography of 105 items.

INTRODUCTION

The social constructionist perspective offers a way to define, understand, and study social problems that is decidedly distinct from previous perspectives. The past decade has witnessed considerable research that, in varying degree, uses or is relevant to the social constructionist or definitional view. In this essay, I review the core statements of this perspective, describe selected research relevant to it, and discuss some of the problems with and insights from using the perspective in research.

PROGRAMMATIC STATEMENTS: MAJOR THEMES

The possibility of a research-based sociology of social problems integrated around a distinct theoretical perspective is not new. More than forty years ago, Waller (1936), Fuller & Myers (1941a, 1941b), and others pursued this goal under the banner of value-conflict theory. A renewed interest in this goal has developed in the past fifteen years (see Tallman & McGee 1971) along with a detailed critique of previous theory and a sharpened conceptualization of what such a sociology of social problems might look like.

While constructionist research and writing has not been the only sociological work on social problems, it arguably constitutes the only serious and sustained recent discussion of social problems theory—a theory *of* social problems distinct from sociological theory used *in* research on undesirable conditions. This latter accurately describes most previous sociological writing and research on social problems, whether it was guided by functionalist, Marxist, conflict theory, or other perspectives. While these latter constitute legitimate sociological work, none informs the question of whether a distinct theory of social problems is possible, what its subject matter might be, or how it might be developed in empirical research. These are precisely the questions Blumer (1971) and particularly Spector & Kitsuse (1973, 1977; Kitsuse & Spector 1973) address.

The question of just what "social problems" means as a sociological concept and how we might study such phenomena has been at the center of the dilemma surrounding this topic since its emergence in the last century. Given this long-lived confusion, Blumer (1971:298) called for a fundamental change in conceptualization to reflect a definition of social problems as "products of a process of collective definition" rather than "objective conditions and social arrangements." Traditional work, he says, reflects a "gross misunderstanding of the nature of social problems" and is virtually useless as a basis for policy since it defines social problems as objective conditions harmful to society. Moreover, sociologists have identified such conditions based on public concern. This is problematic, Blumer says, since many ostensibly "harmful conditions" are not recognized as such by the public, and thus are ignored by sociologists.

Concepts such as "deviance," "dysfunction," and "structural strain" have been "impotent" as guides for research to identify social problems. They can not account for why some conditions fail to become social problems while others do. Sociologists instead "ought to study the process by which a society comes to recognize its social problems" (Blumer 1971:300).

Spector & Kitsuse have called for a similar change, claiming: "There is no adequate definition of social problems within sociology, and there is not and never has been a sociology of social problems" (1977:1). They, like Blumer, critique the familiar functionalist perspective (e.g. Merton & Nisbet 1971) that concentrates on dysfunctional conditions and turns on abstractions such as "latent problems," "collective purposes," society as an "integrated social system," and so on. The sociologist here is a technical expert whose moral vision supersedes that of the people studied. Kitsuse & Spector say this view is empirically problematic, morally infused, and grossly presumptuous. It provides no distinctive subject matter for the sociology of social problems and no effective direction for research.

Kitsuse & Spector endorse the early value-conflict emphasis on the "subjective component" of social problems, but argue that these authors compromised a distinct theory of social problems by their continued attention to objective conditions as a necessary part of the conceptualization. This dualism and confusion as to what social problems are is also found in Blumer's essay, when he speaks of social problems as "products" of collective definitional process, as outcomes, and of objective conditions as a "corrective for ignorance and misinformation" about the "objective makeup of social problems" (Blumer 1971:305). Even Becker's (1966) view of social problems endorses this dualism. This is precisely what Spector & Kitsuse reject. Blumer also cites policy relevance as a criterion to evaluate theory, and implies that public definitions of social problems are somehow inadequate bases for sociological theory (cf. Manis 1984, on "public" definitions). Spector & Kitsuse say that these differences confound the value-conflict approach and thus make it a poor guide for empirical research.

Conventional usage of the term social problems makes it difficult to distinguish what Spector & Kitsuse see as crucial, namely, that it refers to a social process of definition and to the activities that move this process along. For Kitsuse & Spector, participants' definitional activities *constitute* the social problem (Rains 1975, Woolgar 1983), rather than leading to social problems as a product or outcome (cf. Mauss 1975).

Social problems are "*the activities of groups making assertions of grievances and claims with respect to some putative conditions*" (Kitsuse & Spector 1973:415, emphasis in original). Social problems sociology, so defined, should "account for the *emergence and maintenance of claim-making and responding activities*" (Kitsuse & Spector, 1973:415, emphasis in original). Claims making includes: "demanding services, filling out forms, lodging complaints, filing lawsuits, calling press conferences, writing letters of protest, passing resolutions, publishing exposes, placing ads in newspapers, supporting or opposing some governmental practice or policy, setting up picket lines or boycotts. . . ." (Spector & Kitsuse 1977:79). To study the causes of social problems is to examine how such activities come about and how they have been sustained. Toward this end, Spector & Kitsuse, like Fuller & Myers, Blumer, and others, suggest an heuristic, four-stage natural history model.

Stage one comprises "collective attempts to remedy a condition that some group perceives and judges offensive and undesirable. . . . Initial social problems activities consist of attempts to transform private troubles into public issues . . . and . . . the contingencies of this transformation process" (Spector & Kitsuse 1973:148). How claims and grievances are formed and presented, the varieties and nature of the claims and grievances, strategies to press these claims and gain wider attention and support, the power of the group(s) making claims, and the creation of a public controversy are important issues.

Stage two begins with recognition of these claims by "governmental agencies or other official and influential institutions." To continue beyond stage two a social problem must involve "an institution . . . to deal with the claims and complaints concerning the condition in question" (Spector & Kitsuse 1973:154). Social problems thus become routinized in an organization charged with doing something about the putative conditions.

Spector & Kitsuse say that whereas past natural history models end with legitimation and implementation, theirs is open-ended and takes official acceptance as possible grounds for a "new generation" of definitional activities around this official response. When participants claim such response is problematic, *stage three* begins. *Stage four* is marked by claimants' "contention that it is no longer possible to 'work within the system' . . ." and their attempts to develop alternative institutions (Spector & Kitsuse 1973:156).

In their view, sociologists who act as experts on problematic conditions are social problems participants. They become part of the problem rather than analysts of it. Whether he or she "will be treated as a scientist by other participants in the process and accorded the special status of a disinterested and unbiased expert is a problematic empirical question" (Spector & Kitsuse 1977:70). This means sociologists of social problems should not concern themselves with the validity of participants' (their colleagues included) claims about conditions, but with how such claims and definitions are created, documented, pressed, and kept alive. Documenting claims or definitions about conditions constitutes participation. The point is to account for the viability of these claims, not to judge whether they are true. And while social problems participants attribute values to their own and others' activities, sociologists of social problems should not. Gusfield (1984) has characterized this stance as being "on the side" or neutral, rather than choosing "whose side" we are on (Becker 1967).

Besides crediting Fuller & Myers, Becker, and Blumer as important resources in developing their constructionist view, Spector & Kitsuse cite Mauss (1975) and his attention to definitions in his analysis of social problems as social movements. They endorse Ross & Staines's (1971) emphasis on the politics of the definitional process, and they cite as particularly relevant the Hewitt & Hall (1973) analysis of how participants use "quasi-theories" to order problematic situations.

RELEVANT RESEARCH

Containing Trouble and Avoiding Problems

Logically prior to but thus far relatively ignored in research are those diverse definitional activities that occur before professional, bureaucratic, and media categories and personnel become involved. Emerson & Messinger (1977) see such informal reactions as "trouble" and as forerunners of official labeling.

Most research on this informal activity examines how normal others use vernacular categories of mental illness to define troublesome persons. Before Emerson & Messinger (1977) are the well-known studies by Yarrow et al (1955), Sampson et al (1962), Lemert (1962), and Goffman (1959,1969). Goldner (1982) continues this tradition in a study of how others react to "pronoids" in various bureaucratic settings, and Lynch (1983) studied how normals respond to and manage "crazies" in everyday settings.

Research on the origins and development of trouble is not limited to craziness and mental illness. Shearing & Stenning's (1983) study of private security in Canada and the United States shows how owners of mass private property (e.g. shopping malls, apartment complexes, college campuses) define threats to security in precisely such a prebureaucratic, prepublic (in this case precrime) way. Public labeling and processing is something owners usually want to avoid. Private security agents are hired to control anything the owners do not like. This can include behaviors not in violation of the law (e.g. absenteeism, breaches of confidentiality), as well as those that are in violation but not troublesome to owners (e.g. victimless crimes are ignored). By making prevention more important than retribution or restitution, owners and their security forces create a new kind of offender—the employee who allows the theft, damage, or breach to occur. The ultimate wrong is to be nonvigilant in loyalty to owners' interests (see also, Ghezzi 1983, on private control of insurance fraud).

Ball & Lilly (1984) analyze data from a study of a motel used for clandestine sexual encounters to see how motel owners and their staff work to deflect problem-defining activities by three relevant publics: the morally concerned citizenry, the police, and the patrons. The authors show how motel staff attempt to take the role of these three others toward their operations so as to prevent or modify conditions that might become grounds for claims making. They demonstrate that just as conditions are not inherently problematic, neither are they inherently normal. The staff worked hard to create and sustain definitions of the motel as a tolerated and even desirable part of what they saw as a potentially critical environment.

Schneider (1984) studied moral vocabularies used by antismoking and smoking respondents to see how they defined and dealt with trouble around smoking in various public and private settings. He details how antismoke people made claims (or did not) against smokers. While respondents used many negative words to describe smoking and smokers in the interviews, they found confronting bothersome smokers considerably more difficult. The best values to ground their claims were their own health interests and their rights. These claimants and responders were sensitive to the importance of the words they used. Personal dislike alone was considered insufficient grounds for claims.

The language of claims is also important in a study by Cohn & Gallagher (1984) of a social problem involving a gay student group at the University of Maine, a proposed gay conference, a local newspaper, and a group of fundamentalist ministers. Initial claims by the ministers against the University and the gay student group were couched in Biblical terms of sin and immorality. They claimed that the University was condoning such conduct. The University defended itself with a Constitutional and civil rights vocabulary, without mentioning homosexuality or gays. This was strategic. The University thus assured that the issue would not be joined, that they and their critics would not communicate in the ministers' more perilous moral rhetoric. Various sympathetic yet conventional audiences could then support the University while leaving their private opinions about homosexuality unspoken. The case demonstrates how responses are contingent upon, but not determined by initial claims. It also shows that respondents may want not to debate the issue as framed by those initiating claims, particularly if these claims are in unfriendly or difficult vocabularies. Smokers, for instance, felt there was virtually no effective defense against others' health claims.

The Creation, Ownership, and Processing of Problems

The most popular topic for constructionist research has been the creation of bureaucratic and professional categories for problematic conditions, conduct, and persons. Coincidental to Spector & Kitsuse's work, Gusfield (1975,1976,1981), pursuing past interests in the nature of symbolic action (Gusfield 1963,1967), has raised these questions in research on public definitions and policy toward drinking, driving, and accidents in the United States.

Gusfield begins by noting the dominance of one view of this problem: accidents are caused by a category of drivers, "the drunk driver," and their careless and dangerous conduct. Much official data that detail characteristics of the driver, the presence of alcohol, and degree of intoxication have been produced to support this view (cf Kitsuse & Cicourel 1963). Policy has followed accordingly: make drunk drivers control themselves and/or keep them from driving. The laws and public programs that reflect this dominant view, Gusfield argues, contribute to our sense of social order.

To underscore the selective quality of this construction, he details some of what the dominant view omits. Where are such systematic data on vehicle design, the roadway, age and condition of the car, weather, and available emergency assistance as related to "accidents involving alcohol"? How different would definitions and solutions of the problem be were they built on these data?

Gusfield emphasizes connections between the organizational ownership of the problem—a concept he aligns with Becker's (1963) concept, "moral entrepreneur," the construction of supportive scientific facts and causal explanations—and the attribution of political responsibility to "do something about" the problematic condition. This affirms the sociology of knowledge theme in the constructionist approach (see also Aronson 1984) and shows how scientists and experts participate in social problems they purport to analyze. Champions and owners of this favored view of drinking and driving have been The National Safety Council, major auto and life insurance companies, the legal system, the alcoholism industry, and the National Institute on Alcohol Abuse and Alcoholism (NIAAA). Only recently have they been challenged by other groups offering alternate definitions, explanations, and interventions.

Gusfield shows how social context—an important element in constructionist analysis (Woolgar & Pawluch 1985)—facilitates these drunk driver–centered definitions and claims. These favored definitions and explanations allow social drinkers to continue to drive unperturbed and are resources for the alcohol and alcoholism industries to portray the problem of drinking as due to certain sick drinkers rather than the drink. Wiener (1981) examines this social world of alcoholism treatment, policy, and research, and the connections between its participants and their diverse, shifting definitions and claims.

The study of organizational ownership and management of social problems directs attention to how people do this work, to how they handle various kinds of problems and troubles. This parallels earlier work on the organizational processing of deviants and deviance. Recent studies examine how various workers, clients, and others negotiate these definitions. Schwartz & Kahne (1983, Kahne & Schwartz 1978) studied how professionals and clients in a college psychiatric unit negotiated the nature and treatment of students' troubles. Maynard (1982) studied plea bargaining sessions to uncover how court officials use defendants' personal attributes to make sentencing decisions. Miller (1983) examined how workers in a work incentive program used conciliation sessions to reaffirm program morality about responsibility and encourage conformity among troublesome clients. Spencer (1983) examined the familiar probation officer–client relationship and how probation officers negotiate a moral character for their clients to fit the sentencing recommendations they make.

Some studies have focused on how workers, clients, and others use official categories or rules so work can proceed. Joffe (1978) studied how lay abortion counselors balance their ideological support of abortion services with their revulsion at clients who refuse to acknowledge the moral aspects of abortion. McCleary et al (1982) examined how workers in police departments code officers' observations using Uniform Crime Report codes. Pontell et al (1982) studied how California State government reviewed possible fraud and abuse by physicians who used the public medical insurance program. Lynxwiler et al (1983) show how mine inspectors, working for the Office of Surface Mining Reclamation and Enforcement, use discretion in making and processing claims against mining companies. Peyrot (1982) analyzed how community mental health workers used discretion to categorize clients so as to make the best use of scarce resources.

Routinizing and managing people's problems is the essence of the "public interest state"—that complex of federal and state administrative rules, regulations, and personnel that define eligibility for various public endorsements and support (Reich 1964). Spector (1981) says that personnel in these public bureaucracies and programs define troublesome people as "ineligible" to receive benefits (rather than criminal, deviant, or sick) and manage them accordingly.

Public Regulatory Bureaucracies and Legal Institutions

Public regulatory bureaucracies both initiate and receive social problems claims (Chauncey 1980, Randall & Short 1983). Several studies show government agencies as social problems entrepreneurs. Becker's (1963) analysis of how the Treasury Department's Bureau of Narcotics defined the "marijuana problem" is well known (see also Galliher & Walker 1977). Gusfield (1981) and Wiener (1981) point to the NIAAA as a central participant in the world of alcoholism. Nuehring & Markle (1974) and Troyer & Markle (1983, Markle & Troyer 1979) identify the Public Health Service, the Federal Trade Commission, the Civil Aeronautics Board, the Surgeon General, and former Health Education and Welfare Secretary Joseph Califano as important entrepreneurs against smoking.

Chauncey (1980) studied how NIAAA officials tried to convince the nation of the seriousness of teenage drinking. These attempts largely failed because NIAAA was unable to secure endorsement from various private and nonofficial public groups. Public reception ranged from minimal to confused. Specific local teenage drinking programs were few, parents did not buy the definition, doctors did not support it, it had to compete with the drug problem, school officials did not see the problem, and it was rarely reported to police, who, in any case, had little access to special programs. Troyer & Markle (1983) show that antismoking claims made by government agencies have fared considerably better in terms of such grass roots and organization support (see also Ball & Lilly 1982, on the shifting fate of margarine).

When bureaucracies receive citizens' complaints, these claims are transformed by a language that is created and controlled by experts or bureaucrats (cf Latour 1983). Citizens' complaints become part of a system of proper procedures. Murray's (1982) study of the abolition of the short-handled hoe in California farm work makes this clear. While workers and their attorney won the case against managers and the hoe, Murray asks what they did not and could not win, namely, attention to the hazards of all corporate production and to power differences between workers and management. Where claims are made, that is, to whom, can constrain subsequent definitional activities in loosely predictable ways—if one has detailed and current knowledge of the bureaucracy (see also Randall & Short 1983). Without the counsel of legal experts, claimants usually do not possess this knowledge. Murray describes how these experts can control and even change the problem.

Randall & Short (1983) studied a controversy over an Idaho mining company's policy requiring women workers to be sterilized to continue work in an area declared a risk for genetic damage. OSHA initiated claims against the company's policy on behalf of these women. OSHA ultimately lost this case because it could not marshall the necessary external power resources. A court rejected its claims to jurisdiction in such cases, and the Ford Administration was explicitly hostile to all OSHA actions (see also Calavita 1983, and Murray 1982 for similar views of the larger political context and such agencies' claims). The company's claims, definitions, and policy remained intact.

Calavita's (1983) study of the dismantling of OSHA, especially by the Reagan Administration, uncovers the paradox of one part of government making claims against another. By replacing the heads of OSHA (and the FTC) with antiregulators, the Administration was able not only to undermine these agencies and their claims, but to discredit the agency's past work publicly through media stories. Randall & Short say such public agencies are able to make claims, propose general remedies, and gain legitimacy all in one set of activities, effectively collapsing Spector & Kitsuse's first and second stages.

Kitsuse et al (1984) studied the *kikokushijo mondai*—returning student problem—in Japan. In contrast to the Randall & Short case, their study shows how a receptive context—the highly stratified educational system that is considered an essential prerequisite to career success in Japan as a Japanese—can be used to enhance the viability of claims made to a government bureaucracy. This problem consisted of definitional activities by diplomatic, academic, and corporate parents about the educational deficiencies they felt their school-age children experienced upon returning to Japan from foreign residence and education. The authors detail the many and varied ways this problem has become institutionalized, both in the Japanese educational system and in the larger society, while alternative, positive definitions of the returning students' situation (they are "broadened" and "internationalized") have foundered.

Filing a law suit is a common form of claims making today. People, groups, and institutions, including the state, attempt to transform various troubles into legal issues. Such claims making allows us to observe how social problems participants use social structure as a resource.

One topic of study is how various devalued people and their lawyers have challenged owners by invoking the Constitution. Kitsuse (1980) describes how these people have "come out" to demand their civil rights and integrity. Spector (1981) describes these claims as demands to government for "entitlements." These deviants have gone beyond deviance to create new social problems, sometimes with radical social and political implications (see Weitz 1984).

Civil rights, public interest, and consumer law have grown apace. The law here becomes a set of official symbolic categories for making claims to effect social change (cf Gusfield 1981). Using this law, attorneys for black people, the poor, consumers, juveniles, mental patients, prisoners, and others, have attacked a variety of traditional definitions and practices in our public life.

Feminists have been one such challenging group, and rape a particularly important object of their attention. Rose (1977) calls the social problem of rape "a by-product of the feminist movement" and details how women's groups have attacked traditional rape laws and police and court treatment of rape victims. These feminist criticisms offer new definitions of rape (e.g. Brownmiller 1975) and an analysis of its source in traditional gender roles. Alternate institutions run for women by women, some who are themselves rape victims, have grown. As with gay activists and reformed alcoholics, these claimants have taken ownership of the problem away from traditional experts and bureaucrats and made it the object of their and others' routine work (see also Tierney 1982, on the battered women problem).

Spector (1981) and Spector & Batt (1983) compare criminal and civil court procedures concerning rape. These two legal institutions offer victims distinct experiences and opportunities. To define rape as a crime makes the conflict one between the state and the accused. Rape victims sometimes do not even participate in the state's case, which is controlled by lawyers and the judge. If they do, they act as witnesses for the state rather than in their own interests. Spector & Batt use Christie's (1977) idea of conflicts as property to argue that criminal categories, procedures, and professionals steal this conflict from rape victims and transform it into a legal case that seems little related to the victim's experience. By contrast, civil law defines rape as a wrong done to an individual. The state provides the formal setting, judge, and rules to guide the claims-making process. Lawyers (ideally) advise rather than manipulate clients. Rape victims can own their conflicts and express moral outrage against offenders. Spector & Batt examined 31 civil rape cases since the turn of the century and found evidence that rape victims' experiences, compared with those of victims in criminal proceedings, support their analysis.

In another study of legal change, Frank (1983) shows how civil law has replaced criminal law in problems of health and safety in the workplace and the environment since the turn of the century. Through detailed attention to major participants, definitions, and contests in this history, Frank effectively challenges "'knee-jerk' applications of conflict theory" that portray this change as a simple function of corporate capitalist power (see also Donnelly's 1982 study of the origins of the Occupational Safety and Health Act of 1970).

Medicalizing Problems and Troubles

Much recent research on the medicalization of deviance draws on the constructionist perspective. This work examines the implications of these new medical meanings and personnel for participants and the society, and the ownership struggles between professional and lay claims makers. In an early paper, Conrad (1975) draws on Becker (1963), Freidson (1970), and Zola (1972) to describe the origins, rise, and legitimacy of the medical diagnosis hyperkinesis at the hands of a small number of medical researchers, two drug companies, a Congressional Subcommittee on Privacy, and the Association for Children with Learning Disabilities. Conrad contrasts the implications of these medical definitions and interventions around children's troublesome behavior with those contained in the deviant labels "bad" or "problem" child. These new definitions solve problems for teachers and parents responsible for children's difficult behavior, and displace social contextual explanations potentially critical of the educational status quo.

Pfohl's (1977) analysis of child abuse also identifies professional moral entrepreneurs: a few pediatric radiologists who created the new diagnosis, "Battered Child Syndrome." Context is again important in that these radiologists saw this "discovery," says Pfohl, as a welcome opportunity to do significant, career-enhancing work.

The Conrad and Pfohl studies highlight an important kind of professional claims making: scientific publication in a respected professional journal. Such publication is usually not seen as relevant social problems data. These studies also show that those outside medicine can use medical definitions to their own ends, which experts may see as contrary to their own. When professionals become social problems participants, they often must share definitional prerogatives with diverse individuals and groups (see Wiener 1981). Ownership does not always ensure complete control.

Schneider (1978) studied the viability of the "humanitarian" disease concept of alcoholism and found that medical experts in fact were not the primary entrepreneurs. Alcoholics Anonymous, a few scientists and "recovered alcoholics," research centers at Yale and Rutgers Universities, the National Council on Alcoholism, and the NIAAA were the most active political champions of this disease definition (cf Wiener 1981). Similarly, Johnson & Hufbauer (1982) found parents of Sudden Infant Death Syndrome (SIDS) victims were the most active claimants behind new scientific and Congressional awareness and research support for SIDS. These lay champions used scientific research, official medical statements, and public sympathy as important contextual resources to establish the viability of their claims. Troyer & Markle (1983, 1984) reiterate this kind of lay participation around problems of smoking and coffee drinking.

Conrad & Schneider (1980; Schneider & Conrad 1980) studied mental illness, alcoholism, opiate addiction, children's deviant behavior, and homosexuality as prime cases where medical definitions and technology have been championed over sin and crime designations. They used medical journals, professional speeches, editorials, news stories, popular magazines, autobiographies, historical studies, and court cases as sources of data. They identified the actors behind these historic changes and how this definitional work was done. Those who could establish their prerogatives to define the problem and designate who should be responsible for it were powerful figures in these social dramas (cf Gusfield 1975, Latour 1983, Peyrot 1984).

Lay persons can be critics as well as champions of professional owners' definitions and can even win this ownership. The demedicalization of homosexuality illustrates this. Following Spector (1977), Conrad & Schneider (1980) show how gay liberation advocates, with the support of a few insider psychiatrists, challenged the medical disease diagnosis of homosexuality. Using the psychiatrists' own medical, scientific culture, these lay challengers scored a definitional victory that led ultimately to gays themselves becoming the new owner-experts of homosexuality as a "lifestyle." McCrea (1983) studied how a few doctors championed the "deficiency disease" of menopause and a treatment of estrogen replacement. They were effectively challenged by feminists, who used independent scientific research on the link between cancer and estrogen therapy, who defined menopause as a natural part of women's lives, and who claimed that the disease view was sexist. Troyer & Markle's (1984) study of the definition of coffee reiterates the importance of sympathetic professionals and/or supportive research for such challenge. This research enlightens us about how stage three claims are made and successfully pursued.

Studies of the medicalization of deviance also illustrate how professionals create the problems they own and treat (see Hughes 1971, Freidson 1970). In doing this, they make moral judgments both in the technical language of the profession and in the popular moral meanings so far as this language often incorporates popular moral meanings. This second kind of morality seems to be a useful resource for critics, as McCrea's (1983) study demonstrates. Billings & Urban's (1982) analysis of the medical construction of transsexualism and the transsexual shows how doctors became dupes of well-schooled patients who effected key diagnostic criteria to gain treatment, which they later criticized. Loseke & Cahill (1984) describe and criticize—that is, participate in the social problem of—the way experts on battered women label the women who remain in such relationships as unable to control their lives and in need of experts' counsel.

Pawluch's (1983) analysis of the history of pediatrics shifts attention from problematic individuals to how some pediatricians responded to a declining professional market. As childhood diseases and problems of baby feeding were controlled, pediatricians had both less work and less medically worthwhile work to do. Some began to champion new definitions of the baby doctor's role to include, as one advocate said, "shades of difference between health and disease, conditions whereby the child is not invalided, but his social and individual efficacy is decreased" (Pawluch 1983:457; see also Riessman 1983, on women as vulnerable to such medical definitions).

Such professional claims making about problematic conditions in the society is found in science more generally. Aronson's (1982) study of the origins and institutionalization of nutrition research shows how conditions outside science that were seen to threaten powerful interests provided an opportunity for scientist-entrepreneurs to gain financial support and legitimacy by defining themselves and their science as a solution to those "problems." Nutrition's leading late nineteenth-century advocate, Wilbur Atwater, argued he could solve the problem of labor unrest over wages by teaching workers to buy and prepare food in a more economical and healthy way. Such claims appealed to capitalist owners, who sought a productive and cooperative workforce without raising wages. Nutrition advocates finally won official endorsement from Congress, with an appropriation to support their research in US Agricultural Experiment Stations.

Aronson says this case shows some of the conditions under which scientists will make such activist, "social problems interpretive claims" (Aronson 1984) to groups and organizations outside science. When resources to support research are scarce and the opportunity for public funding exists, such enterprising activities might be expected. Johnson & Hufbauer's (1982) study of SIDS shows a contrasting situation in which demands from parents for more research were important as both a direct and indirect impetus to a new medical research community (see also Wiener 1981, on alcoholism research). Latour (1983) makes the most bold argument here, citing the history of Pasteur's capture of the anthrax problem in late nineteenth century France to show how distinctions between science and society, upon close scrutiny, virtually disappeared in the face of compelling scientific facts. Clearly, problems in the larger society and problems in science are often linked, with significant consequences for social organization.

Social Problems and the News Media

Social problems participants usually hope the news media will help them publicize claims and thus enhance their legitimacy. Research shows, however, that the media do not function simply as mirrors claimants can use to reflect "what is really going on." Rather, they decidedly shape the images they convey. Newsworkers are, in short, the true "newsmakers" (Glasgow University Media Group 1980, Fishman 1980), and relevant questions include the following: What happens to claims and definitions that go to media organizations? How do they emerge? What is the place of the media in the social problems process? Do media communicate claims and definitions of their own, quite aside from what other claims makers say?

Fishman (1978) shows that a crime wave against the elderly reported by three New York City media organizations was, in fact, a growing, overlapping media coverage. He details how editors created this news theme to solve routine problems of news work. The theme became a media wave when it was reiterated in other news reports. Fishman calls crime news ideological because it reports crime as the police see it (e.g. street crimes and violent crimes) and because routine newswork produces stories that convey meanings all their own. For instance, news workers recognize good and newsworthy stories by using criteria that systematically filter out things that are not (see also Wiener, 1981:207–211, discussion of media coverage of the Rand Report).

News reporters' routine dependence for information on official owners of problems effectively discourages interpretations foreign to or in conflict with those interpretations on which owner organizations rest. This is what Randall & Short (1983) suggest about the link between OSHA and other official bureaucracies and the media. These agencies are a news beat; they regularly provide the information reporters use to do their work.

Gitlin's (1980) study of how the media covered the New Left and the antiwar movement of the 1960s describes how claims makers who challenge dominant institutions fare in encounters with the media. He studied coverage of antiwar activity by the *New York Times* and CBS News in 1965. When movement spokespersons sought to use the media to convey their views of American society and the war, they found to their dismay that what came out usually gave short shrift to important ideas, but gave full play to conflict, the dramatic, and the bizarre. Individuals in action were important to reporters, who are taught that objectivity and balance are produced by quoting spokespersons for various sides. Gitlin shows how the media created these spokespersons, how they made them "movement leaders" and then celebrities who, overwhelmed by the spotlight, became less concerned with conveying movement claims. The agendas that shape rudimentary news work, then, augur poorly for seriously conveying protest arguments.

Tierney's (1982) research on wife beating reiterates Gitlin's point about what media cover. Wife beating was a topic that was new and controversial, contained violence, was timely and serious, and touched on the familiar themes of feminism, equality, and family life; all of these could still be handled in an entertaining way. Tierney argues that as definitions of wife beating were publicized, social service agencies responded to the conditions described.

Cohn & Gallagher (1984), in the study noted above, detail an incident in which a "conservative" Maine newspaper was involved in a social problem concerning a homosexual group and a planned gay conference at the University of Maine. Fundamentalist ministers attacked the University for allowing the student group on campus and for hosting the conference, after they read about it in the paper (one wonders if a Regents' board meeting was a news beat). The newspaper became a forum for and reporter of the controversy. The editors pursued a delicate balance between their sense of the paper's responsibility to the community, good journalism, and local definitions of the kind of paper theirs was (it did not cause news or stir up trouble). Once the problem developed, it had to be covered, but in a way that would not harm the University and its elite trustees—important figures in the community. By reporting the University's Constitutional defense and the ministers' demands that the University be punished by a legislative budget cut, the paper helped channel the problem. The ministers became the threat against whom the University and community had to be protected.

It is particularly revealing, Cohn & Gallagher say, that, coincidental to this controversy, a major revision of the Maine Criminal Code that decriminalized homosexual intercourse was being voted into law. A second gay conference was planned at the University for a year later. There was no coverage of and virtually no public attention directed to either. Asked about this lack of coverage, editors said that good news stories were about conflict and controversy. There were none around either event; they were not newsworthy. By using these journalistic criteria and their sense of being a responsible paper, editors precluded more social problems concerning homosexuality.

PROBLEMS WITH AND INSIGHTS OF THE PERSPECTIVE

Problems

CONDITIONS AND SOCIAL PROBLEMS An important source of both confusion and disagreement among those using the constructionist perspective is the question of how conditions should figure in social problems analysis. As Rains (1975) focused attention on the "deviant behavior" that societal reaction theory keeps in the background, there has been much comment on Spector & Kitsuse's argument that conditions, as regarded by the sociologist, are irrelevant to a definitional analysis. That these difficulties beset both the labeling and constructionist perspectives suggests that the confusion is perhaps in part a product of the perspective's requirements.

Woolgar (1983), and Woolgar & Pawluch (1985) appropriately note the tension in some constructionist research between a view that sees the natural world, especially in the form of social context, giving rise to various or alternative accounts of what *is* (the "mediative" position), and the view that these accounts, definitions, and claims are "constitutive" of reality (cf Berger & Luckmann 1966). This is the same tension Rains (1975) identifies in labeling work. The criticism is justified for many of the studies identified as constructionist and discussed here.

Sociologists are members of the society they study. The perspective requires them as analysts to suspend both commonsense commitments about what social problems are—e.g. undesirable conditions—and their own scientific judgments about which claims and definitions about these putative conditions are true. The latter proves to be especially difficult (see Gusfield 1984; Aronson 1984). Moreover, as Gusfield (1984) notes, being on the side (that is, standing aside) in the study of social controversies (especially involving differentially powerful participants) has become professionally unpopular as well as personally unsatisfying.

Social problems participants, however, typically neither treat conditions as putative nor suspend their moral convictions, although the perspective does not preclude this possibility. Instead, they see social problems definitions as reflective of the objective reality (Woolgar 1983) in which the problem resides. The sociologist's problem is to avoid participation and, especially, to avoid defending or challenging claims and definitions about putative conditions. This includes avoiding an ironic stance toward some participants' definitions. Few of the authors considered here maintain this distinction consistently in their research. Some make no attempt to do so, even though they call their work definitional.

CLAIMS, DEFINITIONS, AND VIABILITY Spector & Kitsuse's emphasis on claims and claims making has been broadened. They encourage this in their examples (how "floods" and "morons" are products of the social problems process) and by use of the word definitional. Clearly, some of the activities studied fit the definition of claim the authors cite (Spector & Kitsuse 1977:78), but much is described more accurately as definitional. Researchers should consider as data all verbal and nonverbal behavior that conveys meaning about the problematic condition or object of attention. The import of language and how it shapes interpretations and conduct is here enormous. Definitional activities should be treated as an inclusive but carefully grounded concept.

The concept *viability*, important to judging social problems development, should be clarified. Spector & Kitsuse say that viable claims and definitions are those that "live" and that claimants can "get away with." A clear definition of viability is necessary for accurate data collection and to compare the development of various problems. Viability is evident when participants give credibility to claims and definitions, when they treat them as valid. Viability is often produced by media coverage. It is produced when officials and professionals warrant definitions, implement them, and accept responsibility for problematic conditions. We need a clearer understanding of precisely how participants' activities affect the viability of claims and definitions.

NATURAL HISTORY The concept *natural history* is heuristic and directs attention to loose similarities across cases. It leads easily, however, to premature generalization and prediction (R. J. Troyer 1983, unpublished manuscript). Since generalizing is an essential part of scientific work, a cautious strategy would be to examine case studies from similar settings (see Peyrot 1984). One might study problems involving public regulatory bureaucracies. What generalizations might be made about how the news media figure in social problems? What casts of characters emerge at various points in this process? One pitfall to avoid here is the ad hoc, overly topical quality of so much past social problems writing. By using comparative, analytic categories defined by their effects on viability, or examining how the definitional process is moved along by the activities in question (J. I. Kitsuse 1984, personal communication), this might be avoided.

Wiener (1981), in her study of the politics of alcoholism, argues that the sequential aspect of natural history models probably misleads us about the definitional process. She believes a more accurate view is one of "overlapping," simultaneous, "continuously ricocheting interaction" (Wiener 1981:7). A natural history model may encourages us to overstate the extent to which kinds of activities occur only at certain points. This seems likely for Spector & Kitsuse's stage one and stage three activities. Wiener's view reinforces Spector & Kitsuse's argument that the social problems process is open-ended rather than moving to some logical end point (see also Peyrot 1984).

SOCIAL MOVEMENTS SOCIOLOGY VS SOCIAL PROBLEMS SOCIOLOGY? A recent question is whether or not the definitional perspective on social problems is sufficiently distinct from social movements theory to warrant continued attention. Mauss (1984 and unpublished observations) argues it is not, and that social problems are always outcomes of social movements. To study the latter is to study the former.

R. Troyer (1984, unpublished manuscript) uses both definitional and social movements theory and notes the similarities and differences between the definitional approach, the standard structural social movements view, and the more recent resource mobilization perspective on social movements. A traditional social movements approach (e.g. Smelser 1963), with its emphasis on structural strain (to explain grievances) and on organizational considerations and membership recruitment, is contrasted by Troyer with the constructionist view of social problems. Troyer sees the differences as substantial. He also compares the latter with the resource mobilization view (Oberschall 1973, McCarthy & Zald 1973, 1977). While there are general similarities, resource mobilization's emphasis on structural conditions, social movement organizations, and successful outcomes, and its neglect of meaning lead to research agendas quite distinct from those described here. Rather than argue, as Mauss does, that social problems theory should be subsumed by social movements theory, we might better argue that social movements are an example of the social problems process. Moreover, the topics and data of the research cited here seem to challenge the conclusion that the definitional view simply reproduces social movements research.

Insights

The insights of the constructionist perspective as detailed by Spector & Kitsuse appear intact, criticisms notwithstanding. We can still ask, where is a theoretically integrated, empirically based, original research tradition in social problems sociology prior to the work cited here? Have researchers used the core statements and subsequent research to form new and promising questions, as a sociology of social problems? The work described here seems to support an affirmative reply—quite aside from how this or that study could be improved, or whether elements of the core statements are vague or undeveloped. On the other hand, research based ostensibly on a condition-focused approach, or even on a subjective/objective elements approach to social problems has given us few distinct insights. Like the modest claims made by the founders of labeling theory, the definitional view should be judged more by what it has called for and stimulated than what it ignores. Unlike the labeling tradition, Spector & Kitsuse have proposed bold changes. Rather than offering merely another view of social problems sociology, they and others have launched a new speciality and stimulated a sizeable body of work. Whether or not this work would have been done as social movements, Marxist, or conflict sociology we cannot say.

New questions have been asked about what social problems are and how they should be studied. This approach avoids, moreover, some of the major criticisms of labeling by giving attention to the political and historical quality of collective definitional process, and by rejecting an oversocialized view of deviants as "helpless, hapless" victims (see Conrad & Schneider 1980, Kitsuse 1980; Spector 1981). One who carefully reviews this and similar work can hardly reiterate these familiar criticisms (but see Piven 1981).

The perspective and much of the research reaffirms a major strength of labeling, namely, the independence of meaning from the objects to which it is or may be attached by sentient actors as they create, recreate, and are created by social life (cf Matza, 1969, Giddens 1976). Quite contrary to Piven's critique (1981), actors' agency is the source of social action in the constructionist's world.

Finally, this and future work may breathe new life into deviance sociology, particularly as it breaks down old divisions and creates new, more theoretically coherent ones. What might a sociology of trouble or a sociology of morality look like, distinct from theory and research that concentrate on why people behave in ways that happen to break rules or on the social distribution of this behavior and how to control and punish it? I do not say this pejoratively but rather on the assumption that success in these diverse endeavors might be enhanced if we concentrate on the questions our theories ask and on where these theories are incomplete rather than attacking each other because we pursue different questions.

ACKNOWLEDGMENTS:

This review benefited from conversations with John Kitsuse, Malcolm Spector, and Ronald Troyer. Thanks to them. They of course bear no responsibility for my interpretations.

Literature Cited

Aronson, N. 1982. Nutrition as a social problem: A case study of entrepreneurial strategy in science. *Soc. Probl.* 29:474–86

Aronson, N. 1984. Science as a claims-making activity: Implications for social problems research. In *Studies in the Sociology of Social Problems*, ed. J. W. Schneider, J. I. Kitsuse, pp. 1–30. Norwood, NJ: Ablex

Ball, R. A., Lilly, J. R. 1982. The menace of margarine: The rise and fall of a social problem. *Soc. Probl.* 29:488–98

Ball, R. A., Lilly, J. R. 1984. When is a 'problem' not a problem?: deflection activities in a clandestine motel. See Schneider and Kitsuse 1984, pp. 114–39

Becker, H. S. 1963. *Outsiders*. New York: Free

Becker, H. S., ed. 1966. *Social Problems: A Modern Approach*. New York: Wiley

Becker, H. S. 1967. Whose side are we on? *Soc. Probl.* 14:239–47

Berger, P., Luckmann, T. 1966. *The Social Construction of Reality*. New York: Doubleday

Billings, D. B., Urban, T. 1982. The socio-medical construction of transsexualism: An interpretation and critique. *Soc. Probl.* 29:266–82

Blumer, H. 1971. Social problems as collective behavior. *Soc. Probl.* 18:298–306

Brownmiller, S. 1975. *Against Our Will: Men, Women and Rape*. New York: Simon & Schuster

Calavita, K. 1983. The demise of the Occupational Safety and Health Administration: A case study in symbolic action. *Soc. Probl.* 30:437–48

Chauncey, R. L. 1980. New careers for moral entrepreneurs: Teenage drinking. *J. Drug Issues* 10:45–70

Christie, N. 1977. Conflicts as property. *Br. J. Criminol.* 17:1–15

Cohn, S. F., Gallagher, J. E. 1984. Gay movements and legal change: Some aspects of the dynamics of a social problem. *Soc. Probl.* 32:72–86

Conrad, P. 1975. The discovery of hyperkinesis: Notes on the medicalization of deviant behavior. *Soc. Probl.* 23:12–21

Conrad, P., Schneider, J. W. 1980. *Deviance and Medicalization: From Badness to Sickness*. St. Louis: Mosby

Donnelly, P. G. 1982. The origins of the Occupational Safety and Health Act of 1970. *Soc. Probl.* 30:13–25

Emerson, R. M., Messinger, S. L. 1977. The micro-politics of trouble. *Soc. Probl.* 25:121–35

Fishman, M. 1978. Crime waves as ideology. *Soc. Probl.* 25:531–43

Fishman, M. 1980. *Manufacturing the News*. Austin, Texas: Univ. of Texas Press

Frank, N. 1983. From criminal to civil penalties in the history of health and safety laws. *Soc. Probl.* 30:532–44

Freidson, E. 1970. *Profession of Medicine* New York: Dodd Mead

Fuller, R., Myers, R. 1941a. Some aspects of a theory of social problems. *Am. Sociol. Rev.* 6:24–32

Fuller, R., Myers, R. 1942b. The natural history of a social problem. *Am. Sociol. Rev.* 6:320–28

Galliher, J. F., Walker, A. 1977. The puzzle of the social origins of the Marijuana Tax Act of 1937. *Soc. Probl.* 24:367–76

Ghezzi, S. G. 1983. A private network of social control: Insurance investigation units. *Soc. Probl.* 30:521–31

Giddens, A. 1976. *New Rules of Sociological Method: A Positive Critique of Interpretive Sociologies*. New York: Basic

Gitlin, T. 1980. *The Whole World Is Watching: Mass Media in the Making and Unmaking of the New Left*. Berkeley, Calif: Univ. of Calif. Press

Glasgow University Media Group. 1980. *More Bad News*. London: Routledge & Kegan Paul

Goffman, E. 1959. The moral career of a mental patient. *Psychiatry* 22:123–42

Goffman, E. 1969. The insanity of place. *Psychiatry* 32:357–388

Goldner, F. H. 1982. Pronoia. *Soc. Probl.* 30:82–91

Gusfield, J. 1963. *Symbolic Crusade*. Urbana, Ill: University of Ill. Press

Gusfield, J. 1967. Moral passage: The symbolic process in the public designations of deviance. *Soc. Probl.* 15:175–88

Gusfield, J. 1975. Categories of ownership and responsibility in social issues: Alcohol abuse and automobile use. *J. Drug Issues* 5:285–303

Gusfield, J. 1976. The literary rhetoric of science: Comedy and pathos in drinking driver research. *Am. Sociol. Rev.* 41:16–34

Gusfield, J. 1981. *The Culture of Public Problems: Drinking Driving and the Symbolic Order*. Chicago: Univ. of Chicago Press

Gusfield, J. 1984. On the side: Practical action and social constructivism in social problems theory. See Schneider & Kitsuse pp. 31–51

Hewitt, J. P., Hall, P. M. 1973. Social problems, problematic situations, and quasi-theories. *Am. Sociol. Rev.* 38:367–74

Hughes, E. C. 1971. *The Sociological Eye*. Chicago: Aldine

Joffe, C. 1978. What abortion counselors want from their clients. *Soc. Probl.* 26:112–21

Johnson, M. P., Hufbauer, K. 1982. Sudden infant death syndrome as a medical research problem since 1945. *Soc. Probl.* 30:65–81

Kahne, M. J., Schwartz, C. G. 1978. Negotiating trouble: The social construction and management of trouble in a college psychiatric context. *Soc. Probl.* 25:461–75

Kitsuse, J. I. 1980. Coming out all over: Deviants and the politics of social problems. *Soc. Probl.* 28:1–13

Kitsuse, J. I., Cicourel, A. V. 1963. A note of the uses of official statistics. *Soc. Probl.* 12:131–9

Kitsuse, J. I., Spector, M. 1973. Toward a sociology of social problems: Social conditions, value-judgments, and social problems. *Soc. Probl.* 20:407–19

Kitsuse, J. I., Murase, A. E., Yamamura, Y. 1984. *Kikokushijo:* The emergence and institutionalization of an educational problem in Japan. See Schneider & Kitsuse 1984, pp. 162–79

Latour, B. 1983. Give me a laboratory and I will raise the world. In *Science Observed: Perspectives on the Social Study of Science*. ed. K. D. Knorr-Cetina, M. Mulkay, pp. 141–70. Beverly Hills, Calif.: Sage

Lemert, E. M. 1962. Paranoia and the dynamics of exclusion. *Sociometry* 25:2–20

Loseke, D. L., Cahill, S. E. 1984. The social construction of deviance: Experts on battered women. *Soc. Probl.* 31:296–310

Lynch, M. 1983. Accommodation practices: Vernacular treatments of madness. *Soc. Probl.* 31:152–64

Lynxwiler, J., Shover, N., Clelland, D. A. 1983. The organization and impact of inspector discretion in a regulatory bureaucracy. *Soc. Probl.* 30:425–36

Manis, J. G. 1984. *Serious Social Problems*. Boston: Allyn & Bacon

Markle, G. E., Troyer, R. J. 1979. Smoke gets in your eyes: Cigarette smoking as deviant behavior. *Soc. Probl.* 26:611–25

Matza, D. 1969. *Becoming Deviant*. Englewood Cliffs, NJ: Prentice-Hall

Mauss, A. L. 1975. *Social Problems as Social Movements*. Philadelphia: Lippincott

Mauss, A. L. 1984. The myth of social problems theory. *Social Problems Theory Division Newsletter*. Summer, 1984. Buffalo, NY: Society for the Study of Social Problems

Maynard, D. W. 1982. Defendant attributes in plea bargaining: Notes on the modeling of sentencing decisions. *Soc. Probl.* 29:347–60

McCarthy, J. D. Zald, M. N. 1973. *The Trend of Social Movements in America: Professionalization and Resource Mobilization*. Morristown, NJ: General Learning Press

McCarthy, J. D. Zald, M. N. 1977. Resource mobilization and social movements: A partial theory. *Am. J. Sociol.* 82:1212–41

McCleary, R., Nienstedt, B. C., Erven, J. M. 1982. Uniform crime reports as organizational outcomes: Three time series experiments. *Soc. Probl.* 29:361–72

McCrea, F. B. 1983. The politics of menopause: The "discovery" of a deficiency disease. *Soc. Probl.* 31:111–23

Merton, R. K., Nisbet, eds. 1971. *Contemporary Social Problems*. New York: Harcourt Brace Jovanovich

Miller, G. 1983. Holding clients accountable: The micro-politics of trouble in a work incentive program. *Soc. Probl.* 31:139–51

Murray, G. L. 1982. The abolition of *el cortito*, the short-handled hoe: A case study in social conflict and state policy in California agriculture. *Soc. Probl.* 30:26–39

Nuehring, E., Markle, G. E. 1974. Nicotine and norms: The re-emergence of a deviant behavior. *Soc. Probl.* 21:513–26

Oberschall, A. 1973. *Social Conflicts and Social Movements*. Englewood Cliffs, NJ: Prentice-Hall

Pawluch, D. 1983. Transitions in pediatrics: A segmental analysis. *Soc. Probl.* 30:449–65

Peyrot, M. 1982. Caseload management: Choosing suitable clients in a community mental health agency. *Soc. Probl.* 30:157–67

Peyrot, M. 1984. Cycles of social problem development: The case of drug abuse. *Sociol. Q.* 25:83–96

Pfohl, S. J. 1977. The "discovery" of child abuse. *Soc. Probl.* 24:310–23

Piven, F. F. 1981. Deviant behavior and the remaking of the world. *Soc. Probl.* 28:489–508

Pontell, H. N., Jesilow, P. D., Geis, G. 1982. Policing physicians: Practitioner fraud and abuse in a government medical program. *Soc. Probl.* 30:117–25

Rains, P. 1975. Imputations of deviance: A retrospective essay on the labeling perspective. *Soc. Probl.* 23:1–11

Randall, D. M., Short, J. F. 1983. Women in toxic work environments: A case study of social problem development. *Soc. Probl.* 30:410–24

Reich, C. A. 1964. The new property. *Yale Law J.* 73:733–87

Riessman, C. K. 1983. Women and medicalization: A new perspective. *Soc. Policy* 14:3–18

Rose, V. M. 1977. Rape as a social problem: A byproduct of the feminist movement. *Soc. Probl.* 25:75–89

Ross, R., Staines, G. L. 1971. The politics of analyzing social problems. *Soc. Probl.* 18:18–40

Sampson, H., Messinger, S. L., Towne, R. D. 1962. Family processes and becoming a mental patient. *Am. J. Sociol.* 68:88–96

Schneider, J. W. 1978. Deviant drinking as disease: Alcoholism as a social accomplishment. *Soc. Probl.* 25:361–72

Schneider, J. W. 1984. Morality, social problems, and everyday life. See Schneider & Kitsuse 1984, pp. 180–205

Schneider, J. W., Conrad, P. 1980. The medical control of deviance: Contests and consequences. *Research in the Sociology of Health Care* 1:1–53. Greenwich, Conn: JAI

Schneider, J. W., Kitsuse, J. I., eds. 1984. *Studies in the Sociology of Social Problems*. Norwood, NJ: Ablex

Schwartz, C. G., Kahne, M. J. 1983. Medical help as negotiated achievement. *Psychiatry* 46:333–50

Shearing, C. D., Stenning, P. C. 1983. Private security: Implications for social control. *Soc. Probl.* 30:493–506

Smelser, N. J. 1963. *Theory of Collective Behavior*. New York: Free

Spector, M. 1977. Legitimizing homosexuality. *Society* 14:20–24

Spector, M. 1981. Beyond crime: Seven methods to control troublesome rascals. In *Law and Deviance*. H. L. Ross, ed., pp. 127–157. Beverly Hills, Calif: Sage.

Spector, M., Batt, S. 1983. *Toward a more active victim*. Unpublished manuscript. Department of Sociology, McGill University, Montreal, Quebec, Canada

Spector, M., Kitsuse, J. I. 1973. Social problems: A reformulation. *Soc. Probl.* 20:145–59

Spector, M., Kitsuse, J. I. 1977. *Constructing Social Problems*. Menlo Park, Calif: Cummings

Spencer, J. W. 1983. Accounts, attitudes, and solutions: Probation officer-defendant negotiations of subjective orientations. *Soc. Probl.* 30:570–81

Tallman, I., McGee, R. 1971. Definition of a social problem. In *Handbook of the Study of Social Problems*, E. Smigel, ed., pp. 19–59. Chicago: Rand McNally

Tierney, K. J. 1982. The battered women movement and the creation of the wife beating problem. *Soc. Probl.* 29:207–20

Troyer, R. J., Markle, G. E. 1983. *Cigarettes: The Battle Over Smoking*. New Brunswick, NJ: Rutgers University Press

Troyer, R. J., Markle, G. E. 1984. Coffee drinking: An emerging social problem? *Soc. Probl.* 31:403–16

Waller, W. 1936. Social problems and the mores. *Am. Sociol. Rev.* 1:922–34

Weitz, R. 1984. From accommodation to rebellion: Tertiary deviance and the radical redefinition of lesbianism. See Schneider & Kitsuse 1984, pp. 140–61

Wiener, C. 1981. *The Politics of Alcoholism: Building an Arena Around a Social Problem*. New Brunswick: Transaction

Woolgar, S. 1983. Irony in the social study of science. In *Science Observed: Perspectives on the Social Study of Science*. K. D. Knorr-Cetina, M. Mulkay (eds.), pp. 239–66. Beverly Hills, Calif: Sage

Woolgar, S., Pawluch, D. 1985. Ontological gerrymandering: The anatomy of social problems explanations. *Soc. Probl.* 32: (forthcoming)

Yarrow, M. R., Schwartz, C. G., Murphy, H. S., Deasy, L. C. 1955. The psychological meaning of mental illness in the family. *J. Soc. Issues* 11:12–24

Zola, I. K. 1972. Medicine as an institution of social control. *Sociol. Rev.* 20:487–504

[6]

Media Constructions of Crime

By VINCENT F. SACCO

ABSTRACT: The news media are a vital part of the process by which individuals' private troubles with crime—as victims or offenders—are transformed into public issues. The social construction of crime problems may be understood as reflecting the types of relationships that link news agencies to their sources, and the organizational constraints that structure the news-gathering process. The ways in which the news media collect, sort, and contextualize crime reports help to shape public consciousness regarding which conditions need to be seen as urgent problems, what kinds of problems they represent, and, by implication, how they should be resolved. While much attention has been focused on the ways in which media attention to crime influences the fear of crime, it is likely that the most significant effects of media reporting are broadly ideological rather than narrowly attitudinal. By restricting the terms of discussion, the news media facilitate the marginalization of competing views regarding crime and its solution.

Vincent F. Sacco is a professor of sociology at Queen's University. Prior to this appointment, he was a faculty member of the School of Criminology at Simon Fraser University. He has published numerous books and articles in the areas of criminal victimization, crime prevention, and fear of crime. Along with Leslie W. Kennedy, he is the author of a recently published criminology text, The Criminal Event.

CRIME, like an economic recession, a lack of affordable housing, or inadequate health care, is experienced as both a private trouble and a public issue. Quite obviously, for victims, a criminal offense and the resulting loss or injury present problems of a highly personal nature. For victims and nonvictims alike, however, the "plague of drugs," the "epidemic of random violence," and other manifestations of the crime problem are matters for intense public discussion and political debate.

While the distinction between private troubles and public issues is an important one, these dimensions are not independent.[1] Citizens' personal troubles with crime provide the building blocks out of which public issues are constructed. On the other hand, the warnings of danger implicit in public pronouncements about the seriousness and pervasiveness of crime problems may be a source of private trouble if they exacerbate the fear of crime among those who have routine exposure to such pronouncements.

Central to the interplay between individuals' private troubles with crime and the social issue of crime are the mass media. The news media, in particular, provide an important forum in which private troubles are selectively gathered up, invested with a broader meaning, and made available for public consumption. The dynamic character of these processes and the consequences that they have for public understanding of crime and its solution invite close scrutiny.

FROM PRIVATE TROUBLE . . .

Numerous studies of media content have documented the fact that crime reports are a durable news commodity.[2] While news about crime figures prominently in all types of media, important differences exist between print and electronic media, between more elite and more popular media, and between media markets. Because of this variability, estimates of the proportion of total news that is devoted to crime coverage range from 5 to 25 percent.[3]

News about crime is most frequently news about the occurrence or processing of private trouble in the form of specific criminal events. In her study of crime and justice news in Chicago in the late 1970s, Doris Graber found that while attention to crime varied across media, reports of individual crime dominated for all media.[4] With respect to the three newspapers studied, the coverage of individual crimes surpassed the coverage of Congress and the presidency and equaled or surpassed election coverage.

1. C. Wright Mills, *The Sociological Imagination* (New York: Oxford University Press, 1959), pp. 9-11.

2. See, for example, James Garofalo, "Crime and the Mass Media: A Selective Review of Research," *Journal of Research in Crime and Delinquency*, 18:319-50 (1981); Ray Surette, *Media, Crime and Criminal Justice* (Pacific Grove, CA: Brooks/Cole, 1992); Joseph R. Dominick, "Crime and Law Enforcement in the Mass Media," in *Deviance and Mass Media*, ed. Charles Winick (Beverly Hills, CA: Sage, 1978), pp. 105-28.

3. Surette, *Media, Crime and Criminal Justice*, p. 62.

4. Doris A. Graber, *Crime News and the Public* (New York: Praeger, 1980).

Analyses of media content demonstrate that the news provides a map of the world of criminal events that differs in many ways from the one provided by official crime statistics. Variations in the volume of news about crime seem to bear little relationship to variations in the actual volume of crime between places or over time.[5] Whereas crime statistics indicate that most crime is nonviolent, media reports suggest, in the aggregate, that the opposite is true.[6] While crime news tends to provide only sparse details about victims and offenders, that which is provided is frequently at odds with the official picture. Both offenders and victims, for instance, appear less youthful in media reports than they do in statistical records.[7] In addition, news content does not reflect and frequently even reverses the relationship that, according to much social scientific evidence, exists between minority group membership and criminal offending.[8] With respect to gender, however, both crime statistics and crime news portray offending as predominantly a male activity.[9]

News reports also distort the relationship between crime and legal control. In the news, the police appear to be more effective in apprehending offenders than police data would suggest they are.[10] Moreover, while the activities of the police are prominently featured, the functioning of other actors in the criminal justice system is much less visible.[11] This probably reflects a professional judgment that criminal events are most newsworthy immediately following their occurrence and thus when they are in the early stages of justice system processing, when police activity is prominent.[12]

These images of crime, the criminal, and the victim that appear with patterned regularity in print and broadcast news emerge quite logi-

5. F. James Davis, "Crime News in Colorado Newspapers," *American Journal of Sociology*, 57:325-30 (1952); Wesley G. Skogan and Michael G. Maxfield, *Coping with Crime: Individual and Neighborhood Reactions* (Beverly Hills, CA: Sage, 1981).

6. Garofalo, "Crime and the Mass Media"; Skogan and Maxfield, *Coping with Crime*; Philip Schlesinger, Howard Tumber, and Graham Murdock, "The Media of Politics, Crime and Criminal Justice," *British Journal of Sociology*, 42:397-420 (1991).

7. Margaret T. Gordon and Stephanie Riger, *The Female Fear* (New York: Free Press, 1989), p. 70; Roy Edward Lotz, *Crime and the American Press* (New York: Praeger, 1991).

8. Lotz found, for instance, that in newspapers in New York, Miami, and Philadelphia, white offenders outnumbered black offenders by 7 to 1 in those news reports that allowed for the identification of race. Lotz, *Crime and the American Press*, p. 114.

9. M. A. Bortner, "Media Images and Public Attitudes toward Crime and Justice," in *Justice and the Media*, ed. Ray Surette (Springfield, IL: Charles C Thomas, 1984), pp. 15-30.

10. Harry L. Marsh, "A Comparative Analysis of Crime Coverage in Newspapers in the United States and Other Countries from 1960 to 1989: A Review of the Literature," *Journal of Criminal Justice*, 19:67-80 (1991); Bob Roshier, "The Selection of Crime News by the Press," in *The Manufacture of News: Social Problems, Deviance and the Mass Media*, ed. Stanley Cohen and Jock Young (London: Constable, 1973), pp. 28-39.

11. Steven M. Gorelick, " 'Join Our War': The Construction of Ideology in a Newspaper Crimefighting Campaign," *Crime and Delinquency*, 35:421-36 (1989).

12. Sanford Sherizen, "Social Creation of Crime News: All the News Fitted to Print," in *Deviance and Mass Media*, ed. Charles Winick (Beverly Hills, CA: Sage, 1978), pp. 203-24.

cally from the organizational processes of news production. News stories are most useful to news organizations when they are gathered easily from credible sources; for this reason, policing agencies have become the principal suppliers of these stories.[13] In short, relationships involving news organizations and policing agencies allow the collection of news about common crime to be routinized in a manner that uses the resources of news agencies efficiently.[14] In addition, the public view of the police as apolitical crime experts imbues police-generated crime news with authority and objectivity.

Ease of access to authoritative news is not the only advantage that police-generated crime stories offer, since such stories are consistent with several other professional values that structure the news production process. Much of what we call news consists of reports of specific incidents that have occurred since the publication of the previous day's newspaper or the airing of the previous night's newscast. As discrete incidents that occur at particular times and places, individual crimes conform closely to this requirement of periodicity.

Stories about individual crimes—with their characteristic portrayals of villains and victims—also have dramatic value. The dramatic potential is heightened when the victim or offender is a celebrity, when the incident is of a very serious nature, or when the circumstances of the offense are atypical. In addition, the routine crime story is a rather uncomplicated matter, and it is unnecessary for news workers to assume that readers or viewers require an extensive background in order to appreciate the story. The lack of factual complexity associated with the ordinary individual crime story generally means that it can be easily written and edited by news workers whose professional activities are consistently regulated by rigid deadlines.

The elastic character of the crime news supply offers a further advantage. On any given day, particularly in large metropolitan areas, there is an almost limitless supply of crimes that could be the object of media attention. However, from day to day, or from week to week, the demand of the news agency for crime news may vary due to other events that are seen to demand coverage. Depending on the size of the news hole, crime coverage may be expanded or contracted in compensatory fashion. A study by Sanford Sherizen of crime news in Chicago newspapers found, for instance, that crime reports were often located on the obituary pages so that

13. Steve Chibnall, *Law-and-Order News: An Analysis of Crime Reporting in the British Press* (London: Tavistock, 1977); Mark Fishman, "Police News: Constructing an Image of Crime," *Urban Life*, 9:371-94 (1981); Richard V. Ericson, "Patrolling the Facts: Secrecy and Publicity in Police Work," *British Journal of Sociology*, 40:205-26 (1989).

14. In comparison to interpersonal crimes like homicide or robbery, corporate crimes are covered with greater difficulty. Generally, corporate crimes are more complex and more difficult to personalize, and well-established source-reporter relationships do not exist for corporate crime as they do for common crimes. Coverage of corporate, white-collar, and organized crime is more common, however, than is sometimes thought. See, for instance, Donna Randall, "The Portrayal of Business Malfeasance in the Elite and General Public Media," *Social Science Quarterly*, 68:281-93 (1987).

layout difficulties resulting from the inability to plan these pages could be overcome through the use of crime news filler.[15]

Over the last several years, a number of changes in local and national media environments have altered the nature and extent of crime coverage. The growth of cable stations, for instance, has increased the carrying capacity for news generally and for crime news specifically. More stories can be covered, and those that are judged to be particularly newsworthy can be covered in greater detail. The live television coverage of court proceedings—as in the case of the Menendez brothers, Lorena Bobbit, or O. J. Simpson—has become commonplace. The increasing sophistication of news gathering, surveillance, and home video technologies has meant that it is no longer unusual to capture thefts, robberies, or even homicides on tape. One consequence of the diffusion of these technologies has been to raise to national prominence stories with no real national significance. Crime stories that would have been a purely local affair in an earlier period now attract much wider attention because a videotape of the incident is available for broadcast.

The last two decades have also witnessed a redefinition of what can be considered an appropriate subject for news reporting. Changes in mores relating to public discussion of sex and violence have allowed respectable media outlets to report crimes that would have previously been seen as taboo and to do so at a level of detail that would once have been considered lurid. At the same time, the politicization of crimes such as sexual assault and domestic violence has broadened the range of crime stories that, it can be argued, legitimately require coverage.[16]

Programmatic developments in commercial broadcast media have magnified the impact of these changes. The proliferation of newsmagazines, daytime talk shows, docudramas, and various other forms of infotainment has ushered in a programming cycle that is heavily dependent on crime news and victim accounts. The frequent reliance of many of these programs on dramatic reenactments of real events and their mixing of factual reports with rumor and speculation blurs the basic distinctions that analysts of crime content have traditionally drawn between news and entertainment media.[17]

. . . TO PUBLIC ISSUES

Public issues grow up around private troubles when the experiences of individuals are understood as exemplifying a larger social problem, and the news media play a vital role in the construction of such problems.[18] Most notably, professional judgments of newsworthiness and the selective use of news sources allow some

15. Sherizen, "Social Creation of Crime News," p. 221.

16. Keith Soothill and Sylvia Walby, *Sex Crime in the News* (London: Routledge, 1991), p. 6.

17. Graeme R. Newman, "Popular Culture and Criminal Justice: A Preliminary Analysis," *Journal of Criminal Justice*, 18:261-74 (1990).

18. Joel Best, ed., *Images of Issues: Typifying Social Problems* (Hawthorne, NY: Aldine de Gruyter, 1989); Joseph R. Gusfield, "Construct-

groups, rather than others, the opportunity to express a view about what is and what is not a problem and how any such problem should be managed. By implication, the relationships that link the police to news agencies serve law enforcement as well as media interests. The police role as the dominant gatekeeper means that crime news is often police news and that the advancement of a police perspective on crime and its solution is facilitated.[19] It has been argued that this results in the adoption of an uncritical posture with respect to the police view of crime and the measures necessary to control it.[20] More generally, the frame of reference offered by a government bureaucracy or other recognized authority with respect to crime problems may only infrequently be called into question and, as a consequence, competing perspectives may become marginalized.

This tendency may be no less true of in-depth issue coverage than of routine news reporting. Henry Brownstein maintains that during the 1980s, there was relatively little reporting that took issue with the official version of the drug problem constructed by government experts.[21] In a similar way, Philip Jenkins has noted how experts of the Federal Bureau of Investigation were able to present themselves as the authorities on the subject of serial murder and how they made themselves available to journalists who reciprocated with favorable coverage of the agency.[22]

It would be incorrect, however, to suggest that news media are merely the passive conveyors of the claims about problems offered up by government bureaucracies, political candidates, or other self-interested groups, since any such claims must be transformed to meet the requirements of the medium in question. In an analysis of television network news coverage of threats to children, Joel Best argued that "inevitably, network news stories distort the problems they explore"[23] in large part because news conventions impose severe constraints on how stories are covered. Stories must be told in a few minutes, frequently by reporters who may have little more than a surface familiarity with the complexities of the problem at hand. Moreover, the topic must be viewed as serious enough and as visual enough to be chosen over competing issues. Best found, in

ing the Ownership of Social Problems: Fun and Profit in the Welfare State," *Social Problems*, 36:431-41 (1989); Joseph W. Schneider, "Social Problems Theory: The Constructionist View," *Annual Review of Sociology*, 11:209-29 (1985).

19. Fishman, "Police News"; Ericson, "Patrolling the Facts."

20. Richard V. Ericson, "Mass Media, Crime, Law and Justice," *British Journal of Sociology*, 31:219-49 (1991); Marjorie S. Zatz, "Chicano Youth Gangs and Crime: The Creation of a Moral Panic," *Contemporary Crises*, 11:129-58 (1987).

21. Henry H. Brownstein, "The Media and the Construction of Random Drug Violence," *Social Justice*, 18:85-103 (1991).

22. Philip Jenkins, *Using Murder: The Social Construction of Serial Homicide* (Hawthorne, NY: Aldine de Gruyter, 1994), pp. 212-13.

23. Joel Best, "Secondary Claims-Making: Claims about Threats to Children on the Network News," *Perspectives on Social Problems*, 1:277 (1989).

the case of child victimization, that the stories used frightening and dramatic examples to typify the problem and that they emphasized the existence of a consensus among knowledgeable experts regarding its scope and seriousness.

In other instances, news media may more actively engage in problem construction. Investigative reporting, or the coverage of an event judged to be especially newsworthy, may contribute to the establishment of a media agenda that finds expression in the reporting of further stories or in more detailed features. A study by David L. Protess and his colleagues revealed how one Chicago newspaper set its own media agenda after an extensive investigative series on rape.[24] The researchers found that while the series did not appear to have a substantial impact on the perceptions of policymakers or the general public, there were significant changes in the extent and depth of rape coverage after the series ended, even though police reports of rape were unchanged. In a related way, during the summer of 1994, the O. J. Simpson case provided an opportunity for sidebar stories relating to the prevalence and causes of domestic violence, the inadequacy of justice system responses, and pending federal and state legislation. Such coverage contextualized the original incident in a way that helped construct the social issue of violence against women at the same time that it legitimated continuing, detailed attention to the original story.

24. David L. Protess et al., "Uncovering Rape: The Watchdog Press and the Limits of Agenda Setting," *Public Opinion Quarterly*, 49:19-37 (1985).

The content of crime problems

Media constructions of crime problems address both the frequency and the substance of private trouble with crime. Rhetoric regarding both of these dimensions serves to impress on readers and viewers the gravity of particular crime problems and the need to confront them in particular ways.

Large numbers of problems provide convincing evidence that problems exist. This is perhaps most evident in the case of crime waves, when it is argued that crime is becoming more frequent. A study by Steven Gorelick, for instance, of an anticrime campaign sponsored by a New York daily newspaper found that crime in the city was frequently described as a "mushrooming cloud," a "floodtide," a "spreading cancer," or in similar terms.[25] Sometimes these claims about the numbers of people affected have greater specificity in that some particular segment of the population is claimed to be experiencing rapidly increasing risks of offending or victimization.[26]

Yet, with respect to many crime waves, it is the belief that crime is increasing, rather than crime itself, that is really on the rise.[27] A study by Mark Fishman of a 1976 New York

25. Gorelick, " 'Join Our War,' " p. 429.

26. Much has been made in the popular press about, for instance, crime waves that victimize the elderly. See Fay Lomax Cook and Wesley G. Skogan, "Agenda Setting and the Rise and Fall of Policy Issues: The Case of Criminal Victimization of the Elderly," *Environment and Planning C: Government and Policy*, 8:395-415 (1990).

27. Mary Holland Baker et al., "The Impact of a Crime Wave: Perceptions, Fear, and Confidence in the Police," *Law and Society Review*, 17:317-34 (1983).

crime wave against the elderly described how crime waves may be "things of the mind."[28] Fishman found that there was no compelling evidence to indicate that the criminal victimization of the elderly actually increased during the study period. Instead, the crime wave originated in the efforts of journalists to organize individual crime stories around a compelling news theme. The theme of crime against the elderly was elaborated as competing news organizations responded to each other's coverage of the issue. In addition, the police, in their role as gatekeepers of crime news, reacted to the increased media interest by making available more stories that reflected and reinforced the crime-against-the-elderly theme.

A more recent example of a journalistic construction of rapidly rising crime is provided by James D. Orcutt and J. Blake Turner.[29] Their analysis focused on the way in which graphic artists in the national print media transformed survey data, which showed modest yearly changes in drug use, into evidence of a "coke plague." While the numbers were real, their graphical presentation in the weekly periodical under study was misleading. As in the case described by Fishman, the dynamics of competitive journalism created a media feeding frenzy that found news workers "snatching at shocking numbers" and "smothering reports of stable or decreasing use under more ominous headlines."[30]

Claims about statistical frequency are not restricted to reports about how the numbers are increasing, however. With respect to the problem of violence against women, for instance, it is argued that the numbers have always been very high but that the failure to police such incidents, the stigma associated with victimization, and an institutional unwillingness to believe the accounts of victims have resulted in statistical counts that dramatically underestimate the problem. Thus, whether or not the numbers are going up is defined as less salient than the observation that they have always been higher than we have thought.

According to Neil Gilbert, outrageous claims about the prevalence of problems sometimes make their way into news reports in part because of journalists' general inability to evaluate the data supplied to them.[31] Too often, they lack the technical sophistication to critically assess claims about the frequency of crime or victimization in an independent fashion. Instead, they collect and validate information by talking to experts who are expected to offer informed opinions. However, in the case of emergent problems, it is often the problem advocate, interested in advancing a particular point of view, who may be among the first to collect and publicize empirical evidence. As a result, the estimates yielded by advocacy research may be the only ones

28. Mark Fishman, "Crime Waves as Ideology," *Social Problems*, 25:531 (1978).

29. James D. Orcutt and J. Blake Turner, "Shocking Numbers and Graphic Accounts: Quantified Images of Drug Problems in the Print Media," *Social Problems*, 40:190-206 (1993).

30. Ibid., p. 203.

31. Neil Gilbert, "Miscounting Social Ills," *Society*, 31:24-25 (1994).

available at the earliest stages of problem development. Philip Jenkins has argued that the emergence of serial murder as a social issue in the early 1980s was spurred by "epidemic estimates" that placed the number of serial murder victims at between 20 and 25 percent of American homicides.[32] While such numbers continue to circulate through popular and journalistic accounts, more reasoned analysis suggests that the number of serial murder victims is closer to 2 percent of American homicides.

The emergence of crime problems is related not only to claims about the frequency of criminal events but also to claims about their character. Exactly what types of events such incidents are thought to be and who is thought to be typically involved in them matter as much as does the rate at which they are thought to occur.

Any particular social problem can be framed in many ways, and these various frames imply different causal attributions and prospective solutions.[33] Because they are able to legitimate some views and to marginalize others, the news media are an important part of this framing process. Depending on the sources accessed or the type of coverage, rape can be framed as a sex crime or as a crime of violence; the "drug problem" as a product of pushers who hook their victims or as an example of the overreach of criminal law; and violence on the part of youths as a condition necessitating either swift punishment or comprehensive community development.

More generally, when private troubles are constructed as a crime problem of any sort, they are framed in ways that assign primary responsibility for their solution to the criminal justice system. Joel Best has shown how crime problem interpretations of the 1987 freeway shooting incidents in California competed in the relevant news coverage with other interpretations of the incidents.[34] Whereas the crime problem frame implied the need for increased patrols, better investigation, and more effective prosecution, other definitions of the issue—as a gun problem, a traffic problem, or a courtesy problem—suggested other solutions.

In a related way, the social distributional character of victimization is frequently ignored by news coverage that stresses the random character of victimization. While the best social science literature indicates that the risks of crime, like the risks of other misfortunes, are not equally shared, media images often convey a different message. According to Brownstein, for instance, much of the coverage of the drug issue in New York City between 1986 and 1990 emphasized the random character of drug violence even though police statistics indicated that the risks of such violence were extremely low.[35]

32. Jenkins, *Using Murder*, p. 22.

33. Gusfield, "Constructing the Ownership of Social Problems"; Schneider, "Social Problems Theory."

34. Joel Best, " 'Road Warriors' on 'Hair-Trigger Highways': Cultural Resources and the Media's Construction of the 1987 Freeway Shootings Problem," *Sociological Inquiry*, 61:327-45 (1991).

35. Brownstein states, for example, that of the 1051 homicides reported in New York City in 1991, less than 2 percent could be catego-

Themes relating to randomness serve the interests of both news workers and others who seek to frame crime problems. News stories about random crimes have great dramatic value, as the media frenzies that surround serial murders illustrate. Moreover, the advocates to whom news workers have access during the early stages of problem development often stress the random nature of a particular form of victimization since problems must be seen as more urgent when everyone is threatened.

While much routine crime reporting can be understood as maintaining established crime problem frames, new problems are always being discovered as old problem paradigms expand or as novel elements come together with established news themes. The discovery of new problems provides a journalistic opportunity to tell a story that has not been told before, but such stories are told most effectively when they resonate with existing cultural themes. In the 1970s, the problem of crime against the elderly brought together in one package an already familiar concern about crime in the streets and victims' rights with an emerging concern about the aging population.[36] The problem of satanic crime, which received extensive media coverage in the 1980s, combined familiar news themes relating to religious cults, child abuse, and juvenile crime.[37] Media attention to date rape and stalking extends earlier news themes relating to violence against women.

The transition from private troubles to public issues is not always a linear process since media interest in particular crime problems can vary in intensity or decline over time. The 1987 shootings on California freeways never became a well-established problem, despite a strong start.[38] In the case of crimes against the elderly, Fay Lomax Cook and Wesley Skogan observe that while the issue achieved a prominent position on media and other agendas during the early 1970s, by the decade's end, it had declined precipitously.[39] On the other hand, Fishman has argued that as long as police departments are the routine sources of crime news, the media will reinforce a climate of opinion that keeps the attention of the police focused on "crime in the streets." He concludes that while social problems may come and go, "law-and-order news is here to stay."[40]

. . . AND BACK AGAIN?

There can be little doubt that media consumers have broad and regular exposure to crime news.[41] What

rized as random. Brownstein, "Media and the Construction of Random Drug Violence," p. 95.

36. Cook and Skogan, "Agenda Setting and the Rise and Fall of Policy Issues."

37. Ben M. Crouch and Kelly R. Damphousse, "Newspapers and the Antisatanism Movement: A Content Analysis," *Sociological Spectrum*, 12:1-20 (1992); Philip Jenkins and Daniel Maier-Katkin, "Satanism: Myth and Reality in a Contemporary Moral Panic," *Crime, Law and Social Change*, 17:53-75 (1992).

38. Best, " 'Road Warriors' on 'Hair-Trigger Highways.' "

39. Cook and Skogan, "Agenda Setting and the Rise and Fall of Policy Issues."

40. Fishman, "Police News," p. 389.

41. Garofalo, "Crime and the Mass Media"; Skogan and Maxfield, *Coping with Crime*.

are the consequences of this exposure? One potential consequence that has generated considerable interest relates to the deleterious effects that media attention to crime problems may have on audience members' fear of victimization. On the surface, arguments about such effects seem plausible. Public fear of crime is pervasive, and it outstrips measured levels of victimization. By implication, public anxieties would appear to be rooted in vicarious rather than direct experiences, and since messages about crime are so prevalent in the media, it seems reasonable to conclude that much public fear originates in media coverage of crime problems. At issue is whether experience with media treatments of crime as a public issue contributes to fear as a personal trouble. There is a large body of empirical evidence that bears on the relationship between audience exposure to mass media and fear of crime. In the aggregate, however, the findings are equivocal regarding the strength of such a relationship or even whether such a relationship exists.[42]

Some of the inconsistency in this respect is methodological in nature. Considerable variation exists regarding the ways in which crime news, crime news exposure, and fear of crime have been operationalized in the research literature.[43] In addition, since people not only read or watch crime news but also talk about it with friends and neighbors, measured variations in media exposure are not necessarily indicative of exposure to crime news.[44] Nor is it reasonable to assume for research purposes that people are always able to keep clear and report to researchers what is learned in which information channel.[45] Even when such methodological limitations are taken into account, however, the research indicates that the effects of media exposure on fear of crime are less significant than any naive hypothesis would suggest.

Several factors explain this apparent paradox. To begin with, it would

42. For a range of views, see James M. Carlson, *Prime Time Law Enforcement: Crime Show Viewing and Attitudes toward the Criminal Justice System* (New York: Praeger, 1985); Guy Cumberbatch and Alan Beardsworth, "Criminals, Victims and Mass Communications," in *Victims and Society*, ed. Emilio C. Viano (Washington, DC: Visage Press, 1976), pp. 72-90; Anthony N. Doob and Glen E. Macdonald, "Television Viewing and Fear of Victimization: Is the Relationship Causal?" *Journal of Personality and Social Psychology*, 37:170-79 (1979); Garofalo, "Crime and the Mass Media"; George Gerbner et al., "The Demonstration of Power: Violence Profile No. 10," *Journal of Communication*, 10:177-96 (1979); Garrett J. O'Keefe, "Public Views on Crime: Television Exposure and Media Credibility," in *Communication Yearbook 8*, ed. Robert N. Bostrom (Beverly Hills, CA: Sage, 1984), pp. 514-35; Richard Sparks, *Television and the Drama of Crime* (Buckingham, England: Open University Press, 1992); Vincent F. Sacco, "The Effects of Mass Media on Perceptions of Crime: A Reanalysis of the Issues," *Pacific Sociological Review*, 25:475-93 (1982).

43. Glenn G. Sparks and Robert M. Ogles, "The Difference between Fear of Victimization and the Probability of Being Victimized: Implications for Cultivation," *Journal of Broadcasting and Electronic Media*, 34:351-58 (1990).

44. Anthony N. Doob, "The Role of Mass Media in Creating Exaggerated Levels of Fear of Being the Victim of a Violent Crime," in *Confronting Social Issues: Applications of Social Psychology*, ed. Peter Stringer (Toronto: Academic Press, 1982), pp. 145-59.

45. Gordon and Riger, *Female Fear*, p. 85.

be inappropriate to assume that audience members respond passively to the warnings of danger issued by omnipotent news media. Instead, as Paul Williams and Julie Dickinson note, news consumers are actively involved in investing the news with meaning.[46] Audience members bring to the reading and viewing experience their own predispositions, which influence what crime news means for them. These predispositions may include personal experiences with crime or violence,[47] perceptions of the credibility of news media,[48] or the extent of prior concern about personal safety.[49] In the context of cross-sectional research, these predispositions suggest the possibility that the correlation between media usage and fear of crime may be more indicative of selective exposure than of media influence.[50]

While people avidly read and watch crime news, it is unclear that in so doing they extract lessons relating to their own safety. Such lessons, it appears, are more effectively learned in other contexts. The relevant research indicates that the news about crime that travels through interpersonal channels may be more likely to induce fear than is the news that travels through mass channels.[51] To learn about crime by talking to one's neighbors is to learn about victims whose experiences cannot be easily dismissed because they are nameless or faceless or live somewhere else.

By contrast, the typical media crime story is stripped of much of its emotional character and is likely to involve victims about whom the viewer or reader has no personal knowledge. In addition, the average news story may provide readers and viewers with so little information about the victim, the setting in which the crime occurred, or other circumstances of commission that it may be irrelevant to any assessment of personal victimization risks.[52] Most crime news is nonlocal and therefore far removed from judgments that must be made regarding the safety of the immediate environment. Not surprisingly, there is research that suggests that fear is, in fact, related to crime news exposure when local random violent crimes are reported in prominent fashion.[53] Taken together,

46. Paul Williams and Julie Dickinson, "Fear of Crime: Read All about It: The Relationship between Newspaper Reporting and Fear of Crime," *British Journal of Sociology*, 33:34 (1993).

47. Philip Schlesinger et al., *Women Viewing Violence* (London: BFI, 1992), p. 165.

48. O'Keefe, "Public Views on Crime."

49. Sacco, "Effects of Mass Media," p. 483.

50. Williams and Dickinson, "Fear of Crime," p. 51; Dolf Zillmann and Jacob Wakshlag, "Fear of Victimization and the Appeal of Crime Drama," in *Selective Exposure to Communication*, ed. Dolf Zillmann and Jennings Bryant (Hillsdale, NJ: Lawrence Erlbaum, 1987), pp. 141-56.

51. Skogan and Maxfield, *Coping with Crime*; Susan J. Smith, "Crime in the News," *British Journal of Criminology*, 24:289-95 (1984); Tom R. Tyler, "Assessing the Risk of Crime Victimization: The Integration of Personal Victimization Experience and Socially Transmitted Information," *Journal of Social Issues*, 40:27-38 (1984).

52. Gordon and Riger, *Female Fear*, p. 75; Tyler, "Assessing the Risk of Crime Victimization," p. 34.

53. Linda Heath, "Impact of Newspaper Crime Reports on Fear of Crime: Multimethodological Investigation," *Journal of Personality and Social Psychology*, 47:263-76 (1984); Allen E. Liska and William Baccaglini, "Feeling Safe

these findings are consistent with a more general body of research that indicates that people may be less dependent on news media when they seek information about matters close to home.[54]

Overall, it would appear that as crime news relates to matters of personal safety, consumers appear to exercise a healthy dose of skepticism.[55] As Dennis Howitt observes, newspaper readers do not necessarily think that crime rates are going up just because the number of column inches devoted to crime increases.[56] They are more likely to put what is learned from the media in the context of what they learn from other sources, and they may be well aware when media are behaving in a highly sensationalist manner.[57]

CONCLUSION

If the news business is concerned with the production of crime problems, then the private troubles of criminal offenders and crime victims are the raw materials. These troubles are not simply reported on, however, since they are fundamentally transformed by the news-gathering process. Screened through a law enforcement filter, contextualized by advocacy claims and culturally resonant news themes, and shaped and molded by the conventions and requirements of commercial media, these private troubles become public issues.

While news media coverage of crime may not have a powerful influence on the concern for personal safety, this should not obscure other, perhaps more significant effects. Such effects are not narrowly attitudinal or behavioral but are broadly ideological.

Some critics argue that the police perspective implicit in so much crime news reporting dramatically restricts the parameters of discussion and debate about the problem of crime. As a consequence, the causes of offending are individualized and the relationships that link crime to broader social forces are left largely unexplored.[58] Correspondingly, traditional law-and-order responses are reaffirmed as the most efficient way to manage crime problems. A study of media coverage of attacks against women in Toronto found that explanations of the phenomenon tended to focus attention on the ways in which victims placed themselves in conditions of risk, on offender pathology, and on the need for a more coercive criminal justice response.[59] The

by Comparison: Crime in the Newspapers," *Social Problems*, 37:360-74 (1990). Interestingly, these studies also suggest that coverage of nonlocal violence may decrease fear among news consumers by allowing them to feel safer by comparison.

54. Philip Palmgreen and Peter Clarke, "Agenda-Setting with Local and National Issues," *Communication Research*, 4:435-52 (1977).

55. Jack Katz, "What Makes Crime 'News'?" *Media, Culture and Society*, 9:60 (1987).

56. Dennis Howitt, *The Mass Media and Social Problems* (Oxford: Pergamon, 1982), pp. 125-26.

57. Williams and Dickinson, "Fear of Crime," p. 50.

58. Gorelick, " 'Join Our War' "; Drew Humphries, "Serious Crime, News Coverage and Ideology: A Content Analysis of Crime Coverage in a Metropolitan Newspaper," *Crime and Delinquency*, 27:191-205 (1981).

59. Sophia E. Voumvakis and Richard V. Ericson, *News Accounts of Attacks on Women: A Comparison of Three Toronto Newspapers* (Toronto: University of Toronto, Centre of Criminology, 1984).

authors note that while these terms of reference were not unreasonable, the attention they received left little room for alternative interpretations of the problem, particularly those interpretations that link the victimization of women to structures of gender inequality.

When crime problems are successfully constructed, a consensus emerges regarding what kinds of public issues private troubles represent.[60] Yet the development of such a consensus—regarding what the problems are, who is responsible for them, and how they should be resolved—should not be understood in conspiratorial terms. While both news workers and their sources are interested in offering a convincing and credible construction of reality, for many in the media, the construction of these problems is not a matter of activism but just another day at the office.[61]

As news workers observe and influence each other, and as the line between news and entertainment becomes more confused, public discussion of crime problems reflects and reinforces this consensus, and popular views of these problems begin to assume a taken-for-granted character. Inevitably, but regrettably, the emergence of such a consensus relegates to the margins the search for alternative ways of thinking about crime and its solution.

60. Gusfield, "Constructing the Ownership of Social Problems," pp. 434-36.

61. Stephen Hilgartner and Charles L. Bosk, "The Rise and Fall of Social Problems: A Public Arenas Model," *American Journal of Sociology*, 94:57 (1988).

[7]

The Media's Role in the Definition of Crime

Ray Surette and Charles Otto

What is considered a crime is historically both fixed and evolving. In this chapter, we will examine the question of how new crimes come into existence. Why is it, for example, that in certain periods of history consuming alcohol was a crime and in others it was not? We will argue that the media have played a powerful role in the crime definition process and today comprise the primary engine in the criminalization and decriminalization process.

Examine Figure 8.1, a simple representation of the conjunction of crimes and law-abiding behaviors. At the center are sets of behaviors that are nearly universally defined cross-culturally and cross-temporally as crimes. Throughout recorded history and across varying cultures, the unprovoked killing of a complete stranger has been considered a crime. Incest, theft, and rape are other acts that fall into this fixed definition of crime and receive broad social support for their continued criminalization. The social definition of these types of behaviors as crimes has been nearly constant, and only in special circumscribed situations are they decriminalized. Thus, governments sometimes decree that killing complete strangers is acceptable or even mandated such as during a war or execution.

The second ring of behaviors in Figure 8.1 are those that are currently defined as crimes but for which there is not deep and consistent support. These crime definitions vary across time and culture. For example, in the United States it is a criminal act to consume marijuana for nonmedical purposes. However, in other countries and cultures, the recreational use of marijuana is not a crime. Also, time is a factor. Marijuana use was legal in the United States until its criminalization in the 1930s. Along the same lines, recently in the United States driving while under the influence of alcohol has been made into a more serious crime with much harsher penalties.

The third ring of actions in Figure 8.1 are those that are considered deviant

Figure 8.1 Crime and Deviance Consensus Continuum

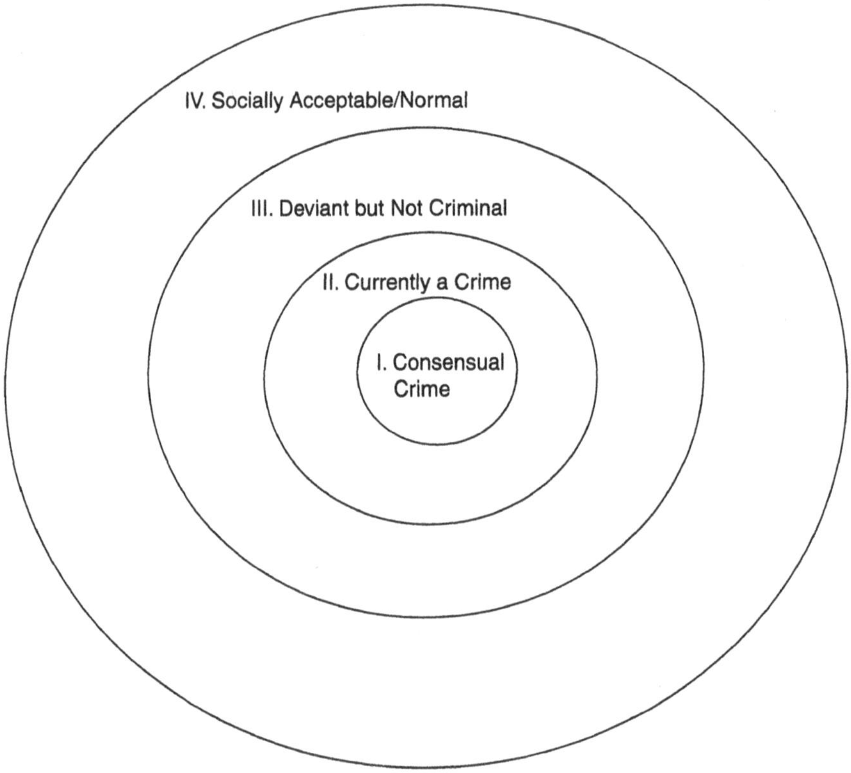

but not criminal. For example, it is seen as deviant to make a romantic gesture to your mother-in-law, but it is not a criminal act. Note that those actions that are considered deviant but not criminal also tend to vary over time and across cultures. In other words, sometimes actions are labeled as deviant but not as criminal; in other situations, times, or cultures, they are considered crimes.

Or the shift may be outward toward the forth ring, where once deviant behavior is seen as socially acceptable and normal. Reading this book is considered to be socially acceptable and normal; however, reading this book at a relative's funeral may not be considered criminal, although it would likely be considered deviant. However, reading it aloud in a library could be a criminal act depending on the laws of the state where the library was located. Again, activities that are usually considered normal may be classified as deviant in some settings or socially abnormal at some point in the future, or they may even be considered criminal in special circumstances or times.

The main point is that the behaviors move between the rings of figure 8.1. Behaviors in the second, third, and fourth groups migrate, and even the core consensually perceived criminal behaviors are decriminalized in special circumstances. Our focus will be on the migration of behaviors among the outer rings and the role that the contemporary mass media plays in the migration. This collective three set group of behaviors are variously defined as crimes, deviant but noncriminal, or normal-acceptable behavior. The observation of this migration has been cited as evidence of the relativism of crime—that whether a behavior is considered a crime is relative. For every behavior, sometimes it is a crime; sometimes it is not.

In contemporary America, the media will have the most impact on the definition and movement of the nonconsensual crimes. Admittedly, the media may have very little influence on the classification of incest as a crime and would be hard-pressed to cause its decriminalization. But the media do have a substantive impact on the legalization, deviantization, and criminalization of the vast set of behaviors that comprise figure 8.1's second, third, and fourth rings. One need only to recall the history and social perception of varied recreational drugs to sense the media's importance.

PRIOR APPROACHES TO CONCEPTUALIZING THE CRIME DEFINITION PROCESS HAVE IGNORED THE MEDIA'S ROLE

Prior approaches to understanding the definition of the crime process have either explicitly or implicitly acknowledged the evolution of these definitions but have until recently ignored the media as having an important role in the definitional process (Lanier and Henry 1998). Thus, the moral consensus view describes the process as the reaction of a common public conscience causing moral outrage and the defining of selected behaviors as serious offenses against society (Burgess 1950; Durkheim [1893] 1933; Roshier 1989). While generally viewed as stable and independent of the need for formal criminal justice system recognition, the ability of the common conscience to vary by culture and time is conceded. Crime definitional changes, however, are expected to be slow and generational in this perspective. The likelihood of rapid transformation (or migration) of a behavior from one status to another is seen as low. In its defense, most of the theoretical development in the moral consensus view precedes the late twentieth century and the emergence of the current postmodern global mass media. Developed prior to a significant mass media, this perspective best applies to a pre–mass media era.

In contrast to the moral consensus view, relativists and others here argued for a more rapidly changing definition environment. In their competitive and conflicting social environment, political power plays an essential role in the crime definition process (Becker 1963; Chambliss and Seidman 1971; Quinney 1973; Tifft 1995). In this perspective, political power is crucial in rendering some behavior criminal and in keeping other harmful behaviors invisible and noncriminal. Here the media are seen as playing a role in the definition process, but they are secondary to political power and are perceived only as manipulated tools for those wielding political power. Those without power are perceived as effectively shut out from access to the media, and the media themselves are seen as substantially controlled by the powerful. Hence, significant broad-based media access, influence of media content by groups and individuals not of the political elite, or the media as independent actors in the crime definition process are not seriously considered in the moral consensus perspective.

However, in the 1960s, corresponding with the social impact of the first pervasive electronic mass medium, television, the concept of social competition was borrowed from the political power perspective and social constructionism emerged (Meyrowitz 1985). The social constructionist perspective saw the process of defining crime and other social realities as both competitive and free wielding. With social constructionism, for the first time access to the media and skill in utilizing media emerge as significant factors in the crime definition process (Barak 1994; Pfuhl and Henry 1993; Schur 1965, 1980; Surette 1998). The media are no longer seen as minor elements reflecting other long-term social processes, nor are they perceived solely as manipulated tools of political power or totally controlled by any single social group. They have become something more.

Constructionist improvements on the earlier somewhat unidimensional views of the crime definition process have produced a virtual geometry of crime definition models. Thus, one finds in the literature Young's (1997) "Square of Crime," Henry and Milvanovic's (1996) "Constitution of Crime," Hagan's (1985) "Pyramid of Crime," and Henry and Lanier's (1998) "Prism of Crime." Within this geometric development, initially the media were not explicitly incorporated. Their effects were first expressly included via the concept of visibility (Henry and Lanier 1998). Visibility is important because it raises the question of how the public becomes aware that social acts are socially harmful and therefore in need of criminalization (Henry and Lanier 1998: 619). The linkage via visibility between the media and crime definitions is seen as the comparative visibility of crimes reflecting the interests of the powerful rather than the inherent social harm of a behavior. The politically powerful are seen as capable of keeping some harmful behaviors invisible to the public by keeping them out of the media and simultaneously inordinately raising the visibility of other behaviors by having the media dwell on them. The politically powerful's interests are also seen as related to the mass media's commercial interests. In this view, the coalescing of the media, business, and politically powerful interests in turn contains and limits the definitional social construction of crime (Barak 1994; Surette 1996).

This initial and limited vision of the media role as serving only the interests of the economically and politically powerful has expanded within the social constructionist perspective. It now includes unanticipated effects from the plethora of entertainment images of crime and justice found in the popular culture and the news media sensationalization of "true crimes." Both popular culture and true crime sensationalization are seen as affecting the visibility of other possible social behaviors for criminalization (Henry and Lanier 1998: 619, citing Ermann and Lundman 1995; Poveda 1994). In its simplest conceptualization, the predatory crime that dominates popular culture and the true-crime genre simply crowds out other candidates from public consideration (Surette 1998).

As it has evolved, the most recent conceptual development of the definitional process of crime, Henry and Lanier's prism of crime explicitly includes the media as a crucial factor in the process. At one apex of the prism, "highly visible crimes" are recognized and emphasized by the media in both its news and entertainment content and at the other vector are "obscured crimes" that lack media attention but are not without social harm. For Henry and Lanier (1998: 623):

> The position of crimes in the prism varies over time. As vocal dominant groups and mass-mediated culture focus on different issues, so the public awareness of what counts as crime is formed and reformed. Acts are recognized as more or less visible, more or less serious, and more or less harmful. For example, the positions of domestic violence and sexual harassment have changed: Both recently have begun to move from the lower to the upper half of the prism. In contrast, other acts that formerly were located in the upper half, such as some religious offenses (e.g. working on Sunday), have become so common as to be hidden, are relatively harmless, and elicit neither public sentiment nor societal response.

The visual image is that of a lava lamp, with behaviors drifting upward and downward from criminal to noncriminal definitions and back again. It is our contention that the heat energy for this social crime definition lamp is largely provided by the media. Their attention provides the heat energy to raise behaviors to criminalization levels, and their lack of attention denies the necessary energy to nonconsensual crime behaviors to keep them in the upper half of the prism. Lacking the heat of media attention, these behaviors will drift down through declining visibility, benign sanctions, and eventual nonenforcement and decriminalization. As currently constituted, collectively the contemporary mass media are the thermal engine for the migration process. They are today so crucial that we argue that behavior cannot be criminalized without media attention and that intense media attention can result in the rapid movement of a behavior within the prism. Such rapid movements are indicative of an accelerated social construction process of crime definitions. To understand this criminalizing and legalizing media impact, it is first necessary to comprehend the social construction of reality process.

THE SOCIAL CONSTRUCTION OF REALITY PROCESS

Understanding the theoretical perspective known as the social construction of reality or social constructionism helps to better understand the impact of a pervasive mass media on crime definitions. Under this theoretical view, people create reality—the world they believe exists—based on their individual knowledge and from knowledge gained from social interactions with other people. This view is the opposite of the dominant Western tradition of logical empiricism, which views social knowledge as independent of social processes and grounded totally in events in the world. Knowledge of the world in logical empiricism is objective and uninfluenced by social processes. An objective social reality exists that is uninfluenced by social perceptions, and social perceptions can only distort one's perception of reality. Social knowledge reflects social facts that are, in turn, tied directly and objectively to social events that are (or should be) recorded identically by different observers.

Social constructionism differs in that it views knowledge as something that is created by humans, and this knowledge may or may not mirror an objective reality. This perspective does not question the physical reality of the world or the fact that social events actually occur but rather focuses on human relationships within the world and the way personal relationships affect how people perceive reality. Understanding of the world is sought by studying its shared meanings. Shared meanings are, in turn, the result of active, cooperative social enterprises. The degree to which a given constructed reality prevails is not directly dependent on its objective empirical validity but is instead strongly influenced by the shifting forces of social trends and interactions. The perspective recognizes the fact that social conditions become major social problems and then subside, without the physical situations they concern having undergone any significant change. Therefore, regarding the defining of crime, not only can social behaviors be criminalized or decriminalized independently of social conditions, but in social constructionism such occurrences are not unusual. It is expected that behaviors may be criminalized and decriminalized without the actual social level or conditions of those behaviors changing.

Within the social construction process the perceptions of conditions change as social knowledge about those conditions change. People acquire knowledge from four sources: personal experiences, significant others (peers, family, friends), other social groups and institutions (schools, unions, churches, government agencies), and the mass media. The first source, also termed *experienced reality*, is one's directly experienced world—all the events that have happened to you. Knowledge gained from experienced reality is relatively limited but has a powerful influence on one's constructed reality. Thus, personal victimization is the most powerful source for defining one's view of what constitutes a crime and how serious a crime is. Fortunately, even in a society fixated with crime like the United States, personal victimization remains comparatively uncommon. Serious victimization tends to concentrate in a high-risk group of citizens composed mostly of lower-income and minority persons (Koppel 1987).

The next three sources of knowledge are shared symbolically and collectively form one's symbolic reality. All the events you didn't witness but believe occurred, all the facts about the world you didn't personally collect but believe to be true, all the things you believe to exist but haven't seen, make up your symbolic reality. The difference between experienced and symbolic reality can be shown by a few questions: How many believe the moon exists? Why? Because you can see it directly—you have experienced-reality knowledge of its existence. How many believe the moon has an atmosphere? Why not? Because you've been told it has no air, you've read it has no air, and you've seen pictures of men in space suits on the moon. It is because so much of our social knowledge is gained symbolically that there is concern over its content and correctness, particularly its use of deception. Not surprisingly, the media are centrally involved in our symbolic reality knowledge formation. Regarding the definitional process of crime, it is from our symbolic reality that we obtain the vast majority of our crime-defining knowledge. In large, advanced, industrialized societies like the United States, the mass media dominate our symbolic reality, overwhelming the information we receive via conversations with significant others and our limited experienced reality. What we see as crimes tend to be described, delimited, and defined in the mass media.

The role of the media in the social construction of knowledge is diagrammed in figure 8.2, which presents the phases of social constructionism. In phase 1 we have the actual physical world we live in. In phase 2 is competition over how to define the physical world. This phase involves a number of theoretical concepts significant for social constructionism, including claims and claims makers, ownership, and linkage. Claims are the descriptions, typifications, and assertions regarding the extent and nature of phenomena in the physical world. These statements are promoted as facts about the world. For example, "Crime is out of control" is a claim about the factual physical condition of crime in society. "Cocaine is a dangerous drug whose use and sale must be criminalized" is a factual claim about what substances should be against the law.

Claims makers are the promoters, activists, professional experts, and spokespersons involved in forwarding specific claims about a phenomenon. They hope to have their claims accepted as the dominant social construction of reality. If the dominant social construction becomes "Crime is out of control," then those who have made that claim can consider themselves to have been successful. When the president states that the culture of violence in our schools must be addressed, he is forwarding a claim about the world that also incorporates a response to the claimed conditions of the world. New laws and policies directed against the "culture of school violence" would indicate the success of the president's construction of a new social problem.

In the United States, four frames compete in the media for domination of the crime definition process (Sasson 1995). The first frame, a faulty criminal justice system, holds that crime is a problem because of excessive due process procedures. The second frame, blocked social and economic opportunities, posits that crime is the result of individuals having opportunity unjustly withheld from

Figure 8.2 Phases of Social Construction

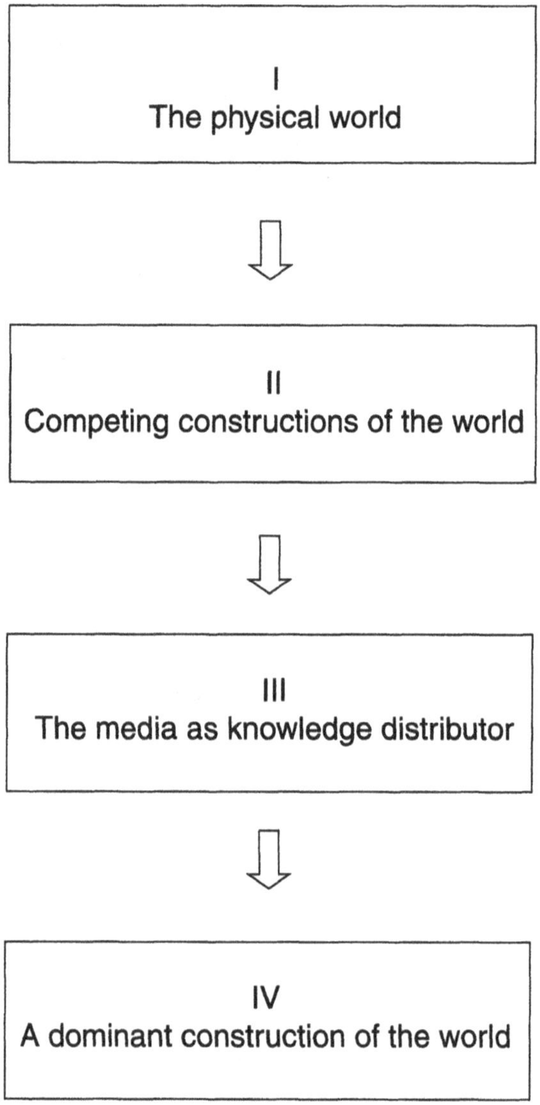

them. The third frame, social breakdown of family and community life, contends that crime is the result of the traditional family structure deteriorating. The fourth frame, an oppressive and racist criminal justice system, argues that crime is the result of an oppressive and racist society. Most crime and justice news stories fall into one of the four frames, and criminal justice policies tend to reflect one frame or another (Beckett and Sasson 2000).

Ownership is the identification of a particular phenomenon with a particular set of claims makers who come to own the issue in that they are sought out by the media for pronouncements regarding its nature and the reasonableness of competing social policies directed toward it. Some groups—by virtue of their superior power, finances, status, organization, technology, or access to the media—have greater resources to make their constructions appear legitimate, to make their version of reality stick, and to take effective ownership of an issue. The NRA, for example, is one of a group of claims makers that are vying for ownership of the gun access issue. While the NRA is striving to not have gun access further criminalized, other groups, such as Handgun Control, headed by Sarah Brady, work to have gun access further criminalized with the passage of the Brady Bill.

Lastly, linkage involves the typing or association of an issue with other issues. For example, drugs are often linked to other social problems such as crime. The linkage of one social phenomenon to another generally seen as more harmful raises the concern and importance of the linked issue. Thus, the social importance of drug abuse is heightened when drugs are linked to other social problems, and the same linkage makes other correlates of crime appear less significant. Hence, gun access is linked to school violence and makes both issues more pressing.

In the third phase, the media filter out the various claims and claims makers. This is where the media play their most powerful role. By giving some claims more credibility and coverage than other claims, the media make it hard for some claims makers to gain legitimacy and to affect the social construction of reality process. Claims makers who are not adept with the media are not able in most circumstances to get their claims and social constructions coverage. This effectively shuts them out of the social construction competition. For example, disorganized, poor, crime-ridden neighborhoods are frequently unable to get their community problems successfully constructed as serious criminal issues (Skogan and Maxfield 1981).

The final phase is the emergence of a dominant construction of the world. Since most of us have very little direct experience with crime and justice reality, the media play an important role in our conceptualization of crime and the reality construction that eventually wins the social construction competition. This dominant construction is the reality that most people accept as valid. For crime and justice, it will include those behaviors that have been accepted as criminal, deviant but noncriminal, and law-abiding. A social behavior will be perceived as a crime, or it will not.

For crimes and the definition of them, the social construction of reality process is therefore crucial, and the media are crucial for the process. The shared meanings of what social acts are considered normal, deviant, or criminal are socially constructed, constantly contested, and evolving. We believe that the mass media have emerged as both key players and crucial playing fields in the crime definition process. As claims makers, the media sometimes are directly involved in the construction competition, forwarding a specific new crime definition. When not involved as claims makers, the media provide the social arena in which other claims makers promote their constructions and compete in the reality-defining process. The next section discusses some examples of the application of the media-based social constructionism to crime definitions.

RECENT EXAMPLES OF MEDIA INFLUENCE ON THE CONSTRUCTION OF CRIME DEFINITIONS

Three Strikes and You're Out

Our first example demonstrates how various groups can use the media to affect the crime definition process—in this case, the "three strikes and you're out" legislation.[1] Serious crime was redefined in the process to include an explicitly quantitative element. The reaction to the initial idea of three strikes in the mid-1980s was not enthusiastic, and criminal justice professionals rejected the need for an expanded definition beyond the existing habitual offender laws. However, in 1988, Diane Ballasiotes was abducted and stabbed to death in Washington state by a convicted rapist who had been released from prison. In reaction to this crime, a group called "Friends of Diane" formed to seek harsher penalties for sex crimes. This group eventually joined forces with another Washington state policy group that was advocating for three-strikes legislation. Despite their combined efforts, however, through 1992 there was little legislative or criminal justice professional interest in three strikes in Washington state. The proposed legislation was perceived as similar to a habitual offender law already on the books, and a petition drive to get three strikes on a statewide ballot failed (Gest 1994).

It is important to note that Friends of Diane and the three strikes group did not have significant access to the media. In this sense, they were unable to forward a dominant construction of reality by being a claims maker that the media relied on to frame various crime stories. Although there was some media coverage, a receptive media environment was not in place.

In 1993, however, the three-strikes group (renamed the Washington Citizens for Justice) allied with the National Rifle Association and succeeded in getting the proposition on the November ballot. Despite some opposition from elements of the criminal justice community, 77 percent of Washingtonians approved the three-strikes law. As the Washington vote approached, a young girl in California, Polly Klass, was abducted and murdered, and a three-strikes campaign took off in California. Unlike in prior years, media coverage was extensive, and this time politicians and citizens across the nation and the political spectrum embraced three strikes (Surette 1996).

A number of social constructionist concepts clearly come to play in the three strikes saga. With the alliance of the NRA, Friends of Diane was able to become a much more powerful claims maker—the NRA was a group that the media would readily contact. Also, with the kidnapping and murder of Polly Klass, the three strikes stakeholders had a symbolic event that they were able to use to define the crime problem and influence policy. Symbolic events in the crime definition process are crucial because they ensure media access for claim makers, while providing dramatic evidence of the behavior that must be criminalized. In three strikes, the Polly Klass murder became the symbolic element that could absorb the media, focus heat and power, lifting the new crime-defining legislation in the social crime prism (Wilkie 1994).

Highway Violence

In our second example, we look at how the media define a new crime. The media do not usually take on this role as much as they act as a filter and playing field among various claims makers, but an example of a media-created crime definition can be seen in their treatment of highway shootings. Joel Best (1991) analyzed imagery concerning highway violence from several major newspapers and television stations. He found that, after an initial story dealing with highway violence appeared, the media began constructing a number of different types of highway incidents as indicative of a new social phenomenon of highway violence today known as "road rage." Best (1991: 332) summarized this situation by stating:

> In short, the media described freeway shootings as a growing problem, characterized by random violence and widespread fear. Without official statistics or public opinion polls bearing on the topic, reporters relied on interviews with their sources to support these claims. Thus, the eleven network news stories used thirty-eight clips from interviews: eleven with law enforcement officials promising to take action or advising caution; thirteen victims describing their experiences; ten person-in-the-street interviews revealing public concern; and four experts offering explanations.

Best further found that the media tried to explain and interpret the problem. The media would say, for example, that highway congestion coupled with the anonymity of the car could trigger these violent outrages in people. The media also offered competing frames for the problem of highway violence. Some interpreted it as a crime problem, suggesting that more law enforcement was the solution to the problem. Others saw it as a traffic problem. Freeway violence would be lessened if the roads were not so congested. Other frames were that freeway violence was a gun access problem or a lack-of-courtesy problem. Best concludes that in this case the media were the primary claims maker in the definition of road rage, taking on this role in part because the summer of 1987 was a slow news period. Needing a new crime, the news media went out and constructed one, in the process raising highway violence from a low-visibility event to a high-visibility "new" crime phenomenon.

Predatory Criminality and Serial Killers

An example of the media constructing a crime issue without constructing a new crime is provided by the historic role that predatory criminality plays in the U.S. media. The media in both its entertainment and its news components have defined predatory criminality by strangers as the dominant and most pressing crime problem in the nation (Surette 1995). The history of the media reveals that the image of the predator criminal has dominated news and entertainment for at least the last one hundred years. The repeated message is that predatory individuals who are basically different from the rest of us perpetrate crime and that criminality stems from individual problems. Media criminals have become more animalistic, irrational, and predatory and their crimes more violent, senseless, and sensational. Because of the media's efforts, the crimes that dominate the public consciousness and policy debates are not the common crimes but the rarest ones. The mass media have raised the visibility of the predator criminal from a minor character to a common, ever-present image. The public is led by the media to see violence and predation between strangers as a way of life (Scheingold 1984). Serious crime has been defined to symbolize the uncertainties of modern life, that criminals are evil, abnormal people (Cavender and Bond-Maupin 1993).

The genesis of the "serial killer" as a significant new type of crime in the 1980s epitomizes the news and entertainment media definition of predatory criminality as the most serious U.S. crime problem. Philip Jenkins (1988) reported that although there was some evidence of a small increase in the number of active serial killers, in total, serial killers account for no more than three hundred to four hundred victims a year, or 2 to 3 percent of all U.S. homicides. Media coverage of serial murderers and the success of fictional books and films about serial killers, however, have resulted in serial killers being redefined and accepted as the dominant homicide problem in the United States and symbolic of a society being overwhelmed by rampant violent predatory criminality (Kappeler, Blumberg, and Potter 1993; Surette 1995).

The effects of this dominant-constructed definition of serious criminality were crucial for subsequent criminal justice policies and legislation, especially the shift toward individual-focused retributive polices during the 1970s and 1980s (Beckett and Sasson 2000; Doppelt and Manikas 1990; Surette 1992). Criminal justice policy was transformed into a war being fought by semihuman monsters against society (Jenkins 1988). The resultant media-induced "serial killer panic" of the 1980s was embraced because media sensationalism and media manipulation by government agencies resulted in a societal quest against an "evil predator criminal foe." As a result, public resources and law enforcement efforts were heavily diverted to address the newly defined social menace (Jenkins 1988). The media-promulgated definition and image of predator crime has also helped to make the United States one of the most punitive countries on the planet (Beckett and Sasson 2000). In the final analysis, the media project the horrendous crime as the norm and maintain the predator criminal at the top of the crime definition prism (Elias 1986).

The Criminalization of Driving under the Influence

A final example of how the media influences the crime definition process in terms of raising the perception of a crime's seriousness can be seen with drinking and driving. Driving under the influence was something that has been legally defined as a crime for a long time. However, until recently it was an act that most closely fit into the second ring of behaviors. It was a deed that was defined as a crime, but there was not broad, consistent support for its criminalization, and, not surprisingly, enforcement was lax and haphazard.

Rick Inmon (1999) examined the media's construction of DUI and found that prior to the 1980s, it was constructed primarily as a rehabilitation problem. News accounts told of how lawmakers wanted to lessen the penalties for DUI. During this period, lawmakers rationalized that the current penalties were too harsh and that the imposition of stiff penalties such as license revocation would interfere with the offender's abilities to care for their families. Inmon also found that, during this time, the media used nonpejorative words such as *errant* to describe the actions of those convicted of DUI.

Craig Reinarman (1988) has also concluded that groups like MADD (Mothers against Drunk Driving) have impacted the dominant social construction of the drunk driver. Previously, drunk drivers were seen as troubled individuals. Socially reconstructed, currently they are seen as individuals who cause trouble. MADD could not have done this without waging successful media campaigns that, in turn, affected how crime is defined.

At the beginning of the eighties, therefore, DUI came to be constructed as a much more serious crime. The drunk driver was now characterized as a "killer drunk" and one of society's worst problems. There was clearly a shift in the media's depiction of drinking and driving and subsequently how society viewed drinking and driving. No longer was it viewed as an individual problem. Now, it was constructed as a menace to society, and support grew for much stricter DUI laws and nondiscretionary enforcement. DUI has shifted in figure 8.1 from the outside edge of ring 2 (criminal but no broad support) to close to ring 1 (consensually criminal). It became and is now an act that most people view as a serious crime.

CONCLUSION

We have argued that the media play a central role in the crime definition process because of the social construction of reality process. Most people do not have any substantial experiential reality to rely on when it comes to defining crime, so they rely on the media. The examples show that the media usually filter information from various claims makers, as they did with the three strikes legislation; they sometimes become the primary claims maker, as they did with the highway violence issue; they also raise rare criminal acts to disordinate public visibility and concern, as they did with serial murder; and they increase the seriousness with which a crime is perceived. The media can also have the opposite crime-defining effects. They can decriminalize behavior by ignoring or trivializing its prevalence and effects; they can block access to the public by crime constructing claims makers; they can keep significant and harmful social and harmful conditions invisible; and they can, by lack of attention, fail to validate and acknowledge truly new crime forms.

What is it that makes the difference between whether something becomes part of the dominant social construction? The answer is complex. Regarding the media, they cannot be simply tagged as manipulating mechanisms that force criminal justice policies and crime definitions down the public's throat. Nor can they be dismissed as objective neutral bystanders in the public policy arena. The reality is that the media play an indispensable but not independent role in the crime definition.

In the large, the media will not have much influence on our core set of crime beliefs. The media have its greatest impact on the crime definition process for those behaviors that are not fixed across time and culture. The limited set of anecdotal case studies suggests that they most easily influence the criminalizing of acts that were once considered deviant or socially acceptable. Because media attention provides visibility-raising energy, the media appear more effective and quicker at criminalizing than decriminalizing behaviors. Because of inertia in the criminal justice system, the removal of media attention needs a longer time period to cool off a behavior, allowing it to sink in visibility, than media attention needs to impart buoyancy to a behavior. Media-criminalizing attention can be achieved in a short time, while the cooling effects of nonattention appear to take longer. This likely explains a deficiency of decriminalization examples in the research literature. Rare, they remain largely undocumented and unstudied.

Speculating on the future, we forecast that as the media technologically develop and we become a mediated global society in the next millennium, the media's role in the crime-defining process will increase. The media-generated rapid escalation of behaviors into the criminalized sphere will be common. The ultimate concern is that reasoned public debate of the merits of defining some behaviors as crimes and others as not crimes will be replaced by a media-based, audience-share standard. Instead of addressing its most harmful behaviors as crimes, society will repeatedly chase a series of media-defined crime specters.

NOTE

1. A television commentator coined the slogan "three strikes, you're out" to denote a policy in which anyone who had been convicted of two serious crimes would subsequently face life without parole if convicted of a third nonmisdemeanor (Surette 1996, citing Gest 1994).

REFERENCES

Barak, G., ed. 1994. *Media, Process and the Social Construction of Crime: Studies in Newsmaking Criminology*. New York: Garland.

Becker, H. S. 1963. *Outsiders: Studies in the Sociology of Deviance*. New York: Free Press.

Beckett, K., and T. Sasson. 2000. *The Politics of Injustice: Crime and Punishment in America*. Thousand Oaks, Calif.: Pine Forge.

Best, J. 1991. "Road Warriors on Hair-Trigger Highways: Cultural Resources and the Media's Construction of the 1987 Freeway Shootings Problem." *Sociological Inquiry* 61: 327–45.

Burgess, E. 1950. "Comment to Hartung." *American Journal of Sociology* 56: 25–34.

Cavender, G., and L. Bond-Maupin 1993. "Fear and Loathing on Reality Television." *Sociological Inquiry* 3: 305–17.

Chambliss, W., and R. Seidman. 1982. *Law, Order and Power*. 2d ed. Reading, Mass.: Addison-Wesley.

Dopplet, J., and P. Manikas. 1990. "Mass Media and Criminal Justice Decision Making." In *The Media and Criminal Justice Policy*, ed. R. Surette. Springfield, Ill.: Thomas, pp. 129–42.

Durkheim, E. [1893] 1933. *The Division of Labor in Society*. New York: Free Press.

Elias, R. 1986. *The Politics of Victimization*. New York: Oxford University Press.

Ermann, D., and R. Lundman, eds. 1995. *Corporate and Government Deviance*. New York: Oxford University Press.

Gest, T. 1994. "Reaching for a New Fix to an Old Problem." *U.S. News and World Report* (7 February): 9.

Hagan, J. 1985. *Modern Criminology*. New York: McGraw-Hill.

Henry, S., and M. Lanier. 1998. "The Prism of Crime: Arguments for an Integrated Definition of Crime." *Justice Quarterly* 15: 609–27.

Henry, S., and D. Milovanovic. 1996. *Constitutive Criminology*. London: Sage.

Inmon, R. 1999. "Drunk Driving Constructed in the United States." Unpublished manuscript, University of Central Florida.

Jenkins, P. 1988. "Myth and Murder: The Serial Murder Panic of 1983–1985." *Criminal Justice Research Bulletin* 3: 1–7.

Kappeler, V., M. Blumberg, and G. Potter. 1993. *The Mythology of Crime and Criminal Justice*. Prospect Heights, Ill.: Waveland.

Koppel, H. 1987. *Lifetime Likelihood of Victimization*. Bureau of Justice Statistics Technical Report, U.S. Department of Justice. Washington, D.C.: U.S. Government Printing Office.

Lanier, M., and S. Henry. 1998. *Essential Criminology*. Boulder, Colo.: Westview.

Meyrowitz, J. 1985. *No Sense of Place*. New York: Oxford University Press.

Pfuhl, E. H., and S. Henry. 1993. *The Deviance Process*. 3d ed. Hawthorn, N.Y.: Aldine de Gruyter.

Poveda, T. G. 1994. *Rethinking White Collar Crime*. Westport, Conn.: Praeger.

Quinney, R. 1973. *Critique of the Legal Order*. Boston: Little, Brown.

Reinarman, C. 1988. "The Social Construction of an Alcohol Problem: The Case of Mothers against Drunk Drivers and Social Control in the 1980s." *Theory and Society* 17: 91–120.

Roshier, B. 1989. *Controlling Crime: The Classical Perspective in Criminology*. Philadelphia: Open University Press.

Sasson, T. 1995. *Crime Talk*. Hawthorne, N.Y.: Aldine de Gruyter.

Scheingold, S. 1984. *The Politics of Law and Order*. White Plains, N.Y.: Longman.

Schur, E. M. 1976. *Crimes without Victims: Deviant Behavior and Public Policy*. Englewood Cliffs, N.J.: Prentice-Hall.

———. 1980. *The Politics of Deviance: Stigma Contests and the Uses of Power*. Englewood Cliffs, N.J.: Prentice Hall.

Skogan, W., and M. Maxfield. 1981. *Coping with Crime: Individual and Neighborhood Reactions*. Newbury Park, Calif.: Sage.

Surette, R. 1992. *Media, Crime, and Criminal Justice: Images and Realities*. Pacific Grove, Calif.: Brooks/Cole.

———. 1998. *Media, Crime, and Criminal Justice: Images and Realities*. 2d ed. Pacific Grove, Calif.: Brooks/Cole.

———. 1996. "News from Nowhere, Policy to Follow: Media and the Social Construction of Three Strikes and You're Out." In *Three Strikes and You're Out*, ed. D. Shichor and D. Sechrest. Thousand Oaks, Calif.: Sage, pp. 177–202.

———. 1995. "Predator Criminals as Media Icons." In *Media, Process, and the Social Construction of Crime: Studies in Newsmaking Criminology*, ed. G. Barak. New York: Garland, pp. 131–58.

Tifft, L. L. 1995. "Social Harm Definitions of Crime." *Critical Criminologist* 7: 9–13.

Wilkie, D. 1994. "Polly's Slaying Now Just Politics." *San Diego Union-Tribune*, 21 October, A1, A25.

Young, J. 1997. "Left Realism: The Basics." In *Thinking Critically about Crime*, ed. B. D. MacLean and D. Milovanovic. Vancouver, Canada: Collective, pp. 28–36.

[8]

"THE ICE AGE" THE SOCIAL CONSTRUCTION OF A DRUG PANIC

PHILIP JENKINS
Pennsylvania State University

In 1989 and 1990 there was much media and political concern about use of the drug "ice," or smokable crystal methamphetamine, which was believed to pose a social threat potentially as great as that of crack cocaine. This concern was not sustained, however, and references to the topic diminished sharply within a few months. The incident thus offers a valuable opportunity to trace the history of a drug panic from its origins to its eclipse. Particular emphasis is placed on the role of domestic political divisions, especially in Hawaii, in citing the panic. It is suggested that this incident illustrates both the manner in which local problems come to be projected on the national political arena and the limitations inherent in such a process. The paper explores the rhetorical devices used to create a sense of impending menace around the supposed danger, and the reasons why such an apparently plausible danger failed to gain more public attention or credence.

Research in illicit drugs has often emphasized the disparity between the perceived threat of a substance and the actual social harm involved. A distinguished literature deals with successive drug "panics," which have focused on marijuana in the 1930s, amphetamines in the 1950s, glue sniffing in the 1960s, and crack cocaine in the last decade (Brecher 1972; Musto 1973; Reinarman and Levine 1989; Goode 1984; 310-34). This is not to argue that any of these substances is harmless or (necessarily) socially acceptable, but in each case, the extravagant claims permit us to employ the term *panic.*

Drug scares generally follow broadly similar patterns in which it is suggested, for example, that the drug in question is currently enjoying an explosive growth in popularity; that it is extremely addictive, and that even occasional use can cause severe physical addiction; and that it is destructive to the user or to others, threatening health or encouraging bizarre and violent behavior. Such claims are buttressed in a number of ways, including the use of exemplary cases and the parading of what appear to be objective statistics and scientific studies; the latter often turn out to be rather questionable on further examination. In addition, claims makers usually demonstrate a certain historical amnesia, often rediscovering problems which in fact are well-established while failing to note how thoroughly earlier panics were discredited.

Social scientists have explained such periodic waves of concern in various ways. Many emphasize the role of political or bureaucratic interest groups seeking to enhance their claims on resources and status. Others stress the role of factors in the broader society, such as ethnic or generational tension and hostility, which come to be symbolized by the drug in question. In this sense it is almost irrelevant whether the claims presented by the rhetoric of a "panic" are well-founded or wholly spurious: the panic itself is valuable in itself for what it suggests about the perceptions of a society as a whole, and specifically of policy makers and legislators. The incident thus has great significance for understanding the social construction of crime and deviance.

Some claims are widely accepted and have the effect of remolding law and public policy: the crack issue has done so in the last decade (Reinarman and Levine 1989). Other issues, however, are more ephemeral, and the claims appear to enjoy far less success. In recent years we have witnessed a dramatic example of such a short-lived panic in the public reaction to the alleged boom in the use of the drug "ice," or smokable methamphetamine. During 1989 and early 1990, it was widely claimed that this substance was becoming enormously popular in certain regions, and that it had the potential to "sweep the nation" in a few months or years. Dramatic statistics were offered to support these claims; it was suggested that ice was uniquely dangerous in combining extremely addictive qualities with the advantages of cheapness, easy access, and domestic manufacture. The media panic about ice found its focus in Congressional hearings during October 1989 and January 1990. The stage seemed to be set for a repetition of the crack "explosion" of 1986.

This concern about ice was not sustained, however, and media references to the topic diminished sharply within a few months. Outside a few cities and regions, the issue either has ceased to exist or is dormant. The incident thus offers an unusual opportunity to trace the creation of a drug panic from its inception to its eclipse. In understanding the phenomenon, we must emphasize that "ice" originated as a very localized event, confined largely to Hawaii, and that the words *epidemic* and *explosion* arose from partisan and bureaucratic rivalries within that state. The projection of this local concern onto the national stage was made possible by a number of factors, including the existence of specialized agencies and investigative bodies focusing on drug issues, and the intensification of public expectations and fears following the crack scare. I suggest that all these elements still exist and are likely to lead in future to other ephemeral drug panics. The "ice" incident is likely to be repeated in various forms.

THE METHAMPHETAMINE INDUSTRY

Methamphetamine is a stimulant of the central nervous system which, as a street drug, is often known as "speed" or "crank" (Graham 1976; Grinspoon 1975; *Methamphetamine Abuse* 1989; Miller and Kozel 1991). The illegal manufacture of methamphetamines began in the early 1960s, and networks of clandestine laboratories emerged to produce several synthetic drugs. During the 1970s, such laboratories tended increasingly to shift their production towards methamphetamine and away from other synthetics such as PCP (Jenkins 1992b). Between 1981 and 1984, methamphetamine producers represented half of all laboratory seizures; by 1988 they exceeded 80 percent (*U.S. Congress: Laboratories* 1980; *U.S. Congress: Re-emergence* 1990:25, 90-91).

The attractions of the industry were obvious. The manufacturing process required little expertise; several cheap "hands-on" manuals were available to provide detailed instruction. A laboratory could make as much as five to 10 pounds of methamphetamine in a week, and the pure substance usually was "cut" repeatedly for street sale. The annual production of a laboratory thus might be worth several million dollars (Jenkins 1992b). In 1989 a Dallas police officer remarked, "We think the profit is much greater when we look at methamphetamine production, as compared to heroin or cocaine. We know that an investment of $3000 to $4000 in chemicals, in glassware, can turn a profit of $25,000 to $30,000." (*U.S. Congress: Re-Emergence* 1990:39).

One appeal of methamphetamine was that the substance was manufactured in the United States and did not need the sophisticated importation and distribution networks required for heroin or cocaine. Laboratories needed no elaborate facilities or natural resources beyond an ample supply of electricity, and distribution demanded little more than convenient access to the interstate highway network (Skeers 1992; Weingarten 1989; Witkin 1989).

During the 1980s, methamphetamine manufacture tended to become strongly regionalized. In the late 1970s and early 1980s, the Philadelphia area was said to be "the speed capital of the world," with networks of hundreds of laboratories in the southern and eastern parts of the state (Jenkins 1992b; *U.S. Congress: Profile* 1983). By the mid-1980s, the city of Eugene, Oregon was believed to enjoy a similar role in manufacturing; other law enforcement sources emphasized the importance of San Diego and the San Francisco Bay area (*Organized Crime in California*

1989:55; Wiedrich 1987). In 1987 and 1988 more than 300 methamphetamine laboratories were seized in the San Diego area alone. Centers of methamphetamine use included Denver, Portland (Oregon), Dallas, and Phoenix; some problems also were observed in Los Angeles, San Francisco, and Seattle (*Arrestee Drug Use* 1990:6; *U.S. Congress: Re-Emergence* 1990:37, 46). Though it is hard to assess the extent of methamphetamine use, there appears to be substantial demand in many parts of the nation (Isikoff 1989; Miller and Kozel 1991; Morgan 1992; *Methamphetamine* 1989).

THE EMERGENCE OF ICE

Like other drugs, methamphetamine can be taken in various ways: either injected, smoked, or ingested orally. The dominant mode of use tends to reflect the tastes and traditions of local subcultures. In view of the highly regional nature of manufacture and distribution, suppliers do not find it difficult to accommodate these local tastes, and it is natural to find wide disparities in patterns of use. Fashions that emerge in one city or region can become dominant in that area without making much impact elsewhere. In short, there is no such thing as a national market in methamphetamines.

During the 1980s, a vogue for smokable crystal methamphetamine developed in Hawaii and some western states under the common nickname *ice* (Cho 1990; Pennell 1990). A similar, though somewhat less pure, product called *glass* also made its appearance in California. The manufacturing process has been described as follows:

> Two basic methods are used to produce crystal meth. The first and most common method is the reaction of phenyl-2-propanone (P2P or phenylacetone) and methylamine. The second method uses ephedrine as a precursor. The second method uses a simple formula and does not require the use of controlled precursors. It is known as the ephedrine/red phosphorus method and requires the use of a hydrogenator. It takes two to four days to make a batch of ice . . . .
>
> In Honolulu, crystal meth is most commonly smoked with a glass pipe, the bowl of which becomes coated with a milky white, brownish or black residue, depending on the form of crystal meth used. A gram of ice sells for $250 to $400 in Honolulu right now, with a 1/10 gram paper going for $50 to $75. It is inexpensive to produce, so the profit margin is tremendous. (*U.S. Congress: Re-Emergence* 1990:74-75).

The drug itself had long been known and used in this crystal form, but apparently the specific process used to make the extremely pure ice was not yet in use in the United States itself. Instead the substance, like the fashion for its use, had been imported from the Pacific Rim. Amphetamines, specifically methamphetamines, had long been popular in Japan and other east Asian countries. In that region, illicit markets were supplied by sizable narcotic networks with roots in organized crime among both Chinese triads and Japanese *yakuza* (Delfs 1991). During the 1970s and 1980s, such networks had collaborated in a variety of activities, including product counterfeiting and trafficking in guns and prostitutes in addition to narcotics; we have much evidence of cooperative endeavors, based (for example) in Taiwan or South Korea (Buruma and McBeth 1984-85; Posner 1988). For methamphetamines, the *yakuza* had developed manufacturing facilities in South Korea; these supplied much of east Asia, though the triads also were active in Hong Kong (Kaplan and Dubro 1986:198-200; *U.S. Congress: Re-Emergence* 1990:11, 99). Entrepreneurs and distributors might be nationals of any of a dozen Asian countries.

Though illegal, the amphetamine drug "family" was stigmatized far less severely than opiates, cocaine, or even marijuana. Most estimates place the number of regular amphetamine (*shabu*) users in Japan at more than half a million. In the 1980s, smokable methamphetamine became the drug of choice among upwardly mobile urban dwellers in several Pacific Rim nations, especially Taiwan, South Korea, and the Philippines (Delfs 1991; McBeth 1989; Savadove 1991).

Therefore it is not surprising to find a similar habit developing in Hawaii, which has so many cultural and economic affinities with the Pacific Rim, and in which Japanese organized crime had developed a strong foothold. In fact, Kaplan and Dubro's (1986) study of the *yakuza* calls Hawaii the "forty-eighth Prefecture," an annex to the 47 administrative units of the Japanese home islands. *Yakuza*-supplied amphetamines were identified in the state during the 1970s, and Korean-manufactured methamphetamines appeared in the following decade (Shoenberger 1989). Beginning in 1987, island authorities had described an "ice problem," linked in part to Filipino youth gangs and Korean groups (*U.S. Congress: Re-Emergence* 1990:5).

DISCOVERING A PROBLEM

By 1989, law enforcement agencies were finding evidence of localized use of smokable methamphetamine, originally in Hawaii and subsequently in and around San Diego. The perceived "wave" of new activity was epitomized by a series of federal drug raids on 20 laboratories in southern California during March, and by a series of smaller raids over the next year (Ford 1990; Reza 1989). Concern about the drug in Hawaii was given a new focus in March 1989 by the arrest of a substantial ice-importation ring headed by one Paciano Guerrero (*U.S. Congress: Drug Crisis* 1990:74-75; *U.S. Congress: Re-Emergence* 1990: 70-72).

It might be thought that the perceived boom in the smokable drug reflected strictly local conditions, unlikely to be replicated in other areas. Even in Hawaii, the problem was confined largely to Oahu (*U.S. Congress: Drug Crisis* 1990:56, 205, 215). Now, however, there began a media campaign to emphasize the perils of the "new" drug, and the danger that this would soon be reflected across the nation. A headline in the *Los Angeles Times*, for example, read "Potent Form of Speed Could Be Drug of 90s" (Corwin 1989). The *Economist* noted that ice could make crack seem almost benign ("Drugs: Ice Overdose" 1989). Rep. Charles Rangel coined the alliterative description "the narcotics nemesis of the nineties" (*U.S. Congress: Re-Emergence* 1990:59).

The theme was taken up by all the major regional newspapers and national newsmagazines, as well as more specialized publications serving the medical and pharmaceutical communities (Cho 1990; "Illicit Methamphetamine" 1991; Zurer 1989). Between September and December 1989, major stories appeared in the *New York Times* (Bishop 1989), *The Washington Post* (Thompson 1989), *The Atlanta Constitution* (Curriden 1989), *The Economist* ("Drugs; Ice Overdose" 1989), *The Boston Globe* (Howe 1989; Tabor 1989), *The Chicago Tribune* (Weingarten 1989), *The Christian Science Monitor* (Larmer 1989), and *Newsweek* (Lerner 1989). The tone of the coverage was epitomized by the *New York Times* headline "Fear Grows Over Effects of a New Smokable Drug" (Bishop 1989). This story was printed on the front page; equal prominence was given to ice related stories on the front pages of the *Los Angeles Times* (Corwin 1989) and *The Chicago Tribune* (Weingarten 1989). In October the *Los Angeles Times* presented a series of four stories on ice within a nine-day period (Corwin 1989; Essoyan 1989; Shoenberger 1989; Zamichow 1989). Clearly, pronouncements about the new drug were finding a ready and enthusiastic market in the mass media.

The jeremiads about ice were heard most frequently in the last quarter of 1989, though a few stories appeared in early 1990, and television news shows such as *60 Minutes* sustained the focus on methamphetamines in general for a few months more ("Meth" 1990). The height of the panic, however, can be identified clearly between about September 1989 and February 1990 (See Table 1 for a chronology of media accounts).

The peak of public concern can be associated with Congressional hearings on this topic; Rep. Rangel's Subcommittee on Narcotics Abuse and Control held a session titled "The Re-Emergence of Methamphetamine" in October. A follow-up session, the "Drug Crisis in Hawaii," was held in Honolulu the following January (*U.S. Congress: Re-Emergence* 1990; *U.S. Congress: Drug Crisis* 1990. For criticisms of the latter session as a Congressional junket, see Anderson and Van Atta 1990). Taken together with the media accounts, the hearings became the chief vehicle for the burgeoning panic about ice. Here it will be useful to analyze the language and rhetoric employed to present the new phenomenon as a major problem.

THE RHETORIC OF ICE

Certain themes and expressions recur with striking regularity. Ice was new, potent, and dangerous, and had acquired high prestige as the new "in" drug. Taken together, these features meant that the use of ice apparently was about to expand rapidly and to create a national menace at least comparable to crack cocaine.

The experience of Hawaii was recounted often, as in a *Boston Globe* story titled "Ice in an Island Paradise" (Tabor 1989). The use of ice, in the words of a Congressional report, "has escalated in such leaps and bounds that we have not been able to keep pace" (*U.S. Congress: Re-Emergence* 1990:2). Generally such accounts suggested that what such areas were experiencing today would be the fate of the whole country in a few months or years. Honolulu police chief Douglas Gibb told the story of a New York City Korean gang that had flown some members to Honolulu to attack some local Samoans. "The whole purpose . . . was to come into town to establish a connection for ice, a line for ice to take back to New York" (*U.S. Congress: Re-Emergence* 1990:8). "It is probably only a matter of time until other parts of the country start to see crystal meth and its attendant problems . . . we fully expect the Ice Age to spread east from Hawaii" (p.77).

The idea that ice was gradually penetrating areas of the mainland gave a local angle to media reporting of the drug in cities such as Atlanta (Curriden 1989), Boston (Howe 1989), and Philadelphia (Durso 1992). In the Congressional hearings, this was a frequent theme. One subcommittee member noted, "We have got ice in Virginia . . . it is for sure coming our way and we had better get ready for it" (*U.S. Congress: Re-Emergence* 1990:19). Another member stated, "Reports are already filtering in of ice use in New York and

Table 1. Chronology of Media Accounts, 1989-1991

	1989	
September		
First ice related stories in mainland newspapers		
Sept. 16	*New York Times*	(Bishop 1989)
October		
Oct. 1	*Boston Globe*	(Howe 1989)
Oct. 8	*Los Angeles Times*	(Shoenberger 1989)
Oct. 14	*Los Angeles Times*	(Essoyan 1989)
Oct. 16	*Los Angeles Times*	(Essoyan 1989)
Oct. 16	*Los Angeles Times*	(Zamichow 1989)
Oct. 24	Congressional hearings, *The Re-Emergence of Methamphetamine*	
November		
Nov. 6	*Chemical and Engineering News*	(Zurer 1989)
Nov. 21	*Washington Post*	(Thompson 1989)
Nov. 27	*Newsweek*	(Lerner 1989)
Nov. 30	*Atlanta Constitution*	(Curriden 1989)
December		
Dec. 2	*The Economist*	("Drugs: Ice Overdose" 1989)
Dec. 8	*Boston Globe*	(Tabor 1989)
Dec. 8	*Christian Science Monitor*	(Larmer 1989)
Dec. 18	*Jet*	(Carthane 1989)
	1990	
January		
Jan. 13	Congressional hearings, on *The Drug Crisis in Hawaii*	
February		
Feb. 8	*Rolling Stone*	(Sager 1990)
February	*Good Housekeeping*	(Holland 1990)
April		
April 22	CBS news program *60 Minutes* broadcasts story on methamphetamine trafficking ("Meth" 1990).	
May		
May 23	*Journal of the American Medical Association*	(Cotton 1989)
August		
Aug. 10	*Science*	(Cho 1990)
	1991	
March		
March 6	*Journal of the American Medical Association*	(Hong, Matsuyama, and Nur 1991)
May		
May 9	*Washington Post*	Holley, Venant, and Essoyan 1991)
June		
June 30	*Emergency Medicine*	("Illicit Methamphetamine" 1991)

Washington DC" (*U.S. Congress: Drug Crisis* 1990:3). A lengthy investigative account in *Rolling Stone* quoted law enforcement officials, who believed that the Hawaii "epidemic" soon would sweep the mainland and that the drug would surpass both heroin and cocaine, marking a new and still more deadly era in drug abuse (Sager 1990).

One paradox was that ice, by its nature, negated some of the obvious advantages of methamphetamine: as an imported drug for example, it encountered the obstacles and expense involved in crossing national borders. The witnesses at the hearings, however, emphasized repeatedly that it would only be a matter of time before domestic manufacturers learned to reproduce Asian techniques; at that point, ice would begin to conquer the American "speed" market. In the words of a Dallas police official, "We have cooks, we have numerous cooks scattered throughout the country, literally thousands of persons who are qualified to make methamphetamine. So, we have the processes in place to make ice. I think we also have a ready consumer market out there, individuals who want the drug. I have no doubt that ice will come to the United States" (*U.S. Congress: Re-Emergence* 1990:39-40).

Particularly evocative was the word *epidemic* which was employed in most of the accounts, with its implications of plague, disease, and uncontrollable spread (compare Reinarman and Levine 1989). During the Congressional hearings, U.S. Attorney Daniel Bent described Hawaii ice use as already an "epidemic" (*U.S. Congress: Re-Emergence* 1990:5). When a DEA spokesman was quoted as having denied the validity of the "epidemic," he was taken to task by members of the committee, especially Florida Rep. Tom Lewis, who described the opinion as "irresponsible" and "lackadaisical" (p.17). "Epidemic" was a politically valuable concept that would not be abandoned easily.

Other significant terms included *deluge*, *plague*, and *crisis*. Congressman Rangel remarked that Honolulu police were "deluged" by ice (*U.S. Congress: Re-Emergence* 1990:1). Sociologist Elliott Currie spoke of "this hidden methamphetamine plague" (p.44). The word *crisis* was much used, generally in the context of an "emerging" crisis, to suggest that what had gone before was trivial compared to what would come in future (p.61). As has been noted, the January hearings of the Narcotics Subcommittee were devoted explicitly to the drug crisis in Hawaii.

The term *ice* offered great potential for writers, suggesting as it did the phrase *ice age* and thus implying that the drug somehow could dominate American society so strongly that it could give its name to an era. The phrase *The Ice Age* was employed both by Douglas Gibb and Hawaii Rep. Daniel Akaka in the Congressional hearings (*U.S. Congress: Re-Emergence* 1990:3, 77). It was used subsequently for major investigative accounts in *Rolling Stone* in

1990 and in the *Washington Post* in 1991 (Holley, Venant, and Essayan 1991; Sager 1990; compare LaBianca 1992). "Ice" also suggested "chilling" in the metaphorical sense of "extremely frightening;" it was used in this sense by several journalists. In late 1989, for example, the *Atlanta Constitution* carried the headline "Police Chilled By New In-Drug: Ice" (Curriden 1989). Within two weeks, the *Christian Science Monitor* warned similarly, "Ice Chills US AntiDrug Officials" (Larmer 1989).

In addition, these arguments were stated by individuals and agencies with great expertise in the field. Every news story was buttressed by the opinions of prominent and credible law enforcement officials, police, and prosecutors from California and Hawaii, together with academics and other experts. In the Congressional hearings, major witnesses included Daniel Bent, the U.S. Attorney for Hawaii; Douglas Gibb, the police chief of Honolulu; and David Westrate of the DEA; all were prestigious and experienced officials. Other presentations were made by reputable doctors and academics. The potential "ice epidemic" thus appeared both plausible and threatening.

ICE AND COCAINE

One potent element of the attack on ice involved the analogy with cocaine. In seeking to portray a new problem as serious or dangerous, one well-known rhetorical device is to stimatize that problem by associating it with another, already familiar issue, thus placing into an existing context. Problem construction is a cumulative or incremental process in which each issue is built, to some extent, on its predecessors. As Best remarks.

> As an acknowledged subject for concern, a well established social problem becomes a resource, a foundation upon which other claims may be built. Rather than struggling to bring recognition to a new problem, claimants may find it easier to expand an existing problem's domain. These new claims take the form (new problem) X is really a type of (established problem) Y (1990:65-66).

Issue (X) therefore demands the array of responses and reactions that already have been judged appropriate for Problems (Y). This is the process described by Hall et al. (1978:223) as "convergence:"

> [C]onvergence occurs when two or more activities are linked in the process of signification so as to implicitly or explicitly draw parallels between them. Thus the image of "student hooliganism" links student protest to the separate problem of hooliganism—whose stereotypical characteristics are already part of socially available knowledge. . . . In both cases, the net effect is amplification, not in the real

events being described but in their threat potential for society (1978:223).

By 1989 cocaine, especially crack cocaine, had been invested with an enormous amount of "threat potential," suggested, for example, by the "drug war" rhetoric, which was then at its height. President Bush had made the "drug war" a major part of his domestic policy; his commitment to drug eradication was symbolized by the appointment of William Bennett as "drug czar." During 1989, American activism against international drug traffickers contributed to the near-civil war in Colombia, beginning in August, and to the invasion of Panama in December. Media coverage in the latter part of the year featured almost daily news of violence and conflict associated with these incidents. In September, President Bush made a nationally televised address on drug control strategy, in which he stated, "All of us agree that the gravest domestic threat facing our nation today is drugs . . . our most serious problem today is cocaine and in particular crack." Producing a sample of crack, which he said had been purchased close to the White House, the president continued, "It's as innocent looking as candy, but it is turning our cities into battle zones, and it is murdering our children. Let there be no mistake, this stuff is poison" ("Text" 1989). President Bush argued that the drug control budget for the coming year should be raised by more than one-third from the 1989 figure, to $8 billion.

If crack was indeed "the gravest domestic threat," then it was a highly effective strategy to suggest that ice was associated somehow with the better-known drug. Superficial parallels also existed. It could be suggested, for example, that crack was an especially virulent and addictive form of powder cocaine, while ice bore a similar relationship to "regular" methamphetamine. Also, the two substances were similar in general appearance and means of ingestion. The ice threat was amplified by its association with crack, an association pursued most vigorously on the Narcotics Subcommittee by Rep. Akaka. From the viewpoint of the media, the analogy with crack made ice an attractive subject because its dangers and thus its social significance could be comprehended easily; thus the drug would be likely to excite public concern and fear.

Ice was said to cause as much social damage as cocaine, in terms of overdoses and emergency room admissions (Gross 1988; "Illicit Methamphetamine" 1991). Rep. Akaka stated that in Hawaii, ice contributed to the problems that elsewhere were linked to crack: "ice-addicted babies, gang activities, turf battles and hospital emergency cases of overdoses . . . this drug has the capacity to drag our country even deeper into the dark abyss created by crack"

(*U.S. Congress: Re-Emergence* 1990:3). "It doesn't make any difference whether it is ice, crack, crank, cocaine. We are losing kids. We are corrupting our police departments. We are corrupting our political arena. We are breaking up families" (p.17).

U.S. Attorney Daniel Bent stated that ice was "in presenting the same problems to Hawaii as crack cocaine has in areas of the Continental United States in terms of its popularity, availability, addiction potential and destructiveness" (*U.S. Congress: Re-Emergence* 1990:64). It was alleged to stimulate violent behavior even more sharply than did crack; Hawaii, it was said, was seeing the birth of a generation of "crystal meth babies" (*U.S. Congress: Drug Crisis* 1990:2, 226-33; *U.S. Congress: Re-Emergence* 1990:66, 76; for the idea of the "crack baby," however, see Jacobs 1991). Such remarks made the two drugs appear all but indistinguishable; in fact, Rep. Akaka even asked a witness, "Can you explain to me the differences between crack, crank, ice and croak . . . ?" (*U.S. Congress: Re-Emergence* 1990:54).

In some ways, ice could be made to appear even more dangerous than crack. First, it was superior to crack because of its lower cost and its longer-lasting high. The effects were reported to last from four to 14 hours, as opposed to a few minutes for crack (Carthane 1989; Holley et al. 1991). Also, ice did not necessarily have to be imported from overseas (though it was imported currently); therefore it did not encounter the stringent restrictions imposed by Customs and the Coast Guard as part of the current "war on drugs." In addition, ice lacked the features that might safeguard individuals from experimenting with other substances. It did not require injection, as did heroin, and did not yet have the destructive associations of crack cocaine. By 1989, crack had acquired undesirable connotations that deterred many people from using it: it was associated with cultures of violence and extreme urban poverty, and was linked especially with racial minorities.

In contrast, methamphetamine generally was linked to hard work. Insofar as it had any racial overtones, it tended to be favored by white users (*Methamphetamine* 1989; Miller and Kozel 1991). Nationally, said the congressional account, "the typical methamphetamine user is a white male 22 to 26 years of age, who is employed in a blue-collar job. The most frequently cited occupations are in construction trades and the trucking industry" (*U.S. Congress: Re-Emergence* 1990:87). In the San Diego region, "abusing populations are predominantly white, lower middle income, high school educated, young adults ranging in age from 18-35 years" (p.111). A Texas police officer stated, "The persons who we most often encounter in Dallas, the users we most often encounter are primarily Caucasian, primarily lower income" (p.39).

Ice users tended to fit a similar profile. In Hawaii, ice was "'popular in the workplace, particularly among blue collar workers, people who do mechanical tasks, and it has also spread into office workplaces as well . . . (it is) the drug of choice for on the job use in Honolulu. . . . It is generally in the blue collar community and the service community" (*U.S. Congress: Re-Emergence* 1990:6-7-9). In short, ice could appeal to white or Asian middle-class people; teenagers especially were at risk. The title of a *Good Housekeeping* article described ice as "a New Drug Nice Kids Can Get Hooked On" (Holland 1990). Women also were believed to be particularly vulnerable: "In Honolulu, most ice users range in age from the late teens to the early thirties. The drug is popular with young women, perhaps because users tend to lose weight" (*U.S. Congress: Re-Emergence* 1990:75).

It was suggested that ice might able to wreak havoc in all sections of society, not merely in the inner cities. Rep. Rangel thus was tapping into potent fears when he write, "[W]e shudder to think of what would happen in this country if the devastation of the crack crisis were doubled or even tripled by adding on a whole new layer of illicit drug abuse" (*U.S. Congress: Re-Emergence* 1990:59). This rhetoric was even more powerful in the context of current developments in the "drug war" at home and overseas.

WHATEVER BECAME OF ICE?

"Ice" thus was attracting quite fervent interest. One might suggest that it had the potential to attract the same kind of fear as crack. The recent precedent of crack cocaine provided a set of stereotyped images and rhetoric on which ice could build readily, with the added "bonus" that ice threatened to reproduce these disturbing images outside the African-American urban community. Ice (it appeared) could cause the same kind of havoc as crack in geographical, social, and ethnic settings still untouched by ice or any other "hard" drug. It would not be difficult to imagine that the new problem could thrive through the use of ethnic and xenophobic stereotypes: the substance was imported from Asia, and had Japanese connotations. *Yakuza* drug dealers might easily acquire the stigma that had adhered earlier to gangsters from immigrant ethnic groups such as Jews and Italians.

In addition, it has been argued that intense media attention to a particular drug might tend to incite interest in the substance, and to lead to experimentation. Prophecies of an "epidemic" thus might be self-fulfilling in that they could unwittingly generate the problem that activists were seeking to avoid (MacDonald and Estep 1985; compare Young 1971). In the 1960s this kind of imitation caused glue sniffing to spread at "incredible speed . . . the enemies of glue-sniffing popularized the custom all by themselves" (Brecher 1972:326, 332). In the 1980s it was suggested that media portrayals of the effects of crack cocaine might have excited interest among users of powdered cocaine. With these precedents in mind, observers of ice warned that ice was being "beautifully advertised by the media" to cocaine users (Cotton 1990). The *Journal of the American Medical Association* warned, "News articles describing (ice) as like 'ten orgasms pronto' are working like paid ads. . . . If the media says it's an epidemic, drug adventurers say everybody's using it so I've got to try it" (Cotton, 1990).

The ice danger, however, did not materialize as a national crisis, and the prospective "plague" faded rapidly in early 1990. Media accounts became far less frequent from February onwards, and virtually none appeared between August 1990 and spring 1991 (see Table 1). In part this silence reflected the new concern of the media with political affairs in Iraq and the Persian Gulf, but the ice panic had been declining sharply for several months before the August invasion of Kuwait. The rather sudden eclipse of the ice problem requires explanation.

Some observers had been skeptical even during the height of the panic, and witnesses at the October hearings faced criticism for their use of the term *epidemic*. The evidence presented also contained clear contradictions— for example, in the damage caused by ice. Early reports of the testimony quoted Chief Gibb's statements that "since 1985, there have been 32 deaths in Honolulu attributed to ice," including eight homicides and seven suicides. (*U.S. Congress: Re-Emergence* 1990:76). Gibb, however, also stated that "32 people were confirmed to have crystal methamphetamine in their system at the time of deaths," which does not necessarily establish a causal link between the drug and the fatality (pp. 7-8). Hawaii's Governor Waihee placed the number of deaths at 36, of whom "three died as a direct result, and 32 had traces of the drug in their systems" (p. 80). It was embarrassing when Gibb was publicly challenged on his statistics; as a result, the early claims about the impact of the drug, even in Hawaii, were reduced substantially. Thus it was even more difficult to claim that ice presented a potential national menace.

During the October hearings, one DEA spokesman commented, "I can confirm there is a drug out there called ice, which is certainly bad news. But D.E.A. agents are not looking for it yet . . . . It will take a while for ice to proliferate. When we get reports from police departments that ice has gotten to be at the epidemic state, such as crack did in 1985, then we will move in" (*U.S. Congress: Re-Emergence* 1990:17). Such a drug "explosion" seemed remote, however. In early 1990, testing of arrestees confirmed considerable amphetamine use in San Diego, Portland, Phoenix, and San Jose, but the figures did not appear to be growing.

Moreover, ice as such had made few inroads among the arrestees, though a substantial majority knew the substance by reputation: the media were cited overwhelmingly as the main source. Even in San Diego, almost 70 percent of those who knew about ice based their knowledge on media accounts rather than on information provided by friends or dealers. Nationwide the proportion who admitted ever having used ice nowhere exceeded 3 percent (though no community in Hawaii was included in the survey) (*Arrestee Drug Use* 1990:6; Pennell 1990). This picture was confirmed by other survey data. Among male hustlers and sex workers in San Francisco, for example, ice had made very limited inroads, even among heavy users of methamphetamine. Moreover, the number of habitual ice users in such groups remained negligible (Lauderback and Waldorf 1992).

Largely on the basis of such data and of the reexamination of the drug's impact in Hawaii itself, law enforcement and DEA officials soon were saying that the danger of ice had been substantially overstated. Media rhetoric subsided within a few months of the Congressional hearings. Ice continues to be popular in some regions, but the language of epidemic no longer seems realistic—if it ever did.

THE CONSTRUCTION OF THE ICE DANGER

In retrospect it seems certain that the menace of ice was considerably overstated, and we might well ask how such a misperception could emerge. A considerable literature exists on the origins of such scares and perceived social problems; some of the explanations suggested by that literature seem relevant here. Many researchers, for example, follow some form of what is generally known as the "moral entrepreneur" theory. The classic discussion of this term comes from Becker, who emphasized the role of a particular individual in the formulation of American narcotics policy in the 1930s:

> Wherever rules are created and applied we should be alive to the possible presence of an enterprising individual or group. Their activities can properly be called "moral enterprise" for what they are enterprising about is the creation of a new fragment of the moral constitution of society, its code of right and wrong (1963:145).

Such entrepreneurs might have diverse motives. In the case of a drug panic, for example, we might find activism by an interest group or a bureaucratic agency that was seeking to portray a serious social danger in order to focus public attention on issues falling within its scope of activity. This effort would permit the agency to expand its influence and resources, and might allow local authorities and law enforcement agencies to justify and request for federal funding and other support. In such circumstances, we often find a cyclical pattern in which greater concern causes more resources to be devoted to a problem; the result is more detection and more vigorous prosecution of the activity in question. This process in turn generates statistical evidence that can be used to intensify public concern, and thus to argue for still more resources. "Epidemics" thus can be self-sustaining.

Such bureaucratic concerns may have played some role in the case of ice. One recurrent theme of the hearings was the need to strengthen still further the numbers and resources of the DEA (*U.S. Congress: Re-Emergence* 1990:8-9). This agency had grown in numbers from 1,900 in 1980 to 2,900 in 1989. Currently it was requesting 160 new agents, chiefly for international enforcement in Latin America and the Pacific Rim (34-35). An ice panic therefore served the interests of the DEA, but it certainly cannot serve as a full explanation. As we have seen, the DEA was strongly critical of the exaggerated claims made for ice, and during 1990 was instrumental in damping down the nascent panic. In January, for example, the head of the Honolulu office wrote that ice was still confined largely to Hawaii and "very limited West Coast areas;" otherwise, he reported, "we know of no ice samples (having) been analyzed elsewhere in the United States" (*U.S. Congress: Drug Crisis* 1990:76).

Instead of examining national groups and controversies, it would be more profitable to consider the needs of the political and bureaucratic interests in Hawaii that sponsored most of the extravagant claims about ice and first identified an "epidemic." For example, the major claims makers heard by the Congressional committees included two of the leading figures in the state's law enforcement bureaucracy, police chief Douglas Gibb and U.S. Attorney Daniel Bent. The evidence offered by these two witnesses accounted for more than one-third of the total testimony presented during the October hearings, and both men emphasized the "epidemic" quality of the ice threat. As in the case of the DEA, an ice panic would enhance the reputation of local police agencies as well as increasing their access to resources. In addition, the powerful office of U.S. Attorney often provides any incumbent with the opportunity to win prestige and visibility that can be translated subsequently into a wider political career. This is not to suggest that either individual was insincere in his claims about the ice problem, but both had clear bureaucratic interests in formulating the issue in a particular way.

Electoral politics also played a role in shaping official claims and statements. At the opening of the 1989 hearings, which did so much to put ice on the map of American social problems, Congressman Rangel emphasized that the impetus for concern came chiefly from the Hawaii Congressional delegation of Representatives Daniel Akaka and Patricia Saiki. Both in fact had a strong vested interest in appearing to be active and interested in drug issues, and in adopting hard-line antidrug stances. Therefore they stood to benefit from making ice seem as perilous and as threatening as possible; both can be viewed as classical moral entrepreneurs.

This political context can be observed if we describe recent developments in Hawaii, traditionally one of the most loyally Democratic states in the nation (Smith and Pratt 1992). In the 1980s, for example, both of the Democratic U.S. senators could count regularly on receiving 70 to 80 percent of the votes cast, and the powerful governor's office remained firmly in Democratic hands throughout these years (Benenson 1991). Republicans were placed extremely poorly; they won offices chiefly when Democratic factions were split, as when Republican Patricia Saiki won the First Congressional District. By 1989 she had retained this position in two elections, but with progressively slimmer majorities. Democrat Daniel Akaka had remained firmly in control of the Second District in every contest since 1976.

Saiki's presence as a Republican representative therefore might appear anomalous, but the Republicans had one major point of potential strength, namely in the general area of law and order. Throughout the decade, Democratic authorities had been involved in a series of scandals; these had exposed alleged links between organized crime and the labor unions, which play so crucial a role in Hawaii Democratic politics. These incidents reached a climax in 1984 with the investigation by Charles F. Marsland, the Republican Honolulu city/county prosecutor, into a series of gangland murders that included the killing of Marsland's own son. Marsland targeted a prominent political ally of Democratic Governor George Ariyoshi as the alleged "godfather" of organized crime in the state (Turner 1984a, 1984b). The ensuing scandals and lawsuits did not destroy Democratic power. In fact, the next governor, elected in 1986, was a close associate of Ariyoshi, but the incident suggested one area in which Democrats were politically vulnerable: Daniel Akaka himself had been an Ariyoshi protegé. In addition, he is of native Hawaiian descent, and thus could potentially be associated with Larry Mehau, the ethnically Hawaiian "godfather."

In the following years, Saiki and Akaka emerged as powerful figures in Hawaii politics, and they clashed on crime-related issues. In the U.S. Congress, Saiki voted for a measure to extend the death penalty to major drug dealers, which Akaka opposed. The rivalry between the two was especially significant in 1989, when it became increasingly likely that soon they would be vying for a U.S. Senate seat in Hawaii. The junior senator's position currently was held by Spark Matsunaga, a very popular figure first elected in 1972, but a series of health crises beginning in 1984 made it unlikely that Matsunaga would run again in 1990, even if he completed his current term.

Therefore it was likely that within a year, Saiki would challenge Akaka for the hitherto solidly Democratic Senate seat, but the balance in this apparently unequal match could be tipped in a number of ways. One would be the ethnic factor. As noted above, Akaka is a native Hawaiian. The strongest faction in his Democratic party, however, is Japanese-American, a group to which Saiki could be expected to appeal. In addition, it would be natural to portray the relatively liberal Akaka as soft on crime and drugs, and possibly not sufficiently vigorous in the war on local organized crime. As a result, it was important for Akaka to rebut such charges; his membership on the House Subcommittee on Narcotic Abuse provided an ideal opportunity.

Both representatives therefore needed to appear strong on drug issues, and ideally both needed national media credentials as antidrug crusaders. Local ethnic and partisan alignments, however, circumscribed the kinds of rhetoric that would be appropriate in such a campaign. Although organized crime in general could be denounced, it is significant that none of the ice rhetoric focused on the specifically Japanese component of drug manufacture and distribution or on the role of the *yakuza* described so frequently by other law enforcement agencies and investigators. One might suggest that the nature of the forthcoming Hawaii elections made such accusations too sensitive to be presented at that time, for fear of perpetrating ethnic slurs against one of the most influential communities in the islands.

In fact, both Akaka and Saiki succeeded in gaining significant political capital from the ice issue. Saiki earned credit for having brought the problem to national attention and for requesting increased resources, but Akaka also shared the credit, and was not portrayed as soft on the crime issue in any sense. Akaka first used the term *ice age* in the hearings, and drew some of the starkest analogies between ice and crack. Both confirmed their role as standard-bearers of their respective parties. When Senator Matsunaga died a few months later, in April 1990, Akaka was the natural choice to fill the unexpired portion of his term. Both he and Saiki easily won their parties' nominations or the November election ("Hawaiian Politics" 1990). That contest normally would have been a Democratic walkover, but Saiki had established her prestige so firmly that she made it a close race, and lost only narrowly to Akaka. He thereby became the first native Hawaiian to be represented in the U.S. Senate (Saiki went on to head the federal Small Business Administration) (Reinhold 1990; Richburg 1990).

Domestic politics in Hawaii thus made it likely that the state representatives would seek to focus on a crime or drug problem of local significance. It was by no means apparent, however, that these issues would come to wider attention, especially when conditions and controversies in Hawaii so rarely attract the attention of the national media. The opportunity was provided by Akaka's service on the House Narcotics Subcommittee, where he was aided by another representative with a strong record in drug issues and a long career as a "moral entrepreneur." This was a Pennsylvania representative named Lawrence Coughlin, from the thirteenth district in suburban Montgomery County, outside Philadelphia. Coughlin, the ranking Republican on the Narcotics Subcommittee, was instrumental in bringing Akaka's views to Rangel's attention. His advocacy was significant in showing that ice was causing concern far outside Hawaii, and legitimately could be presented as a national issue.

Other agendas, however, may have been at work here as well. Coughlin's interest in methamphetamine issues dated back at least to the late 1970s, when he had been one of the most active supporters of the theory that Philadelphia was the "speed capital of the world" (Jenkins 1992a, b). To illustrate this questionable assertion, Coughlin had publicized stories from local Montgomery County newspapers as if they represented conditions throughout the state or the nation, and in effect had generated a mythology about the prevalence of speed in southeastern Pennsylvania. In 1980, largely at Coughlin's behest, the Narcotics Select Committee had been persuaded to hold special hearings in Philadelphia, where local issues and investigations received national attention (*U.S. Congress: Laboratories* 1980). The campaign to link Philadelphia with speed was so successful that it became the focus of the popular 1985 film *Witness*, whose plot concerns a huge shipment of the precursor chemical P2P. Coughlin thus emerges as a long-standing protagonist of a "speed menace." As a result, it is scarcely surprising to see the limited experience of Hawaii extrapolated to the entire nation in the 1989-1990 hearings, just as had happened with conditions in Philadelphia in 1980.

TRANSFORMING LOCAL ISSUES INTO NATIONAL PROBLEMS

In studying social problems, one critical theme is the relationship between local and national perceptions, and the way in which some (but by no means all) local phenomena come to be regarded as issues of far wider significance. The panic about ice serves to remind us that drug problems are extremely localized, and that in crime, as in so much else, it is difficult to generalize about the American experience. Drug problems rarely strike the nation in a regular or homogeneous way. Much has been written about the "crack epidemic" that swept the United States in the mid-1980s, but we must always remember that this phenomenon was highly localized. The "epidemic" initially was centered in the major cities of the east and west coasts, but scarcely penetrated large sections of the midwest until the early 1990s. This situation has many possible explanations—the strength of local traditions and subcultures, patterns of law enforcement vagaries of manufacture and supply, the interests of criminal groups—but the point is that a "panic" might be well under way in one area years before it is felt elsewhere, and it is by no means inevitable that it ever will move beyond the original region (for the localized nature of drug cultures, see, for example, Weisheit 1992).

On the other hand, certain extraneous factors demand that a local problem should be viewed in a national context, and that policy responses should be developed accordingly. One important element in this regard is the mass media, which had come, during the 1980s, to treat drug-related stories as events of major significance. newspapers assigned journalists to cover such stories as their sole or major responsibility; thus the papers had a vested interest in the constant generation of newsworthy items in this area.[1] One way to achieve this goal was to focus on local concerns or incidents, but to project them as if they were of wider, even national significance. A

[1] I am indebted to one of the anonymous reviewers for raising this point when I originally submitted this article to *Justice Quarterly*.

notorious example appeared in 1986 in the CBS television documentary *48 Hours on Crack Street*. This program presented the (then) essentially New York City problem of crack cocaine as if it were already a national epidemic, with vials littering the streets and parks of virtually every community across the country (Reinarman and Levine 1989). Though largely spurious, this account had enormous influence in generating fears of a national crack epidemic.

In the early 1980s, before the advent of crack, the media often presented the localized PCP problem in Washington, DC in such a way as to suggest that it soon would become a national crisis. (Such "extrapolations" are not confined to drug issues: witness the suggestions, at about that time, that Los Angeles's distinctive gang problems were spreading to cities throughout the nation.) Once the media present a problem in this way, Congressional hearings permit the issue to be discussed in another national forum, with the certainty that national news coverage will reinforce perceptions of a widespread crisis.

This process of "nationalization" gives rich opportunities to local activists, moral entrepreneurs, or claims makers who wish to draw attention to a particular issue, and who do so by presenting it as more dangerous or more important than it may be in fact. One natural way to do this is to suggest that a local issue either is national in scope or has a strong potential to become so in the very near future: in short, that it is about to "sweep the nation." This process enhances the importance of local campaigns; it also offers the local moral entrepreneurs the opportunity to acquire the status of national leaders and experts, should their analysis be accepted. This enhancement, in turn, can reinforce the position of local figures in their home areas.

The panic about ice is a model example of this process. The use of the drug was a local phenomenon; the national concern about the drug in 1989 derived chiefly from Hawaii's elected officials and law enforcement agencies with a definite political agenda. For two specific reasons, they were relatively successful in projecting their concerns. First, the recent experience of crack made it easy for them to represent ice, in effect, as part of the same problem; this process is known by the rhetorical term *convergence*. The ice phenomenon occurred at precisely the right time, when the rhetoric about crack was still fresh in the public mind and when the "drug war" was reaching a crescendo. It is difficult to imagine that the ice issue would have arisen at all if public expectations had not been conditioned by these recent precedents.

Second, the intense public focus on drug issues during the 1980s had created bureaucracies and political frameworks able to publicize information and opinion about drugs. These groups, such as the DEA, the NIDA, and the Narcotics Subcommittee itself, had excellent media ties and could be relied on to provide newsworthy stories about crime and drug abuse. In the case of the Congressional committee, it is inevitable that members of any political organization charged with investigating drug problems will attempt to attract as much publicity as possible by presenting themselves as concerned, active, well-informed guardians of the public good. There are few better opportunities to do so than by recognizing a problem at an early stage to prevent it reaching crisis proportions. The case of Hawaii offered the committee members the chance to investigate and combat a drug problem in a proactive, farsighted way.

No significant risk was involved in this strategy. If an "ice epidemic" occurred, the committee earned credit for having predicted it and for urging preemptive action; if it faded away, the committee could claim that its forethought had prevented a drug crisis. Conversely, there was much to be lost by cautious or skeptical reactions to an incipient crisis. If the predicted menace actually materialized, an agency or an administration stood to attract most of the blame for the ensuing problems.

None of the factors that produced the ice panic has changed significantly since 1989, or is likely to change significantly in the near future. Therefore it is probable that local drug fads will be presented once again as potential crises, likely to spread rapidly across the entire country. Social scientists must recognize and publicize the social and political factors that generate such misleading expectations.

REFERENCES

Anderson, J. and D. Van Atta (1990) "Big Plane Junket for Hill Spouses." *Washington Post*, January 10, p. 3.

Arrestee Drug Use (1990) National Institute of Justice, Research in Action. Washington, DC: U.S. Government Printing Office.

Becker, H. (1963) *Outsiders*. New York: Free Press.

Benenson, B. (1991) "Democrats Reassert Primacy in Hawaii Politics." *Congressional Quarterly*, October 12.

Best, J. (1990) *Threatened Children*. Chicago: University of Chicago Press.

Bishop, K. (1989) "Fear Grows over Effects of a New Smokable Drug." *New York Times*, September 16, p. 4A.

Brecher, E.M. (1972) *Licit and Illicit Drugs*. Boston: Little, Brown.

Buruma, I. and J. McBeth (1984-85) "An East Side Story . . . ." *Far Eastern Economic Review*, 27 December/3 January, pp. 15.

Carthane, A. (1989) "Will New Drug 'Ice" Freeze Hope in Black Communities?" *Jet*, December 18.

Cho, A.K. (1990) "Ice: A New Dosage Form of an Old Drug." *Science* (249): 631-34.

Corwin, M. (1989), "Potent Form of Speed Could Be Drug of 90s." *Los Angeles Times*, October 8, pp. 1A.

Cotton, P. (1990) "Medium Isn't Accurate Ice Age Message." *Journal of the American Medical Association* (263):2717.

Curriden, M. (1989) "Police Chilled by New In Drug: Ice." *Atlanta Constitution*, November 30, p. 1.

Delfs, R. (1991) "Cocaine Surge." *Far Eastern Economic Review*, November 21, pp. 7.

"Drugs: Ice Overdose" (1989), *Economist*, December 2, pp. 29-30.

Durso, C. (1992) "Powerful Drug 'Ice' Is Found at Lab" *Philadelphia Inquirer*, August 14, p. 1B.

Essoyan, S. (1989) "Use of Highly Addictive 'Ice' Growing in Hawaii." *Los Angeles Times*, October 16, p. 3A.

Ford, A. (1990) "Federal, Local Police Raid House in San Diego." *Los Angeles Times*, July 26, p. 7A.

Goode, E. (1984) *Drugs in American Society*. 2nd ed. New York: Knopf.

Graham, J.M. (1976) "Amphetamine Politics on Capital Hill." In W.J. Chambliss and M. Mankoff (eds.), *Whose Law? What Order?*, pp. 107-22. New York: Wiley.

Grinspoon, L. (1975) *The Speed Culture: Amphetamine Use and Abuse in America*. Cambridge, MA: Harvard University Press.

Gross, J. (1988) "Speed's Gain in Use Could Rival Crack." *New York Times*, November 27, p. A9.

Hall, S., Critcher, C., Jefferson, T., Clarke, J. and Roberts, B. (1978) *Policing the Crisis*. London: Macmillan.

"Hawaiian Politics: Ethnic Pineapple Salad" (1990) *Economist*, October 20, pp. 32.

Holland, L. (1990) "All about Ice: New Drug Nice Kids Can Get Hooked On." *Good Housekeeping*, February, pp. 215-16.

Holley, D., E. Vernant, and S. Essoyan (1991) "The Ice Age." *Washington Post*, May 9, pp. 1A.

Hong, R., E. Matsuyama, and K. Nur (1991) "Cardiomyopathy Associated with the Smoking of Crystal Methamphetamine." *Journal of the American Medical Association* (265):1152-54.

Howe, P.J. (1989) "Ice Worse Than Crack, Officials Warn." *Boston Globe*, October 1, p. 2.

"Illicit Methamphetamine: Street Drug on the Rise" (1991) *Emergency Medicine*, June 30, pp. 13-17.

Isikoff, M. (1989) "Rural Drug Users Spur Comeback of Crank." *Washington Post*, February 20, p. 3A.

Jacobs, J. (1991) "Debunking the Crack Baby Myths." *Centre Daily Times*, State College, Pa, August 11, p. 6A.

Jenkins, Philip (1992a) "Narcotics Trafficking and the American Mafia: the Myth of Internal Prohibition." *Crime, Law and Social Change* 18: 303-318.

Jenkins, Philip (1992b) "The Speed Capital of the World: Organizing the Methamphetamine Industry in Philadelphia 1970-1990." *Criminal Justice Policy Review* 6(1): 17-39.

Kaplan, D.E. and A. Dubro (1986) *Yakuza*. Reading, MA: Addison-Wesley.

LaBianca, D.A. (1992) "The Drug Scene's New Ice Age." *USA Today*, January, pp. 54-56.

Larmer, B. (1989) "Ice Chills US Anti-Drug Officials." *Christian Science Monitor*, December 8, p. 7.

Lauderback, D. and D. Waldorf (1992) "Whatever Happened to Ice?" Paper presented at meetings of the American Society of Criminology, New Orleans.

Lerner, M.L. (1989) "The Fire of Ice." *Newsweek*, November 27, p. 26.

MacDonald, P.T. and R. Estep (1985) "Prime Time Drug Depictions." *Contemporary Drug Problems* 12(3):419-38.

McBeth, J. (1989) "The Junkie Culture: Supercharged Speed is Scourge of Manila's Smart Set." *Far Eastern Economic Review*, November 23, pp. 23-25.

"Meth" (1990) Report broadcast on *60 Minutes*, April 22.

Methamphetamine Abuse in the United States. (1989) Rockville, MD: U.S. Department of Health and Human Services.

Miller, M.A. and N.J. Kozel (1991) *Methamphetamine Abuse: Epidemiological Issues and Implications*. Rockville, MD: U.S. Department of Health and Human Services.

Morgan, J.P. (1992) "Amphetamine and Methamphetamine during the 1990s." *Pediatrics in Review* 13(9):330-336.

Musto, D. (1973) *The American Disease: Origins of Narcotic Control*. New Haven: Yale University Press.

Organized Crime in California: Annual Report to the California Legislature. (1989) State of California: Department of Justice.

Pennell, S. (1990) "Ice: DUF Interview Results from San Diego." *NIJ Reports* 221:12-13.

Posner, G.L. (1988) *Warlords of Crime*. New York: McGraw-Hill.

Reinarman, C. and H.G. Levine (1989) "The Crack Attack: Politics and Media in America's Latest Drug Scare." In Joel Best (ed.), *Images of Issues*, pp. 115-37. Hawthorne, NY: Aldine.

Reinhold, R. (1990) "Hawaii Race Tests Democratic Hold." *New York Times*. November 1, pp. 9B.

Reza, H.G. (1989) "Raids Shut 23 Drug Labs." *Los Angeles Times*, March 20.

Richburg, K.B. (1990) "For Hawaii Democrats, Anxiety Over Safe Seats." *Washington Post*, November 1, p. 7A.

Sager, M. (1990) "The Ice Age." *Rolling Stone*, February 8, pp. 53-57.

Savadove, B. (1991) "High Society: Growing Drug Abuse Reflects Economic Changes." *Far Eastern Economic Review*, September 12, pp. 45-46.

Shoenberger, K. (1989) "South Korea Seen as Major Source of Ice Narcotic." *Los Angeles Times*, October 14, pp. 9A.

Skeers, V.M. (1992) "Illegal Methamphetamine Drug Laboratories." *Journal of Environmental Health* 55(3):6-9.

Smith, Z.A. and R.C. Pratt, eds. (1992) *Politics and Public Policy in Hawaii*. Albany: SUNY Press.

Tabor, M. (1989) "Ice in an Island Paradise." *Boston Globe*, December 8, p. 7.

"Text of President's Speech on Drug Control Strategy" (1989) *New York Times*, September 6, p. 4A.

Thompson, L. (1989) "Ice: New Smokable Form of Speed." *Washington Post*, November 21, p. 2.

Turner, W. (1984a) "Hawaii Criminal's Pledge to Talk Seen as Door to Underworld." *New York Times*, July 24, p. 11A.

___ (1984b) "Inquiry on Murders in Hawaii Brings Governor and Prosecutor into Conflict." *New York Times*, August 28, pp. 7A.

U.S. Congress: Drug Crisis (1990) *Drug Crisis in Hawaii: Hearing before the Select Committee on Narcotics Abuse and Control House of Representatives 101st Congress, Second Session, January 13, 1990*. Washington, DC: U.S. Government Printing Office.

U.S. Congress: Laboratories (1980) *Illicit Methamphetamine Laboratories in the Pennsylvania/New Jersey/Delaware Area: Hearing before the Select Committee on Narcotics Abuse and Control, U.S. House of Representatives, 96th Congress, Second Session, July 7, 1980*. Washington, DC: U.S. Government Printing Office.

U.S. Congress: Profile (1983) *Profile of Organized Crime: Mid-Atlantic Region: Hearings before the Permanent Subcommittee on Investigations of the Committee on Governmental Affairs, United States Senate, 98th Congress, First Session, February 15, 23, and 24, 1983*. Washington, DC: U.S. Government Printing Office.

U.S. Congress: Re-Emergence (1990) *The Re-Emergence of Methamphetamine: Hearings before the Subcommittee on Narcotics Abuse and Control, U.S. House of Representatives, 101st Congress, First Session, October 24, 1989*. Washington, DC: U.S. Government Printing Office.

U.S. Congress: Small Business (1988). *Impact of Clandestine Drug Laboratories on Small Business: Hearings before the Subcommittee on Regulation and Business Opportunities of the Committee on Small Business, U.S. House of Representatives, 100th Congress, Second Session. Eugene, Oregon, May 13, 1988*. Washington, DC: U.S. Government Printing Office.

Weingarten, P. (1989) "Profits, Perils, Higher for Today's Bootleggers." *Chicago Tribune*, September 14, p. 16.

Weisheit, R.A. (1992) *Domestic Marijuana: A Neglected Industry*. Westport, CT: Greenwood.

Wiedrich, B. (1987) "San Diego Has Become National Center for Manufacture of Methamphetamine." *Chicago Tribune*, April 20, pp. 11.

Witkin, G. (1989) "The New Midnight Dumpers." *U.S. News and World Report*, January 9, p. 23.

Young, J. (1971) "Drugs and the Media." *Drugs and Society* 2(1):14-18.

Zamichow, N. (1989) "Navy Hopes Drug Test Will Detect, Deter Meth Users." *Los Angeles Times*, October 16, p. 6A.

Zurer, P.S. (1989) "Federal Officials Plot Strategy to Stop Methamphetamine Spread." *Chemical and Engineering News*, November 6, pp. 13-16.

[9]

another look at moral panics: the case of satanic day care centers

Mary deYoung
Grand Valley State University, Allendale, Michigan, USA

Moral panics reveal something of interest about social structure, social process, and social change, and the satanic day care moral panic of the 1980s certainly is no exception. This article begins by presenting an overview of that moral panic, using data from a sample of 15 of the over 100 day care centers that comprised it, to illustrate salient points about its timing, trigger and target, content, spread, and denouement. The article then asserts that the satanic day care moral panic also reveals that classical moral panic theory is in need of some revision if it is to retain its explanatory and analytical power in a complex, modern, social world. Specifically, an updated theory needs to account for empowered folk devils, pluralistic social reactions, and symbolic and contradictory social ends.

The term "moral panic" was coined by Cohen (1972) to describe a collective response, generated by unsettling social strain and incited and spread by interest groups, toward persons who are actively transformed into "folk devils" and then treated as threats to dominant social interests and values. Through the use of highly emotive claims and fear-based appeals, a moral panic tends to orchestrate cultural consent that something must be done, and quickly, to deal with this alleged threat. The increased social control that typically follows from such consent ends up preserving and reasserting the very hegemonic values and interests that purportedly are being undermined by the folk devils. A

Received 14 July 1997; accepted 8 September 1997.

The author wishes to thank Tammi Niven for her invaluable assistance in the collection of archival data on the day care cases.

Address correspondence to Mary deYoung, 245 Ausable Hall, Department of Sociology, Grand Valley State University, Allendale, MI 49401. E-mail: deyoungm@gvsu.edu moral panic, then, serves a distinct stabilizing function at a time of unsettling social strain.

Why and how a moral panic arises, the types of people it demonizes, and the methods by which it ends up defining what Durkheim (1938) refers to as the normative contours and moral boundaries of a given society at any historical moment have been of considerable interest to sociologists. The concept has been used to analyze, among other things, the witch-hunts in Europe and America (Ben-Yehuda 1980; Erikson 1966); temperance movements and drug panics (Goode 1990; Gusfield 1963; Wilkins 1994); anti-pornography and censorship crusades (Greek and Thompson 1992; Shuker 1986); the mugging and garrotting scares of the 19th century (Adler 1996; Sindall 1987); and law and order campaigns throughout the western world (King 1987; Williams 1993; Zatz 1987).

The term also is used to describe the collective response to new folk devils who were demonized in the 1980s—day care providers who, it was claimed, were abusing their very young charges in satanic rituals that included such horrific practices as blood-drinking, cannibalism, and human sacrifices. Between 1983 and 1991, in fact, over a hundred day care centers in major urban areas and small towns across the country were investigated for what quickly came to be known as satanic ritual abuse (Nathan and Snedeker 1995). These investigations created deep and often irreparable breaches in the communities where they occurred and resulted in scores of arrests, often long and costly criminal trials, many convictions despite the absence of any corroborating and material evidence, usually draconian prison sentences and, over recent years, many reversals of those convictions upon appeal (deYoung 1994).

The satanic day care scare had all of what Goode and Ben-Yehuda (1994) set out as the defining characteristics of a moral panic: it was widespread, overreactive, volatile, hostile, and largely irrational. But another look at this moral panic, and at the day care cases that are the stuff of it, reveals some interesting refinements that are needed in classical moral panic theory if it is to retain its explanatory and analytical power in the contemporary social world.

It is the purpose of this present article to offer that look. First, the article presents an overview of the satanic day care moral panic. Then, it uses data from a sample of 15 day care cases, some more notorious than others, to advance and illustrate a

TABLE 1 Day Care Center, Year of Investigation Initiation, and Location

Day Care Center	Year	Location
McMartin	1983	Manhattan Beach, CA
Country Walk	1984	Miami, FL
Small World	1984	Niles, MI
Fells Acres	1984	Malden, MA
Georgian Hills	1984	Memphis, TN
Rogers Park Jewish Community	1984	Chicago, IL
Manhattan Ranch	1984	Manhattan Beach, CA
Craig's Country	1985	Clarksville, MD
Felix's	1985	Carson City, NV
East Valley YMCA	1985	El Paso, TX
Glendale Montessori	1987	Stuart, FL
Old Cutler	1989	Miami, FL
Little Rascals	1989	Edenton, NC
Faith Chapel	1989	San Diego, CA
Fran's	1991	Austin, TX

discussion of the areas of classic moral panic theory in need of refinement and updating. It should be noted that for the purposes of this article, a day care case was included in the sample if it met all of the following criteria: (1) an investigation led to the arrest of one or more day care provider; (2) allegations of satanic ritual abuse; that is, of the sexual abuse of children carried out during, or as part of, the ceremonial worship of Satan were actively investigated and publicly reported, even if they were not introduced into criminal trial; and (3) there are sufficient archival data in the form of court transcripts, legal briefs, investigative reports, interview transcripts, and local and national news articles to assess the case. Information that further identifies the 15 cases in the sample is presented in Table 1.

THE SATANIC DAY CARE MORAL PANIC

A basic analysis of any moral panic must account for its timing, target and trigger, content, spread, and denouement (Goode and Ben-Yehuda 1994). Each of these factors will be examined in turn to provide a necessarily brief overview of the satanic day care moral panic of the 1980s.

Timing of the Moral Panic

By the 1980s, a number of social, ideological, professional, and political forces had contributed to a growing cultural anxiety about satanic menaces to children (Richardson, Best, and Bromley 1991; Victor 1993). From concerns about demonic influences in heavy metal music, fantasy role-playing games, tarot cards and ouija boards; to urban legends about mysterious satanists abducting fair-haired, blue-eyed children from shopping malls; to rumors of covert satanic cults filming child pornography; to tales about satanic child sex rings, that decade was rife with "mini-moral panics" about satanic menaces to children, and ripened by them for more.

Target and Trigger of the Moral Panic

Coincident with that concern about the protection of children was another one about their daily care. The economic strains that made participation in the market economy a necessity, and the ideological force of the women's movement that made it an increasingly accessible alternative to unpaid housework, combined in that decade to put more and more women with young children into the labor market. In 1980, in fact, a record 45% of them were working outside of the home and using public and private day care centers for daily child care (Hofferth and Phillips 1987).

Most working parents were doing so with more than a little anxiety, however, and considered day care centers a change for the worse from the stay-at-home child care of their parents' generation (Hutchison 1992). That anxiety was heightened by the impact of other types of economic strains. Deep cuts in federal funding that over half of the public day care centers had received just a few years before closed down many of them, and left the remaining centers with high enrollment fees, too many enrollees and, because of low wages, too few providers and high staff turnover (Hofferth and Phillips 1987). Trapped as they were between necessity and contingency, working parents reluctantly began transforming the almost sacred covenantal duty of caring for their young children into businesslike contractual arrangements with day care providers.

The tension created by this imbrication of covenant and contract made that most innocuous of social institutions, the local day care center, the target of a moral panic. But a trigger was yet needed, some kind of spark that in the words of Adler (1996) "would link ethereal sentiment to focused activity" (p. 262).

That spark was lit in 1983 at the McMartin Preschool. A 2.5 year-old enrollee made a statement, vaguely suggestive of sexual abuse, that eventually was worked into an allegation of satanic ritual abuse by social workers who already had some experience as claims makers in the mini-moral panics about satanic menaces to children (deYoung 1997).

Content of the Moral Panic

Eventually, 369 more current and past enrollees of the McMartin Preschool were identified as victims. Their claims, elicited over repeated and suggestive interviews by social workers now convinced of a satanic influence in the case, came to define the still unfamiliar term of satanic ritual abuse and, in doing so, gave the ensuing moral panic its content. The children described, among other ghastly things, the ritualistic ingestion of urine, feces, blood, semen, and human flesh; the disinterment and mutilation of corpses; the sacrifices of infants; and orgies with their day care providers, costumed as devils and witches, in classrooms, tunnels under the center, and in car washes, airplanes, mansions, cemeteries, hotels, ranches, neighborhood stores, local gyms, churches, and hot air balloons. In the accusatorial atmosphere of this nascent moral panic, they named not only the seven McMartin day care providers as their satanic abusers, but local businesspeople and city officials, world leaders, television and film stars, and even their own family members (Nathan and Snedeker 1995).

Spread of the Moral Panic

The same social strains that accounted for the timing of the onset of the satanic day care moral panic also created an engendering environment for its rapid spread across the country. The role of interest, professional and grassroots groups in sustaining both the drama and the exigency of this moral panic, however, cannot be underestimated.

As in all contemporary moral panics, the news media emerged as a major interest group. The McMartin Preschool case, and all of the "little McMartins" as the well over a hundred ensuing cases it triggered were euphemistically called, fit all of the criteria for newsworthiness set out by Soothill and Walby (1991). They had ample complexity to warrant daily coverage from different angles; nearly intolerable horror to evoke and sustain intense emotional responses; enough familiarity in terms of location, key claims-makers, and even prime suspects to spark interest; real enough folk devils in the roles of day care providers to demonize; and sufficient exigency to elicit feelings that something must be done, and to focus action in doing it.

The news media hardly were monolithic as an interest group, however. While the nearly hysterical tone of reportage set in local coverage of the McMartin Preschool case was mimicked in local news media in other cases across the country, as well as in the mass media, it was tempered considerably in the national press and quelled completely in a few investigative reports in large circulation newspapers (Charlier and Downing 1988; Reinhold 1990). And, as both the McMartin Preschool case and many, although certainly not all, of the other satanic day care cases that followed began to fall apart as criminal charges were dismissed, children recanted, or day care providers were exonerated in courts of law, the tone of even local news coverage changed to one of skepticism, criticism, and even excoriation (Sauer 1993; Shaw 1990).

One eventual target of that excoriation was the very professionals who, in the role of what Becker (1963:145) so aptly described as "moral entrepreneurs," had triggered and spread the satanic day care moral panic. During its nearly decade-long duration, with many of their activities funded and endorsed by the National Center for Child Abuse and Neglect, these social workers, mental heath professionals, attorneys and law enforcement officers acted as the chief claims-makers in not only the local and national news media, but also on network television talk shows and primetime news magazines. The social workers and mental health professionals, in particular, became captains of a burgeoning "sexual abuse industry," as Goodyear-Smith (1993) referred to it, and took to the lecture circuit, addressed child protection conferences, conducted workshops, consulted with professionals involved in other cases, and testified as expert witnesses in the criminal and civil trials of the day care providers.

Their claims about satanic day care centers also were voiced in sworn testimony in high profile government hearings. The social worker who interviewed most of the children in the McMartin Preschool case, for example, added a touch of conspiracy to the satanic day care cases when in late 1984 she testified before Congress that an organized operation of "child predators" was using day care centers "as a ruse for a larger, unthinkable network of crimes against children. If such an operation involves child pornography, or selling children, as is frequently alleged, it may have greater financial, legal and community resources at its disposal than those attempting to expose it" (Brozan 1984: A-21).

Rhetoric like that may be enough to ignite a moral panic, but rhetoric backed up by "facts" is more combustible (Best 1990). To make more persuasive claims, both about the satanic day care problem and their expertise in it, professionals developed and widely disseminated a wholly synthetic diabolism out of materials haphazardly borrowed from eclectic sources on satanism, the occult, mysticism, paganism and witchcraft (Mulhern 1991). They constructed "indicator lists" to assist other professionals, both here and abroad, in identifying child victims, and "symptom lists" to guide the course of their therapy. Little of what passed for facts about satanic ritual abuse in day care centers was the result of well designed and controlled empirical studies or even systematic case studies, and little of the exchange of facts was taking place in the formal arena of peer-reviewed professional journals, but a burgeoning critical literature was, thus deeply dividing the professional field into claims-makers and counterclaims-makers, believers, and skeptics.

Parents of the allegedly victimized children were unabashed believers, and they constitute the grassroots group that spread the satanic day care moral panic. Like the professionals, and sometimes in conjunction with them, the parents were very vocal and, given their outrage and grief, very pitiable claims-makers. Many of them became keenly politicized as well. Some of the parents in the Little Rascals case, for example, formed an organization called Citizens Against Child Abuse to raise money to assist prosecutors in bringing the seven day care providers to trial. Believe the Children, a group formed by a coterie of McMartin Preschool parents, established a clearinghouse on satanic ritual abuse replete with a speakers' bureau, support groups for parents, police, and prosecutors involved in other day care cases, and a referral list of sympathetic professionals.

As another example, a legislative group called CLOUT was formed by parents in the aftermath of the Manhattan Ranch case. It successfully lobbied the California legislature for "child-friendly" changes in criminal trial procedures in which young children testified as witnesses, changes that were well into place when the long-delayed McMartin Preschool case finally came to trial. The rapid adoption across the country of these and other courtroom innovations, such as shielding child witnesses by allowing them to testify on videotape, closed-circuit television, behind screens, or with their backs to the defendants have not been without legal controversy since they violate the defendants' First and Sixth Amendment rights to a public trial in which accusatory witnesses can be confronted (Montoya 1995).

Denouement of the Moral Panic

The satanic day care moral panic effectively ended in 1991 but its denouement is no more a matter of coincidence than was its onset nearly a decade before. Several factors contributed to its demise. The overweening cultural anxiety about satanic menaces to children largely had been debunked and many of its most vocal claims-makers had retreated into silence (Victor 1993). Changing economic conditions over that decade only increased the number of women in the labor force and the concomitant increase in the use of day care may have worked to integrate this service even more thoroughly into the culture, thus reducing the conflict associated with its use (Hofferth and Phillips 1987).

Changes in day care over the decade of the moral panic, and largely in reaction to it, also acted to pare down any residual conflict about its use. State licensing agencies tightened day care regulations and by legislative fiat were given more teeth to enforce them. As a result, allegations of any kind were promptly, even aggressively, investigated and the licenses of day care centers in noncompliance were suspended or revoked. In the immediate wake of the Georgian Hills case, for example, 15 local day care centers were investigated for sexual abuse (Mydans 1994), and in the months after the McMartin Preschool case was made public, nine other centers in the small bedroom community of Manhattan Beach were closed down when investigations were launched (Fisher 1989). Significant day care reforms also took place on a state level. After the Country Walk case, as another example, the Governor of Florida held public hearings on the accessibility and quality of day care, and then asked the state legislature for $30 million to reform the system (Ynclan 1984).

In the accusatorial atmosphere of the moral panic, day care providers also took measures to protect themselves from false allegations (Bordin 1996). They installed video cameras to record their activities, opened up private spaces to public view, and kept physical contact with their young charges to a necessary minimum. They adopted open-door policies and invited parents to drop in without notice to talk with staff, observe their children or even spend time with them. The net effect of these and other changes was not only to make day care centers more accessible to worried parents, but more like families, thus further minifying the anxiety about their use (deYoung 1997).

What also certainly played a role in the denouement of the moral panic was the fact that the satanic day care cases, so reprehensible in the court of public opinion, nonetheless did not fare well in courts of law. As Table 2 shows, in many cases in the sample charges were dropped against day care providers and convictions eventually overturned. Although this is certainly due to the fact that the pubic requires a lower standard of evidence, for lack of a better term, to develop an impression about a case than a court does to adjudicate it, the considerable clash between public opinion and judicial reaction made it difficult to sustain the drama and the exigency of the satanic day care moral panic.

Finally, the schism within the claims-making professional groups that widened over the years of the moral panic also played a role in its demise. The satanic day care center was the site upon which an almost gothic professional struggle for social, political, and moral meaning had taken place, yet no consensus about that meaning was ever reached. The intra-professional dispute about the satanic day care cases, the inter-professional criticism of how they were handled, coupled with the growing public discontent with the expansion of clinical authority into families, institutions, and courts of law very well may have led to the construction of a new folk devil—the overzealous, short-sighted professional, bent on proving sexual abuse of any kind—and a new moral panic, colloquially known as "the backlash," now being directed against them (Myers 1994).

RETHINKING MORAL PANICS

The classic theory of moral panic has enjoyed a quite long and lively tenure in the discipline of sociology, but the satanic day

TABLE 2 Disposition Details for 38 Defendants in the Sample of 15 Day Care Cases

Day Care Center Defendant	Verdict	Sentence
McMartin Preschool		
Raymond Buckey	Not Guilty	—
Peggy Buckey	Not Guilty	—
Virginia McMartin	Charges Dropped	—
Peggy Ann Buckey	Charges Dropped	—
Betty Raidor	Charges Dropped	—
Babette Spitler	Charges Dropped	—
Mary Ann Jackson	Charges Dropped	—
Country Walk		
Frank Fuster	Guilty	6 life terms
Ileana Fuster	Pled Guilty	10 years
Small World		
Richard Barkman	Guilty	50–75 years. Conviction overturned, pled guilty to lesser offense in lieu of re-trial, 5 years probation
Fells Acres		
Gerald Amirault	Guilty	30–40 years
Violet Amirault	Guilty	8–20 years. Conviction overturned, re-trial ordered. Superior Court denied re-trial and reinstated original sentence; that ruling overturned by state Supreme Court which overturned conviction and ordered re-trial
Cheryl LeFave	Guilty	8–20 years. Conviction overturned, re-trial ordered. Superior Court denied re-trial and reinstated original sentence; that ruling overturned by state Supreme Court which overturned conviction and ordered re-trial
Georgian Hills		
Betty Stimpson	Charges Dropped in Trial	—
Jeff Stimpson	Not Guilty	—
Frances Ballard	Guilty	5–35 years. Conviction overturned; charges dismissed
Paul Shell	Charges Dropped	—

Rogers Park Jewish		
Deloartic Parks	Not Guilty	—
Manhattan Ranch		
Michael Ruby	Not Guilty	—
Craig's Country		
Sandra Craig	Guilty	10 years. Conviction overturned; charges dismissed
Jamal Craig	Charges Dropped in Trial	—
Felix's		
Martha Felix	Guilty	3 life sentences. Conviction overturned; charges dismissed
Francisco Ontiveros	Guilty	Life. Conviction overturned; charges dismissed
East Valley YMCA		
Michelle Noble	Guilty	Life plus 311 years. Conviction overturned; retried, not guilty.
Gayle Dove	Guilty	20 years. Conviction overturned, charges dismissed
Glendale Montessori		
James Toward	Pled Guilty	27 years
Brenda Williams	Pled No Contest	10 years
Old Cutler		
Bobby Fijnje	Not Guilty	—
Little Rascals		
Robert Kelly	Guilty	12 life sentences. Conviction overturned, re-trial ordered; charges dismissed
Betsy Kelly	Pled Guilty	7 year suspended sentence
Dawn Wilson	Guilty	Life. Conviction overturned, re-trial ordered; charges dismissed
Willard Privott	Pled Guilty	10 year suspended sentence
Shelly Stone	Charges Dropped	—
Darlene Harris	Charges Dropped	—
Robin Bynum	Charges Dropped	—
Faith Chapel		
Dale Akiki	Not Guilty	—
Fran's		
Fran Keller	Guilty	48 years
Dan Keller	Guilty	48 years

care moral panic of the 1980s reveals that some refinement and updating of the theory is needed. Specifically, another look has to be given to folk devils, the societal reaction to a moral panic, and the social ends it serves. Each of these will be examined in turn with data from the sample of 15 satanic day care cases used for illustration.

Folk Devils

Every moral panic needs folk devils, those individuals or groups who, in the inflammatory rhetoric of the various claims-makers, are held responsible for the very social strains and concerns that fomented the moral panic in the first place. Their alleged deviance, amplified by repeated claims that divest them of any positive characteristics and invest them with negative, folk devils become in the cultural imagination "quintessentially evil" (Cohen 1972:43).

What makes their demonization so nearly effortless is that the folk devils of classic moral panic theory tend to be already marginalized individuals and, as such, have neither the credibility nor the resources to counter the claims against them. Whether the menially situated women of the witch-hunts (Ben-Yehuda 1980), the unemployed racial minorities of the mugging and garrotting scares (Hall et al. 1979; Sindall 1987), or the disenfranchised teenagers of the youth violence and the drug panics (Cohen 1972; Goode 1990), folk devils tend to be located on the edges of society.

Not so with the day care providers who were the folk devils of the satanic day care moral panic. As surrogate parents to the country's youngest children, they not only provided a much in demand service but in other senses of the term were well integrated into their communities. A few examples from the sample of 15 satanic day care cases will illustrate this point. Deloartic Parks who was alleged to have boiled babies in the basement of the Rogers Park Jewish Community Day Care Center, was a devout Christian and a deacon in his Baptist church (Arndt 1984); Bobby Fijnje, the 14 year-old day care volunteer at the Old Cutler Church who was said to have forced children to eat feces and drink urine, was a popular high school student (Viglucci and Evans 1990); and Sandra Craig who was accused of torturing children in satanic rituals and burying them alive in the woods was a community activist and successful entrepreneur (Leff 1987).

Demographically, the day care employees were unremarkable. The 16 men and 22 women criminally charged in the 15 satanic day care cases in the sample ranged in age from 14 to 77 years, with a mean age of 38 years (SD 14.77). Thirty-one were White, 4 Latino, and 3 African American; 24 were married at the time of their arrest, 10 single, 3 divorced, and 1 widowed.

Far from being the defenseless, ineffectual folk devils of classic moral panic theory, many of the 38 day care providers in the sample took active measures not only to assert their innocence, but resist their demonization. Their integration into their respective communities afforded them access to the kinds of resources that made it possible to do so. Again, a few examples from the sample will illustrate this point. Michael Ruby, the 17-year-old playground aide at the Manhattan Ranch Preschool, took advantage of the media interest in his case and gave an interview in which he not only denied having abused children in satanic rituals conducted in sewers and haunted houses, but also assured everyone that he bore no hatred against the young children who had falsely accused him (Feldman and Needham 1984). Others took advantage of the courts. When the Fells Acres center was closed by the state after her son was arrested for abusing a child, owner Violet Amirault immediately filed suit to remove the emergency suspension of the center's license and to prevent state officials from holding meetings with the parents of other enrolled children to inform them of the on-going investigation (Bennett 1984). And Virginia McMartin, matriarch of the preschool that triggered the moral panic, successfully sued the parent of one of her alleged victims for slander when he publicly labeled her a satanic ritual abuser. Although the judge awarded her only $1 in damage, she claimed a pyrrhic victory. "I got what I wanted—the truth to come out," she told the press. "I didn't care a snip about the money. I wanted him to shut-up" (McGraw 1991: B-1).

The lack of marginality of the satanic day care folk devils has two implications for an updated theory of moral panic. First, it suggests that the targets of moral panics may not be just the expediently constructed folk devils of classic theory, but also those akin to what Watney (1987: 41) once described as "monstrous representations," those whose appearance of conformity and normalcy is believed to hide more than it reveals. The creation of such monstrous representations seems to be more a process of pathologizing then demonizing and certainly would be enhanced if, as in the case of the satanic day care moral panic, the primary claims-makers are well versed in the language of psychology and their claims are made in a culture that is as well.

The attempt by Finkelhor and Williams in *Nursery Crimes* (1988), a highly regarded scholarly treatise on sexual abuse in day care, to explain why so many women providers were arrested for the horrific crime of satanic ritual abuse, illustrates this process of pathologizing. Acknowledging that women rarely commit sexual crimes against children and that these women, in particular, often were "highly regarded in their communities as church and civic leaders, intelligent businesswomen, and generally law-abiding citizens" (p. 41), they go on to create monstrous representations. In the absence of any reliable life history data or psychiatric evaluations, they conjecture that the women's own histories of sexual abuse or sexual repression must have caused them to see their own sexuality as evil or demonic, and that this led to a hatred of children whose sexuality is pure and innocent. They go on to speculate that the women must have "identified with evil" during their own childhoods in rigidly moralistic families and that this caused them to "discover a sense of power and spiritual fulfillment in a doctrine [of satanism] that celebrates participation in intentionally evil acts" (p. 64).

Second, the lack of marginality of the targets of the satanic day care moral panic suggests that a refined theory must take into account how the empowerment of folk devils impacts the course of the moral panic over time, shapes public discourse about the strains and concerns that engendered it, and challenges efforts at social control. An updated theory also would bring more analytical focus to the interactions between empowered folk devils and those interest groups, particularly the media and the courts, that are resources for presenting and defending their interests even while they play a major role in spreading the moral panic.

Societal Reaction

In classic moral panic theory, the societal reaction to a moral panic generally is described as invariable. Indeed, this allegedly monolithic response is a theoretical necessity in that it helps explain both how and why a moral panic tends to spread with such alacrity. Yet this assumption that societal reaction is hegemonic, to borrow a term from Hall et al. (1979), certainly also has led theorists to overlook counterclaims and counternarratives, and to underestimate their role in shaping the course of the moral panic.

The satanic day care moral panic was rife with those very counterclaims and counternarratives. They took the form not only of the protestations of innocence by the accused day care providers, but of the views of skeptics that were juxtaposed with those of the primary claims-makers routinely in the national media and occasionally even in the local media. Within the professional groups, claims and counterclaims were so vociferously and angrily made that Putnam (1991) urged mental health professionals to resolve their conflict over satanic ritual abuse in day care or risk stalling the considerable progress they already had made in the area of sexual abuse. In the criminal trials of the day care providers, counterclaims and counternarratives not only were offered by expert witnesses for the defense, but by community people personally touched by the moral panic. Two of the satanic day care cases in the sample illustrate just how diverse local reactions to the moral panic really were. In the Faith Chapel case, two ministers testified that it was nothing more than a "wave of hysteria" that had swept over their own parishioners, resulting in the arrest of day care volunteer Dale Akiki for abusing children in satanic rituals that included the sacrifice of an elephant and a giraffe, and the murder of a baby (Wolf 1993). And in the Old Cutler case, over 800 parishioners offered to testify as character witnesses for teenage church day care aide Bobby Fijnje who was facing life in prison (Evans 1990).

In a couple of instances, counterclaims and counternarratives almost certainly played a major, but admittedly difficult to measure, role in shaping societal reactions both to specific day care cases and the satanic day care moral panic. A series of scathing editorials critical of the Fells Acres case, published in the *Wall Street Journal,* continues to dominate public discourse on this still legally unresolved case (Rabinowitz 1995a, 1995b, 1995c, 1997a, 1997b, 1997c). And a series of investigative reports on the Little Rascals case, aired by PBS on its primetime documentary "Frontline," is credited with turning around national opinion on this controversial case.

The assumption of classic moral panic theory that societal reaction is hegemonic is called into question by the satanic day care moral panic. Rather than opting for theoretical convenience, an updated theory needs to take into account the plurality of reactions that inevitably will arise in a complexly differentiated society, and to assess the impact of those counterclaims and counternarratives on the course and content of the moral panic.

Social Ends

In classic theory, moral panics are described as working on behalf of the dominant social order. Through their use of emotive rhetoric and fear-based appeals, and their demonization of folk devils, moral panics tend to orchestrate social consensus that something must be done, and quickly, to deal with the imminent threat. The increased social control that usually follows not only is aimed at the threat, but also acts to preserve and reassert those very values and interests that purportedly are being undermined. Goode (1990), for example, discusses how the drug panic of the 1980s defined the moral boundaries of American society by prompting the passage of stricter drug laws, imposing longer prison sentences on dealers and users, and developing drug prevention programs aimed at socializing children into the value of a drug-free way of life.

Although it also is true that some moral panics never achieve any discernible social ends and, in the words of Cohen (1972:28), just devolve into "folklore and collective memory," an updated theory must consider the possibility that the ends achieved are more symbolic than real. Consider the satanic day care moral panic's legacy in law. Like every moral panic, this one needed the authority of the law to legitimate its claims and activities and restore the social order so threatened by its folk devils. Over the 1980s, the satanic day care moral panic provoked a dozen states to either revise existing criminal codes to include references to ritual abuse, or propose new legislation that specifically criminalizes the ritual abuse of children. Although at first blush all of this appears to be in service of increased social control, the irony is that the very behaviors that are alleged to comprise satanic ritual abuse—sexual assault, kidnapping, torture, murder—already are prohibited by criminal and child protection laws (Ogloff and Pfeifer 1992). These reiterative new laws, then, have more symbolic than actual value, and it is symbolic social ends such as this that an updated theory of moral panic must anticipate and analyze.

On an ideological level, the satanic day care moral panic

actually achieved contradictory social ends. By the early 1980s, an emerging feminist ideology of sexual abuse was shaping discourse on this once taboo topic and setting out a controversial agenda for sexual politics. Noting the stark asymmetry in gender in its perpetration and victimology, the feminist ideology redefined sexual abuse in terms of male dominance and contextualized it within the routinized, culturally sanctioned interactions between men and women, parents and children, fathers and daughters. And by situating childhood within a moral and political frame, the feminist ideology gave voices to once culturally silenced children and treated them as credible witnesses to their own victimization.

The satanic day care moral panic, on the one hand, served as a courier for dominant interests and values that were threatened by this emerging feminist ideology (deYoung 1996). More of its folk devils were women than men, thus weakening the link between sexual abuse and male dominance, and forging a new one between bizarre and sadistic sexual abuse and women as perpetrators. It loosened the embeddedness of sexual abuse within the routine and the familiar by mystifying its context with claims that children were being abused not only in their day care centers but in other unusual or unrecognizable places, during the course of meaningless rituals and incomprehensible ceremonies performed not only by their day care providers but by robed and hooded strangers. The moral panic also delegitimated the voices of children. Their allegations of satanic ritual abuse most often were the products of months, even years, of such relentless interrogation by therapists, police, prosecuting attorneys, and parents that it is impossible to discern just whose voice really is telling the tale (Bruck and Ceci 1995; Montoya 1995).

On the other hand, the satanic day care moral panic had the antithetical effect of actually advancing the feminist ideology of sexual abuse, and it is the possibility of this kind of achievement of contradictory social ends that an updated theory must anticipate. In response to counterclaims critical of their decorum in the satanic day care cases, professional organizations developed standards of practice for interviewing, evaluating, and treating any child or adult with a history of sexual abuse (American Academy of Child and Adolescent Psychiatry 1988). These not only serve as a check and balance against the beliefs, values, and assumptions of professionals that in the case of the satanic day care moral panic so obviously occluded the assessment process, but act to bring more common, albeit prosaic, cases of sexual abuse into the public realm. In doing so, these standards of practice lead to the identification of cases that lend some legitimacy to the still emerging, but no less controversial, feminist ideology about sexual abuse.

Although most mainstream child protection agencies such as the Child Welfare League and the International Society for the Prevention of Child Abuse and Neglect remained stonily silent on the topic of satanic ritual abuse, beleaguered claims-makers responded to criticisms about their expertise in dealing with the satanic day care cases by forming the American Professional Society on the Abuse of Children (APSAC). With its mission that "everyone affected by child abuse and neglect receive the best possible professional response," APSAC also brings the maltreatment of children into the social and political arena, thus challenging the dominant social interests and values that for generations had worked to keep discussion and action on this issue to a minimum. APSAC is legislatively active, provides professional education, promotes research, and develops practice guidelines for those involved in any number of ways with cases of alleged child maltreatment. Ironically, though, this organization that began in response to the satanic day care moral panic, and whose early leadership roster was a veritable "who's who" of the panic's most vocal moral entrepreneurs, published a carefully worded fact sheet a few years after its denouement informing members that after all the dramatic claims-making there actually is little, if any, reliable evidence that there even is such a thing as satanic ritual abuse (APSAC Fact Sheet 1995).

CONCLUSION

In his groundbreaking study, Cohen (1972) concluded that moral panics reveal something of interest about social structure, social process, and social change. The satanic day care moral panic of the 1980s certainly is no exception. From its origin in the structurally generated strains and anxieties peculiar to that decade, to its emotive rhetoric that transformed day care providers into folk devils, to the social processes of its spread by varied interest groups, and finally to its denouement and institutional and ideological legacy, the satanic day care moral panic is, in every sense of the term, a revealing moral panic.

One of the things this moral panic also reveals is that the classic theory of moral panic is in need of updating and refinement. First, an updated theory must anticipate that the folk devils of some moral panics may be as empowered as the day care providers were in the satanic day care moral panic. With access to a variety of resources that will allow them to protest their innocence and resist their demonization, such empowered folk devils inevitably will impact the course of the moral panic, shape public discourse, and challenge efforts at social control in ways that an updated theory must take into account and analyze. Second, an updated theory also must anticipate that in a complex, differentiated society, reactions to a moral panic may be far from uniform. That certainly was the case in the satanic day care moral panic. Throughout its nearly decade-long course, its claims were criticized, belittled, and rejected, and the impact of such counterclaims on the course and the content of the moral panic must be considered. Finally, an updated theory must bring some analysis to the possibility that the social ends achieved by a moral panic may be as institutionally symbolic and ideologically contradictory as those achieved by this one.

If the satanic day care moral panic is at all predictive of what future panics will resemble, then it also suggests a future approach to sociological analysis. That analysis must take careful consideration of the multi-mediated nature of the complexly differentiated social worlds that will be the contexts of future moral panics. The intricate web of relations between various interest groups, the kinds of claims they make, and the media that present and contest them, must be part and parcel of future analysis. And so must be the many audiences that receive them. Either overlooked completely or treated as little more than passive dupes in classic analysis, these audiences must be seen and appreciated for their imaginative and active roles in moral panics. Whether as actors, observers, readers, or listeners, audiences actively appropriate and decode the "facts" of the claims of moral panics and act in relation to them. They do so as well with the ideological underpinnings of those claims. Future analysis, therefore, must include a critical examination of the ideology of moral panics, how it resonates with the lived experiences of those audiences, how it acts to recruit them, and how it retains them often long after the "facts" of the claims have been disputed and debunked.

The satanic day care moral panic is a fascinating slice of

American cultural history. It was as widespread, overreactive, volatile, hostile, and irrational as any moral panic that preceded it, but a great deal more revealing than most. What it reveals is that it is time to take another look at classic moral panic theory.

REFERENCES

Adler, Jeffrey. S. 1996. "The Making of a Moral Panic in 19th Century America: The Boston Garroting Hysteria of 1865." *Deviant Behavior 17*:259–278.

American Academy of Child and Adolescent Psychiatry. 1988. *Guidelines for the Clinical Evaluation of Child and Adolescent Sexual Abuse.* Washington, DC: Author.

APSAC Fact Sheet. 1995. "Ritual Abuse." Chicago, IL: Author.

Arndt, Michael. 1984. "Portrait of Janitor Clashes with Abuse Charge." *Chicago Tribune* May 2: II–8.

Becker, Howard. 1963. *Outsiders.* New York: Free Press.

Bennett, Philip. 1984. "Judge Denies Request to Reopen Day Care Center." *Boston Globe* September 14: 17, 24.

Ben-Yehuda, Nachman. 1980. "The European Witch Craze of the 14th and 17th centuries: A Sociological Perspective." *American Journal of Sociology 86*:1–31.

Best, Joel. 1990. *Threatened Children: Rhetoric and Concern about Child-Victims.* Chicago, IL: University of Chicago Press.

Bordin, Judith A. 1996. "The Aftermath of Unsubstantiated Child Abuse Allegations in Child Care Centers." *Child and Youth Care Forum 25*:73–87.

Brozan, Nan. 1984. "Witness Says She Fears 'Child Predator' Network." *New York Times* September 18: A–21.

Bruck, Maggie and Stephen Ceci. 1995. "Amicus Brief for the Case of *State of New Jersey v/Michaels* Presented by the Committee of Concerned Social Scientists." *Psychology, Public Policy and Law 1*:272–322.

Charlier, Tom and Shirley Downing. 1988. "Justice Abused: A 1980's Witch-hunt" (Series). *Memphis Commercial Appeal* January.

Cohen, Stanley. 1972. *Folk Devils and Moral Panics: The Creation of the Mods and the Rockers.* Oxford, England: Basil Blackwell.

deYoung, Mary. 1994. "One Face of the Devil: The Satanic Ritual Abuse Moral Crusade and the Law." *Behavioral Sciences and the Law 12*:389–407.

——— 1996. "Satanic Ritual Abuse: Exploring the Controversies." Paper presented to the 11th International Congress on Child Abuse and Neglect. August, Dublin, Ireland.

——— 1997. "The Devil Goes to Day Care: McMartin and the Making of a Moral Panic." *Journal of American Culture 20*: 19–26.

Durkheim, Emil. 1938. *The Rules of Sociological Method.* Trans. Sarah Solovay and John H. Mueller. Ed. George E. G. Catlin. Chicago, IL: University of Chicago.

Erikson, Kai T. 1966. *Wayward Puritan: A Study in the Sociology of Deviance.*

New York: Wiley.

Evans, Christine. 1990. "Church Sex-Abuse Trial Opens Today." *Miami Herald* September 17: B–1.

Feldman, Paul and John Needham. 1984. "Victim of 'Witch-Hunt,' Accused Molester Says." *Los Angeles Times* November 30: 1, 8.

Finkelhor, David and Linda Meyer Williams. 1988. *Nursery Crimes*. Newbury Park, CA: Sage.

Fisher, Mary A. 1989. "A Case of Dominoes?" *Los Angeles Magazine* October: 126–135.

Goode, Erich 1990. "The American Drug Panic of the 1980's: Social Construction or Objective Threat?" *International Journal of the Addictions 25*:1083–1098.

Goode, Erich and Nachman Ben-Yehuda. 1994. *Moral Panics*. Cambridge, MA: Blackwell.

Goodyear-Smith, Felicity. 1993. *First Do No Harm: The Sexual Abuse Industry*. Auckland, New Zealand: Benton-Gay.

Greek, Cecil E. and William Thompson. 1992. "Anti-Pornography Campaigns: Saving the Family in America and England." *International Journal of Politics, Culture and Society 5*:601–616.

Gusfield, Joseph. 1963. *Symbolic Crusade*. Urbana, IL: University of Illinois.

Hall, Stuart, Charles Critcher, Tony Jefferson, John Clark and Brian Roberts. 1979. *Policing the Crisis: Mugging, the State, and Law and Order*. London, England: MacMillan.

Hofferth, Sandra L. and Deborah A. Phillips. 1987. "Child Care in the United States: 1970–1995." *Journal of Marriage and the Family 49*:559–571.

Hutchison, Elizabeth D. 1992. "Child Welfare as a Woman's Issue." *Families in Society 73*:67–77.

King, Peter. 1987. "Newspaper Reporting, Prosecution Practice, and Perceptions of Urban Crime: The Colchester Crime Wave of 1765." *Continuity and Change 2*:423–454.

Leff, Lisa. 1987. "Day Care Owner Denies Abuse." *Washington Post* March 28: C–1.

McGraw, Carol. 1991. McMartin Figures Win $1 in Civil Trial." *Los Angeles Times* May 8: B–1.

Montoya, Jean. 1995. "Lessons from *Akiki* and *Michaels* on Shielding Child Witnesses." *Psychology, Public Policy and Law 1*:340–369.

Mulhern, Sherril. 1991. "Satanism and Psychotherapy: A Rumor in Search of an Inquisition." Pp. 145–172 in *The Satanism Scare*, edited by J. T. Richardson, J. Best, D. G. Bromley. Harthorne, New York: Aldine deGruyter.

Mydans, Seth. 1994. "Grand Jury Rips Sex-Abuse Prosecution, Says Parents, Therapists Influenced Kids." *Memphis Commercial-Appeal* June 3: A–1.

Myers, John E. B. 1994. *The Backlash: Child Protection Under Fire*. Newbury Park, CA: Sage.

Nathan, Debbie and Michael Snedeker. 1995. *Satan's Silence: Ritual Abuse and the Making of a Modern American Witch Hunt*. New York: Basic.

Ogloff, James R. P. and John E. Pfeifer. 1992. "Cults and the Law: A Discussion of the Legality of Alleged Cult Activities." *Behavioral Sciences and the Law* *10*:117–140.

Putnam, Frank W. 1991. "Commentary: The Satanic Ritual Abuse Controversy." *Child Abuse & Neglect 15*:175–180.

Rabinowitz, Dorothy. 1995a. "A Darkness in Massachusetts." *Wall Street Journal* January 15: A–10.

Rabinowitz, Dorothy. 1995b. "A Darkness in Massachusetts II." *Wall Street Journal* March 14: A–14.

Rabinowitz, Dorothy. 1995c. "A Darkness in Massachusetts III." *Wall Street Journal* May 12: A–12.

Rabinowitz, Dorothy. 1997a. "Justice and the Prosecutor." *Wall Street Journal* March 21: A–18.

Rabinowitz, Dorothy. 1997b. "Massachusetts Justice." *Wall Street Journal* March 26: A–18.

Rabinowitz, Dorothy. 1997c. "The Amiraults' Trial Judge Reviews His Peers." *Wall Street Journal* April 10: A–14.

Reinhold, Robert. 1990. "How Lawyers and the Media Turned the McMartin Case into a Tragic Media Circus." *New York Times* January 25: D–1.

Richardson, James T., Joel Best and David G. Bromley. 1991. *The Satanism Scare*. Hawthorne, New York: Aldine deGruyter.

Sauer, Mark. 1993. "Decade of Accusations: The McMartin Preschool Case Launched 100 Others—And a Vigorous Debate on How to Question Youngsters." *San Diego Union Tribune* August 29: D–1.

Shaw, David. 1990. "Reporter's Early Exclusives Triggered a Media Frenzy." *Los Angeles Times*. January 20: A–1.

Shuker, Roy. 1986. "'Video Nasties': Censorship and the Politics of Popular Culture." *New Zealand Sociology 1*:64–73.

Sindall, Rob. 1987. "The London Garrotting Panics of 1856 and 1862." *Social History 12*:351–358.

Soothill, Keith and Sylvia Walby. 1991. *Sex Crime in the News*. London, England: Routledge.

Victor, Jeffrey S. 1993. *Satanic Panic*. Chicago, IL: Open Court.

Viglucci, Andress and Christine Evans. 1990. "Regular Kid Accused of the unthinkable." *Miami Herald* March 4: 1–B.

Watney, Simon. 1987. *Policing Desire: Pornography, AIDS and the Media*. London, England: Methuen.

Wilkins, Leslie. T. 1994. "Don't Alter Your Mind—It's the World That's Out of Joint." *Social Justice 21*:148–153.

Williams, Brian. 1993. "Bail Bandits: The Construction of Moral Panics." *Critical Social Policy 13*:104–112.

Wolf, Lisa. 1993. "Satanism at Issue in Akiki Trial. Frenzy of Rumors at Church Recalled." *San Diego Union Tribune* August 14: B–1, B–2, B–4.

Ynclan, Nery. 1984. "Legislature May Convene on Child Abuse." *Miami Herald* September 16: B–1.

Zatz, Marjorie S. 1987. "Chicano Youth Gangs and Crime: The Creation of a Moral Panic." *Contemporary Crises 11*:129–158.

[10]

Beyond folk devil resistance: Linking moral panic and moral regulation

Sean P. Hier, Dan Lett, Kevin Walby and André Smith
University of Victoria, Canada

Abstract
This article is a contribution to widening the focus of moral panic studies. Our aim is to advance recent attempts to link moral panic studies to the criminological literature on moral regulation. We argue that moral panics should be conceptualized as volatile expressions of long-term moral regulation processes. To substantiate these conceptual and theoretical arguments, we examine claims-making activities about the threat posed by British youth who don hooded tops in public places.

Keywords
anti-social behavior, claims making, folk devils, moral panic, moral regulation

Introduction

Moral panic research traces to Jock Young's (1971) study of the social meaning of drug taking and to Stanley Cohen's (1972) canonical investigation of the construction of the mods and rockers. Moral panic research developed through the 1970s and 1980s, focusing primarily on the role that claims makers, moral guardians, and the media play in the construction, amplification, and exaggeration of deviance. Significant contributions appeared in the 1990s that stimulated interest in moral panics (e.g. DeYoung, 1998; Goode and Ben-Yehuda, 1994; Hunt, 1997; McRobbie, 1994; McRobbie and Thornton, 1995; Thompson, 1998), and recent contributions have critically assessed moral panic in the context of broader theoretical formulations (e.g. Critcher, 2008, 2009; Garland, 2008; Hier, 2003, 2008; Rohloff, 2008; Rohloff and Wright 2010; Ungar, 2001).

Corresponding author:
Sean P. Hier, Department of Sociology, University of Victoria, Victoria, British Columbia, V8W 3P5, Canada
Email: shier@uvic.ca

Despite growing interest in moral panic analyses across sociology and criminology (see Hier, 2011), the full explanatory potential of moral panic studies has yet to be realized. Many scholars continue to conceptualize moral panics as exceptional rather than ordinary constructions of deviance to explain irrational and disproportionate reactions to exaggerated threats. One consequence of conceptualizing moral panic in this manner is that the explanatory power of moral panic studies has been minimized if not dismissed in wider investigations of routine moral regulation processes (Hunt, 1999; Moore and Valverde, 2000). A small number of contributions to moral panic studies has started to demonstrate how moral panics are rational, routine features of everyday life that contribute to ongoing processes of moral regulation within and beyond the State (e.g. Critcher, 2008; Hier, 2008; Rohloff, 2008). Nevertheless, efforts to 'widen the focus' (Critcher, 2009) of moral panic studies have only started to make an impact on the direction of research, analysis, and argumentation.

Our aim in this article is to contribute to ongoing debates about widening the focus of moral panic studies by examining the relationship between the criminologies of moral panic and moral regulation. We argue that moral panic scholars have correctly emphasized tendencies for folk devils and their supporters to resist both typification and regulation (Hier, 2002a, 2002b; McRobbie, 1994; McRobbie and Thornton, 1995). We argue, however, that the scope of moral panic analyses must extend beyond the episodic nature of resisting primary definitions to assess the broader foundations that give rise to and sustain ongoing processes of moral regulation. Although folk devils and their supporters can and do fight back, their resistance to dominant claims can be subverted, particularly when primary claims are integral to the validation of (especially state-based) regulatory programs. In other words, moral panics represent episodes of contestation and negotiation that emerge from and contribute to or reinforce broader processes of moral regulation.

To substantiate these conceptual and theoretical arguments, we examine the emergence of 'hoodies' as an assumed indicator of moral decline among youth in contemporary Britain. Our specific focus is on claims-making activities in the British press after a shopping center in Kent placed a ban on hooded tops. On 11 May 2005, the Bluewater shopping center implemented a code of conduct forbidding attire that conceals customers' facial features from the gaze of nearly 400 closed-circuit television cameras distributed throughout the complex. The ban prevented anyone wearing a hooded top (aka 'a hoodie') from entering the mall. Given that the garment is a popular mode of attire for British youth, the ban functioned to exclude groups of young people from gathering in the mall. Our focus is not on the Bluewater ban per se but rather the extensive national newspaper and television media coverage that the ban incited.

Although moral regulation vis-à-vis the signification of hoodies garnered momentum from an established cultural impulse to moralize the activities of youth (Cohen, 1972; Coleman, 2005; Thornton, 1994), discourses opposing the ban appeared in the mass and alternative media. British government officials invoked the hoodies signifier to address assumed youth tendencies towards anti-social behavior, and to justify legislative attempts to impose regulatory measures on British youth. Media reports used the 'hoodies' signifier as a rhetorical device to ascribe blame for a range of crime and anti-social behaviors. These processes were indicative of what Hall et al. (1978) conceptualized as a signification spiral: a mode of signifying events by the convergence of a newly identified concern with other social problems and issues, escalating the perceived threat of the emergent events beyond the thresholds of societal tolerance. However, diverse interest groups 'fought back' against the problematization of the hoodies in mainstream and alternative media counter claims. The struggle to define the problem of the hoodies occurred in the context of an established debate concerning the British government's Anti-Social Behavior Act of 2003 (ASBA) and the emergence of the Anti-Social Behavior Order (ASBO) as state-based techniques to enact forms of moral regulation.

Our purpose in this article is to neither quantify the regularity of ASBO deployment by authorities nor account for the legal technicalities of ASBOs; a burgeoning literature on youth and crime in the UK has already made these contributions (see Crawford, 2006, 2007, 2009; Millie, 2008; Pearson, 2006; Simester and Von Hirsch, 2006). Nor is our purpose to examine the origins of the Bluewater ban. Rather, our aim is to conceptualize the debate about hoodies as a volatile manifestation of long-term regulatory processes. Although several theorists of moral regulation have distanced regulatory projects from moral panic theory on the grounds that the latter imports a negative normative judgment, Hier (2002a, 2003, 2008; and see Critcher, 2009) has demonstrated that much can be made of a *convergence* of moral panic and moral regulation literatures. Whereas the moral panic literature has hitherto been concerned to show how contestation of primary definitions and dominant claims making is possible, we demonstrate how resistance efforts are themselves undermined with reference to New Labour's 'Reform and Respect Agenda'. Our analysis is thus important in the context of Waiton's (2008) argument that the contemporary politics of anti-social behavior has ushered in the era of amoral panics, insofar as we demonstrate how seemingly 'amoral' politics of managing anti-social behavior is linked to both volatile and long-term forms of moralization.[1]

Moral Regulation and the Volatility of Panics

Analyses of moral panic regularly begin with the arguments presented in Stan Cohen's (1972) *Folk Devils and Moral Panics*. For Cohen (1972: 41), every moral panic has its folk devil: the personification of evil who is (or that are) susceptible to recognition based on 'unambiguously unfavorable symbols'. The source of moral panic is not the folk devil itself; rather the folk devil serves as the ideological embodiment of the moral panic. When folk devils are revealed to the public in a stereotypical fashion through mainstream media reporting, they are constructed as threats to the social/moral fabric requiring immediate regulatory intervention (see Young, 2009). Often the symbolic folk devil correlates approximately to certain individuals and groups, but it is primarily a mode of representation that functions as a proxy for the harmful other in discourses about crime, law, and order.

Cohen's framework corresponds to what Goode and Ben-Yehuda (1994: 124–143) describe as the 'interest group' theory of moral panic – one of three traditional models of moral panic. In this model, moral panic is explained as the unintended outcome of moralizing projects undertaken by interest groups in an effort to draw public attention to a specific 'moral evil'. Goode and Ben-Yehuda distinguish the 'interest group' from the 'elite-engineered' model. The elite engineered model conceives of moral panic as the outcome of manufactured campaigns that are designed to divert attention away from real social crises. Hall et al. (1978), for example, argue that moral panic is a mechanism utilized by the ruling class to mystify deeper crises in the capitalist system. In contrast to the interest group and elite-engineered models, Goode and Ben-Yehuda (1994) propose a third model: grassroots. The grassroots model stipulates that moral panic originates with the general public. In the grassroots model, moral panic is understood to provide release for a reservoir of social insecurity.

The three traditional models of moral panic continue to influence moral panic studies, but subsequent efforts to 'rethink' moral panic theory have called into question the assumptions of the three foundational models. They have done so to develop alternative ways to explain moral panic. It has been argued that most contemporary political strategies are media strategies, and that the relationship between processes of claims making and social control is less circumscribed than past formulations concede (McRobbie and Thornton, 1995). For example, DeYoung (1998) argues that the daycare providers who became the focal point of satanic daycare panics through the 1980s were well integrated into their communities, and that they lacked the social marginality of traditional folk devils. Thornton's (1994) study of British club cultures reveals that fanzines, pirate radio, websites, and email distribution lists are among the plethora of media outlets regularly used to counter moralizing discourses. And Hier's (2002b) study of attempts to ban raves in the City of Toronto highlights the role of heterogeneous media outlets involved in the construction and contestation of moral panic.

The volatility of moralization

Efforts to rethink (and move beyond) traditional models of moral panic provide many progressive insights into the nature of moralization, and they have partially influenced the direction of theorization and empirical study. One of the problems with efforts to rethink moral panic, however, is that they have led to the deconstruction of traditional models without a reconstruction of alternative modes of explanation. In most moral panic research, there is an assumption that the harm believed to be posed by folk devils is disproportional to the harm that actually exists, which speaks to a tendency in moral panic studies to impose a negative normative judgment on explanations of volatile moralizing discourses as 'irrational' evaluations of the threat(s) posed (see Hier, 2008). Even though revisionist efforts have problematized the empirical bases through which these analytic judgments are rendered, analysts are forced to rely on normative value judgments to render assessments pertaining to the 'irrationality' of public beliefs (see Doran, 2008).

To remedy these theoretical difficulties, Hier (2008) draws from the sociology of governance studies to conceptualize 'moralization' (i.e. moral regulation) in terms of dialectic constructions of self and other that are transmitted through everyday discourses of risk management and harm avoidance. Conceptualized in this way, moralization references a liberal conception of 'the moral' that values individual rights. The deployment of contemporary liberal rights functions as a proxy for moralization, and one central, shared liberal moral value in an age of apparent moral relativism is to ensure one's right to freedom from harm (Hier, no date). As everyday activities become moralized in the form of judgments pertaining to what is right and wrong in terms of the negative consequences for other people, moralization finds expression through the proxies of risk, harm, and personal responsibility. One common feature of moralization in everyday life is that people are called upon to engage in responsible forms of individual risk management that exist in tension with collective subject positions of 'harmful others' (also see Hunt, 2003). On a conceptual level this implies that moralization is dialectical: individualizing discourses calling upon people to take personal responsibility to manage risk (e.g. drinking responsibly) are situated against collectivizing discourses representing the subject position of harm (e.g. the drunk driver).

The volatility of moralization brings into play a different nexus of values and emotions (Hier, 2008; Walby and Spencer, 2011). Through the deployment of a set of sensational discourses that erupt suddenly, and subside quickly, the moral dialectic that situates individualized risk management against a collective dimension of harm is inverted. Discourses that call upon individuals to engage in responsible forms of self-conduct to manage risk are transposed into collectivizing discourses of risk management. The latter take the form of defensive group reactions against what is represented as an immediate dimension of harm posed by 'irresponsible' others: those who fail to engage in individual risk management. As a volatile disturbance in the course of moral governance, 'moral panics' are short-lived disturbances focused on limiting the agency of 'folk devils'. Where conventional moral panic studies are often concerned with the 'origins' of each 'episode' of moral panic in terms of a particular event, claim or other 'tipping point' with causal primacy, the conceptual model we employ focuses on the implications of volatile moralization for the development of different regulatory approaches.

Anti-Social Behavior Orders and Regulating British Youth

Although moral regulation projects in Britain are attendant to the activities of a wide range of people, 'no age group is more associated with risk in the public imagination than that of "youth"' (Thompson, 1998: 43; also see Fionda, 2006). Not only are British youth represented as a social group 'at risk' from harms posed by child abusers and pedophiles (e.g. Critcher, 2002; Hay, 1995; Jenkins, 1992), but they are also identified as a *source* of risk (e.g. Cohen, 1972; Hay, 1995). The contemporary preoccupation with youth as particularly risky can be explained in relation to the primary mode of moralization – responsibilization. Responsibilization presupposes rational, liberal subjectivity, which is a developmental rather than inherent characteristic of human beings. Long-term efforts to regulate British youth over the past decade have manifested in moral-legal regulatory apparatuses institutionalized to counteract 'anti-social behavior'. We conceptualize these mechanisms of regulation in terms of governmental and extra-governmental attempts to responsibilize youth conduct in public spaces by encouraging certain modes of dress and behavior. By explicating the ways that moral regulation is currently enacted in relation to British youth, we conceptualize the events that followed the ban of hooded tops by representatives of the Bluewater shopping center.

British youth, law, and order

In 2003, the Home Office introduced the Anti-Social Behavior Act (ASBA). Applicable to England and Wales, the ASBA facilitated the regulation of 'anti-social behaviors' through the deployment of Anti Social Behavior Orders (ASBOs) and Acceptable Behavior Contracts (ABCs). The Home Office defines ASBOs as:

> civil orders that exist to protect the public from behaviour that causes or is likely to cause harassment, alarm or distress. An Order contains conditions prohibiting the offender from specific anti-social acts or entering defined areas and is effective for a minimum of two years. (Home Office, 2003: 9)

Whereas the purpose of ASBOs is to act on the conduct of moral transgressors after the fact, ABCs are pre-emptive, non-legally binding agreements between offenders and police. The Home Office defines ABCs as:

> an intervention designed to engage the individual in recognising their behaviour and its negative effects on others ... An ABC is a written agreement between an anti-social behaviour perpetrator and their local authority, Youth Inclusion Support Panel, landlord or the police ... ABCs are not legally binding, but can be cited in court as evidence in ASBO applications or in eviction or possession proceedings (Home Office, 2003: 9).

Together, ASBOs and ABCs act as a two-step prohibition (Simester and Von Hirsch, 2006). Despite the fact that neither ASBOs nor ABCs are exclusively applicable to youth, their primary target is youth transgression, which Crawford (2009b) argues follows the logic of de-differentiation insofar as all youth are problematized as probable sources of harm. The ASBA is also designed to enable spatial regulation – Section 30 of the ASBA invokes the notion of dispersal zones and orders. Crawford and Lister (2007) describe how dispersal orders are used to target youth simply on the basis of their presence in particular urban spaces (e.g. shopping centers). Millie (2008) comments on how ASBOs are used to regulate disparate forms of activity, which means there is no clear-cut definition of anti-social behavior. The application of ASBOs, argues Millie, is often based on aesthetics.

> When New Labour introduced the Crime and Disorder Act (CDA) of 1998, government rhetoric problematized simultaneously the behaviour of youth and the existing institutional measures to counteract youth irresponsibility.

> An excuse culture has developed within the youth justice system. It excuses itself for its inefficiency, and too often excuses the young offenders before it, implying that they cannot help their behaviour because of their social circumstances. Rarely are they confronted with their behaviour and *helped to take more personal responsibility for their actions*. The system allows them to go on wrecking their own lives and disrupting their families and communities. (Home Office, 1997: Preface, *emphasis added*)

The institutionalization of the CDA signified a wider ideological shift in the regulation of British youth from a 'minimum intervention' approach that predominated in the

1990s to a preventative 'early intervention' approach (see Crawford, 2009a; Squires, 2008). As Bottoms and Dignan (2004) explain, the reason for this shift was the perceived failures of the Conservative Party's so-called 'new-orthodoxy' that prevailed among youth justice workers in the period 1985–1997. The 'new orthodoxy' adopted two discernable governing principles: first, a retreat from carceral strategies based on the belief that institutionalization and the 'official processing of juvenile delinquents' (Bottoms and Dignan, 2004: 33) was both harmful to youth and conducive to establishing more long-term criminal tendencies in young offenders; second, the endorsement of the 'age-crime curve' (see Rutherford, 2002) – an assertion that the majority of young offenders naturally 'grow out of crime' over time. The CDA was facilitated by the Audit Commission's report on the youth justice system, which found that much of the £1bn spent annually on processing young offenders 'was wasted through lengthy and ineffective court procedures' (Muncie, 1999: 150). The Audit Commission (1996: 96) recommended a shift to preventative policy, concluding: 'the present arrangements are failing young people – who are not being guided away from offending to constructive activities'. Jones (2001) argues the 1996 audit influenced the rise to prominence of ASBOs as mechanism of legal regulation in Britain and Wales.

For Coleman (2005: 133), ASBOs and ABCs converge under the auspices of 'entrepreneurial urbanism': hybrid public/private regulatory projects negotiated between businesses and state agencies that wield control over the 'normative-cultural dimensions' extending beyond criminality. When youth skateboarders dodge the gaze of cameras, or when working class youth gather outside malls, these actions are met with fines, bans, and curfews. It is at the antagonistic intersection of entrepreneurial urbanism and youth cultural expression that the problematization of hoodies is articulated (Burney, 2005; Crawford, 2008; Pearson, 2006; Walsh, 2002). Even though ASBOs are mechanisms of legal regulation, they depend on extra-governmental partnerships to be applied. State agencies must extend themselves through public/private partnerships and spaces (Button, 2003; Crawford, 2006; Raco, 2003). Bluewater is an example of private regulation in a quasi-public space, which leads to post hoc forms of state agency regulation in the application of ASBOs (see Crawford, 2008; Wakefield, 2008).

Problematizing Hoodies and the Bluewater Ban

In this section, we explain how volatile moralization emerged where long-term regulatory efforts aimed at youth were perceived to be in a state of breakdown. We draw from two data sources. The first data source consists of newspaper stories in the mainstream newspaper media. We sampled six of the most widely circulated national newspapers in Britain: *The Times*, the *Guardian*, the *Express*, the *Daily Mail*, the *Sun*, and the *Mirror*. These sources were sampled to include coverage in quality broadsheets, middle-of-the-road tabloids, and redtop tabloids (Critcher, 2003). We do not present a detailed content or discourse analysis. We illustrate how the dominant discourse in the mainstream press and political debate was countered in the context of a web of media relations and social activism. Legislation was enacted even in the absence of consensus, which is important to analyses of moralization of youth because it demonstrates how folk devils and their supporters fight back, but also how these counter claims can be reversed.

Primary definition

On 12 May 2005, the day following the Bluewater ban, the *Express* ran front-page coverage under a headline reading, 'Shopping centre bans hoody yobs: Britain's biggest mall has had enough of menacing gangs' (Fagge, 2005). The article frames the Bluewater ban in the wider context of a moral decline in youth behavior: 'prowling gangs of "hoody" hooligans who plague our high streets and malls'; 'yobs who deliberately strike fear by skulking behind hooded tops'; and 'gangs of thugs have plagued the venue … making shopping a terrifying experience'. The following day, the *Mirror* (13 May 2005) proclaimed that, 'the sight of youths kitted out in [hoodies] strikes fear in law-abiding citizens'; 'in their Grim Reaper-style headgear, "hoodies" have become the reviled and feared bogeymen of modern Britain' (Roberts and Allen, 2005). The *Daily Mail* (18 May 2005) invoked the imagery of 'The feral gangs who rule our streets' (Seamark, 2005) to characterize youth who don hooded tops in public space. And the 'hoodies' signifier was adopted to denote a range of deviance and crime: '"Hoody" thug mugs pregnant woman in front of shoppers' (Ginn, 2005), 'Evil hoody battered me black and blue' (Hamilton, 2005), 'Fond farewells … and then a vicious attack by hoodies' (Moriarty, 2005), and 'Hoodies' rampage on train' (*Sunday Mirror*, 2005).

Following the Bluewater ban, Prime Minister Tony Blair and his deputy, John Prescott, laid claim to the problematic nature of youth behavior. Speaking in support of the ban, Blair argued that 'People are rightly fed-up with street corner and shopping centre thugs' (Fagge and Chapman, 2005), and he openly supported the banning of hooded tops (*The Guardian*, 12 May 2005). Prescott, too, endorsed the ban, reinforcing his support by recollecting a personal encounter with a group of 'hoodies' when he was surrounded and 'menaced' at a motorway service station; he reported that it was 'very intimidating' to be confronted by 'ten people wearing hoods – you know, these covers with hoods on' (Fagge and Chapman, 2005). The claims made by Blair and Prescott were articulated in the context of an established governmental discourse concerning anti-social behavior invoked in government rhetoric since the introduction of the ASBA.

Deviance amplification

Emerging from the initial problematization of hoodies, newspaper coverage amplified the severity of the problem by linking hoodies to a range of crimes. For instance, under a headline reading, 'Hunt for hoodies', the *News of the World* (10 July 2005) reported that, 'a teenager may be blinded in one eye after an unprovoked attack by hoodies'. When Phil Carroll, a building site engineer, was attacked outside his house and left 'fighting for his life' in a coma (Seamark, 2005), newspaper coverage identified a 'feral, drunken and abusive hoodie gang' as the culprit. Three days later, the *Daily Mail* ran a front-page story about Alan Irwing, a 72-year-old pensioner who was beaten to death on his doorstep, adding: 'the area had been plagued by gangs of youngsters wearing "hoodies"'. In the span of two months, the repertoire of deviance attributed to hoodies included the rape of an 11-year-old girl (Sulaiman, 2005), underage drinking and sex (Mackay, 16 May 2005), murder (Taylor, 2005), 'binge-drinking' (Fagge and Chapman, 2005), and, somewhat contradictory, a '"Hoodies" nude riot' (Express, 2005b).

The escalating coverage on hoodies exemplifies what Hall et al. (1978) conceptualize as a signification spiral, which designates the symbolic escalation of harm posed by deviants through a process that inflates the volume and magnitude of deviance attributed to signifying categories. This signification spiral is demonstrated by the newspaper media's conflation of hoodies and 'happy slapping': an ambush-style physical attack – sometimes a slap, but variously a punch, stab, or attack with a weapon, possibly in conjunction with a robbery – which is recorded on a hand-held video device for the amusement of the attackers or distribution via the Internet and mobile telephony networks. Happy slapping entered the inventory of deviance through the claims-making activities of primary definers and 'experts'. The Deputy Prime Minister, recounting his confrontation with a gang of 'hoodies', proclaimed: 'not only did they come with these kinds of uniforms but they had a movie camera to take a film of any such incident' (Fagge and Chapman, 2005). The 'expert' opinions of crime-control officers were drawn upon in efforts to link happy slaps to hoodies:

> Police have now identified so-called 'hoody' culture as a major concern, as yobs lurk in our streets and shopping malls with their faces hidden behind hoods and baseball caps ... innocent members of the public are being targeted in the latest craze for 'happy slapping' in which children randomly attack complete strangers just for fun. (Knapp, 2005)

According to Hall et al. (1978), signification spirals precipitate the symbolic amplification of deviance across certain 'thresholds' of societal tolerance. Primary indicators of threshold breach in the hoodies discourse came in the form of increasing calls for regulatory action vis-à-vis the growing perception of an 'out-of-control' situation. The repetition of nomenclature including 'feral', 'yob culture', 'running riot', and 'culture of disrespect' attests to the perception of a widespread breakdown in the behavioral code, summarized by Lord Stevens (2005), ex-chief of the Metropolitan Police:

> After terrorism, the biggest single crime crisis facing this country is juvenile yobbery. It is a raging social cancer tearing away at Britain – but currently we are treating this terrible sickness with the moral and social equivalent of a sticking plaster ... I've been a policeman for 43 years, and have never seen such fear and helplessness about juvenile crime in our communities.

Before long, news sources called for new regulatory responses. Demands such as 'hooded thugs and happy slappers should get longer sentences than other criminals, a former senior policeman said yesterday' (Roberts, 23 May 2005), calls for 'compulsory national community service' (*Express*, 2005a), and a 'nationwide ban' of hoodies (Fagge and Chapman, 2005) followed.

The amplification of the harm posed by hoodies involved numerous converging factors. While the Bluewater ban was not the first prohibition of hooded tops or baseball caps in a UK shopping precinct, previous actions in Essex, Hampshire, Cornwall, and Devon (Coleman, 2005) did not lead to the level of coverage and debate that followed the Bluewater ban. One feature that was absent from earlier clothing regulations was the lack of concerted attempt by primary definers to articulate the ban in the context of wider social problems. Although governmental claims contributed to the intensification of concern – and indicated attempts to seek consent for their proposed expansion of regulatory measures under the auspices of the ASBA – the newspaper media further imbued the hoodies signifier with a dimension of risk. Although it is important not to deny the seriousness of the real crimes and acts of violence reported by the media – which the term 'amplification' may appear to do – it is nevertheless justified to use the term amplification because of the array of unrelated crimes and offenses that are attributed to a singular subject position with little evidence.

'Fighting Back' against Primary Definition

In this section, we examine forms of contestation that emerged in opposition to the dominant hoodies discourse to empirically demonstrate how folk devils and their supporters fight back (McRobbie, 1994). Sociologists of risk, such as O'Malley (2006), contend that problematization engenders contestation among targets of regulation. Such contestation often takes forms that appear unorganized (Moore, 2007), as is the case with many of the examples discussed below. Opportunities to participate in the production of media messages have increased, due in part to technological means such as the Internet and the proliferation of desktop publishing software (Downey and Fenton, 2003). The increasing array of 'interpretive agents who are constructing our view of the world' (Vattimo, 2004: 17) weaken media claims to objectivity, and authoritative versions of events give way to numerous interpretations.

Problematization shifted somewhat from youth socialization to the Government's youth regulation policies. We provide an illustration of a heterogeneous oppositional movement that emerged following the Bluewater ban and that gained the attention of mainstream journalists. We also draw on data from Internet news publications and forums to show how alternative media enabled marginalized communities to enter into the debate about hoodies. The influence of diverse claims in the mainstream media, oppositional claims making outside the press, and alternative media messages combined to precipitate a re-articulation of the hoodies discourse. However, it was not enough to halt the continuation of attempts to regulate youth through legislative activity.

Problematizing state typifications: Counter claims and alternative frames

The *Daily Mail* has long been associated with moralization as a standard mode of reporting (Hill, 2002). Following the Bluewater ban, coverage in the *Daily Mail*, instead of individualizing moral culpability through the hoodies signifier, invoked youth transgression as a platform from which to criticize Tony Blair's government. Playing on the language of Blair's 'Reform and Respect' agenda, the *Mail on Sunday*'s 'Respect? Surely you abolished it, Mr. Blair' (Hitchens, 2005) attributed causality for anti-social behavior to an ideological shortfall inherent to Left-liberal governance: 'The liberal Left have been on a long march through this country, destroying old-fashioned authority. They believe deference and respect are wrong and bad and repressive.' Under a headline reading, 'When will our politicians wake up to the fact that it's THEY who have done more than anyone to create this culture of yobbery?' (Stevens, 2005), it was argued, 'disorder and threatening behaviour are a modern plague, and whole communities are under siege from crime and yobbery'. The problematization of New Labour in the *Daily Mail* was attributed to a retreat from authoritarianism on behalf of the liberal Left that is responsible for 'the destruction of the family' (ibid.). By holding the Government culpable for the erosion of 'traditional' family values, including responsibility toward others and the behavior of British youth, the dominant discourse was countered by retaining the hoodies signifier. The newspaper subverted primary definitions to implicate New Labour as morally misaligned with public opinion.

The *Guardian* attacked the initial framing of hoodies as an attempt to draw attention away from the failure of the State's education and social order policies: 'the new concern for boys' underachievement, hoodies and chavs parallel fears of a black rap culture … like "gangstas", the "dumbed down" are turning away from learning' (Ainley, 2005). At the same time, the *Guardian* remained reflexive about the role of the media: 'the latest moral panic over hoodies echoes the last one over chavs … Manufactured moral panic, or last stand of the lost tribe of the white working class?' (Ainley, 2005). As McRobbie and Thornton (1995) contend, since the early 1990s 'moral panic' has entered the lexicon of mainstream society and media. Hay (1995) commented that the standardization of moral panics as ordinary modes of news reporting has heralded in the age of the 'reflexive moral panic'. Media opposition to the dominant discourse was buttressed by enlisting 'experts' to counter the vilifying claims. Angela McRobbie was recruited as an expert sociologist by the *Guardian* in the interests of normalizing hoodies: 'nowadays it is the norm among young people to flag up their music and cultural preferences in this way, hence the adoption of the hoodie by boys across the boundaries of age, ethnicity and class' (McLean, 2005).

Perhaps sensing the opportunity to align with a growing tide of populist dissent against representations of youths, the leader of the UK Conservative Party, David Cameron delivered a 'hug a hoodie' speech to the Centre for Social Justice on 9 July 2006. Cameron's speech sought to undermine New Labour's approach to youth regulation and presented an alternative interpretation of hooded clothing:

> Because the fact is that the hoodie is a response to a problem, not a problem in itself. We – the people in suits – often see hoodies as aggressive, the uniform of a rebel army of young gangsters. But, for young people, hoodies are often more defensive than offensive. They're a way to stay invisible in the street. In a dangerous environment the best thing to do is keep your head down, blend in, don't stand out … For some, the hoodie represents all that's wrong about youth culture in Britain today. For me, adult society's response to the hoodie shows how far we are from finding the long-term answers to put things right.

Fighting back for folk devils

McRobbie (1994: 111) acknowledges that – once the sole torch-bearer for the defense of 'moral minorities' – the academic is now bolstered and even surpassed by 'a new band of experts' in the form of skilled representatives from pressure groups and voluntary organizations. Below we focus on how the dominant framing of hoodies was countered by activist groups, making no claims about the success of these attempts at fighting back. In 2005, attempts to deflect a general demonization of youth were made by organizations such as the British Youth Council (*The Guardian*, 13 May 2005a), the Children's Society Charity (*The Mirror*, 20 May, 2005a), and the charity NCH (*Mirror*, 3 June 2005) who went on record to decry the ban. The British Youth Council commissioned a report that found youths increasingly alienated by negative portrayals, and they circulated a press release recommending fairer media coverage, and greater political involvement opportunities for youth. The Children's Rights Alliance for England (CRAE) also raised questions about human rights violations.

Among organized attempts to counter negative typifications of youth through the hoodies signifier, the renowned subversive artists Gilbert and George produced *Hooded*, a work of art depicting the artists standing alongside two hooded youth (Kennedy, 2005). Two headmasters introduced attire codes including hooded tops as official school uniform (Harper, 2005; 20 May 2005) – each was quoted opposing the government-endorsed clothing bans. The most direct example of successful contestation involved the Scottish Socialist Party (SSP) and the subsidiary Scottish Socialist Youth (SSY) (see 'Young hoodies fight ban with street protest', O'Kane, 2005). In response to plans by businesses of the Eastgate Centre in Inverness to follow suit with Bluewater, SSY volunteers canvassed stores in the mall and publicized a Saturday demonstration against the ban. On 2 June, the mall released a statement retracting their plans, a decision the SSY attribute to their pressure. The Lambeth and Southwark Respect Coalition – a London-based activist group – coordinated a similar action at the Elephant and Castle mall in London. Although they failed to prevent the ban, they attracted the support of local community groups and formed an allegiance with the civil-liberties organization ASBO Concern.

Contestation involved the use of alternative media. While 'mass' media are regularly conceptualized as a monolith in analyses of public policy formation, it is important to consider texts that fall on the periphery of customary conceptions of the 'mass' media. Dominant, state-sponsored claims may be countered, or bypassed by particular efforts originating in micro, niche, or alternative media (Couldry and Corran, 2002; McRobbie, 1994) or through an engagement with the 'mass' media by organized groups who seek to subvert dominant discourses.

Dedicated communicative networks condensed around hoodies. The libertarian community 'libcom', for example, opened a forum dedicated to hoodies that yielded a critical discourse negotiating the politics of negative youth depictions and was subject to over 5000 views. The popular 'flikr', an online photograph hosting site, featured a 'hoody moral panic' area where the public could upload positive photographs of hooded clothing to stimulate political discussion. The 'G-Rime' musician, Lady Sovereign, began an online 'save the hoodie' campaign, inviting viewers to sign a petition opposing the ban that Sovereign would present to the Prime Minister. Although this coincided with the imminent release of Sovereign's 'Hoodie' single, the petition received over 1500 signatures and attracted attention in the mainstream and 'alternative' media. Collectively, these strategies of contestation managed to partially shift the onus of problematization from youth transgression to governmental regulation. However, while studies of moralization have hitherto been concerned to demonstrate how contestation may be enacted, scholars interested in moralization have not pressed further to explore state agency responses to counter claims making.

The Reform and Respect Agenda

The response of state agencies can be understood in two forms: a symbolic alignment with wider sentiments to legitimate further regulatory legislation, and the deployment of existing regulatory measures to intervene directly in the behavior of those failing to self-regulate. On 17 May 2005, six days after the Bluewater ban went into effect, New Labour's 'Reform and Respect Agenda' was announced in the Queen's Address at the State Opening of Parliament. The Prime Minister legitimized the agenda with reference to anti-social behavior: 'It is time to reclaim the streets for the decent majority'; and later, cited in the 'Respect Action Plan': 'I am pleased that an ASBO is now a household expression – synonymous with tackling anti-social behaviour' (Home Office, 2006b). The agenda included 45 bills and five drafts that introduced new measures to regulate anti-social behavior. In January 2006, the agenda was expanded to include additional regulatory measures, including fines for the parents of 'anti-social children', a new mandate allowing the judiciary to ban people from their own dwelling places for recidivist anti-social activity, and the introduction of 'on the spot' fines levied by patrolling police. The 'Respect Task Force' – tasked with delivering the Respect Agenda – was launched in January 2006 by Home Secretary Charles Clarke with this address:

> Tackling disrespect in our society is an absolute priority for the Government and this new task force will play a vital role in improving our communities and the lives of people in them. From bad behaviour in schools and poor parenting to binge drinking and noisy neighbours, disrespect for others can take many forms. … We all have the right to live our lives free from harassment. But with those rights come responsibilities, and we all need to play a part in tackling disrespect and unacceptable behaviour.

Regardless of whether New Labour acted to stimulate the hoodies discourse, the agenda's political efficacy lay in its linkage with an established discourse of anti-social behavior, and stylized representations of declining behavioral standards among the polis – youths in particular. Language employed by state spokespersons to legitimize the new legislation drew on the typifications of youth behavior in the media following the Bluewater action. While the long-term project of morally regulating youth hinges upon a call for rational risk subjects to self-regulate, the hoodies discourse is indicative of a temporary breakdown of moral regulation, whereby the agency of youth came under scrutiny and subsequent regulation.[2] Claims making by politicians and law and order officials ascribed blame to youth in terms of an 'irresponsible' retreat into a 'culture of disrespect'.

Discussion and Conclusion

The individualization of harm has thus far been conceptualized in moral panic theory through signification of 'folk devils'. The folk devil concept, as 'unambiguously unfavorable symbols' (Cohen, 1972: 41), fails to account for the contingency by which harm becomes attributed to individual bodies in urban spaces. The temporary inversion of the dialectic that operates in the moralization in everyday life involves a conceptual shift from individualized discourses governing responsible and ethical self-conduct against a collective dimension of harm to collectivizing discourses that individualize responsibility for harm (Hier, 2008). The Bluewater ban opened possibilities for the articulation of familiar, cultural artifacts and the very *mise-en-scène* of urban spaces with a symbolic dimension of harm. The symbolic dimension of harm articulated with pre-existing discourses of risky behavior through media sensationalism, retaining as an element certain signifiers originating in representations of commonplace phenomena of the cultural realm (e.g. hooded clothing, groups of congregating youths). Problematization of youth behavior thus involved the inscription of a dimension of harm into established cultural texts, which came to represent a range of risks associated with contemporary urban spaces in Britain. The hoodie emerged as a dialectical articulation of risk and harm in the context of a series of highly recognizable cultural motifs to negotiate the management of risks in localized settings.

Arguments to the effect that folk devils can contest regulatory efforts owe much to a conception of political power as the aggregate of dispersed forces. Folk devils and their supporters can and do 'fight back'; the opportunities to participate in and subvert problematization are opening up to more variegated publics. Although the contestation we discussed above was subverted by New Labour's 'Reform and Respect Agenda', these efforts and their ramifications for understanding moral panic should not be discounted. We have also shown that the volatility of moralization hinges upon the amenability of cultural representations to link up with pre-existing, or emergent, themes of risk (also see Hier, 2008). Such representations are tied to long-term political and moral projects, and they are not simply irrational, isolated episodic articulations.

A critical insight we draw from the integration of the studies of moral panic and moral regulation is that episodes of moral panic involve a unique political dynamic of 'double problematization'. While moral panic scholars focus primarily on the reasons for and implications of sensationalized representations of folk devils, they pay less attention to the fact that moral panics also involve problematization of existing regulatory measures. Claims, counter-claims, and resistance represent struggles over the ascription of blame, but also simultaneous struggles over the proper regulatory responses to matters of crime and law-and-order.

Notes

1. We conceptualize 'the moral' in terms of a flexible set of normative understandings about what is right and wrong that operates through interactive circuits. Circuits do not determine but rather exercise an interactive effectivity with other circuits including economics and politics. We are interested in examining the various ways that moral phenomena are inscribed in and modified through everyday ethical practices that intersect with political and governmental practices and processes of self-formation (see Hier, 2002b, no date). Waiton (2008), by contrast, works with an assumed moral domain that cannot account for shifting forms of moralization.
2. Existing measures, combined with those introduced under the auspices of the Reform and Respect Agenda, have been brought to bear on specific youth behavior problematized through the hoodies signifier. To enforce this increasing array of conditions, ASBOs and ABCs are supplemented by Individual Support Orders (ISOs), Parenting Orders, Dispersal Orders and Injunctions, which Crawford (2009a) argues target not only youth but also their support networks. The breaching of ASBOs and other orders results, in many cases, with immediate detention for youths. Common to each of the orders mentioned above are the imposition of restrictions on actions, movements through space, and even gestures (also see Millie, 2008).

References

Ainley P (2005) Open your arms. *Guardian*, 14 June. Available at: http://www.guardian.co.uk/education/2005/jun/14/furthereducation.socialexclusion.

Audit Commission (1996) *Misspent Youth*. London: Audit Commission.

BBC News (2006, July 10). 'Cameron Hoodie speech in full' Available at http://news.bbc.co.uk/2/hi/uk_news/politics/5166498.stm (retrieved March 6, 2011).

Bottoms A and Dignan J (2004) Youth justice in Great Britain. *Crime and Justice* 31: 21–183.

Burney E (2005) *Making People Behave: Anti-Social Behavior, Politics and Policy*. Cullompton: Willan.

Button M (2003) Private security and the policing of quasi-public space. *International Journal of the Sociology of Law* 31(3): 227–237.

Cohen S (1972) *Folk Devils and Moral Panics*. London: MacGibbon & Kee.

Coleman R (2005) Surveillance in the city: Primary definition and urban spatial order. *Crime, Media, Culture* 1(2): 131–148.

Couldry N and Corran J (2002) *Contesting Media Power: Alternative Media in a Networked World*. Toronto: Rowman & Rowman.

Crawford A (2006) Networked governance and the post-regulatory state. *Theoretical Criminology* 10(4): 449–479.

Crawford A (2008) Dispersal powers and the symbolic role of anti-social behavior legislation. *Modern Law Review* 71(5): 753–784.

Crawford A (2009a) Governing through anti-social behavior: Regulatory challenges to criminal justice. *British Journal of Criminology* 49(6): 810–831.

Crawford A (2009b) Criminalizing sociability through anti-social behavior legislation: Dispersal powers, young people and the police. *Youth Justice* 9(1): 5–26.

Crawford A and Lister S (2007) *The Use and Impact of Dispersal Orders: Sticking Plasters and Wake-Up Calls*. Bristol: Policy Press.

Critcher C (2002) Media, government and moral panic: The politics of paedophilia in Britain 2000–1. *Journalism Studies* 3(4): 521–535.

Critcher C (2003) *Moral Panics and the Media*. London: Open University Press.

Critcher C (2008) Moral panic analysis: Past, present, future. *Social Compass* 2(4): 1127–1144.

Critcher C (2009) Widening the focus: Moral panics as moral regulation. *British Journal of Criminology* 49(1): 17–34.

DeYoung M (1998) Another look at moral panics: The case of satanic day care centres. *Deviant Behaviour* 19(3): 257–275.

Doran N (2008) Decoding 'encoding' moral panics, media practices and Marxist presuppositions. *Theoretical Criminology* 12(2): 191–221.

Downey J and Fenton N (2003) New media, counter publicity and the public sphere. *New Media & Society* 5(2): 185–202.

Express (2005a) Slapping craze must end. *Express*, 21 May, p. 12.

Express (2005b) 'Hoodies' nude riot. *Express*, 2 July, p. 31.

Fagge N (2005) Shopping centre bans hoody yobs: Britain's biggest mall has had enough of menacing gangs. *Express*, 12 May, pp. 1, 7.

Fagge N and Chapman J (2005) Ban hooded thugs from our streets. *Express*, 13 May, pp. 1, 4.

Fionda J (2006) *Devils and Angels: Youth Policy and Crime*. Oxford: Hart Publishing.

Gallagher P (2005a) Buys in the hood: Massive surge in business at shops mall that outlawed hoodies. *Mirror*, 20 May, pp. 8–9.

Garland D (2008) On the concept of moral panic. *Crime, Media and Culture* 4(1): 9–30.

Ginn K (2005) 'Hoody' thug mugs pregnant woman in front of shoppers. *Daily Mail*, 15 June, p. 13.

Goode E and Ben-Yehuda N (1994) *Moral Panics: The Social Construction of Deviance*. London: Blackwell.

Guardian (2005, May 12). 'Blair pledges crackdown on yobs'. Available at www.guardian.co. uk/uk/2005/may/12/politics.society (retrieved August 5, 2010).

Hall S, Critcher C, Jefferson T, Clarke J and Robert B (1978) *Policing the Crisis: Mugging, the State, and Law and Order*. London: Macmillan.

Hamilton M (2005) Evil hoody battered me black and blue. *News of the World*, 15 May, p. 1.

Harper J (2005) Head: Hoodies for school uniform. *Sunday Mirror*, 15 May, p. 40.

Hay C (1995) Mobilization through interpellation: James Bulger, juvenile crime and the construction of a moral panic. *Social and Legal Studies* 4(3): 197–223.

Hier S (2002a) Conceptualizing moral panic through a moral economy of harm. *Critical Sociology* 28(3): 311–334.

Hier S (2002b) Raves, risks and the ecstasy panic: A case study in the subversive nature of moral regulation. *Canadian Journal of Sociology* 27(1): 33–57.

Hier S (2003) Risk and panic in late-modernity: Implications of the converging sites of social anxiety. *British Journal of Sociology* 54(1): 3–20.

Hier S (2008) Thinking beyond moral panic: Risk, responsibility and the politics of moralization. *Theoretical Criminology* 12(2): 173–190.

Hier S (ed.) (2011) *Moral Panic and the Politics of Anxiety*. London: Routledge.

Hier S (no date) Linking the sociologies of moral panic and moral regulation. Unpublished manuscript.

Hill A (2002) Acid house and Thatcherism: Noise, the mob, and the English countryside. *British Journal of Sociology* 53(1): 89–105.

Hitchens P (2005) Respect? Surely you abolished it, Mr. Blair. *Mail on Sunday*, 22 May, p. 2.

Home Office (1997) *No More Excuses: A New Approach to Tackling Youth Crime in England and Wales*. Cm. 3809. London: The Stationery Office.

Home Office (2003) *A Guide to Anti-Social Behaviour Orders and Acceptable Behaviour Contracts*. London: Home Office.

Home Office (2006a) *Tackling Anti-Social Behaviour: 2005 Survey Results*. London: Home Office.

Home Office (2006b) *Respect Action Plan*. Ref. 272299. London: Home Office.

Hunt A (1997) Moral panic and moral language in the media. *British Journal of Sociology* 48(4): 629–648.

Hunt A (1999) *Governing Morals: A Social History of Moral Regulation*. Cambridge: Cambridge University Press.

Hunt A (2003) Risk and moralization in everyday life. In: Ericson R, Doyle A (eds) *Risk and Morality*. Toronto: University of Toronto Press, 165–192.

Jenkins P (1992) *Intimate Enemies: Moral Panics in Contemporary Great Britain*. New York: Aldine de Gruyter.

Jones D (2001) 'Misjudged youth': A critique of the Audit Commission's report on youth justice. *British Journal of Criminology* 41(2): 362–380.

Kennedy M (2005) Hoodie art unveiled Gilbert and George's new fashion statement. *Guardian*, 23 May, Home Pages, p. 1.

Knapp M (2005) Living in fear of ferals. *Sunday Express*, 22 May, p. 31.

Lakeman G (2005b) Hoodie 2-shoes. *Mirror*, 20 May, p. 9.

Mackay C (2005) Battered to death: Thugs use planks in birthday beating. *Mirror*, Scottish Edition, 16 May, p. 24.

McLean G (2005) In the hood: On the meaning of the hoodie. *Guardian*, 13 May, G2, p. 2.

McRobbie A (1994) Folk devils fight back. *New Left Review* 203(January–February): 107–116.

McRobbie A and Thornton S (1995) Rethinking 'moral panic' for multi-mediated social worlds. *British Journal of Sociology* 46(4): 559–574.

Millie A (2008) Anti-social behavior, behavioral expectations and an urban aesthetic. *British Journal of Criminology* 48(3): 379–394.

Mirror (2005) Now head bans kids in hoodies. *Mirror*, 3 June, p. 7.

Moore D (2007) *Criminal Artefacts: Governing Drugs and Users*. Vancouver: University of British Columbia Press.

Moore D and Valverde M (2000) Maidens at risk: 'Date rape drugs' and the formation of hybrid risk knowledges. *Economy & Society* 29(4): 514–531.

Moriarty R (2005) Fond farewells … and then a vicious attack by hoodies. *Express*, 18 May, p. 2.

Muncie J (1999) Institutionalized intolerance: Youth justice and the 1998 Crime and Disorder Act. *Critical Social Policy* 19(2): 147–175.

News of the World (2005) Hunt for hoodies. *News of the World*, 10 July, p. 1.

O'Kane R (2005) Young hoodies fight ban with street protest. *Express*, 2 June, p. 32.

O'Malley P (2006) *Risk, Uncertainty and Government*. London: Glasshouse Press.

Pearson G (2006) Disturbing continuities: 'Peaky blinders' to 'hoodies'. *Criminal Justice Matters* 65(1): 6–7.

Raco M (2003) Remaking place and securitising space: Urban regeneration and the strategies, tactics and practices of policing in the UK. *Urban Studies* 40(9): 1869–1887.

Roberts B (2005) Reclaim our streets: Hoodies jail plea. *Mirror*, 23 May, p. 28.

Roberts B and Allen V (2005) Reclaim our streets: Hoodies and baddies. *Mirror*, 13 May, pp. 8–9.

Rohloff A (2008) Moral panics as decivilizing processes: Towards an Eliasian approach. *New Zealand Journal of Sociology* 23(1): 66–76.

Rohloff A and Wright S (2010) Moral panic and social theory: Beyond the heuristic. *Current Sociology* 58(3): 403–419.

Rutherford A (2002) *Growing Out of Crime: The New Era*. Winchester: Waterside.

Seamark M (2005) The feral gangs who rule our streets. *Daily Mail*, 18 May, p. 1.

Simester A and Von Hirsch A (2006) Regulating offensive conduct through two-step prohibitions. In: Von Hirsch A, Simester A (eds) *Incivilities: Regulating Offensive Behavior*. Oxford: Hart Publishing, 173–194.

Squires P (2008) The politics of anti-social behavior. *British Politics* 3(3): 300–323.

Stevens L (2005) Lord Stevens has the cure for yobs. *News of the World*, 22 May, Leader, p. 1.

Sulaiman T (2005) Girls' rape 'filmed by teenagers on mobile'. *The Times*, 18 June, p. 2.

Sunday Mirror (2005) 'Hoodies' rampage on train. *Sunday Mirror*, 12 June, p. 28.

Taylor, B. (2005, May 21) 'Beaten to death on his doorstep'. Daily Mail, p. 1.

Thompson K (1998) *Moral Panics*. London & New York: Routledge.

Thornton S (1994) Moral panic, the media and British rave culture. In: Ross A, Rose T (eds) *Microphone Fiends: Youth Music, Youth Culture*. London: Routledge, 176–192.

Ungar S (2001) Moral panic versus the risk society: The implications of the changing sites of social anxiety. *British Journal of Sociology* 52(2): 271–292.

Vattimo G (2004) *Nihilism & Emancipation: Ethics, Politics and Law*. New York: Columbia University Press.

Waiton S (2008) *The Politics of Antisocial Behavior: Amoral Panics*. London: Routledge.

Wakefield A (2008) Private policing: A view from the mall. *Public Administration* 86(3): 659–678.

Walby K and Spencer D (2011) How emotions matter to moral panics. In: Hier S (ed.) *Moral Panic and the Politics of Anxiety*. London: Routledge, Forthcoming.

Walsh C (2002) Curfews: No more hanging around. *Youth Justice* 2(2): 70–81.

White M (2005) PM attacks yob culture and pledges to help bring back respect. *Guardian*, 13 May. Available at: http://www.guardian.co.uk/politics/2005/may/13/ukcrime.immigrationpolicy.

Young J (1971) *The Drugtakers: The Social Meaning of Drug Use*. London: McGibbon & Kee.

Young J (2009) Moral panic: Its origins in resistance, ressentiment and the translation of fantasy into reality. *British Journal of Criminology* 49(1). 4–16.

Biographies

Sean P. Hier is Associate Professor and Chair, Department of Sociology, University of Victoria. Recent books include *Moral Panic and the Politics of Anxiety* (ed., Routledge, 2011) and *Panoptic Dreams: Streetscape Video Surveillance in Canada* (UBC Press, 2010).

Dan Lett is a PhD candidate, Department of Sociology, University of Victoria. His recent publications include an article in the *Canadian Journal of Sociology* (2010, with S. Hier and K. Walby) and *Racism and Justice: Critical Dialogue on the Politics of Identity, Inequality, and Change* (ed., 2009, Fernwood Press, with S. Hier and B. Singh Bolaria).

Kevin Walby is an Assistant Professor, Department of Sociology, University of Victoria. Peer reviewed articles include *Antipode* (2011, with R. Lippert), *International Sociology* (2011, with S. Hier), *Punishment & Society* (2011, with J. Piché), *Social Movement Studies* (2011, with J. Monaghan), *Qualitative Research* (2010), the *British Journal of Criminology* (2010, with J. Piché), and *Criminology and Criminal Justice* (2010, with N. Carrier). He is co-editor of *Emotions Matter* with A. Hunt and D. Spencer (forthcoming, University of Toronto Press). He is the prisoners' struggles editor for the *Journal of Prisoners on Prisons*.

André Smith is an Assistant Professor, Department of Sociology, University of Victoria. He has interests in the areas of aging, mental health, deviance, and discourse analysis. Smith has worked on research investigating the social construction of psychiatric disorders and the pharmaceutical discourse on aging and dementia. He has contributed articles to the *Journal of Deviant Behavior* and *Dementia: The International Journal of Social Research and Practice*.

[11]

THE SOCIAL CONSTRUCTION OF CRIME AND CRIME CONTROL

NICOLE HAHN RAFTER

A number of disciplines have been deeply affected in recent years by constructionism, an approach that analyzes the processes by which social information is produced, disseminated, "verified," and "disconfirmed." Criminal justice too has developed a constructionist tradition, albeit mainly through attracting scholars from other fields into its terrain. This article traces the accumulation of the constructionist tradition within criminal justice by examining work in four areas: social histories of criminal justice practice and theory; critical criminology; research on the victimization of females; and feminist theory about the contribution of criminal justice to understandings of gender. If the constructionist approach continues to develop within criminal justice, it may lay the basis for a sociology of knowledge in the field.

Applied to criminal justice, the social constructionist approach investigates how the facts of crime and crime control are produced. Asking how we arrive at knowledge within the field, it explores relationships among social structures, law, criminal acts, and perception. This type of inquiry focuses on the origins and effects of social theory, social movements, and social practices, aiming at understanding not *how* to control crime but rather *why* we engage in different types of crime control at various times and places. Constructionism is simultaneously historical, political, and epistemological, seeking to explicate the interplay between specific circumstances and the meanings they engender.[1]

In recent years, the constructionist approach has thrived in other fields, notably cultural anthropology, history, literary criticism, some areas of political science and psychology, and sociology. Criminal justice lags behind for several interrelated reasons. One lies with its dominant professional model, which ties it to agency needs and the solution of immediate, practical problems. Another rests with the current mood of political conservatism, which values outcome-assessment over critical inquiry. A third is the field's adherence to a fairly narrow, scientific positivism that conceives of social facts as inert and independent, like fragments of ancient pottery, and that instructs social scientists to dig up, reassemble, and evaluate these "facts" without reference to the civilization that produced them.[2] Criminal justice has also been blocked from considering the broader, more theoretical issues of constructionism by its lack of historical perspective and by the ethno- and androcentric biases that permeate the field.

Despite these impediments, constructionism has evolved sufficiently to constitute, at the very least, a valuable supplement to traditional approaches to criminal justice. It enables us to relativize practices usually taken for granted, to problematize received wisdom, and to historicize otherwise unquestioned assumptions. As indicated by Starr's (1987) essay on "The Sociology of Official Statistics," which takes "statistics [and] their sources as an *object* of analysis" (p. 7; emphasis in original), the constructionist approach can lead to a greater self-consciousness and epistemological sophistication about what we do. It is the first step toward a sociology of knowledge.[3] Furthermore, constructionism enables us to distinguish academic from administrative criminal justice: Instead of defining the discipline as a mere creature of the system, it expands our work to include questions about social control and relationships between criminal justice and the broader society. Finally, this type of inquiry can improve our understanding of the nature of the criminal justice professions, at present one of the vaguest and least analyzed aspects of the discipline.

In what follows, I trace the emergence of constructionism within criminal justice on four fronts: social histories of criminal justice practice and theory; critical criminology; work on the victimization of females; and recent feminist theory about the role played by criminal justice in our interpretation of gender. The four categories are not mutually exclusive, nor do they fully cover constructionist contributions.[4] However, they suffice to give an overview of the development of the constructionist tradition within criminal justice.

SOCIAL HISTORIES

The social history of criminal justice began with stories, often quite simple accounts of past practices. Although most of these were unanalytical narratives, some indirectly raised constructionist issues. For example, studies of the execution of Black men for allegedly raping White women encouraged questions about the nature of punishment: Was it merely a response to crime, or might it also reflect and reinforce racial stereotypes?

The social history of criminal justice became more sophisticated with the advent of labeling theory. Becker's (1963) momentous words, "social groups create deviance by making the rules whose infraction constitutes deviance"

(p. 9), had the effect of a starting gun at a race track: Historical sociologists took off in a rush to discover where the rules came from. The next few years brought us *Symbolic Crusade*, Gusfield's (1963) analysis of the social struggles that produced the temperance movement and Prohibition, and *Wayward Puritans*, Erikson's (1966) account of how the Puritans' efforts to maintain their identity generated waves of deviance and religious persecution. While these and other early historical investigations in the sociology of deviance often shied away from structural explanations, they posed an entirely new set of questions: Who are likely to become moral entrepreneurs, and why do they undertake their criminalization crusades? What steps do moral entrepreneurs take, en route to legislation, to persuade others of the righteousness of their cause? How does law create and preserve social class divisions? These were constructionist questions.

Rothman's (1971) *Discovery of the Asylum* was one of the first in a line of institutional histories that forced us to probe deeper into the relations between law, deviance, and society. These accounts of the origins of entire institutional systems—the juvenile justice and juvenile reformatory systems (Platt 1969; Schlossman, 1977), the British and French penal systems (Ignatieff 1978; O'Brien 1982), the network of residential hospitals for the insane and mentally retarded (Dwyer 1987; Grob 1973; Tomes 1984; Tyor and Bell 1984), and the poorhouse system (Katz 1986)—focused attention on that pivotal point in the early 19th century when Western nations began to use institutions to manage deviants. Why, numerous researchers asked, did the switch occur at that particular point in time? Their answers, though varied, drew attention to broad structural factors—industrialization, urbanization, immigration, and class relationships—as possible influences on criminal justice. The answers also forced us to ask whether earlier historians had been naive in presenting the evolution of criminal justice as a story of progress. If the result of reforms was not necessarily improvement, how should we interpret reformers' efforts? Might something other than good intentions be shaping the course of events? (Social control from a historical perspective is discussed in Pisciotta 1981; also see various essays collected in Cohen and Scull 1983.)

Thinking about these issues was further complicated by a series of histories on female institutions. Brenzel's (1983) study of the first reform school for girls, Freedman's (1981) research on those who founded the first prisons for women, and my own (Rafter 1985b) history of the women's prison system indicated that institutions were molded by gender roles and that their social functions could include enforcement of gender and racial hierarchies. It became clear that criminal justice was more than a simple matter of dealing with offenders; rather, definitions of criminals and their appropriate treatment could be shaped by preconceptions of which officials were completely unaware. It also became clear that our *understanding* of past practices was distorted by accounts which, like Rothman's, ignored the influence of gender and race (Rafter 1985a). We began to see that not only past realities but our *perceptions* of them were socially constructed.

In general, social historians have paid little attention to criminological theory.[5] Biological determinism has provided the main exception to this rule, no doubt because it starts by assuming that it itself is immune to social influences.[6] Through its claims to neutrality and scientific objectivity, biological determinism has cast itself in the role of a smart-aleck, taunting "Catch me if you can"—a challenge gladly met by historians, including scholars mainly involved in hard science. The evolutionary biologist Stephen Jay Gould (1981), for example, produced *The Mismeasure of Man*, a critique of criminal anthropology and the psychometrics that heavily influenced early 20th-century criminology. Gould quickly goes for the jugular, writing that the issue is not determinism *versus* antideterminism nor nature *versus* nurture but rather

> the myth that science itself is an objective enterprise, done properly only when scientists can shuck the constraints of their culture and view the world as it really is. . . . My message is not that biological determinists were bad scientists or even that they were always wrong. Rather, I believe that science must be understood as a social phenomenon. (p. 21)

Gould's book was followed by *Not in Our Genes*, in which an evolutionary geneticist, a neurobiologist, and a psychologist analyzed the social processes through which biological determinism has been built. These authors faulted sociobiology (including sociobiological theories of crime) for both scientific and epistemological weaknesses. Sociobiologists, they argued, can perform their measurements only by treating processes as fixed properties:

> Aggression and intelligence are seen not as processes that emerge from a situation . . . but rather . . . like reservoirs each of defined amount, inside each of us, to be turned on or off. . . . [R]eified verbs, like aggression, are assumed to be rigid, fixed things that can be reproducibly measured. Like height, they will not vary much from day to day. (Lewontin, Rose, and Kamin 1984, p. 91)

In *White Trash* (Rafter 1988), I took this epistemological approach one step further by applying discourse analysis to a series of turn-of-the-century sociobiological studies of criminalistic families. My aim was to show how the family studies authors constructed not only their biological variables but a powerful myth, that of the bad family itself, endlessly passing its evil protoplasm through the generations. This myth continues to shape criminological theory today, partly because it meshes easily with another of our favorite stories: that of the ability of science to produce naked truth. With other historians of biological determinism, I argue that the emperor is never naked; "truth" is always swathed in the gauze of social preconception (also see Kaye 1986).

It was Foucault (1977), in *Discipline and Punish*, who introduced poststructuralist theory into criminal justice history. Poststructuralists focus on knowledge, "the understanding produced by cultures and societies of human relationships" (Scott 1988, p. 2)—in our case, mainly (but not solely) relationships among criminals, social controllers, and the rest of us. Knowledge, for the poststructuralists, includes concepts (e.g., career criminals and deterrence), agencies and institutions, laws, rituals, the way by which we reach decisions, and everyday practices (e.g., the writing of pre-sentence reports and the measurement of variables). Such knowledge is constantly changing: We adopt a new method for classifying inmates; whereas yesterday we dichotomized "race," today we include other categories. Knowledge changes, in this view, because it is an arena for political contest: We discard long-form in favor of short-form pre-sentence investigations because the latter leave less room for racial and other biases, a political consideration; political pressure from feminists forces us to stop classifying female inmates by male criteria. Knowledge neither precedes nor follows social organization but is *itself* that organization. Knowledge includes what we do, what we write, and how we derive our "findings." Thus poststructuralism also directs us to examine the rhetoric of the discipline.

Foucault's *Discipline and Punish*, of course, is concerned above all with power, with the way in which the nascent prison system redistributed power and control through society, intensifying the surveillance not only of individuals by the state but of individuals by themselves. Foucault's concern with power leads him directly to perception; for him, the two are indivisible. Thus he analyzes the disciplinary power of institutions and the significance of that power, its influence on discourse and meaning. Garland (1985) sets himself similar tasks in *Punishment and Welfare*, the best poststructuralist history of crime control of the 1980s and a work that takes major steps toward defining the criminal justice professions.

All of these social histories raise constructionist issues for criminal justice, but each type addresses a somewhat different problem. Social historians working within the tradition of labeling theory pose the question: How is criminal law created, and why? For the institutional historians, a basic question is: Where did our institutions come from? Those who have concentrated on biological determinism ask: How are these theories built? And for the poststructuralists, the basic issue is: What are the origins and effects of knowledge and power?

Another route toward establishment of the constructionist tradition was taken by critical criminologists of the 1970s, who asked: How does social structure affect criminal justice?

CRITICAL CRIMINOLOGY[7]

Critical criminology—the movement, strongest in the 1970s, to reformulate the basic issues of criminal justice in Marxist terms—contributed to constructionism primarily by analyzing the influence of social class on criminal justice. It conceptualized crime and crime control as instruments of class struggle that create and maintain inequities in wealth and power. Law, in its view, is largely the creature of the most powerful class or classes, a means of social control that has symbolic as well as instrumental effects.

Critical criminology faltered as a disciplinary *movement* for reasons that are now fairly clear. A victim of conservative trends, it also suffered from self-inflicted wounds. It overprivileged social class as an analytic category and was so androcentric in its interpretation of "class" that it lost otherwise natural adherents among feminists. It tended to confuse empiricism with scientism, attacking the two indiscriminantly. Analytically, it sometimes adhered to a determinism as crude as that of sociobiology. And its leaders lacked the vision to take the next logical step: analyzing how power is created (see Melossi 1985).[8]

Although critical criminology stumbled as a movement, it made important contributions to constructionist analysis, through which it may have its most enduring influence. It made the obvious—"crime," for example—seem problematic. It forced us to locate crime control in the broader context of social control. Rejecting the dominant professional model, it stepped back from agency needs to pose more "sociological" questions about the effects of social structure on criminal justice. Although its attacks on empiricism were occasionally befuddled, it sensitized us to the political processes through which the "facts" of criminal justice are established. And critical criminology produced a generation of teachers and scholars who later, as neo-Marxists, continued to ask constructionist questions—and provide more sophisticated answers.

WORK ON THE VICTIMIZATION OF FEMALES

Research in the two areas reviewed thus far—the social history of criminal justice and critical criminology—originated within the academy. In contrast, work on the victimization of women and girls began with grassroots organizations. For those who have focused on this third area, the basic issue has been: How are victims defined?

Changes in the interpretation of rape exemplify the way in which a number of crimes against females have been redefined over the past two decades and the theoretical results of that redefinition. In the early 1970s, feminists began working to change the legal definition of rape. Common law (and hence most of our statutes) had defined rape as a crime committed by a man against a woman other than his spouse and against her will. Critics of this traditional definition raised a host of constructionist questions: Why did the definition ignore the obvious—that men can rape men? Why did it permit husbands legally to rape their wives? Why did it include the phrase "against her will" when for all other offenses, we assume the victim is unwilling? These criticisms led, eventually, to redefinition of rape as, simply, sexual assault—irrespective of the sex of or relationship between victim and offender. It also led to a new formulation of the old question: Where does law come from? and to an answer—from men—that now had a new edge to it. If law can function to maintain male domination, perhaps one of its aims is not justice but the preservation of power. This aim, moreover, need not be part of a conscious design—indeed, historically, it clearly was a product not of a plot but rather of power itself.

Meanwhile, community groups working to establish support services for victims of rape, wife battering, and (somewhat later) incest began to critique the criminal justice process. Why were police officers trained to ignore such victims or to question their motives? Why did court processes (however unintentionally) put victims, instead of offenders, on trial? It began to appear that not only law but the criminal justice system was implicated in the construction and maintenance of male power.

These suspicions eventually crept into the academy, where irreverent questions were raised about conventional criminological studies of crimes with female victims. By this point, community activists had accumulated pools of victims against whom the data of such studies could be measured for accuracy. Evidently, Amir (1971) had been wrong when he suggested that many rape victims were willing or deserving. Perhaps there was something faulty with his methodology, which drew on police records. Perhaps the traditional image of incest victims as teenage girls who wander around in their underwear was incorrect. Perhaps criminology itself was part of the structure of male domination.

Let us step back from the specifics to inquire how efforts on behalf of female victims contributed generally to the constructionist approach. Most important, they awakened people to the political nature of criminal justice. A system of state power justified by the help that it supposedly provided to victims turned out, instead, unintentionally to protect certain groups of offenders and delegitimize their victims. We could recognize the politics in this situation only by socially constructing new ways of seeing. Second, this work demonstrated—again outside as well as within the academy—that crime, offenders, and victims are social artifacts. Third, through its awareness of the way in which the system can encourage offender self-excuse and victim self-blame, this work showed that criminal justice is involved in how we define ourselves as male or female—how we internalize male privilege. In sum, it reinforced the realization that the name of the game may be not justice but power, the power to define.

FEMINIST THEORY

One strain of feminist theory, that which deals with the creation of meanings associated with gender, has been the source of some of the most recent and radical efforts to apply constructionism to criminal justice. According to the formula used previously, the basic question here should be: How does gender affect criminal justice? But this formulation is incompatible with the focus of feminist theory, which asks: How does criminal justice contribute to the social construction of gender? Gender itself has been central in feminist work in two areas: the processing of offenders and criminological theory.

Research of the past two decades has produced a sizable literature on sex differentials in the processing and treatment of those accused or convicted of crime (for an overview, see Simpson 1989; also see Chesney-Lind 1986; Parisi 1982). For our purposes, what is most interesting about this literature is that it moved from the original, fairly simple equity issue—are females treated more leniently or harshly than males?—to complex explanations of sex differentials in terms of gender-related factors.

Researchers in this area examined the influence on criminal justice processes of gendered attitudinal perceptions—chivalry and paternalism, for example (Parisi 1982)—and of deeply entrenched cultural symbols, such as those of the good girl and the dark lady (Rafter and Stanko 1982) and the madonna and the whore (Feinman 1980). They analyzed ways in which criminal justice works to control female sexuality—through (a) antiprostitution campaigns (Connelly 1980; Rosen 1982); (b) subjecting girls to vaginal exams, irrespective of charges (Chesney-Lind 1981); and (c) repression of female premarital sexual activity (Rafter 1990; Schlossman and Wallach 1978). Working to untangle the complicated interactions of race and gender, these researchers distinguished between processing reactions to Black and White women. They found that marital status and "family" status (whether or not a defendant has dependent children) also affect court processing (Daly 1987, 1989), indicating that the system reacts to "the degree to which women are subjected to formal versus informal social control in their everyday lives" (Simpson 1989, p. 614). Even prison architecture has been revealed as gendered (Rafter 1990). In short, through this research, we are now aware of a number of gender-related variables that can influence the social construction of offenders and the treatment they receive.

Feminists differ over how to react politically to these findings. Some call for identical treatment of the sexes, while others insist on parity—equal treatment that would allow for sex-based differences (Parisi 1982; Rafter 1989). But policy is not the central issue here. More to the point is the implication of this work for our understanding of how (to borrow Scott's [1988] words about her own discipline of history) criminal justice "operates as a site of the production of gender knowledge" (p. 10).

The same issue is raised by feminist analyses of criminology (for reviews, see Daly and Chesney-Lind 1988; Gelsthorpe 1988; Simpson 1989), which criticize traditional criminology for focusing exclusively on male delinquency and crime. They also take purportedly feminist criminological theories, especially those of Adler (1975) and Simon (1975), to task for promulgating the (erroneous) notion that women's "liberation" is a cause of crime. However, these critics disdain "the 'add women and stir' approach" (Chesney-Lind 1986, p. 84). Instead, they are working to understand female crime in its own right, distinct from male crime, and to develop new methods of analysis.[9] They are, moreover, examining criminological discourse itself as an aspect of the construction of gender. They argue not that criminology is incomplete without women but rather that it, like criminal justice processing, contributes to understanding of gender and hence of ourselves as included or excluded, dominant or subordinate, central or peripheral.

CONCLUSION

Although the four areas of research and theory reviewed here—social history, critical criminology, work on the victimization of females, and feminist theory—are diverse, their commonalities are at least as significant as their differences. All four are concerned less with offenders and their control than with the processes through which offenders and mechanisms of control are produced. All explore relationships among law, society, and perception. Each investigates power (the power to punish, to marginalize, and to define), and in recent years, each has tended toward discourse analysis, examining the conflicts through which meaning and knowledge emerge. Taken together, these common elements comprise a constructionist tradition within criminal justice research and theory, albeit one that has developed haphazardly and on the discipline's margins.

Constructionism is sometimes misconstrued as a rejection of empiricism and knowable "reality." To some extent, this misapprehension has been fostered by adherents who contrast the "subjectivist" approach of constructionism with "objectivist definitions" (e.g., Best 1989, "Introduction"). Yet it is inaccurate to equate constructionism with subjectivism, as the works reviewed here demonstrate: All start with the belief that there is a world "out there" and that we can apprehend it. Constructionism *does* claim that apprehension is influenced by social position (class, gender, and race) and historical circumstance. But that claim is based on data, and it is falsifiable. Moreover, constructionism does not hold that all versions of reality are equally accurate: If I claim to have killed Lizzie Borden's parents, you can prove me wrong. It does insist, however, that we pay attention to the *politics* of verification—of theories as well as of killers. While it challenges the notion of value-free science, it does so on the basis of empirical evidence and in order to enhance, not obscure, understanding of the world. It may make us uncomfortable by noting that ultimate truth is hard to attain, but that observation, too, is based on evidence.

Having examined the evolution of the contructionist tradition within criminal justice, we can conclude by considering some of its implications for the future of the discipline. One of these concerns the optimal composition of the discipline's academic leadership.

Criminal justice was perforce interdisciplinary in its origins, drawing together lawyers, economists, psychologists and social psychologists, system workers, and policymakers, but it is in the process of losing its interdisciplinarity. The first generation of Ph.D.'s has produced a second. Just as in Boston, the Lowells speak only to the Cabots and the Cabots only to God, specialists in criminal justice now swap ideas mainly with those of similar background. In large part, constructionism has been developed by scholars who have come to criminal justice from other fields, and this approach will probably survive the discipline's growing insularity. However, if we wish to nurture it, we will have to reaffirm our original commitment to interdisciplinary work by inviting more "outsiders" to join our faculties. We will also have to make sure that our courses in theory and methods include constructionist research.

A second implication of constructionism for the future concerns conceptualization of the type of work that criminal justice involves. Constructionism has the potential to overcome a problem noted earlier: our lack of a clear sense of criminal justice as a profession or group of professions. As an academic discipline, we are young enough to remember our immediate roots. But the criminal justice professions that gave birth to the discipline are much older, and—in contrast to law, medicine, and social work—they have received little historical or sociological attention. As a result, those who belong to or affiliate with such professions lack occupational identity, a sense of how their work has evolved, what (generally speaking) it entails, and how it fits into the broader picture of social control. Constructionism, focused as it is on origins, relationships, and the production of information, could be the vehicle that carries us to a firmer comprehension of the nature of the criminal justice professions.

Last, constructionism has significance for the future because through it we may develop a sociology of knowledge within criminal justice.[10] This sociology of knowledge would enable us to theorize our work more systematically. It would force us critically to examine our practices, texts, and methods of producing information. By developing it, we could join other fields in their current scrutiny of their disciplinary underpinnings. It would help us to distinguish criminal justice as discipline from criminal justice as profession. However, the field is unlikely to succeed in establishing its foundations in a sociology of knowledge if it remains resistant to the constructionist approach.

NOTES

1. For expositions of constructionism and its debates within the closely related field of sociology, see Best (1987, 1989), Schneider (1985), Spector and Kituse (1987), and Woolgar and Pawluch (1985).

2. Criminal justice, of course, is not the only field to suffer from this problem, which is endemic in the sciences. Todd (1989) explains the "inflexibility" of "the scientific method of fact-finding" in terms of its "commitment to an external reality that is discoverable cumulatively through the application of objective methods. Historical connections and human influences are not considered part of science" (p. 107).

3. Although constructionism and the sociology of knowledge are sometimes equated, it is important to distinguish between them. The sociology of knowledge is more systematic, more

concerned with methodology and epistemology (cf. Berger and Luckman 1967, p. 14). It focuses more clearly on (a) signs, symbols, and signification; (b) the diffusion and distribution of knowledge; and (c) the foundations of disciplines. Nevertheless, it presupposes a more general constructionist approach, such as that exemplified in this article.

4. I chose these four categories because I am most familiar with their literature. This leads me to slight, in particular, contributions of the sociology of law. In what follows, the social history literature receives the most'attention because it is most diverse.

5. This situation will probably change rapidly in the near future. For a harbinger of the change, see Laub and Sampson (forthcoming).

6. "One of the problems for the study of science as a social construction is the prevailing view . . . that it is not socially constructed" (Todd 1989, p. 104).

7. There is debate over the most appropriate label (see Sparks 1980). I use "critical criminology" here because it most clearly denotes the phenomenon that I am analyzing: the development of a *critical* perspective on criminal justice theory and practice.

8. Richard Quinney (1970), in fact, *had* this vision in his early work, *The Social Reality of Crime*, which was strongly epistemological in approach, emphasizing the "formulation of criminal definitions" and "the portrayal of crime in personal and mass communications" (pp. 22-23). But by the mid-1970s, Quinney (1974) had rejected this emphasis, criticizing "social constructionist thought" for "a failure to provide an image of what a new world should look like" (p. 8).

9. For what these new methods might entail, see Harding (1986, chap. 6) and Smith (1987, chap. 3); also see Simpson (1989, pp. 608-9).

10. This may seem axiomatic. "(T)he sociology of knowledge," according to Berger and Luckman (1967), "is concerned with the social construction of reality" (p. 3). But the reverse is not necessarily true: Constructionism does not lead automatically to a sociology of knowledge. We have the first, at least as a tradition of inquiry; its results will depend on how we develop it.

REFERENCES

Adler, Freda. 1975. *Sisters in Crime*. New York: McGraw-Hill.

Amir, Menachem. 1971. *Patterns in Forcible Rape*. Chicago: University of Chicago Press.

Becker, Howard S. 1963. *Outsiders: Studies in the Sociology of Deviance*. New York: Free Press.

Berger, Peter L. and Thomas Luckmann. 1967. *The Social Construction of Reality*. New York: Anchor/Doubleday.

Best, Joel. 1987. "Rhetoric in Claims-Making: Constructing the Missing Children Problem." *Social Problems* 34(2):101-21.

———, ed. 1989. *Images of Issues: Typifying Contemporary Social Problems*. New York: Aldine de Gruyter.

Brenzel, Barbara. 1983. *Daughters of the State: A Social Portrait of the First Reform School for Girls in North America, 1856-1905*. Cambridge: MIT Press.

Chesney-Lind, Meda. [1977] 1981. "Judicial Paternalism and the Female Status Offender: Training Women to Know Their Place." Pp. 354-66 in *Women and Crime in America*, edited by Lee H. Bowker. New York: Macmillan.

———. 1986. "Women and Crime: The Female Offender." *Signs* 12(1):78-96.

Cohen, Stanley and Andrew Scull, eds. 1983. *Social Control and the State: Historical and Comparative Essays*. Oxford: Martin Robertson.

Connelly, Mark Thomas. 1980. *The Response to Prostitution in the Progressive Era*. Chapel Hill: University of North Carolina Press.

Daly, Kathleen. 1987. "Discrimination in the Courts: Family, Gender and the Problem of Equal Treatment." *Social Forces* 66:152-75.

———. 1989. "Rethinking Judicial Paternalism: Gender, Work-Family Relations, and Sentencing." *Gender and Society* 3(1):9-36.

Daly, Kathleen, and Meda Chesney-Lind. 1988. "Feminism and Criminolgy." *Justice Quarterly* 5(4):497-535.

Dwyer, Ellen. 1987. *Homes for the Mad: Life Inside Two Nineteenth-Century Asylums.* New Brunswick, NJ: Rutgers University Press.

Erikson, Kai T. 1966. *Wayward Puritans: A Study in the Sociology of Deviance.* New York: Wiley.

Feinman, Clarice. 1980. *Women in the Criminal Justice System.* New York: Praeger.

Foucault, Michel. 1977. *Discipline and Punish: The Birth of the Prison.* New York: Pantheon.

Freedman, Estelle B. 1981. *Their Sisters' Keepers: Women's Prison Reform in America, 1830-1930.* Ann Arbor: University of Michigan Press.

Garland, David. 1985. *Punishment and Welfare: A History of Penal Strategies.* Brookfield, VT: Gower.

Gelsthorpe, Loraine. 1988. "Feminism and Criminology in Britain." *British Journal of Criminology* 28(2):93-110.

Gould, Stephen Jay. 1981. *The Mismeasure of Man.* New York: Norton.

Grob, Gerald N. 1973. *Mental Institutions in America: Social Policy to 1875.* New York: Free Press.

Gusfield, Joseph R. 1963. *Symbolic Crusade: Status Politics and the American Temperance Movement.* Urbana: University of Illinois Press.

Harding, Sandra. 1986. *The Science Question in Feminism.* Ithaca, NY: Cornell University Press.

Ignatieff, Michael. 1978. *A Just Measure of Pain: The Penitentiary in the Industrial Revolution.* New York: Pantheon.

Katz, Michael B. 1986. *In the Shadow of the Poorhouse: A Social History of Welfare in America.* New York: Basic Books.

Kaye, Howard L. 1986. *The Social Meaning of Modern Biology: From Social Darwinism to Sociobiology.* New Haven, CT: Yale University Press.

Laub, John H. and Robert J. Sampson. Forthcoming. "On the Social Constitution of Criminological Knowledge: The Sutherland-Glueck Debate." *American Journal of Sociology.*

Lewontin, R. C., Steven Rose, and Leon J. Kamin. 1984. *Not in Our Genes: Biology, Ideology, and Human Nature.* New York: Pantheon.

Melossi, Dario. 1985. "Overcoming the Crisis in Criminology: Toward a Grounded Labeling Theory." *Criminology* 23(2):193-208.

O'Brien, Patricia. 1982. *The Promise of Punishment: Prisons in Nineteenth-Century France.* Princeton, NJ: Princeton University Press.

Parisi, Nicolette. 1982. "Are Females Treated Differently?" Chap. 9 in *Judge, Lawyer, Victim, Thief: Women, Gender Roles, and Criminal Justice,* edited by Nicole Hahn Rafter and Elizabeth Anne Stanko. Boston: Northeastern University Press.

Pisciotta, Alexander W. 1981. "Corrections, Society, and Social Control in America: A Metahistorical Review of the Literature." *Criminal Justice History* 2:109-30.

Platt, Anthony M. 1969. *The Child Savers: The Invention of Delinquency.* Chicago: University of Chicago Press.

Quinney, Richard. 1970. *The Social Reality of Crime.* Boston: Little, Brown.

———. 1974. *Critique of Legal Order.* Boston: Little, Brown.

Rafter, Nicole Hahn. 1985a. "Gender, Prisons, and Prison History." *Social Science History* 9(3):233-47.

———. 1985b. *Partial Justice: Women in State Prisons, 1800-1935*. Boston: Northeastern University Press.

———. 1988. *White Trash: The Eugenic Family Studies*. Boston: Northeastern University Press.

———. 1989. "Gender and Justice: The Equal Protection Issue." Chap. 6 in *The American Prison: Issues in Research and Policy*, edited by Lynne Goodstein and Doris MacKenzie. New York: Plenum.

———. 1990. *Partial Justice: Women, Prisons, and Social Control*. New Brunswick, NJ: Transaction.

Rafter, Nicole Hahn and and Elizabeth Anne Stanko, eds. 1982. *Judge, Lawyer, Victim, Thief: Women, Gender Roles, and Criminal Justice*. Boston: Northeastern University Press.

Rosen, Ruth. 1982. *The Lost Sisterhood: Prostitution in America, 1900-1918*. Baltimore, MD: Johns Hopkins University Press.

Rothman, David J. 1971. *The Discovery of the Asylum: Social Order and Disorder in the New Republic*. Boston: Little, Brown.

Schlossman, Steven L. 1977. *Love and the American Delinquent: The Theory and Practice of "Progressive" Juvenile Justice, 1825-1920*. Chicago: University of Chicago Press.

Schlossman, Steven L. and and Stephanie Wallach. 1978. "The Crime of Precocious Sexuality: Female Juvenile Delinquency in the Progressive Era." *Harvard Educational Review* 48(1): 65-94.

Schneider, Joseph W. 1985. "Social Problems Theory: The Constructionist View." *Annual Review of Sociology* 11:209-29.

Scott, Joan Wallach. 1988. *Gender and the Politics of History*. New York: Columbia University Press.

Simon, Rita James. 1975. *Women and Crime*. Lexington, MA: Lexington Books.

Simpson, Sally S. 1989. "Feminist Theory, Crime and Justice." *Criminology* 27(4):605-31.

Smith, Dorothy E. 1987. *The Everyday World as Problematic: A Feminist Sociology*. Boston: Northeastern University Press.

Sparks, Richard F. 1980. "A Critique of Marxist Criminology." Pp. 159-210 in *Crime and Justice: An Annual Review of Research*, vol. 2, edited by Norval Morris and Michael Tonry. Chicago: University of Chicago Press.

Spector, Malcolm and John I. Kituse. 1987. *Constructing Social Problems*. New York: Aldine de Gruyter.

Starr, Paul. 1987. "The Sociology of Official Statistics." Pp. 7-57 in *The Politics of Numbers*, edited by William Alonso and Paul Starr. New York: Russell Sage.

Todd, Alexandra Dundas. 1989. *Intimate Adversaries: Cultural Conflict Between Doctors & Women Patients*. Philadelphia: University of Pennsylvania Press.

Tomes, Nancy. 1984. *A Generous Confidence: Thomas Story Kirkbride and the Art of Asylum-keeping, 1840-1883*. Cambridge: Cambridge University Press.

Tyor, Peter L. and Leland V. Bell. 1984. *Caring for the Retarded in America: A History*. Westport, CT: Greenwood Press.

Woolgar, Steve and Dorothy Pawluch. 1985. "Ontological Gerrymandering: The Anatomy of Social Problems Explanations." *Social Problems* 32:214-27.

[12]

Inventing Criminal Justice
Myth and Social Construction

Victor E. Kappeler

The phrase "criminal justice" invokes powerful images and understandings. It conjures images of uniformed police officers pursuing dangerous criminals down dark alleys or detectives meticulously combing over crime scenes collecting evidence for criminal identification. The phrase can prompt dramatic courtroom scenes where magistrates sit in black flowing robes high above courtroom participants, dispensing equal justice for all. Or it can evoke darker images of crowded places of confinement where dangerous jumper-clad inmates pay their debts to society and pass the time planning new crimes or violent escapes. We might even think of criminal justice as a unified and seamless system that responds to the threat of crime through various agencies dedicated to making society safer and administering justice in a fair and impartial fashion. All these images, however, are constructed mystifications of the reality of criminal justice in U.S. society.

When we think of criminal justice, we usually don't think of police officials falsifying crime statistics to secure resources for their agencies. We don't think about detectives clearing stacks of unsolved cases by pinning crimes on their latest suspect despite no evidence of guilt. Seldom does the image of prosecutors and defense attorneys bargaining to dispose of entire dockets of criminal cases in the backrooms of courthouses come to mind. Nor do we think of attorneys trading the futures of defendants to enhance the possibility of a judicial appointment or magistrates handing down sentences for purposes of political advancement. Seldom do we think about the children left behind when inmates are sentenced to prison for drug possession or whether inmates really emerge from prison rehabilitated. Our attention is directed away from these alternative images of criminal justice by an array of social actors and myths.

Images of justice are not happenstance. While it is comforting to think of criminal justice as a fixed reality void of political and ideological influences, nothing could be further from the truth. Criminal justice, like crime, is a social construction that shifts with intellectual perspective, political influence, social sentiment, cultural values, and the interests of powerful groups in society. The very notion that criminal justice constitutes a "system" distinct from the larger social context in which it operates is a powerful myth that masks vested interests and contradictions. Likewise, to think of the criminal justice system as protecting us from criminals and evildoers is to misunderstand the powerful forces that construct our reality of justice. By merely invoking the phrase "criminal justice system," we limit our conception of justice. In doing so, we reduce social harm to the behaviors defined as criminal. Likewise, the phrase compels us to view criminal justice as a naturally occurring or even organic functional response to crime. Alternative conceptions of justice are blocked from consideration by preconceived notions.

Learning Criminal Justice Myths

Where do myths come from and how are they learned? Criminal justice myths are collective presentations of reality. Everyone we come into contact with can add a bit of myth to our understanding of criminal justice. We learn about crime myths from our parents, when we are in church, socializing with friends, and from our teachers. Many of our criminal justice practices are based on false conceptions created by the mass media, urban legend, ideology, or pure political power. The process of producing this unified vision is social construction. The largest and most powerful contributors to the social construction of criminal justice are the mass media and government.

The media have a vested interest in the promotion of criminal justice myths. First, the public is fascinated by sensational crime. Crime has become a media product that sells perhaps better than any other media commodity. Attracting a larger audience translates into more advertising dollars. Simply put, the more viewers or readers, the more money a television station or newspaper makes. Second, alternative explanations of criminal justice rarely resonate with the viewers—and a loss of viewers equals a loss of dollars. Third, expression of views that contradict official government positions can lead to enhanced regulation of the industry and a loss of news sources. Media depictions of criminal justice are intertwined with government, money, and ideology. The media are therefore compelled to present a very simplistic, standardized view of justice that does not alienate those who either control or consume it.

The government makes a significant contribution to the social construction of criminal justice. The government is a powerful mythmaker with a vested interest in maintaining the existing definitions of crime, protecting the current operation and public perception of criminal justice, and extending formal social control to groups and behaviors that are perceived to be a threat to the existing social order. These interests extend to seeing that the current response to crime is not significantly altered in purpose or function. Dramatic changes in criminal justice are never implemented because the status quo serves the interests of government, crime-control agencies, and social elites. We build more prisons, mete out longer prison terms, reinstate the death penalty, and move more offenders through the criminal justice system at faster speeds.

The government controls, directs, and molds messages about criminal justice for public consumption. The government can suppress information for national security reasons; it can punish "obscenity"; and it can reward the media for presenting official versions of crime myths. Shaping the content of messages and rewarding the media for myth presentation are frequently done under the guise of public service announcements, controlled press briefings, and the release of state-sponsored research reports.

The government is also a form of media. The government controls extensive print publication resources, commissions and funds research, operates radio stations, and exposes the television-viewing audience to government-sponsored messages. With great regularity governmental agencies like the Federal Bureau of Investigation (FBI), the Bureau of Justice Statistics (BJS), and the National Institute of Justice (NIJ) distribute press releases about criminal justice to the media. One must remember that these press releases are written by the same people who fund the research and decide what statistics should be collected and shared with the public. While much of the research that these agencies release provides basic and needed information, it is often oversimplified and sometimes designed to elicit social concern—at a minimum, it is filtered through a process shaped and controlled by political interests.

In addition to providing the media and public with distorted statistics on crime, the government also disseminates a highly selective ideology of crime and justice. The media need constant sources of information to feed their demand for news products. Convenient sources like police officials and political leaders respond eagerly to media inquiries. Favorite sources for journalists' inquiries are often those who are readily available or those who reliably provide quotable statements.

In this pipeline to the media, governmental officials, criminal justice practitioners, and politicians have a distinct advantage over researchers and scholars. Michael Welch, Melissa Fenwick, and Meredith Roberts (1998) examined the sources major newspapers used to craft their feature crime stories. These researchers found a striking ideological difference between governmental and academic sources. Generally, governmental spokespersons were more likely to advance a crime-control ideology, whereas academics were more likely to discuss crime causation. Likewise, politicians and criminal justice practitioners were more likely to construct crime in terms of deterrence and the personal pathology of criminals, whereas academics were more likely to discuss the social factors that contribute to crime. Additionally, governmental spokespersons were more likely to advocate stringent crime-control efforts packaged in slogans like "three strikes and you're out" and "get-tough-on-crime," while their academic counterparts subscribed to crime-control measures like education, the provision of social services, and reducing economic disparity and racism. "Reporters' dependence on authorities makes them—and by extension media consumers—particularly vulnerable to deliberate attempts to mislead by governments and agencies" (Hynds, 1990, p. 6).

Media depictions of criminal justice in the United States represent a form of knowledge construction where crime and the response to it is a hybrid product of governmental ideology and media distortion. The media and the government, whether independently or in concert, focus public attention on criminal justice problems, but perhaps more importantly they set the boundaries of thinkable solutions. These two powerful entities establish the seriousness of problems and inform the public of viable solutions. In the process, they sow the seeds of criminal justice myths and teach us how to think about crime and criminal justice.

Myths, Contradictions, and Criminal Justice

Many of our views of criminal justice are based on myths that either hide or attempt to reconcile social contradictions. Myths are conceptual schemes that assist us in interpreting reality and organizing our thoughts and beliefs about reality. Myths let us make sense of the world, reconcile contradictions, and explain processes and events we cannot readily understand. Myths tend to support the status quo by organizing the way we see reality. Myths, in this sense, are sources of authority and power because they allow us to adhere steadfastly to contrived belief systems even when reality contradicts them.

Myths tell us where in society problems reside, where we should look to find solutions, and what solutions are acceptable. Most of us learn that stealing is wrong. When people take property that does not belong to them, it is much easier to remember our early lessons and to label anyone who violates those teachings as criminals and wrongdoers than it is to question an economic system in which many live in poverty. It is comforting to attribute theft to individual greed without ever questioning the role culture and socialization play in creating the powerful desire to accumulate wealth. In this construction, criminal justice becomes the system that protects us from greedy and evil people rather than a system that maintains the economic order.

All myths contain fictions but are used as if they were true accounts of issues or events. The power of myths comes not from their ability to reflect reality accurately but from their repeated presentations. Myths gain power and take on new meanings as they are told and retold—and at some point evolve into truth for many people. The fiction in criminal justice myth comes not only from the fabrication of events but also from the transformation and distortion of ideas about criminal justice into common-sense truths. Crime myths are so powerful and can become so compounded in their public presentations that they shape our thoughts about and reactions to almost any issue related to criminal justice (Kappeler & Potter, 2005). A lifetime's exposure to criminal justice myths make them seen reasonable and natural—just plain common sense.

Myths provide a conceptual framework from which to identify behaviors needing a criminal justice response, to develop our personal opinions about justice, and to apply ready-made solutions to problems. Myths support and maintain prevailing views of criminal justice and strengthen the tendency to rely on established conceptions of crime. Myths reinforce the current designation of conduct as criminal, support criminal justice practices, and provide the background assumptions for our social response to crime. In a sense, society becomes intellectually blinded by the mythology of criminal justice (Kappeler & Potter, 2005).

Myths can be restricted to specific criminal events, always presented as occurring regularly or with increasing frequency. Many myths cluster around stalkers, serial killers, or murderers who hide in the back seat of cars at shopping malls. They can tell us about mythical gang initiation rights that require members to victimize innocents (Best & Hutchinson, 1996), they may instruct us about depraved people who dispense poisonous candy to children at Halloween, or they may recount the bravery of cops on mean streets. Myths can broaden their scope by explaining the reasons people commit crime or by supporting our social response to crime. Depraved and evil people commit crime because our criminal justice system is too soft on criminals; the failure to prevent crime is the result of too few laws, police, judges, or prisons.

Myths of Crime and Human Nature

Myths of criminal justice are related to broader social myths about human behavior and society. These broad social myths make our constructions of criminal justice and response to crime seem all the more reasonable and unchallengeable. The way we construct and understand criminal justice is by promoting a series of powerful myths that guide us in interpreting reality in a very narrow fashion. Let's consider some of the broad myths that organize our thoughts about human behavior and criminal justice. These myths create a collective belief system—a powerful ideology—that hides contradictions.

Perhaps the most powerful and sustained social construction of criminal justice is the myth of the "divine lawgiver" and the "sanctity of law." This myth and its derivatives can be traced throughout recorded history from the pharaohs of ancient Egypt, through the divine rights of kings, and even to the founding fathers' declaration of independence. The myth holds that law is not the product of men; it is imbued with a divine quality, making it unquestionable and infallible. Transgressors against divine law are, if not evil, at least sinners in need of redemption, correction, or punishment. The truth, regardless of one's religious beliefs, is that law has no divine source. People just as fallible as the rest of us create law.

Modern mystifications of the law in this fashion include assertions like "the law protects us and grants us our freedom," and "we live in a nation of laws not men." Law has little to do with divinity and freedom. Law is a man-made social construction that protects vested interests and limits, not expands, freedom. The atrocities committed by the Nazis during World War II, the racism of apartheid in South Africa, and the treatment of women under the Taliban in Afghanistan were legally sanctioned. The myth of the divinity of lawgivers and law, however, masks this fact and begs for unquestioned obedience. When the state, its leaders, and their legislation are constructed as something greater than a human product, questioning becomes unthinkable.

Another equally powerful myth explains criminal behavior. According to the myth of human rationality, criminal behavior is a matter of individual choice; criminals are solely responsible for their actions. Crime is not the product of social, political, or economic conditions nor is it the product of the laws that have been passed defining crime. This construction of criminality ignores the fact that society is not just an aggregate of individuals who voluntarily engage in uninfluenced behavior. We all make decisions, think, and behave in a social context. The criminal justice system, especially in the courtroom, goes to great pains to exclude any consideration of the social, historical, political, or economic influences on people.

Some laws are created for the purpose of constructing the "impartiality of the state judiciary and preserving the appearance of the impartiality of the state judiciary . . . because it preserves public confidence in the judiciary" (see *Republican Party of Minnesota v. White*, 2002, p. 9). Likewise, criminal behavior is isolated to the moment in which it occurs and to the individual criminal. The myth focuses our attention on criminal "events" and directs our criminal justice response to these events. The view of individuals as having free will to make rational choices means criminals are also rational social actors who must face the consequences for deliberately violating the law. However, most media presentations of crime, and the vast majority of political speech on crime, are not about rational calculating criminals; they are about senseless random acts of violence. In essence everyone who commits a crime is a rational actor for purposes of punishment. For purposes of generating fear of crime and building the criminal justice system, society is painted as beset by irrational acts of violence.

The myth of human rationality is more about the generation and maintenance of social order than it is about the empirical reality of human behavior. It has very little to do with why people behave the way they do. The myth doesn't explain atrocities, but it does allow us to punish all transgressors without questioning the fundamental fairness or acceptability of the model from which punishment is generated. Breaking the law is the sole criterion.

We seldom ask why some socially harmful acts are regulated, some criminalized, and others not addressed at all.

A related myth of rationality and criminal justice is the notion that crime can be deterred by the threat and administration of punishment. In this line of reasoning, it follows that the more certain and severe the punishment, the less likely people are to commit crime. This myth focuses once again on the individual rather than on the social order and reinforces punishment as the most appropriate criminal justice response. The myth is contradictory even if we accept its premise. If criminals are rational actors, then they will not commit crime because of fear of punishment. The high recidivism rates reported in nearly every study of punishment highlight the glaring inaccuracy of this construction of human behavior. The myth has another inherent contradiction. If everyone is individually responsible for their behaviors and social influences and conditions do not direct human behavior, how can punishment—determined and administered by society—prevent crime? In addition, the myth ignores the fact that the threat of punishment is not the reason most people abstain from crime. Ask yourself this question: If all the laws, police, and courts were abolished tomorrow would you go out and murder, rob, steal, or rape? It is not the threat of punishment that makes us conform.

Although most myths deny the role of social influences, one contemporary myth about the causes of crime is that crime is related to a deterioration or breakdown in certain social institutions. The sustained and frequent commission of crime is said to be a product of the failure of the family, religious institutions, the poor socialization of youth, or even moral decay. This myth contradicts the construction of crime as the product of individual choice and the construction of criminals as free-willed, rational actors who are uninfluenced by their social conditions, and it ignores the fact that criminality is the product of how crime is defined by people with the power to affect laws. Myths divert our attention to street crime and to crimes by strangers, while simultaneously evoking laudatory images of family and religious institutions. Given the number of crimes often committed within these institutions—domestic violence; child abuse, rape, and murder; sexual abuse by the clergy—this type of myth hides one reality while attempting to explain another. The myth is that no social institution is responsible for the social conditions in which we live or the failure of the justice system to adequately address social harm. While we can assign individual blame for criminal conduct, we ignore the social conditions and institutions that generate crime. In this myth, justice is something other than the collective decisions of legislators, judges, police officers, and corrections officials, and the public accepts the system as it is constructed—contradictions and all.

A Convergent Core Myth

A vast majority of the public believes that the criminal justice system generally and judges specifically are soft on crime and criminals. This myth is predicated on the myth of deterrence. It is often argued that if the police caught more criminals, if more people were convicted of crimes, and if judges handed down longer prison sentences, criminal behavior would be reduced. It is, however, a myth that the criminal justice system in the United States is soft on crime. We have the highest rate of citizens convicted of crime by the courts, and we incarcerate and kill more of our citizens than any other Western industrialized democracy (United Nations, 2001). We incarcerate over 756 persons for every 100,000 residents in the population (Sabol, West, & Cooper, 2009). This is a rate more than five times greater than that of England, France, and Germany; 10 times greater than Sweden; 12 times higher than Japan; and twice the rate of South Africa (Walmsley, 2009). The United States has one of the highest rates of incarceration in the entire world surpassing even Russia. The United States has become even more severe in its treatment of offenders in recent years, even while crime is declining. The trend toward increased incarceration is not a universal phenomenon. Both Denmark and England have developed policies that are designed to reduce the number of prison inmates. Yet these countries have considerably lower crime rates than the United States. Still, we continue to move in the opposite direction. In fact, in 2008 7.3 million people were under the control of the criminal justice system (Bureau of Justice Statistics, 2010)—awaiting death, incarcerated in prison or jail, or under probation or parole.

The United States is the only Western industrial nation that continues to execute criminals. Canada, Great Britain, Australia, New Zealand, and all the nations of Western Europe have halted this practice. In many societies, capital punishment was abolished long ago. Most jurisdictions in the United States, however, have not followed suit. It is hard to believe that a society that incarcerates and kills more of its citizens than any other Western industrialized nation is soft on crime. The myth seems to persist because of a continued and unfounded belief in the logic of deterrence and its reinforcement by government officials, the media, and political leaders. So the solution to crime continues to be a system built on flawed logic and contraction that supports the existing social and economic order.

The Costs of Justice Myths

The construction of a social reality of criminal justice based on myths has consequences. While some myths are harmless, myths associated with the criminal justice system have profound consequences for individuals and society at large. Myths direct our attention toward certain social problems and solutions. They also obscure reality and direct our attention away from other social problems and solutions that could have a more meaningful impact on the human condition. The major detriment of myths isn't even that cherished traditions and beliefs have unintended consequences. The problem is that myths hide or help us ignore consequences. Instead of rethinking the premise, energies are directed to explain why appearances to the contrary do not attack the foundation.

Myths hide contradictions in logic and reality, and they obscure the role of powerful groups in society to protect their vested interests. We hire more police officers to detect criminals, employ more judges and lawyers to administer justice, and build more prisons to punish those we deem criminal based on a flawed ideology. We conceptualize criminality not as the presence or absence of poverty, not as the presence or absence of racism in our social institutions, and not as the political construction of those with power but as individual deviation. Because of these myths, changes to the current system seem unthinkable or even unpatriotic. We don't want to admit that a hallowed symbol can be flawed; therefore, we ignore the complications that inevitably accompany implementation. Myths simplify issues that are too complex—that involve reflections we don't want to make and risks we aren't willing to take—whether we don't want to engage in the rigorous, extensive reflection required to confront problems or don't want to sacrifice personal gain to protect someone else's human rights.

All the myths we've discussed give rise to perhaps the most important myth for sustaining the criminal justice practice. This is the myth that no one is responsible for the social conditions in which we live or the failure of the justice system to adequately address social harm. While we assign individual responsibility for criminal conduct, we ignore responsibility for the social conditions that generate crime, the failures of the criminal justice system to prevent crime, and crimes linked to our social institutions. In this myth, criminal justice is something other than the decisions of legislators, judges, police officers, and corrections officials—and the public that participates in and accepts the social construction of the system as an immutable given. The ultimate power of the social construction of criminal justice by myth is its ability to determine what is and is not thinkable.

References

Best, J., & Hutchinson, M. M. (2006). The gang initiation rite as a motif in contemporary crime discourse. In G. W. Potter & V. E. Kappeler (Eds.), *Constructing crime: Perspectives on making news and social problems* (2nd ed., pp. 95–114). Long Grove, IL: Waveland Press.

Bureau of Justice Statistics. (2010). Key facts at a glance: Correctional populations. Retrieved March 19, 2010, from http://www.bjs.ojp.usdoj.gov/content/glance/tables/corr2tab.cfm

Hynds, P. (1990). Balance bias and critical questions. *Media & Values*, 50, 5–7.

Kappeler, V. E., & Potter, G. W. (2005). *The mythology of crime and criminal justice* (4th ed.). Long Grove, IL: Waveland Press.

Republican Party of Minnesota et al. v. White, Chairperson, Minnesota Board of Judicial Standards, et al. No. 01–521. 536 U.S. (2002). Argued March 26, 2002—Decided June 27, 2002.

Sabol, W. J., West, H. C., & Cooper, M. (2009, December). *Prisoners in 2008* (NCJ 228417). Washington, DC: Bureau of Justice Statistics.

United Nations. (2001). Surveys of crime trends and operations of criminal justice systems, covering the period 1990–2000. United Nations Crime Reduction and Analysis Branch Office for Drug Control and Crime Prevention.

Walmsley, R. (2009). *World prison population list* (8th ed.). London: King's College, University of London. Retrieved January 14, 2010, from http://www.kcl.ac.uk/depsta/law/research/icps

Welch, M., Fenwick, M., & Roberts, M. (2006). State managers, intellectuals, and the media: A content analysis of ideology in experts' quotes in feature newspaper articles on crime. In G. W. Potter & V. E. Kappeler (Eds.), *Constructing crime: Perspectives on making news and social problems* (2nd ed., pp. 70–91). Long Grove, IL: Waveland Press.

[13]

THE COLUMBINE EFFECT AND SCHOOL ANTIVIOLENCE POLICY

Glenn W. Muschert and Anthony A. Peguero

ABSTRACT

Purpose – *This chapter explores the problem of school shootings as a source of anxiety and fear in schools. Such fear has generated calls for security in schools and has been a catalyst for the development and deployment of antiviolence policies in schools.*

Methodology/approach – *The chapter begins by examining the development of the Columbine Effect, which is a set of emotions surrounding youth social problems, particularly violence in schools. This Columbine Effect is then explored in relation to its role in the development of policies to mitigate the problem of school violence. These purposes are linked using a multilevel typology of school violence and their sources, created by Henry (2009).*

Findings – *The chapter explores the levels of violence addressed by six antiviolence policies: crime prevention through environmental design (CPTED), zero tolerance, anti-bullying programming, emergency management planning, peer mediation, and school climate programming. The analysis indicates the level(s) of violence each type of policy is designed to address and identifies research evidence regarding the efficacy of each policy. The analysis also focuses on the unintended consequences*

New Approaches to Social Problems Treatment
Research in Social Problems and Public Policy, Volume 17, 117–148

of school antiviolence policies, especially those which reduce violence on one or more levels, while exacerbating the problem on other levels.

Research limitations/implications – *The analytical approach was selective, rather than exhaustive. Nonetheless, the analysis has suggested a number of ironies concerning the unintended consequences of antiviolence programming in schools. This suggests the need for broader analysis in this area.*

Practical implications – *The analysis identifies a number of detrimental effects that have resulted from school violence policy initiatives ranging from the socialization of youth toward a society of control and authority. In addition, the chapter helps to clarify the (often negative) effects of hype about violence in schools.*

Originality/value of chapter – *Although not often connected, this chapter explores the intersection between the discourse of school violence (typically, a social problems framing concern) and the development of school antiviolence policies (typically, an applied social scientific concern).*

INTRODUCTION

Over the past decade, given the continued occurrences of school-related shootings, it has become widely understood that schools may be risky places for youth. In the same year that the Columbine shootings occurred, Beck (1999) posited the emergence of a world risk society, one in which our technological and social systems were out of control. Thus, each member of society is potentially at risk for human or technical accidents that are the "normal" outgrowth of complex social systems. While traditional conceptions of such fears derived from moral panics connected to a group of folk devils (see e.g., Cohen, 1972 or Goode & Ben-Yehuda, 1994), a new conception developed which viewed terrible events as deriving from systematic complexity (Ungar, 2001). From this point of view, school shootings are something that people have to live with and tolerate. Thus, the best that can be done is to reduce the risk of such events or to deal with them more effectively when they occur. Although school shootings are undoubtedly very rare events, they nonetheless exert strong leverage on the discourse about and responses to school violence. While school shootings remain a source of fear, the risk tolerance for these events is very low, if not nil. Such a general consensus about the intolerability of school shootings has led to wide-scale policy treatments for managing this and related social problems.

This chapter examines school violence from the point of view of the fear and anxiety it motivates, particularly related to school shootings. Our primary foci lie in the examination of the fear generated by school shooting events and in exploring how that fear has been translated through the development of policy outcomes. In this regard, there is much to tell about what is sometimes termed the "Columbine Effect," a term that refers to how rampage shootings change the way we think about school violence and security. These changes have deep impacts on the way we conceptualize the juvenile delinquent and his or her act and are associated with an increased level of fear about such attacks.

One development is that this fear serves as a potent motivator for implementation of school antiviolence policies, although as we shall demonstrate there is often mixed evidence that such policies are efficacious. Often, although certainly not always, such policies have been punitive, as opposed to restorative or aimed at mediation, in their efforts to control violence. In the sociology of social problems, scholars have noted that policy makers tend to search for a "silver bullet" solution, one that will solve problems without causing unintended consequences (Marx, 1995). To the contrary, sociologists as far back as Max Weber have pointed out that social policies have, almost invariably, latent unintended consequences. Indeed, one grave irony comes when those policies intended to ameliorate the problem are themselves the cause of an increase in the violence or fear they are entrusted to control (Marx, 1981). In this chapter, we examine a number of school antiviolence policies at various levels and examine the unintended negative consequences of these policies.

THE DISCOURSE OF SCHOOL VIOLENCE AND RISK

Of course, Columbine is not the only cause of increased fear in schools, although the Columbine Effect may be part of this dynamic. In a longitudinal study of mass media framing, Altheide (2002) noted that news discourse about children converged with the discourse of fear, peaking in 1994. This timing coincided with well-documented high rates of violence crimes perpetrated by youth (Office of Juvenile Justice and Delinquency Prevention, 2008). Shortly thereafter, in 1997, rampage-type school shootings gained salience as a social problem of national proportions, peaking in 1999 with the Columbine shootings (Muschert & Carr, 2006).

Given these preconditions, when the Columbine shootings occurred in 1999, it was not only something of a media spectacle but also the catalyst for a national discussion about the state of American society, and the ascendant social problem of school violence.

As one of the most closely followed stories of the late 1990s (Pew Research Center for the People and the Press, 1999), the discourse about Columbine became a battleground for efforts to define the problem of school violence in the public arena. Following the O. J. Simpson car chase, Columbine was the second most closely followed emergent news story in the 1990s (Muschert, 2002). Some scholars concluded that the mass media tended to associate the problem of school violence with insufficient control of firearms (Haider-Markel & Joslyn, 2001; Lawrence & Birkland, 2004), and that the mass media has acted as a catalyst for the occurrence of such events (Lawrence & Birkland, 2004; Samuels, 2000). Although the exact framing of the problem, and thus solutions, for school violence was contested, Columbine still looms large as a "problem-defining event, as it has come to characterize the problem of youth violence and the general understanding of youth social problems" (Muschert, 2007a, p. 351). Examining Columbine's role in problem definition of youth violence teaches sociologists of social problems and public policy "how dramatic news events are defined in the news in ways that contribute to the social construction of public problems" (Lawrence, 2001, p. 92). In this chapter, we discuss Columbine not as an historical event but as metaphorical "keyword for a complex set of emotions surrounding youth, fear, risk, and delinquency in 21st century America" (Muschert, 2007a, p. 365).

Since Columbine, other events have occurred that mesh with this Columbine-centered discourse of fear. Altheide (2009) argues that the discourse of fear surrounding school violence has merged into an overarching discourse of control about terrorism. For example, the 2001 terror attacks on U.S. soil raised fears that schools might be selected as targets in terror attacks (Casella, 2003), such that many schools combined internal security efforts with antiterror efforts. Despite the institution of antiviolence policies, school shootings continue to happen in the United States, and they also seem to be spreading to other countries, including Australia, Argentina, Canada, Finland, and Germany. Although this chapter focuses on the policies instituted in primary and secondary schools in the United States, we also observe school shootings seem to be occurring more commonly at universities, which are also active in the development of antiviolence policies (Fox & Savage, 2009).

Given that many causes for these events stem from combinations of relatively "garden variety" social conditions (see Muschert, 2007b for a review), perhaps some of these anxieties about the risks of school rampages may not be entirely unfounded. However, the annual number of fatalities (including both homicide and suicide) in all U.S. primary and secondary schools combined has steadily remained between 20 and 50 per year, over the last quarter century (Dinkes, Cataldi, Kena, Baum, & Snyder, 2006, p. 7). Nonetheless, fear of victimization in schools remains, and the findings of recent studies about such fear may seem counterintuitive. A quasi-experimental study of U.S. students aged 12–17 found that the fear of crime in schools was not significantly different after Columbine (Addington, 2003), and another study drawing from 1,500 schools indicated that students felt that their own schools were safer than other schools (Chapin & Coleman, 2006). If school-aged children are not overly fearful for their own safety, school antiviolence policies are frequently developed as administrators respond to concerned parents' calls to schools (Snell, Bailey, Corona, & Mebane, 2002). Thus, parental concern for children's safety in school seems to drive much policy development in this area.

An apparent conundrum lies in the discrepancy between the low level of tolerance for risk in schools and the comparatively higher acceptance of risk for children in other areas, such as abuse at home by family members. Some conceptual exploration might serve here to clarify the difference. One useful distinction is between compositional risk, which is an evaluation of the frequency of events, and degree of risk, which refers to the severity of misfortune that will result should the risk be realized. For example, compositional risk of airplane crashes is low, but the degree of risk is perceived to be extremely high. In comparison, the compositional risk of auto accidents is higher than for plane crashes, while the degree of risk for auto accidents is lower than for plane crashes. School shootings seem to fit in the category of events similar in risk perception to plane crashes where the chance of their occurrence is low, but the effect of the occurrence is horrific. When school shootings have occurred, numerous people may die, and this degree of risk is viewed as intolerable.

THE "COLUMBINE EFFECT" AS CATALYST FOR SOCIAL CONTROL

Although we may generally live in a risk society (Beck, 1992, 1999; Furudi, 1997), no risk is tolerable when it comes to children in schools. Taken together, fear and the expectation of risk are common features of contemporary public life (Altheide & Michalowski, 1999), but fear in schools is reflexively driven by a low tolerance for this variety of risk. This drives a call for safety in schools (where *safety* is defined as "an acceptable level of risk") through the institution of school security measures (where *security* is defined as the "process of achieving acceptable levels of risk"; Vestermark, 1996, p. 108, cited in Addington, 2009). In popular terms, this process has sometimes been called the "Columbine Effect" and seems the catalyst for development of many recent school antiviolence policies.

The term "Columbine Effect" first appeared as the title of a December 6, 1999, article in *Time* magazine in which the author discussed the post-Columbine movement toward increased punitive measures in schools (Cloud, 1999). Later, the term was prominently featured on a *Time* cover for an issue discussing the March 5, 2001, high school shooting in Santee, California. The cover featured a picture of a blue backpack typical of many used by American students. In the backpack's open pockets were books, a pen, a pencil, and a handgun. Such an image suggested the cultural discord about extreme forms of violence in schools, implying that the implements of schooling and the implements of violence should not exist in proximity. Since that time, the term has appeared in numerous places in the news media, popular presses (e.g., Matera, 2001), and academic discourse (e.g., Addington, 2003).

Although the idea represented by the term "Columbine Effect" may seem discordant at first glance, it is useful to illustrate the symbolic confluence of two previously unrelated cultural currents. Empirical research has indicated that there has been an association between the discourse of fear and the concept of youth (Altheide, 2002). In this context, the backpack with a gun is not so discordant at all but stands as a visual depiction of the "complex set of emotions surrounding youth, fear, risk, and delinquency" (Muschert, 2007a, p. 365). In fact, terror (as an emotion separate from the current connotation about terrorism) was an important component of the media coverage of the Columbine shootings (Muschert, 2002). Surprisingly, discussion of terror was not associated with the suffering of the victims and the community. Rather, references about terror and other emotional words were associated with reactions to the shootings that were occurring in various communities across the United States (Muschert, 2009). Thus, the terror of Columbine referred to the anxiety that it generated in communities across the nation. In such an emotionally charged context, the larger fear of youth as potential victims and victimizers (especially in schools) allows mechanisms of social control to expand.

There may be various catalysts for control mechanisms to expand within the context of the Columbine Effect, and these include various overlapping and potentially contradictory dynamics. The first dynamic may involve the perceived spread of school violence from urban areas to suburban and rural areas. Before the Columbine shootings, the spatial framing of school violence as a social problem was localized (Muschert & Carr, 2006), but the expansion in the problem frame to include a national scope coincided with highly publicized school violence incidents (mostly school shootings) that occurred in suburban and rural locales. Thus, the perceived migration of school violence into new areas is related to the development of antiviolence policies to mitigate the putative spatial expansion in school violence.

Second, the cultural shifts related to the increasing complexity and scale of society stimulate anxiety and systematic responses to threats to public safety. Bureaucratic practice in complex systems leads to an increasing focus on mitigation of risk through a crisis management approach. Thus, school safety increasingly becomes an issue of crisis management, which includes a multiple-stage focus on prevention and response to threats to school security. This dynamic includes the related, if often contradictory, trajectories about the control of risk and the beneficent desire to protect and nurture youth. Beyond this, school districts have an organizational interest in controlling liability, and as a result may apply an actuarial logic when approaching school safety. Here, in an effort to keep all threats to safety and accidents within controllable parameters, the focus may fall on security and social control.

As an overlapping issue, there is a sincere concern for the well-being of children. For example, school staff members maintain a bona fide interest in the caring and nurturance of pupils in their communities. In addition, parents and other community members may express fear for the safety of children in school, especially when they are exposed through mass media to shocking crimes in other, similar schools. Communication between parents and school staff often is related to their shared concern for the youth in their care, and school antiviolence policies are most commonly instituted after discussions between administrators and parents (Snell et al., 2002)

The difficulty in understanding the catalysts for school antiviolence policy development is that the line between caring and undue control is unclear. Socially, we have seen little legal or ethical debate concerning what sort of limitations we should place on efforts to maintain security in schools. In the next sections, we explore a number of school antiviolence policies and their outcomes. Although the policies examined are not entirely in response to high profile school shootings, events such as Columbine do exert a high leverage in the discourse about school violence.

CONCEPTUALIZING SCHOOL VIOLENCE

The discussion of the Columbine Effect leads to a discussion of various antiviolence policies implemented in response to violence within schools. There is an interactive relationship between school violence and the policies implemented, and we draw on Stuart Henry's (2009) multilevel framework to define and understand school violence and the associated school antiviolence policies. However, it is essential to first discuss the relative and constructed definition of school violence. The National Institute of Education (NIE) (1978) *Safe School Study* report to Congress is one of the first studies to focus on assessing the level of violence occurring within U.S. schools. The landmark *Safe School Study* suggests that violence occurring within schools is not prominently committed by "outsiders" but rather the students themselves. Thus, the NIE *Safe School Study* clearly denotes that the school administrators and policymakers can indeed implement policies to ameliorate violence occurring within schools and among members of the school community. The *Safe School Study* suggests policies that can facilitate an administrator's objective of reducing violence at school. These include increasing efforts in student governance and rule through enforcement, treating students fairly and equally, improving the relevance of subject matter to suit students' interests and needs, and reducing class size. The study also presents results reflecting that unemployment, poverty, and neighborhood conditions are not imperative factors toward the violence occurring within a school, but rather, school characteristics such as size of student enrollment, student–teacher ratios, principal's fairness, firmness, and consistency of discipline are more relevant in reducing school violence (Champion 1997; Lawrence, 2006; NIE, 1978).

Since the 1978 NIE *Safe School Study* report to Congress, researchers have continued to explore the possible causes, related factors, and consequences of school violence. As researchers began to scrutinize the landmark study, the relative definitions of school violence and the associated policies have changed. Conventional research, such as the 1978 NIE *Safe School Study*, utilized a definition of school violence that is founded on legal statutes of crime such as murder, rape, assault, robbery, and theft. However, many argue that the definition of school violence that typically applies to the adult realm is an inappropriate framework toward identifying, understanding, and addressing youth violence within schools. Given different psychological and sociological circumstances, the effects of victimization and harm from violence that youth endure are comparatively more damaging to children's development than to adults (Finkelhor, 2008; Henry, 2000). Research clearly indicates that youth have limited mental capacity and are less able to defend and protect themselves than adults (Finkelhor, 2008). Thus, a less severe instance of harm of victimization may cause a child to suffer emotional, mental, and physical injury where an adult would not (Finkelhor, 2008). This new perspective from developmental researchers draws into question the school's culture of tolerance for behaviors such as school bullying and sexual harassment. Such behaviors are consequently no longer tolerated as a normal part of the childhood school experience, but rather tend to be more strongly scrutinized than in the past (Olweus, 1993; Olweus & Limber, 1999; Spivak & Prothrow-Stith, 2001).

Although many research studies still follow the conventional wisdom established by the NIE (1978) *Safe Study* that school violence falls strictly within the purview of the school, many scholars argue it is also quite important to examine the forces external of the school contributing to the occurrence of violence within schools (Henry, 2000). Because the definition of school violence varies across schools and communities in this nation, we utilize a framework conceptualized by Stuart Henry (2009) to discuss a comprehensive view of school violence and the antiviolence policies implemented in response to the various forms and levels of school violence.

Levels of School Violence

Henry (2000, 2009) is critical of the conventional definitions of violence within schools that construct their definitions concentrating on overt student-on-student or student-on-teacher physical violence. Because subtle harm and injury for youth can seriously impede their emotional and educational development, a broader understanding and definition of school violence is necessary to conceptualize effective policies to address the many forms and levels of school violence. Henry (2009) suggests there are five levels of school violence, spanning from the individual to the societal/cultural level.

Individual violence (Level 1) encompasses behavior that originates specifically from the student, teacher, or administrator and includes actions such as fighting, vandalism, theft, or harassment with the victims either being fellow students, faculty, administration, staff, or the school. The defining characteristic of violence on this level involves the individual use (or abuse) of power by an individual student, teacher, or administrator toward another individual or group.

Group school violence (Level 2) stems from a collective or group. This group can be a clique or group of students who collectively bully other students, teachers, and staff. This also includes groups of teachers who cooperatively victimize other students, parents, teachers, and staff. Examples of group school violence are school faculty and staff neglect, prejudice, or discriminatory behavior in interactions with parents and parents' verbal abuse of school faculty, administration, and staff.

Institutional/organizational school violence (Level 3) refers to institutional practices that may injure individuals or groups. For example, such violence may reinforce societal oppression, marginalization, and privilege based on race, ethnicity, gender, sexual orientation, and ability that can undermine students' educational success and social progress. Institutional harms may include creating a prisonlike environment of control within a school and instituting invasive disciplinary practices. On a cultural level, the organizational exclusion or suppression of cultures, identities, beliefs, and views, while the privileging of others reflected in the curriculum and sanctions practices as a result of the local school board also exemplifies this level of violence. For example, when a local school district denies students permission to form "gay straight alliances" or organizations to curb and address the harassment and bullying of lesbian, gay, bisexual, and transgender (LGBT) students, the local school district is committing additional harm, injury, and victimization of LGBT youth within schools.

Communal/neighborhood school violence (Level 4) is reflective of the political, social, and economic tensions between the school and the community/neighborhood. Educational policies, juvenile justice policies, and local business exploitation of students are some examples reflective of this level of school violence. For example, many researchers, educators, parents, and community stakeholders have clearly protested against the *No Child Left Behind Act of 2001* (NCLB), a U.S. federal law, because it can marginalize some youth within U.S. public schools and their communities/neighborhoods. There are a number of ways reported that NCLB has victimized public schools and the associated students, families, and communities that they serve (see Meier & Wood, 2004 for further details). Underfunding of a number of extracurricular programs and detrimental educational effects on disabled and students with limited English proficiency is associated with NCLB (Meier & Wood, 2004).

Societal and cultural school violence (Level 5) is defined as the harmful cultural or social processes that may pervade each of the preceding four levels. This level of school violence highlights the historical, structural, systemic, and the overarching discourse our nation has in relationship to school violence. Such factors include the glorification of masculinity and infamy in popular culture, the widespread availability of guns, and the promotion of competition in school environments. As suggested earlier in this chapter, the Columbine Effect has thrust the phenomenon of school violence into a higher level of salience, such that it is perceived as a serious social problem threatening this nation's youth. In this sense, the Columbine Effect operates on this level and is intimately linked to policy developments intended to mitigate the victimization of youth on levels one through four of the multilevel model. The fear of harm, injury, and victimization by children, parents, faculty, and all stakeholders in the educational system is overarching and ubiquitous in our society. Thus, the importance of providing a safe school for children is often perceived as an urgent issue, and exploration of school policies in the following section helps to clarify how school antiviolence polices may be understood through this multilevel framework.

EXPLORING SCHOOL ANTIVIOLENCE POLICIES

School antiviolence policies are initiatives instituted to prevent, control, or mitigate violence in schools. While many such policies concentrate on student-based violent behavior (Level 1), we also consider antiviolence policies to include programs designed to address victimization on one or more of Henry's (2009) five levels, including programs designed to reduce psychological and symbolic harm. For illustrative purposes, we explore a number of school antiviolence policies that address the varying levels of school violence, including environmental design, zero tolerance, anti-bullying programs, emergency management planning, peer mediation, and initiatives to influence school climate. Following a discussion of some unintended detrimental consequences of such policies, we conclude the section with a reflection on the evolution of antiviolence policies in schools.

Crime Prevention through Environmental Design

Crime prevention through environmental design (CPTED) is an antiviolence approach founded on the notion that the physical environment is a significant predictor of crime in a given location (Crowe, 1990, 2000; Newman, 1972; Wilcox, Augustine, & Clayton, 2006) – in this case, the school. CPTED primarily addresses four aspects of school physical environment associated with Levels 1 and 3 school violence: surveillance, access control, target hardening, and territorial reinforcement.

Control through surveillance is based on the assumption that potential offenders will be deterred because their acts can be quite observable. Enhanced visibility can be addressed in a number of ways by a school: for example, school buildings can be designed with clear lines of sight and monitoring across the structure. Given greater visibility, the possible occurrence of violence can be identified and addressed expeditiously. The process of enhancing visibility can of course also be supplemented using electronic surveillance measures in school common areas.

School access control is based on the concept that restricting access to potential victims of violence maintains greater safety among all in the school. For instance, school buildings can be designed to implement a centralized point of entry. This controls the access of the school because visitors must enter and leave through the same entrance, which directs any visitors through or near the administration area.

School target hardening is enhancing the physical defense of school participants while on school grounds. This can be accomplished through window locks, security bars over classroom windows, alarms for unauthorized opening of school doors, school fences and gates that border campus, and metal detectors. Similarly, the school territorial reinforcement suggests that all these CPTED factors must be clearly visible to deter potential offenders. The physical presence and visibility of these safety and antiviolence measures promotes a perception of control that discourages violence. In other words, such measures are effective as target hardeners, when it is clearly visible that the school territory is reinforced and protected.

Although a number of researchers have suggested that implementing CPTED antiviolence policies within schools would be effective (Crowe, 1990, 2000; Schneider, Marschall, Roch, & Teske, 1999; Toby, 1994), few scholarly studies have specifically focused on the implementation of CPTED antiviolence policies within schools. Astor and colleagues (Astor, Meyer, & Behre, 1999; Astor & Meyer, 2001) hypothesize there are "subcontexts" or "hot spots" within the school where the incidence of crime is relatively higher due to physical and environmental characteristics, including hallways, cafeterias, and parking lots. Because these high traffic locations on campus have higher rates of violence, increased monitoring and restricted access can mitigate violence in these locations. Astor and colleagues

(Astor et al., 1999; Astor & Meyer, 2001) report that these school areas are perceived as "unowned" by students or school faculty, and administration, a perception that may facilitate violent behavior in these locales.

In an extensive analysis of the effectiveness of CPTED on school violence, Wilcox et al. (2006) reveal limited relationships between CPTED and the occurrence of violence on school grounds. They suggest that the social structure (i.e., student enrollment, percent free lunch, percent racial and ethnic minority, and percent male) of the school is more relevant in terms of the occurrence of school crime (Wilcox et al., 2006). Moreover, they find that the school physical structure (i.e., main office territoriality, hallway territoriality, exterior territoriality, and surveillance in the main office, hallways, and exterior areas), after controlling for school social structure, is not related to student-based measures of school crime. However, the school physical structure is related to teacher-based measures of school crime. Teacher-witnessed misconduct is negatively associated with hallway territoriality and exterior area surveillance, and in contrast, hallway territoriality and exterior area surveillance are found to be the only features of the physical environment to be (negatively) associated with teacher-based perceptions of school crime after controlling for school social structure (Wilcox et al., 2006).

Zero Tolerance Policies

No other school antiviolence policy has received as much social scrutiny as zero tolerance (Verdugo, 2002). Zero tolerance school antiviolence policy attempts to ameliorate Level 2 school violence by establishing clear and transparent guidelines of student punishment. Zero tolerance school antiviolence policy intends to restrict the discretion from school administrators and faculty to ensure unbiased application of student discipline punishments for violent acts within school (Arum, 2003; Morrison & Skiba, 2001; Skiba, Michael, Nardo, & Peterson, 2002; Verdugo, 2002).

Similar to mandatory sentencing guidelines implemented within the criminal justice system, zero tolerance school policies are intended to remove, or at least minimize, discretion from school administrators and faculty to ensure unbiased application of the punishments associated with school antiviolence policies (Arum, 2003; Morrison & Skiba, 2001; Skiba et al., 2002; Verdugo, 2002). The U.S. Customs Agency developed zero tolerance in the 1980s to target the booming drug trade (Martinez, 2009; Skiba et al., 2002; Verdugo, 2002). In partial response to the tragic events that occurred at Columbine, this zero tolerance philosophy and policy was legislatively indoctrinated into this nation's public school systems during President Clinton's administration with the Gun-Free Schools Act (Martinez, 2009; Skiba et al., 2002; Verdugo, 2002). Congress passed this law to address the issue of school violence, requiring schools to institute a zero tolerance policy for students and enforcing a minimum of 1 year of expulsion to students who bring a firearm on campus; otherwise, schools lose federal funds that the Elementary and Secondary Education Act (1965) provides (Martinez, 2009; Skiba et al., 2002; Verdugo, 2002); hence, the pervasiveness of zero tolerance school antiviolence policies has grown exponentially since.

It is estimated that over 90% of public schools have a zero tolerance antiviolence policy in place (Verdugo, 2002; Skiba et al., 2002). Most state and local school administrators have established zero tolerance antiviolence policies with mandatory expulsions or suspensions (Verdugo, 2002). Violent or criminal behaviors such as fighting, rape, assault, indecent exposure, sexual assault and harassment, vandalism, and destruction of school property often result in mandatory student expulsion or suspension (Arum, 2003; Kupchik & Monahan, 2006; Morrison & Skiba, 2001; Verdugo, 2002). Zero tolerance school antiviolence policies, however, also encompass nonviolent student misbehavior. For example, gambling, spitting, verbal harassment, disobedience, truancy, and obscene language fall within some zero tolerance antiviolence policy parameters that mandate expulsion or suspension for the aforementioned student behavior on school grounds (Arum, 2003; Kupchik & Monahan, 2006; Morrison & Skiba, 2001; Verdugo, 2002). Schools across the nation have implemented zero tolerance antiviolence policies that are not entirely in response to school shootings but more in response to various less severe events.

The effectiveness of zero tolerance antiviolence school policies is questionable at best. Even though school administrators continue to practice zero tolerance antiviolence policies, there is minimal research to support that the amelioration of school violence results from this antiviolence school policy. It is reported that zero tolerance school antiviolence polices do make students, teachers, staff, and school community participants "feel safer" and thus may have and influence improved behavior among school participants (Martinez, 2009; Verdugo, 2002). As with many antiviolence school policies, however, the majority of evidence that is utilized to promote the success of zero tolerance antiviolence policies are based on testimonials from schools and school administrators who advocate for the continued use of zero tolerance (Martinez, 2009; Morrison

& Skiba, 2001; Skiba et al., 2002; Verdugo, 2002). On the contrary, there is evidence that suggests zero tolerance school antiviolence policies are not only ineffective but problematic. Even though zero tolerance antiviolence policies are common place since the past decade, the rate of seriously injured victims of violence occurring within schools remains consistent (Kupchik & Monahan, 2006; Martinez, 2009). On the contrary, expulsions and suspensions have exponentially increased as a result of zero tolerance antiviolence policies (Martinez, 2009; Morrison & Skiba, 2001; Skiba et al., 2002; Verdugo 2002). Zero tolerance school antiviolence policies socialize and marginalize students toward social exclusion, educational failure, and economic depression (Kupchik & Monahan, 2006; Morrison & Skiba, 2001; Noguera, 2003; Verdugo, 2002; Wacquant, 2001).

Bullying Prevention Policies

Bullying has two key components: repeated harmful acts and an imbalance of power. It involves repeated physical, verbal, or psychological attacks or intimidation directed against a victim who cannot properly defend himself or herself because of size or strength, or because the victim is outnumbered or less psychologically resilient (American Association of University Women Educational Foundation, 2001; Olweus, 1993; Olweus & Limber, 1999; Smith, Twemlow, & Hoover, 1999). Basically, bullying occurs when a student being victimized is exposed repeatedly over time to intentional injury or discomfort inflicted by one or more other students. It may include physical contact, verbal assault, making obscene gestures or facial expressions, and being intentionally excluded.

In recent years, there has been an effort to scrutinize traditionally defined minor forms of victimization, such as bullying and harassment within schools, and to redefine them as forms of school violence. Although conventional wisdom often portrayed bullying as normative within the youth experience, research findings indicated that many victims of bullying sustained long-lasting detrimental social, psychological, and educational effects (American Association of University Women Educational Foundation, 2001; Olweus, 1993; Olweus & Limber, 1999; Smith et al., 1999). Thus, bullying prevention polices are designed to send a message that bullying violence will not be accepted or tolerated. Addressing Levels 1 and 2 categories of school violence, well-designed and implemented bullying prevention programs are based on educating staff and students to recognize and respond to instances of bullying.

The *Olweus Bullying Prevention Program* (OBPP) is the most prevalent blueprint that school antiviolence policies have utilized to address school bullying. The OBPP is a school-based program designed to prevent or reduce school bullying violence, identifying and focusing on three levels of the school to decrease bullying: school-wide, classroom, and the individual. At the school level, the first step of the program is to identify bullies and bullying victims. School faculty and staff administer the Olweus Bully/Victim Questionnaire to students to assess the prevalence and characteristics of bullying occurring among the student body. Then, school faculty and staff establish a committee to implement training for all faculty and staff members to address bullying. Finally, faculty and staff develop curricula for all students that highlight the school-wide rules against bullying, while promoting the importance of mutual respect and healthy relations among students. Within the classroom, teachers deliver a number of anti-bullying lessons or oversee student meetings about school bullying and peer relations. Teachers also extend communication and discussions about school bullying violence with parents. On the individual level, students may be individually identified as a bully or bullying victim to have regularly scheduled meetings to discuss and address why the bullying is occurring and what can be done to resolve the violence. Through these mechanisms, the OBPP school antiviolence program attempts to reorganize the existing school climate to decrease the occurrence of bullying violence (Olweus,1993; Olweus & Limber, 1999; Smith et al., 1999).

Although the OBPP is generally viewed by school administrators as successful, there have been limited studies that examine the effectiveness and the limitations of anti-bullying programs, and inconsistent findings in these studies are common (see, e.g., Mishna, 2008; Smith, Ryan, & Cousins, 2007). Because the definition of bullying is complex and relative (Crick & Grotpeter, 1995; Hand & Sanchez, 2000; Vaillancourt et al., 2008), the OBPP may not address all forms of perceived bullying. In this context, the perception of violence, injury, and victimization is primarily based on adult definitions and understandings of bullying, which may lead to under- or over-monitoring of violent student behavior (Safran, 2007; Vaillancourt et al., 2008). In other words, school administrator, faculty, and staff interpretations may influence the utilization of bullying prevention policies. Intimidation based on race, ethnicity, gender, religion, socioeconomic status, social class, physical ability, and sexual orientation is sometimes excluded from definitions of bullying and are therefore not addressed by anti-bullying policies (Espelage & Swearer, 2003, 2004; Simmons, 2002). For instance, there are reports of schools underutilizing bullying definitions that include homophobic harassment among the student body for fear of the perception that parents and community will interpret this action as supportive of homosexuality (Swearer, Turner, Givens, & Pollack, 2008). Furthermore, there is a clear gender gap between how bullying is defined, identified, and addressed by male and female faculty as well as a variation by the gender of the bully and bullying victim (Espelage & Swearer, 2004). Of course, this may be complicated by the relative and subjective definitions of each student, teacher, administrator, and parent's view of bullying. Thus, a "universal" or standardized approach toward addressing bullying behavior is difficult to maintain (Espelage & Swearer, 2003).

Emergency Management Planning

Given contemporary risk perception in general, schools have become sites of anxiety for a number of threats, including natural disasters, terrorist attacks, and of course violent attacks. At the time of the 2001 terrorist attacks on the United States, schools were comparatively well prepared for attacks, due to the perception that school rampages were palpable risks in schools (Muschert, 2007b). Such awareness has led to the development of crisis management plans in schools, as 97% of schools have in place a plan to prepare for, respond to, and recover from a major crisis, and 87% of schools with plans provided training on crisis response to faculty and staff in the past 2 years (Schuster, 2009). Emergency readiness is intended to address the sources of violence on the institutional plane (Level 3), when implemented on the level of the individual school. When implemented on the community scale, crisis management plans address the sources of violence in communities (Level 4).

Although many such plans have not been tested in practice, there are some indicators that suggest the presence of such plans may not be solution to extreme threats they are intended to be. For example, 51% of school resource officers (SROs) surveyed indicated that the emergency management plans in place were inadequate, and 67% indicated that the emergency plans were not practiced on a regular basis in their schools (Schuster, 2009). Despite these possible challenges, the National Institute of Justice continues to provide resources and training related to critical incident responses including a school safety plan generator, resources for creating a critical incident response team, and how to deal with an on-campus active shooter. Following the 2007 Virginia Tech shootings, the perception of such risk on postsecondary campuses has grown, and numerous universities have formed similar crisis management plans and have formed campus-wide incident response teams. On all levels of education, faculty, staff, and administration are typically aware of the existence of emergency management plans; however, students are often unaware that such plans exist.

Peer Mediation Policy

Although a number of school antiviolence policies exclude student voices in addressing violence in their own environments, there is a growing implementation of peer-led school antiviolence policies. Peer mediation programs are negotiation-based conflict resolution strategies that promote student mediators as a means of resolving disagreements among peers. This variety of policy centers on students as conflict managers who apply problem-solving strategies to assist peers in settling disputes and is intended to address the sources of violence on Level 1, the individual level. Peer mediation cultivates an alternative set of skills that students use to avoid violent situations and, with effective implementation and oversight, helps provide students with alternatives to violence in solving personal problems or resolving interpersonal conflict (Bodine & Crawford, 1998; Johnson & Johnson, 1996; Trujillo, Bowland, Myers, Richards, & Roy, 2008).

Peer mediation policies have been implemented in response to a number of Level 1 school violence situations; however, there are variations. Some peer mediation only addresses informal violent situations among students (e.g., minor school yard harassment), while others have implemented approaches to bring peer mediation programs into the classroom for resolving student disputes. Some schools have utilized formal and structured approaches with peer mediation such as establishing a "mediation office" in which all mediation occurs. Although there are various ways that these programs have been implemented, there are three common elements to peer mediation: First, *planning*, before implementing a peer mediation school antiviolence policy and program within a school. This involves choosing students, the structure and scheduling of the peer mediation, clear and transparent objectives for peer mediation, and the type of violence and conflict that fall within the scope of the program. Second, programs require *training*, in which students learn the basic principles of conflict resolution and how to implement these principles in a respectful and effective manner. This aspect is vital toward the success of a peer mediation program. Third, the program requires *on-going implementation*, involving monitoring and evaluation of the efficacy. Beyond these three commonalities, most iterations of peer mediation fall within two broad categories: the *cadre* approach, in which a few students receive training to serve as peer mediators for an entire school, or the *holistic* school approach, in which all students in a school or in a class are taught how to manage conflicts constructively and are given the opportunity to be a mediator (Bodine & Crawford, 1998; Johnson & Johnson, 1996; Trujillo et al., 2008).

As with many other school antiviolence policies, there is limited research evaluating the effectiveness of peer mediation across schools. Commonly, individual school or district administrators laud the successes of peer mediation. Some programs dictate that only students who are enrolled in peer mediation elective courses can serve as mediators, thus limiting the number of mediators and restricting the schedule of times during which mediation can be offered (Lupton-Smith, Carruthers, Flythe, Goettee, & Modest, 1996). Additionally, the depth of training and frequency of support for mediators and coordinators may face structural pressures on resources (Lupton-Smith, 2004). Johnson and Johnson (1996) argue that for peer mediation school to be effective, a "holistic" approach must be implemented, in which *all* students are taught the conflict resolution methods and *all* have the opportunity to become mediators. They further note that the strength of the holistic approach to mediation is that each student learns about managing conflict and violence constructively. Through this channel, schools can facilitate inclusive peer mediation programs that reduce violence in schools by socializing and teaching students to negotiate and mediate conflict in more healthy and creative ways (Johnson & Johnson, 1996).

School Climate Policy

Gottfredson and colleagues (Gottfredson & Gottfredson, 2001; Gottfredson, Gottfredson, Payne, & Gottfredson, 2005) argue that creating strong communal school organization is an effective and efficient approach toward providing a safe and healthy school climate for students. Defined as the organization of a school as a community, key characteristics include supportive relationships among teachers, administrators, and students all of whom share a common set of goals and norms, collaboration, and involvement (Gottfredson & Gottfredson, 2001). Strong communal school organization is found to reduce student drug use, delinquency, misbehavior, and dropouts and to increase levels of student academic interest, motivation, achievement, and interpersonal empathy (Gottfredson & Gottfredson, 2001; Gottfredson et al., 2005; Payne, Gottfredson, & Gottfredson, 2003;

Payne, 2008; Phaneuf, 2006). The importance of establishing good relationships among all school members is a relatively new approach to ameliorating the school violence; however, it is not a new approach within educational research.

Bryk and Driscoll (1988) argue that schools are a "community" because they reflect many of the social mechanisms, bureaucratic practices, cultural values (e.g., focus on education), and behavioral patterns present in communities at large. As in communities, school participants share common activities, routines, and symbiotic interactions that influence one another and an "ethos of caring" (Bryk & Driscoll, 1988). Collective relationships between administrators, teachers, and students create a sense of trust and belonging for a larger school community that influences a school's overall climate, effectiveness, efficiency, and safety (Battistich & Solomon, 1997; Payne et al., 2003). Verdugo and Schneider (1999) highlight that there is fine line between creating safe and quality schools and the risk that schools with a culture centered on security and control will have detrimental consequences for the all participants. Schools with increased security and control may promote distrust among all participants because they are fearful of violence, thereby distracting administrators, parents, teachers, and students from focusing on educational progress (Noguera, 2003; Verdugo, 1999; Verdugo & Schneider, 1999).

This recent holistic school antiviolence policy approach, as a means of addressing the occurrence of school violence on multiple levels (here, Levels 1, 2, and 3), has yielded early positive research results. Epstein (2002) indicates that "healthy" and functional relationships between school administrators, teachers, students, parents, and the community are influential upon the overall climate and effectiveness of that school. Hazler (2000) indicates that schools that implement programs that promote social issues awareness (e.g., AIDS, violence, or homelessness) have yielded positive results such as increased school attachment, bond, attendance, and engagement among all members of the school community. Hoy and Sabo (1998) note that teachers and administrators who focus on establishing a learning climate that strives for academic excellence often positively influence the school's cultural attitude toward learning. That pursuit of academic excellence is argued to be "contagious" among students, teachers, and administrators in schools that promote such scholastic virtue (Hoy & Sabo, 1998). Epstein and Sanders (1998) discuss how relationships between the school administrators, teachers, and the students directly and indirectly promote learning and safety. School policies and programs that focus on promoting the importance of educational achievement, attainment, and success improve the overall school climate as well as making it safer (Noguera, 2003; Payne et al., 2003; Payne, 2008; Skiba & Peterson, 2000).

IRONIES IN THE DEVELOPMENT OF SCHOOL ANTIVIOLENCE POLICIES

While our review of school antiviolence policies in the previous section has been selective, we nonetheless note some unintended consequences resulting from these efforts to mitigate the problem. Indeed, many of these ironies are best understood as situated within the historical development of school antiviolence policies.

Reflecting on the Evolution of School Antiviolence Policies

The development in school antiviolence policies in recent decades reveals that policies are not monolithic, and their implementation is not uniform. The implementation, utilization, and enforcement of school antiviolence policies and subsequent school punishment are influenced by school characteristics (e.g., size, locale, region, demographics, and economic affluence) and student factors (e.g., race, ethnicity, gender, and socio-economic status) (Arum, 2003; Kupchik & Monahan, 2006; Morrison & Skiba, 2001; Verdugo, 2002; Skiba et al., 2002). As school size increases, so does the number of school antiviolence policies instituted, and although school antiviolence policies have been adopted across all schools, urban schools have the highest proportions of school antiviolence policies relative to schools in rural and suburban locations. Regionally, school antiviolence policies are practiced more in western and southeastern regions of the country, and schools with higher proportions of racial and ethnic minority students have more school antiviolence policies. Furthermore, schools with higher levels of students who receive free or reduced price lunches also have increased likelihood of having school antiviolence policies in place. Regarding individual student characteristics, racial and ethnic minority, poor, and male students are more likely to be suspended or expelled from school as a result of zero tolerance policies. These findings suggest that school antiviolence policies, as well as the associated school violence discourse, have a longer history in urban areas within racial and ethnic minority and poor communities. As suggested earlier in this chapter, however, it is also evident that the school violence discourse and subsequent antiviolence policies have more recently seized suburban, predominately white, and affluent schools.

It is not surprising that the definition, parameters, and implementation of school antiviolence policies and programs vary because the phenomenon of school violence is a complex, socially constructed, historically contingent, and politically driven issue influenced by myriad of diverse factors. The social construction and the perception of school violence fundamentally stemming from students is apparent in many school antiviolence policies and programs; however, it is also evident that there is growing consensus that indicates multilevel, holistic, inclusive, and community approaches toward addressing the many forms of school violence is vital. "At the end of the day all violence prevention programs come down to relationships: our ability to listen to ourselves, to recognize others' experience and use this information to solve problems, to learn and be creative together" (Twemlow & Cohen, 2003, p. 121).

Clearly, the broad categories of school violence vary significantly across schools as well as which types of violence are defined as a clear and present danger to all school participants that needs to be addressed. Of course, one school antiviolence policy cannot address all the variegated aspects and levels of the issue. Thus, a singular and populist view that students are the sole source of violence occurring within schools leading to the social and physical control of students as a practical antiviolence response has detrimental consequences.

Some Unintended Consequences

The policies we have reviewed here certainly address school violence on various levels; however, we do note that a policy designed to address the sources of violence on one level may in turn create additional challenges on the same level or on other levels of violence. From our review of selected policies, there are noteworthy ironies. First, CPTED may address some contributing causes of interpersonal violence (Level 1 violence), yet might contribute to an overall prisonlike feel associated with contemporary school design. This prisonlike feel becomes a source of violence on the institutional level (Level 3 violence). Second, zero tolerance policies are intended to reduce discretion in the administration of penalties, and therefore to reduce individual (Level 1 violence) or organizational (Level 3 violence) inequalities that may contribute to violence. In turn, zero tolerance policies might increase inequality by disproportionately affecting certain groups (Level 2 violence) and by contributing to the punitive atmosphere in the institution (Level 3 violence). Third, anti-bullying programs are intended to reduce violence on the individual (Level 1) and group (Level 2) planes. Cultural or individual differences of opinion regarding what constitutes bullying might unfortunately disregard (or amplify) the victimization of vulnerable individuals or groups, thereby magnifying the problem in some senses on the same individual (Level 1) and group (Level 2) planes. Fourth, emergency management planning is intended to address causes of violence emerging from the institution (Level 3) or the community (Level 4). Even when effectively implemented, such plans may stimulate a sense of fear among faculty and staff, emotionally undermining the sense of security such plans might instill. In this case, addressing the sources of violence on Levels 3 and 4 could damage the school environment (Level 3) or individual relationships (Level 1). Fifth, peer mediation programs (intended to reduce violence on the individual and group levels, Levels 1 and 2) if implemented ineffectively might exclude participants from mediation, thereby potentially amplifying violence on the same levels. Finally, school climate policies, intended to address violence on the institutional plane (Level 3), have been demonstrated sometimes to cause mistrust on individual (Level 1) and group (Level 2) planes.

The development of school antiviolence polices have created what has been called the "New American school" as an institution of socialization toward a life of social control and fear (Hirschfield, 2008; Kupchik & Monahan, 2006; Noguera, 2003; Wacquant, 2001). Noguera (1995) argues that schools are increasingly oriented as an institution of control and that implementation of rigid social control measures establishes a "prison-like," "lock-down" environment for students (Noguera, 1995, p. 190). Wacquant (2001) argues that schools have gradually transformed into "institutions of confinement" that socialize youth for an adult life of control, security, and restricted access. Nineteen percent of high schools and 40% of large urban high schools have full-time law enforcement officials on campus (Heaviside et al., 1998; National Center for Education Statistics, 2005), and the number of schools with full-time SROs is growing rapidly (Beger, 2002: Kupchik & Monahan, 2006). Twenty-five percent of high schools have surveillance cameras and most of new schools built in 2000 are designed with surveillance objectives in mind (Small et al., 2001). Metal detectors, video recording, internet tracking, biometrics, transparent lockers and book bags, and security and drug dogs are just some of the security measures implemented as a result of school antiviolence policies that are becoming part of students' daily experience (Kupchik & Monahan, 2006; Verdugo, 2002).

Because schools are institutions of education and socialization where youth learn about their current and future roles in society, the school's environment, in terms of the presence of control and security, may be socializing youth to perceive security, fear, and social control as normative (Kupchik & Monahan, 2006). Indeed, the increasing level of social control (e.g., zero tolerance and security) within schools deteriorates the educational experience of all students (Noguera, 1995). In turn, school antiviolence policies may merely respond to the symptoms of a more pervasive social problem, while ignoring the core issue – the nation's eroding school communities (Kozol, 1991; Noguera, 2003; Verdugo, 2002).

School exclusion (i.e., suspension and expulsion) has exponentially increased as a result of many school antiviolence policies (Arum 2003; Verdugo 2002; Skiba et al., 2002). Zero tolerance policies are socializing and marginalizing students toward social exclusion, poor educational attainment, and economic disadvantage (Arum, 2003; Kupchik & Monahan, 2006; Verdugo, 2002; Morrison & Skiba, 2001). School exclusions place students on a path toward academic disengagement and failure (Skiba & Peterson, 2003; Skiba & Rausch, 2006; Noguera, 2003; Wacquant, 2001). As a result of being suspended or expelled, students are being deprived of the benefits of the educational system, a process that then detrimentally impacts their life chances (Skiba & Peterson, 2003; Sprague & Walker, 2000; Skiba & Rausch, 2006), and those who are suspended or expelled are also more likely to drop out of high school and terminate education (Skiba & Peterson, 2003; Skiba & Rausch, 2006). Students excluded from school no longer perceive education as a viable institutional mechanism for success, and because of their restricted access, these youth are at increased risk to become involved in misbehavior, delinquency, drug use, and future adult criminality (Dunham & Alpert, 1986; Morrison & Skiba, 2001).

Regarding school security, research findings are inconsistent and potentially counterintuitive. Schreck, Miller, and Gibson (2003) find that a high level of school security is not associated with a decrease in school violence. To the contrary, school security practices such as checking student lockers are related to increased stress, anxiety, and victimization (Schreck et al., 2003). In another study, Wilcox et al. (2006) report that increased school surveillance is not associated with lower levels of school violence, and in fact, some indicate that school security surveillance may instill fear for all members of the school community (Schreck et al., 2003; Phaneuf, 2006). In turn, student fear is associated with school disengagement, avoidance of particular places within school, psychological and emotional instability, and educational failure (Phaneuf, 2006; Verdugo, 1999; Verdugo & Schneider, 1999). Although there is debate regarding whether school antiviolence policies are achieving their proposed objective to provide safe and healthy learning environment for students, it appears that these policies "facilitate the criminalization of poor students in order to establish and maintain a criminal class to legitimate systems of inequality" (Kupchik & Monahan, 2006, p. 628).

Perhaps a more generalized irony is that the Columbine Effect itself might contribute to school violence. While this review of policy responses does include those addressing the sources of violence on a variety of levels, we note that no policy developments appear oriented toward ameliorating violence on Level 5, the sociocultural level. Henry (2009) notes that various cultural dynamics may operate to exacerbate school violence problems, including mass media hype about violence. The Columbine Effect is as example of mass media hype, and in this case, the dynamic has become pervasive and nestled within the broader context of fear in a risk society. The Columbine Effect is a discourse of anxiety about school violence that acts as a catalyst for antiviolence policy development, much of which is oriented toward control of student behavior. Ironically, we note that as a justification for antiviolence policy development, the Columbine Effect might serve to exacerbate violence on a number of other levels. Notably, we have observed an expansion in the geographical reach and penetration of such policies, and such an expansion leads to the increased expansion of the types of unintended consequences we have illustrated.

The symbolic leverage exerted by Columbine-type events seems strongly related to the institution of policies that have a low threshold in their response to violent behaviors. Although rare in themselves, rampage school shootings are an extreme end on a broad continuum of violent behaviors in schools, one that exerts disproportionate influence on calls for security in schools. As Columbine-type events somewhat typify school violence in the public discourse, the understandably low risk tolerance for school shootings has bled over to other, less grave, forms of school violence. Thus, we observe a high level of sensitivity to school violence, one which elicits a serious and increasingly formal response to school violence on all levels. Our concern remains that many of the most vulnerable students might suffer disproportionately from this sensitivity, although there may be a light at the end of the tunnel as antiviolence policies begin to respond to more comprehensive aspects of the problem.

CONCLUSION

The discourse of school violence known as the Columbine Effect has resulted in an increasing number of school administrators implementing school antiviolence policies as strategies to address school violence (Kupchik & Ellis, 2008; Stanley, Juhnke, & Purkey, 2004). Policies that primarily or singularly focus on responding to the ubiquitous discourse of school violence by increasing control without considering the core problem of eroding school and learning communities will only continue to socially, culturally, and educationally marginalize all students, especially those who are most vulnerable. These school antiviolence policies have suggested that the key to reducing the dilemma of school violence centers on social control to create safe schools; however, most of these policies disregard the importance and allocating resources for improving the overall communal school organization (Gottfredson & Gottfredson, 2001). "Safe" and "learning" environments are not mutually exclusive concepts but rather symbiotic ideas of thinking about providing what school antiviolence policies are ideally pursuing to provide to all students – safe and healthy learning environments that promote educational success as well as instilling the importance of citizenship, respect, and justice for all youth.

Simply "fortifying" schools is not an effective policy toward establishing and sustaining a "healthy" learning environment (Noguera, 1995; Verdugo, 1999; Verdugo & Schneider, 1999). The unfortunate reality within schools across this nation is that, indeed, school antiviolence policies are "normalizing" control and socializing fear, a dynamic that clearly impedes the educational process and youth development. Additionally, this discourse of the fear of school violence is also impacting the school administrators, teachers, and staff. No longer can administrators and teachers base daily interactions, informal passing by, and hallway chats on the pursuit of establishing rapport and camaraderie but rather are charged with tasks to survey, restrict, and control social behavior. This further erodes the communal school organization by fostering distrust and suspicion (Gottfredson & Gottfredson, 2001; Payne, 2008).

The perceived sense of control derived from efforts to securitize schools may not be worth the negative tradeoffs, and a grave irony is the possibility that in the effort to create safe schools, we may be magnifying risks in other areas. For example, security measures may cause students to experience increased anxiety/angst in general. The potential pitfall here is socializing children toward compliance through efforts to mitigate risk, as the movement toward safety and control in schools may move beyond efforts to create security. Social control measures often demonstrate a tendency to expand or take on autonomy of their own, a dynamic that may complicate the contradiction between caring and control. We question whether children ought to be treated as objects of control. Scholars of the social problem of school violence and related policies must conceptualize and investigate policies that improve communal school organization as the most effective way to reduce school violence and foster educational success, healthy school relationships, and a safe learning environment for youth. Such policies must balance needs for security on individual, group, and institutional levels with the rights and interests of individual students, particularly those who are most vulnerable.

ACKNOWLEDGMENTS

The authors would like to acknowledge Tirth Bhattta for research assistantship and the following colleagues for their comments on a draft of this manuscript: Fauzia Ahmed, J. Scott Brown, Jennifer Bulanda, Ronald Bulanda, Heidi Ewen, and Stephen Lippmann.

REFERENCES

Addington, L. A. (2003). Students' fear after Columbine: Findings from a randomized experiment. *Journal of Quantitative Criminology*, *19*(4), 367–387.

Addington, L. A. (2009). Cops and cameras: Public school security as a policy response to Columbine. *American Behavioral Scientist*, *52*(10), 1426–1446.

Altheide, D. L. (2002). Children and the discourse of fear. *Symbolic Interaction*, *25*, 229–250.

Altheide, D. L. (2009). The Columbine shootings and the discourse of fear. *American Behavioral Scientist*, *52*(10), 1354–1370.

Altheide, D. L., & Michalowski, R. D. (1999). Fear in the news: A discourse of control. *Sociological Quarterly*, *40*, 475–503.

American Association of University Women Educational Foundation. (2001). Hostile hallways: Bullying, teasing, and sexual harassment in school hallways, AAUW Education Foundation, Washington, D.C.

Arum, R. (2003). *Judging school discipline: The crisis of moral authority*. Cambridge, MA: Harvard University Press.

Astor, R. A., & Meyer, H. A. (2001). The conceptualization of violence-prone school subcontexts: Is the sum of the parts greater than the whole? *Urban Education*, *36*, 374–399.

Astor, R. A., Meyer, H. A., & Behre, W. J. (1999). Unowned places and times: Maps and interviews about violence in high schools. *American Educational Research Journal*, *36*, 3–42.

Battistich, V., & Solomon, D. (1997). Caring school communities. *Educational Psychologist, 32*(3), 137–151.

Beck, U. (1992). *Risk society: Towards a new modernity*. Newbury Park, CA: Sage.

Beck, U. (1999). *World risk society*. Malden, MA: Polity Press.

Beger, R. (2002). Expansion of police power in public schools and the vanishing rights of students. *Social Justice, 29*, 119–130.

Bodine, R., & Crawford, D. (1998). *The handbook of conflict resolution education: A guide to building quality programs in schools*. San Francisco: Jossey-Bass.

Bryk, A., & Driscoll, M. (1988). *The school as community: Shaping forces and consequences for students and teachers*. Madison, WI: National Center on Effective Secondary Schools.

Casella, R. (2003). The false allure of security technologies. *Social Justice, 30*, 82–93.

Champion, D. (1997). *The Roxbury dictionary of criminal justice*. Los Angeles: Roxbury.

Chapin, J., & Coleman, G. (2006). Knowledge is power: A theory-based approach to reducing school violence. *Journal of Family Violence, 21*, 381–386.

Cloud, J. (1999). The Columbine effect. *Time*, December 6. Available at http://www.time.com/time/magazine/article/0,9171,992754,00.html. Retrieved on December 15, 2008.

Cohen, S. (1972). *Folk devils and moral panics: The creation of mods and rockers*. London: MacGibben and Kee.

Crick, N., & Grotpeter, J. (1995). Relational aggression, gender and social–psychological adjustment. *Child Development, 66*, 710–722.

Crowe, T. (1990). Designing safer schools. *School Safety* (Fall), 9–13.

Crowe, T. (2000). *Crime prevention through environmental design: Applications of architectural design and space management concepts* (2nd ed.). Boston: Butterworth-Heinemann.

Dinkes, R., Cataldi, E. F., Kena, G., Baum, K., & Snyder, T. D. (2006). *Indicators of school crime and safety*. Washington, DC: U.S. Departments of Education and Justice.

Dunham, R., & Alpert, G. (1986). Keeping marginal youth in school: A prevention model. *Youth and Society, 17*, 346–361.

Epstein, J. L. (2002). *School, family, and community partnerships: Preparing educators and improving schools*. Boulder, CO: Westview Press.

Epstein, J., & Sanders, M. (1998). What we learned from international studies of school family-community partnerships. *Childhood Education, 74*, 392–394.

Espelage, D., & Swearer, S. (2003). Research on school bullying and victimization: What have we learned and where do we go from here? *School Psychology Review, 32*(3), 365–383.

Espelage, D., & Swearer, S. (2004). *Bullying in American schools: A social-ecological perspective on prevention and intervention*. London: Lawrence Erlbaum.

Finkelhor, D. (2008). *Childhood victimization: Violence, crime and abuse in the lives of young people*. New York: Oxford University Press.

Fox, J. A., & Savage, J. (2009). Mass murder goes to college: An examination of changes on college campuses following Virginia Tech. *American Behavioral Scientist, 52*(10), 1465–1485.

Furudi, F. (1997). *Culture of fear: Risk-taking and the morality of low expectations*. London: Cassell.

Goode, E., & Ben-Yehuda, N. (1994). *Moral panics: The social construction of deviance*. Cambridge, MA: Blackwell.

Gottfredson, G., & Gottfredson, D. (2001). What schools do to prevent delinquency and promote safe environments. *Journal of Educational and Psychological Consultation, 12*(4), 313–344.

Gottfredson, G., Gottfredson, D., Payne, A., & Gottfredson, N. (2005). School climate predictors of school disorder: Results from the national study of delinquency prevention in schools. *Journal of Research in Crime and Delinquency*, *42*(4), 412–444.

Haider-Markel, D. P., & Joslyn, M. R. (2001). Gun policy, opinion, tragedy, and blame attribution: The conditional influence of issue frames. *Journal of Politics*, *63*, 520–543.

Hand, J., & Sanchez, L. (2000). Badgering or bantering? Gender differences in experience of, and reactions to, sexual harassment among U.S. high school students. *Gender and Society*, *14*, 718–746.

Hazler, R. (2000). When victims turn aggressors: Factors in the development of deadly school violence. *Professional School Counseling*, *4*, 105–112.

Heaviside, S., Rowand, C., Williams, C., Farris, E., Burns, S., & McArthur, E. (1998). *Violence and discipline problems in U.S. public schools: 1996–1997*. Washington, DC: National Center for Education Statistics.

Henry, S. (2000). What is school violence? An integrated definition. *Annals of the American Academy of Political and Social Science*, *567*(1), 16–30.

Henry, S. (2009). School violence beyond Columbine: A complex problem in need of an interdisciplinary analysis. *American Behavioral Scientist*, *52*(9), 1246–1265.

Hirschfield, P. (2008). Preparing for prison? The criminalization of school discipline in the USA. *Theoretical Criminology*, *12*(1), 79–101.

Hoy, W., & Sabo, D. (1998). *Quality middle schools: Open and healthy*. Corwin Press, Inc: Thousand Oaks, CA.

Johnson, D. W., & Johnson, R. T. (1996). Conflict resolution and peer mediation programs in elementary and secondary schools: A review of the research. *Review of Educational Research*, *66*, 459–506.

Kozol, J. (1991). *Savage inequalities: Children in America's schools*. New York: Crown.

Kupchik, A., & Ellis, N. (2008). School discipline and security: Fair for all students? *Youth and Society*, *39*(4), 549–574.

Kupchik, A., & Monahan, T. (2006). The new American school: Preparation for post-industrial discipline. *British Journal of Sociology of Education*, *27*, 617–632.

Lawrence, R. (2006). *School crime and juvenile justice* (2nd ed.). New York: Oxford University Press.

Lawrence, R. G. (2001). Defining events: Problem definition in the media arena. In: R. P. Hart & B. H. Sparrow (Eds), *Politics, discourse, and American society: New agendas* (pp. 91–110). Lanham, MD: Rowman and Littlefield.

Lawrence, R. G., & Birkland, T. A. (2004). Guns, Hollywood, and school safety: Defining the school-shooting phenomenon across the public arenas. *Social Science Quarterly*, *85*, 1193–1207.

Lupton-Smith, H., Carruthers, W., Flythe, R., Goettee, E., & Modest, K. (1996). Conflict resolution as peer mediation: Programs for elementary, middle and high school students. *The School Counselor*, *43*, 374–391.

Lupton-Smith, H. S. (2004). Peer mediation. In: E. R. Gerler (Ed.), *Handbook of school violence*. Binghamton, NY: Haworth Press.

Martinez, S. (2009). A system gone berserk: How are zero-tolerance policies really affecting schools? *Preventing School Failure*, *53*(3), 153–157.

Marx, G. T. (1981). Ironies of social control: Authorities as contributors to deviance through escalation, nonenforcement and covert facilitation. *Social Problems*, *28*(3), 221–246.

Marx, G. T. (1995). The engineering of social control: The search for the silver bullet. In: J. Hagan & R. D. Peterson (Eds), *Crime and inequality* (pp. 225–246). Stanford, CA: Stanford University Press.

Matera, D. (2001). *A cry for character: How a group of students cleaned up their rowdy school and spawned a wildfire antidote to the columbine effect*. Paramus, NJ: Prentice Hall.

Meier, D., & Wood, G. (2004). *Many children left behind: How the no child left behind act is damaging our children and our schools*. Boston: Beacon Press.

Mishna, F. (2008). An overview of the evidence on bullying prevention and intervention programs. *Brief Treatment and Crisis Intervention*, *8*(4), 327–341.

Morrison, G., & Skiba, R. (2001). Predicting violence from school misbehavior: Promises and perils. *Psychology in the Schools*, *38*, 173–184.

Muschert, G. W. (2002). *Media and massacre: The social construction of the Columbine story*. Doctoral Dissertation, University of Colorado at Boulder.

Muschert, G. W. (2007a). The Columbine victims and the myth of the juvenile superpredator. *Youth Violence and Juvenile Justice*, *5*(4), 351–366.

Muschert, G. W. (2007b). Research in school shootings. *Sociology Compass*, *1*(1), 60–80.

Muschert, G. W. (2009). Frame-changing in the media coverage of a school shooting: The rise of Columbine as a national concern. *Social Science Journal*, *46*(1), 164–170.

Muschert, G. W., & Carr, D. (2006). Media salience and frame-changing across events: Coverage of nine school shootings, 1997–2001. *Journalism and Mass Communication Quarterly*, *83*, 747–766.

National Center for Education Statistics (2005). *Students report of bullying: Results from the 2001 school crime supplement to the national crime victimization survey*. Washington, DC: U.S. Government Printing Office.

National Institute of Education (NIE) (1978). *Violent schools, safe schools: The safe school study report to congress*. Washington, DC: U.S. Government Printing Office.

Newman, O. (1972). *Defensible space: Crime prevention through urban design*. NewYork: Macmillan.

Noguera, P. (1995). Preventing and producing violence: A critical analysis of responses to school violence. *Harvard Educational Review*, *65*, 189–212.

Noguera, P. (2003). Schools, prisons, and social implications of punishment: Rethinking disciplinary practices. *Theory into Practice*, *42*, 341–350.

Office of Juvenile Justice and Delinquency Prevention (2008). *Juvenile arrests 2006*. Washington, DC: U.S. Department of Justice Office of Justice Programs.

Olweus, D. (1993). *Bullying at school: What we know and what we can do*. Malden, MA: Blackwell Publishers.

Olweus, D., & Limber, S. (1999). *Blueprint for violence prevention: Book nine. Bullying prevention program*. Denver, CO: C and M Press.

Payne, A. (2008). A multilevel analysis of the relationships among communal school organization, student bonding, and delinquency. *Journal of Research in Crime and Delinquency*, *45*(4), 429–455.

Payne, A., Gottfredson, D., & Gottfredson, G. (2003). Schools as communities: The relationships among communal school organization, student bonding, and school disorder. *Criminology*, *41*, 749–778.

Pew Research Center for the People and the Press. (1999). Columbine shooting biggest news draw of 1999, Pew Research Center for the People and the Press. Available at http://people-press.org/reports/display.php3?ReportID = 48. Retrieved on December 13, 2005.

Phaneuf, S. (2006). *School security practices: Investigating their consequences on student fear, bonding, and school climate*. Doctoral Dissertation, University of Maryland.

Safran, B. (2007). Bullying behavior, bully prevention programs, and gender. *Journal of Emotional Abuse*, *7*(4), 43–67.

Samuels, R. (2000). From Columbine to professional wrestling: Psychoanalysis of postmodern media violence. *Journal for the Psychoanalysis of Culture and Society*, *5*, 312–318.

Schneider, M., Marschall, M., Roch, C., & Teske, P. (1999). Heuristics, low information rationality, and choosing public goods: Broken windows as shortcuts to information about school performance. *Urban Affairs Review*, *34*, 729–741.

Schreck, C., Miller, J., & Gibson, C. (2003). Trouble in the school yard: A study of the risk factors of victimization at school. *Crime and Delinquency*, *49*(3), 460–484.

Schuster, B. (2009). Preventing, preparing for critical incidents in schools. *NIJ Journal*, *5*(262), 42–46.

Simmons, R. (2002). *Odd girl out: The hidden culture of aggression in girls*. Harcourt: New York.

Skiba, R., Michael, R., Nardo, A., & Peterson, R. (2002). The color of discipline: Sources of racial and gender disproportionality in school punishment. *The Urban Review*, *34*(4), 317–342.

Skiba, R., & Peterson, R. (2000). School discipline at a crossroads: From zero tolerance to early response. *Exceptional Children*, *66*, 335–346.

Skiba, R., & Peterson, R. (2003). Teaching the social curriculum: School discipline as instruction. *Preventing School Failure*, *47*(2), 66–73.

Skiba, R., & Rausch, M. (2006). Zero tolerance, suspension, and expulsion: Questions of equity and effectiveness. In: C. Evertson & C. Weinstein (Eds), *Handbook of classroom management: Research, practice, and contemporary issues*. Mahwah, NH: Erlbaum.

Small, M., Jones, S., Barrios, L., Crossett, L., Dahlberg, L., Albuquerque, M., Sleet, D., Greene, B., & Schmidt, E. (2001). School policy and environment: Results from the school health policies and programs study 2000. *Journal of School Health*, *71*, 325–334.

Smith, J., Ryan, W., & Cousins, J. (2007). Antibullying programs: A survey of evaluation activities in public schools. *Studies in Educational Evaluation*, *33*, 120–134.

Smith, J., Twemlow, S., & Hoover, D. (1999). Bullies, victims and bystanders: A method of in-school intervention and possible parental contributions. *Child Psychiatry and Human Development*, *30*(1), 29–37.

Snell, C., Bailey, C., Corona, A., & Mebane, D. (2002). School crime policy changes: The impact of recent highly-publicized school crime. *American Journal of Criminal Justice*, *26*, 269–285.

Spivak, H., & Prothrow-Stith, D. (2001). The need to address bullying: An important component of violence prevention. *Journal of the American Medical Association*, *285*, 2131–2132.

Sprague, J., & Walker, H. (2000). Early identification and intervention for youth with antisocial and violent behavior. *Exceptional Children*, *66*, 367–379.

Stanley, P., Juhnke, G., & Purkey, W. (2004). Using an invitational theory of practice to create safe and successful schools. *Journal of Counseling and Development*, *82*, 302–311.

Swearer, S., Turner, R., Givens, J., & Pollack, W. (2008). 'You're so gay!': Do different forms of bullying matter for adolescent males? *School Psychology Review*, *37*(2), 160–173.

Toby, J. (1994). Everyday school violence: How disorder fuels it. *American Educator*, *17*(4), 4–9, 44–48.

Trujillo, M., Bowland, S., Myers, L., Richards, P., & Roy, B. (2008). *Re-centering culture and knowledge in conflict resolution practice*. Syracuse, NY: Syracuse University Press.

Twemlow, S., & Cohen, J. (2003). Stopping school violence. *Journal of Applied Psychoanalytic Studies, 5*(2), 117–124.

Ungar, S. (2001). Moral panic versus the risk society: Implications of the changing sites of social anxiety. *British Journal of Sociology, 52*, 271–291.

Vaillancourt, T., McDougall, P., Hymel, S., Krygsman, A., Miller, J., Stiver, K., & Davis, C. (2008). Bullying: Are researchers and children/youth talking about the same thing? *International Journal of Behavioral Development, 32*(6), 486–495.

Verdugo, R. (1999). Safe schools: Theory, data, and practices. *Education and Urban Society, 31*, 267–276.

Verdugo, R. (2002). Race-ethnicity, social class, and zero-tolerance policies: The cultural and structural wars. *Education and Urban Society, 35*(1), 50–76.

Verdugo, R., & Schneider, J. (1999). Quality schools, safe schools: A theoretical and empirical discussion. *Education and Urban Society, 31*, 286–308.

Vestermark, S. D. (1996). Critical decisions, critical elements in the effective school security program. In: A. M. Hoffman (Ed.), *Schools, violence, and society*. Westport, CT: Praeger.

Wacquant, L. (2001). Deadly symbiosis: When ghetto and prison meet and mesh. In: D. Garland (Ed.), *Mass imprisonment: Social causes and consequences* (pp. 82–120). London: Sage.

Wilcox, P., Augustine, M., & Clayton, R. (2006). Physical environment and crime and misconduct in Kentucky schools. *The Journal of Primary Prevention, 27*(3), 293–313.

Part II
Social Constructionist Related Theories

[14]

NOTES ON THE SOCIOLOGY OF DEVIANCE

KAI T. ERIKSON
University of Pittsburgh

It is general practice in sociology to regard deviant behavior as an alien element in society. Deviance is considered a vagrant form of human activity, moving outside the more orderly currents of social life. And since this type of aberration could only occur (in theory) if something were wrong within the social organization itself, deviant behavior is described almost as if it were leakage from machinery in poor condition: it is an accidental result of disorder and anomie, a symptom of internal breakdown.

The purpose of the following remarks will be to review this conventional outlook and to argue that it provides too narrow a framework for the study of deviant behavior. Deviation, we will suggest, recalling Durkheim's classic statement on the subject, can often be understood as a normal product of stable institutions, a vital resource which is guarded and preserved by forces found in all human organizations.[1]

I

According to current theory, deviant behavior is most likely to occur when the sanctions governing conduct in any given setting seem to be contradictory.[2] This would be the case, for example, if the work rules posted by a company required one course of action from its employees and the longer-range policies of the company required quite another. Any situation marked by this kind of ambiguity, of course, can pose a serious dilemma for the individual: if he is careful to observe one set of demands imposed upon him, he runs the immediate risk of violating some other, and thus may find himself caught in a deviant stance no matter how earnestly he tries to avoid it. In this limited sense, deviance can be regarded a "normal" human response to "abnormal" social conditions, and the sociologist is therefore invited to assume that some sort of pathology exists within the social structure whenever deviant behavior makes an appearance.

This general approach is clearly more concerned with the *etiology* of deviant behavior than with its continuing social *history*—and as a result it often draws sociological attention away from an important area of inquiry. It may be safe to assume that naive acts of deviance, such as first criminal offenses, are provoked by strains in the local situation. But this is only the beginning of a much longer story, for deviant activities can generate a good deal of momentum once they are set into motion: they develop forms of organization, persist over time, and sometimes remain intact long after the strains which originally produced them have disappeared. In this respect, deviant activities are often absorbed into the main tissue of society and derive support from the same forces which stabilize other forms of social life. There are persons in society, for example, who make career commitments to deviant styles of conduct, impelled by some inner need for continuity rather than by any urgencies in the immediate social setting. There are groups in society which actively encourage new deviant trends, often prolonging them beyond the

Paper read at the 55th annual meetings of the American Sociological Association, New York, 1960.

[1] Emile Durkheim, *The Rules of Sociological Method* (translated by S. A. Solovay and J. H. Mueller), Glencoe: The Free Press, 1958.

[2] The best known statements of this general position, of course, are by Robert K. Merton and Talcott Parsons. Merton, *Social Theory and Social Structures* (revised edition), Glencoe: The Free Press, 1957; and Parsons, *The Social System*, Glencoe: The Free Press, 1951.

point where they represent an adaptation to strain. These sources of support for deviant behavior are difficult to visualize when we use terms like "strain," "anomie," or "breakdown" in discussions of the problem. Such terms may help us explain how the social structure creates fresh deviant potential, but they do not help us explain how that potential is later shaped into durable, persisting social patterns.[3] The individual's need for self continuity and the group's offer of support are altogether normal processes, even if they are sometimes found in deviant situations; and thus the study of deviant behavior is as much a study of social organization as it is a study of *dis*organization and anomie.

II

From a sociological standpoint, deviance can be defined as conduct which is generally thought to require the attention of social control agencies—that is, conduct about which "something should be done." Deviance is not a property *inherent in* certain forms of behavior; it is a property *conferred upon* these forms by the audiences which directly or indirectly witness them. Sociologically, then, the critical variable in the study of deviance is the social *audience* rather than the individual *person,* since it is the audience which eventually decides whether or not any given action or actions will become a visible case of deviation.

This definition may seem a little indirect, but it has the advantage of bringing a neglected sociological issue into proper focus. When a community acts to control the behavior of one of its members, it is engaged in a very intricate process of selection. Even a determined miscreant conforms in most of his daily behavior—using the correct spoon at mealtime, taking good care of his mother, or otherwise observing the mores of his society—and if the community elects to bring sanctions against him for the occasions when he does act offensively, it is responding to a few deviant details set within a vast context of proper conduct. Thus a person may be jailed or hospitalized for a few scattered moments of misbehavior, defined as a full-time deviant despite the fact that he had supplied the community with countless other indications that he was a decent, moral citizen. The screening device which sifts these telling details out of the individual's over-all performance, then, is a sensitive instrument of social control. It is important to note that this screen takes a number of factors into account which are not directly related to the deviant act itself: it is concerned with the actor's social class, his past record as an offender, the amount of remorse he manages to convey, and many similar concerns which take hold in the shifting moods of the community. This is why the community often overlooks behavior which seems technically deviant (like certain kinds of white collar graft) or takes sharp exception to behavior which seems essentially harmless (like certain kinds of sexual impropriety). It is an easily demonstrated fact, for example, that working class boys who steal cars are far more likely to go to prison than upper class boys who commit the same or even more serious crimes, suggesting that from the point of view of the community lower class offenders are somehow more deviant. To this extent, the community screen is perhaps a more relevant subject for sociological research than the actual behavior which is filtered through it.

Once the problem is phrased in this way, we can ask: how does a community decide what forms of conduct should be singled out for this kind of atten-

---

[3] Cf. Daniel Glaser and Kent Rice, "Crime, Age, and Employment," *American Sociological Review,* 24 (1959), pp. 679-86.

tion? And why, having made this choice, does it create special institutions to deal with the persons who enact them? The standard answer to this question is that society sets up the machinery of control in order to protect itself against the "harmful" effects of deviance, in much the same way that an organism mobilizes its resources to combat an invasion of germs. At times, however, this classroom convention only seems to make the problem more complicated. In the first place, as Durkheim pointed out some years ago, it is by no means clear that all acts considered deviant in a culture are in fact (or even in principle) harmful to group life.[4] And in the second place, specialists in crime and mental health have long suggested that deviance can play an important role in keeping the social order intact —again a point we owe originally to Durkheim.[5] This has serious implications for sociological theory in general.

III

In recent years, sociological theory has become more and more concerned with the concept "social system"—an organization of society's component parts into a form which sustains internal equilibrium, resists change, and is boundary maintaining. Now this concept has many abstract dimensions, but it is generally used to describe those forces in the social order which promote a high level of uniformity among human actors and a high degree of symmetry within human institutions. In this sense, the concept is normatively oriented since it directs the observer's attention toward those centers in social space where the core values of society are figuratively located. The main organizational principle of a system, then, is essentially a centripetal one: it draws the behavior of actors toward the nucleus of the system, bringing it within range of basic norms. Any conduct which is neither attracted toward this nerve center by the rewards of conformity nor compelled toward it by other social pressures is considered "out of control," which is to say, deviant.

This basic model has provided the theme for most contemporary thinking about deviance, and as a result little attention has been given to the notion that systems operate to maintain boundaries. Generally speaking, boundaries are controls which limit the fluctuation of a system's component parts so that the whole retains a defined range of activity—a unique pattern of constancy and stability—within the larger environment.[6] The range of human behavior is potentially so great that any *social* system must make clear statements about the nature and location of its boundaries, placing limits on the flow of behavior so that it circulates within a given cultural area. Thus boundaries are a crucial point of reference for persons living within any system, a prominent concept in the group's special language and tradition. A juvenile gang may define its boundaries by the amount of territory it defends, a professional society by the range of subjects it discusses, a fraternal order by the variety of members it accepts. But in each case, members share the same idea as to where the group begins and ends in social space and know what kinds of experience "belong" within this domain.

For all its apparent abstractness, a social system is organized around the movements of persons joined together in regular social relations. The only material found in a system for marking boundaries, then, is the behavior of its participants; and the form of be-

[4] Emile Durkheim, *The Division of Labor in Society* (translated by George Simpson), Glencoe: The Free Press, 1952. See particularly Chapter 2, Book 1.

[5] Emile Durkheim, *The Rules of Sociological Method, op. cit.*

[6] Cf. Talcott Parsons, *The Social System, op. cit.*

havior which best performs this function would seem to be deviant almost by definition, since it is the most extreme variety of conduct to be found within the experience of the group. In this respect, transactions taking place between deviant persons on the one side and agencies of control on the other are boundary maintaining mechanisms. They mark the outside limits of the area in which the norm has jurisdiction, and in this way assert how much diversity and variability can be contained within the system before it begins to lose its distinct structure, its unique shape.

A social norm is rarely expressed as a firm rule or official code. It is an abstract synthesis of the many separate times a community has stated its sentiments on a given issue. Thus the norm has a history much like that of an article of common law: it is an accumulation of decisions made by the community over a long period of time which gradually gathers enough moral influence to serve as a precedent for future decisions. Like an article of common law, the norm retains its validity only if it is regularly used as a basis for judgment. Each time the community censures some act of deviance, then, it sharpens the authority of the violated norm and re-establishes the boundaries of the group.

One of the most interesting features of control institutions, in this regard, is the amount of publicity they have always attracted. In an earlier day, correction of deviant offenders took place in the public market and gave the crowd a chance to display its interest in a direct, active way. In our own day, the guilty are no longer paraded in public places, but instead we are confronted by a heavy flow of newspaper and radio reports which offer much the same kind of entertainment. Why are these reports considered "newsworthy" and why do they rate the extraordinary attention they receive? Perhaps they satisfy a number of psychological perversities among the mass audience, as many commentators have suggested, but at the same time they constitute our main source of information about the normative outlines of society. They are lessons through which we teach one another what the norms mean and how far they extend. In a figurative sense, at least, morality and immorality meet at the public scaffold, and it is during this meeting that the community declares where the line between them should be drawn.

Human groups need to regulate the routine affairs of everyday life, and to this end the norms provide an important focus for behavior. But human groups also need to describe and anticipate those areas of being which lie beyond the immediate borders of the group—the unseen dangers which in any culture and in any age seem to threaten the security of group life. The universal folklore depicting demons, devils, witches and evil spirits may be one way to give form to these otherwise formless dangers, but the visible deviant is another kind of reminder. As a trespasser against the norm, he represents those forces excluded by the group's boundaries: he informs us, as it were, what evil looks like, what shapes the devil can assume. In doing so, he shows us the difference between kinds of experience which belong within the group and kinds of experience which belong outside it.

Thus deviance cannot be dismissed as behavior which *disrupts* stability in society, but is itself, in controlled quantities, an important condition for *preserving* stability.

IV

This raises a serious theoretical question. If we grant that deviant behavior often performs a valuable service in society, can we then assume that society as a whole actively tries to promote this resource? Can we assume, in other words, that some kind of active recruitment process is going on to assure society of a steady volume of deviance? Sociology has not yet developed a conceptual language in which this sort of question can be discussed without a great deal of circularity, but one observation can be made which gives the question an interesting perspective—namely, that deviant activities often seem to derive support from the very agencies designed to suppress them. Indeed, the institutions devised by human society for guarding against deviance sometimes seem so poorly equipped for this task that we might well ask why this is considered their "real" function at all.

It is by now a thoroughly familiar argument that many of the institutions built to inhibit deviance actually operate in such a way as to perpetuate it. For one thing, prisons, hospitals, and other agencies of control provide aid and protection for large numbers of deviant persons. But beyond this, such institutions gather marginal people into tightly segregated groups, give them an opportunity to teach one another the skills and attitudes of a deviant career, and even drive them into using these skills by reinforcing their sense of alienation from the rest of society.[7] This process is found not only in the institutions which actually confine the deviant, but in the general community as well.

The community's decision to bring deviant sanctions against an individual is not a simple act of censure. It is a sharp rite of transition, at once moving him out of his normal position in society and transferring him into a distinct deviant role.[8] The ceremonies which accomplish this change of status, usually, have three related phases. They arrange a formal *confrontation* between the deviant suspect and representatives of his community (as in the criminal trial or psychiatric case conference); they announce some *judgment* about the nature of his deviancy (a "verdict" or "diagnosis," for example); and they perform an act of social *placement*, assigning him to a special deviant role (like that of "prisoner" or "patient") for some period of time. Such ceremonies tend to be events of wide public interest and ordinarily take place in a dramatic, ritualized setting.[9] Perhaps the most obvious example of a commitment ceremony is the criminal trial, with its elaborate ritual and formality, but more modest equivalents can be found almost anywhere that procedures are set up for judging whether or not someone is officially deviant.

An important feature of these ceremonies in our culture is that they are almost irreversible. Most provisional roles conferred by society—like those of the student or citizen soldier, for instance—include some kind of terminal ceremony to mark the individual's movement back out of the role once its temporary advantages have been exhausted. But the roles allotted to the deviant seldom make allowance for this type of passage. He is ushered into the special position by a decisive and dramatic ceremony, yet is retired from it with hardly a word of public notice. As a result, the deviant often returns home with no proper license to resume a normal life in the com-

7 For a good description of this process in the modern prison, see Gresham Sykes, *The Society of Captives*, Princeton: Princeton University Press, 1958. For views of two different types of mental hospital settings, see Erving Goffman, "The Characteristics of Total Institutions," *Symposium on Preventive and Social Psychiatry*, Washington, D. C.: Walter Reed Army Institute of Research, 1957; and Kai T. Erikson, "Patient Role and Social Uncertainty: A Dilemma of the Mentally Ill," *Psychiatry*, 20 (1957), pp. 263-74.

8 Talcott Parsons, *op cit.*, has given the classical description of how this role transfer works in the case of medical patients.

9 Cf. Harold Garfinkel, "Successful Degradation Ceremonies," *American Journal of Sociology*, 61 (1956), pp. 420-24.

munity. From a ritual point of view, nothing has happened to cancel out the stigmas imposed upon him by earlier commitment ceremonies: the original verdict or diagnosis is still formally in effect. Partly for this reason, the community is apt to place the returning deviant on some form of probation within the group, suspicious that he will return to deviant activity upon a moment's provocation.

A circularity is thus set into motion which has all the earmarks of a "self-fulfilling prophecy," to use Merton's fine phrase. On the one hand, it seems obvious that the apprehensions of the community help destroy whatever chances the deviant might otherwise have for a successful return to society. Yet, on the other hand, everyday experience seems to show that these apprehensions are altogether reasonable, for it is a well-known and highly publicized fact that most ex-convicts return to prison and that a large proportion of mental patients require additional treatment after once having been discharged. The community's feeling that deviant persons cannot change, then, may be based on a faulty premise, but it is repeated so frequently and with such conviction that it eventually creates the facts which "prove" it correct. If the returned deviant encounters this feeling of distrust often enough, it is understandable that he too may begin to wonder if the original verdict or diagnosis is still in effect—and respond to this uncertainty by resuming deviant activity. In some respects, this solution may be the only way for the individual and his community to agree what forms of behavior are appropriate for him.

Moreover, this prophecy is found in the official policies of even the most advanced agencies of control. Police departments could not operate with any real effectiveness if they did not regard ex-convicts as an almost permanent population of offenders, a constant pool of suspects. Nor could psychiatric clinics do a responsible job if they did not view former patients as a group unusually susceptible to mental illness. Thus the prophecy gains currency at many levels within the social order, not only in the poorly informed attitudes of the community at large, but in the best informed theories of most control agencies as well.

In one form or another, this problem has been known to Western culture for many hundreds of years, and this simple fact is a very important one for sociology. For if the culture has supported a steady flow of deviant behavior throughout long periods of historical evolution, then the rules which apply to any form of functionalist thinking would suggest that strong forces must be at work to keep this flow intact. This may not be reason enough to assert that deviant behavior is altogether "functional"—in any of the many senses of that term—but it should make us reluctant to assume that the agencies of control are somehow organized to prevent deviant acts from occurring or to "cure" deviant offenders of their misbehavior.[10]

This in turn might suggest that our present models of the social system, with their clear emphasis on harmony and symmetry in social relations, only do a partial job of representing reality. Perhaps two different (and often conflicting) currents are found within any well-functioning system: those forces which promote a high over-all degree of conformity among human actors, and those forces which encourage some degree of diversity so that actors can be deployed throughout social space to

[10] Albert K. Cohen, for example, speaking for most sociologists, seems to take the question for granted: "It would seem that the control of deviant behavior is, by definition, a culture goal." In "The Study of Social Disorganization and Deviant Behavior," Merton, et al., editors, *Sociology Today*. New York: Basic Books, 1959, p. 465.

mark the system's boundaries. In such a scheme, deviant behavior would appear as a variation on normative themes, a vital form of activity which outlines the area within which social life as such takes place.

As Georg Simmel wrote some years ago:

> An absolutely centripetal and harmonious group, a pure "unification," not only is empirically unreal, it could show no real life process. . . . Just as the universe needs "love and hate," that is, attractive and repulsive forces, in order to have any form at all, so society, too, in order to attain a determinate shape, needs some quantitative ratio of harmony and disharmony, of association and competition, of favorable and unfavorable tendencies. . . . Society, as we know it, is the result of both categories of interaction, which thus both manifest themselves as wholly positive.[11]

V

In summary, two new lines of inquiry seem to be indicated by the argument presented above.

First, this paper attempts to focus our attention on an old but still vital sociological question: how does a social structure communicate its "needs" or impose its "patterns" on human actors? In the present case, how does a social structure enlist actors to engage in deviant activity? Ordinarily, the fact that deviant behavior is more common in some sectors of society than in others is explained by declaring that something called "anomie" or "disorganization" prevails at these sensitive spots. Deviance leaks out where the social machinery is defective; it occurs where the social structure *fails* to communicate its needs to human actors. But if we consider the possibility that deviant persons are responding to the same social forces that elicit conformity from others, then we are engaged in another order of inquiry altogether. Perhaps the stability of some social units is maintained only if juvenile offenders are recruited to balance an adult majority; perhaps some families can remain intact only if one of their members becomes a visible deviant or is committed to a hospital or prison. If this supposition proves to be a useful one, sociologists should be interested in discovering how a social unit manages to differentiate the roles of its members and how certain persons are "chosen" to play the more deviant parts.

Second, it is evident that cultures vary in the way they regulate traffic moving back and forth from their deviant boundaries. Perhaps we could begin with the hypothesis that the traffic pattern known in our own culture has a marked Puritan cast: a defined portion of the population, largely drawn from young adult groups and from the lower economic classes, is stabilized in deviant roles and generally expected to remain there for indefinite periods of time. To this extent, Puritan attitudes about predestination and reprobation would seem to have retained a significant place in modern criminal law and public opinion. In other areas of the world, however, different traffic patterns are known. There are societies in which deviance is considered a natural pursuit for the young, an activity which they can easily abandon when they move through defined ceremonies into adulthood. There are societies which give license to large groups of persons to engage in deviant behavior for certain seasons or on certain days of the year. And there are societies in which special groups are formed to act in ways "contrary" to the normal expectations of the culture. Each of these patterns regulates deviant traffic differently, yet all of them provide some institutionalized means for an actor to give up a deviant "career" without permanent stigma. The problem for sociological theory in

---

[11] Georg Simmel, *Conflict* (translated by Kurt H. Wolff), Glencoe: The Free Press, 1955, pp. 15-16.

general might be to learn whether or not these varying patterns are functionally equivalent in some meaningful sense; the problem for applied sociology might be to see if we have anything to learn from those cultures which permit re-entry into normal social life to persons who have spent a period of "service" on society's boundaries.

[15]

Crime as Social Interaction

Leroy C. Gould, Gary Kleck, and Marc Gertz

One of the most popular semantic problems posed to first-year philosophy students is "Is there 'sound' when a tree falls in the forest and there is no person within earshot to hear it?" This problem is sometimes paired with another: "Is there 'sound' when a psychotic person 'hears' voices that no one else hears?" The answer, of course, is "It depends on the definition of 'sound.' " If the definition focuses on objects producing pressure waves in the air, then there is sound in the first example, but not in the second; if the definition focuses on human perception, then there is sound in the second, but not in the first.

Although people are free to choose whichever definition they want, the choice makes a difference. Defining sound as pressure waves in the air places emphasis on the physical properties of sound and is more likely to attract the attention of physicists than of psychologists. Defining sound as human perception places the study of sound primarily within the domain of psychology.

And so it is with the definition of "crime." Although criminologists are free to define crime however they like, their choice affects the aspects of crime they will study and the academic discipline that is best equipped to study it.

BACKGROUND

When criminology began, with the publication of the essay *On Crimes and Punishments* by Cesare Beccaria ([1764] 1963), the emphasis was the law and its enforcement (Jeffrey [1959] 1960). Some criminologists—for example, Gary Becker (1968) and Isaac Ehrlich (1981)—still think of crime this way. For the vast majority of criminologists, however, the concept "crime" refers not to the law but to the behavior of offenders. As Matza (1964: 3) described the situation:

> The most celebrated and thus the most explicit assumption of positive [scientific] criminology is the primacy of the criminal actor rather than the criminal law as the

major point of departure in the construction of etiological theories. The explanation of crime, according to the positive school, may be found in the motivational and behavioral systems of criminals. Among these systems, the law and its administration are deemed secondary or irrelevant. This quest for explanation in the character and background of offenders has characterized all modern criminology, irrespective of the particular causal factors espoused.

At the time Matza was writing these words, several criminologists were in the process of changing this focus. Wilkins (1964), for example, showed that the availability of automobiles was an important determinant of the volume of theft from automobiles. Biderman (1966) argued that prosperity, which creates increases in the amount of property, influences rates of property crime. Gould (1969, 1971) and Mansfield, Gould, and Namenwirth (1974) showed that rates of automobile theft and bank robbery are highly correlated with rates of automobile ownership and the amount of money available in banks to be stolen.

These studies, which shifted attention from offenders to victims and crime targets, first came to be known as "criminal opportunity theory" (Cook 1986: 2) and then as "routine activities theory" (Felson 1987). Other important works in this tradition include Boggs (1965), Luckenbill (1982), Ziegenhagen and Brosan (1985), Stark (1987), Kleck and Sayles (1990), and Kleck and DeLone (1991).

The purpose of this chapter is to suggest a conception of crime that includes elements from each of these criminological traditions. It is a conception that views crimes as interactions among three distinct elements: offenders, agents of social control, and crime targets. It is a conception that accommodates different theories of "crime." It suggests that the most productive criminological question is not "Why do certain people commit crimes?" but rather "Why do crimes occur?" Crimes occur, the argument goes, partly because people are motivated to commit them, partly because they are not deterred from committing them, and partly because there are opportunities for their commission.

CRIMINAL EVENTS

Albert Cohen (1985: 86) was among the first criminologists to make a distinction, theoretically, between crime as a social event and crime as the behavior of individual offenders:

> Even the most profound and lucid understanding of the actor's state of mind and of the motives and the history that led him to do what he did, however useful it may be for establishing guilt and doing justice, does not explain the occurrence of the criminal act. It may explain the actor's part in or contribution to the criminal act, which may be important to know, but it does not equal an explanation of the act. If we want to explain the criminal act, we must start with the appropriate question.

That question is not, "Why would somebody do something like this?" but rather "What made it happen?"

At the same time, Hirschi and Gottfredson (1987: 958) were working along similar lines:

> We have been developing a general theory of crime designed to account for the distribution of all forms of criminal behavior (Hirschi and Gottfredson, 1986 and 1987; Gottfredson and Hirschi, 1987). This emerging theory starts from a distinction between crimes as events and criminality as a characteristic of people. Whereas traditional positivistic theories begin by looking at offenders, we begin by looking at crime.

Crediting an earlier, unpublished, paper by Hirschi and Gottfredson, Wilson and Herrnstein (1985: 22–23) defined a "crime" in their book *Crime and Human Nature* as an "act committed in violation of a law that prohibits it and authorizes punishment for its commission." "Criminality," in contrast, "refers to stable differences across individuals in the propensity to commit criminal (or equivalent) acts" (1985: 23). There is a difference, in other words, between people's propensity to commit criminal acts (criminality) and the acts themselves (crimes). Indeed, Wilson and Herrnstein went on to say that their book was more "concerned with criminality than with crime" (1985: 23).

Like Cohen, Hirschi and Gottfredson, and Wilson and Herrnstein, we hold the point of view in this chapter that an important distinction must be made between criminal behavior and criminal events. Although the behavior of individual offenders is an important component of criminal events, it is, as Cohen (1985) suggests, only one of several important components. Also important are crime targets, victims, law enforcement officials, and other members of society.

CRIMINAL EPISODES

What is being argued here is that the unit of analysis of criminology needs to change. The unit of analysis should not be the individual offender. Neither, however, should it be the law or crime targets. Rather, the unit of analysis should be the criminal event itself. Indeed, the criminal event may even be too narrow a focus. *Criminal episode* might be a better term. In addition to the immediate, overt interaction among offenders, victims, law enforcement officials, and other members of society implied by the term *event*, the term *criminal episode* would include various overt and symbolic interactions among these actors that precede and follow the event itself. Casing several liquor stores before robbing one, for example, would represent an interaction between potential offenders and potential crime targets that preceded a robbery. Tracking robbers down, bringing them to trial, convicting them, and sentencing them to prison would involve interactions between offenders and law enforcement agents that follow a robbery. This broader context is important to criminology for it includes activities, both those that precede an event and those that follow, that can play an important role in whether an event occurs. If a potential robber concludes after casing several liquor stores, for example, that robbing a liquor store is not likely to result in very much money or is too risky, he or she may decide to rob another type of target—for example, a convenience store—or not to engage in robbery at all. A potential robber's estimate of risk, in turn, will depend on her or his expectation of what will happen during and after the robbery: "Does the manager keep a gun? Will he or she use it? Will I be seen leaving the store? How long will it take for the police to get there? Will I be captured? How much time does a person do for robbery?" Things that the potential offender anticipates might happen during and after the event, in other words, play a role in whether the event will occur.

The importance of interactions leading up to and following criminal events does not end with potential offenders. A liquor store owner, for example, will decide to keep (or not to keep) a gun on the premises, in part because he or she thinks it will or will not deter robberies, in part because of the risk a gun poses to customers and employees, in part because of the law, and in part because of the presumed effectiveness of the police and other criminal justice agencies in preventing robbery.

The actions of law enforcement officers, in turn, may be influenced by their conceptions about the robber, the victim, and the crime target. Whether the police will intervene while a robbery is in progress or wait until the robber leaves the store, for example, will depend in part on whether the police believe the robber, or the store clerk, is armed with a gun and whether either is likely to use it.

Criminal episodes, in other words, are complex social phenomena that take place over extended periods of time. They involve not only a criminal event but also social interactions that precede and follow the event itself. To understand why criminal events occur, then, it is necessary to understand the motivations and actions of offenders, victims, and official agents of social control, before, during, and after the event.

The Interactionist Approach

Thinking of crimes as social, rather than as individual, units of analysis implies not only that criminal episodes are multifaceted—involving the actions several people—it also implies that they are interactive. Indeed, the "interactive" component of criminal episodes may be their most important conceptual characteristic (see Cohen 1985). Criminal episodes contain many potential interactions. There are potential interactions between offenders and crime targets. There are potential interactions between offenders and agents of social control. There are potential interactions between agents of social control and crime targets. There are potential interactions among offenders, victims, law enforcement agents, and those who witness criminal events. There are also potential interactions among offenders themselves, when a criminal episode involves more than one offender, just as there may be interactions among more than one victim, more than one law enforcement agent, and more than one observer of a crime. These interactions may be overt, symbolic, or both (Mead 1934). That is, they may involve both the anticipated and the direct interplay among the various actors in the drama.

The cast of characters in a criminal episode may become quite large, and each character may play more than one role. Even the distinction between the offender and the victim sometimes does not become apparent until well into the episode (Wolfgang 1957; Luckenbill 1977). This is particularly true of crimes like assault or murder. Victims may play not only the role of crime target, as in crimes against persons; they also may play the roles of social control agent and witness. Similarly, police officers sometimes play the dual roles of observer and control agent.

All of these interactions, among many individuals playing several roles, are components of criminal episodes. To conceive of criminal episodes in ways that do not include all of these individuals and all of these interactions is to miss much that is important about crime. This complexity, however, is exactly what traditional criminological conceptions of crime—those that conceive of crimes as violations of law or as the actions of criminal offenders—overlook.

THE CONCEPT "CRIME" IN EVERYDAY LIFE

This complexity, although sometimes overlooked by criminologists, is not overlooked by ordinary people. Consider, for example, Gary Fineout's description of a criminal episode that appeared in the 26 April 1989, *Florida Flambeau:*

> The state attorney's office has subpoenaed 12 more members of the Pi Kappa fraternity of Florida State University in the ongoing investigation into the possible sexual battery of an 18-year-old female student found unconscious from intoxication in a fraternity house. A medical report found she had been "sexually violated by more than one person." A Pi Kappa Alpha fraternity member spoke to officials Monday while the other 11 will talk to a representative of the state attorney's office this afternoon. All 12 live on the third floor of the "Pike" house, which the victim said was the site of the alleged sexual assault. Also subpoenaed by the state attorney's office were four women, two of whom belong to the Delta Delta Delta sorority. One of the four is a member of the Alpha Delta Pi sorority. . . . FSU police spokesman Lt. Jack Handley would not comment directly on any of those subpoenaed. Handley said FSU police and the state attorney are continuing their investigation.
>
> "We spent a good part of today doing interviews," FSU police spokesman Lt. Jack Handley said. "We will be continuing tomorrow. We are obtaining new information

from those individuals. We hope to conclude this investigation in the near future." The latest subpoenas follow last week's grand jury investigation in which seven members of the fraternity and the fraternity adviser were summoned before the state grand jury. FSU officials, members of FSU police, and three female students went before the grand jury last week. . . .

The state grand jury released an interim report late Thursday claiming Pi Kappa Alpha members were "evasive" and "uncooperative" with investigating police and that "some evidence of witness intimidation existed." The grand jury is investigating the March 5 incident in which the woman was found abandoned in the hallway of the Theta Chi fraternity house with a "life-threatening" blood-alcohol level. Theta Chi was cleared of any wrongdoing in the incident but FSU police began an investigation in conjunction with the state attorney's office, which continues at this time.

The interim report said the woman testified that she met a Pi Kappa Alpha fraternity member whom she knew at the Late Night Library bottle club where she had been drinking beer and tequila. He invited her back to the third floor of the Pi Kappa Alpha house, she said. Her host then offered her a bottle of wine which she drank. At that point, she said, the fraternity member sexually assaulted her and she passed out.

The woman was found by FSU police at 5:30 a.m. on March 5 with bruises, scratches, and crude words and a fraternity symbol written on her thighs. Medical tests showed that she had been "sexually violated by more than one person."

One day after the grand jury released their report FSU officials suspended the fraternity pending a hearing to be held Wednesday at 2 p.m. But while the fate of the fraternity as a whole won't be decided until then, FSU police and the state attorney's office has been continuing its investigation. . . . The Pi Kappa Alpha fraternity will go before FSU officials in a hearing Wednesday. The charges specifically being directed at the fraternity are violations of two sections of the student code.

Those two sections read: "Obstructs or interferes with the reprimand, discipline, or apprehension of another person who is involved in the commission of an offense under this rule, Board of Regents rules, or Florida Statutes . . ." or "Intentionally acts to impair, interfere with or obstruct the orderly conduct, processes, and sanctions of the University."

This account was one in an ongoing series of articles that appeared in the *Florida Flambeau* and the *Tallahassee Democrat* describing a criminal episode that occurred in Tallahassee, Florida. Earlier articles described the criminal event that occurred in early March; later articles reported such developments as the expulsion of the Pi Kappa Alpha fraternity from the university and the arrest of several of its members and an out-of-town visitor on charges of sexual battery.

Crime Stories

The particular kind of episode described in these articles may not be common, but articles like these are. They are "crime stories." Such stories have several common characteristics.

First, they describe a single criminal episode. The sexual battery case described by the Tallahassee newspapers began on 5 March when a member of the Pi Kappa Alpha fraternity had illegal sexual contact with a woman whom he had invited to his fraternity house. It continued when some of his fraternity brothers also had illegal sexual contact with the women and then left her, unconscious, in another fraternity house.

Although the primary criminal event ended here, the criminal "episode" did not. Following the initial crime, the police were called and medical help was summoned. The police, the state attorney, and university authorities initiated investigations, both of the precipitating incident of sexual battery and of subsequent attempts by members of Pi Kappa Alpha fraternity to impede official investigations. Eventually a state grand jury was impaneled, people were arrested, trials were held, and at least one person went to prison.

The point is this: to the average citizen—to those who write crime stories for the newspaper as well as to those who read them—crimes are singular phenomena. They are not various violations of the law, as they might be to a legal scholar, nor are they a series of individual illegal acts committed by individual offenders, as they are to many criminologists. Rather, they are singular social episodes that happen in social time and space. As in the example cited here, individual criminal events can become chapters in longer criminal episodes involving protracted dealings with the criminal justice system and the community. Although their characterizations may change as new information or interpretations of events come to the fore, these episodes nevertheless retain a singularity over their entire life spans.

COMPONENTS OF CRIMINAL EPISODES

Criminal episodes may involve more than one violation of law (charge), more than one offender, more than one victim, and several law enforcement agencies. The sexual battery case described earlier began when the fraternity member offered alcoholic beverages to someone who already had been drinking and may well have had too much to drink. To offer alcohol to someone who is already drunk is a violation of law.

The case continued when the fraternity member had sex with the victim. Whether this sexual was an "assault," as the victim reported, is immaterial; having sex with someone who is too drunk to give informed consent is sexual battery according to Florida law. This, therefore, was the second violation of law. As additional fraternity brothers had sex with the victim, additional violations of law occurred and additional offenders entered the episode.

As the police and the university pursued the investigation, members of the Pi Kappa Alpha fraternity were uncooperative and tried to intimidate witnesses, which are violations of Florida law and university regulations. Indeed, as the episode continued to unfold, many agencies of social control became involved: the Tallahassee Police, the Florida State University Police, the state attorney, a grand jury, and a Florida State University hearing panel. Eventually, the court and the penal system were called on as well.

Overall, this one criminal episode (newspaper reporters would call it a "story;" the police and state attorney's office would call it a "case") included many violations of law, many offenders, several victims (including those who were "intimidated"), many witnesses, and several agencies of social control. In addition, it involved several newspaper reporters, writing several newspaper articles, read by thousands of Tallahassee residents.

The case illustrates the point that although criminal events usually occur at one rather well-defined time and place, they also usually have histories and ramifications that transcend the immediate events themselves. This means that a crime, in the broadest sense of the term, consists not only of an immediate illegal event (or events) but also of the forethought and human interactions that led up to the event and the considerable drama that often follows the event. In its fullest sense, then, a crime begins with planning and premeditation and ends with the administration of criminal justice (see Black 1989).

Interactions

Episodes of crime usually involve many elements. Most of these elements are persons or the things that persons do. More specifically, they are things that persons do to other persons. They are social interactions. Since criminal episodes involve human interaction, crimes (if crimes are defined as criminal episodes) are social phenomena, by definition. Although the actions of each individual actor in a criminal episode could be thought of, reasonably, as individual personal events, the episode itself is most reasonably thought of as a social phenomenon: a series of social interactions to which the actors, and others, give singular meaning.

Social interactions may be either overt or implicit (what sociologists would call "symbolic"). Overt interactions involve people acting in such a way that their actions affect the subsequent actions of other people. Having sex is an overt interaction. A symbolic interaction does not involve overt behavior; rather it involves "expectations." When one person alters his or her behavior because of what she or he thinks another person will do (or might do or should do), the two are engaging in "symbolic" interaction (Mead 1934). What the fraternity brother thought the woman in the bottle club would do, or "might do" or "had in mind," as he invited her to the fraternity house, in other words, probably played a role in what he and the other fraternity members did later.

Typification

There was no doubt in the mind of the newspaper reporter who wrote about the incident of sexual battery described previously that the incident was criminal. In other times or other places, it might not have been so categorized. Sex, per se, is not viewed as a crime by most people, and most residents of Tallahassee probably would not even consider sex between unmarried adults to be illegal, although some would consider it wrong.

What made this incident particularly noteworthy was the fact that more than one man had sex with the same woman on the same occasion and that the woman was too drunk to resist (or, indeed, even to say no). It was an incidence of rape according to Florida law. The event became a crime, however, not simply because it occurred but because members of the community in which it occurred viewed it as criminal. The incident became a rape, first, because the Florida legislature had defined these kinds of interactions as rape but also because the victim, the medical examiner, and the police depicted the event in such a way that it could not be construed as some lesser infraction, such as adultery or lascivious carriage, or as no infraction at all.

The newspaper article also went to some length to report that the offenders were members of a fraternity and that the victim was a sorority member. (Other articles noted that members of this particular fraternity had been in trouble with the law or with university authorities on other occasions.) This identified the principal actors in the drama as university students. Attempts by members of the fraternity to impede the investigation, as well as the university's appointment of a hearing panel, indicate how important the event was to the reputations of these organizations. Criminal episodes, then, depending on how they are depicted, may become matters of concern not only to offenders, victims, and agents of social control but to others in the community as well. How a crime is depicted, then, becomes an important component of the event itself.

CRIME, CRIMINALITY, AND CRIMINAL BEHAVIOR

As discussed earlier, classical criminologists referred to crimes as violations of law, whereas positivist criminologists used the term to describe certain forms of human behavior. The central contention of this chapter is that neither should be called a crime. Rather, each should be considered as a component of a crime. A violation of law, more commonly referred to as a charge or an offense, is a particular kind of interaction between a person and a crime target that is proscribed by law. Criminal behavior is the proscribed action on the part of the offender.

Victims and Targets of Crime

It is useful to distinguish between a crime target and a crime victim. The *target* of a crime is what an offender wants. The *victim* of a crime is the person, persons, or institutions that are harmed by the crime, because they either own the target, as in the case of burglary, or are the target, as in the case of sexual battery.

Not all crimes have a victim. Indeed, criminologists use the special category "victimless crimes" for these kinds of offenses (see Schur 1965).

It would appear, however, that all crimes have a target. The target of a drug crime is drugs. The target of assault is another person. The target of theft is money or property. The victim, in this latter case, is the owner of the crime target. In the case of drugs, there is no victim, per se.

Including a victim in the definition of a crime would be a mistake because it would imply, first, that the presence of a victim is inherent in the "nature" of crime and, second, that crimes are inherently "predatory." The fact that some societies have made things such as gambling and drug use illegal attests to the fact that neither the presence of a human victim nor predation are necessary prerequisite for societies to deem certain activities to be criminal.

Including a victim as part of the conception of crime also has the effect of obscuring the various, and quite different, roles that victims may play in criminal episodes. Not only is the victim the aggrieved party, as in theft or assault, but often he or she is the person who reports the crime to the police and sometimes also may act, independent of the police, as an agent of social control.

Agents of Social Control

Until the development of the modern state, responsibility for crime control rested primarily with the crime victim or the victim's kin. There were no police, no lawyers, no full-time judges, and no prisons. If a party were aggrieved, it was that party's responsibility to secure amends (see Kittrie 1971).

In modern societies, formal agencies of crime control—police, courts, prisons—perform many of these functions. This does not mean, of course, that victims play no role in controlling crime. Owners of property, for example, contribute significantly to whether their property is stolen by where they locate it and how well they guard it (Kleck 1988). Similarly, people increase or decrease the risk of being assaulted by where they go and what they do (Cohen, Kluegel, and Land 1981).

When discussing crime control in modern societies, it is necessary to differentiate between individual, private control, usually administered by the victim or the potential victim, and public control, administered by agencies of the state. Those who administer the former are often referred to as "informal agents of social control" and the latter as "formal agents of social control" (or as law enforcement agents or officers of the law). Given that Americans spend more money each year on private than on public protection (Cook 1986: 10–14), informal social control is probably more important than formal, state control.

STUDYING CRIME

From the point of view put forth in this chapter, a theory of criminal behavior is not the same thing as a theory of criminal episodes. Since criminal behavior is only one of several elements that make up criminal episodes, knowing why such behavior occurs is not the same thing as knowing why criminal episodes occur. Crimes, in other words, occur for several reasons, only some of which involve offenders.

Criminologists, therefore, should be very precise when they specify which aspects of criminal episodes their particular theory applies to. Is it a theory of law, criminality, criminal behavior, criminal events, or criminal episodes? Although a comprehensive theory of criminal episodes—that is, a comprehensive theory of crime—will include theories of law, criminal behavior, and criminality, it will also include theories of criminal opportunity and theories of social control.

This chapter does not propose such a comprehensive theory. Such a proposal, at this time, is surely premature; criminology does not yet know enough about each of the components of criminal episodes, let alone the interactions among the components, to develop a comprehensive theory of crime.

Nevertheless, the conception of crime outlined here may be a useful guide for studying crime. It should direct attention to questions not addressed by conventional criminological theories and raise doubts about some of the assumptions concerning the nature of crime and the nature of social control employed by policymakers. If the chapter does these two things, it will have accomplished its mission.

Prospects for Theoretical Integration

Conceptualizing "crime" as social episodes opens new avenues for investigation and provides a mechanism by which the several seemingly disparate (and sometimes quarreling) schools of criminology might be united. The conceptualization is quite consistent with labeling theory, critical criminology, economic theory, and opportunity theory; indeed, it grew in part from each of these traditions. The conceptualization is consistent also with the more traditional American positivist approach in that it acknowledges that the criminality of offenders is one component of criminal episodes.

To say that the conception of crimes as social episodes is consistent with each of these different criminological traditions, however, does not resolve the theoretical differences among them. It does not, for example, resolve the conflict between economic (or classical) theory, which assumes that differences in the propensity of individuals to commit crimes (criminality) is unimportant when it comes to explaining variations in crime rates, and traditional positivist criminology, which assumes that these differences can account for essentially all such variation. Rather, the conception leaves the question open.

Nevertheless, by acknowledging that crimes involve both the actions of offenders and the actions (or potential actions) of agents of social control, the conception implies that both of these factors probably have a causal role to play in crime. In the same way, by acknowledging that crimes also involve crime targets, the conception implies that characteristics of potential crime targets (how many there are, what they are worth, how well they are guarded, etc.) also play a causal role in crime. The conception implies, in other words, that variations in crime rates, across social time and social space, cannot be explained fully by knowing how inclined people are to commit crimes, how effective agents of social control are in deterring them, or how many opportunities there are to commit crimes; rather, variations in crime, which involve each of these factors (and perhaps others) will be explained well only if all are taken into account in a single model.

No school of criminology presently offers such a comprehensive model. Indeed, different schools of criminology still focus on different aspects of crime. Traditional American positivist criminologists, including Gottfredson and Hirschi, focus on offenders. Opportunity theorists focus on crime targets. Critical criminologists focus on the law. Economic theorists focus on applications of the law. Labeling theorists focus on the consequences of these applications. This does not mean that these different approaches to criminology are incompatible; it means only that they have been studying different aspects of crime. What now needs to be done is to integrate these various approaches.

Conceiving of crimes as social episodes is one means by which these different branches of criminology might be brought together. If crimes are thought to include the actions of rule makers, rule enforcers, offenders, and victims, then the work of criminologists who have been investigating these different aspects of crime all become legitimate parts of an integrated explanation of crime. If crimes are thought of more narrowly, as they have been in the past, there is no compelling reason that these different points of view should be combined.

REFERENCES

Becker, Gary. 1968. "Crime and Punishment: An Economic Approach." *Journal of Political Economy* 78:169–217.

Beccaria, Cesare. [1764] 1963. *Essay on Crimes and Punishments*. Indianapolis: Bobbs-Merrill.

Biderman, Albert D. 1966. "Social Indicators and Goals." In *Social Indicators*, ed. R. A. Bauer. Cambridge: MIT Press.

Black, Donald. 1989. *Sociological Justice*. New York: Oxford University Press.

Boggs, Sarah L. 1965. "Urban Crime Patterns." *American Sociological Review* 30: 899–908.

Cohen, Albert. 1985. "An Offense-Centered Approach to Criminological Theory." In *Victimology: International Action and Study of Victims*, ed. Zvonimir P. Separovic Zagreb, Yugoslavia: n.p. (Papers given at the Fifth International Symposium on Victimology.)

Cohen, Lawrence E., James R. Kluegel, and Kenneth Land. 1981. "Social Inequality and Predatory Criminal Victimization: An Exposition and Test of a Formal Theory." *American Sociological Review* 46: 505–24.

Cook, Philip J. 1986. "The Demand and Supply of Criminal Opportunities." In *Crime and Justice: An Annual Review of Research*, vol. 7, ed. Michael Tonry and Norval Morris. Chicago: University of Chicago Press.

Ehrlich, Isaac. 1981. "On the Usefulness of Controlling Individuals: An Economic Analysis of Rehabilitation, Incapacitation, and Deterrence." *American Economic Review* 71: 307–22.

Felson, Marcus. 1987. "Routine Activities and Crime Prevention in the Developing Metropolis." *Criminology* 25: 911–31.

Fineout, Gary. 1989. "Court Might Extradite Victim in Pike Rape Case." *Florida Flambeau*, 28 September, 1*ff*.

Gottfredson, Michael, and Travis Hirschi. 1988. "A Propensity–Event Theory of Crime." In *Advances in Criminological Theory*, vol. 1, ed. William S. Laufer and Freda Adler. New Brunswick, N.J.: Transaction.

———. 1990 A *General Theory of Crime*. Stanford, Calif.: Stanford University Press.

Gould, Leroy C. 1969. "Who Defines Delinquency: A Comparison of Self-Reported and Officially-Reported Indices of Delinquency for Three Racial Groups." *Social Problems* 16: 325–36.

———. 1971. "Crime and Its Impact in an Affluent Society." In *Crime and Justice in American Society*, ed. Jack Douglas. Indianapolis: Bobbs-Merrill.

Hirschi, Travis, and Michael Gottfredson. 1987. "Causes of White-Collar Crime." *Criminology* 25: 949–74.

———.1986. "The Distinction between Crime and Criminality." In *Critique and Explanation: Essays in Honor of Gwynn Nettler*, ed. Timothy F. Hartnagel and Robert Silverman. New Brunswick, N.J.: Transaction.

Jeffery, Clarence Ray. [1959] 1960. "The Historical Development of Criminology." In *Pioneers in Criminology*, ed. Hermann Mannheim. Montclair, N.J.: Patterson Smith.

Kittrie, Nicholas N. 1971. *The Right to be Different*. Baltimore: Johns Hopkins University Press.

Kleck, Gary. 1988. "Crime Control through the Private Use of Armed Force." *Social Problems* 35: 1–21.

Kleck, Gary, and Miriam DeLone. 1991. *Victim Resistance and Offender Weapon Effects in Robbery*. Tallahassee: Florida State University School of Criminology and Criminal Justice.

Kleck, Gary, and Susan Sayles. 1990. "Rape and Resistance." *Social Problems* 37: 149–62.

Luckenbill, David F. 1977. "Criminal Homicide as a Situated Transaction." *Social Problems* 25: 176–86.

———. 1982. "Compliance under Threat of Severe Punishment." *Social Forces* 60: 811–25.

Mansfield, Roger, Leroy C. Gould, and J. Zvi Namenwirth. 1974. "A Socioeconomic Model for the Prediction of Societal Rates of Property Theft." *Social Forces* 52: 462–72.

Matza, David. 1964. *Delinquency and Drift*. New York: Wiley.

Mead, George Herbert. 1934. *Mind, Self, and Society*. Chicago: University of Chicago Press.

Schur, Edwin. 1965. *Crimes without Victims*. Englewood Cliffs, N.J.: Prentice Hall.
Stark, Rodney. 1987. "Deviant Places: A Theory of the Ecology of Crime." *Criminology* 25: 893–909.
Wilkins, Leslie T. 1964. *Social Deviance*. London: Tavistock.
Wilson, James Q., and Richard J. Herrnstein. 1985. *Crime and Human Nature*. New York: Simon & Schuster.
Wolfgang, Marvin. 1957. "Victim-Precipitated Criminal Homicide." *Journal of Criminal Law, Criminology, and Police Science* 58: 317–24.
Ziegenhagen, Edward A., and Dolores Brosan. 1985. "Victim Responses to Robbery and Crime Control Policy." *Criminology* 23: 675–95.

[16]

The Labelling Perspective Forty Years On

Ken Plummer

The stream of thought flows on; but most of its segments fall into the bottomless abyss of oblivion.
William James: The Principles of Psychology Ch. XVI

Developing throughout the earlier twentieth century, labelling theory became prominent in the 1960's, reached its heyday in the 1970's and thereafter has more or less gently faded away. Its brief history spans one or two generations of criminologists at most. In this article I briefly review this history, examine the current status of labelling theory and suggest some links to what I call generational theory. As a partial focus, I also revisit an earlier article which I wrote on labelling theory during the 1970's – at the peak of labelling awareness.

Labelling Theory and Perspectives: A Brief Generational History

At base, labelling theory highlights social responses to crime and deviance and moves away from the standard – even 'boring' – questions of aetilogy. As I claimed in my earlier paper (Plummer 1979), labelling theory can be seen as having two forms: a narrow version and a broader, paradigmatic version. The narrow version asks what happens to criminals after they have been labelled testing the hypothesis that crime is heightened (even caused by) criminal sanctions. Sending an offender to prison may work to criminalize him or her further, and stigmatizing minor infractions at too early an age may lead a young offender into a criminal career. The clearest controversies within this narrow version were in the key debate by Scheff and Gove on the labelling theory of mental illness. (Scheff, 1967; Gove, 1979). In contrast, the perspective or paradigmatic version claims that criminology has given too much attention to the commonsense, pedestrian and almost banal focus upon criminals as types of people and too little attention to the panoply of social control responses to deviance – from the law and the police to media and public reactions. Yet surely these reactions are symbiotic with crime? Giving each other their social shapes reactions and crime emerge together dialectically. And in an earlier paper, I claimed that this *labelling perspective* had a fourfold problematic:

1. What are the *characteristics* of labels, their variations and forms?
2. What are the *sources* of labels, both societal and personally?
3. How, and under what *conditions*, do labels get applied?
4. What are the *consequences* of labelling? (Plummer 1979: 88)

The word label here might now be better translated as the whole gamut of social reactions. Labelling theory, I suggest, is best seen as a useful set of key problems designed to re-orientate the criminological mainstream to the consideration of the nature, emergence, application and impact of social reactions to crime and deviance. It establishes the problematic of social reactions.

My early paper arose from two key sources. Firstly, I was a member of the then every exciting movement of the National Deviancy Conference (NDC) where new ideas in deviancy theory and criminology were being proposed as a challenge to mainstream orthodoxies (cf Cohen, 1971; Taylor and Taylor, 1974). Secondly, I was doing my own Ph.D. on homosexuality at the time, and labelling made enormous sense of this emergent field of enquiry. I spent on and off about five years writing the paper – presenting it at an NDC Conference in Cardiff in 1976 – and it was finally published in *Deviant Interpretations* (Downes & Rock 1979), which was meant implicitly as a riposte to the gathering momentum of the new criminology, critical criminology and the realist criminology of the time. (In that early article I set myself three main tasks. The first was to briefly situate the theory in its time and complexity. The second was to make a broad distinction between labelling as a specific theory, and labelling as a paradigm or perspective. And the third was to defend the theory against a number of its critics).

My view then – and now – is that labelling theory is "most usefully conceived as a perspective whose core problems are the nature, emergence, application and consequences of labels" (Plummer 1979: 86). These questions can be approached by a range of theories, though I was clear then, as I still am that "*my own preference.... is for an interactionist theory of labelling*" (cf Plummer 1979:92-94). But of course interactionism itself has moved on and has become capable of being a much more political and varied position (e.g. Denzin 1979; Plummer 2000; Denzin 2010).

At the heart of much earlier labelling work was an interest in the politics of naming and control: of the trouble that labels can cause, of 'Leviathan and Ban' (Matza, 1969). It is present of course in Becker's (1963) account of moral enterprise where the focus is placed on who has the power to name. And it is there in many of the key processes studied by theorists at the time; how conducts became criminalized; how 'problems in living' became medicalized; how many problem behaviours were cast into the net of the law; how problems had become the province of professionalization and expert systems. All these showed power at work in the shaping of crime and deviance problems. And the thrust of much of this early work was to critique this power from above and champion power from below; the move was towards positions of decarceration, deinstitutionalization, demedicalization, deprofessionalization and overall decategorization. And it led simultaneously to a major intellectual and political interest in the politics of social movements and identities.

Labelling Theory: Generational Histories

It is possible to trace basic ideas of labelling back a long way (Pearson 1975). But as a criminological theory it starts its public and symbolic journey in the 1930's (possibly with Tannebaum and some members of the Chicago School like Clifford Shaw), and by mid-century its writings and research abound. As I said in my 1979 article:

> In the early sixties it was seen as a 'radical, underground' theory, attracting the 'young Turks' of sociology who used it as a basis for developing critiques of the dominant paradigms in deviancy analysis… By the late sixties (in America at any rate), the theory had been co-opted into the mainstream of sociological work–enshrined in formal statements, texts, readers and Ph..D. theses, taught widely on undergraduate sociology and criminology programmes, and absorbed into much 'positivistic' social research… In just ten years, labelling theory has moved from being the radical critic of established orthodoxies to being the harbinger of new orthodoxies to be criticized (Plummer, 1979: 85).

Even by the time that I wrote my review article, the theory was already fading. Taylor Walton and Young's highly influential *The New Criminology* (published in 1973), and which contained a chapter outlining its key problems, was perhaps the turning point. It is hard after that time to find many self-proclaimed labelling theorists (there are a few of course).

Since then, Labelling Theory has become canonized in the history of institutionalized criminology, and by 1994 its obituary had been written (Sumner, 1994). Indeed it is hard to subsequently find much evidence of either proponents or research moving under that name after that heady early period. Textbook treatments usually only cite earlier work—it is part of the history of criminology, not its contemporary life. I briefly researched all volumes of the journal *Theoretical Criminology* and found no mention of labelling per se (there were early articles on 'careers' though; and some mention of 'moral panics'). Google and Amazon searches found unusually little that was not part of the classic canon.

86 The Labelling Perspective Forty Years On

The core labelling theory reader by Rubington and Weinberg (which ran through eight editions between 1968 and 2001) was rarely updated with new research – except in the field of mental health, where it does seem to have had a minor continuing underlife. And all those key researchers of the 1960's who were so identified moved on to other things. Edwin Lemert (1912-1996) later went on to the study of 'evil'. Howard S. Becker is still extremely prominent as a cultural sociologist but did very little further work on either crime or labelling after his famous compilation (1963) book (Most of his work has been on culture, art, photography and music). Crime effectively is part of his much more general view of life as 'doing things together' (Becker, 1986). Erving Goffman became the leading microsociologist of the twentieth century but never identified himself clearly as labelling theorist. Edwin Schur is a bit of an exception: after his influential *Crimes without Victims* (1963) he worked assiduously to develop a research programme for labelling theory – producing a programmatic statement (Schur, 1971), a textbook (1979), a policy statement on *Radical Non Intervention* (1973) and, in 1980, *The Politics of Deviance* which showed the importance of struggles and protests over definitions and 'stigma contests' (1980). In 1983, he applied labelling theory to women. But he has since retired with no further interest, and sadly he is no longer widely cited. David Matza and Kai T. Erickson are both identified with one key influential book on labelling (*Becoming Deviant* 1969 and *Wayward Puritans* 1966) but neither continued with or developed labelling theory any further. John Lofland's brilliant *Deviance and Identity* (1969) became a lost masterpiece even as it was published (but has been recently partially rediscovered a little (Lofland 1969/2002). Stanley Cohen and Jock Young have become very prominent world criminologists – and they have not, as far as I know, rejected labelling theory: but they have certainly gone on to many other things. Paul Rock has been a quiet champion of it (Rock 1972). On a much lesser scale, I have also used labelling throughout my work (Plummer, 1975; 1981); but I have rarely explicitly returned to it. I think of myself as a critical humanist and symbolic interactionist for sure and it deeply shapes my work on sexual stories and intimate citizenship) Plummer 1975; 2003); but rarely in the past thirty years have I called myself a labelling theorist.

Criminological generations?

Labelling theory – like all theories, including criminological theories—might usefully be seen as a generational theory. In a powerful and major exposition, Randall Collins (1998) has charted the significance of communities and interaction ritual chains as world intellectual movements throughout global history claiming that an approximate life of thirty years – maybe two overlapping generations – is the period that most theories survive within these chains. All knowledge – including criminological knowledge – is shaped by and dwells within generational structures which are always moving on. There is now a significant social science literature on the sociology of knowledge, memory, historical time lines, age cohorts, and generations which makes allied claims. In the work of Gramsci (1971), Mannheim (1936; 1952), Halbwachs (1992), Edmunds and Turner (2002) and Collins (1998) and others we can see this grounded and age linked base of knowledge. I have discussed it elsewhere (Plummer 1981; 2010).

Basically, the stories we tell of all of social life –including those of crime – are bound up with the generations we live in: we tell *generational narratives*. These can be seen as perspectives or standpoints on social worlds. The criminology literature is littered with such generational tales of crime – accounts come and go, theories rise and fall with different generations. Often reading a criminology textbook is a little like reading a history of the attempts of different generations to try and understand what crime is. Each generation has its own multiple narratives, rhetorics, key references, foundational stories and the like (see Bennett 1981). We all live with pluralised pasts and invented memories of crime storie told in earlier times. And so the crime theories of each generation rise and fall: the stories of crime do not usually last more than several generations and rarely more than thirty years. That said, there are often deep continuities between past and present; and the past comes to dwell in the present in new forms. Like all narratives, they are always multiple and plural (Plummer 2009).

In criminology, the liturgies of seemingly dead theories are somewhat astounding. We rehearse the arguments of cultural transmission, learning theory, differential association, status frustration theory, anomie theory, and Chicago ecology to each generation of students less they forget their pasts: but it is hard to find proponents of them today. The theories move on and take new forms and names. Dick Hebdidge's almost cult like book on *Subcultures* was the key book of its time, but in my view was always a thin book and was woefully ignorant of much earlier theorizing on subcultures from from Frederick Thrasher, Albert Cohen and Cloward and Ohlin to John Barron Mays and David Downes. And in their turn, these days, new 'post subculture' theories move on new languages once again ignoring their past (though others see it too located in the past. (Huq 2006; Brabazon 2005; Gelder 2007).

This is all as it should be – especially in the social sciences where the world being studied is itself in constant flow and change. It is world of continual permutations of actions (Strauss 1993) and with this theories and meanings are always on the move. Theories come; theories go; everything changes; nothing changes. We could not expect labelling theory to last: little does.

21st Century Labelling Theory? Contemporary Developments

There are, then, very few proponents today of what I have called the narrow version of labelling theory. Indeed, I am not sure it has actually ever had that many followers in its tight and limited form. In what follows I briefly review some recent putative contributions to both labelling *theory* and the labelling *perspective*. It is with the latter that I see the biggest contribution.

Labelling as a limited theory

The most prominent area for testing the theory has been that of mental illness. In what came to be known as the Scheff-Gove debate, a number of studies have continued this old controversy about mental health. Although in the main this field is now dominated by genetic and biological thinking, there are some who still argue that stigma and labelling have profound impacts on the career of those designated mentally ill. Scheff himself has long moved on to the study of emotions and shame; Goffman moved on to language and frames. Thomas Szasz may be the key exception – but he keeps repeating the same old story in new books which do not really advance on his key formative arguments. Yet empirical studies do still appear which make clear the significance of this tradition. For example Bruce Link and others in a series of empirical studies have found that the rejection of people with mental illness has profound consequences on their sense of self and subsequent responses and actions. (Link et al 1989; 2001). Others have found that social rejection is a persistent cause of stress (Wright et al 2000).

At the same time, in a major, detailed and important new book, Allan Horowitz and Jerome C. Wakefield's *The Loss of Sadness*, devote their research to showing "how psychiatry transformed normal sorrow into depressive disorder". Yet they dismiss Scheff's work in a scant reference (2007:19). The study seems to me to be a major exemplar of the labelling theory of mental illness – yet they ignore, or even deny, it. I am not sure why they do not see their study as part of the labelling tradition, but they seem not to.

Another tradition which could be relevant is that of "life course criminology" of which the rich research work of Laub and Sampson (2003) is most prominent. Their core problem is the 'persistence or desistance' of criminality in a life; their method is the life history; and their theoretical tradition connects to rich seams of social control and attachment theory. But again, as a recent work, there is no mention of labelling theory even though they do give a detailed focus on how involvements with the justice system "reverberated over the life course" (2003:51). Many factors shape a persistent criminal life – and one of them is incarceration.

Labelling Theory and the significance of societal reaction

The narrow version of labelling has never been the prime concern of labelling theorists. It is useful to return to the canonical statements to remind ourselves ultimately what labelling theory is all about. These statements act as a kind of *Greek Chorus of Labelling theory*, repeated everywhere. Here they are again:

> An older sociology tended to rest heavily on the idea that deviance leads to social control. I have come to believe that that the reverse idea i.e. that *social control leads to social deviance* is equally tenable and the potentially richer premise for studying deviance in modern society (Lemert 1967: 22)

> Deviance is not a property inherent in certain forms of behaviour; it is a property conferred upon these forms by the audiences which directly or indirectly witness them. Sociologically, then, *the critical variable is the social audience* (Erikson 1962: 308)

> Social groups create deviance by making the rules whose infraction constitutes deviance and by applying these rules to particular people and labelling them as outsiders. From this point of view, deviance is not a quality of the act the person commits, but rather *a consequence of the application by others of rules and sanctions to an 'offender'*. "The deviant is one to whom that label has successfully been applied; *deviant behaviour is behaviour that people so label"* (Becker 1963:9)

The italicized phrases are mine and not the original. What is striking about these statements is that they never suggest a simple-minded propositional positivistic testable hypothetic-deductive style of theory for labelling: what they provide instead is a broad orientation, a paradigm push, a perspective, a set of puzzles and problems. And the essential core of this approach is the turn away from the criminal per se which has usually preoccupied mainstream criminology and a major move towards studying societal reactions, in the widest sense, and their relation to crime. It is this I believe which is at the heart of the tradition and which has been taken on in contemporary work, even as the significance of early labelling work is often, even usually, ignored.

90 The Labelling Perspective Forty Years On

Labelling Theory Today

So labelling theory is dead: long live labelling theory. This epanalepsis captures the dilemma. In effect, how could anyone *ever* take a criminology seriously that did not take into account societal reactions and labels? And there is indeed a long history of this line of thought. But the specific variety that came into being under that name in Western criminology in the middle twentieth century was a specific and distinct historical form that had both its moment and its generation. Its ideas are then carried on in new movements, fashions, and languages by new generations. Labelling theory becomes – as all theories do- 'old fashioned', out of their own time and their own generation. But the significance of societal reactions for any intellectual, critical or practical work on crime or deviance can never go away. When we look for signs of it in more recent work, we can find it everywhere.

Once phrased this way, we can see the diffuse impact of labelling theory everywhere. Here are just twelve instances which come swiftly to mind and which could be amplified further id space allowed. The problematic of labelling theory is alive and well and dwelling within:

1. Moral panic theory. This focus on hysteria and panic around crimes has indeed become a major contemporary and highly influential theory of crime and problem awareness.
2. Sociology of everyday crime and dramatisation. This sees the ubiquity of the millions of ordinary everyday crimes (boring crimes) which in effect need dramatic social responses to become significant.
3. Studies of public attitudes to crime. We now study the origins and nature of 'fear of crime', with a key example being penal populism
4. Research on discourses around crime. From Foucault and govermentality to critical discourse analysis, we look at the interventions of state discourse in assembling crime.
5. Shaming and stigmatization studies. We look at the ways in which shame may be implicated in the prevention and generation of crimes.
6. Studies of stereotype. There is a long history of the study of stereotypes and it still continues. Linked here too are phenomenological questions of categorizations.
7. Neutralization and denial studies. In a sense the other side of labelling, this is the concern with *not* labeling. Harking backoften to Sykes and Matza's techniques of neutralization (1957), there remains a key interest in accounting and denial.

8. The construction of social problems arguments. This is a strand that has taken many permutations since the 1970's but which is still very much around (Loeske 2003).
9. The State and Social exclusion theory. This id often lined to studies of poverty and inequality, but shows the roles of the state in excluding many people in the criminal process.
10. Crime, Media and Culture: This new journal, of this very name, flags the growth and significance of media theory and its links to the shaping of crime problems
11. Cultural criminology. More generally, this focuses on media and everyday responses to crime.
12. Cultures of control and their impact. The whole field of social control –police, courts, prisons etc.-- gives a clear focus to reactions to crime.
13. Governance theory. This focuses on the myriad little activities (the micro-circuits of power) in which psychologists, psychiatrists, criminologists, social workers, prison officers, engineer and manage 'the human soul'. The hand of Foucault is clearly at work here (cf Miller and Rose 2008).
14. Queer theory. This has a major interest in deconstructing social reaction categories to sex, sexuality and gender and leads to new thinking about sex crimes.
15. Postmodernism with its concern with reaction signs, simulacrums and significations.

In a short article I cannot follow up all these connections but I will follow a few as suggestive and indicative.

Towards a Sociology of Social Reactions to Crime & Deviance

Since the halcyon days of labelling theory, major new – and critically important – domains of sociological inquiry have been developed. Although rarely called this, we might even see this as *a sociology of societal reactions* (cf. Garland 2008). Here I simply suggest just three areas of reaction, all now major fields and all informed by labelling.

1 The reactions of media: Back in the 1960's, the pioneering work of Jock Young and Stan Cohen on media in their respective PhD's led to a quite striking grasping of the ways in which modern media played critical roles in the shaping of crime. It culminated in their highly influential *The Manufacture of News* (1973).

Now it has developed into a well-developed field (with its own courses and even degrees) which marks out the significance of media constructions of crime: its audiences, representations and industries. It even has its own journal: *Crime Media Culture* which started in 2005. The late modern world of crime now simply cannot be understood without placing it within the reactions of modern media which so strikingly help to assemble it. (e.g. Carrabine, 2008; Jewkes, 2004).

2 The reactions of publics: Famously, it was Durkheim who told us of the power of the public response to crime. In the early labelling writing (such as Erikson, 1968/2004 and Scott 1972), Durkheim loomed large:

> We have only to notice what happens, particularly in a small town, when some moral scandal has just occurred. Men stop each other on the street, they visit each other, and they seek to come together to talk of the event and to wax indignant in common. From all the similar impressions which are exchanged, and the anger that is expressed, there emerges a unique emotion, more or less determinate according to the circumstances, which emanates from no specific person, but from everyone. This is the public wrath.......Crime brings together honest men and concentrates them. (Emile Durkheim *The Division of Labor in Society)*

The issue of taking seriously the attitudes of the public to crime has now become a major part of the criminologist's task. In the U.K., *The British Crime Survey* (of victims responses and public perceptions of crime) started in 1980 and is now an annual event. The very concept of 'fear of crime' can now be traced and analysed in the process of generating social anxiety. (cf. Lee, 2006; Lee and Farrall 2008; Farrall et al, 2009).

A good instance of this is the awareness of (and research into) what has become known as the practice and theory of penal populism (Pratt, 2007). Penal populism is associated with the decline in public deference to the criminal justice establishment and their furious (if often misplaced) alarm that crime is out of control. Pratt argues that new media technology is helping to spread national insecurities and politicians are not only encouraging such sentiments but are also being led on by them. Penal populism explains to have most influence in the development of policy on sex offenders, youth crime, persistent criminals and anti-social behaviour.

3 The reactions of control cultures: Traditionally, many labelling theorists were concerned with the excessive encroachment of technology, bureaucracy and the state upon the personal life–often in its grossest forms such as the increasing medicalisation of deviance, the bureaucratisation of the control agencies and the concomitant dehumanisation of the lives of their 'victims', as well as the direct application of technology in the service of control. With the continuing political shift to the right in many Western democracies since the 1980's, such concerns were co-opted as part of a market based laissez faire liberalism which aimed to roll back the state and introduce privatization into social control. New patterns of governance have emerged which examine the new 'rationalities' and 'technologies' which regulate our 'subjectivities' (Miller and Rose 2008). These are not so much reactions as part of the daily circuits of power we all inhabit.

Theorising Social Reactions

Back in my 1979 paper, I tried to show that whilst there may have been a common sense of a major problematic appearing in the work of the labelling theorists, there was little if any theoretical consensus between them. The theory certainly connects well to the sociological ideas of Durkheim, G. H. Mead, the Chicago School, some interpretations of Marx and conflict theory, as well as Symbolic Interactionism – drawing upon both the idea of a 'self-fulfilling prophecy' and the dictum of W.I. Thomas that 'when people define situations as real they become real in their consequences'. But I have to stress again that that labelling theory is actually a rag bag of different theories – often incompatible with each other, and sharing no common identity with the name: but nevertheless sharing common substantive and often theoretical problems. As I said in 1979:

> None of the [early] theorists above actually began by identifying ... as a labelling theorist: rather ironically, they had that label thrust upon them by others and only later came to incorporate it into their own sociological identities. Thus neither Becker nor Lemert seems at all happy with being identified as a labelling theorist; neither used this tag in his earlier work. Indeed, by the early 1970s Becker was publicly stating his preference for being known as an interactionist rather than a labelling theorist (Becker, 1974 p. 44), while Lemert was disassociating himself from the 'conceptual extrusions' and 'crudities' of labelling theory (Lemert 1972 p. 6). Goode's review of the field also concludes that Becker and Lemert (as well as Erickson and Kitsuse) 'cannot be called labelling theorists' (Goode, 1975 p. 571). It is important to stress both this lack of self-recognition by labelling theorists and their diverse theoretical concerns: *for the labelling perspective has only emerged from the retrospective selection of a few select themes largely from diverse theoretical projects.* They are united by some common substantive problems but not common theories. There are often much wider discrepancies than overlaps. Erickson's brand of functionalism can hardly be equated with Cicourel's ethnomethodology, while Lemert's focus on putative deviation (which implies a

non-putative or objective deviance) jars markedly with Kitsuse's relativistic 'imputed deviance' (which denies an objective reality of deviance).

Labelling theories have in fact long genealogies and many contrasting routes. Like all theoretical work, the construction of the social reaction/labelling perspective is a messy business of pluralising pasts and contested concepts. We can trace a number of earlier theoretical positions within labelling to include functionalism, many variants of Marxism and critical conflict criminologies, hermeneutics, feminisms and cultural theories. We can also see intellectual affinities with the work of many social psychologists on processes of stigmatization and stereotyping. It is probably most at home – has an intellectual affinity with -- the phenomenologists, the discourse theorists (including Foucault), the conversational analysts, and of course the symbolic interactionists. And in recent times, we could suggest how many more contemporary theories would benefit from a partial focus on labelling and social reaction: the globalization of labelling, surveillance as labelling, the habitus of social reactions, reactions as flow and mobilities (cf Urry 2007), intersectional labelling, queer labelling, and its strong links with cultural criminology (cf Ferrell, Hayward & Young). The ideas of labelling theory could flourish in many theories and there are many ideas here that are worth exploring. Here to conclude are a few final examples.

1. Social constructionist theory.

This is the major term under which much recent labelling theory has moved. We can trace this back to at least Berger and Luckman's key 1966 work, which by 1970 had helped to shape Richard Quinney's crucial (but now ignored) *The Social Reality of Crime* (1971). This has been a popular framework that has been used to examine the social construction of social problems. My earliest recollection of this was the work of Herbert Blumer, John Kitsuse and Malcolm Spector. The latter focused on the changing psychiatric definitions of homosexuality in the mid-1970's and extended in their 1977 classic *Constructing Social Problems*. This has subsequently grown into a full scale theory, as exemplified in Donileen Loseke's (1999/2003) textbook which outlines its shape: the focus is on claims making, claims makers, audience and competition. She contrasts two views: "Objectivism" which makes claims about social problems that they believe are real and stem from objective conditions of social life, while "constructionism" by contrast argues about the claims-making processes occurring in and around these things. This is an approach in sociology which argues that 'conditions must be brought to people's notice in order to become social problems' (Best 1990: 11). Once again closely allied to Becker's notion of moral enterprise, it looks at the ways individuals, groups and societies come to label certain phenomena as problems and how others then respond to such claims. Joel Best (1990) for instance has traced the 'rhetoric and concern about child victims', whilst Philip Jenkins (2004) has traced the child molester problem. Broadly, there is seen to be a 'social problems marketplace' in which people struggle to own social problems: these theories continue to examine the rhetorics, the claims and the power struggles behind such definitional processes. In this area there is now a massive amount of continuing work even if it often fails to note its roots.

2. Boundary and classification theory

At its heart, labelling theory surely raises long standing classical problems of boundaries. Such theoretical problems will never go away. It was Durkheim who has most clearly seen the bond between the normal and the pathological: twin processes bound up with the conditions for social life. This basic classification of the normal and the pathological serves to mark out moral boundaries, unite people against common enemies and establish that there is a 'we' and the 'other'. It is hard to find instances of societies which do not do this. There were several labelling theorists of the 1960's and 1970's who revisited this key idea; most famously Ericksons's classic *Wayward Puritans*; Robert Scott's (1970.) celebrated analysis, and very prominently, in the work of Mary Douglas on purity and taboo (1966; 1970).

Here the problems are outlined of how boundaries are bound up with social life, of how there is always stuff that is 'inside' and stuff that is 'outside'. All societies dwell in multiplicities of flux are in persistent need of classification systems (Bowker and Starr 2007). Boundaries and classifications are never fixed, they are always on the move. Classification of the normal and the abnormal, the natural and the unnatural, the criminal and the non-criminal are best seen as flows, as continual permutations of classifications being reworked through by groups. Politically, social movements are a prime mover of such boundaries.

Here we also have a sense of what is a key problem of postmodernity and crime. 'Order is what is not chaos; chaos is what is not orderly. Order and chaos are *modern* twins' (Bauman 1991:4). It is a problem that I have addressed in more detail more recently (see Plummer 2007).

3. Moral Panic Theory

The concerns with media, publics and control cultures come together in the study of moral panics -- a term gestating in Becker's work over the initial concern with drugs in the USA. brought to prominence in Young's research on drug use in Notting Hill (1971) and Cohen's study (1972) of the teenage panics of Mods and Rockers on English Bank Holiday beach resorts in the 1960's and Hall's study of race relations in the UK and the fear of the 'black mugger', it has subsequently been absorbed into the lexicons of mainstream criminological and sociological research. It is by far the most widespread and most apparent legacy of those early labelling theorists.

The study of moral panics has been applied to many areas and has become a staple feature of research with a stream of research investigations (satanic panic, child molesters, single mothers, drug users, working class males, violent schools, hyperactive children, welfare scroungers, computer games, pornography, guns, street stabbings, the sexualization of girls, ASBO's, drugs of all kinds – including binge drinking and 'ecstasy parties', panic, obesity- or 'fat' people, and – of course, refugees and immigrants. It has developed its own canonical textbooks and even conferences. It is a standard entry in textbooks, dictionaries and seen as a 'key idea' in sociology. A Google search can cheerfully bring up 450,000 entries (e.g. Ben-Yehuda & Goode, 1994/2009; Jenkins, 2004; Critcher, 2003/2006; Thompson, 1998). If labelling theory is manifestly alive anywhere today it is in this branch of moral panic theory. It has now even entered the public imagination and become part of common sense (Garland 2008; Altheide 2009 see also the debate at the British Academy Lectures in 2007: 'Moral Panics: The and Now' by Stan Cohen, David Garland & Stuart Hall at http://britac.studyserve.com/home/default.asp).

4. Shame theory and Reintegration theory

A further illustrative example could be Braithwaite's book *Crime, Shame and Reintegration* (1989) demonstrated that current criminal justice practice tends to stigmatize offenders, making the crime problem worse. Braithwaite argued that restorative justice enables both offenders and citizens, by way of mediation, to repair the social harm caused by crime. Some societies have higher crime rates than others because of their different processes of shaming wrongdoing. Shaming can be counterproductive, making crime problems worse. But when shaming is done within a cultural context of respect for the offender, it can be an extraordinarily powerful, efficient and just form of social control. Braithwaite identifies the social conditions for such successful shaming. If his theory is right, radically different criminal justice policies are needed – a shift away from punitive social control toward greater emphasis on moralizing social control.

5. Intersectional theory and the inequalities of labelling

At the heart of much of the earlier labelling theory was a concern with the way social class, race and age were major factors in shaping decisions around deviance. Race famously in the work of Stuart Hall played a key role in 'moral panics' – andmany panics were about youth. Likewise, decision making studies of police and courts could often show how class biases worked. In more recent research on

Inequalities – heavily shaped b feminist theory and critical race theory (Crenshaw 1995; Collins 1990), a much greater emphasis has come to be placed on the ways in which these vectors of inequality and oppression intersect with each other. Inequalities should be located at the intersection of class, ethnicity, gender, age, disability, sexuality and nationhood. Lives are shaped by these inequalities, and so are the contingencies which organize the labelling of criminals and deviants. Recent theories bring these once disparate features together. Acts of labelling lie at the intersections of class, race, age – and even sexuality and health—and need to be understood within this framework.

6. The state and social exclusion theory

Many writers from the 1990s onwards have pointed to the significance of the state and social exclusion from a wide range of political, policy and theory positions (e.g. Byrne, 2005). Within criminology, Jock Young in the U.K. and Loic Wacquant in France and the U.S. have, amongst others, made the process of exclusion a key to grasping the crime process. Young is concerned with 'the demonization and creation of monstrosity', how societies 'essentialise the other', how we vomit out our deviants, casting them beyond the social order in a so called "purification process" (Young, 1999). Late capitalist modernity makes us live with these extreme bifurcations. Likewise, Wacquant's studies of global inner cities speaks explicitly of 'urban outcasts', to the creation of the hyperghetto, of 'territorial stigmatization', the 'great confinement' and the rise of 'punitive panopticism' (Wacquant, 2004/9;2008). Now it would be crude to say these are twenty-first century labelling theorists. But their concerns with the way in which the neo-liberal state works to split the social order and exclude a growing group of people lies at the heart of their accounts and certainly echoes the heady days of the labelling theorists (of which of course Jock Young's, 1971, first book was a major part).

Moving Ahead: The Continuing Relevance of Reactions and Labelling

Generations may change but intellectual puzzles have to be repeatedly confronted. What is clear is the contemporary world is just as amenable to problems of labelling now as it was fifty years ago. We now have the existence of sex offender registers (and Meagan's law in the U.S and Sarah's law in the U.K.) which raises major human rights issues of permanent life-long stigmas being applied. We have even more of the over reach of law and medicine into the private sphere of personal problems, especially in the new shapes of 'Youth crime' and new community offences appear and the net of surveillance casts wider. We have the hyper-categorisation of problems and a proliferation of new categories from

ASBOS to ADHD. The control apparatus continues to grow and takes on ever new forms, sucking in more crimes and problems. Deviancy amplification, and what Pratt has called the sorcerer's apprentice, continue to magnify the symbiotic relation of crime and control. The media has become a pivotal agent in constructing the problems of crime and it oozes the daily air we breathe. And still people experience the problems of labelling on a daily basis in many institutions. I had could go on.

My argument here, then, has been a very simple one. Forty years on from the gestation of my original article, we can see that labelling theory may well have had its own criminological generation and its heyday. Theories inevitably come and go. But I have also argued here that labelling theory brings an important and abiding set of concerns for sociologists and criminologists. Its fall from explicit prominence in the twenty-first century does not make the issues it raises any less significant. What I have tried to do is outline just a few preliminary number of issues where we can see how labelling theory's continuing problematic and questions are re-fashioning themselves for yet another new generation. I am not concerned with defending its old positions and arguments or the terminology of labelling, but seek instead to show that the problems it raised in the 1960's and the 1970's are still alive with us today and continue to demand attention. We should never forget the key problems of criminology and the works of earlier generations in confronting them.

Bibliography

Aas, Katja Franko (2007): Globaliztion and Crime, London.

Altheide, David (2009): Moral Panic: From Sociological Concept to Public Discourse, in Crime, Media, Culture 5: 79-99.

Bauman, Zygmunt (1991): Modernity and Ambivalence, Cambridge

Becker, Howard S. (1963). Outsiders: Studies in the Sociology of Deviance, New York.

Becker, Howard S. (Ed.) (1964). The Other Side. New York.

Becker, Howard S.(Ed.) (1986). Doing Things Together. Evanston.

Ben-Yehuda Nachman & Eric Goode (1994/2009 2nd ed.). Moral Panics: The Social Construction of Deviance, Oxford.

Bennett, James. (1981). Oral History and Delinquency: The Rhetoric of Criminology, Chicago..

Berger, Peter and Thomas Luckmann. (1966). The Social Construction of Reality. Harmondsworth.

Best, Joel. (1990). Threatened Children: Rhetoric and Concern about Child Victims. Chicago.

Bordua, David. J. (1967). Recent Trends: Deviant Behavior and Social Control. Annals of the American Academy of Political and Social Science, 57: 149-63.

Brabazon, Tara (2005): From Revolution to Revelation: Generation X, Popular Memory and Cultural Studies, Aldershot.

Bowker, G. & Lee Starr (2000): Sorting Things Out, Cambridge, MA

Braithwaite, John. (1989): Crime, Shame and Reintegration, Cambridge.

Byrne, David. (2005). Social Exclusion (2nd ed.), Milton Keynes.

Carrabine, Eamonn. (2008): Crime, Culture and Media. Cambridge: Polity Press.

Cohen, Stanley. (Ed.) (1971): Images of Deviance, Harmondsworth.

Cohen, Stanley. (1972; 2002): Folk Devils and Moral Panics. 3rd ed. London.

Cohen, Stanley. (1985): Visions of Social Control, Cambridge.

Cohen, Stanley and Jock Young. eds. (1973). The Manufacture of News, London.

Collins, Patricia Hills (1990): Black Feminist Thought, London.

Collins, Randall. (1998): The Sociology of Philosophies: A Global Theory of Intellectual Change, Cambridge.

Conrad, Peter & Joseph Schneider. (1980): Deviance and Medicalization: From Badness to Sickness, Philadelphia.

Critcher, Chas. (2003): Moral Panics and the Media, Milton Keynes

Critcher, Chas. (Ed.) (2006): Moral Panics and the Media: Critical Readings, Milton Keynes

Denzin, Norman K. (1991): Cultural Studies and Symbolic Interaction. Oxford.

Denzin, Norman K. (2010): The Qualitative Manifesto: A Call to Arms, Walnut Creek.

Douglas, Mary. (1966): Purity and Danger: An Analysis of the Concepts of Purity and Taboo, London.

Douglas, Mary. (1970): Natural Symbols: Explorations in Cosmology, London.

Downes, David & Paul Rock (Eds.) (1979): Deviant Interpretations, Oxford.

Edmunds, June & Bryan S. Turner. (2002): Generations, Culture and Society. Milton Keynes.

Erikson, Kai T. (1962): Notes on the Sociology of Deviance, in: Social Problems, 9:307-314.

Erikson, Kai T. (1968/2004). Wayward Puritans. 2nd ed., Upper Saddle River.

Farrall, Stephen D., Jonathan Jackson & Emily Gray. (2009): Social Order and the Fear of Crime in Contemporary Times, Oxford.

Garland, David. (2002). The Culture of Control, Chicago.

Garland, David. (2008): On the Concept of Moral Panic, in: Crime, Media, Culture. 4(1): 9-30.

Gelder, Ken (2007): Subcultures: Cultural Histories and Social practice, London.

Goffman, Erving (1961): Asylums. New York.

Goffman, Erving (1963): Stigma, New Jersey.

Goode, Eric (1975): On Behalf of Labeling Theory, in Social Problems, 22: 570-83.

Goode, Eric & Nachman Ben-Yehuda. (1994; 2009): Moral Panics: The Social Construction of Deviance, 2nd ed. Oxford.

Gove, Walter. (1975; 1980): The Labeling of Deviance (2nd ed.), Beverley Hills.

Gouldner, Alvin. (1968). The Sociologist as Partisan, in: American Sociologist. 3(2):103-116.

Gramsci, Antonio. (1971). Selections from the Prison Notebooks, London.

Gusfield, Joseph R. (1981): The Culture of Public Problems: Drinking-Driving and the Symbolic Order, Chicago.
Halbwachs, Maurice. (1992): On Collective Memory. Chicago.
Hammack, Phillip L. & Bertram J. Cohler (Eds.) (2009): The Story of Sexual Identity: Narrative Perspectives on the Gay and Lesbian Life Course, Oxford.
Huq, Rupa (2006): Beyond Subculture: Pop, Youth and Identity in a Postmodern World, London.
Jenkins, Phillip. (2004): Moral Panic: Changing Concepts of the Child Molester in Modern America, Newhaven.
Jewkes, Yvonne. (2004): Media and Crime. London.
Lee, Murray. (2006): Inventing Fear of Crime: Criminology and the Politics of Fear. Cullompton.
Lee, Murray & Stephen Farrall (Eds.) (2008): Fear of Crime: Critical Voices in an Age of Anxiety, London.
Lemert, Edwin. (1967): Human Deviance, Social Problems and Social Control. Englewood Cliffs, NJ.
Loeseke, Donileeen (1999/2003): Thinking about Social Problems: An Introduction to Constructionism 2nd ed, New York.
Lofland, John. (1969; 2002): Deviance and Identity. Clinton Corners.
Mannheim, Karl. (1936): Ideology and Utopia, London.
Mannheim, Karl. 1952: The Problem of Generations, Pgs 276-320 in Collected Works of Karl Mannheim, Vol 5, London.
Mankoff, Milton (1971): Societal Reaction and Career Deviance, in: Sociological Quarterly, 12: 204-218.
Matza, David. (1969): Becoming Deviant, Englewood Cliffs, NJ.
Miller, Peter & Nikolas Rose (2008): Governing the Present, Cambridge.
Pearson, Geoffrey (1975): The Deviant Imagination, London.
Plummer, Ken (1975): Sexual Stigma: An Interactionist Account, London.
Plummer, Ken. (1979): Misunderstanding Labelling Perspectives, in David Downes & Paul Rock, eds. Deviant Interpretations. Oxford.
Plummer, Ken. (Ed.) (1981): The Making of the Modern Homosexual, London..
Plummer, Ken. (1983/2001): Documents of Life: An Invitation to a Critical Humanism. 2nd ed. London.
Plummer, Ken. (1995): Telling Sexual Stories: Power, Change and Social Worlds. London.
Plummer, Ken. (2000): Symbolic Interactionism in the Twentieth Century, in Bryan S. Turner ed, The Blackwell Companion to Social Theory. 2nd edition. Oxford.
Plummer, Ken. (2003): Intimate Citizenship: Private Decisions and Public Dialogues, Seattle.
Plummer, Ken. (2007): The flow of boundaries: gays, queers and intimate citizenship, in David Downes et al., Crime, Social Control and Human Rights: Essays in Honor of Stanley Cohen, Cullompton.
Plummer, Ken. (2009): On Narrative Pluralism, Pgs.. vii-xiv in P.L. Hammack & B. J. Cohler eds., The Story of Sexual Identity: Narrative Perspectives on the Gay and Lesbian Life Course, Oxford.
Plummer, Ken. (2010): Generational Sexualities: Subterranean Traditions, and the Haunting of the Sexual World: Some Preliminary Remarks, in: Symbolic Interaction. 33: 163-190.

Ken Plummer 101

Pratt, John. (2007). Penal Populism. London.
Quinney, Richard (1970): The Social Reality of Crime, Boston.
Reiman Jeffrey & Paul Leighton (1979, 2009): The Rich Get Richer and the Poor Get Prison, Boston.
Rock, Paul (1973): Deviant Behaviour. London.
Rubington, Earl & Martin S. Weinberg. (1968/2001): Deviance: The Interactionist Perspective, Oxford.
Schur, Edwin. (1965): Crimes without Victims. Englewood Cliffs, NJ.
Schur, Edwin. (1971): Labeling Deviant Behavior. London.
Schur, Edwin. (1973): Radical Non-Intervention. Englewood Cliffs, NJ.
Schur, Edwin. (1979): Interpreting Deviance. London.
Schur, Edwin. (1980): The Politics of Deviance. Englewood Cliffs, NJ.
Schur, Edwin. (1983): Labeling Women Deviant, Philadelphia.
Scheff, Thomas J. (1966): Being Mentally Ill. New York: Aldine
Scheff, Thomas J. (2007): Goffman Unbound: A new Paradigm for Social Science, Boulder.
Scott, Robert A. (1972): A Proposed Framework for Analyzing Deviance as a Property of Order, pp. 9-36 in: R.A. Scott & J. Douglas, Theoretical Perspectives on Deviance, New York.
Spector, Malcom & John Kitsuse (1976; 2000): Constructing Social Problems. New York.
Strauss, Anselm (1993): Continual Permutations of Action, New York.
Sumner, Colin. (1994): The Sociology of Deviance: An Obituary. Milton Keynes.
Sykes, Gresham & David Matza (1957): Techniques of Neutralization, in American Sociological Review 22: 664-670.
Szasz, Thomas (2007): The Modernization of Everyday Life, New York.
Tannenbaum, Frank. (1938): Crime and the Community. Boston.
Taylor, Ian & Laurie Taylor: (1973). Politics and Deviance. Harmondsworth.
Taylor, Ian, Paul Walton & Jock Young. (1973). The New Criminology. London.
Thompson, Kenneth (1998): Moral Panics, London.
Urry, John (2007): Mobilities, Cambridge.
Wacquant, Loic. (2004/2009): Punishing the Poor: The Neoliberal Government of Social Insecurity. Durham.
Wacquant, Loic. (2008): Urban Outcasts: A Comparative Sociology of Advanced Marginality, Cambridge.
Young, Jock. (1971): The Drugtakers. London.
Young, Jock. (1999): The Exclusive Society. London.
Young, Jock. (2007): The Vertigo of Late Modernity. London.

[17]

CONDITIONS OF SUCCESSFUL DEGRADATION CEREMONIES

HAROLD GARFINKEL[1]

ABSTRACT

Communicative work directed to transforming an individual's total identity into an identity lower in the group's scheme of social types is called a "status degradation ceremony." To reconstitute the other as a social object, the denouncer must get the witnesses to appreciate the perpetrator and the blameworthy event as instances of an extraordinary uniformity, in dialectical contrast to ultimately valued, routine orders of personnel and action. The denouncer must publicly claim and manage the status of bona fide representative of the group of witnesses. From this position he must name the perpetrator an "outsider." Organizational variables will determine the effectiveness of a program of degradation tactics.

Any communicative work between persons, whereby the public identity of an actor is transformed into something looked on as lower in the local scheme of social types, will be called a "status degradation ceremony." Some restrictions on this definition may increase its usefulness. The identities referred to must be "total" identities. That is, these identities must refer to persons as "motivational" types rather than as "behavioral" types,[2] not to what a person may be expected to have done or to do (in Parsons' term,[3] to his "performances") but to what the group holds to be the ultimate "grounds" or "reasons" for his performance.[4]

The grounds on which a participant achieves what for him is adequate understanding of why he or another acted as he did are not treated by him in a utilitarian manner. Rather, the correctness of an imputation is decided by the participant in accordance with socially valid and institutionally recommended standards of "preference." With reference to these standards, he makes the crucial distinctions between appearances and reality, truth and falsity, triviality and importance, accident and essence, coincidence and cause. Taken together, the grounds, as well as the behavior that the grounds make explicable as the other person's conduct, constitute a person's identity. Together, they constitute the other as a social object. Persons identified by means of the ultimate "reasons" for their socially categorized and socially understood behavior will be said to be "totally" identified. The degradation ceremonies here discussed are those that are concerned with the alteration of total identities.

It is proposed that only in societies that are completely demoralized, will an observer be unable to find such ceremonies, since only in total anomie are the conditions of degradation ceremonies lacking. Max Scheler[5] argued that there is no society that does not provide in the very features of its organization the conditions sufficient for inducing shame. It will be treated here as axiomatic that there is no society whose social structure does not provide, in its routine features, the conditions of identity degradation. Just as the structural conditions of shame are universal to all societies by the very fact of their being organized, so the structural conditions of status degradation are universal to all societies. In this framework the critical

[1] Acknowledgment is gratefully made to Erving Goffman, National Institute of Mental Health, Bethesda, Maryland, and to Sheldon Messinger, Social Science Research Council pre-doctoral fellow, University of California, Los Angeles, for criticisms and editorial suggestions.

[2] These terms are borrowed from Alfred Schutz, "Common Sense and Scientific Interpretation of Human Action," *Philosophy and Phenomenological Research*, Vol. XIV, No. 1 (September, 1953).

[3] Talcott Parsons and Edward Shils, "Values, Motives, and Systems of Action," in Parsons and Shils (eds.), *Toward a General Theory of Action* (Cambridge: Harvard University Press, 1951).

[4] Cf. the writings of Kenneth Burke, particularly *Permanence and Change* (Los Altos, Calif.: Hermes Publications, 1954), and *A Grammar of Motives* (New York: Prentice-Hall, Inc., 1945).

[5] Richard Hays Williams, "Scheler's Contributions to the Sociology of Affective Action, with Special Attention to the Problem of Shame," *Philosophy and Phenomenological Research*, Vol. II, No. 3 (March, 1942).

question is not whether status degradation occurs or can occur within any given society. Instead, the question is: Starting from any state of a society's organization, what program of communicative tactics will get the work of status degradation done?

First of all, two questions will have to be decided, at least tentatively: *What are we referring to behaviorally when we propose the product of successful degradation work to be a changed total identity?* And *what are we to conceive the work of status degradation to have itself accomplished or to have assumed as the conditions of its success?*

I

Degradation ceremonies fall within the scope of the sociology of moral indignation. Moral indignation is a social affect. Roughly speaking, it is an instance of a class of feelings particular to the more or less organized ways that human beings develop as they live out their lives in one another's company. Shame, guilt, and boredom are further important instances of such affects.

Any affect has its behavioral paradigm. That of shame is found in the withdrawal and covering of the portion of the body that socially defines one's public appearance—prominently, in our society, the eyes and face. The paradigm of shame is found in the phrases that denote removal of the self from public view, i.e., removal from the regard of the publicly identified other: "I could have sunk through the floor; I wanted to run away and hide; I wanted the earth to open up and swallow me." The feeling of guilt finds its paradigm in the behavior of self-abnegation—disgust, the rejection of further contact with or withdrawal from, and the bodily and symbolic expulsion of the foreign body, as when we cough, blow, gag, vomit, spit, etc.

The paradigm of moral indignation is *public* denunciation. We publicly deliver the curse: "I call upon all men to bear witness that he is not as he appears but is otherwise and *in essence*[6] of a lower species."

The social affects serve various functions both for the person as well as for the collectivity. A prominent function of shame for the person is that of preserving the ego from further onslaughts by withdrawing entirely its contact with the outside. For the collectivity shame is an "individuator." One experiences shame in his own time.

Moral indignation serves to effect the ritual destruction of the person denounced. Unlike shame, which does not bind persons together, moral indignation may reinforce group solidarity. In the market and in politics, a degradation ceremony must be counted as a secular form of communion. Structurally, a degradation ceremony bears close resemblance to ceremonies of investiture and elevation. How such a ceremony may bind persons to the collectivity we shall see when we take up the conditions of a successful denunciation. Our immediate question concerns the meaning of ritual destruction.

In the statement that moral indignation brings about the ritual destruction of the person being denounced, destruction is intended literally. The transformation of identities is the destruction of one social object and the constitution of another. The transformation does not involve the substitution of one identity for another, with the terms of the old one loitering about like the overlooked parts of a fresh assembly, any more than the woman we see in the department-store window that turns out to be a dummy carries with it the possibilities of a woman. It is not that the old object has been overhauled; rather it is replaced by another. One declares, "*Now*, it was otherwise in the first place."

The work of the denunciation effects the recasting of the objective character of the perceived other: The other person becomes in the eyes of his condemners literally a different and *new* person. It is not that the new attributes are added to the old "nucleus." He is not changed, he is reconstituted. The

[6] The man at whose hands a neighbor suffered death becomes a "murderer." The person who passes on information to enemies is really, i.e., "in essence," "in the first place," "all along," "in the final analysis," "originally," an informer.

former identity, at best, receives the accent of mere appearance. In the social calculus of reality representations and test, the former identity stands as accidental; the new identity is the "basic reality." What he is now is what, "after all," he was all along.[7]

The public denunciation effects such a transformation of essence by substituting another socially validated motivational scheme for that previously used to name and order the performances of the denounced. It is with reference to this substituted, socially validated motivational scheme as the essential grounds, i.e., the *first principles*, that his performances, past, present, and prospective, according to the witnesses, are to be properly and necessarily understood.[8] Through the interpretive work that respects this rule, the denounced person becomes in the eyes of the witnesses a different person.

II

How can one make a good denunciation?[9]

To be successful, the denunciation must redefine the situations of those that are witnesses to the denunciation work. The denouncer, the party to be denounced (let us call him the "perpetrator"), and the thing that is being blamed on the perpetrator (let us call it the "event") must be transformed as follows:[10]

1. Both event and perpetrator must be removed from the realm of their everyday character and be made to stand as "out of the ordinary."

2. Both event and perpetrator must be placed within a scheme of preferences that shows the following properties:

A. The preferences must not be for event A over event B, but for event of *type* A over event of *type* B. The same typing must be accomplished for the perpetrator. Event and perpetrator must be defined as instances of a uniformity and must be treated as a uniformity throughout the work of the denunciation. The unique, never recurring character of the event or perpetrator should be lost. Similarly, any sense of accident, coincidence, indeterminism, chance, or monetary occurrence must not merely be minimized. Ideally, such measures should be inconceivable; at least they should be made false.

B. The witnesses must appreciate the characteristics of the typed person and event by referring the type to a dialectical counterpart. Ideally, the witnesses should

[7] Two themes commonly stand out in the rhetoric of denunciation: (1) the irony between what the denounced appeared to be and what he is seen now really to be where the new motivational scheme is taken as the standard and (2) a re-examination and redefinition of origins of the denounced. For the sociological relevance of the relationship between concerns for essence and concerns for origins see particularly Kenneth Burke, *A Grammar of Motives*.

[8] While constructions like "substantially a something" or "essentially a something" have been banished from the domain of scientific discourse, such constructions have prominent and honored places in the theories of motives, persons, and conduct that are employed in handling the affairs of daily life. Reasons can be given to justify the hypothesis that such constructions may be lost to a group's "terminology of motives" only if the relevance of socially sanctioned theories to practical problems is suspended. This can occur where interpersonal relations are trivial (such as during play) or, more interestingly, under severe demoralization of a system of activities. In such organizational states the frequency of status degradation is low.

[9] Because the paper is short, the risk must be run that, as a result of excluding certain considerations, the treated topics may appear exaggerated. It would be desirable, for example, to take account of the multitude of hedges that will be found against false denunciation; of the rights to denounce; of the differential apportionment of these rights, as well as the ways in which a claim, once staked out, may become a vested interest and may tie into the contests for economic and political advantage. Further, there are questions centering around the appropriate arenas of denunciation. For example, in our society the tribal council has fallen into secondary importance; among lay persons the denunciation has given way to the complaint to the authorities.

[10] These are the effects that the communicative tactics of the denouncer must be designed to accomplish. Put otherwise, in so far as the denouncer's tactics accomplish the reordering of the definitions of the situation of the witnesses to the denunciatory performances, the denouncer will have succeeded in effecting the transformation of the public identity of his victim. The list of conditions of this degrading effect are the determinants of the effect. Viewed in the scheme of a project to be rationally pursued, they are the adequate means. One would have to choose one's tactics for their efficiency in accomplishing these effects.

not be able to contemplate the features of the denounced person without reference to the counterconception, as the profanity of an occurrence or a desire or a character trait, for example, is clarified by the references it bears to its opposite, the sacred. The features of the mad-dog murderer reverse the features of the peaceful citizen. The confessions of the Red can be read to each the meanings of patriotism. There are many contrasts available, and any aggregate of witnesses this side of a complete war of each against all will have a plethora of such schemata for effecting a "familiar," "natural," "proper," ordering of motives, qualities, and other events.

From such contrasts, the following is to be learned. If the denunciation is to take effect, the scheme must not be one in which the witness is allowed to elect the preferred. Rather, the alternatives must be such that the preferred is morally required. Matters must be so arranged that the validity of his choice, its justification, is maintained by the fact that he makes it.[11] The scheme of alternatives must be such as to place constraints upon his making a selection "for a purpose." Nor will the denunciation succeed if the witness is free to look beyond the fact that he makes the selection for evidence that the correct alternative has been chosen, as, for example, by the test of empirical consequences of the choice. The alternatives must be such that, in "choosing," he takes it for granted and beyond any motive for doubt that not choosing can mean only preference for its opposite.

3. The denouncer must so identify himself to the witnesses that during the denunciation they regard him not as a private but as a publicly known person. He must not portray himself as acting according to his personal, unique experiences. He must rather be regarded as acting in his capacity as a public figure, drawing upon communally entertained and verified experience. He must act as a bona fide participant in the tribal relationships to which the witnesses subscribe. What he says must not be regarded as true for him alone, not even in the sense that it can be regarded by denouncer and witnesses as matters upon which they can become agreed. In no case, except in a most ironical sense, can the convention of true-for-reasonable-men be invoked. What the denouncer says must be regarded by the witnesses as true on the grounds of a socially employed metaphysics whereby witnesses assume that witnesses and denouncer are alike in essence.[12]

4. The denouncer must make the dignity of the supra-personal values of the tribe salient and accessible to view, and his denunciation must be delivered in their name.

5. The denouncer must arrange to be invested with the right to speak in the name of these ultimate values. The success of the denunciation will be undermined if, for his authority to denounce, the denouncer invokes the personal interests that he may have acquired by virtue of the wrong done to him or someone else. He must rather use the wrong he has suffered as a tribal member to invoke the authority to speak in the name of these ultimate values.

6. The denouncer must get himself so defined by the witnesses that they locate him as a supporter of these values.

7. Not only must the denouncer fix his distance from the person being denounced, but the witnesses must be made to experience their distance from him also.

8. Finally, the denounced person must be ritually separated from a place in the legitimate order, i.e., he must be defined as standing at a place opposed to it. He must be placed "outside," he must be made "strange."

These are the conditions that must be fulfilled for a successful denunciation. If they are absent, the denunciation will fail. Regardless of the situation when the denouncer enters, if he is to succeed in degrading the other man, it is necessary to introduce these features.[13]

[11] Cf. Gregory Bateson and Jurgen Ruesch, *Communication: The Social Matrix of Psychiatry* (New York: W. W. Norton & Co., 1951), pp. 212–27.

[12] For bona fide members it is not that these are the grounds upon which we are agreed but upon which we are *alike*, consubstantial, in origin the same.

[13] Neither of the problems of possible communicative or organizational conditions of their effective-

Not all degradation ceremonies are carried on in accordance with publicly prescribed and publicy validated measures. Quarrels which seek the humilitation of the opponent through personal invective may achieve degrading on a limited scale. Comparatively few persons at a time enter into this form of communion, few benefit from it, and the fact of participation does not give the witness a definition of the other that is standardized beyond the particular group or scene of its occurrence.

The devices for effecting degradation vary in the feature and effectiveness according to the organization and operation of the system of action in which they occur. In our society the arena of degradation whose product, the redefined person, enjoys the widest transferability between groups has been rationalized, at least as to the institutional measures for carrying it out. The court and its officers have something like a fair monopoly over such ceremonies, and there they have become an occupational routine. This is to be contrasted with degradation undertaken as an immediate kinship and tribal obligation and carried out by those who, unlike our professional degraders in the law courts, acquire both right and obligation to engage in it through being themselves the injured parties or kin to the injured parties.

Factors conditioning the effectiveness of degradation tactics are provided in the organization and operation of the system of action within which the degradation occurs. For example, timing rules that provide for serial or reciprocal "conversations" would have much to do with the kinds of tactics that one might be best advised to use. The tactics advisable for an accused who can answer the charge as soon as it is made are in contrast with those recommended for one who had to wait out the denunciation before replying. Face-to-face contact is a different situation from that wherein the denunciation and reply are conducted by radio and newspaper. Whether the denunciation must be accomplished on a single occasion or is to be carried out over a sequence of "tries," factors like the territorial arrangements and movements of persons at the scene of the denunciation, the numbers of persons involved as accused, degraders, and witnesses, status claims of the contenders, prestige and power allocations among participants, all should influence the outcome.

In short, the factors that condition the success of the work of degradation are those that we point to when we conceive the actions of a number of persons as group-governed. Only some of the more obvious structural variables that may be expected to serve as predicters of the characteristics of denunciatory communicative tactics have been mentioned. They tell us not only how to construct an effective denunciation but also how to render denunciation useless.

UNIVERSITY OF CALIFORNIA, LOS ANGELES

---

ness have been treated here in systematic fashion. However, the problem of communicative tactics in degradation ceremonies is set in the light of systematically related conceptions. These conceptions may be listed in the following statements:

1. The definition of the situation of the witnesses (for ease of discourse we shall use the letter *S*) always bears a time qualification.

2. The *S* at t_2 is a function of the *S* at t_1. This function is described as an operator that transforms the *S* at t_1.

3. The operator is conceived as communicative work.

4. For a successful denunciation, it is required that the *S* at t_2 show specific properties. These have been specified previously.

5. The task of the denouncer is to alter the *S*'s of the witnesses so that these *S*'s will show the specified properties.

6. The "rationality" of the denouncer's tactics, i.e., their adequacy as a means for effecting the set of transformations necessary for effecting the identity transformation, is decided by the rule that the organizational and operational properties of the communicative net (the social system) are determinative of the size of the discrepancy between an intended and an actual effect of the communicative work. Put otherwise, the question is not that of the temporal origin of the situation but always and only how it is altered over time. The view is recommended that the definition of the situation at time 2 is a function of the definition at time 1 where this function consists of the communicative work conceived as a set of operations whereby the altered situation at time 1 is the situation at time 2. In strategy terms the function consists of the program of procedures that a denouncer should follow to effect the change of state S_{t1} to S_{t2}. In this paper S_{t1} is treated as an unspecified state.

[18]

Ethnomethodology and Criminology: The Social Production of Crime and the Criminal

Stephen J. Pfohl

An ethnomethodological perspective . . . directs the researcher's attention to the theories of delinquency employed by laymen and particularly to theories employed by police, probation, and court officials. What is needed are studies showing how folk theories articulate with actual practice.—Aaron V. Cicourel, *The Social Organization of Juvenile Justice*[1]

During the oral portion of my Ph.D. examinations, one of my examiners asked whether the theoretical claims of the societal-reaction perspective on deviance were not a bit exaggerated. The examiner prefaced his inquiry with several comments on the utility of this perspective as a sensitizing device. He then queried me about the existence of certain types of behaviors that would be considered ''naturally'' deviant in any society or culture—homicide, for example. I responded in the negative.

Homicide is a categorization that removes the act of killing from socially redeemable rationalizations. The behavior is essentially the same: killing the police officer or killing by the police officer; stabbing an old lady in the back or stabbing the unsuspecting war-time enemy; a black slave shooting a white master or a white master lynching a black slave; being run over by the drunken driver or slowly dying of cancer caused by a polluting factory. All are forms of killing. Some are called homicide. Others are excused, justified, or viewed, as in the case of industrial pollution, as environmental health risks. The form and context of what is considered homicide thus appear to vary with social context and circumstance. This is hardly what one would expect from a universally recognized form of crime or deviance.

''Well,'' continued the examiner, ''what about hyperkinesis? Certainly the problems caused by hyperkinetic children cause a universal disturbance in any culture.'' I disagreed. Consider the interpretation of such behaviors in several South Seas island communities. The behavior we normally associate with hy-

I wish to thank Mary Brady, Susan Guarino, and Ron Huff for thoughtful and constructive comments on an earlier draft of this chapter and Sara White for her assistance in preparing the manuscript. I also wish to thank Simon Dinitz. His support and encouragement in developing a diverse range of critical criminological inquiry has been a great catalyst for all of us who studied with him.

perkinesis is revered there with a categorical halo of religious sanctity. Another examiner, an anthropologist who had studied one such community, agreed. "It's no use arguing with you," the first examiner commented.

So what is universal about deviance? It is not its content but the process that gives deviance its social form—the process by which definitions of acts and persons as deviant are socially generated and applied. This was my answer then. My examiner was Simon Dinitz. In this chapter, written for this volume honoring Simon Dinitz, I will expand this response.

My answer is essentially the same now as then. However, it is an answer that attempts to transcend some of the often-cited limitations of the so-called labeling-theory tradition within the societal-reaction perspective. In doing so, it draws attention to a second major but less commonly articulated strand of theorizing within this perspective—ethnomethodology. Specifically, this chapter outlines the contributions of ethnomethodology to the creation of what might be called an interpretive criminology. It briefly traces the theoretical, methodological, and empirical contributions of ethnomethodology to criminology, contrasts it with the more familiar prescriptions of the labeling-factors approach, and suggests its affinity with the concerns of a historically grounded, critical criminological perspective.

Ethnomethodology: Socially Structured Structures

As a sociological perspective, ethnomethodology is generally concerned with the various methods that people, including sociological researchers, use to accomplish a reasonable account of what is happening in social interaction and to provide a sense of structure for the interaction itself. Ethnomethodology differs from other perspectives, which assume the independent existence of a social structure that provides a fairly standardized set of meanings, roles, and normative rules for the individuals who live within them. From the ethnomethodological perspective, social structure is *never* independent of the consciousness of actors who experience its force. A sense that life is governed by standardized meanings, roles, and rules is just that—a sense, common sense. This makes social structure no less forceful. It simply relocates it within, rather than outside, the world of human thinking and doing, talking and acting, working and playing. Structured society is viewed as an accomplished product of concrete social interaction, rather than its overshadowing predecessor.

This is not to say that, from the ethnomethodological vantage point, life is unstructured. Indeed, most ethnomethodologists follow the phenomenological lead of Alfred Schutz in depicting the experience of everyday life as largely taken for granted, prestructured, and shared with others.[2] However, the structures of everyday life experience are never fully independent of the interpretive work that actors do in making sense of this moment and this place in social life.

It is for this reason that ethnomethodologists turn to the small, detailed, practical features of interpretive social interaction for keys to the larger mysteries of structure and of social life in general.

Ethnomethodological Studies of Crime, Criminal, and Criminal Controls

Given its concern with the processes by which people construct believable, acceptable, or defensible accounts of what social life really is, it is no surprise that ethnomethodology has paid particular attention to problems of deviance and crime. In declaring, discovering, or asserting the category of deviance, social actors dramatize the recognizably real boundaries of social life. The recognition of certain acts or actors as outside the accepted rules of structured society permits us ritualistically to pay homage to the reality of both these rules and the structured society that it is assumed is behind them.

The ethnomethodological view of deviance closely resembles certain aspects of Durkheim's description of the boundary-setting functions of crime control.[3] A structured sense of normal social life is produced by apprehending its opposite. George Herbert Mead suggested a similar phenomenon in his classic essay, "The Psychology of Punitive Justice."[4] For Mead, the "majesty of the law," the "solemnity of the criminal court," and the "severity of the penal sanction" combine symbolically to create a sense of belonging for those who ritualistically unite in opposition to crime and the criminal. Once again, a structured sense of rule-governed society is gained by recognizing that which would threaten the way it is organized.

Although certain aspects of the ethnomethodological approach resembles Durkheim's functional and Mead's symbolic interpretations of deviance, its primary focus is on the practical, interpretive work of actors in making imputations of crime and deviance. The theoretical contribution of ethnomethodology in explicating these matters is perhaps best understood by reference to what are conceived as the three central features of all practical interpretive work: indexicality, reflexivity, and documentary interpretation.

Indexicality

The term *indexicality* is used to indicate that all human interpretive work is in certain ways bound to the context in which it occurs. The reality of the same potentially deviant act will be conceived very differently, depending on whether it is viewed from the patrol car of a police department under pressure to make arrests or from the backseat of a fast-moving vehicle full of partying teenagers.

The importance of indexicality is revealed in Sudnow's analysis of the overcrowded and pressurized court context within which public defenders employ commonsense stereotypes about who is and who isn't the "normal" criminal, and who should be offered or refused a certain line of plea-bargaining or defense.[5] A similar analysis of the indexical constraints inherent in the organization of social-control agencies is found in Cicourel's study of juvenile-justice decision-making,[6] Daniels's consideration of psychiatry within the military,[7] and McCleary's examination of career contingencies affecting parole officers' production of "bad records for good reasons."[8]

Reflexivity

Reflexivity refers to the manner in which actors' interpretive accounts (verbal and nonverbal) come to alter the setting in which they are employed. In other words, interpretive accounts are not only bound by the context in which they occur (indexically), but through their very expression they create new contexts and thereby become (reflexively) a part of the phenomenon on which they report.

The omnipresent importance of reflexivity in human interpretive work is increased by its relative inconspicuousness. Reflexive work, once completed, appears to vanish from self-conscious awareness. This unnoticeable character of reflexivity is particularly evident in the production of deviance. The end product of successful imputational work is paradoxically to forget (or at least be inattentive to) the fact that such work was even involved. This reflexive disguising of the created character of deviance is discussed by Melvin Pollner, who suggests: "While a community creates deviance, it may simultaneously mask its creative work from itself."[9]

Empirically, the dynamics of "unnoticed" reflexive work are clearly evident in Weider's study of the inmate code in halfway houses.[10] This code does not operate as an abstract set of rules governing appropriate behavior. Rather, it is invoked as a solution to particular instances of tension. It allows inmates to call one another into question. The code is invoked to order a disorderly situation. In doing so, however, its users divert attention from the subjective, particularistic, or situational nature of conflict. They reflexively recognize, instead, the objective nature of general rules that allegedly cover all situations. Are the rules really like this? No—they are reflexively invoked only when they are strategically useful. This is rarely noticed. The reflexive use of rules to give a sense of structure to life in the halfway house fades as it is enacted.

The paradoxical characteristic of interpretive work is further illustrated in Garfinkel's analysis of the reflexive rule images produced by jurors in the course of deciding a verdict.[11] These quasi-legal rules were announced after the fact, after jurors had already decided a verdict. They were nonetheless reflexively applied backward in time. As such, they came to be viewed by jurors as the standards that had guided their "fair deliberations" from the beginning. A similar hiding of the reflexive character of social-control judgments is revealed in Sacks's analysis of the reality of suicide threats discovered during hot-line crisis conversation[12] and in Douglas's examination of official descriptions of suicide as the cause of death.[13]

Documentary Interpretation

Harold Garfinkel, the central figure in the development of ethnomethodology, uses the term *documentary interpretation* to refer to the manner in which people infer meaningful action patterns from the appearance of simple behaviorial stimuli. Appearances are treated as documents of something deeper, as expressions of underlying patterns or structures. In the words of Garfinkel, "Not only is the underlying pattern derived from its individual documentary evidences, but the individual documentary evidences, in their turn, are interpreted on the basis of 'what is known' about the underlying pattern. Each is used to elaborate the other."[14]

The study of documentary interpretive practices has proved a valuable resource for studying the ascription of criminal or deviant identities. Such practices are evidenced in Egon Bittner's description of the cognitive methods that police use to jump from surface appearances to the recognition of real troublemakers;[15] in Robert Emerson's analysis of the construction of delinquent biographies in juvenile court;[16] in Jacqueline Wiseman's depiction of the typification of individuals charged with public drunkenness;[17] and in my own study of the prediction of dangerousness by psychiatric specialists.[18] In each case, the interpretive work of social-control agents reduces complex and often contradictory social, political, and economic realities into a neatly packaged depiction of the offender as a fixed type of troublesome individual.

Similar observations are made with regard to norms or social rules. The study of documentary interpretations suggests that ideas about fixed norms or rules are also a product of the judgmental work of those who would control the behaviors of others. This is not to say that rules or norms do not exist, but that they exist only as the end product of the interpretive work by which control agents size up a situation, treat it as a document of a more general pattern, and then use this pattern as a device for ordering experience in the present.

From the ethnomethodological perspective, rules are not viewed as existing independent of the documentary interpretations of actors who see them. When understood in conjunction with the principles of indexicality and reflexivity, this aspect of documentary interpretation underscores the ethnomethodological claim that all norms or roles are essentially open or empty until filled in by the context-bound interpretive work of people in the process of social interaction. Through this work, appearances are transformed into patterns, which are then (reflexively) recognized as having a life of their own. According to ethnomethodologists Mehan and Wood, "Without this work a rule has no meaning, no life at all."[19] With this work, social-control agents produce a sense of the world as normative or rule-governed and thereby justify or legitimize their action as required by norms or rules that are independent of the ways they act to restrain, repress, reform, or rehabilitate those who are discovered to be deviant. But are such norms or rules ever fully independent of the interactional occasions in which they are evoked? The ethnomethodological answer is no. Its detailed observations display the interpretive interaction by which believable and justifiable senses of deviance are produced and legitimized. This is its major contribution to the study of crime, deviance, and social control. With such observations, ethnomethodology constructs interpretive or phenomenologically informed criminology.

Ethnomethodology and the Methods of Criminological Inquiry

Ethnomethodology has contributed to several advances in the methods of criminological inquiry. First, it has questioned the uncritical use of official statistics on crime and deviance as reflective of crime itself. According to Garfinkel, Kitsuse and Cicourel, and others, the production of official statistics suggests more about the organizational work of control agencies than it does about the activities of deviants.[20] As Edwin Schur points out, this means "that official statistics should be considered an object of investigation to be explained in their own right. Our primary interest should not be in what they might tell us about the causation of deviance, but rather in exploring the causation of the rates themselves."[21]

A second methodological contribution of ethnomethodology to criminology concerns the issue of exactly what is to be considered criminal or deviant. Criminologists have argued since the inception of the discipline about what should or shouldn't be considered a crime. Should one follow legal, normative, or ethical definitions? The ethnomethodological position is clear. Do not start with any preconceived definition. Focus, instead, on definitions that are used concretely in specific historical circumstances. This follows from ethnomethodology's assumption that, for all practical sociological purposes, there is no crime or deviance independent of the judgmental work of the control agents who see such things. If this is the case, then an actor's own definitional practices must become the starting point for the study of crime in history. Criminologists and sociologists of deviance are thus freed from the problem of trying to decide on the most appropriate conceptualizations of rule breaking. According to Kitsuse:

> Definitions . . . of members . . . must prevail, however 'misinformed,' 'er-

roneous,' or 'misguided' they may appear to be from the sociologist's standpoint. The alternative of invoking the sociologist's definitions as the standard of assessing normative behavior, is to face the problem of accounting, on one hand, for the failure of members to negatively sanction behavior that is 'obviously deviant,' and on the other for the imposition of such sanctions in the absence of 'norm violating' behavior.[22]

A third contribution of ethnomethodology to the canons of criminological inquiry concerns the reflexive nature of the research process itself. Ethnomethodologists recognize that criminologists, like the people they study, are bound in certain ways to the context in which research is done. Similarly, in interpreting the interpretations of others, researchers are forced to employ similar documentary practices. How, then, can they claim any objectivity about their own observations and analyses? The answer is not to be found in the structured havens of survey analysis or fixed-choice questionnaires. These methods also employ situate inferences and context-bound judgments about what is or isn't a likely, plausible, or meaningful answer or response. To claim otherwise is to lie to oneself, to hide behind a false cloak of constructed objectivity. This is a fundamental theme in ethnomethodology's examination of the practical work entailed in doing social research. How, then, can the researcher make any claims as to the objective nature of his or her inquiry?

Ethnomethodology's response is twofold.[23] It acknowledges that objectivity is partial, at best. The task of the disciplined researcher is to approximate objectivity while providing one's audience with a detailed account of the social context and contextual decisions that are a necessary feature of the research process. Two recommendations are made in approximating objectivity: wherever and whenever possible, (1) attempt at least partial replications of one's work and (2) display as much as possible (for example, through verbatim audio or visual transcripts) the verbal or nonverbal actions of those about whose activities one makes interpretative judgments. In other words, display the phenomenon being analyzed. This allows the audience to join the researcher, at least partially, in interpreting the scene being studied. It furthers the quest for objectivity by providing the audience with data by which to reject or modify as well as to accept the researcher's description and analysis.

The second aspect of ethnomethodology's response calls for the criminologist, or any social researcher, to accompany a study of crime, the criminal, or criminal controls with a study of one's study. This is a difficult, time- and paper-consuming task. Yet, once completed and reported on, this analysis of the research project provides a better vantage point from which to assess the empirical claims of the work.

Ethnomethodology and the "Labeling Factors" Tradition

Ethnomethodology is one of two general traditions within the societal-reaction perspective on crime and deviance. This perspective is rooted in Howard

Becker's proposition that "deviance is not a quality of the act the person commits, but rather a consequence of the application by others of rules and sanctions to an 'offender.' "[24] Since the 1963 publication of this statement, there have been numerous applications and critiques of the societal-reaction perspective. Some have usefully advanced, modified, or pointed out its limitations. Others have generated issues that have sidetracked its central contribution—a concern with the processes through which certain acts and people become defined and dealt with as deviant. The centrality of this theme is emphasized by John Kitsuse, who states:

> The distinctive character of the societal reaction perspective . . . leads . . . to a consideration of how deviants come to be differentiated by imputations made upon them by others, how these imputations activate systems of social control, and how these control activities become legitimated.[25]

The concerns of ethnomethodology coincide directly with this distinctive character of the societal-reaction perspective. The same is not true for what might be called the labeling-factors of tradition. Its arguments as to the primacy of social (as opposed to behavioral) factors in the imputation of criminal or deviant labels and its allowance for the possibility of "secret" and "falsely accused" deviants has generated a series of intellectual debates, sidetracking the essential thrust of the perspective. The primacy of social factors has been contested by researchers who claim, instead, the primacy of individual or behavioral factors.[26] This argument has turned into a sort of quantitative debate about which types of factors account for a high percentage of labeling. This debate takes place as if the documentation of influential social factors would mean that acts that were really not deviant had incorrectly come to be labeled as such. Critics appear to argue the opposite—that deviant acts had really occurred and that they were appropriately labeled. Both sides appear to miss the essential thrust of the societal-reaction perspective—that the recognition of deviance is first and foremost a social judgment and that, like any other judgment, a combination of indexical, reflexive, and interpretive processes are constitutive features of what will be seen, acted upon, and legitimized as really deviant. In other words, the process is essentially social, not incidentally social. It is not incidentally social because, when operationalized, such things as race, class, gender, or presence of a good lawyer account for more labeling than a person does. It is essentially social because knowledge of what a person does is an accomplished product of the interactional processes whereby control agents assess the likelihood that someone is, in facts produced in the assessment itself, really a deviant.

The labeling-factors tradition remains bogged down in assessing the correctness of labels, thus lending credence to the assumption that there are basic social norms that define deviance independent of the interaction process through which control agents do their imputational work. Gibbs is quick to point this out regarding the concepts of secret and falsely accused deviance.[27] On what grounds do labeling-factor theorists make such claims regarding the incorrectness of labeling? Obviously, they must assume a certain normative character of deviance that is independent of what control agents see or don't see. From within the labeling-factors tradition, the societal-reaction perspective appears contradictory and weak. How can it be both ways—defining deviance in terms of controlling reactions and yet arguing that some reactions are incorrect, that they miss or mislabel deviance?

The ethnomethodological perspective is more radically interpretive. Its concern is not with the correctness but with the success of labeling. It discards the implicit assumption of normativity found in the labeling-factors tradition. It offers a more consistent conceptual structure for the societal-reaction perspective as a whole. The correctness issue becomes a nonissue. Attention is directed, instead, to the essential interactional processes through which imputations of deviance emerge, are applied, and are rationalized as reflective of a legitimate reality independent of the imputer. As Kitsuse argues, ''The contention is not that agents of control act without regard to the behavior of the one labeled, but that in labeling, rule breaking behavior is imputed by others to the deviant.''[28]

Power, Identity, History, and Interpretive Criminology

Human reality is a product of concrete social interaction. There is no reality independent of what people do to make interpretive sense of life in the here and now. These are fundamental principles of ethnomethodology. They are also the source of much criticism. According to critics, ethnomethodology's emphasis on interpretive work is too subjective or too relativistic. It ignores the role of power, the impact of self-concept, or the influence of historical circumstance in shaping the form and content of interpreted reality. As Dreitzel points out, much ethnomethodological writing appears relatively inattentive to the ongoing ''struggle over the rules of interpretation, a struggle . . . dominated by factors alien to the interpretive creativity of the involved parties.''[29]

What is ethnomethodology's response to such criticism? Such matters seem of acute importance with regard to the study of crime, the criminal, and criminal-control work. It is unimaginable that one could articulate a plausible criminology devoid of any reference to power, identity, or history. What, after all, is crime or the criminal but the exercise of the power of the state to control certain behaviors or people believed to have a certain criminal identity within particular historical circumstances?

Ethnomethodology's response is twofold. It is generally true that it has made little explicit or systematic reference to problems of power, self-identity, and history. However, ethnomethodology is not incapable of incorporating these issues into its conceptual framework. Each is implied, if not explicitly developed, within its central theoretical imagery. Moreover, in recent years, such matters have become increasingly recognized in the writings of ethnomethodologists and those who are influenced by this theoretical perspective. Douglas's concern with the impact of differentiated power on the production of social research,[30] Kitsuse and Cicourel's discussion of the organizational constraints guiding the construction of official statistics,[31] Molotch and Lester's analysis of power as producing and being produced by media coverage of the Santa Barbara oil spill,[32] and Daniels's study of the uses of psychiatry in a military setting[33] all point ethnomethodology in this direction. So does my own study of predictions of dangerousness.[34] There I take explicit notice of the ways that self-typified identities and power differentials influence the style and results of diagnostic work. Diagnostic control agents routinely respond or defer to the resistance of powerful others. Power is an ever-present part of the context of indexicality of their interpretive work. The same holds for identity. In their diagnostic work, psychiatric agents produce images or situated identities that they were this or that kind of "professional," "expert," "humanitarian reformer," "good-guy," or whatever. These identities reflexively feed back on the diagnostic work of those who displayed them. Like power, they become intrinsic features of the interpretive imputation of deviance.

Historical circumstance affects interpretive social-control work in a similar fashion. It is never fully outside the documentary interpretations of people who see general patterns or structures behind interactional specifics. Nonetheless, interpretive work is limited by a finite vocabulary of terms to describe a particular event or person at a particular moment in time. It is limited by language that is available in history.

Control agents literally did not see hyperkinesis before the 1960s, because this interpretive control category was not historically available. As suggested by Peter Conrad, seeing hyperkinesis awaited the medicalization of troublesome childhood behaviors.[35] My own analysis of the discovery of child abuse suggests a similar historical grounding of another currently available control category.[36] Today, hyperkinesis and the battered-child syndrome are seen everywhere. This is a matter of historical circumstance. These terms have become part of the interpretive linguistic repertoire of those who would control others. How such terms emerge and become accepted in history has become an increasingly important question for criminologists and students of deviance.

This historical "discovery" of such categorizing devices is often traced, indexically, to powers that reward linguistic or conceptual innovations and to the identities such discoveries produce, reflexively, for those who produce them (for example, the brilliant professional or great reformer). The interpretive use of such concepts, once historically available, further advances or modifies such alignments of power and identity. Historical circumstance passes interpretively into its next moment. Like power and identity, it both shapes and is shaped by the interpretive work of actors in everyday life. Each becomes an additional dimension of the process through which social reality is created, lived within, legitimized, or changed. Regarding crime, the criminal, and criminal controls, each expands ethnomethodology's contributions in creating a criminology that is informed both phenomenologically and by the simultaneous shaping of power, identity, and history.

Concluding Remarks

I began this chapter with a question about what is universal about crime or deviance. Ethnomethodology assists the criminologist in answering this question by drawing attention to interpretive interactional judgments that designate as criminal certain events and people and that activitate and legitimize controlling actions against them. Avoiding certain conceptual pitfalls of the labeling-factors tradition, ethnomethodology has contributed significantly to substantive and methodological aspects of the study of societal reaction to crime. When expanded to include a consideration of power, situated identity, and historical circumstance, ethnomethodology represents a powerful framework for examining what is universal about crime and deviance—the process by which events and people are defined and sanctioned as offenses and offenders.

Notes

1. Aaron V. Cicourel, *The Social Organization of Juvenile Justice* (New York: Wiley, 1969), p. 24.
2. Alfred Schutz, *Collected Papers I: The Problem of Social Reality,* ed. Maurice Natunson (The Hague: Martinus Nijhoff, 1962).
3. Emile Durkheim, *The Rules of the Sociological Method,* trans. Sarah A. Solovay and John W. Mueller, ed. Sir E.G. Catlin (New York: Free Press, 1965), pp. 65–73.
4. George Herbert Mead, ''The Psychology of Punitive Justice,'' *American Journal of Sociology* 23(1918):577–602.
5. David Sudnow, ''Normal Crimes: Sociological Features of the Penal Code in a Public Defender Office,'' *Social Problems* 12(Winter 1965):255–276.
6. Cicourel, *The Social Organization of Juvenile Justice*.
7. Arlene Kaplan Daniels, ''The Social Construction of Psychiatric Diagnosis,'' in *New Sociology No. 2,* ed. Hans Peter Dreitzel (New York: Macmillan, 1970), pp. 182–205.
8. Richard McCleary, ''How Parole Officers Use Records,'' *Social Problems* 24(June 1977):576–589.
9. Melvin Pollner, ''Sociological and Commonsense Models of the Labeling Process,'' in *Ethnomethodology,* ed. Roy Turner (Middlesex, England: Penguin Books, 1974), p. 39.

10. D. Lawrence Weider, "Telling the Code," in *Ethnomethodology*, ed. Roy Turner (Middlesex, England: Penguin Books, 1974), pp. 144–172.

11. Harold Garfinkel, *Studies in Ethnomethodology* (Englewood Cliffs, N.J.: Prentice-Hall, 1967), pp. 104–115.

12. Harvey Sacks, "On Initial Investigation of the Usability of Conversational Data for Doing Sociology," *Studies in Social Interaction*, ed. David Sudnow (New York: Free Press, 1972).

13. Jack D. Douglas, *The Social Meaning of Suicide* (Princeton: Princeton University Press, 1967).

14. Garfinkel, *Studies in Ethnomethodology*, p. 78.

15. Egon Bittner, "The Police on Skid-Row: A Study of Peace Keeping, *American Sociological Review* 32(1969):669–715.

16. Robert M. Emerson, *Judging Delinquents: Context and Process in Juvenile Justice* (Chicago: Aldine, 1969).

17. Jacqueline P. Wiseman, *Stations of the Lost: The Treatment of Skid Row Alcoholics* (Englewood Cliffs, N.J.: Prentice-Hall, 1970).

18. Stephen J. Pfohl, *Predicting Dangerousness: The Social Construction of Psychiatric Reality* (Lexington, Mass: Lexington Books, D.C. Heath and Company, 1978).

19. Hugh Mehan and Houston Wood, *The Reality of Ethnomethodology* (New York: Wiley, 1975).

20. Garfinkel, *Studies in Ethnomethodology*, pp. 186–207; John I. Kitsuse and Aaron V. Cicourel "A Note on the Use of Official Statistics," *Social Problems* 11(Fall 1963):131–139.

21. Edwin M. Schur, *Interpreting Deviance: A Sociological Approach* (New York: Harper and Row, 1979), p. 363.

22. John Kitsuse "The 'New Conception of Deviance' and Its Critics," in *The Labeling of Deviance: Evaluating a Perspective*, ed. Walter Gove (New York: Halstead Press, 1975), p. 278.

23. Stephen J. Pfohl, "Social Role Analysis: The Ethnomethodological Critique," *Sociology and Social Research* 59, 3(April, 1975):243–265.

24. Howard Becker, *Outsiders: Studies in the Sociology of Deviance* (New York: Free Press, 1963), p. 9.

25. Kitsuse, "The 'New Conception of Deviance' and Its Critics," p. 274.

26. Travis Hirschi, "Labelling Theory and Juvenile Delinquency: An Assessment of the Evidence," in *The Labelling of Deviance: Evaluating a Perspective*, ed. Walter R. Gove (New York: Halstead Press, 1975), pp. 181–203; Charles R. Tittle, "Labelling and Crime: An Empirical Evaluation," in *The Labelling of Deviance: Evaluating a Perspective*, ed. Walter R. Gove (New York: Halstead Press, 1975), pp. 157–179; Walter R. Gove "Societal Reaction as an Explanation of Mental Illness: an Evaluation," *American Sociological*

Review 35(October 1970):873–874; A.R. Mahoney, "The Effects of Labeling Upon Youths in the Juvenile Justice System: A Review of the Evidence," *Law and Society Review* 8(1974):583–614.

27. Jack P. Gibbs "Issues in Defining Deviant Behavior," in Robert A. Scott and Jack D. Douglas, eds., *Theoretical Perspectives on Deviance* (New York: Basic Books, 1972), pp. 56–64.

28. Kitsuse, "The 'New Conception of Deviance' and Its Critics." p. 280.

29. Hans Peter Dreitzel, *Recent Sociology No. 2: Patterns of Communicative Behavior* (New York: Macmillan, 1970), p. xviii.

30. Jack Douglas, *Understanding Everyday Life: Toward a Reconstruction of Sociological Knowledge* (Chicago: Aldine Publishing Co., 1920), p. 30.

31. Kitsuse and Cicourel, "A Note on the Use of Official Statistics."

32. Harvey Molotch and Marilyn Lester "Accidental News: The Great Oil Spill as Local Occurrence and National Event," *Americal Journal of Sociology* 81(September 1975):235–260.

33. Daniels, "The Social Construction of Psychiatric Diagnosis."

34. Pfohl, *Predicting Dangerousness*.

35. Peter Conrad, *Identifying Hyperactive Children: the Medicalization of Deviant Behavior* (Lexington, Mass: Lexington Books, D.C. Heath and Company, 1976).

36. Stephen J. Pfohl, "The 'Discovery' of Child Abuse," *Social Problems* 24(February 1977):310–323.

[19]

Ethnomethodological Perspective (on Crime and Deviance)

Robert O. Keel, M.A.
University of Missouri-St. Louis, St. Louis, MO

Ethnomethodology emerged as a distinctive perspective within sociology during the 1960s. It is associated—and confused—with a variety of perspectives (existential sociology, creative sociology, reflexive sociology, interactionism, and, most recently, constructionism). Specifically, ethnomethodology is a part of the tradition of phenomenological sociology established through the work of Alfred Schutz (1962). Although the primary focus of ethnomethodology differs from that of phenomenology, both are centered on describing the emergence of order out of the shared experience of members of particular societies (Zimmerman and Wieder 1970:286–290). This focus on order as a practical accomplishment of the everyday interactions of members of a group produces ethnomethodology's distinctive perspective on deviance in comparison to normative sociologies.[1]

Simply put, deviance in and of itself is not a concern for ethnomethodological analysis. Deviance, as a commonsensical designation employed by societal members and organizations, and as a sociological construct, is viewed as an organizing concept that emerges in interaction. These ongoing constructions produce a sense of order within the world of everyday life. It is within the context of these interactional constructions, where the normal and ordinary are distinguished from the abnormal and strange, that ethnomethodological interest is raised. Here, where the norm is made manifest, the ceaseless interpretive work of societal members which produces a sense of the objective reality of the norm can be observed and described.

Constructions of deviance become convenient windows that allow the observation and description of the interpretational processes that sustain an ongoing sense of an ordered reality for members of a particular group or society. Deviance is a negotiated reality, and through its negotiation members produce a practical sense of an orderly and shared world. This is in stark contrast to traditional sociologies which typically define deviance as disorder, disorganization, or the product of conflict between differing groups—in one way or another an objective reality independent of, and constraining upon, members of a group.

ETHNOMETHODOLOGY AND PHENOMENOLOGY

Phenomenological sociology holds that reality is an intersubjectively shared and socially constructed phenomenon. People act based on the meaning that events and others have for them. Drawing upon the understandings developed by Alfred Schutz (1962), phenomenological sociology focuses on describing the subjective reality understood to be reality by members of society. Schutz suggested that members' subjective experience is a shared reality which draws upon a common stock of knowledge—typifications, recipes, and formulas for accomplishing particular tasks, and commonsense understandings and theories that are shared by members of a group.

Through the processes of socialization, these typifications and understandings are internalized. In interaction, as we strive to produce meaningful accounts of the people and world around us, we apply these understandings in an attempt to order our experience. In doing so, these understandings, and the objects to which we attach them, come to have the appearance of a reality of their own. The externalization of our shared, intersubjective experience results in the objectification of the categories of understanding we have created (Berger and Luckmann 1967). The interactionally produced explanations of deviance and normalcy, good and bad, right and wrong; interpretations of behaviors constructed as a means of making sense out of concrete situations, become "institutionalized versions of social reality . . . (operating) as controls over what we experience as real" (Pfohl 1994:355). Phenomenological analysis seeks to describe this shared, intersubjective reality as it is perceived and defined by societal members in the course of their everyday lives. To do this accurately, phenomenologists "bracket" or suspend their own belief in the objective reality of the world around them.

Ethnomethodology goes further. The structures of objective reality are characterized as being far more fragile and malleable. For the ethnomethodologist there is no shared set of understanding and meaning which members attach to the world around them. There is no shared sense of deviance that can be called upon to order the strange and unusual behavior of others. What members of a group do share are methods for making sense. Schutz's common stock of knowledge is reconceptualized as a shared set of interpretive procedures, sense-making activities, that are invoked and employed continually in interaction. These procedures allow members to produce practical accounts of specific individuals engaged in specific activities in the context of particular situations. Deviance and deviants emerge as particular designations which provide practical understandings of everyday life situations. By constructing a sense that particular people and specific behavior are outside the norm, members produce a shared understanding of the reality of the norm.

By focusing on how deviant labels—symbolic meanings attached to behavior—and norms are constructed through the interpretive work of individuals in everyday life situations, ethnomethodology, along with phenomenological sociology, can be seen as forming a foundation for other interactionist approaches to deviance. However, for ethnomethodologists the idea of an objective social structure (status, roles, groups, institutions, and the cultural system of meaning, values, and norms that support these elements) is no longer conceived of as a determinant of human behavior. Ethnomethodologists suspend belief in (bracket) not only the objective reality of the world, but also the idea that members share symbolic meaning structures. Social structure—conceptualized as a moment-to-moment accomplishment—and its symbolic meanings are analyzed as emerging properties of human interaction. The process of continually negotiating the image of normative boundaries by accomplishing practical accounts of deviant behavior that becomes the focus of the ethnomethodologist.

Significant within the ethnomethodological approach is a focus on how the constraints of the situational context, the biographies of the individuals involved, and the organizational demands placed upon the actors interact with the basic features of interpretive work to produce definitions of behavior (e.g., deviance). There are a variety of interrelated processes that ethnomethodologists analyze in connection with the interpretive work of actors in everyday situations. The spiral of reflexivity and indexicality forms the core of their analysis. Specific interpretational procedures and guidelines such as retrospective interpretation, the rules of consistency and economy, and documentary interpretation, are displayed as basic activities out of which understandings of deviance emerge.

REFLEXIVITY

Once constructed, understandings of deviance become part of the context from which they emerged. The resulting typifications become explained within the context of commonsense theories. These theories, sometimes rooted in folk wisdom, sometimes rooted in science, focus attention on the relevance of specific features of situations as being keys to understanding behavior.

Reflexivity expresses the ethnomethodologist's understanding of the ongoing (re)construction of meaning and the sense of continuity we maintain in our interpretive work. Once defined, a situation or person becomes, in our understanding, the type we have constructed. The objective reality of this type thus created is, paradoxically, understood as a product of the features of the situation rather than of our interpretive process (Pfohl 1994:357).

Theories of deviance, shaped within the historical context of understanding the deviant as simply bad, wicked, or evil—or the more contemporary conceptions of sickness and disease—structure our perceptions and allow us to recognize, for the practical purposes at hand, the meaning of individuals and their behavior. Such understandings, couched in causal terminology, lead to the institutionalization of societal response to deviance. Whether the child molester is electrocuted, chemically castrated, or continually monitored via the Internet is dependent on the prevailing interpretive guidelines of the moment. When officials come to define tobacco as a drug millions of smokers become drug users, and a new campaign against drug use ensues.

Relevant here is the phenomenological concern with the subjective meaning that behavior has for the actor. Identity (a sense of order within the individual) is constructed and embodied in ways similar to the appearance of order out there in society. The individual actor may well become the deviant phenomenon. This social construction of reality produces the context of individual (and group) identity and behavior out of which typifications and commonsense theories emerge.

INDEXICALITY

The central concept of indexicality focuses attention on the (reflexive) sense we make of a particular situation or activity as being a product of our personal biographies (the experiences and expectations we bring to the situation) and of the contingent elements of the situation. Smoking a marijuana cigarette means one thing to the novice, another to an experienced user, and still another to a substance abuse counselor. The reality of being high takes on different significance depending on whether one is entering a rock and roll concert or a calculus exam. Situational constraints and cues continually shape interpretational processes. Commonsense theories, constraints of time and place, appearances, and the practical demands of the moment, organize an actor's response to particular situations. The construction of deviance is always from a particular point of view.

Sudnow (1965) describes how the broader context of the social organization of a public defender's office and the specific features of particular defendants intersect to allow attorneys to arrive at understandings of clients' behaviors as atypical and deserving of special handling, or typical—normal—crimes which can be processed via a set of standard procedures and plea bargaining. The meaning of being a criminal is not contained within the act one commits but emerges from within the context through which one's act is interpreted.

The ongoing spiral of indexicality and reflexivity describes the central interpretive context through which typified understandings of deviance (labels) are produced and applied as practical accomplishments leading to reasonable accounts of particular individuals and their behavior within the confines of specific situations. These accounts are seen as shaping social response that generates new contexts, both official and unofficial, and the process continues.

Through this process, organizations emerge as definers and controllers of deviance, individuals come to be understood as deviant, and oftentimes the individuals come to see themselves as deviant. The important component here is that individuals typically fail to see, or at least forget, that it is through their work that reality and their sense of self is constructed. These come to take on a natural, taken-for-granted character. (See also Pfohl 1994:356–357)

RETROSPECTIVE INTERPRETATION

Retrospective interpretation details a particular process in this social construction of reality. The idea here is that the meaning of behavior, in this case past behavior, and the significance of past events, is continually being reevaluated based on the exigencies of current situations and typified understandings. What was once perhaps confusing or even simply irrelevant for our understanding becomes seen in a new interpretive light.

Garfinkel's (1967) study of jury decision-making processes suggests that jurors arrive at understandings of guilt or innocence through a variety of situational cues. Having arrived at this understanding, the evidence presented in the course of the trial is organized to conform to the already arrived at conclusion. The image of rational decision-making is maintained, but the "facts" are constructed to fit the conclusion (See also Pfohl 1994:358). The point here is that once we arrive at a particular account (explanation) of a situation or person (decision-making based on typifications and commonsense categories indexically tied to the context of the situation), we reflexively reconstruct our understanding of the process so that our decision or definition appears to us as normal, natural, and real.

Sacks (1972) makes a similar claim in his analysis of how suicide threats are constructed out of crisis hotline telephone calls. Describing the process with his "consistency rule," he notes how information from the past, as well as newly encountered information, is interpreted as significant within the context of the now known threat—the individual's conversation is seen to have been leading up to the threat all along. Sacks extends his analysis with the associated interpretational process he calls the "economy rule," which suggests that once actors construct an organized understanding of a particular event they are hesitant to take into account competing explanations or constructions (see also, Liska and Messner 1999:152).

The power of these constructions when they are couched in an assumption of deviant behavior can be so overwhelming as to shape an actor's identity and lead to his or her immersion within a world of deviance. "The former identity, at best, receives the accent of mere appearance . . . What he is now is what, 'after all,' he was all along." (Garfinkel, 1956:422)

Erving Goffman (1963) discusses the process of retrospective interpretation as part of the "moral career" of those defined by deviance. The subjective understandings generated through current experiences allow for turning points during which "the stigmatized individual may single out and retrospectively elaborate experiences which [*then*] serve for him to account for his coming to the beliefs and practices he now has regarding his own kind and normals" (Goffman 1963:9). A disabling event can become reinterpreted as an opportunity to start on a new life path, or an inopportune disclosure that leads to an arrest becomes a call for help. The individual may come to a new understanding of his or her past which then serves to (re)confirm the present. Out of the spiral of indexicality and reflexivity a sense of structure emerges. This structure is a practical accomplishment based on everyday interpretive processes, and it serves to confirm and elaborate deviant identities—subjectively for the individuals involved, and objectively for the organizations which document and respond to these identities.

DOCUMENTARY INTERPRETATION

Documentary interpretation, a special case representing the indexical-reflexive structure of interpretational processes, refers to a procedure through which immediately given information (documents), such as appearance, police reports, past records, and other typifications, is used to infer meaning and motive in the behavior of others.

> *Not only is the underlying pattern derived from its individual documentary evidences, but the individual documentary evidences, in their turn, are interpreted on the basis of "what is known" about the underlying pattern. Each is used to elaborate the other. (Garfinkel 1967: 78).*

Selectively taking bits and pieces of information, those presented informally in interaction and those that are part of the official record, enables the construction of a reasonable account of the individual that then seems to confirm the reading of the documents. Members work back and forth, taking into account particular documents that then are seen as meaningful within the context of commonsense theories of behavior. The theories direct attention to particular documents, and as these contextual elements are taken into account, they become meaningful. Rosenhahn (1973) displays the workings of this process within the context of psychiatric evaluations. What would otherwise be seen as unremarkable statements about such things as occasional arguments and child spankings become interpreted as signs of an underlying mental disorder. The emerging significance of these statements develops based upon the assumption of the subject's underlying mental disorder.

DEVIANCE, NEGOTIATION, AND IMPUTATION OF MOTIVE

Sometimes behavior is normalized, explained away, or even ignored. Members are likely to allow certain types of disrupting behavior to pass, assuming that clarification and understanding will come later. When clarification does not come, or when behavior is too problematic, negotiation occurs. Actors do not always readily succumb to the process of being identified as deviant. The construction of a deviant identity often involves negotiation and bargaining. Information is selectively presented. Actors attempt to enable others to see the world from their particular point of view. Explanations are presented and evaluated. Actors may deny intentional activity, or present other rationalizing accounts: the drug user steals to feed his or her addiction; a victim may "have had it coming;" or an event may be presented as having been an accident. How do we infer whether or not a specific act was planned and chosen by a particular individual? Intention is an important, though not specifically necessary, component in defining a person as deviant. Interpreting an actor's behavior as being determined by forces outside their own control typically leads to more or less nondeviant designations (Jones and Davis 1965). In the context of modern medical (commonsense) theories of behavior, audiences are most likely to arrive at interpretations of sickness. On the other hand, if the audience cannot come to accept the actor's point of view, nor ascribe cause to external contingencies, then deviant intention becomes a defining characteristic of the interaction.

The "facts" established become part of the indexical reality of the situation and reflexively shape the definition constructed. Social response to the deviant, both formal and informal, is based upon the understandings that emerge from such interactions. If deviant definitions do not emerge, the actor in question may be reintegrated within the group. If understanding of the individual or behavior as deviant develops, processes of exclusion, punishment, or treatment may ensue. Members act toward others based on the meaning constructed out of the situation at hand.

ORGANIZATIONAL CONTEXT

The process of constructing images of deviance and deviants takes place at many levels of interaction. At the level of face-to-face interaction, the construction of deviance allows members to account for behavior viewed as problematic and to organize their daily lives. At the more formal level of social organizations, identification and control of deviance becomes a practical activity embedded within the routines of organizational life. The rational demands for efficiency, calculability, predictability, and standardized control produce interpretive guidelines and categorical systems that further routinize the social construction of deviance.

At this formal level the process of negotiation is strained. The fixed categories and interests of the organization influence the decision-making process. Viewed through the constraints of the organization, a variety of behaviors are collapsed and standardized (surveys of illicit drug use which define use during 20 of the past 30 days as daily use, do not distinguish "daily use" at this level from multiple use throughout the day). Once confirmed within a certain type, the action of the control agent toward the deviant is determined by the prescribed routines of the organization of social control (Sudnow 1965). Based on this analysis, the accounts of deviance provided by official agencies of social control (crime rates, prevalence of illicit drug use, etc.) are not viewed by ethnomethodologists as information on the reality of deviant behavior, ". . . but as indicators and reflections of organizational properties and routines" (Liska and Messner 1999:154).

SUMMARY

The perspective of ethnomethodology suggests that deviance and the deviant do not exist independently of the social construction of meaning centered in the situational context of everyday life. The work of ethnomethodologists forms a foundation for understanding how deviant labels and categories are created and applied through the social processes of interpretation, typification, and negotiation. The qualities and attributes of a particular individual become lost or distorted as she or he is located within the context of a particular category of deviance. His or her behavior, and identity, comes to represent the category of deviance, and the category of deviance, in turn, becomes an explanation for the behavior or identity in question.

NOTE

1. The concept "normative sociologies of deviance" as used here to refer to those approaches which define deviance as the violation of social norms and that seek to provide a causal analysis of the social forces which propel individuals into norm violation. Traditional strain theories, social control or social bonding theories, and traditional social disorganization theories all reflect this general approach.

REFERENCES

Berger, Peter and Thomas Luckmann. 1967. *The Social Construction of Reality*. Garden City, New York: Anchor Books.

Garfinkel, Harold. 1956. "Conditions of Successful Degradation Ceremonies." *American Journal of Sociology* 61:420–424.

———. 1967. *Studies in Ethnomethodology*. Englewood Cliffs, NJ: Prentice-Hall.

Goffman, Erving. 1963. *Stigma: Notes on the Management of a Spoiled Identity*. New York: Simon and Schuster.

Jones, Edward E. and Keith E. Davis. 1965. "From Acts to Dispositions: The Attribution Process in Personal Perception." In L. Berkowitz, ed., *Advances in Experimental Social Psychology*, vol. 2. New York: Academic Press.

Liska, Allen and Steven Messner. 1999. *Perspectives on Deviance*, 3rd ed. Englewood Cliffs, NJ: Prentice-Hall.

Pfohl, Stephen J. 1994. *Images of Deviance and Social Control: A Sociological History*, 2nd ed. New York: McGraw-Hill.

Rosenhahn, David. 1973. "On Being Sane in Insane Places." *Science* 179:250–258.

Sacks, Harvey. 1972. "An Initial Investigation of Usability of Conversational Data for Doing Sociology." Pp. 31–74 in David Sudnow, ed., *Studies in Social Interaction*. New York: Free Press.

Schutz, Alfred. 1962. *Collected Papers I: The Problem of Social Reality*, edited by Maurice Natanson. The Hauge: Martinus Nijhoff.

Sudnow, David. 1965. "Normal Crimes." *Social Problems* 12:Winter:255–76.

Zimmerman, Don H. and D. Lawrernce Wieder. 1970. "Ethnomethodology and the Problem of Order: Comment on Denzin." In Jack Douglas, ed., *Understanding Everyday Life*. Chicago: Aldine Publishing Company.

[20]

Phenomenology, Postmodernism, And Philosophical Criminology: A Conversational Critique

David Polizzi, Indiana State University
Department of Criminology and Criminal Justice

and

Bruce A. Arrigo, University of North Carolina, Charlotte.
Department of Criminal Justice and Criminology

INTRODUCTION

For the most part, the theoretical practice of traditional (i.e., modernist) criminology relies on causal and structural formulations to describe and explain the existence of crime. Ultimately, these practices focus on individual-level factors and/or socio-economic conditions to situate and validate any subsequent claims concerning the nature of crime and the manifestation of criminal behavior. Thus, so-called "legitimate" determinations of wrongdoing are wedded to positivistic assertions.

For example, theories that seek to explain offenders and their criminal actions as the product of rational choice or as the result of psychological forces typically endorse a cause-effect (i.e., linear, reductionistic) orientation. Similarly, theories that account for the existence of crime by examining economic or socio-cultural determinants (e.g., Critical Theory), mostly support a foundational (i.e., hierarchical, fixed) logic. However, as Arrigo, Milovanovic, Schehr (2005) assert, "Post-Enlightenment thought in the social sciences brought with it a set of core assumptions that [all] too often have remained unexamined" (p. ix).

The conventional practice of theoretical criminology has been particularly guilty of this charge. In large part, it has ignored or, at the very least, has taken for granted the embedded ideology on which much of its policy direction and focus have

Journal of Theoretical and Philosophical Criminology
2009, Vol 1 (2), 113-145 Polizzi, D, Arrigo, B.

been based. Presuppositions concerning the ontology of the self/society mutuality; the epistemology of race, gender, class and the body; and the ethic or aesthetics of their respective connections to delinquent or criminal behavior are not problematized in any appreciable manner. Indeed, these topics of inquiry - so essential to growing a philosophical criminology - receive only marginal attention in the extant literature (Arrigo and Williams, 2006).

Recently, several volumes have endeavored to better specify the theoretical footing of criminology, criminal justice, and offender treatment by contextualizing the broad field within phenomenological (Polizzi, 2009), existentialist (Crew & Lippens, 2009), and post-structural ((Arrigo & Milovanovic, 2009) frames of reference. While this theoretical realignment has been met with skepticism - especially when the push is for more evidence-based science - this new "conversation" has evocatively added to the debates concerning the role of language, the place of the subject, and the construction of social knowledge in criminological *verstehen*. Interestingly, perhaps some of the most rigorous and productive contributions have emerged from discussions within Continental Philosophy, including those insights traceable to phenomenological and postmodern analyses. Although quite brief, the preceding intellectual history informs the trajectory of the present article.

(The conversation that follows was conducted over a twelve month period with Bruce Arrigo via e-mail where we discussed a variety of theoretical concerns related to Continental Philosophy. After approximately nine months into this conversation, Bruce suggested that we might want to publish our musings as an article that could potentially appear in the Journal of Theoretical and Philosophical Criminology. Given that I had already decided to add a "conversation section" to the journal, which would invite various scholars within criminology, sociology, and psychology to

Journal of Theoretical and Philosophical Criminology
2009, Vol 1 (2), 113-145

discuss their work and related theoretical concerns or observations, I agreed to use our conversation for the current edition of JTPCRIM. Thus, the ensuing conversation inaugurates this new section of the journal.

Our conversation begins with my response to an article titled "Existentialism and the Criminology of the Shadow" which Bruce co-authored with Christopher Williams who teaches at the University of West Georgia. The concept of the criminological shadow, which Arrigo and Williams (2009) define as "...those covert forces that discipline the body, implode the reality-appearance dichotomy, thwart human agency, and undo positive freedom, becomes the theoretical backdrop of this discussion. (pp. 222-3) Ostensibly, our conversation remains focused on that article; however, it quickly moves to a variety of other topics related to the philosophical projects of phenomenology and postmodernism. Included in our exchange is the relationship between phenomenology and postmodernism, as well as specific summary reviews of those authors most identified with these two theoretical frameworks.

Our exchange first examines the Freudian/Marxist perspective generally associated with the work of Fromm (1994, 2003, 2005) and then pivots to a brief discussion of Foucault (1972, 1977), Derrida (1977, 1978) and Lacan (1981, 1985, 2007) in which we assess their respective positions on language and subjectivity. Finally, our focus shifts to a more general critique of the postmodern position relative to phenomenology. Here, we consider the contribuations of Husserl (1962, 1970) Heidegger (1962), and Merleau-Ponty (1964, 1968, 2002). It is important to note that our overarching conversational concern is with the underlying philosophical foundation of the Arrigo and Williams (2009) article. It represents a significant departure from those matters noticeably featured in criminology proper exhaustively debated by its strident positivist adherents. Thus, our exchange probes the

Journal of Theoretical and Philosophical Criminology
2009, Vol 1 (2), 113-145

criminological enterprise, mindful of its (often misguided) ontological, epistemological, ethical, and aesthetical commitments.

Polizzi: Though I have never been all that interested in Freudian-Marxism generally or Fromm specifically, I generally like the discussion even though it tends to essentialize capitalism as the problem and indirectly seems to essentialize Marxism as the solution. It is possible, however, to step outside of this false necessity. (Unger, 1988) Cornelius Castoriadis, also a Freudian-Marxist, does so quite well without evoking a comparison between the two or evoking a demand which insists that a critique of the one demands the support of the other. I'm not sure Fromm's analysis leaves one with a place to stand. Any relationship with the State, regardless its ideological makeup, will have significant impact on the possibility for personal freedom and social responsibility. There is no question that the myth of modernity in general and capitalism specifically, has merely replaced one type of feudal relationship with another. Capitalism certainly freed us from the traditional bonds of feudalism, but in doing so has simply replaced one repressive relationship with another, and in the end proving to be equally problematic for personal freedom or social responsibility. The Marxist state evokes the same dynamic, and recreates the same type of repressive bonds, even though the specific image of these bonds is seemingly different due to ideological considerations. Much like the movement away from feudal societies, which constructed capitalism as the new liberator, Marxism fills a similar role relative to capitalism, and sadly delivers the same distorted sense of identity and self.

I think Foucault provides the best answer to this ideological dilemma: He urges yes not to become overly comfortable with the certainty of our own presuppositions. (Fromm's trinity I think) We must always be willing to challenge that which is closest to us, that which remains most familiar and that which often provides us our greatest sense of comfort. The vigilance to which Foucault eludes seems to me the clearest sense of personal freedom and the most profound sense of social responsibility because it demands that *we never become too comfortable*, (Nietzsche, 1967), never assume that there is not more after the discovery of this liberating fact (Capitalism, Marxism, etc.), and never assume that we can realize the potential of personal freedom or social responsibility without constantly seeking to redefine the truth.

I know we do not agree on Lacan. I prefer the phenomenological Lacan and you the later work that seems to have held serve for a number of decades. I'm not certain that the postmodern critique of phenomenology based on the subject and language actually achieves what it claims or that it actually transcends what Merleau-Ponty's (1964; 1968) later work articulates prior to Derrida, and his intentional misread of Husserl. (Marion, 1998; Derrida, 1973)

I think when the subject of desire and the unconscious is discussed within Lacanian theory, it is important to point out that this is Freudian unconscious of classical psychoanalysis; that is, the unconscious constructed by oedipal desire. (Deleuze and Guattari, 1983). I do not believe that this is a minor point, but is one that is constantly covered over. If the unconscious, that is, the unconscious of Lacan's Real Order, is being discussed, it is impossible to maintain that this unconscious is structured by symbolic categories. If the real is situated outside of the constructing grip of the Symbolic Order, it also lays outside of language as well, unless of course one is privileging language as its own ontological category, which is problematic and fundamentally structuralist in temperament. If in the beginning there was the Word, it is a beginning after existence and not before it.

When Lacan states that language speaks us, it is a "speaking" that is fundamentally and perhaps exclusively situated within the context of the Freudian unconscious. My desire to make whole the lack evoked by the loss of the symbiotic

Journal of Theoretical and Philosophical Criminology
2009, Vol 1 (2), 113-145 Polizzi, D, Arrigo, B.

bond with the mother makes sense within this oedipal structure. The split nature of discourse, again, exists within the consequences of the Freudian unconscious and the process of repression that this structure demands as its artifact. The Freudian unconscious is indeed structured like a language, but it is language which structures the unconscious and gives it its symbolic power.

(Arrigo explores the way in which capitalism through its relationship with the media creates and manipulates the desiring subject and by so doing reduces it to a function of that desire, the state's desire. He then introduces what he has identified as the "criminology of the stranger" which seeks to free the subject from this endless cycle of objectification and toward the possibility for transformation. Within this context, transformation or becoming represents or introduces us to a different type of subject who is not reducible to a set of socially derived categories. Once liberated from the objectifying quality of these categories, the possibility of becoming can be realized insofar as it represents the ontologically unfinished character of being.

Taken from a far less theoretical point of reference, the relationship between imposed social categories and the transformation of the subject is easily witnessed through the image of the criminal. In their work, Revolution in Penology, Arrigo and Milovanovic (2009) point out the way in which the process of imposed categorization continues to imprison the subject in an ever-evolving cycle of otherness that fundamentally denies being the possibility of transformation. Whether these categories evoke essentalized differences related to ethnicity, gender, or socio-economic status, the result is still the same. The individual caught up in the criminal justice system is essentially reduced to those categories imposed by the system or by state, and becomes socially defined by them. Once constructed and coded as criminal, the possibilities for being are greatly restricted; however, such restrictions never completely eliminate or preclude the possibility for transformation and it

Journal of Theoretical and Philosophical Criminology
2009, Vol 1 (2), 113-145

remains possible for the individual to employ a variety of strategies of resistance that can liberate the potential for transformation, the potential for becoming other.)

Arrigo: The chapter "essentializes" the conspicuous consumption of media manufactured capitalism (by way of Baudrillard's insights), mindful of how such ravenousness fosters what Foucault identified as docility in which the subject is panoptically reduced to a functionary of the state. Moreover, the critique draws support by invoking Lacan and his position on the *discourse of the master* and Fromm's analysis on mechanisms of escape.

My view is that the emphasis on "being" rather than "having" is more akin to Aristotle (by way of Fromm), and the emphasis on becoming is closer to Deleuze and Guattari. Chris (Williams) and I don't spell out these transitions other than to invoke the need for a philosophy of the subject or, if you will, a "criminology of the stranger." In my forthcoming book with Dragan Milovanovic titled, *Revolution in Penology: Rethinking the Society of Captives*, how such a transition would occur is much more fully specified. Here, Dragan and I invoke the work of Deleuze, Deleuze and Guattari (e.g., molecular forces; schizoanalysis, rhizomatics; anti-Oedipus), Nietzsche (e.g., overcoming; a will to power), Lacan (e.g., *discourse of the hysteric/analyst*), complex systems science (e.g., stranger attractors; dissipative structures; far-from-equilibrium conditions), Fromm (e.g., positive freedom; spontaneity) and Derrida (e.g., critique of the metaphysics of presence; reversal of hierarchies). Freire's dialogical pedagogy is also employed in parts.

The concern for personal freedom and social responsibility to which you elude is quite important and I agree that Foucault (as you cite him) is instructive. I would further argue, consistent with postmodern or ultramodern sensibilities, that one's presuppositions must be provisional, positional, and relational. I take this to be compatible with Judith Butler's notion of "contingent universalities."

Journal of Theoretical and Philosophical Criminology
2009, Vol 1 (2), 113-145

I like your position on Lacan, even though we differ here. But, of course, Lacan was a Freudian revisionist as you note. So, it follows that the former's observations address the "law-of-the-father" (the Symbolic Order) and not the Real Order. Of course, in his work on *Feminine Sexuality* (1985) Lacan did make a case for an *ecriture feminine*; that is, the variable contexts in which a woman's desire or *pas toute* (not-all) could be reclaimed. I think Luce Irigaray and Julia Kristeva were better in expressing how a reworking of language was but one dimension of this reframing toward an *ecriture feminine*. Consider, for instance, Irigaray's (1985) *This Sex Which Is Not One* or Kristeva's (1980) *Desire in Language*. I don't believe either author would argue that language is an ontological category for the reasons you specify. However, their respective critiques of Lacan seem to understate (misstate?) his view on the topic.

Then, too, Deleuze (1983) - often in collaboration with Guattari - (1984, 1987) helped to demonstrate that desire is not "lack" (unless within a Freudian reworking). Instead, it is productive, transmutating, "becoming other;" or as they proclaimed, "a people yet to come." Once again, language is but one facet of this metamorphosis.

(*Our conversation moves to a more specific exploration of the concepts of Being as discussed by Heidegger in Being in Time and the notion of becoming, as discussed by Deleuze in his text Nietzsche & Philosophy and Lacan's notion of the Other. Arrigo applies his discussion of the Lacanian Other to his concept of the shadow. In part, through its speaking the subject, the Other sustains the shadow and the shadow holds us captive. Whereas I see a more fluid development of these ideas from phenomenology to critical theory, to postmodernism, Arrigo maintains that the movement from critical theory to postmodernism is a more accurate read of this ultramodern condition.*

Journal of Theoretical and Philosophical Criminology
2009, Vol 1 (2), 113-145

This discussion has particular significance for criminology relative to the construction of racism, crime and the criminal other. The liberation of the shadow seems most related to the way in which certain subject positions, be these based on race, gender, or socio-economic class, construct the subject and subjectivity and by so doing, restrict the possibility of becoming. Deconstructing these covert forces that discipline and control social presence, allows subjectivity to free itself from this "diminished milieu" (Deleuze, 1983) or, at the very least, allows for this possibility.)

Polizzi: But wouldn't you say that ultimately the notion of becoming, which comes from Nietzsche (actually, the pre-Socratics, at least in Western thought), is also situated in Heidegger's notion of being/becoming and isn't this same relationship to being/becoming also present in Merleau-Ponty as well and then brilliantly taken up by many writers in the Post-Modern movement? The notion of docility is also present in the work of Castoriadis, which I believe both pre-dates and overlaps the published writing of Foucault. Castoriadis (1988; 1997) is particularly critical of the role of the proletariat, and uses virtually the same language to describe the problem.

I guess my issue with the discourse of the Other is that not only does it evoke the shadow of Heidegger's discussion of authenticy/inauthencity and Heidegger's concept of the They-Self, but also seems to maintain that we can truly free ourselves from the Other. Though I completely agree with Lacan, at least relative to the internal logic of classical psychoanalysis that subjectivity must find a way to speak for itself and not be spoken through by the discourse of the Other, we are never completely free from this relationship. Perhaps this dovetails somewhat into Fromm's notion of personal freedom and social responsibility. (I have not really read that much of his work.)

For personal freedom to be possible it must find a way to not only liberate itself from the desire of the Other or what the Other wants, but also re-establish a

Journal of Theoretical and Philosophical Criminology 2009, Vol 1 (2), 113-145

relationship with this Other, with the Symbolic Order, that does not deny the legitimacy of that freedom. (Lacan, 2007). Right, to have therefore I am, is not a very liberating foundation for human freedom. The conspicuous consumption of media manufactured capitalism, if I understand you correctly, is the discourse of the Other that not only speaks the subject, but limits any real possibility for personal freedom/social responsibility. My point was that Critical Theory in the end, really only offers more of the same and in the end, may simply invite the possibility for a different type of alienated subject.

(Our discussion moves to an exploration of the relationship between phenomenology and postmodernism. Included in this discussion are a variety of theoretical concepts which are not specifically defined. Thrownnnes, a concept introduced by Heidegger (1962), describes the social character of human being. Human being or experience for Heidegger, always finds itself situated or thrown within very specific cultural, historical linguistic or sociological contexts which help to define the possibilities for human being. For example, the possibilities for black experience are fundamentally restricted if "thrown" into a social context of anti-racism, which seeks to criminalize the social presence of blackness. (Polizzi, 2007) The Lacanian concept of the Other represents that aspect of the Lacanian Symbolic registrar that seeks to control desire through its ability to control subjectivity and individual desire. Entry into the symbolic is the entry into language and the confrontation with the desire of the Other.

Within both of these concepts we can witness the way in which the possibility for personal experience and responsibility is confronted by a meaning generating process that seeks to control or configure the contours of human experience. In neither of these conceptualizations is there a complete foreclosing of human

Journal of Theoretical and Philosophical Criminology
2009, Vol 1 (2), 113-145 Polizzi, D, Arrigo, B.

possibility; however, the potentiality for human expression does remain contingent to this undeniable and unavoidable meaning generating dynamic.)

Arrigo: I regretfully confess ignorance on the work of Castoriadis. I need to rectify this as you have referenced his work a number of times in our email, phone, or in-person conversations. Thank you! I agree with the development of thought on being/becoming as you delineate it above.

I also agree that we can never free ourselves entirely from the "Other" as in Heidegger's (1962) notion of "thrownness," or, if you will, as in Buber's notion of the I-Thou relationship. But why would we want to and, more philosophically, why should we? As you correctly point out, the question is the character of this thrownness, the character of the I-Thou relationship (Buber, 1970), the character of the "Other" (when placed in Lacanian psychoanalytic terms), or the character of Heidegger's (1962) *dasein* analytic as in a being-toward-care. And it is here that authenticity or *alethia* (interestingly, for Aristotle it is *eudaimonia* or excellence as in a flourishing of being; as in living a virtuous existence), that comes into play.

Does the critical theory-to-postmodern movement merely substitute one form of alienation for another? Perhaps, however, I think the latter's reading of the "ultramodern" condition is a bit more accurate than any other and, to this extent, makes for a compelling critique of the *zeitgeist* beyond what their philosophical predecessors identified. Of course, this is not to dismiss their predecessors as much as to assess the relative contribution such antecedent philosophy offers in an account of any existing issue. Still, the question is how to confront the crisis that sustains the "shadow" in society and in our lives today. This is a crisis in which the call to personal freedom and social responsibility must be re-conceptualized. From my perspective, this implicates a new theory of the subject or, if you will, a philosophy of the stranger. In part, I believe that *Revolution in Penology* endeavors

Journal of Theoretical and Philosophical Criminology
2009, Vol 1 (2), 113-145

to tackle this very vexing, but prescient, problem. We'll have to see what the reviewers/critics of the book have to say about this.

(A question is raised concerning the philosophical implications toward a postmodern/ poststructural understanding of language. It is argued that such formulations cover over an implicit structuralist understanding of the role of language that, at its worst, reduces existence and subjectivity to that of a collection of epiphenomenal artifacts of this process. For example, the sign, "criminal," can only construct a variety of signification that remains more or less consistent and contingent upon this beginning category, but this process does not and cannot construct the actual presence of the sign, the presence of this actual human being, only its diminished meaning.

This section of the conversation is related in part to the earlier discussion of the shadow in criminology and the need for its transformation; existing categories imposed upon the subject work in concert with the signifying process erected by language, which results in the diminishment of human possibility. To be constructed as offender or even former offender, still carries with it the crippling affects of imposed social meaning. A word or concept like rehabilitation or restorative justice rather than invite the possibility of transformation remains caught within this process of objectified meaning that continues to deny being or subjectivity the full breath of its potential.)

Polizzi: I have a question for you: How do the various postmodernist perspectives (or your own) on language, escape the very obvious essentialism that is explicit in their theorizing? It seems that these types of critiques are caught by an implied or implicit logic that appears to be contradictory to the very project(s) they are attempting to bring forth. These critiques, particularly of phenomenology or at the least, those critiques which identify their target as phenomenology seem to take on

Journal of Theoretical and Philosophical Criminology
2009, Vol 1 (2), 113-145 Polizzi, D, Arrigo, B.

very structuralist proclivities which merely substitute language for subjectivity. Also, (referring to Michelle Brown's article in *Philosophy, Crime and Criminology:* The Aesthetics of Crime) how would Lyotard's description of the sublime differ from a phenomenological exploration of the same concept? People like Foucault maintain that they want to get as far from phenomenology as they can, but yet don't really appear to have moved that far away at all.

(Arrigo clarifies the postmodern position on the role of language. He argues that language carries with it established cultural, social, and political implications that are embedded in the dominant discourse and helps to construct what he calls the person-world dialectic. Though certain deterministic qualities may exist in language this is not due to a linguistic determinism, but the way in which these narratives impose a specific meaning upon the person-world dialectic. Positive Postmodern thinkers—authors who espouse a philosophical practice that is nondogmatic, tentative and nonideological (Rosenau, 1992)—seek to evoke what Arrigo identifies as evolving strategies of re-framing or re-constituting which seeks to liberate the subject from this objectifying cycle reproduced by language.)

Arrigo: Different postmodern theorists provide a response to your question. My view is that language always already serves as a mediating force (variable, factor, and vehicle) for naming the person-world dialectic. This is not the same as linguistic determinism. Many postmodern scholars are keenly aware of the social and material realities (e.g., race/gender/class disparities, access to opportunities, political status) that establish the extant conditions in which people live. However, just as Ricoeur (1973) once observed, in order to shatter and to increase our reality we need to shatter and to increase our language. Affirmative postmodernists want to de-stabilize the implicit values, hidden assumptions, and concealed meanings embedded within

Journal of Theoretical and Philosophical Criminology
2009, Vol 1 (2), 113-145

dominant discourses (e.g., science, law, politics) that linguistically (and socially) structure the person-world dialectic. Moreover, HOW this occurs for affirmative postmodernists is through such things as contingent universalities (Butler); dissipative structures, non-linearity and far-from-equilibrium conditions (chaos theory); non-hierarchical reversal of hierarchies in binary opposition (Derrida); position, relational, and provisional truth claims (Arrigo), the individual as a subject-in-process (Kristeva), a will-to-power and transpraxis (Nietzsche), critical dialogical pedagogy and speaking "true words" (Freire); the discourse of the hysteric/analyst (Lacan); and becoming other/imperceptible, schizoanalysis, and minor literatures (Deleuze & Guattari). In short, rather than linguistic determinism, evolving strategies for "reframing" or re-constituting the self and the social in multiple non-static form is recommended, given the historically contingent political-economy from which we speak and into which we are inserted (a reference to Althusser and his notion of interpellation).

As for your question about Foucault, Lyotard, and the sublime, my reading of Michelle's piece was closer to a cultural and post-structural critique rather than a phenomenological account. I could be incorrect. Part of what I struggle with is that I tend to put phenomenology and structuralism within a similar camp. How they respectively access meaning differs but a foundational "reality" is ascertainable for both of them. Post-structural philosophy does not assess interpersonal and social reality this way; instead, there is an unfolding of meaning that defies closure and is subject to multiple, divergent, and poly-vocal readings. Am I mistaken about phenomenology?

(The conversation moves to a more specific focus concerning the philosophical assumptions underlying phenomenology and postmodernist thought. The current conversation emerges from a discussion of the philosophical notion of the sublime

Journal of Theoretical and Philosophical Criminology
2009, Vol 1 (2), 113-145 Polizzi, D, Arrigo, B.

which is found in Kant and later discussed by Lyotard and Foucault. Within this context, Lyotard's critique of the modernist understanding of the sublime, which includes the transcendental phenomenology of Edmund Husserl, more generally reflects the underlying assumptions of conceptual thought and the self that he finds problematic within modernist formulations.

This conversation raises the more general concerns related to the post-structural assumptions about the so-called structuralist proclivities of phenomenonology. A structuralist perspective assumes the existence of basic underlying "causes" that once uncovered provide a specific objective and systemized structure to social knowledge, the self, consciousness, and its objects, etc. Husserl can be seen as following this structuralist perspective, when he maintains that those aspects of human experience which remain implicit or remain as a background to those objects which appear to consciousness, can become knowable. Husserl puts forward the belief that for human experience to be totally intelligible, that is—for human consciousness to know what is unknowable—it must be able to make these implicit backgrounds or horizons explicit and accessible to consciousness.(Husserl, 1962; Gurwitsch, 1964; Dreyfus, Rabinow, 1983) His answer to this difficult task is found in the transcendental reduction or epoche, which seeks to place the phenomenologist outside of consciousness so as to describe what remains unknowable to that consciousness.(Husserl, 1970; Dreyfus, Rabinow, 1983) Such a methodological adaptation certainly appears rather tenuous at best, if one is intending a complete and total "knowing" of the objects of consciousness; however, such a "failure" but does not necessarily collapse the total project of phenomenology in on itself, unless of course one assumes that there exists only one serious read or critique of phenomenology.

Though phenomenology presumes a subjective point of departure from which the world is perceived as meaningful, this does not also imply a structuralist

Journal of Theoretical and Philosophical Criminology
2009, Vol 1 (2), 113-145

foundation for this process. Consciousness makes sense of the world by the way the world appears to consciousness; however, to assume that this process is not also historically contingent and culturally circumscibed, as well as psychologically contingent is nonsensical and transforms the project of phenomenology into a straw man of postmodern reflection. Perhaps said more simply, the unknowable must remain unknowable, regardless of Husserl's seemingly ultimate goal. Phenomenology, by its recognition of the contingency of existence, the contingency of consciousness, and the contingency of language also sees meaning as unstable, insofar as it would be illogical within this philosophical frame of reference to systematically construct what is essentially provisional at every moment.)

It is also important to note that much of this overlap between phenomenology and postmodernism likely emerges through the shared influence of Nietzsche. Heidegger was greatly influenced by Nietzsche. Thinkers such as Derrida, Foucault, Delueze, and Lyotard were similarly influenced by him as well.)

Polizzi: Let me begin by commenting on your ending observation. I'm not sure how phenomenology could be seen as a structuralist perspective, except perhaps in the earlier work of Husserl and his somewhat problematic conclusions concerning the essence of consciousness and world. (Dreyfus, Rabinow, 1983) His attempt to uncover the essence of consciousness and the objects or presencings which appear to consciousness, seems to me to be an attempt to extend a type of Kantian idealism. Kant does not appear to be interested in determining the exact nature of the thing perceived as a separate philosophical category; whereas Husserl seems to want to discover the absolute essence of both. So if am correct in my reading of Husserl, I would agree that he seems to embrace or approximate a similar structuralist epistemology or inclination that if you take to its conclusion, does

Journal of Theoretical and Philosophical Criminology Polizzi, D, Arrigo, B.
2009, Vol 1 (2), 113-145

appear to breakdown in some very important ways. However, I would still argue that Husserl remains outside of the structuralist camp.

Moving away from Husserl specifically... I would maintain that my reading of phenomenology, generally, sounds very familiar to the project you identify for post-structural reflection. I would see such an unfolding of meaning as being absolutely central to the project of phenomenology, insofar as Being can never be limited or confined by provisional philosophical categories. Nor do I recognize any difficulties or contradictions between my understanding of the way in which phenomenology accesses interpersonal/social reality and the characteristics which you attribute to post-structural perspectives.

Phenomenology, or at least my reading of it, seems predicated on the proposition that consciousness (Husserl) or being-in-the-world (Heidegger and Merleau-Ponty) is in constant flux and meaning is always perspectival and therefore can never be final or complete. However, such a position should not lead one to assume that this perspective ignores the reality of the meaning-generating dynamics of power which can be highly restrictive and oppressive. In fact, this perspective, particularly with Heidegger's notion of thrownness or facticity, is clearly present and must be seen as an aspect or condition that being-in-the-world may seek to overcome.

Such a reality or condition is also a part of this flux of multiple possibilities for meaning, both realized and absent. I really don't understand how meaning could be foreclosed within a phenomenological perspective, except if one attempts to conflate the provisional with the essential, which of course would no longer be phenomenology. Even within a highly restricted notion of thrownness, meaning is not completely foreclosed and certainly cannot be totalized within the confines of that restricted type of being-in-the-world; the possibility for the potentiality of being

Journal of Theoretical and Philosophical Criminology
2009, Vol 1 (2), 113-145

still remains, regardless the limitations imposed upon it by the condition of one's thrownness.

If I could, I would like to shift gears somewhat and respond to Michelle Brown's discussion of Lyotard's concept of the sublime. Lyotard's reading of the sublime really resonates with me for the implications it presents for being. When Lyotard states that the self, "exists in a fabric of relations that is now more complex and mobile than before," he still seems to be seeking in the language of phenomenology. (Lyotard, 1991, p.15) The distinctions that are often raised between postmodernism proper and phenomenology, which I see as the beginning of postmodern reflection, seem rather artificial. To my ear, phenomenology and postmodernism are really in the same key, or at the very least in different keys which share many of the same tones. Any dissonance is marginal and often very appealing.

If language is a mediating force for naming/ appearance then I would agree; but too often this mediating force sounds much more essentalistic and oppressive than is comfortable. For example, language may be a mediating force for naming unconscious processes, but that dynamic is provisional and never complete. The inability of language to define completely this process reflects the limits of language, but not necessarily the limits of existence. The sublime not only represents the ethical limits of the human condition, but also the limits of language and the specific mediating force(s) it represents. Postmodernism(s) chooses to ignore the problem of the transcendental signified identified by Pierce and continues to focus its entire logic on the self-referential character of language, which seems trapped within this never ending dialectical loop. What the postmodern position on language is really proposing is the belief that language must precede signification, which is in the end a structuralist argument. To argue that the sign or signification must follow language presumes a deterministic philosophical position that seems to

Journal of Theoretical and Philosophical Criminology
2009, Vol 1 (2), 113-145

undermine any categorization of these perspectives as post-structural. If language precedes existence, it must also precede meaning as well, which raises a variety of very problematic concerns.

I really need to think about this question more thoroughly and provide a more thoughtful response. But again, what I hear sounds very familiar and the version of phenomenology being critiqued by its postmodern critics unfamiliar and foreign.

(Two brief clarifications concerning the difference between postmodernism and phenomenology are offered. Arrigo argues that postmodernism departs from the sense making categories provided by phenomenology due to belief that such categories inhibit the possibility of transcending being or becoming)

Arrigo: Eloquent response on your end. Thank you! Let me offer just two brief comments.

First, the notion of perspectivity and meaning as lodged in intersubjective renditions of the "knowable" is where phenomenology and postmodernism, at least as I understand it, depart. Postmodernism questions the very categories of sense-making, identity construction, reasoning/affecting, etc., that are "spoken," reified, and legitimized in diverse contexts. Moreover, affirmative postmodernism recognizes that these categories are antithetical to transcending being and to experiencing a becoming, a people yet to come or a becoming imperceptible. It is language, as a mediating force, that helps to unshackle us from the discourses we use to define our very existences. Without this postmodernist-informed position, I do not see, phenomenologically, how our existences can attain Heidegger's notion of authenticity or Sartre's' notion of the *en soi*, which he astutely reminds must be transcended by way of the *pour soi*.

Journal of Theoretical and Philosophical Criminology
2009, Vol 1 (2), 113-145

Second, I agree that in too many instances the postmodernism critique (especially the negative variety) comes off as extreme political correctness, hate politics, and oppression of the radical left; but the version to which I ascribe, finds this version of postmodernism antithetical to the enterprise to which it claims allegiance. Instead, I see an affirmative postmodernism, informed by phenomenology, but extended into chaos theory, cultural criminology, post-structuralism, critical theory, constitutive thought, and psychoanalytic semiotics. I would argue, by way of example, that the language and logic of the psychiatric "consumer movement," "offender reentry initiatives," "restorative justice/ victim offender mediation programs," diversion courts (e.g., mental health/drug) and "therapeutic jurisprudence decision-making, are benignly (and increasingly) part of the systemic pathology (Fromm) problem.

Perhaps phenomenology would agree; I guess I don't know how it would.

(The conversation explores the way in which phenomenology and postmodernism address the problem of language. There appears to be agreement concerning the way in which language constructs certain pathological types of encounters within the practice of criminal justice that are "essential" to those discursive practices. However, it is not clear how these systemic pathologies are somehow less accessible from a phenomenological frame of reference. The presence of systemic pathologies, as identified above, seems easily understood within Heidegger's concept of thrownness, insofar as, not only are we thrown into specific cultural, historical, political, sociological contexts, but are thrown into language as well. For example, the thrownness evoked by the practice of "penal harm, evokes a variety of controlling and objectifying discursive practices which riddle this experience and create the foundation for its constituted meaning; but it appears equally true that being-in-the-world can never be completely removed from the possibility of

resistance to and transformation of some aspect of these emerging systematic pathologies. The discursive practices found in offender rehabilitation, restorative justice, and diversion courts, etc., in their current configuration, certainly evoke the notion of penal harm, but such configurations do not preclude the possibility for being-in-the-world to discover or create other meanings for existence that resist the toxic effects these pathologies provide.

Heidegger's concepts of authenticity/inauthenticity are also discussed. For Heidegger, these concepts reflect the differing potentialities of being that are not meant to reflect differing values of being. Generally speaking, Heidegger's (1962) notion of inauthentic being is tied to his concept of the They-self, which he defines as:

> *Thus the 'they' maintains itself factically in the averageness of that which belongs to it, of that which it regards as valid, and that which it does not, and to that which it grants success and to that which it denies. (p. 165)*

Inauthentic being delivers itself over to the whims of the 'they-self, and allows it to define the meaning for human beings (Heidegger, 1962; Zimmerman, 1981) Authentic being or authenticity is that which defies the 'they", which resists the 'they' and seeks its own way to be; this idea seems greatly influenced by Nietzsche's general description of Will to Power and seems to be theoretically compatible with Deleuze's notion of Active and Reactive Forces as explored in his text, Nietzsche and Philosophy.)

Polizzi: I would like to respond to your last point first. I do not see any great difficulty concerning phenomenology and the problem of language and logic which you connect to systemic pathology. It seems that both positions are possible. Is becoming or an active Will to Power possible within the systemic pathology which

Journal of Theoretical and Philosophical Criminology
2009, Vol 1 (2), 113-145 Polizzi, D, Arrigo, B.

you identify? Of course, if we are to take Deleuze's discussion of reactive and active will seriously. Can this same process be applied to phenomenology? I don't see why not. For example, what does the phenomenology of the court-ordered client look like? It is the artifact of the systemic pathology that you describe, an artifact of objectified being-in-the-world; but it cannot also be argued that such a process completely forecloses the possibility of becoming, the possibility of realizing a "strange new power." For if this was true, the possibility for human experience, for being-in-the-world would be completely foreclosed due to this relationship to these systemic pathologies and escape would be impossible? If you can't get there from here, you can't get there from anywhere.

More generally, I don't think that I would want to give any specific privileged designation to this process of phenomenological knowing and would always want to maintain that this knowledge is never complete or final, or even necessarily accurate in any essentialist way; nor would I want to deny the way in which this knowing is constantly influenced or overwhelmed, and mediated by the situated realities of history, culture, economic status, or future possibilities for human knowledge, etc. I think that the point you raise is more an issue of degree and not of kind. However, does the fact that these sense-making processes or categories occur in diverse contexts invalidate all aspects of this type of knowing or simply help to better inform us of the limits and challenges which are fundamental to human existence? Neither am I sure that I would agree that these categories construct a necessarily false relationship to the possibility of becoming (I also see Heidegger's understanding of being as a becoming; within this context being is a verb and not a noun).

This dialectical formulation of knowing is hardly free of its own internal contradictions, and assumes a dyadic relationship that seems rigid and limiting. I would want to argue that sense-making; regardless its specific manifestation is always provisional. It appears that phenomenology is often constructed by postmodern theorists as a type of solipsistic project, which assumes a hyper-privileging of phenomenological "subjectivity" that then conflates other and world into its solipsistic gaze. Situated existence by its very nature is open, incomplete and continually confronted by all of the sense-making categories which you name and are therefore always overwhelmed by these processes. I would agree that language is indeed the way by which we may unshackle ourselves from subject positions that have become restricted or even annihilated by this oppressive dynamic(s). My dissertation explored this very idea through the multivariant articulations for the meaning of blackness within a racist culture and the way in which Malcolm X indeed unshackled himself from the annihilation blackness represented by anti-black racism. (Polizzi, 2002)

In regard to Heidegger's notion of authenticity... I have always struggled with this idea and really do not believe it is attainable in any complete manner for all of the reasons you maintain; but I don't think one needs to embrace a postmodern perspective by which to realize this point. Heidegger's formulation of this concept seems best situated as a potentiality that is very difficult to obtain. Authenticity would seemingly need to occur outside of the care structure for it truly to be authentic. I recognize that the notion of becoming is probably most attainable through various eastern practices or other non-western approaches that de-centralize not only the knowledge of the ego, but the concept of the ego itself. Within this context, I would agree that certain contexts preclude the possibility of such becoming in it fullest sense. But again these ideas are hardly new, and may simply reflect the fact that the West has finally caught up with Eastern philosophy some two thousand years later. Heidegger apparently read Lao Tzu toward the end of his life and is reported to have admitted that this is what he had been trying to achieve with his philosophy his whole professional life (paraphrase). Similar ideas are certainly present in the Pre-Socratics of whom Heidegger was well versed and

Journal of Theoretical and Philosophical Criminology Polizzi, D, Arrigo, B.
2009, Vol 1 (2), 113-145

where the idea of becoming is clearly situated. It is not surprising to me therefore, that we also find this idea in Nietzsche, and perhaps more indirectly in the work of his student (indirectly of course), Heidegger.

Heidegger's notion of authenticity appears to be a type of being that transcends notions of the they-self and idle talk. Inauthentic being-in-the-world, the type of being most common for human beings, remains trapped within the prison of idle talk and tends to construct these images as the totality of human possibility.

I'll end with the opening verse of my most favorite translation of *The Way of Life: According to Lao Tzu* completed by Witter Bynner (1944).

1

Existence is beyond the power of words

To define:

Terms may be used

But are none of them absolute.

In the beginning of heaven and earth there were no

Words,

Words came out of the womb of matter;

And whether a man dispassionately

Sees to the core of life

Or passionately

Sees the surface,

The core and the surface

Are essentially the same,

Words making them seem different

Only to express appearance.

If name be needed, wonder names them both:

Journal of Theoretical and Philosophical Criminology
2009, Vol 1 (2), 113-145

From wonder into wonder

Existence opens.

(The conversation continues to explore the relationship between phenomenology and postmodernism from the work of Nietzsche.)

Our recent discussions have returned me to Nietzsche, and perhaps more specifically, Heidegger's rather interesting read of Nietzsche's work. I'm not sure that one needs to set up the dichotomy between Being/ becoming in the way that it normally is within this debate. Though I think I understand what Nietzsche is attempting by situating becoming within the context of completed nihilism: the grounding of the notion of value within an all too human context, thereby canceling out any supersensory discussion of Being... He negates a type of metaphysics, but does this need to reject all possibilities for this concept? I'm not sure.

(The concept of becoming is discussed; within this context, becoming is seen as the process by which certain rarified views of the self are transformed and overcome. The notion of becoming signifies for Nietzsche the self that is never complete, never a return of the same. Becoming is always on the way to that which can never be completed; to maintain otherwise would result in new renditions of the self that are equally as fixed and complete.)

Arrigo: My take on Nietzsche (1966, 1967, 1969) is akin to Deleuze (1983) and Deleuze and Guattari's (1984, 1987) reading of Nietzsche. I understand becoming within the context of an overcoming, or a will-to-power that, within it, contains the unspoken but felt conditions for transcending finite (even progressive liberal) renditions of the self (and the social). When mobilized and activated, these conditions transform being into a "person (or people) yet to come" in provisional,

Journal of Theoretical and Philosophical Criminology
2009, Vol 1 (2), 113-145

positional, and relational ways. This is an evolving sense of what could be; it is not fixed or axiomatic. This is not existence or essence per se; rather, this is spirit that represents an active molecular line of flight displacing conventional interpretations of work, family, the "American dream", recovery/restoration, and the like. This notion of becoming is, for Nietzsche, "transpraxis:" an effort to move beyond "being" and our all too human tendencies to foster sameness or a ontological death, if you will. Thus, as Nietzsche proclaims, one's reach must exceed one's grasp (the quote is elaborated on by the poet, William Browning). The tension between being and becoming is a theme addressed within the book, *Revolution in penology: Rethinking the society of captives*.

Polizzi: When Deleuze states: "The notion of values loses all meaning if values are not seen as receptacles to be pierced, statues to be broken open (great metaphors) to find what they contain, whether it is the most noble or the most base"(Deleuze, 1983, p. 55), wouldn't it be possible to say that being-in-the-world, lived-experience, does exactly the same thing for the same reasons without resorting or retreating to a metaphysical stand on Being? If will-to-power is the internal compliment of force (Deleuze, 1983), how do we situate this notion of internal: internal to what?

Arrigo: Ummmm, good question. My reading is that will-to-power (the internal compliment to force) is internal to or juxtaposed against the social/material dimensions of our lives that renders us all too human. I've interpreted will-to-power as an overcoming, mobilized and activated to transcend what "is" (i.e., the self and the social). Is this what you mean when invoking the phenomenological notion of being-in-the-world?

Journal of Theoretical and Philosophical Criminology
2009, Vol 1 (2), 113-145 Polizzi, D, Arrigo, B.

(The conversation attempts to reconcile the positions of phenomenology and postmodern reflection generally.

Polizzi: Yes! I would see being-in-the-world as having the very same interaction with the material/social dimensions that you state. Being-in-the-world has the potentiality to transcend what is, which must include any provisional understanding of self and world. But I would also argue that the will-to-power is not omnipotent, or else it seems to lapse into an untenable idealism, if only indirectly; as Delueze argues, force is always in relation to other manifestations of force which are real and may not surrender simply because I wish it so. I would include here the concept of the They-Self, which I would argue is multilayered and never fixed or complete. The meaning of being-in-the-world can be fundamentally transformed by simply altering this relationship (self/world) to one aspect of the They. I would say that Malcolm X was able to transcend certain aspects of self/world, but certainly did not silence the influence of anti-black racism. The overcoming which you describe can also be situated within the context of the overcoming of an oppressive They-Self, thereby evoking a transcendent moment that may also invite the creation of a different type of person.

I think this can also be explored within Deleuze's reading of Nietzsche's distinction between the Will to Nothingness and the Will to Power. Malcolm seeks to adapt to his diminished milieu after the loss of his parents and it is from this position of reactive force that he is able to perceive the possibility of health, the possibility for an active Will to Power as represented by his involvement with the Nation of Islam. Malcolm is able to deny this Will to Nothing through his recognition of the sublime that becomes perceiveable through his new will to power. (Deleuze, 1983)

Journal of Theoretical and Philosophical Criminology
2009, Vol 1 (2), 113-145

Nietzsche's notion of becoming still remains fully situated in the world, to which it must take some account: the bringer of new values often does so at the risk of great personal loss. (Nietzsche/2009) I'm more concerned with how and where this becoming finds itself in the world: is this a limitless becoming, unconcerned with the world or is it a new interaction with the world?

(The conversation moves to a discussion of Nietzsche's concept of becoming and more specifically, the way in which this "new interaction with the world" represents a new engagement of the world that transcends exiting categories of the self. Stated another way, becoming represents a process by which socially constructed aspects of the self are overcome and transformed.)

Arrigo: I see Nietzsche's becoming as a new interaction with the world because it is not reducible to categorization and because it defies axiomatics. Take the example of race. Typically, race is an artificial, socially constructed category used for purposes of (political/social) exclusion. Moreover, as Deleuze and Guattari explain it, constructions of race are linked to established or recognized forms of libidinal production and capital logic. The notion of becoming, following a Deleuzian interpretation of Nietzsche, is about becoming imperceptible: that moment when we transcend established or routinized constructions. How do we accomplish this? I think Nietzsche's will-to-power finds embodiment is Deleuze and Guattari's notion of schizoanalysis; anti-Oedipus; deterritorializing and reterritorializing the socius; mobilizing molecular, active lines of flight; desire as production (not as the Lacanain lack), etc.

(The conversation ends with a question: once becoming has cleared away calcified and routinized categories of the self, where are we?)

Journal of Theoretical and Philosophical Criminology
2009, Vol 1 (2), 113-145 Polizzi, D, Arrigo, B.

Polizzi: I'm not sure I'm following your distinction between becoming as nonreducible and being-in-the-world as a reducible category. I also see being-in-the-world as including the potentiality for transcending "established or routinized constructions," though this is certainly not guaranteed. I really don't see phenomenology confined or constricted in this way nor is it all that easy to transcend established or rountinized constructions, and when one does so, how does this desiring machine respond to the world? I can transcend certain restrictive constructions, but where does this new child find herself?

CONCLUSION

The preceding conversation represented a preliminary and modest critique. What was contested was the philosophical grounding of our humanity and the suggestive relevance of this grounding for the criminological enterprise. The theoretical contributions of phenomenology and postmodernism remain mostly under-examined, especially within the context of understanding delinquent and criminal conduct and those actors the criminal justice system identifies as offenders. Both perspectives problematize language, the body, the state, power, subjectivity, race/gender/class, and other facets of social reality. The ontological, epistemological, ethical, and aesthetical significances of each warrant further explication. Regrettably, positivistic science takes these constructs for granted and, correspondingly, unreflectively reifies them. As such, our view is that the modernist (causal and structural) intellectual landscape has mostly failed the human project because of this "addictive" and disturbing tendency. Accordingly, we advocate for theory that transcends the limits of the modernist episteme. Phenomenological and postmodern analyses evocatively move in this direction. The challenge that lies ahead is to explore their respective potentials, and to advance a much needed philosophical criminology as a precursor to any programmatic and policy reform.

REFERENCES

Arrigo, B, Milovanovic, D., & Schehr, R.C. (2005). *The French connection in criminology: rediscovering crime, law, and social change*. Albany: State University of New York Press.

Arrigo, B., & Milovanovic, D. (2009). *Revolution in penology: Rethinking the society of captives. Lanham: Rowman & Littlefield*

Arrigo, B. A., & Williams, C. R. (Ed.). (2006). *Philosophy, crime, and criminology*. Urbana/Chicago, IL: University of Illinois Press.

Arrigo, B. A., & Williams, C. R. (2009). Existentialism and the criminology of the shadow. In, D. Crew and R. Lippens (Eds.), *Existential criminology*, (pp. 222-248). UK: Routledge-Cavendish.

Baudrillard, J. (1972). *For a critique of the political economy of the sign*. St. Louis, MO: Telos Press.

Baudrillard, J. (1983). *Simulations.* New York, NY: Semiotext(e).

Brown, M. (2006). Aesthetics of crime. In Bruce A. Arrigo and Christopher R. Williams (Eds.). *Philosophy, Crime, and Criminology*. Urbana and Chicago: University of Illinois Press.

Buber, M. (1970). *I and Thou.* Translated by R.G. Smith. Edinburgh: T &T Clark.

Castoriadis, C. (1987). *The imaginary institution of society*. Cambridge: MIT Press.

Crew, D., & Lippens, R. (Eds.) (2009). *Existentialist criminology*. UK: Routledge-Cavendish.

Deleuze, G. (1983). *Nietzsche's philosophy*. Translated by Hugh Tomlinson. New York: Columbia University Press.

Journal of Theoretical and Philosophical Criminology
2009, Vol 1 (2), 113-145
Polizzi, D, Arrigo, B.

Deleuze, G. & Guattari, F. (1983). *Anti-Oedipus: Capitalism and schizophrenia*. Minneapolis: University of Minnesota Press.

Deleuze, G., Guattari, F. (1987). *A thousand plateaus: Capitalism & schizophrenia*. Translated by Brian Massumi. Minneapolis: University of Minnesota Press.

Derrida, J. (1973). *Speech and phenomena and other essays on Husserl's theory of signs*. Evanston: Northwestern University Press.

Derrida, J. (1977). *Of grammatology*. Baltimore, MC: Johns Hopkins University Press.

Derrida, J. (1978). *Writing and difference*. Chicago: University of Chicago Press.

Dreyfus, H.L., Rabinow, P. (1983). Michel Foucault: Beyond Structuralism and Hermeneutics 2nd edition. Chicago: University of Chicago Press.

Foucault, M. (1972). *The archaeology of knowledge*. New York, NY: Pantheon.

Foucault, M. (1977) *Discipline and punish: The birth of a prison*. New York, NY: Pantheon.

Fromm, E. (1994). *Escape from freedom*. New York, NY: Henry Holt & Co.

Fromm, E. (2003). *The sane society*. New York, NY: Routledge

Fromm, E. (2005). *To have or to be?* London, UK: Continuum International Publishers.

Gurwitsch, A. (1964). *The field of consciousness*. Pittsburgh: Duquesne University Press.

Heidegger, M. (1962). *Being and time*. Translated by John Macquarrie & Edward Robinson. San Francisco: HarperSanFrancisco.

Husserl, E. (1962). *Ideas: General Introduction to pure phenomenology*. New York: Collier Books.

Husserl, E. (1970). *The crisis of European sciences and transcendental phenomenology*. Evanston: Northwestern University Press.

Irigaray, L. (1985). *This sex which is not one*. Ithaca, NY: Cornell University Press.

Kristeva, J. (1980). *Desire in language*. New York, NY: Columbia University Press.

Lao Tzu (1944). *The way of life: According to Lao Tzu*. New York: Perigee Books.

Lacan, J. (1981). *The four fundamental concepts of psychoanalysis*. New York, NY: W. W. Norton.

Lacan. J. (1982). *Feminine sexuality*. Translated by Jacqueline Rose. New York: W. W. Norton Inc.

Lacan, J. (2007). *Ecrits: The first complete edition in English*. Translated by Bruce Fink. New York: W. W. Norton Inc.

Lyotard, JF. (1991). *The postmodern condition: A report on knowledge*. Minneapolis: Minnesota University Press.

Lyotard, JF. (1989). *The Lyotard reader*. Oxford, England: Basil Blackwell Ltd.

Marion, J-L. (1998). *Reduction and givenness: Investigations of Husserl, Heidegger, and phenomenology*. Translated by Thomas A. Carlson. Evanston: Northwestern University Press.

Merleau-Ponty, M. (2002). *Phenomenology of perception*. Translated by Colin Smith. London: Routledge 2nd edition.

Merleau-Ponty, M. (1968) *Visible and the invisible: Followed by working notes*. Translated by Alphonso Lingis. Evanston: Northwestern University Press.

Merleau-Ponty, M. (1964). *Signs*. Translated by Richard C. McCleary. Evanston: Northwestern University Press.

Nietzsche, F. (1967). *The birth of tragedy and the case of Wagner*. Translated by Walter Kaufmann. New York: Random House.

Nietzsche, F. W. (1966). *Beyond good and evil: Prelude to a philosophy of the future*. New York, NY: Vintage

Nietzsche, F. (1967). *The will to power*. Translated by Walter Kaufmann and R.J. Hollingdale. New York: Random House and Vintage Books.

Nietzsche, F. W. (1969). *On the genealogy of morals and ecce homo*. New York, NY:

Journal of Theoretical and Philosophical Criminology
2009, Vol 1 (2), 113-145

Vintage.

Nietzsche, F. 1885/ 2009). *Thus spoke Zarathustra: A book for everyone and nobody*. Translated by Graham Parkes. New York/ Oxford: Oxford University Press.

Polizzi, D. (2002). *The experience of anti-black racism: A phenomenological hermeneutic of the Autobiography of Malcolm X*. (UMI No. 3069293)

Polizzi, D. (2007). The social construction of race and crime: The image of the black offender. *International Journal of Restorative Justice*. Vol 3(1): 6-20.

Polizzi, D. (2009). *Transforming corrections: Humanistic approaches to corrections and offender treatment*. Durham, NC: Carolina Academic Press.

Ricouer, P. (1973). Creativity of language. *Philosophy Today*, 17, 97-112.

Rosenau, P. M. (1992). *Post-Modernism and the social sciences: Insights, inroads, and intrusions*. Princeton: Princeton University Press.

Unger, Mangabeira, R. (1988). *False necessity: Anti-necessitarian social theory in the service of radical democracy*. New York: Cambridge University Press.

Zimmerman, M.E. (1981). *The eclipse of the self: The development of Heidegger's concept of authenticity*. Athens, OH: Ohio University Press.

[21]

Constitutive Criminology: Origins, Core Concepts, and Evaluation

Stuart Henry and Dragan Milovanovic

In the 12 years since Dragan Milovanovic and I first formulated this theoretical perspective, we have received numerous questions (many via e-mail) about various aspects of the theory. Interestingly, these have not come predominantly from academics, but mainly from undergraduate, graduate, and even high school students. In addition, there have been over 25 discussions of the theory in journals and books (for an assessment of these, see Henry and Milovanovic, 1999). Below we will address the issues raised by summarizing the constitutive position and offering an evaluation of its contribution to date.

Origins and Influences

In one sense, constitutive criminology has a long history in that it draws on several well-established critical social theories, most notably symbolic interactionism, social constructionism, phenomenology, ethnomethodology, structural Marxism, poststructuralism, structuration theory, semiotics (for a review of these roots, see Arrigo, 1997; Bak, 1999, 2000). In another sense, it is part of the relatively recent interest in chaos theory and affirmative postmodernism. In particular, it draws on complexity theory (Mandelbrot, 1983; Gregerson and Sailer, 1993; Pickover, 1988), structural coupling (Luhmann, 1992; Teubner, 1993), strategic essentialism (Spivak, 1988; Jessop, 1990), relational sets (Hunt, 1993), critical race theory and intersections (Matsuda et al., 1993), autopoietic systems (Teubner, 1988, 1993; Cornell, 1991), dialectical materialism (Marx, 1975; Sayer, 1979), and topology theory (Lacan, 1961; Milovanovic and Ragland, 2001; Milovanovic, 1996c).

Most recently, constitutive criminology was born of the application of these postmodernist concepts to critical criminology by a relatively small group of critical criminologists whose inner circle comprises Stuart Henry, Dragan Milovanovic, Gregg Barak, and Bruce Arrigo. This group has primarily been

---

Stuart Henry, Ph.D., is Director and Associate Dean, Interdisciplinary Studies Program, College of Life-Long Learning, Wayne State University, 5700 Cass Avenue, Detroit, MI 48202 (e-mail: Stuart.Henry@wayne.edu). **Dragan Milovanovic** is Professor in the Department of Criminal Justice, Sociology, and Social Work, Northeastern Illinois University, 5500 N. St. Louis Avenue, Chicago, IL 60625 (e-mail: D-Milovanovic@neiu.edu) He is the past editor of *Humanity and Society*, *The Journal of Human Justice*, and *The Critical Criminologist*.

responsible for founding the position in criminology and making theoretical innovations. A broader group that is more loosely linked to the constitutive project includes T.R. Young, Rob Schehr, Lisa Sanchez, Vic Kappeler, James Williams, and Mary Bosworth. These scholars have found the theory helpful in explaining particular developments in crime and justice and have pushed the theory in new directions (see Henry and Milovanovic, 1999, for a sampling of their research). The outer circle of this group includes sympathizers who have incorporated aspects of the theory into their analysis, while developing their own theoretical analysis in new directions. There is also a growing body of students who have developed their research around the constitutive position, including Biko Azino, Andrew Bak, and Mark Faccini. Finally, there are critics of the position. Their contributions are included in an evaluation section at the end of this article.

In a more narrow sense, constitutive criminology first emerged in the 1980s in Stuart Henry's studies on crime and social control in the workplace (Henry, 1983; 1985). They were considerably influenced by Peter Fitzpatrick's (1984) theory of "integral plurality" and Anthony Giddens' (1979, 1984) structuration theory, especially in *The Constitution of Society*. Henry outlined a sociolegal theory concerning the relationship between social forms and social action, initially defined as "integrated theory" (Henry, 1983). The actual term "constitutive theory" came from a suggestion by Christine Harrington (1988) in her constructive critique of Henry's 1983 work. It became the motif for subsequent renditions (Henry, 1987a; 1987b) and was incorporated into other work in Brigham and Harrington's series "After the Law" (e.g., Hunt, 1993).

In June 1989, during a chance meeting at the 25th Anniversary meeting of the Law and Society Association in Madison, Wisconsin, Dragan Milovanovic shared similar insights. He had been developing theories in the sociology of law, particularly Lacanian postmodernism and psychoanalytic semiotic approaches (Milovanovic, 1992; 1993a; 1993b; 1994a; 1994b; 1994c), and in his studies on law and the prison (1988; Milovanovic and Thomas, 1989). At that meeting Henry commented that he had read an article by Marty Schwartz (1989) in one of the issues of the then newly founded *Critical Criminologist* that outlined new directions in critical theory. He felt that Schwartz had minimalized the treatment of the human subject in his summary of what he described as "Postmodernist Criminology." Milovanovic, then coeditor of the *Critical Criminologist*, invited Henry to respond: "six pages, double space is all I need," he said. Thus began our collaboration. The very first statement under the title "Constitutive Criminology" was published in *The Critical Criminologist* (Henry, 1989). In 1990, we wrote two preliminary position papers (Henry and Milovanovic, 1991; Milovanovic and Henry, 1991). In 1992, we wrote a third paper (Henry and Milovanovic, 1994). In 1993, we published a short paper dealing with the definition of crime (Henry and Milovanovic, 1993). Henry (1994) then wrote on another key aspect of the theory, "replacement discourse." Independently, and on a convergent track, Milovanovic in 1992 developed and applied the notion of "displacement discourses" to law (1992: 221–222; 256–258). Milovanovic has also dealt with this topic in several recent publications (1993a; 1993b; 1994b; 1994c; 1996a: 205–209; 1996b; 1996c) and he devoted a chapter to it in his *Sociology of Law* (1994a: Chapter 6). The culmination of this work resulted in our first book-length treatment of the topic, *Constitutive Criminology: Beyond Postmodernism* (Henry and Milovanovic, 1996), and, most recently, the edited volume of research by criminologists applying and developing the ideas, *Constitutive Criminology at Work: Applications to Crime and Justice* (Henry and Milovanovic, 1999).

Core Concepts

Constitutive criminology is a theoretical perspective influenced by postmodernism that examines the discursive coproduction of crime by human agents in their interrelation with cultural products, social institutions, and the wider societal structure. Constitutive theory rejects the argument of traditional modernist criminology that crime and offenders can be separated from social processes of societal production and analyzed and corrected in isolation from the whole. Further, crime is not understandable as a determined product of cultures and structures. Instead of setting out to identify factors that "cause" offending, constitutive criminology seeks to examine the relations that coproduce crime, as well as ways to intervene in that coproduction to reduce the harms that are its ongoing outcome.

On Knowledge, Discourse, and Politics

Constitutive criminology incorporates and accepts postmodernists' anarchistic critique that knowledge is political, subjective, and hierarchical. Knowledge is not so much power as it is bodies of discourse continuously constructed and invoked by human subjects to make truth claims for use in the politics of their interaction with others. Knowledge is not value free, objective, or neutral, but a weapon of domination or resistance. Use of knowledge is an expression of power or resistance to power.

We see socially constructed discourse as the basis for organizational activity, institutions, and social structure. Constitutive criminology accepts the need for deconstruction of discourse to expose its constructed nature, assumptions, and contradictions. However, unlike skeptical postmodernists (see Rosenau, 1992), whose analysis comprises largely nihilistic critique, constitutive criminology takes an affirmative perspective. It believes in the political value and social reality of constructions. Constitutive criminology leaves us not in an endlessly deconstructed world, but one in which we acknowledge the constructed nature of the world and the continuous input of energy humans make to maintain it. Constitutive criminology maintains that it is possible to expose, not only the tentative, contingent nature of knowledge and social reality (Butler, 1992), but also to make the politically conscious analysis that some social constructions and ways of constructing reality are more harmful and others are less harmful.

Constitutive criminology takes the position that because crime is conceived of, made meaningful, and acted out through particular discursive forms, an important component in any policy for crime reduction is to change the ways of talking that facilitate its expression. Thus, it proposes the concept of "replacement discourse," which is the attempt to substitute new, less harmful discursive practices and their associated constructions for those that are more harmful. Herein lies the politics of constitutive criminology: to deconstruct harmful constructions, along with the sources and practices of their generation, and to replace them with less harmful discursive forms that are contingent and revisable. Thus, the concept of "replacement discourse," affords the possibility, though not the certainty, of reconstructing a less harmful world by putting energy into creating new social constructions that affect the wider social order and open up the potential for human growth. One way to accomplish this is through an activist engagement with the mass media (Barak, 1993, 1994).

Human Agency's Construction of Order and Order's Construction of Human Agency

Constitutive criminology is founded on the proposition that humans are responsible for actively creating their world with others. They do this by transforming their surroundings through interaction with others, not least via discourse. Through language and symbolic representation humans identify differences, construct categories, and share a belief in the reality of that which is constructed that orders otherwise chaotic states. It is toward these social constructions of reality that humans act.

In the process of investing energy in their socially constructed, discursively organized categories of order and reality, human subjects not only shape their social world, but are also shaped by it. They are coproducers and coproductions of their own and others' agency. Constitutive criminology is about how some of this socially constructed order, as well as some of the human subjects constituted within it, can be harmed, impaired, and destroyed by the process and by what is built during that process: ultimately by each other as fellow subjects.

Constitutive theorists argue that the coproduction of harmful relations occurs through society's structure and culture, as these are energized by active human subjects — not only as offenders, but also as social categories such as victims, criminal justice practitioners, academics, commentators, media reporters and producers of film and TV crime shows, and most generally, as investors, producers, and consumers in the crime business. They look at the psycho-socio-cultural matrix (the cloth of crime) for that which provides the discursive medium through which human agents construct "meaningful" harms to others. The approach taken, therefore, shifts the criminological focus away from narrow, dichotomized issues that focus either on the individual offender or on the social environment. Instead, constitutive criminology uses a holistic conception of the relationship between the "individual" and "society," gives priority to neither, and examines their mutuality and interrelationship. Human subjects are thus not discrete individual entities. They are integrally bound up with the social constructions they and others make. They act toward each other in terms of those constructions as if they were realities. Humans are permeable to their socially constructed world, as it is to them. Yet this is an unequal relationship; the discourse from which their subjectivity is constituted is that which exists as it is produced by others. An implication of this coproduction is that human subjects are contingent, rather than complete; they are subjects in the making. For this reason, we refer to them as "recovering subjects."

The human subject is seen as "recovering" because it is always striving for a final and certain state of being, but never arrives. Such a vision is an important first step in developing a framework that allows for the richness of human potentiality, without foreclosing its endless possibilities. The recovering human subject always has the potential to escape the cages of its own and others' constructions, not least by investing energy in new ones (Barak, Henry, and Milovanovic, 1997: 95).

Power, Harm, and Crime

According to constitutive criminologists, a major source of harmful relations emanates from the nature of its power structure. Unequal power relations, built on the constructions of difference, provide the conditions that define crime as harm. Constitutive criminology defines crime as the harm resulting from humans investing energy in harm-producing relations of power. Humans suffering such "crimes" are in relations of inequality. Crimes are nothing less than people being disrespected. People are disrespected in numerous ways, but all have to do with denying or preventing us from becoming fully social beings. What is human is to make a difference to the world, to act on it, to interact with others, and together to transform the environment and ourselves. If this process is prevented, we become less than human; we are harmed. Thus, constitutive criminologists define crime as "the power to deny others their ability to make a difference" (Henry and Milovanovic, 1996: 116).

Constitutive theory divides crimes that deny humanity's ability to make a deference into two types: "*crimes of reduction*" and "*crimes of repression.*" Harms of reduction occur when offended parties experience a loss of some quality relative to their present standing. They could have property stolen from them, but they could also have dignity stripped from them, as in hate crimes. Harms of repression occur when people experience a limit, or restriction, preventing them from achieving a desired position or standing. They could be prevented from achieving a career goal because of sexism or racism, or meet a promotional "glass ceiling." Considered along a continuum of deprivation, harms of reduction or repression may be based on any number of constructed differences. In Western industrial societies, harms cluster around the following constructed differences: economic (class, property), gender (sexism), race and ethnicity (racism, hate), political (power, corruption), morality, human rights, social position (status/prestige, inequality), psychological state (security, well-being), self-realization/actualization, biological integrity, etc. Whatever the construction, actions are harms either because they move an offended person away from a position or state they currently occupy, or because they prevent them from occupying a position or state that they desire, the achievement of which does not deny or deprive another. This raises the question of whether it is ever legitimate to reduce or repress another, and if legitimate, by what process and substantive criteria, an issue that should be a challenge for future constitutive criminological investigations.

Criminality as a Social Coproduction

This reconception of crime, offender, and victim locates criminality not in the person, the structure, or culture, but in the ongoing creation of social identities through discourse; it thus leads to a different notion of crime causation. To the constitutive theorist, crime is not so much *caused as discursively constructed* through human processes of which it is one.

In such a view, we might consider that the focus on some people as "criminals" is merely an exaggeration of a condition of human existence that we are all subject to: powerlessness to be free from our own constructions. However, there is something uniquely concentrated about those designated as criminals. Whether single human beings or collectives of humans, constitutive criminology sees such people as "excessive investors" in the power to impose order (i.e., discursive constructions) on others. The offender is viewed as an "excessive investor" in the power to dominate others. Such "investors" put energy into creating and magnifying differences between themselves and others. This investment of energy disadvantages, disables, and destroys others' human potentialities. Their "crime" is a concentration of the general tendency to limit others' freedom. Their crime is that they act toward others as objects for domination, such that the subject as victim loses some of their humanity in the process. Victims are more entrenched, more disabled, and suffer loss. Victims "suffer the pain of being denied their own humanity, the power to make a difference. The victim of crime is thus rendered a non-person, a nonhuman, or less complete being" (Henry and Milovanovic, 1996: 116). Rape victims feel something has been taken from them, their humanity and their dignity. Victims of financial fraud feel a loss, not just of money, but a part of themselves. They are less whole than they were because they are reminded that they are vulnerable to extreme domination by others that reduces their humanity, disables, disadvantages, and destroys some aspects of their sense of self as subject. This is what racism, sexism, and ageism do (see, for example, Milovanovic and Russell, 2001). From the constitutive perspective, all are concentrations of the general tendency for humans to relate to one another through relations of domination and subordination. Crime then becomes domination, whether by single humans such as rapists or robbers, collectives such as organized crime or corporate fraudsters, or by state governments such as genocide. Yet these are the extremes of a construction process that is based on the same general principles. Indeed, this is why criminal justice is seen as harm creating; it denies human subjects their freedom to make a difference and contributes to the discursive divisions that fragment society. In the process, the person victimized is rendered a "recovering subject," still with untapped human potential, but with a damaged faith in humanity.

The Contribution of Criminal Justice to Crime

From the constitutive criminological position, criminal justice is part of the problem, not the solution. It is a system whose practitioners act toward the world of crime as though it were a reality. It is a system designed to invest excessively in producing harm, while claiming to protect others. Consciously striving to reconstruct the discourse of the excessive investor at both a societal and a systemic level, crime is fed by the discursive fear of being victimized as well as the system of criminal justice; both ironically expand the discursive production of energy that constitutes crime. Put simply, crime is the coproduced outcome, not only of humans and their environment, but also of human agents and the wider society through its excessive investment, to the point of obsession, in crime, through crime shows, crime drama, crime documentaries, crime news, crime books, crime films, crime precautions, criminal justice agencies, criminal lawyers, and criminologists. All are parasitic on the crime problem, but as constitutive criminology suggests, they also contribute to its ongoing social and cultural production and ongoing reproduction. This is particularly true for crime control and criminal justice.

Conventional crime control efforts, whether in the form of growing criminal justice institutions — police and prisons — or as political rhetoric rehearsed in the media, fuel the engine of crime. Such control interventions take criminal activity to new levels of investment and to self-enclosed innovation. Here the contradictory emotions of brutalized insensitivity, public horror, and outrage call for more investment in control measures that further feed the cycle. In short, crime is an "autopoietic" (self-referential) system that is "self-sustaining" through its absorption of others' reactions to it.

Instead of criminal justice, we believe the central issue should be social justice. This is not social justice in terms of equity principles, but in terms of deconstructing the ways we produce harm so that less is produced.

The Politics of Change Through the Social Justice of Replacement Discourse

The implications of constitutive theory are, first that crime must be deconstructed as a recurrent discursive process, and second, that conscious attempts must be made at reconstruction with a view to preventing recurrence. Given this interrelated nature of social structures and human agents and their social and cultural productions in the coproduction of crime, constitutive criminology calls for a justice policy of reconstruction. This is achieved through *replacement discourse* that:

> is directed toward the dual process of deconstructing prevailing structures of meaning and displacing them with new conceptions, distinctions, words, and phrases, which convey alternative meanings.... Replacement discourse, then, is not simply critical and oppositional, but provides both a critique and an alternative vision (Henry and Milovanovic, 1996: 204–205).

The new replacement constructions are designed to displace crime as moments in the exercise of power and as control. They offer an alternative medium by which social constructions of reality can take place. This is not a unitary medium, but, as Smart (1990: 82) has argued, refers instead to "subjugated knowledges, which tell different stories and have different specificities" and that aim at "the deconstruction of truth" and the power effects of claims to truth. Instead of replacing one truth with another, replacement discourse invokes a "multiplicity of resistances" to the ubiquity of power (*Ibid.*). Beyond resistances, the concept of replacement discourse offers a celebration of unofficial, informal, discounted, and ignored knowledges through its discursive diversity. In terms of diminishing the harm experienced from all types of crime (street, corporate, state, hate, etc.), constitutive criminology talks of "liberating" replacement discourses that seek transformation of the prevailing political-economies and the associated practices of crime and social control. Constitutive criminology thus simultaneously argues for ideological and materialistic change; one without the other renders change only in part.

Replacement discourse can be implemented through attempts by constitutive criminologists to reconstruct popular images of crime in the mass media through engaging in "newsmaking criminology" (Barak, 1994). It can also be induced through "narrative therapy." Narrative therapy developed as part of family therapy to enable offenders (excessive investors in power) to construct more liberating life narratives and, through these, to reconstitute themselves. We (Henry and Milovanovic, 1996: 203–211) have also theorized how a replacement discourse may emerge. Elsewhere, Milovanovic has theorized how a replacement discourse may materialize in integrating Paulo Freire's dialogical pedagogy, Jacque Lacan's psychoanalytic semiotics, and chaos and catastrophe theory: in the context of activist lawyers (1996b), conflict resolution (1999), and in social transformations (1996a: 205–209).

Some sympathetic critics have pointed out, however, that replacement discourse may itself be harm producing, and that while affording a means of resistance, it can also allow new negative constructions to occur (see Sanchez, 1999; Kappeler and Kraska, 1999). In short, constitutive criminology argues for a transpraxis that is deconstructive, reconstructive, and sensitive to the dialectics of struggle.

Summary of the Core Concepts

Elsewhere (Barak, Henry, and Milovanovic, 1997: 93), we have summarized this basic position as follows:

> The essence of the constitutive argument is that crime and its control cannot be separated from the totality of the discursively ordered, structural and cultural contexts in which it is produced.... This new criminology addresses crime's interwoven connections with the wider complexity of social relationships through a synoptic analysis whereby crime is related to the "symbolic," the "imaginary," and the "real." It is an open-ended approach proposing that human subjects are responsible for actively creating their world with others, a world which simultaneously acts back, shaping the subject's own identity. Through social interaction involving language and symbolic representations, people identify and evaluate differences, construct categories, organize their activities to reflect those categories, and share a belief in the reality of that which is constructed. This shared belief gives order to otherwise chaotic states while it also recursively constructs their lives. By investing energy in socially constructed realities, human subjects are not only shaped, but they also help shape the world around them. Constitutive criminology thus furnishes a dynamic conception of social structure as a virtual and infinitely revisable society where human subjects dynamically and contingently interact.

Evaluation of the Perspective

Constitutive criminology has generated considerable interest among theorists, practitioners, and a range of other students of criminology. Among leading criminologists the constitutive idea has now been accepted into the corpus of criminological knowledge as a significant theoretical contribution, and one of the few criminologies illustrative of the postmodernist perspective. Constitutive criminology has been seriously discussed in 11 texts on crime and deviance (see Gibbons, 1994: 160–614; Beirne and Messerschmidt, 1995: 533–535; Einstadter and Henry, 1995: 277–300; Naffine, 1996: 75–77; DeKeseredy and Schwartz, 1996: 275–276; Akers, 1997: 176–179; Lanier and Henry, 1998: 282–285; Deutschmann, 1998: 378; Barak, 1998: 219–234; Vold, Bernard, and Snipes, 1998; Schmalleger, 1999). The initial statement (Henry and Milovanovic, 1991) was cited among nine key works that "have added to the richness of criminological theory," and that "extend the bounds of traditional criminology" (Stitt and Giacopassi, 1992: 6). Our early statement was cited in the development of various theories, including a constitutive theory of law (Harrington, 1988; Hunt, 1993), integral legal pluralism (Fitzpatrick, 1984, 1992), cultural theory of law (Silbey, 1992; Ewick and Silbey, 1998), autopoietic theory of law (Teubner, 1992, 1993), and reflexive criminology (Nelken, 1994). Our later statements also proved to be a considerable influence on Barak's (1998) holistic integrated criminology, and Barak himself joined with us in co-authoring a few constitutive works (Barak and Henry, 1999; Barak, Henry, and Milovanovic, 1997).

In a substantial review, Gibbons (1994: 164) discusses the theory as one of the "new criminologies" that warrants attention, not least for its valid contention that "crime is both in and of society." Most recently, in his attempt to locate the roots and intellectual influences on constitutive criminology, Arrigo (1997: 392–923) proclaimed that, "constitutive thought is now firmly established as a leading conceptual orientation in the sociology of law and in criminology," but he admits that it is "relatively new and not yet fully legitimized." Ruller (1997: 497) predicts that "we can expect a slow and steady infiltration of postmodern elements into the discipline. Indeed, this infiltration is already well underway." However, not all evaluations have been so celebratory. Most commentators have pointed to constitutive theory's relatively unresearched state. Gibbons (1994) questioned the future impact of the theory and, while acknowledging its critical challenge to mainstream approaches, speculated that it was more likely to be incorporated by mainstream criminology than to result in a revolutionary transformation. Similarly, DeKeseredy and Schwartz (1996: 276) conclude that, despite its important presence, it is not yet developed enough to be called a school of thought. Although Colvin (1997: 1449) saw its "most provocative discussions" as "those concerning the definition and causes of crime," Nelken (1994: 13) concluded that it will be difficult for constitutive criminology to reach one of its goals of changing the meaning of crime unless the approach is spelled out in more detail. Critical responses to the constitutive project have taken a variety of forms. Unfortunately, one of the underlying themes shared by critics is their focus on parts of the project rather than on the project as a whole. Indeed, we are somewhat disconcerted that, despite our urging that the harm of crime is a dialectical *coproduction* and that ceasing such production requires a holistic *response at multiple levels*, some commentators have sought to reduce the project to its component "parts." Here we address a variety of such partial evaluations, pointing out that by separating off aspects for analysis, without relating them to the whole project, critics undermine the integrational objective that we and others set out to achieve (see Barak, 1998).

Complexity in Need of Complex Prose

A recurring theme in evaluations of postmodern perspectives in general, and constitutive criminology in particular, is that the prose is seen as excessively complex. One commentator, for example, questioned "whether the complexity (and apparently obscurity) of the terminology and schemata...is fully warranted, and whether the propositions could be more concisely stated" (Friedrichs, 1996: 125). He goes on to say that "this is a difficult work, dense and even bewildering in places, and especially likely to be challenging to those who come to it with no direct familiarity with the work of the various contemporary critical and postmodern writers cited" (*Ibid.*). The same sentiment was echoed by another who said, "the reader not already familiar with postmodern work and its often obscure language...will find it exceedingly difficult to extract the author's ideas" (Colvin, 1997: 1450). In an otherwise very positive assessment, Bohm (1997: 16) concluded, "the most vexing problem awaiting readers...is the esoteric language used."

Interestingly, in their own critique of postmodernism's "semantic challenge," Schwartz and Friedrichs (1994: 227–228) usefully summarize some of the arguments in favor of what they describe as "dense and abstruse...gratuitously obscure, incoherent, and undisciplined" prose. These include its greater responsiveness to complexity and a playfulness that enables readers to construct their own meaning from the text, thereby empowering them. While dismissing these arguments (in favor of addressing the needs of victims suffering the reality of crime), Schwartz and Friedrichs also stumble upon a third argument in favor of complexity: that it may reveal "modes and styles of understanding that are ultimately more valid and more revealing in a changing, endlessly complex world?" (*Ibid.*)

The difficulty in comprehending constitutive theory is not merely unfamiliar prose, but an outcome of the modernist scientific tradition that divides the world into ever-more specialized corpses of knowledge, and then comes to believe that immersion in any one of these language fragments is universal. When theorizing is vested in single disciplines or subdisciplines, it becomes very difficult for those outside to understand. Normally, that presents little difficulty because academics rarely read outside their own discipline and most intradisciplinary prose is understandable; in contrast, most interdisciplinary prose presents problems of comprehension.

These problems are complicated by the challenge postmodernism makes to the modernist practice of dividing knowledge into disciplines and to the myopic and fragmented knowledges such disciplinary division produces. This fragmentation occurs not only between disciplines, but, in the case of multidisciplinary fields like criminology, also within them (Ericson and Carriere, 1994; Barak, 1998). In seeking to integrate insights and build transcending concepts, it has become necessary to incorporate some prose from the diversity of disciplines *and* to invent some overarching concepts designed to capture social life's complexity (Berube, 1997). The result is that the prose becomes largely unfamiliar to the narrowly invested reader.

Indeed, that we have a wide range of disciplinary coverage has been recognized by some of our critics. For example, Friedrichs (1996: 124–215) admits that in "advancing a novel integrative approach," *Constitutive Criminology* incorporates a "vastly ambitious engagement with a wide range of especially challenging and difficult theories in social thought." These include, according to Friedrichs, the familiar mainstream theories and those of several generations of critical scholars, postmodernists, and educationalists, but,

> going wholly outside of the boundaries of social theory and the literature of the humanities, they consider the relevance of innovative theoretical approaches and propositions emanating out of the physical sciences and mathematics, such as chaos theory, quantum mechanics, Godel's theory, catastrophe theory, and topology for the concerns of criminologists! Altogether, the range of exceptionally demanding ideas, concepts, and positions in this book is simply awesome.

Further focusing on where the problem of prose may lay is Ruller's (1997: 496) paradoxical judgment that *Constitutive Criminology* "is hard to understand for a 'modern' (pre-postmodern) reader who believes the world can be characterized in terms of order, perfection, essentialism, causality, and individual autonomy." Yet Ruller also says "[Henry and Milovanovic] describe the traditional or 'modern' criminology with considerable conciseness and clarity" and reiterates that although "the authors write with great clarity," "what they present in this field (about chaos theory, corel sets, etc.) will not be understandable to the great majority of criminologists" (1997: 496–497). So, where precisely is the problem located here? The issue seems not to be that the presentation of constitutive ideas lacks lucidity, but that they reflect the complexity, ambiguity, and uncertainty of the social world and the artificial limits of disciplinarity, itself the hallmark of modernity. It seems that the difficulty is at least partly in the eye of the reader, and yes, reading outside one's discipline would considerably lessen the problem of prose.

In addition, the question of innovative language use has earned the dubious honor of "esoteric" (Ruller, 1997: 497; Bohm, 1997: 16). However, innovative language use has been recognized by those in critical pedagogy as necessary if we are to transcend our present power-knowledge relations. Giroux (1992: 21), for example, has said, "every new paradigm has to create its own language because the old paradigms, through their use of particular language forms, produce knowledge and social relations that often serve to legitimate specific relations of power." He goes on to say that a clarity versus complexity binarism is an artificial construct in that it overlooks "how language and power come together in complex ways to exclude diverse narratives that rupture dominant codes and open up new spaces and possibilities for reading, writing, and acting within, rather than outside of, a democratic politics of difference" (1992: 25). The call for "clarity," therefore, assumes a consensus whose continuous invocation fuels the politics of containment, not liberation.

The Issue of Integration

While different disciplines are seemingly incompatible, so too are different positions within any one discipline. We take the view that integration of knowledge involves complimentarity: contradictory positions are contributory explanatory frameworks, often explaining different aspects or dimensions of an issue. Such positions, which are not limited to two, are co-contributors to the totality and must be examined in themselves, in relation to counter positions, and in relation to the whole of which they are part. We can illustrate this by considering critiques of the constitutive project's notion of the "integration" of structure and agency. For one commentator (Naffine, 1996: 75), we "seem to be suggesting, in Marxist fashion, that economic structures formed by the logic of capital...determine the fate of the individual." This leads to the conclusion that "their criminology appears to be pure instrumental Marxism." Naffine continues, "but then they endeavor to complicate their account of power by suggesting that the economic and social structures which oppress are the products of our imagination, which we can therefore reimagine," a position that leads them, unlike Foucault, to deny the reality of power (*Ibid.*: 76). Further:

> As Marxist materialists, however, Henry and Milovanovic evidently are not persuaded that the life of the mind can have real effects. It is the economy that is real, while our understanding of the world — our "imaginings" — can never be truly constitutive of reality. So while they flirt with Foucault, at heart Henry and Milovanovic seem unconvinced by the Foucauldian account of power as knowledge, preferring an oddly adapted Marxist formulation of power and its relation to crime (*Ibid.*).

Union, it seems, is difficult to sustain when some readers are intent on separation. The idea that both of these notions are co-constitutive, as we clearly and categorically assert, is not enough. There needs to be certainty, commitment, and essentializing; no "flirting" *a la* Matza (1964: 28) is allowed. Similarly, we find an essentialist and reductionist position in Howe (1997), who indicates that any crossover to modernist thinking from poststructuralist thought is equivalent to sleeping with the enemy. In short, this "wedding," Howe (1997: 89) tells us, cannot be a happy one.

Such essentializing is troubling. However, others reading the constitutive project seem to find a different truth, one reflective of a non-essentializing position. For example, compare Bohm's comments with Naffine's reading of us as "Marxist materialists." Bohm (1997: 15) argues that "by focusing on the linguistic production of reality, the authors tend to downplay (but do not ignore) the material conditions of production (e.g., the ownership of private property and wealth)." Indeed, in a succinct statement of our basic position, he demonstrates that *Constitutive Criminology*:

> assumes that human beings socially construct their world primarily through language and symbolic representation but, at the same time, are also shaped by the world they create. Two contradictions of this process are that people come to "reify" the world they create...and that the institutions and structures people create frequently become the source of social constraint and domination, as do attempts to oppose them. The optimism of Henry and Milovanovic's theory lies in the belief that, as creators, human beings are capable of changing the institutions and structures that dominate and constrain them. For Henry and Milovanovic, people are the "co-producers" of reality and their actions can be both constraining and liberating (*Ibid.*).

In spite of this empathetic reading of our position, the notion that such seemingly contradictory ideas, and even the integration of insights from diverse disciplines, can be mutually constructive, let alone constitutive, is rejected by many of those committed to particular disciplines. Indeed, the unwillingness to accept that disciplines can provide contributory insight to our understanding of the totality is not confined to the structure versus agency debate. From a feminist postmodernist perspective, Howe (1997) rejects any notion of marrying modernism with postmodernism and sees our constitutive project as fundamentally flawed: "criminology offers no insights into crime. Postmodern theories cannot be happily wedded with the modernist, positivistic paradigms of criminology.... [T]hat is what I tell my students" (*Ibid.*: 89). Howe asks, "Can criminology and postmodern feminism meet and have a nice day?" She replies, "I don't think so" (*Ibid.*: 92). Yet it is precisely such a wedding that others wish to arrange (Barak, 1998). We find much work sympathetic to this thrust in recent theorizing in critical pedagogy, "border pedagogy," and "postmodern pedagogy." Giroux (1992), for example, advocates that intellectuals become "border crossers." "Borderlands," he observes, "should be seen as sites for both critical analysis and as a potential source of experimentation, creativity, and possibility" (1992: 34). Indeed, Lippens (1998, 1999), who applies these ideas to criminology, asks: Who owns this discipline and who claims to police its borders? He states:

> my performed (b)orders of criminology — even if I once have clothed them with the sign "borderless" (see Lippens, 1998) are just that: partial and ever-fallible attempts at control and mastery, born out of contingency and undecideability, of which they bear all the traces, and which turns them into unstable, shaky constructions that will simply always be in need of *suppléments*; which, in other words, will always and ever be dependent on their '*constitutif extérieur*' (2000).

Lippens argues that border policing constitutes the discipline, but in so doing, it limits our understanding of the issue.

Logic and Causality

The tendency among those invested in particular disciplines or theoretical positions to divorce agency and structure, and to separate modernism and postmodernism, is reflected in readings of the constitutive take on causality. Several commentators highlight the point that *Constitutive Criminology* is not content to settle for traditional conceptions of linear causality. For example, Croall (1996) says that the constitutive project "rejects uni-causal theories, recognizes that there are no determined structures, rejects the social construction of crime, and sees those attracted to crime as being affected by multiple influences in a socioeconomic and cultural context." She goes on to claim that much of this has long been recognized in more "modernist" critiques. If that is the case, it must be news to leading mainstream modernist theorists like Akers (1997: 178), who complains that "constitutive criminology has not yet offered a testable explanation of either crime or criminal justice" and who treats our rejection of mainstream criminology's traditional search for the causes of crime, while simultaneously accepting the notion that crime is "codetermined," as reflecting "some internal logical inconsistencies" (*Ibid.*: 177). He rhetorically asks:

> If the search for causes must be abandoned, as clearly stated by Henry and Milovanovic, or if crime does not exist as an objective reality in the discursive process as they may imply, then how can crime be enabled and constrained...and at the same time have reciprocal "shaping" effects on social structure...? It would seem that constitutive criminology has not really abandoned the search for causes, because crime, victims, and control are "shaped" by both micro-level events...and macro-level structural arrangements (*Ibid.*).

Why should it be contradictory to consider the relevant contributions of mutually interrelated events, activities, arrangements, and structures? As we have repeatedly stated, the concept of causality that seems best able to capture this notion of duality is that of dialectical interrelationships or coproduction. Indeed, rather than reject social construction, as Croall claims, we consider the social construction process to be critical. As Colvin's (1997: 1449) reading of *Constitutive Criminology* explains:

> these processes comprise relationships that are not deterministic, but dialectical, a dialectic that assumes nonlinear development and a movement, through human agency, toward instability of social forms.... Whether a particular situation or interrelationship will result in criminality cannot be determined with any precision since the dynamics of human relations are indeterminate, can be altered by seemingly small events, and are part of a historically situated, ongoing process that is also indeterminate (*Ibid.*).

It is unclear whether critics are made uncomfortable by the indeterminacy of social life itself or by constitutive criminology's reflection of that indeterminacy. What should be clear is that *Constitutive Criminology*, "assumes that the very notion of 'cause is problematic' and...importantly, while not totally abandoning the notion of causation...dialectically assemble[s] causality from the perspective of 'mutual influences,' 'structural couplings,' 'strategic essentialisms,' 'relational sets,' 'psychoanalytic semiotics,' 'gendered analyses,' and 'chaotic transformations'" (Barak, 1996: 157), to which we would add, "contingent universality" and "nonlinear iteration."

Unlike many of modernism's dualisms, such as free will versus determinism, conflict versus consensus, and order versus chaos, constitutive theory sees each as operative. Indeed, according to the insights generated by chaos theory, we can have order and disorder in the same system. This does not mean despair, resignation, or nihilism; rather, it poses new challenges to the ways we conceptualize complexity. Thus, the challenge will be to further integrate ideas such as nonlinearity, feedback, fractal geometry, attractors, phase space, self-similarity, indeterminacy, and iterations into our scholarly horizons. It is not that the affirmative postmodern approach of constitutive criminology rejects the gains of the past. Rather, it builds on what has been in creating new conceptual tools for future analysis and offers new visions of change, such as those painted by postmodernist feminists like Cornell (1991) and Butler (1990, 1996).

Our own development of causality is built on various perspectives drawn from *both* the modernist and postmodernist initiatives. In *Constitutive Criminology*, for example, we developed the idea of constitutive interrelational sets. These can be conceived of as historically situated, relatively stabilized configurations of coupled iterative loops that may follow nonlinear causal principles (i.e., extreme sensitivity to initial conditions, disproportional effects, order and disorder existing not as dichotomies but side by side, etc.) and can be best conceptualized by fractal, not Euclidean, geometry. It is not, therefore, that complexity cannot be understood, but that it cannot be captured solely within the prevailing categories of much of modernist thought. The idealization of prediction cannot be our goal either. Constitutive criminology is an ongoing search for understanding complexity over time. This is not to say that we cannot develop useful conceptualizations that can provide the basis of social action. To this end, modernist and postmodernist insights need to be critiqued *and* integrated. At best, we can offer only "contingent universalities." Anything more is tantamount to creating potentially reified structures; anything less is to regress to the nihilistic forms of postmodern analysis.

Crime as a Constructed Reality

Related to the problematic nature of causality is the nature of the reality of what is constituted through the dialectical process. Some commentators seem to assume that because *Constitutive Criminology* sees crime as socially constructed, this necessarily denies that it has real effects. For example, Akers (1997: 176–177) argues that constitutive criminology seems to "take the extreme position that denies crime as such really exists. Crime exists only because it is a 'discursive production,' that is, a product not only of the interaction of offenders, control agents, criminologists, or other people, but also simply by their talking about it.... This implies that there is no such thing as crime as an objective behavioral reality to be explained.... Does this mean that criminal behavior would not exist if we did not talk about it?"

At issue here is what is meant by "talk," or, more precisely, "discursive practices" in the social construction of reality. The critics assume there is a neat separation between reality and our talk about it. We argue that practices are part of the process that produces what then seems to be a separate reality. However, the critical issue for criminology is not whether the discursively produced representations have some underlying and independent existence, but that people act toward them *as if* they possess this quality. As such, categories based on socially constructed difference become invested with energy from those who treat them as real. Investors then act toward these categories to defend their interest in that reality or oppose others' notion of reality. It is people's (and agency's) actions that produce harm. To be clear, it is not that the harm of crime is unreal, but that the constructions that lead to its effects are the outcome of discursive practices.

Consider race, ethnicity, sexuality, gender, and class, all socially constructed, reified categories produced by the creation of distinctions based on perceived difference. Actions of people based on these differences (e.g., impositions, reductions, repressions, etc.), whether men against women, straights against gays, etc. (all themselves constructed categories), produce avoidable harms. Crime, as we have said, is the expression of the power to create harm based on socially constructed differences. The pain of that expression is real; its constitution is socially constructed. Thus, we are not arguing that crime (as harm) will disappear if we stop talking about it, but that harm will cease to be the outcome of a world that does not invest in the realities of difference. This leads directly to the problem of policy.

A Question of Policy

The fundamental policy problem confronting the constitutive project is how, as a society, it is possible to stop investing in structures of oppression whose manifestation channels and sustains the very use of the power to harm, without at the same time exercising power. A related problem is how, given the nature of power and social structure, is it possible to change the reified products of discourse that we take to be structure, culture, nature, and so on.

In responding to these policy questions, some believe the constitutive project meets its Waterloo:

> Most disappointing is the discussion of how to overcome the problem that local action cannot transform wider structural, state, and institutional systems. While [Henry and Milovanovic] argue that superliberalism and chaos theory can create an "empowered" democracy, they provide few practical strategies to indicate how this can be achieved...and many of the strategies seem little more than old wine in new bottles (Croall, 1996).

In considering policy, the connection between resistance and reconstruction is vital. Unlike some relevant critiques levied against the nihilistic forms of postmodern analysis — "its skepticism about 'progress,' its deconstruction of the concept of crime, its antipathy towards grand theory, mean that it can too easily lead towards nihilism, cynicism, and conservatism" (Matthews and Young, 1992: 13) — our affirmative version sees deconstruction *and* reconstruction as necessary foci; separate one from the other and the roads to nihilism or romanticism are seductively inviting.

Given that the basis of crime (as harm) is the socially constructed and discursively constituted exercise of power through difference, it follows that human subjects whose investment in power relations harms others have the potential to reconstitute their use of human agency to be less harmful or have the potential to be reconstituted through interactive relations with the wider culture or structure. Such a perspective, as Colvin (1997: 1450) comments, "opens the possibility for transformation of human subjects and the social structures we construct."

One means for achieving this reconstruction is through replacement discourse that fuels positive social constructions. Replacement discourse is designed to displace harmful moments in the exercise of power with discourses that tell different stories about the world. This is not simply saying that if we stop talking about crime it will go away. Rather, it is to say that if human discursive practices cease to construct differences as a basis of power (see Cornell, 1991), the site for investment will be deconstructed and investment and defense of it as a reality will be less possible. This is because the perception of people as less than fellow human subjects, as "others," will be dissipated. Harming others will be tantamount to harming oneself. This is why we advocate a policy of "social judo," in which the use of power is turned away from harm production and toward reinvesting in positive connections with a relationally oriented community of fellow human subjects. As Bohm (1997: 16) comments, "the judo metaphor is apt here because, on the one hand...using power to reduce the power of others only replaces one excessive investor with another. On the other hand, when using judo as a means of self-defense, the power of the aggressor is turned back against the aggressor."

The problem of policy, then, is not one of merely applying strategies, but of teaming deconstruction and reconstruction so that appreciation of difference, rather than domination based on difference, pervades the spirit of social life.

Difference without domination is to be celebrated (see Cornell's point about an "ethical feminism," 1991). The classical economic equivalency principle should not be quickly embraced either, because subsuming difference within notions of formal equality is to deny the variability and polyvocality of the human condition, as well as to ride roughshod over substantive inequality. The problem is not to remove existing institutional and social structures that reproduce differences whose investment with power results in oppression and inequality. Instead, the problem is how to cease our unreflexive rebuilding of these social forms and structures while reinvesting energy in alternative, connective interrelational social forms. That we are doing just the opposite is symbolized in the current prison-building program, as if by building prisons we are not deeply harming ourselves as well as those incarcerated (Milovanovic and Henry, 1991). That this is taking place in 21st-century America indicates how far we are from dealing with the fundamental issue and why societal and structural transformation require continuous and relentless struggle.

We are suggesting that "dissipative structures" — structures that are extremely sensitive to their environment and to its perturbations, and consequently undergo continuous change while still providing provisionally stable horizons for social action — have much in common with the notion of "contingent universalities" (Butler, 1990). Here provisional truths may become the basis of political action and social policy. However, these are always contingent and subject to change, refinement, substitution, and deletion when faced with historical conditions and further reflective investigation. In short, in our view the problem of policy should remain a problem; there are no answers, only working solutions.

REFERENCES

Akers, Ronald
1997 *Criminological Theories: Introduction and Evaluation*. Los Angeles: Roxbury.

Arrigo, Bruce
1997 "Review of Stuart Henry and Dragan Milovanovic's Constitutive Criminology." *Theoretical Criminology* 3: 392–396.

Bak, Andrew
2000 "Assessing Henry and Milovanovic's *Constitutive Criminology*." R. Schehr (special issue editor), "Re-Mapping American Criminology." *Postmodern Criminology* 7: www.tryoung.com/journal-pomocrim/vol-7-remap/002bak.html.
1999 "Constitutive Criminology: An Introduction to the Core Concepts." Stuart Henry and Dragan Milovanovic (eds.), *Constitutive Criminology at Work: Applications to Crime and Justice*. Albany, NY: SUNY Press.

Barak, Gregg
1998 *Integrating Criminologies*. Boston: Allyn and Bacon.
1996 "Review of Stuart Henry and Dragan Milovanovic's Constitutive Criminology." *Social Pathology* 2: 154–159.
1994 *Media, Process, and the Social Construction of Crime: Studies in Newsmaking Criminology*. G. Barak (ed.). New York: Garland.
1993 "Media, Crime, and Justice: A Case for Constitutive Criminology." *Humanity and Society* 17,3: 272–296.

Barak, Gregg and Stuart Henry
1998 "An Integrative-Constitutive Theory of Crime, Law, and Justice." Bruce Arrigo (ed.), *Social Justice/Criminal Justice: The Maturation of Critical Theory in Law, Crime, and Deviance*. Belmont: West/Wadsworth: 152–175.
Barak, Gregg, Stuart Henry, and Dragan Milovanovic
1997 "Constitutive Criminology: An Overview of an Emerging Postmodernist School." B. MacLean and Dragan Milovanovic (eds.), *Critical Criminology*. Vancouver: Collective Press.
Beirne, Piers and James Messerschmidt
1995 *Criminology*. Second edition. Fort Worth, TX: Harcourt Brace.
Berube, Michael
1997 "In Praise of Obscurity." *The Chronicle of Higher Education* (February 21): B4.
Bohm, Robert M.
1997 "Review of Stuart Henry and Dragan Milovanovic's *Constitutive Criminology*." *The Criminologist* 22: 15–16.
Butler, Judith
1996 *Excitable Speech: A Politics of the Performative*. New York: Routledge.
1992 "Contingent Foundations: Feminism and the Question of 'Postmodernism.'" J. Butler and J.W. Scott (eds.), *Feminists Theorize the Political*. London: Routledge.
1990 *Gender Trouble*. New York: Routledge.
Colvin, Mark
1997 "Review of Stuart Henry and Dragan Milovanovic's *Constitutive Criminology*." *American Journal of Sociology* 102: 1448–450.
Cornell, Drucilla
1991 *Beyond Accommodation: Ethical Feminism, Deconstruction, and the Law*. New York: Routledge.
Croall, Hazel
1996 "Crime: Understanding More and Condemning Less?" *Reviewing Sociology* 10,3.
DeKeseredy, Walter and Martin D. Schwartz
1996 *Contemporary Criminology*. Belmont: Wadsworth.
Deutschmann, Linda B.
1998 *Deviance and Social Control*. Second edition. Toronto: IPC.
Einstadter, Werner and Stuart Henry
1995 *Criminological Theory: An Analysis of Its Underlying Assumptions*. Fort Worth, TX: Harcourt Brace.
Ericson, Richard and Kevin Carriere
1994 "The Fragmentation of Criminology." David Nelken (ed.), *The Futures of Criminology*. London: Sage.
Ewick, Patricia and Susan S. Sileby
1998 *The Common Place of Law: Stories from Everyday Life*. Chicago: University of Chicago Press.
Fitzpatrick, Peter
1992 *The Mythology of Modern Law*. London: Routledge.
1984 "Law and Societies." *Osgoode Hall Law Journal* 22: 115–138.
Friedrichs, David 0.
1996 "Critical Criminology and Progressive Pluralism: Strength in Diversity for These Times." *Critical Criminology* 7: 121–128.
Gibbons, Donald C.
1994 *Talking About Crime and Criminals: Problems and Issues in Theory Development in Criminology*. Englewood Cliffs, NJ: Prentice Hall.
Giddens, Anthony
1984 *The Constitution of Society: Outline of the Theory of Structuration*. Oxford: Polity Press.
1979 *Central Problems in Social Theory: Action, Structure, and Contradiction in Social Analysis*. London: Macmillan.

Giroux, Henry
1992 *Border Crossings: Cultural Workers and the Politics of Education*. New York: Routledge.

Gregerson, H. and L. Sailer
1993 "Chaos Theory and Its Implications for Social Science Research." *Human Relations* 46: 777–802.

Harrington, Christine
1988 "Moving from Integrative to Constitutive Theories of Law: Comments on Itzkowitz." *Law and Society Review* 22: 963–967.

Henry, Stuart
1994 "'Newsmaking Criminology' as Replacement Discourse." Gregg Barak (ed.), *Media, Process, and the Social Construction of Crime: Studies in Newsmaking Criminology*. New York: Garland Press.
1989 "Constitutive Criminology: The Missing Paradigm." *The Critical Criminologist* 1,3: 9, 12.
1987a "The Construction and Deconstruction of Social Control: Thoughts on the Discursive Production of State Law and Private Justice." John Lowman, Robert Menzies, and Ted Palys (eds.), *Transcarceration: Essays in the Sociology of Social Control*. Aldershot: Gower Press.
1987b "Private Justice and the Policing of Labor." Clifford Shearing and Phillip Stenning (eds.), *Private Policing*. Beverly Hills: Sage: 45–71.
1985 "Community Justice, Capitalist Society, and Human Agency: The Dialectics of Collective Law in the Co-operative." *Law and Society Review* 19: 303–327.
1983 *Private Justice*. London: Routledge and Kegan Paul.

Henry, Stuart and Dragan Milovanovic
1999 *Constitutive Criminology at Work: Applications to Crime and Justice*. Albany, NY: SUNY Press.
1996 *Constitutive Criminology: Beyond Postmodernism*. London: Sage.
1994 "The Constitution of Constitutive Criminology: A Postmodern Approach to Criminological Theory." D. Nelken (ed.), *The Futures of Criminology*. London: Sage.
1993 "Back to Basics: A Postmodern Redefinition of Crime." *The Critical Criminologist* 5,2–3: 1–2, 6, 12.
1991 "Constitutive Criminology." *Criminology* 29: 293–316.

Howe, Adrian
1997 "Criminology Meets Postmodern Feminism (and Has a Nice Day)." Brian D. MacLean and Dragan Milovanovic (eds.), *Thinking Critically About Crime*. Vancouver: Collective Press.

Hunt, Alan
1993 *Explorations in Law and Society: Toward a Constitutive Theory of Law*. New York: Routledge.

Jessop, Bob
1990 *State Theory: Putting the Capitalist State in Its Place*. Cambridge, U.K.: Polity Press.

Kappeler, Victor E. and Peter B. Kraska
1999 "Policing Modernity: Scientific and Community-Based Violence on Symbolic Playing Fields." Stuart Henry and Dragan Milovanovic (eds.), *Constitutive Criminology at Work: Applications to Crime and Justice*. Albany, NY: SUNY Press.

Lacan, Jacques
1961 *The Seminar of Jacques Lacan: Book IX: Identification 1961–1962*. Translated by Cormac Gallageur (unpublished).

Lanier, Mark M. and Stuart Henry
1998 *Essential Criminology*. Boulder, CO: Westview Press.

Lippens, Ronnie
2000 *Who Owns Criminology? A Short Note on Gaps, Divides, and Bridges*. At http://www.tryoung.com/journal-pomocrim/lippens.html.
1999 "Into Hybrid Marshlands." *International Journal for the Semiotics of Law* 34: 59–89.
1998 *Grenze/n/loze Kriminologie* (transl. *Borderless Criminology*). Ghent, Belgium: Academia Press.
Luhmann, Niklas A.
1992 "Operational Closure and Structural Coupling: The Differentiation of the Legal System." *Cardozo Law Review* 13: 1419–1441.
Mandelbrot, B.
1983 *The Fractal Geometry of Nature*. New York: W.H. Freeman.
Marx, Karl
1975 *Early Writings*. Translated by Rodney Livingstone and Gregor Benton. New York: Random House/Vintage.
Matsuda, M.J., C.R. Larence, R. Delgado, and K.W. Crenshaw (eds.)
1993 *Words That Wound*. San Francisco: Westview Press.
Matthews, Roger and Jock Young
1992 "Reflections on Realism." Jock Young and Roger Matthews (eds.), *Re-Thinking Criminology: The Realist Debate*. London: Sage.
Matza, David
1964 *Delinquency and Drift*. New York: Wiley.
Milovanovic, Dragan
1999 "Catastrophe Theory, Discourse, and Conflict Regulation: Generating the 'Third Way.'" B. Arrigo (ed.), *Social Justice/Criminal Justice: The Maturation of Critical Theory in Law, Crime, and Deviance*. Belmont: Wadsworth: 203–223.
1996a *Chaos, Criminology, and Social Justice*. D. Milovanovic (ed.). Westport, CT: Praeger.
1996b "Rebellious Lawyering." *Legal Studies Forum* 20,3: 295–321.
1996c "Postmodern Criminology." *Justice Quarterly* 13: 567–610.
1994a *Sociology of Law*. Second edition. Albany, NY: Harrow and Heston.
1994b "The Postmodern Turn: Lacan, Psychoanalytic Semiotics, and the Construction of Subjectivity in Law." *Emory International Law Review* 8,1: 67–98.
1994c "The Decentered Subject in Law: Contributions of Topology, Psychoanalytic Semiotics, and Chaos Theory." *Studies in Psychoanalytic Theory* 3,1: 93–127.
1993a "Lacan's Four Discourses." *Studies in Psychoanalytic Theory* 2,1: 3–23.
1993b "Borromean Knots and the Constitution of Sense in Juridico-Discursive Production." *Legal Studies Forum* 17,2: 171–192.
1992 *Postmodern Law and Disorder: Psychoanalytic Semiotics, Chaos, and Juridic Exegeses*. Liverpool, U.K.: Deborah Charles.
1988 "Jailhouse Lawyers and Jailhouse Lawyering." *International Journal of the Sociology of Law* 16: 455–475.
Milovanovic, Dragan and Stuart Henry
1991 "Constitutive Penology." *Social Justice* 18: 204–224.
Milovanovic, Dragan and Ellie Ragland (eds.)
2001 *Topologically Speaking*. New York: Other Press.
Milovanovic, Dragan and Katheryn Russell (eds.)
2001 *Petit Apartheid in Criminal Justice*. Durham, NC: Carolina Academic Press.
Milovanovic, Dragan and J. Thomas
1989 "Overcoming the Absurd: Legal Struggle as Primitive Rebellion." *Social Problems* 36,1: 48–60.
Naffine, Ngaire
1996 *Feminism and Criminology*. Philadelphia: Temple University Press.
Nelken, David (ed.)
1994 *The Futures of Criminology*. London: Sage.

Pepinsky, Hal and Richard Quinney (eds.)
1991 *Criminology as Peacemaking*. Bloomington, IN: Indiana University Press.

Pickover, C.
1988 "Pattern Formation and Chaos in Networks." *Communication of the ACM* 31: 136–151.

Rosenau, Pauline
1992 *Postmodernism and the Social Sciences*. Princeton, NJ: Princeton.

Ruller, Sibo van
1997 "Review of Stuart Henry and Dragan Milovanovic's *Constitutive Criminology*." *Contemporary Criminology* 26: 496–497.

Sanchez, Lisa
1999 "Sex, Law, and the Paradox of Agency and Resistance in the Everyday Practices of Women in the 'Evergreen' Sex Trade." Stuart Henry and Dragan Milovanovic (eds.), *Constitutive Criminology at Work: Applications to Crime and Justice*. Albany, New York: SUNY Press.

Sayer, Derek
1979 *Marx's Method*. New York: Humanities Press.

Schmalleger, Frank
1999 *Criminology Today: An Integrative Introduction*. Second edition. Upper Saddle River, NJ: Prentice Hall.

Schwartz, Martin D.
1989 "The Undercutting Edge of Criminology." *The Critical Criminologist* 1: 1, 2, 5.

Schwartz, Martin D. and David 0. Friedrichs
1994 "Postmodern Thought and Criminological Discontent: New Metaphors for Understanding Violence." *Criminology* 32: 221–246.

Silbey, Susan S.
1992 "Making a Place for the Cultural Analysis of Law." *Law and Social Inquiry* 17: 39–48.

Smart, Carol
1990 "Feminist Approaches to Criminology, or Postmodern Woman Meets Atavistic Man." L. Gelsthorpe and A. Morris (eds.), *Feminist Perspectives in Criminology*. Milton Keynes: Open University Press.

Spivak, G.
1988 "Can the Subaltern Speak?" C. Nelson and L. Grossberg (eds.), *Marxisms and the Interpretation of Culture*. London: Macmillan.

Stitt, B. Grant and David J. Giacopassi
1992 "Trends in the Connectivity of Theory and Research in Criminology." *The Criminologist* 17: 1, 3–6.

Teubner, Guenther
1993 *Law as an Autopoietic System*. Oxford: Blackwell.
1992 "The Two Faces of Janus: Rethinking Legal Pluralism." *Cardozo Law Review* 13: 1443–1462.
1988 *Autopoietic Law: A New Approach to Law and Society*. New York: Walter de Gruyter.

Vold, George B., Thomas J. Bernard, and Jeffrey B. Snipes
1998 *Theoretical Criminology*. Third edition. New York: Oxford University Press.

Name Index